CONTENTS

KEY MAP

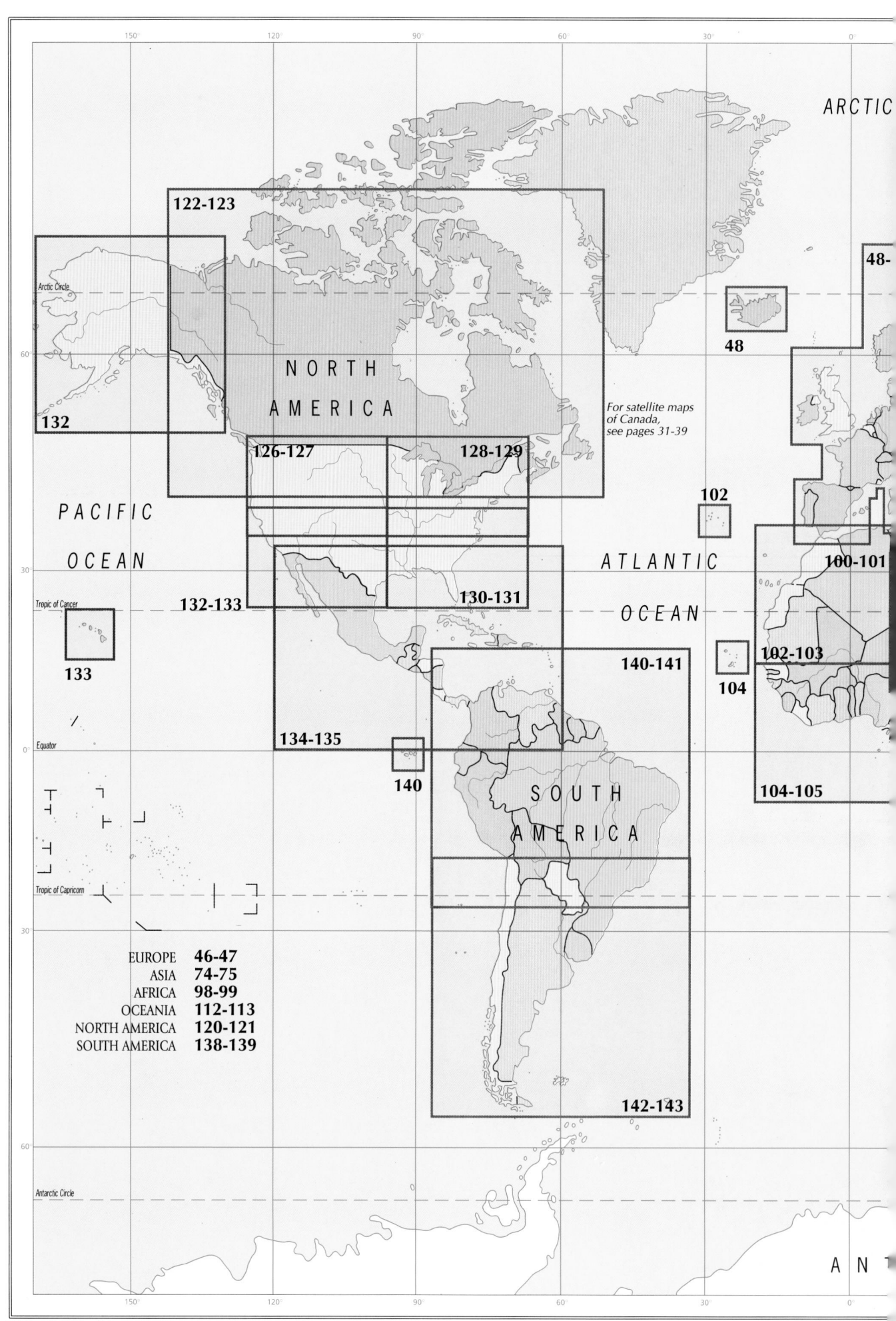

ARCTIC

122-123

Arctic Circle

NORTH

AMERICA

132

*For satellite maps
of Canada,
see pages 31-39*

48-

48

126-127   **128-129**

PACIFIC

OCEAN

102

100-101

ATLANTIC

132-133

Tropic of Cancer

130-131

OCEAN

133

102-103

104

140-141

134-135

Equator

140

SOUTH

AMERICA

104-105

Tropic of Capricorn

EUROPE	**46-47**
ASIA	**74-75**
AFRICA	**98-99**
OCEANIA	**112-113**
NORTH AMERICA	**120-121**
SOUTH AMERICA	**138-139**

142-143

Antarctic Circle

AN T

© Helicon Publishing Ltd

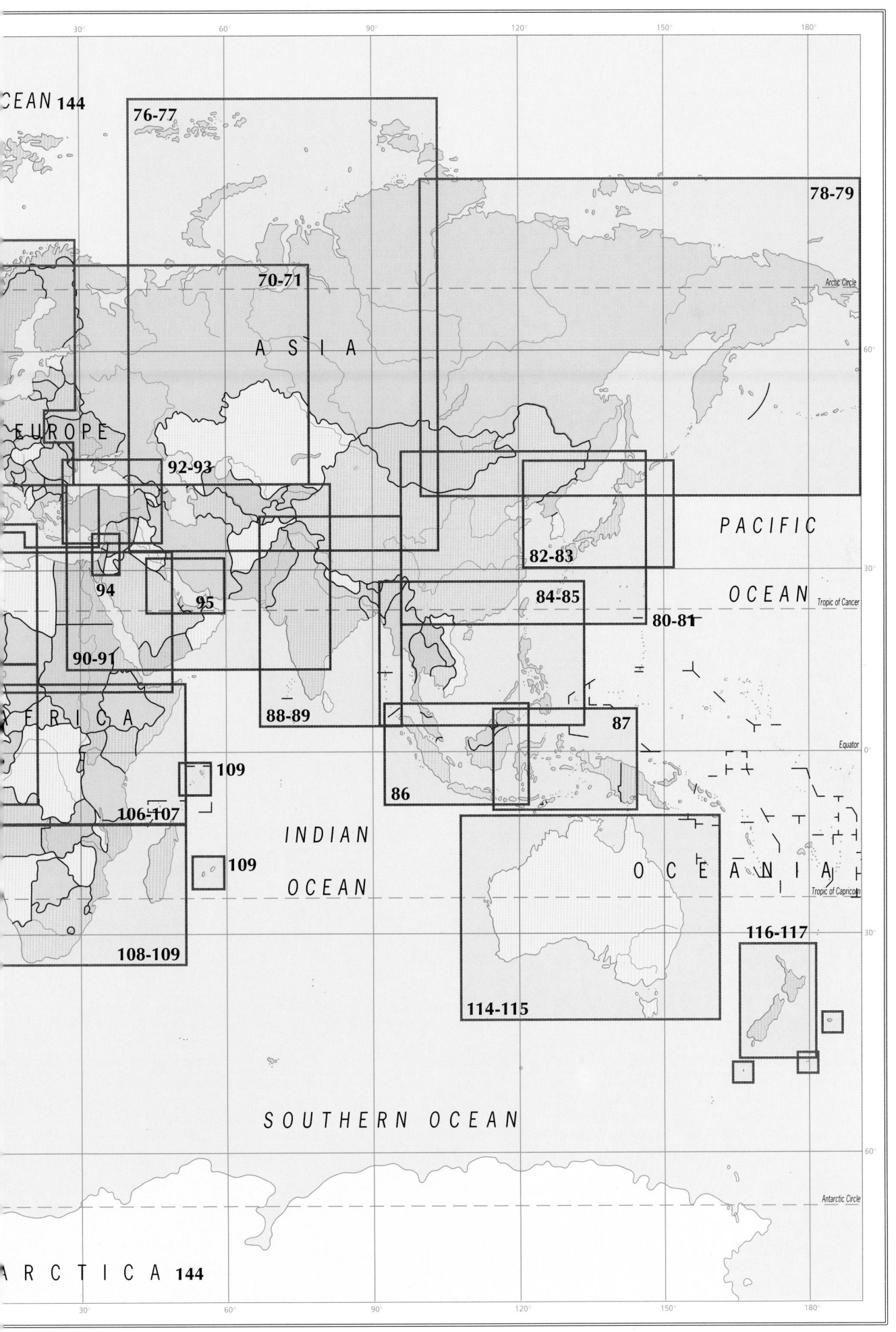

OCEAN **144**

76-77

78-79

Arctic Circle

60°

A S I A

70-71

EUROPE

92-93

PACIFIC

82-83

OCEAN

Tropic of Cancer

94

95

84-85

30°

80-81

90-91

88-89

87

FRICA

86

Equator

0°

109

INDIAN

106-107

OCEAN

O C E A N I A

Tropic of Capricorn

109

30°

116-117

108-109

114-115

SOUTHERN OCEAN

60°

Antarctic Circle

ARCTICA **144**

30°   60°   90°   120°   150°   180°

THE CHANGING WORLD

OUR STAR & OUR NEIGHBOURS

THE EARTH IS ONE MEMBER of a Solar System of nine planets orbiting our local star – the Sun. All these bodies formed from a single cloud of gas and dust around 4.5 billion years ago as it was compressed, possibly by shockwaves from a giant supernova explosion. The centre of the cloud collapsed most rapidly, becoming denser and attracting more material until eventually it reached a point so hot and dense that nuclear reactions began inside it. These reactions continue today and are the source of the sunlight that heats our planet and sustains life. The Sun is critical to the regulation of our climate and environment – fine alterations in Earth's orbit are thought to cause periodic ice ages, so we are fortunate that the Sun is not likely to change drastically for another 5 billion years.

On a shorter scale, the Sun's output does have slight fluctuations. A cycle of sunspot formation (comparatively cool regions of the Sun's surface caused by magnetic activity), reaches a maximum every 11 years. From 1645–1705 almost no sunspots were seen, a dip in solar activity which coincided with a 'mini-Ice Age' of unusually low temperatures on Earth.

Once the Sun had formed, a disk of material would have been left outside the newly-formed star, which condensed to form the planets. Particles in the gas and dust cloud collided and stuck together, becoming increasingly larger bodies. Eventually these 'proto-planets' were pulled into a spherical shape by their increasing gravity.

The Solar System we see today reflects the composition of that gas and dust cloud, and divides into two regions. The inner portion contains the four terrestrial (Earth-like) planets – from Mercury orbiting close to the Sun, through Venus and Earth, to Mars. Beyond the orbit of Mars lies the asteroid belt, a ring of rocky debris, outside which are the gas giants, enormous planets created where the cloud bulged with huge quantities of gas.

The inner rocky worlds

The terrestrial planets are all very different. Mercury is a small, baking world, quite similar to our own Moon, and covered in craters. Venus is shrouded in a thick atmosphere of carbon

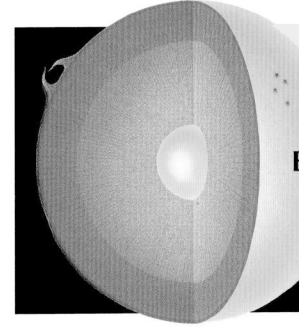

▶ **THE SUN**
The Sun is a massive ball of hydrogen gas **[B]**, *1.39 million km across. Energy is generated at its heart, where temperatures exceed 15 million°C, by nuclear fusion – the joining together through a chain reaction of two hydrogen atoms to form one helium. In the process, a large amount of excess energy is released, carried to the surface of the Sun in giant convection cells, and then radiated across the Solar System from the top of* the 'photosphere' – the visible disk of the Sun, with a temperature of 5500°C.

◀ **THE SOLAR SYSTEM**
The solar system consists of 9 planets **[A]**: *Pluto [1], the smallest, is the furthest away from the Sun, though once in every 248.6 years its orbit crosses inside Neptune's path. Neptune [2], the outermost of the gas giants, has a* diameter of 49,400km, and orbits every 164.8 years.

Uranus [3] is similar in size to Neptune and orbits every 84 years. All the gas giants have ring systems, but Uranus's are second only to Saturn's. The planet is tilted at over 98° to the plane of the dioxide and toxic molecules, with a surface pressure 95 times that of Earth's atmosphere, and temperatures of 470°C. Beyond the Earth's orbit, Mars is famous as the Red Planet – a colour given by rust in its surface dust. Although smaller than Earth, there is evidence that Mars once had a thick atmosphere, and that water ran on its surface – although now it is frozen into polar ice-caps.

The gas giants

The outer Solar System contains worlds quite different from those nearer the Sun – the gas giants. Largest of these is Jupiter, more massive than all the other planets in the Solar System put together, with churning weather systems that include the Great Red Spot, a storm large enough to engulf Earth. Beyond Jupiter lies Saturn, with its spectacular ring system of icy particles, and then the smaller giants Uranus and Neptune. Space probes have shown that Jupiter, Uranus and Neptune also have thin ring systems, although these are nothing to match Saturn's spectacle.

All four of these worlds have large families of moons orbiting round them. Jupiter has a vast family of moons, including Io, the most volcanic body in the Solar System, whose eruptions launch yellow plumes of sulphur into space, scarring its surface with streaks. The most interesting member of Uranus's satellite system is Miranda – a small, deeply-cratered world which displays so many variations in terrain that it must have suffered some great cataclysm in the past. Neptune's giant satellite Triton has active geysers shooting water, ammonia and methane 8km above its surface.

surface in its past. Next in towards the Sun is our own blue planet, the Earth [8], with a diameter of 12,700km. Within the orbit of the Earth lies its near twin Venus [9], circling the Sun in 225 days, and with a diameter of 12,100km. The atmosphere of Venus, however, is a poisonous mixture of carbon dioxide and other gases, with clouds of sulphuric acid.

Mercury [10] is the second smallest planet with a diameter of only 4,880km, and a solar orbit that lasts 88 days. Its proximity to the Sun (58 million km) makes it a scorched world with no atmosphere, and a cratered surface similar to that of the Moon. It orbits the Sun once every 88 days.

Solar System, so it seems to roll around its orbit. Saturn [4] is noted for its spectacular ring system – the planet has a diameter of 105,000km, while the rings stretch out to 300,000km. It orbits the Sun every 29.5 years, and has a huge family of satellites.

Jupiter [5] orbits the Sun every 11.9 years. With a diameter of 137,400km it is the largest planet in the Solar System. It has complex weather systems, including the Great Red Spot, a storm with a diameter larger than the Earth's.

Between Jupiter and Mars is the asteroid belt [6], rocky debris left over from the Solar System's formation. Inside it lie the terrestrial planets. Mars [7], the red planet, circles the Sun in 1.9 years, and has a diameter of 6790km. Its surface is scoured by massive dust storms, and it shows evidence of running water on the

◀ The Sun is just one of over 200 billion stars in the vast spiral of the Milky Way galaxy, like every other star that we see with the naked eye in the night sky. It lies roughly two-thirds of the way towards the edge of the galactic disc, orbiting the centre at a speed of 250 kilometres per second, taking 200 million years to complete each revolution. This view is what the galaxy would look like to an observer outside. But because of our position in the plane, we see the dense star clouds as a pale band across the sky.

THE EARTH & THE MOON

THE EARTH'S SATELLITE, THE MOON, IS SO LARGE by comparison with our own world (at 3746km, it is over one-quarter the Earth's diameter) that astronomers consider the two together as a 'double planet'. This massive size and proximity means that the Moon has a great influence on the Earth itself, for example through the tides.

The origins of the Moon are open to debate – some believe that the Moon is a chunk of debris flung off when the still-molten Earth collided with another body the size of Mars, in the early days of the Solar System. Since then, the two bodies have had very different histories. The Moon's small size meant that it cooled more quickly and its low gravity made it unable to hold onto an atmosphere – the factor which has been crucial in shaping our own planet's terrain. In fact, the Moon has altered so little that it provides valuable information about the history of the early Solar System. The lack of an atmosphere also means that, unlike Earth, the Moon is not shielded from the extremes of heat from the Sun. Temperatures at noon climb to 150°C, while at night they can plummet to -200°C. These acute differences can even cause moonquakes as the surface stretches and contracts.

A familiar face

The Moon's surface divides into two distinct types of terrain, which can be easily distinguished with the naked eye from Earth. The bright highlands are highly cratered areas created more than 4 billion years ago during an era of bombardment by rock particles from space. The numbers of these particles dwindled until only a few massive chunks were left, which created enormous impact basins as they crashed into the Moon's surface. The gnarled highlands contrast sharply with the smoother, darker Maria (from the Latin for seas). After the cratering had died away, the Moon seems to have undergone a brief period of intense volcanic activity. Red-hot fissures opened up across its surface, out of which huge volumes of lava poured, flooding low-lying areas. These lava lakes solidified to form the Maria, marked by only a few, very small craters.

Lunar attraction

The changing direction of the Sun and Moon from Earth cause our monthly cycle of tides. Twice a month, at full and new moon, the high Spring Tides occur, with Moon and Sun lined up, or directly opposed, so the tidal effect is at its strongest. Such tidal effects have influenced the Earth-Moon system as a whole. Over millions of years, the friction of the oceans' movement has slowed the lunar 'day', so it now lasts exactly as long as the time the Moon takes to orbit Earth, with the result that it always keeps the same face turned towards us. Fossil records show that there were once 400 days in each Earth year, so the same effect must also be

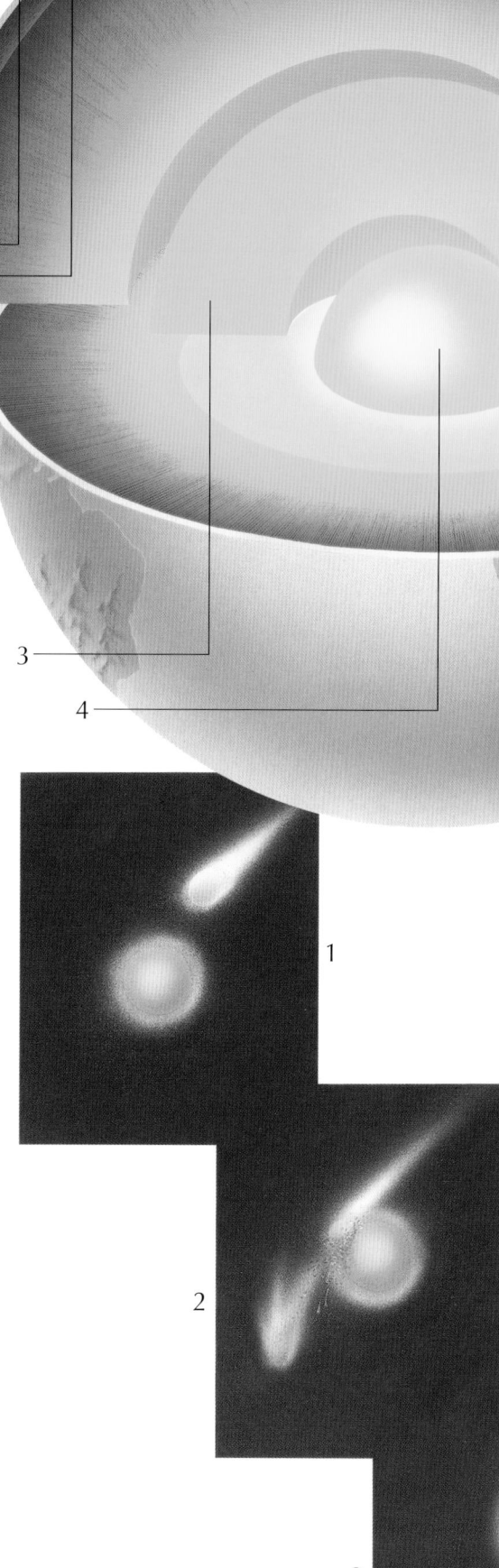

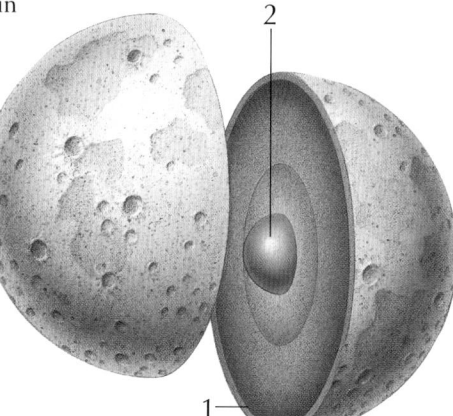

▶ **STRUCTURE OF THE MOON**
The Earth's satellite, the Moon **[B]**, has a structure that reflects its different size, and possibly origin. Because it is a much smaller body – around one-twentieth the volume of the Earth – it has a higher surface area to volume ratio. It cooled down more rapidly early in the history of the Solar System, and is now inactive. The lunar crust [1] is actually thicker than Earth's – an average of 70km, though it is thinner on the Earth-facing side, possibly due to the tidal effects of the Earth's gravity. This could be a possible explanation of why the smooth 'seas' are found far more on this side, formed from eruptions of lava through the thin crust. Beneath this lie layers of solidified, cold rock, which decrease in rigidity. At the centre there may be a cold core [2], although its existence is still debated.

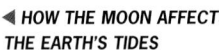

▶ THE EARTH'S SEASONS

The Poles of the Earth are tilted at 23.5° [C]. As it orbits the Sun, different parts of the globe receive a varying amount of sunlight through the year-long cycle of the seasons [3]. For six months of the year, the Northern Hemisphere is tilted towards the Sun, which therefore appears higher in the sky, giving warmer temperatures and longer days [1]. Six months later, when the Northern Hemisphere is tilted in the other direction, the days are shorter and the Sun stays closer to the horizon [2]. The situation is reversed in the Southern Hemisphere. The Tropics of Cancer and Capricorn are lines around the globe at the lines of latitude +/- 23.5°. They mark the northernmost and southern-most points where the Sun appears directly overhead.

Spring

Winter

Sun

Autumn

Summer

◀ THE STRUCTURE OF THE EARTH

The Earth has the shape of a squashed ball or a spheroid [A]. It has a diameter at the poles of 12,703km, but is wider at the Equator, thrown outward by the rapid daily spin which causes a 'bulge'. The crust [1], on which lie the continents and oceans, is a thin layer of rock varying in depth between 10 and 20km. Below this lies a mantle [2], divided into two regions. The upper mantle extends down to 3000km, and divides into the mainly solid lithosphere and the mostly molten aesthenosphere. Beyond this, the molten rock of the upper and lower mantle extends down towards the molten outer [3] and solid inner [4] cores of iron and nickel, around 7000km across, at the centre of the Earth. It is the rotation of this core that is believed to generate the Earth's magnetic field, in an effect similar to that of a dynamo.

slowing its rotation as well. Hence in the distant future, the spin of the Earth could be so slow that its day and year are equal, so that one scorched side of the planet will permanently face the Sun.

Complete coverage

Very occasionally, as the Moon orbits around the Earth and it in turn moves around the Sun, all three bodies – Sun, Earth and Moon – line up exactly and an eclipse is seen. If the Earth blocks out the Sun shining onto the full Moon, a rather unspectacular lunar eclipse happens. Far more spectacular are solar eclipses, when the new Moon passes right across the face of the Sun. By chance the Moon and Sun have discs in the sky that are almost the same size. This means that total solar eclipses can only be seen for short periods of time from tiny regions of the Earth. The effect is breathtaking as the Moon covers the bright central disk of the Sun, and reveals the wispy white corona of gas streaming out from the Sun's surface.

D

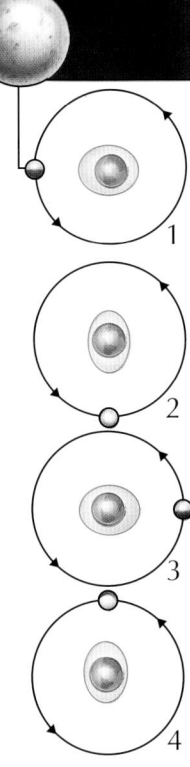

◀ HOW THE MOON BEGAN

The Moon orbits too far from the Earth to be a captured asteroid. Instead, it is thought to have been formed when a body the size of Mars collided with the still-molten Earth during the formation of the Solar System, some 5 billion years ago [1].

The collision resulted in a stream of debris being thrown off into orbit round the Earth [2], and this eventually condensed to form the Moon [3]. The iron-rich cores of the two original bodies combined and remained within the Earth, becoming its very dense central region, whilst the Moon formed from the two lighter outer sections.

This may explain why the Earth is thought to have a more complicated structure than the Moon, and also the lack of iron in Moon rock.

◀ HOW THE MOON AFFECTS THE EARTH'S TIDES

The proximity of the Moon to the Earth, coupled with its size, causes strong gravitational forces between the two worlds, which is shown in the tides [D].

As the Moon exerts a gravitational pull on the Earth, it draws the seas towards it, and creates a bulge in the seawater on one side of the planet. At the same time, the Earth itself is attracted towards the Moon, pulling it away from the sea on the opposite side of the globe and creating a smaller tidal bulge on the opposite side. Because the Moon is relatively slow-moving, the tidal bulges in the sea remain in almost the same place, while the Earth rotates under them [1,2,3,4]. As each bulge passes a point on the Earth roughly once each day, seashores experience two high and two low tides each day (although the shape of an inlet can alter their spacing). As the Moon circles the Earth once a month, the tides occur at different times each day.

▼ During the brief minutes of the eclipse, the corona of the Sun can be seen.

Normally this is an invisible halo, made up of two distinct regions of gas which overlap, the K-corona and the F-corona. The latter reaches out many millions of kilometres from the Suns surface while the K-corona extends for a mere 75,000km.

A WORLD IN MOTION

WE THINK OF THE GROUND AS BEING STEADY AND IMMOVABLE: in fact the surface of the Earth is in a constant state of movement, propelled by the intense heat of the interior. Although our planet is 12,700km wide, the crust on which the continents and oceans lie is only a few tens of kilometres thick at its deepest. This thin crust is broken into slabs or plates, which float on top of an inner molten layer, the mantle. Where these plates collide with each other or slowly draw apart are areas of violent activity, subject to earthquakes and studded with volcanoes. This drama is not restricted to dry land: satellite photography has shown that the two-thirds of Earth's surface under the ocean is just as fascinating, with features such as chains of volcanic mountains that stretch for 60,000km around the globe.

The idea that the continents are slowly moving was first put forward to explain how the coastlines of different continents appear to fit together like pieces of a jigsaw puzzle. For example, the eastern coast of South America nestles snugly into the western coast of Africa. Such continental drifts can be traced back to a point around 250 million years ago, when all the land masses on Earth were joined into a supercontinent called Pangaea (from the Greek for all earth), surrounded by a single vast sea, the Tethys Ocean. This supercontinent slowly disintegrated into the major land masses we know today.

Geologists call their model for the movements of the Earth's crust plate tectonics. This describes the surface, both continents and ocean floor, as being split into plates whose movements are driven by the churning of the molten rock in the inner mantle. The largest plates are as wide as the Pacific Ocean, while others are much smaller. Their thickness varies from around 10km beneath the oceans, to 30km under major land masses, and up to 60km where a plate has to support the weight of a mountain range. In general, ocean floor plates are made of dense basaltic rocks, while the continents are formed from less dense granite.

Earthquakes

Most of the areas where plates are separating are hidden beneath the ocean. At the fault between the plates molten rock wells up through a fissure and solidifies, creating new ocean floor. Only in a few places can this process be seen on dry land, notably in the volcanoes of Iceland, which sits on a fault called the Mid-Atlantic Ridge.

Plates can meet in a number of ways. At earthquake zones they grind past each other in opposite directions, being compressed so that they store huge amounts of energy. This is released in calamitous movements of the ground – earthquakes. The most famous earthquake zone of all, the San Andreas Fault in California, is a region where the North American and Pacific Plates are moving past each other. Earthquake prediction hinges on the theory that major quakes are preceded by 'quiet' periods during which the plates lock together, and store up the energy. Not all the plate boundaries are earthquake or volcano zones – the Himalayas are the result of a head-on collision between the relatively fast-moving Indo-Australian Plate, and the Eurasian Plate. These two continental plates buckled upwards, forming the mountain range, and halting the Indo-Australian plate's movement.

Conversely, not all volcanoes are at plate boundaries. The volcanic Hawaiian Islands, for

▼ PANGAEA

The continents of the world have not always looked as they do today [**A**]. The process of plate tectonics means that that they have migrated across the surface of the Earth. 200 million years ago, in the Jurassic era, all the land masses were joined in a single supercontinent, Pangaea [1].

Eventually, 120 million years ago, Pangaea split in two, the northern Laurasia made up of present-day North America and Eurasia, and the southern Gondwana, comprising South America, Africa, Australia and India [2].

By 40 million years ago the world had taken on a familiar look, although India had yet to collide with Eurasia (and create the Himalayas in the process) and Australia was still located very close to Antarctica [3].

A

1

2

3

▼ PLATE TECTONICS

The processes of plate tectonics can be seen most clearly on a section of ocean floor [**B**]. At a subduction zone [1], an oceanic plate meets a much thicker continental plate and is forced down into the Earth's upper mantle. The heat in this zone melts the upper basalt layer of the oceanic plate, forming liquid magma which then rises to the surface and is vented through volcanoes.

At a mid-oceanic ridge [2] new crust is constantly being generated where two plates are separating. Magma rises up from the Earth's mantle, forcing its way through cracks in the crust, and solidifying.

As the cracks expand, a striated ocean floor is formed. When the new crust solidifies, traces of iron in it align with the Earth's magnetic field and so preserve a record of the various reversals in the field over millions of years.

A hot spot volcano [3] forms where the crust thins above a hot plume rising from the inner mantle. It is only the latest in a string of volcanoes that form as the oceanic plate moves over the stationary plume. The earlier volcanoes become extinct, subsiding to volcanic islands with coral fringes, and eventually become atolls, where only the ring of coral remains above the surface of the ocean.

B

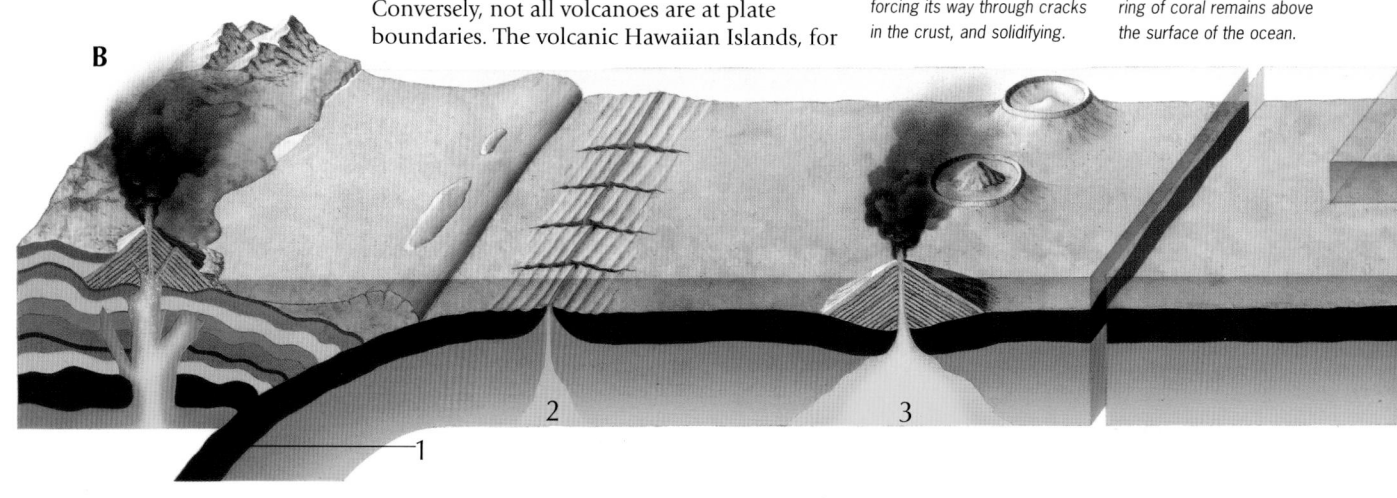

1   2   3

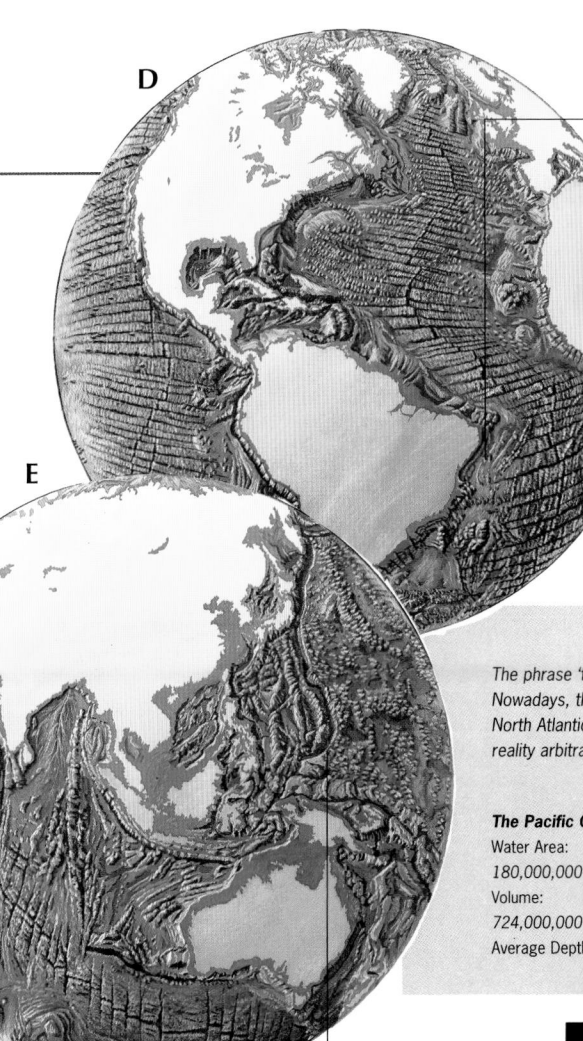

D — Mid-Atlantic Ridge

◀ THE ATLANTIC AND THE PACIFIC

The floors of the two largest oceans reveal important differences in their structures.

The Atlantic Ocean [D] is divided by the Mid-Atlantic Ridge that runs for its entire length, from Greenland down to the Antarctic Plate. This is a region where the Earth's crust is stretching, new floor being pumped out so that the Atlantic is gradually widening. As the rock is pulled apart, large slabs sink, creating the series of rifts that run parallel to the ridge along its length. Only in a few places does the ridge emerge above the sea, most spectacularly in Iceland, the shape of which is constantly being redefined by volcanic activity.

In contrast, the floor of the Pacific Ocean [E] shows signs of many different seismic activities. It is surrounded by the so-called 'ring of fire' – volcanic zones where the oceanic plates dive below continental ones and create volcanoes. At other places, oceanic plates converge, creating trenches where one plate dives below the other, such as the Marianas Trench, the deepest place on Earth.

THE SEVEN SEAS

The phrase 'the seven seas' dates back to the seas known to Muslim voyagers before the fifteenth century. Nowadays, the waters of the world are divided into seven oceans – the North Pacific, the South Pacific, the North Atlantic, the South Atlantic, the Indian, the Arctic and the Antarctic. But divisions such as these are in reality arbitrary, as all these waters can just as easily be considered as parts of one continuous global ocean.

The Pacific Ocean
Water Area:
180,000,000 square kilometres
Volume:
724,000,000 cubic kilometres
Average Depth: 3940 metres

The Atlantic Ocean
Water Area:
106,000,000 square kilometres
Volume:
355,000,000 cubic kilometres
Average Depth: 3310 metres

The Indian Ocean
Water Area:
75,000,000 square kilometres
Volume:
292,000,000 cubic kilometres
Average Depth: 3840 metres

Marianas Trench

▼ SEA CHANGE

A coastal region [C] is shaped by the forces of longshore drift. Sand is pushed along the shore by ocean currents to build up spits [1], bars [2] and sometimes enclosing bays to form lagoons.

A river carries vast amounts of sediment out to sea, which is deposited to form a delta [3]. Under the sea, the accumulation of sediment forms the continental shelf [4], a region that slopes gently out from the coastline for about 75km, to depths of 100-200m. In places it is cut through by submarine gorges, formed either by rivers when the sea level was lower or by the undercutting effect of river currents flowing out to sea. The shelf gives way to the steep continental slope, which dives to depths of several kilometres. From the base of the slope, the continental rise extends up to 1000km from the coast into the ocean.

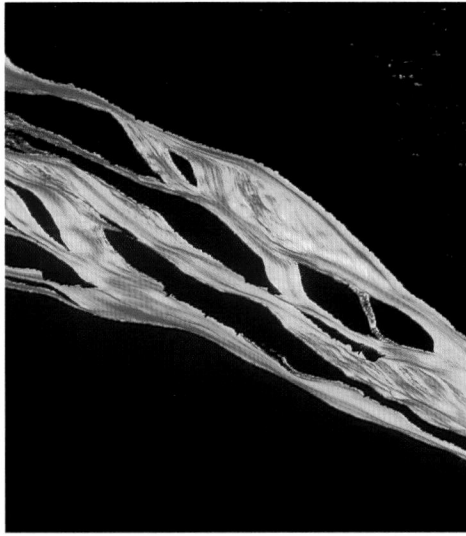

◀ Lava which erupts from the earth's surface can take on a number of forms Aa, or block lava, is runny, and quickly forms a hard pastry-like crust when it cools. Pahoehoe lava has a sheen to it like satin and often consolidates in rope-like forms. When this kind of lava comes into contact with the sea it takes on the form of a jumbled heap of pillows, hence its name pillow lava.

C

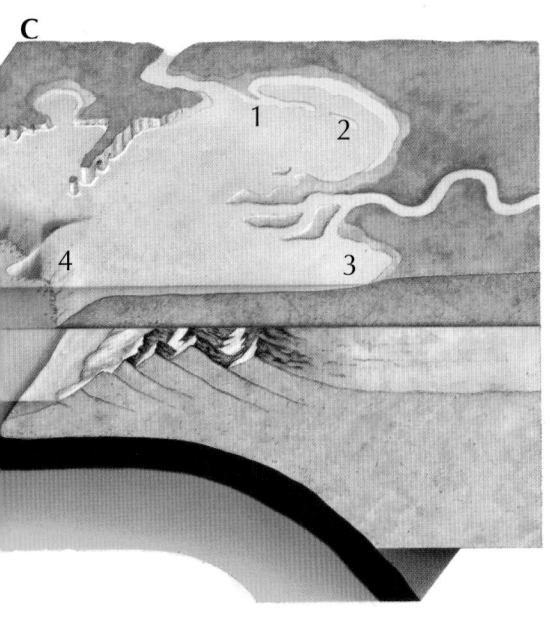

instance, lie in the middle of the Pacific Plate. This chain of volcanic mountains is caused by a semi-permanent 'hot spot' where molten magma rises from the depths of the mantle through the crust, and spews out of a volcano. Although the hot spot in the mantle is stationary, the Pacific Plate, and with it the volcano, is continually moving. Hawaii itself is only the most recent in a chain of 107 volcanic vents formed by the plume. As the plate moves on, each volcano becomes extinct, and a new one forms further along the chain. Many thousands of these 'hot spot' volcanoes are known – mostly beneath the ocean surface – so there must be hundreds of hot plumes in the mantle to have created them all.

While plates are being destroyed in the subduction zones where they collide, new plate material is being produced all the time deep beneath the ocean surface. The sea floor is just as geologically fascinating as the continental land surface, and is still awaiting full exploration.

Occasionally, the volcanic activity of the mid-oceanic ridges reaches the surface, and forms islands. At other places, hot gases venting from the depths of the Earth create pools of warmth on the ocean floor, where life can flourish.

SHAPING THE EARTH

OVER BILLIONS OF YEARS, THE HARSH landscape created by geological activity such as plate tectonics and volcanism has been softened and sculpted by the eroding forces of ice, water and air. Glaciers have ground out valleys, and rivers have carved huge gorges, including America's Grand Canyon. At the same time the steady pounding of the seas and oceans eats away and remodels coastlines.

Studies of the changing climate in the past show that the Earth has gone through periodic 'ice ages' when the ice-caps pushed into temperate regions closer to the Equator. These periods were critical in shaping the landscape that we see today – during the last Ice Age, which ended 10,000 years ago, an ice sheet covered most of Northern Europe, Asia and North America. The ice ages can be dated by drilling out an ice core from a polar cap. Each year a layer of new ice is laid down, which in colder years – during ice ages – is thicker. These records surprisingly reveal that over the last 4 million years, successive ice ages have gripped Earth for longer than the warmer periods in between.

Variations in the Earth's climate are thought to be the result of cyclical changes in its orbit, which becomes more, then less, elongated. According to these models the Earth's average temperature should currently be on the increase – which means that the measured increases in temperature cited as evidence of global warming and the greenhouse effect may have a natural cause.

Getting in shape

During the ice ages, massive glaciers formed across the globe. As these vast, slow-moving rivers of ice rolled forward, the sheer weight of ice ground down rocks in their paths, leaving a softened, altered landscape once they had retreated. These forces are still at work today: on Greenland and in Antarctica there are many glaciers which eventually find their way to the sea, where they break up into icebergs.

Although glaciers are the most dramatic form of erosion, there are others: over longer periods, rivers and seas can cut through rock and carve out valleys. Even rain has a profound cumulative effect on rock. Raindrops dissolve gases from the atmosphere and become dilute acid, chemically attacking igneous rocks formed from volcanic lava. In time, the particles broken off build up to great depths and are converted by pressure and heat into sedimentary rocks such as limestone. When these are subjected to the intense heat of the Earth's crust they become metamorphic rocks, such as marble and slate.

▼ **A WOBBLING WORLD**
The climate of the Earth is not constant but gradually varies over time in cycles of thousands of years [**B**]. The shape of the Earth's orbit around the Sun can vary between an almost perfect circle [1] and a pronounced ellipse [2] over a cycle of around 100,000 years. When the orbit is more elliptical, the climate of the Earth is more extreme. At the same time, another cycle changes the angle of tilt of the planet between a minimum 21.8° and a maximum 24.4° [**C**]. At the maximum inclination, every 22,000 years, the climate is most extreme, and the seasons are especially marked, with the Poles pointing further away from the Sun during winter. When the effects of these cycles are combined, they lead to ice ages of varying severity, the last of which ended around 10,000 years ago.

▶ **EARTH SCRAPER**
Glaciers [**A**] are dramatic rivers of ice slowly creeping down valleys and carving mountain ranges into a series of sharp peaks. They usually originate where ice or hard-packed snow builds up in a cirque [1], a basin near a mountain top. After a sufficient mass has built up, it will start to move under its own gravity, wearing down rocks by pressure, scraping and frost action, to form glacial spoil called 'moraines'. The boulders of moraine underneath the glacier act as abrasives, scouring the landscape. Lateral moraines [2] are rocks cut away and pulled along at the sides of the glacier. Where two ice-rivers meet, the lateral moraines can join to form a medial moraine [3] – a stripe of rubble down the centre of the glacier. As the glacier grinds along over rocks and boulders, the stresses induced can open up deep and jagged splits called crevasses [4]. A glacier terminates at a snout [5] which may empty into the sea, or a great lake. On dry land the shape of the snout depends on the climatic conditions, and especially the rate at which the snout melts compared with the rate at which the glacier advances. If the the two rates are exactly

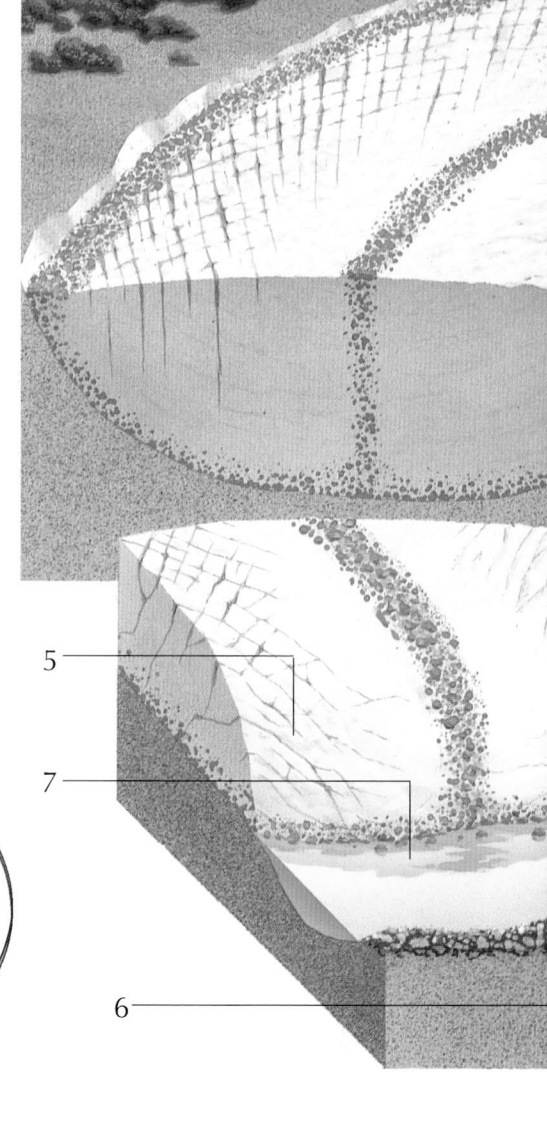

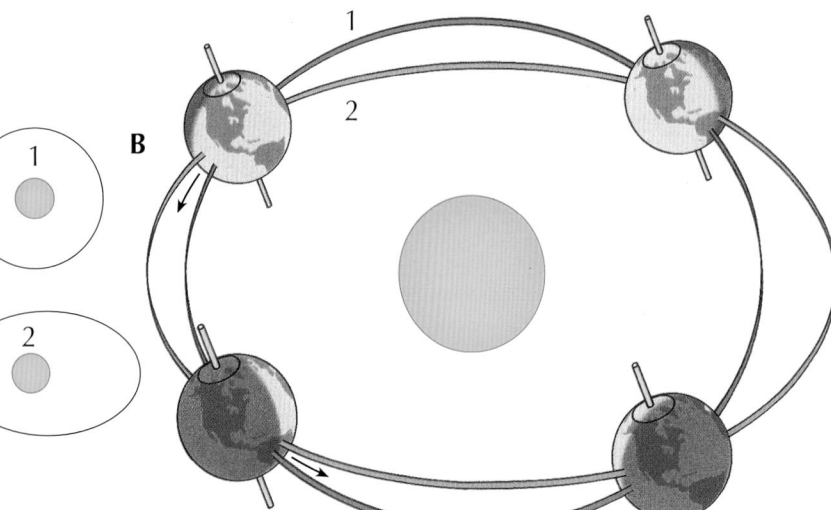

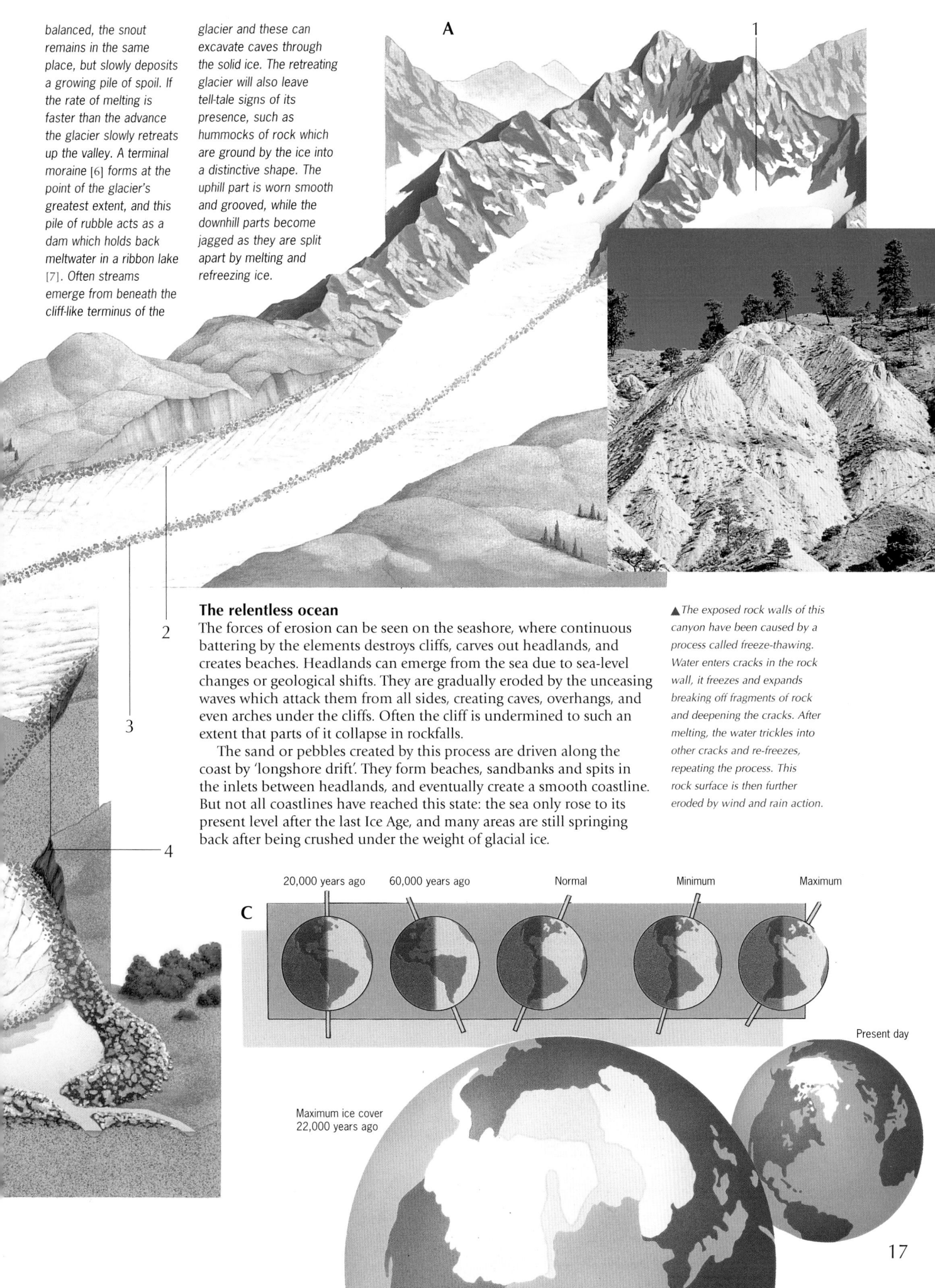

balanced, the snout remains in the same place, but slowly deposits a growing pile of spoil. If the rate of melting is faster than the advance the glacier slowly retreats up the valley. A terminal moraine [6] forms at the point of the glacier's greatest extent, and this pile of rubble acts as a dam which holds back meltwater in a ribbon lake [7]. Often streams emerge from beneath the cliff-like terminus of the glacier and these can excavate caves through the solid ice. The retreating glacier will also leave tell-tale signs of its presence, such as hummocks of rock which are ground by the ice into a distinctive shape. The uphill part is worn smooth and grooved, while the downhill parts become jagged as they are split apart by melting and refreezing ice.

A

1

2

3

4

The relentless ocean

The forces of erosion can be seen on the seashore, where continuous battering by the elements destroys cliffs, carves out headlands, and creates beaches. Headlands can emerge from the sea due to sea-level changes or geological shifts. They are gradually eroded by the unceasing waves which attack them from all sides, creating caves, overhangs, and even arches under the cliffs. Often the cliff is undermined to such an extent that parts of it collapse in rockfalls.

The sand or pebbles created by this process are driven along the coast by 'longshore drift'. They form beaches, sandbanks and spits in the inlets between headlands, and eventually create a smooth coastline. But not all coastlines have reached this state: the sea only rose to its present level after the last Ice Age, and many areas are still springing back after being crushed under the weight of glacial ice.

▲ The exposed rock walls of this canyon have been caused by a process called freeze-thawing. Water enters cracks in the rock wall, it freezes and expands breaking off fragments of rock and deepening the cracks. After melting, the water trickles into other cracks and re-freezes, repeating the process. This rock surface is then further eroded by wind and rain action.

C

20,000 years ago   60,000 years ago   Normal   Minimum   Maximum

Present day

Maximum ice cover 22,000 years ago

CONTRASTING CONDITIONS

WE TALK SO MUCH ABOUT THE WEATHER because of its infinite changeability. As the Sun's radiation heats up the Equatorial zones of the planet much more than the Polar regions, it creates wide temperature contrasts. The hottest places on Earth can be a blistering 50°C in the shade, while in the depths of an Antarctic winter, levels as low as -70°C have been recorded. This variable heat produces hot air at the Equator, which rises, while cooler air further north and south sinks under it, producing wind patterns that stretch across the globe. These in turn create swirling eddies of air that can absorb water vapour over the sea, forming clouds, and deposit it as rain over land. Such air currents couple with the variable heat of the Sun to produce the wide variety of climates found on Earth, ranging from hot, rainless deserts to cool, wet, temperate coastal regions.

The atmosphere of the Earth just after it formed was an unbreatheable mixture of hydrogen and helium. In time this was replaced by an equally unbreatheable mixture belched out from volcanoes, which in turn has been modified by lifeforms to the air we breathe today. This is made up of 78 per cent nitrogen, 21 per cent oxygen, and a small proportion of carbon dioxide, which plants then recycle into oxygen. The remainder of the atmosphere is water vapour and small traces of other gases. The balance is a delicate one, perfectly suited to life as it has evolved, and the entire planet – both living things and minerals – is needed to maintain it.

The outer limits of the atmosphere stretch 2400 km above the surface, but the lower 15km, the troposphere, is the densest, holding nearly all the atmosphere's water vapour – which condenses under different conditions to create clouds. Beyond this region, up to 40 km high, lies the stratosphere, which contains a thin ozone layer that blocks out harmful ultraviolet radiation.

Climate types

Land near the Equator has weather patterns typified by those of southern Asia. For six months of the year cold dry winds blow from the land out to sea, giving arid conditions and little rain. In the summer the wind reverses direction and starts to blow warm air off the ocean. This air is heavy with water vapour and triggers torrential rainstorms over land.

Weather in the temperate latitudes of northern Europe is dominated by the jet stream, a band of high winds at altitudes of about 12km. It forms where warm air from the tropics meets cold Polar air, creating a jet of air travelling at speeds around 200kmh in summer, 400kmh in winter. The jet stream's direction develops in a similar way to a slowly flowing river, meandering and forming eddies. These are seen as high-pressure anticyclones, wind systems that create clear, dry weather, or low pressure depressions with associated clouds and weather fronts.

The circulation patterns of the oceans are just as important in regulating climate. In general, the oceans circulate in large eddies, clockwise in the Northern Hemisphere, anticlockwise in the Southern. One of the

Hadley cell

A

▲ CREATING WINDS

The amount of heat absorbed at the Equator is much greater than at the Poles. The temperature difference creates giant circulation cells which transfer heat from the Equator to the Poles [A]. The Hadley cell is driven by hot air rising from the Equator which cools and returns to the surface at 30° latitude. Some of this returning air is drawn back towards the Equator, creating the trade winds. The Ferrel cell guides warm air towards the Poles, creating winds which
the Earth's rotation skews to become the Westerlies. Where these winds meet cold air blowing directly from the Pole, frontal depressions form giving unsettled weather. At the cell boundaries jet streams form – channels of high winds which encircle the planet. This circulation from the Equator to the Poles is complicated by the Earth's rotation, creating the Coriolis force which bends winds to the right in the Northern Hemisphere, and to the left in the Southern Hemisphere.

▶ *Deserts can be created in many ways, and they may be hot or cold. The Antarctic, being one of the driest places in the world, is classed as a cold desert. The Sahara and the Arabian Deserts are classic examples of hot deserts. The photograph shows a sand dune system in the Namib Desert in Southern Africa. Winds blowing over the land constantly shift dunes in ever changing patterns.*

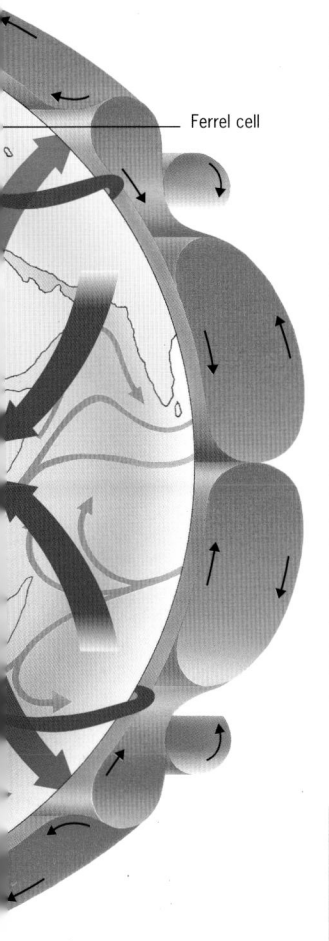

Ferrel cell

▶ *A tornado can form during a very severe thunderstorm* **[C].** *Hot air evaporating off land or sea rises rapidly through the atmosphere, condensing to form clouds. As surface air rushes inward the low pressure at the centre of the storm, the spin of the Earth makes the whole complex spin, producing a typhoon or hurricane (right). Tornadoes occur when the fast-rising thermals, which create a storm, begin to spin even more quickly, perhaps in response to the local geography. As the thermal winds up on itself, it draws a funnel of cloud down from the bottom of the storm towards the ground, where the winds often exceed 200kmh. The extreme low pressure sucks up material from the ground, flinging it out at the top of the tornado, sometimes to land several kilometres away. Waterspouts are similar vortices that form over water.*

C

▶ **VARIETY OF CLIMATE**
The patterns of rainfall and temperature around the world divide the Earth into different regions of vegetation **[B].** *Seven cities around the world illustrate the wide variety of weather these produce.*

New York has an east coast continental climate, with cold winters, hot summers and steady rainfall all year round. London's climate is marine west coast, similarly wet to New York's but with less variation between summer and winter temperatures. Omsk has typical steppe climate, with low rainfall and very cold winters followed by hot summers. Singapore's tropical climate gives almost constant hot and very wet weather. Manaus in Brazil's region of tropical savanna has constant high temperatures, with very dry summer months. A desert climate like that of Alice Springs has very high average temperatures (with a slight dip during the southern winter months), but almost no rain throughout the year. The Nigerian capital, Lagos, has a constantly hot tropical rainforest climate, characterized by its extremely wet summer months.

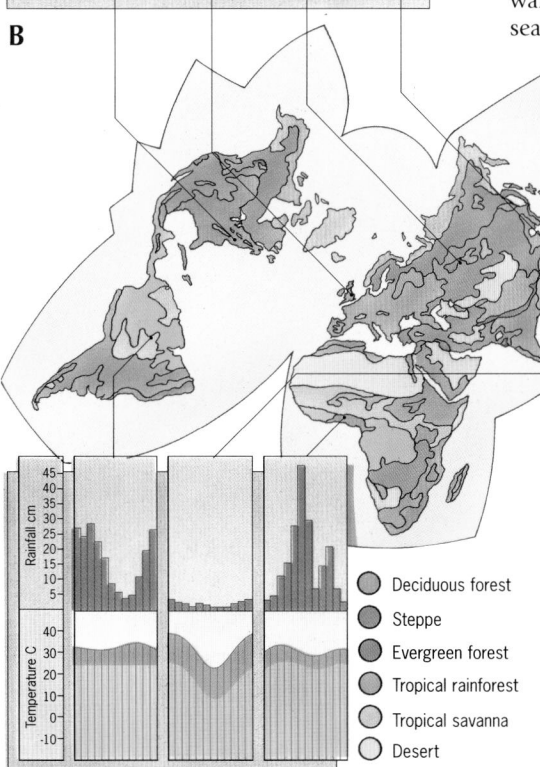

New York — London — Omsk — Singapore

Rainfall cm: 45 40 35 30 25 20 15 10 5

Temperature C: 40 30 20 10 0 -10

B

Rainfall cm: 45 40 35 30 25 20 15 10 5

Temperature C: 40 30 20 10 0 -10

Manaus — Alice Springs — Lagos

● Deciduous forest
● Steppe
● Evergreen forest
○ Tropical rainforest
○ Tropical savanna
○ Desert
○ Tundra

best-known currents is the Gulf Stream, which crosses the Atlantic towards northern Europe, moderating the climate with warm water carried from the Gulf of Mexico, counteracting the Polar air blowing over the rest of the continent.

Another example of the oceanic effect on the weather is El Niño. Normally, the circulation of the Pacific Ocean creates cold, dry weather on the west coast of South America, and rain on the east coast of Australia. Air and water currents circulate warm surface water westwards to Australia, raising sea levels and creating an upwelling of deep cold water off South America. But as the warm water spreads eastwards it destabilizes the trade winds, which reverse their direction. The ocean circulation reverses as well, with warm water off South America preventing the cold upwelling which brings up nutrients vital to fish stocks. On land, Australia experiences drought, and South America suffers torrential rain. Such drastic climatic changes show how delicate the balance is between climate and the environment.

Major volcanic eruptions can also affect the climate, throwing dust particles high into the upper atmosphere, where they block out sunlight. Sudden climate changes are believed to have caused mass extinction of life on Earth in the past, and as yet there is little humanity can do to counter, or even predict, these changes.

PEOPLING THE GLOBE

THE ORIGINS OF HUMANKIND ARE VERY HARD TO DETERMINE. The fossil record of our ancestors is very patchy, and thus the story involves large amounts of guesswork. Archaeologists believe that between 7 and 10 million years ago, a human ancestor, called Ramapithecus, developed from the same stock as chimpanzees and gorillas. The route from these creatures to modern man can be traced in terms of changing skeletons. Bipedal motion required a sturdy pelvis, while the increasing intelligence of these progenitors can be followed through increasing brain capacities. Ramapithecus was succeeded by Australopithecus, whose later form is named Homo habilis, the handy man, because fossil evidence shows that it used simple tools.

Homo erectus appeared in Africa 1.7 million years ago and spread to the rest of the world roughly 1 million years ago. They were almost as tall as modern humans, with skull capacities twice as large as Homo habilis. This species lived longer in Asia than in Africa – it includes Peking Man, who lived 250,000 years ago. It was gradually succeeded by our species, Homo sapiens, which appeared in Africa more than 500,000 years ago. The expansion was a slow drift as bands of hunter-gatherers followed prey animals. There can have been no population pressure: 10,000 years ago the world population was between 5 and 10 million, about the population of New York City today. As people settled in various places, climate and food sources led them to evolve differently. For example, those in very hot Equatorial countries kept a dark skin to protect them from ultraviolet sunlight; those in colder climates developed lighter skins to maximize the effect of a weaker sun – vitamin D, essential to bone growth, is gained from sunlight.

At first only Africa, Asia and the warmer parts of Europe were colonized: America and Australia remained empty for thousands of years. Movement between continental land masses was made possible by climate changes. During the last Ice Age, much of the world's water was locked into the ice caps. Sea levels dropped dramatically, what is now the Bering Strait became a land passage, and vast stretches of ocean became navigable by small boats.

Hunters to farmers

For two million years, human ancestors lived as hunter-gatherers, following a nomadic pattern of life, with a diet of animals and seasonal fruits. This changed between 20,000 and 10,000 years ago with the development of agriculture. About 15,000 years ago, as temperatures rose, primitive

▼ THE ICE AGE

In the Ice Age, parts of Europe were covered in glacial sheets and the North Sea was a great plain [A]. The climate and terrain were very like Alaska today, and herds of reindeer roamed the area. These were a main food source for groups of hunter-gatherers, traces of whom have been found in Europe, mostly in the warmer areas (southern Spain, south-west France and along main rivers). These people followed the deer herds on their grazing migrations, augmenting their diet with small game as well as vegetables, berries and grains. As the climate became warmer various groups settled near coasts to become fisher-gatherers.

A

● Hunter-gatherers
● Fisher-gatherers

◄ HOMO SAPIENS

From central and southern Africa Homo sapiens spread out to populate the whole world [B]. The first migration spread from Africa eastwards across to Asia. Routes branched off to northern Africa and southern Europe. A second wave occurred 15,000 years ago, when glaciation provided a land bridge across the Bering Strait, allowing movement from northern Asia to the Americas.

B

● Evidence of Homo sapiens

▲ Prehistoric Americans

C

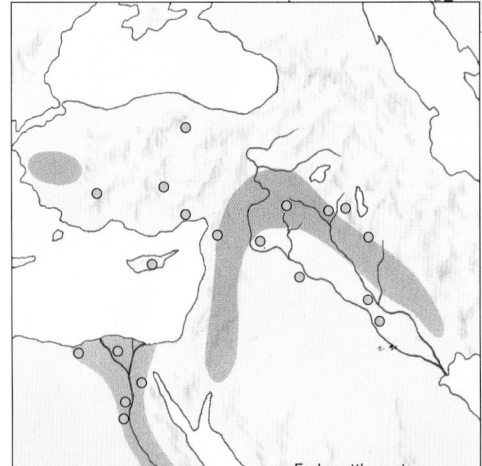

○ Early settlements

◄ THE FIRST FARMERS

The first farming settlements, which developed into the first cities, were probably founded around 10,000 years ago in the 'Fertile Crescent' [C], a band of land stretching from the Mediterranean to the rivers Tigris and Euphrates, in modern Jordan, Lebanon, Syria, Turkey and Iraq. Civilisation also flowered along the banks of the river Nile, similarly suited to agriculture. From simple farmsteads grew villages, towns, cities and eventually whole civilisations.

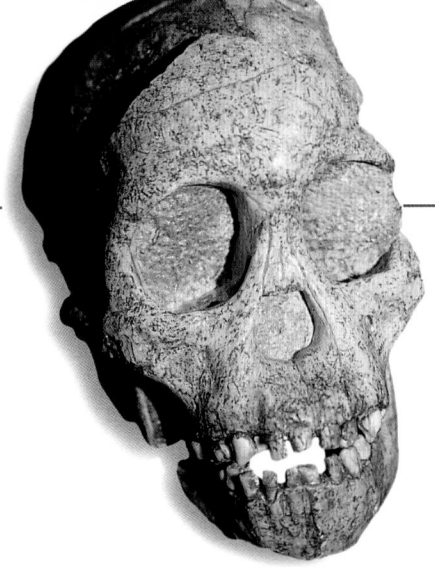

▲ This skull of Australopithicus africanus *is over 2 million years old.* Africanus *was the first hominid to leave the forest for the open plain.*

farming practices began to appear wherever the climate allowed it. The most important of these were Mesopotamia, the crescent between the rivers Tigris and Euphrates in modern Iraq, south-eastern Turkey and eastern Syria, the Nile valley, Central America and north-east China. Once wandering groups settled down the population soared, increasing from 5 to 300 million in 8000 years.

Small farming settlements developed into villages, then towns, then cities. Social and political organisations developed to control large groups of people. Gradually, the great civilisations grew, in the fertile fields of these first settlements. Along the Nile Valley, the Egyptians started to build a sophisticated culture around 3000BC, at the same time as the Sumerians were developing a system of city states in Mesopotamia. Similar civilisations appeared in China and Central America. Influences from these civilisations rippled outwards, laying down the pattern for the shape of the modern world.

▶ **OUT OF AFRICA**
It is now considered that the ancestors of humankind first appeared in Africa **[D]**. As well as indications of early Homo sapiens, the evidence for Africa's claims to be the cradle of humanity comes from fossils of Australopithecus and Homo erectus found in South Africa, Olduvai Gorge in Kenya, and Ethiopia. These are older than any others so far discovered in the world and so it seems likely that the human beings who evolved in Africa gradually spread out to

other parts of the world. This is corroborated by fossils of a later date found in India, Java and China which indicate the direction of migration out of Africa. Early Homo sapiens fossils have also been found in China, southern Europe, North and South America and the Middle East. In Europe, the fossils found so far are confined to early forms of Homo sapiens and Neanderthal man, whose traces have been found in Germany, Hungary, France, Belgium, Greece, Czechoslovakia, Russia and the Middle East.

D

△ Homo erectus
▲ Homo habilis
● Australopithecus
■ Early paleolithic

E

○ Caucasian
○ Mongol
○ Negroid
○ Indian/Caucasian
○ Aboriginal
○ Caucasian/Mongol
○ Negroid/Caucasian

▲ **FIRST MIGRATIONS**
Human beings it seems could not stay long in one place **[E]**. At first, migrations were slow and took place over thousands of years. From their African prototype, people adapted physically, in response to extremes of climate, gradually evolving

into the various races that populate the world today. These races developed in certain areas, as shown on the map above, however, the forces of the modern world from the age of discovery onwards created later movements that have spread people around the world. These modern migrations, some voluntary, others enforced as in the slave trade, are also shown.

THE POPULATION EXPLOSION

THERE ARE 6 BILLION PEOPLE IN THE WORLD TODAY. This figure is rising at a rate of 140 million each year, an increase of more than the population of Japan. But until comparatively recently, the rate of increase of the world population was low. Two thousand years ago, there were an estimated 300 million people on Earth; by 1650 this had increased to a mere 500 million. Then in only 200 years this number had doubled, and in the 150 years since then it has increased five-fold. In spite of recurrent famine and war, the world population seems set on an inexorable upward curve, doubling every 39 years.

This population explosion is a result of social developments since the Industrial Revolution. Proportionally there are the same number of births each year – or perhaps fewer. But the advances of improved sanitation and nutrition made possible by the industrial and scientific advances of the 18th and 19th centuries meant that fewer babies died at birth and that people lived longer.

At first these changes were confined to the countries of the developed world, in Europe and America, but as they have spread around the world, the population has ballooned. Now in most European countries the population remains stable, mainly because of the availability of reliable contraception. Indeed, in some countries the birth rate has fallen below the number needed to maintain stability; this will result in a top-heavy 'age pyramid', with too many grandparents and not enough grandchildren to support them. Some countries, such as France and Sweden, have tried to encourage people to have more babies through maternity payments and tax discounts for large families.

In the developing world the situation is different. There are many cultural and religious objections to the use of contraception. In a traditional agricultural community, too, a large family was desirable. As well as ensuring that the parents would have surviving children to look after them, many children provided a workforce to farm the land. But fewer people now live on the land, as farming becomes mechanized; and a large family in an urban industrialized setting just creates more mouths to feed. China, the most populated country in the world, has solved the problem, rationing families to one child each.

The rush to the cities

All over the world, more people live in cities than in the country, because it is no longer possible to make a living working on the land.
As a consequence cities have proliferated. The process is not a new one: after the Industrial Revolution industrial towns gradually expanded until they merged to form huge conurbations. In terms of population density, a vast swathe of northern Europe

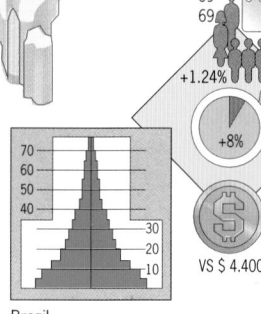

United States
VS $ 28.020

59
69
+1.24%
+8%
Brazil
VS $ 4.400

▲ GLOBAL POPULATION
The global population is distributed in clumps and clusters around the world. In hotter countries, most people live on a narrow ribbon along the coast, leaving vast arid inner tracts of land underpopulated. In cooler countries, the population is able to spread itself more evenly about the landmass. The map makes clear the huge numbers of people living all across China and India, in contrast with the comparatively sparse population of much of the United States. The graphics around illustration [A] show for each continent the rate of population growth, the average longevity of men and women, the gross national product per capita (a measure of wealth), and the calorific intake per

head as a percentage of an adult's average daily requirement. These illustrate the gap in health and wealth between the developed world and the developing nations.

B
>100 — No of people per sq. km.
11-100
8-10
<2
A

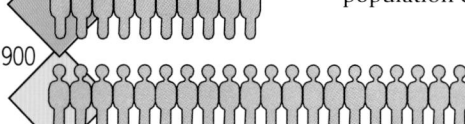

1750
1900
2000
D

▲ GROWTH 1750–2000
The growth of the human population can be shown [D] by demonstrating the number of people that would occupy each 2km² of land of the Earth's surface at various eras: 1750, 1900 and an estimation of the figure for the year 2000.

▶ POPULATION GROWTH
The Earth's population has swollen from a mere 250 million 1000 years ago (roughly the present-day population of the United States) to 6 billion today.

For most of the intervening period growth was very slow, and there were even slight declines caused by plagues

such as the Black Death. However, from about the time of the Industrial Revolution the rate of growth increased, accelerating further with each improvement in hygiene and healthcare.

A graph of world population growth over the past 300 years [C] can be split to show how the relative increases in

each continent have been staggered. Throughout recorded history, the population of Asia has been greater than that of all the other continents combined. However, during the 19th century the population of Europe grew at twice the rate of Asia's, thanks mainly to the improvements in living conditions brought about by

scientific advances and the Industrial Revolution. This rate of growth has slowed in Europe this century, whereas that of Asia has accelerated spectacularly – its population seems likely to have tripled in the fifty years from 1950. Over the last two centuries the populations of North and South America have been

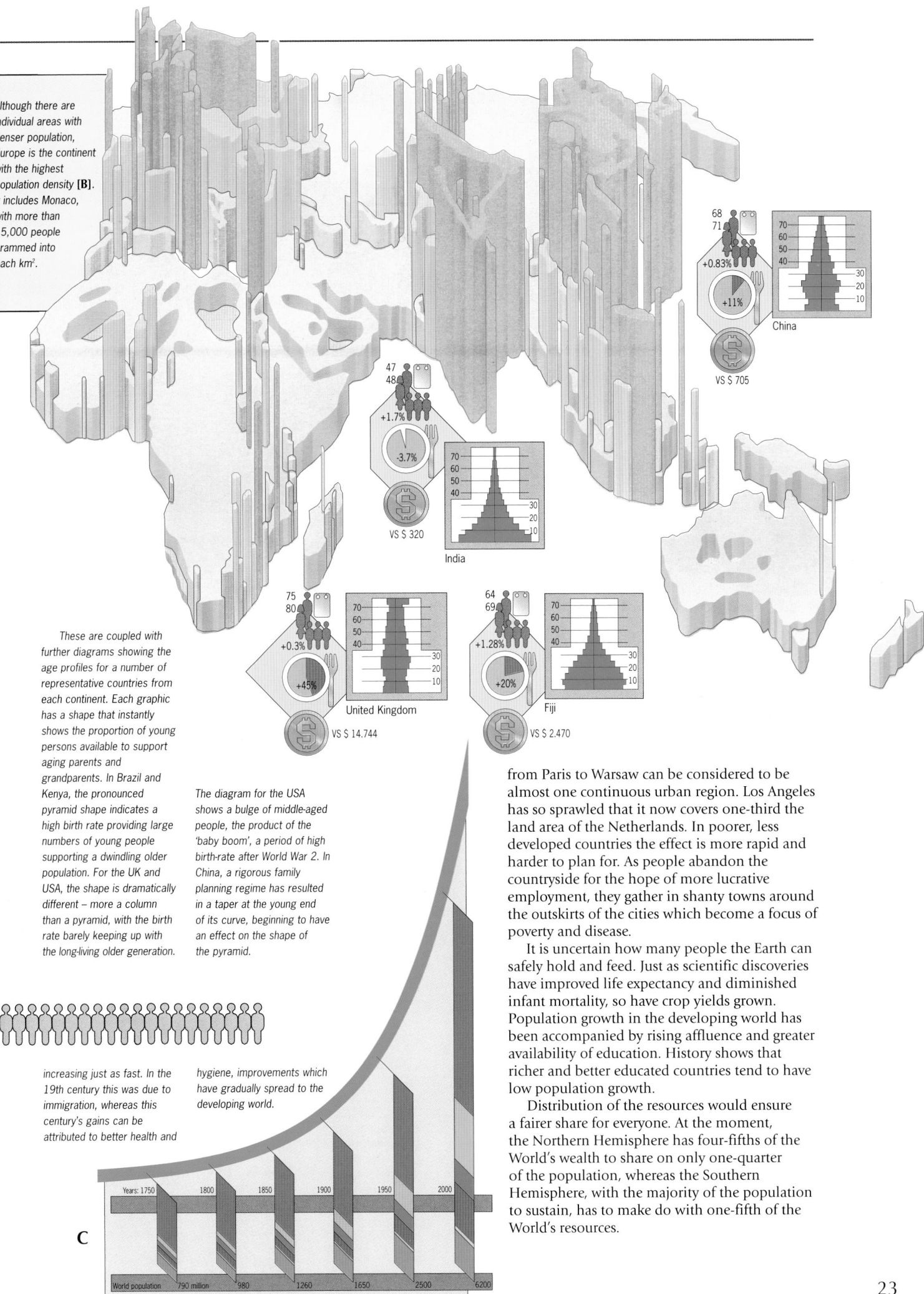

[B]

Although there are individual areas with denser population, Europe is the continent with the highest population density [B]. It includes Monaco, with more than 15,000 people crammed into each km².

These are coupled with further diagrams showing the age profiles for a number of representative countries from each continent. Each graphic has a shape that instantly shows the proportion of young persons available to support aging parents and grandparents. In Brazil and Kenya, the pronounced pyramid shape indicates a high birth rate providing large numbers of young people supporting a dwindling older population. For the UK and USA, the shape is dramatically different – more a column than a pyramid, with the birth rate barely keeping up with the long-living older generation.

The diagram for the USA shows a bulge of middle-aged people, the product of the 'baby boom', a period of high birth-rate after World War 2. In China, a rigorous family planning regime has resulted in a taper at the young end of its curve, beginning to have an effect on the shape of the pyramid.

increasing just as fast. In the 19th century this was due to immigration, whereas this century's gains can be attributed to better health and hygiene, improvements which have gradually spread to the developing world.

China — 68 / 71 — +0.83% — +11% — VS $ 705

India — 47 / 48 — +1.7% — -3.7% — VS $ 320

United Kingdom — 75 / 80 — +0.3% — +45% — VS $ 14.744

Fiji — 64 / 69 — +1.28% — +20% — VS $ 2.470

from Paris to Warsaw can be considered to be almost one continuous urban region. Los Angeles has so sprawled that it now covers one-third the land area of the Netherlands. In poorer, less developed countries the effect is more rapid and harder to plan for. As people abandon the countryside for the hope of more lucrative employment, they gather in shanty towns around the outskirts of the cities which become a focus of poverty and disease.

It is uncertain how many people the Earth can safely hold and feed. Just as scientific discoveries have improved life expectancy and diminished infant mortality, so have crop yields grown. Population growth in the developing world has been accompanied by rising affluence and greater availability of education. History shows that richer and better educated countries tend to have low population growth.

Distribution of the resources would ensure a fairer share for everyone. At the moment, the Northern Hemisphere has four-fifths of the World's wealth to share on only one-quarter of the population, whereas the Southern Hemisphere, with the majority of the population to sustain, has to make do with one-fifth of the World's resources.

C

Years:	1750	1800	1850	1900	1950	2000
World population	790 million	980	1260	1650	2500	6200

MODERN COUNTRIES HAVE BEEN SHAPED POLITICALLY by many forces and movements, the most important being religion and language. Religion has been a central aspect of human society since before the earliest written records – fertility sculptures dating from the Ice Age indicate a need to recognize and pacify a spirit that brought forth the sun and rain, made crops grow and ensured a plentiful supply of food. The ancient Near-Eastern civilisations, particularly Egypt, had a multitude of different gods for each aspect of human life or death. This polytheism was continued in the Greek and Roman traditions, in contrast with monotheism, belief in a single all-powerful god, exemplified by Judaism and first recorded around 1200BC.

Today there are eleven major formal religions in the world: Christianity; Judaism; Islam; Hinduism; Buddhism and Jainism; Zoroastrianism; Confucianism; Taoism; Shinto and Sikhism. Of these Christianity is the most widespread, with over a billion followers. It has three major divisions: Roman Catholic, Protestant and Greek Orthodox, and 300 different denominations.

Christianity staked a political claim very early in the history of the developed world, being adopted as the official religion of the Roman Empire in AD324 by the emperor Constantine. The religion instantly changed from being a local Near-Eastern cult to the majority religion of Europe. It became more widespread over 1000 years later through the zeal of European colonists. The Portuguese and Spanish took Catholicism to South America, while the French, English and Dutch brought a variety of denominations to North America. The British took Anglicanism to Africa, India and China and the Dutch took Calvinism to South Africa and Malaysia.

More than words

There are over 3000 spoken languages in the world, a figure that does not include dialects. Of these, just over 100 have more than a million speakers, and only 13 have over 50 million speakers. Some of these are spoken by very large numbers of people (more than 800 million people speak Mandarin Chinese) concentrated in one country. Others – notably Portuguese, Spanish and English – are spoken in many places as a result of the colonial past. Just as explorers brought their religion with them, they also brought their language. Languages spread across the world through different mechanisms today. The growth of international trade has meant that a few languages – mostly English, and to a lesser extent French, Spanish and German – have become standard for business.

The film, television and music industries have been instrumental in making American English understood almost worldwide. American English is also the language of electronics and computing.
As electronic communication grows through the Internet and other networks, it is interesting to speculate on what will happen to language in the freedom of cyberspace; perhaps a new, worldwide lingua franca of the Internet will emerge, allowing everyone to communicate as long as they have the technology.

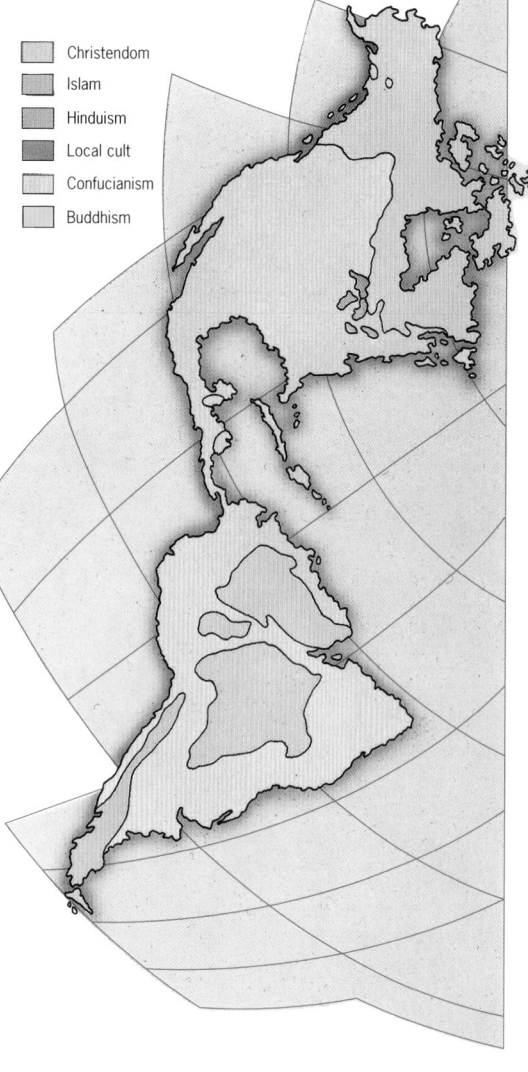

▲ MAIN BELIEF SYSTEMS
The main illustration shows the distribution of the adherents to the main belief systems of the world [A]. The areas that carry no shading are not dominated by any of these main systems of belief: this does not mean that they are free of religion, merely that they are dominated by local or tribal traditions.

Key:
- Christendom
- Islam
- Hinduism
- Local cult
- Confucianism
- Buddhism

► SPREAD OF RELIGIONS
The great religions all originated in a comparatively small area of the globe [B], but have spread in different directions to be practised by the majority of the world's population.

Hinduism and Buddhism are the world's oldest religions. Hinduism arose in prehistoric India. Strictly speaking it is not a single religion, but a group of different bodies of belief. Today there are roughly 733 million Hindus worldwide.

Buddhism was founded in the 6th century BC, also in India, but spread eastwards and is now practised in various forms all over East Asia with large numbers of adherents in Tibet, China and Japan. The number of Buddhists in the world has been estimated at 315 million.

Judaism can be traced from before 1200BC. Jewish people have spread sorldwide from Israel, partly driven by periodic persecution. In particular, during the Nazi holocaust, 6 million Jews perished. Today Jews number 18 million worldwide.

Islam was was created in Arabia in the 7th century, and spread through migration, conversion and conquest. There are an estimated 1 billion Muslims worldwide.

Christianity, which also began in Palestine as a Jewish sect, has spread most around the world, through conquest and conversion. Today it is the most popular religion worldwide, the different denominations numbering 1.8 billion adherents.

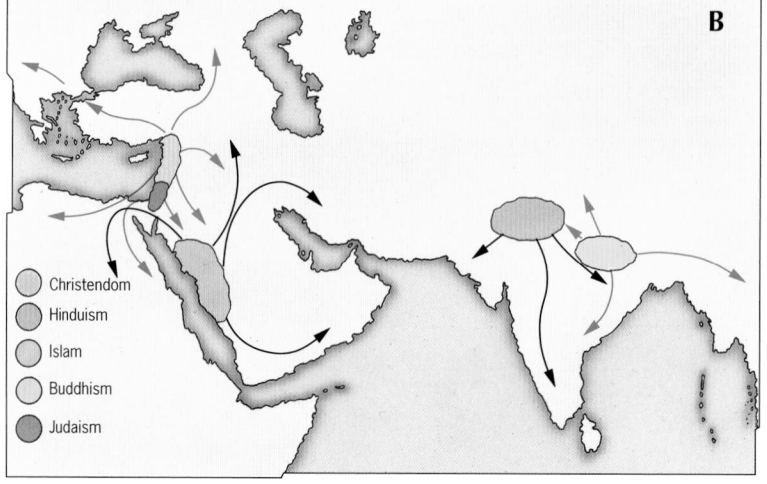

B

Key:
- Christendom
- Hinduism
- Islam
- Buddhism
- Judaism

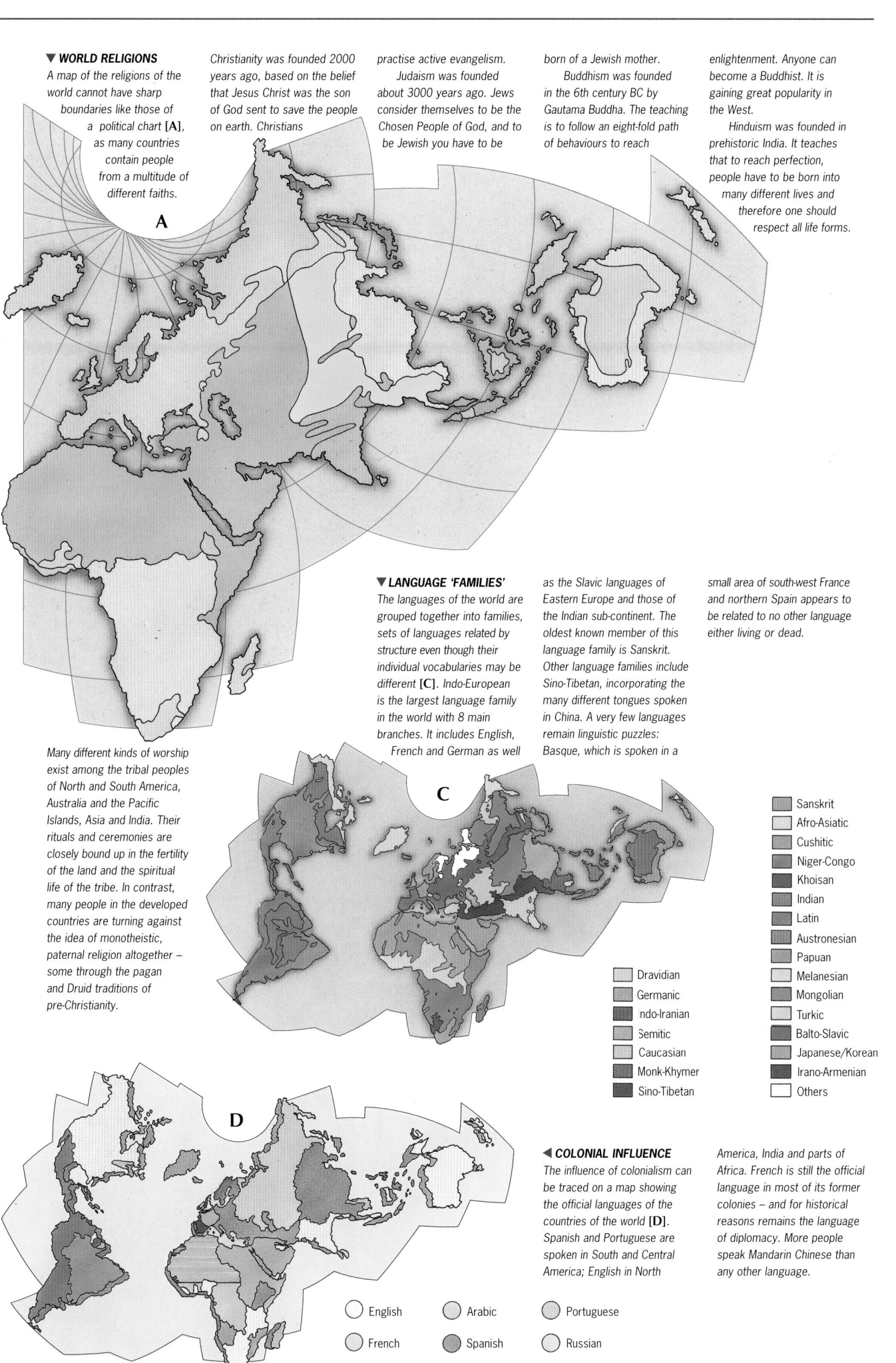

▼ WORLD RELIGIONS

A map of the religions of the world cannot have sharp boundaries like those of a political chart [A], as many countries contain people from a multitude of different faiths.

A

Christianity was founded 2000 years ago, based on the belief that Jesus Christ was the son of God sent to save the people on earth. Christians practise active evangelism.

Judaism was founded about 3000 years ago. Jews consider themselves to be the Chosen People of God, and to be Jewish you have to be born of a Jewish mother.

Buddhism was founded in the 6th century BC by Gautama Buddha. The teaching is to follow an eight-fold path of behaviours to reach enlightenment. Anyone can become a Buddhist. It is gaining great popularity in the West.

Hinduism was founded in prehistoric India. It teaches that to reach perfection, people have to be born into many different lives and therefore one should respect all life forms.

Many different kinds of worship exist among the tribal peoples of North and South America, Australia and the Pacific Islands, Asia and India. Their rituals and ceremonies are closely bound up in the fertility of the land and the spiritual life of the tribe. In contrast, many people in the developed countries are turning against the idea of monotheistic, paternal religion altogether – some through the pagan and Druid traditions of pre-Christianity.

▼ LANGUAGE 'FAMILIES'

The languages of the world are grouped together into families, sets of languages related by structure even though their individual vocabularies may be different [C]. Indo-European is the largest language family in the world with 8 main branches. It includes English, French and German as well as the Slavic languages of Eastern Europe and those of the Indian sub-continent. The oldest known member of this language family is Sanskrit. Other language families include Sino-Tibetan, incorporating the many different tongues spoken in China. A very few languages remain linguistic puzzles: Basque, which is spoken in a small area of south-west France and northern Spain appears to be related to no other language either living or dead.

C

- Dravidian
- Germanic
- Indo-Iranian
- Semitic
- Caucasian
- Monk-Khymer
- Sino-Tibetan

- Sanskrit
- Afro-Asiatic
- Cushitic
- Niger-Congo
- Khoisan
- Indian
- Latin
- Austronesian
- Papuan
- Melanesian
- Mongolian
- Turkic
- Balto-Slavic
- Japanese/Korean
- Irano-Armenian
- Others

D

◀ COLONIAL INFLUENCE

The influence of colonialism can be traced on a map showing the official languages of the countries of the world [D]. Spanish and Portuguese are spoken in South and Central America; English in North America, India and parts of Africa. French is still the official language in most of its former colonies – and for historical reasons remains the language of diplomacy. More people speak Mandarin Chinese than any other language.

- English
- French
- Arabic
- Spanish
- Portuguese
- Russian

THE WORLD AT WORK

THE DEVELOPMENT OF SOCIETY can be looked at as a series of industrial revolutions, as man has learned to use the Earth's resources. Ancient history divides up into three such stages: the Stone Age, when humans first learned to make stone tools and began to practise agriculture; the Bronze Age, when pure metals were first refined and used; and the Iron Age, when man discovered how to extract iron from rock and cast or forge it into tools and weapons.

The greatest industrial leaps have come in the past three centuries. New scientific discoveries led to the construction of the first steam engines, which transformed industry as well as transport. Iron was then overtaken by steel, and the chemical and electrical industries developed. Plastics, electrical transistors and silicon chips became part of everyday life. Each new wave of industries has had a far-reaching effect on society: employment rises and falls, new methods of transport become available and global trade opens up. With each 'revolution' a world economy is brought closer, fuelling an ever-increasing demand for energy.

The source of power

The first Industrial Revolution depended on coal to produce the iron and fire the steam engines. Today, the vast majority of the world's energy still comes from fossil fuels such as coal, oil and natural gas which are a finite resource. Coal is still burnt to generate electricity, supplying about 28 per cent of our total energy needs. The internal combustion engine has created an insatiable demand for petroleum. Today, oil reserves supply 40 per cent of the world's energy, and natural gas 20 per cent. As well as being a finite resource, fossil fuels are a major source of pollution, contributing to the greenhouse effect and the global warming that it brings. In the long term, other sources of energy will have to be found.

Energy alternatives

Nuclear power comes from the splitting of heavy uranium atoms, accompanied by the release of energy in a process called 'fission'. In many countries this energy has been harnessed to electricity needs, but there are many problems, particularly the long-term storage of waste products. Research continues into nuclear fusion, the process which powers the Sun. Although much more difficult to achieve, this could be a cleaner way of generating cheap energy. There are pollution-free energy sources. Hydro-electric power is used in countries such as Switzerland, where water provides more than half of all energy requirements, but it can have a great impact on the environment, flooding valleys and destroying eco-systems. Tidal power exploits the energy of the sea in a similar way. Windmills were one of our earliest sources of power. Today, wind-farms are sited on exposed coasts or on offshore spits, and some countries hope to be able to generate 10–20 per cent of energy needs in this way in the next decade or so. California, for instance, has tens of thousands of wind turbines.

The demand for energy is highest in the USA and western Europe, which are heavily industrialized and also have a large consumer society. At the same time, increasing consumption of oil has led to the rise in power and wealth of Middle-Eastern countries where two-thirds of the world's reserves are located.

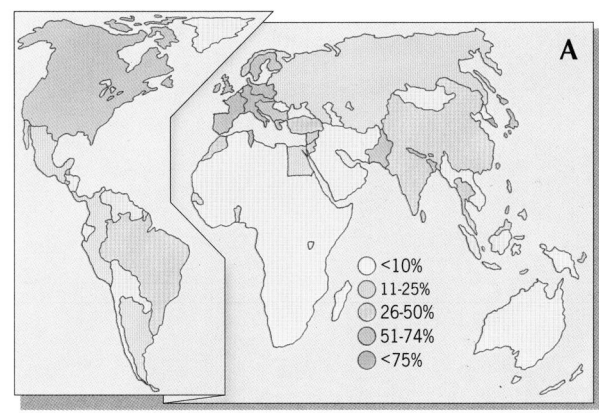

A

○ <10%
◐ 11-25%
◑ 26-50%
◕ 51-74%
● <75%

▲ **THE GLOBAL ECONOMY**
The engine-houses of today's global economy are those countries that produce the most consumer goods. Map **[A]** is shaded according to the percentage of each country's total exports that are manufactured goods. It clearly demonstrates that the most successful manufacturing economies are concentrated in the richer northern hemisphere of the world. Almost the whole of Europe and North America have figures over 50%, but the best performers are in Central Europe and the Far East. These include traditionally industrial nations, such as Germany and Japan, as well as fast -growing economies like Korea, Taiwan and the

Czech Republic.
The world's biggest producers of food are its largest countries in terms of area and population. However, although there is an overall excess of food, some countries, particularly in Africa, are still susceptible to famine. The reasons for this are both political and environmental. Traditionally farmed areas of land are often cleared to make way for so-called 'cash crops', and instead of using the land for self-sufficiency, an export-driven economy is created, with newly-displaced farmers to support. At the other extreme, the United States farms staple crops successfully on a massive scale, producing surpluses which can then be sold on to smaller countries.

◀ **ENERGY**
The driving-force of an economy is energy, **[B]** so the balance between the energy a country produces – in the form of coal, oil and other fuels – and the amount it consumes is vital. This table shows the ratio for the main regions of the world. In many areas the balance is even, but some, such as Europe, produce 12% of world energy, but consume 17%.

▲ Wind turbines, pictured here in Palm Springs in California USA, are being viewed as an increasingly viable way of producing energy. Europe, especially Holland and Germany, has a number of these eco-friendly farms.

Product of Consumption

United States	— Consumption — Product
Russia	
Asia	
Europe	
Middle East	
Japan	▪ Coal
Africa	▪ Gas
Australia	□ Oil
	□ Water
	▤ Nuclear energy

B

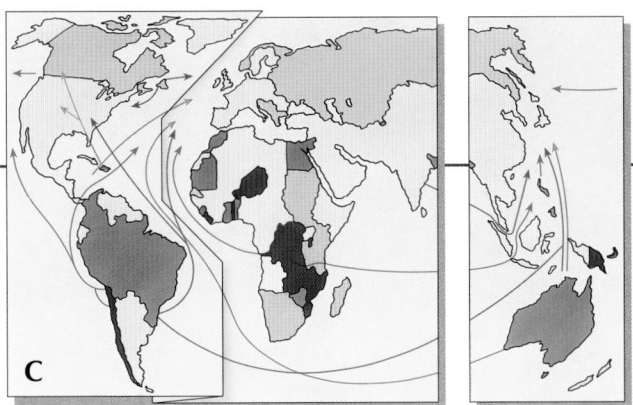

Copper →
Iron →
Bauxite →

| 5-9% | >50% |
| >5% | 10-49% |

C

▲ MINERALS

Mineral deposits can often be the key to a nation's economy **[C]**. Jamaica has extensive bauxite and alumina deposits – the raw material for the production of aluminium – which account for almost half the country's total exports.

Mineral deposits are not only valued for their practical uses: gemstones can also bring in considerable income. Central and Southern Africa were the world's largest producers but are now threatened by the deposits in Australia, and those in Russia which have yet to be fully exploited, but which could flood and destabilize the market. If in the future the market is flooded with Russian diamonds, the market could collapse.

Many other minerals and metal ores are concentrated only in rocks which have undergone extensive weathering, or around mountain ranges, which have seen intense metamorphic processes in the past.

The Industrial Revolution, which began in Britain, soon spread through the rest of Europe. Apart from America, the industrialisation of the rest of the world was the result of investment by colonial European powers, taking advantage of cheap labour and raw materials, and faster, cheaper transport which turned the world into a single complex economy.

In the last fifty years the rest of the world has also developed major industries, overtaking the West. Japan became one of the world's great economic powers by heavy investment in new technology, and other nations are following its example. The pattern is now reversed as Far-Eastern companies open manufacturing plants in the West to provide goods for the lucrative consumer markets. Often, these plants assemble imported components, but they also provide access to the major economic blocs, such as the United States and the European Union, which impose quotas and tariffs on imported goods.

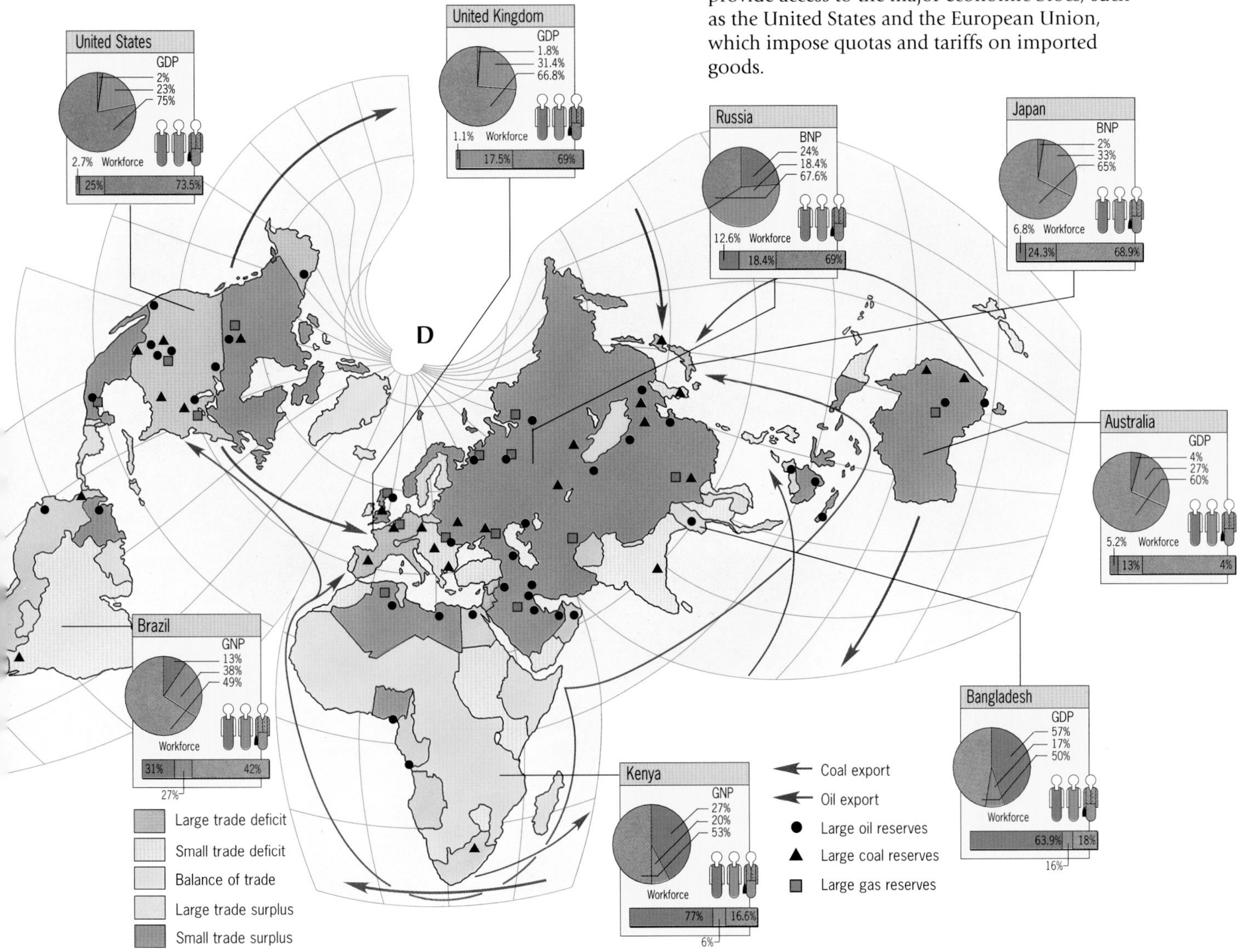

United States
GDP
2%
23%
75%
2.7% Workforce
25% | 73.5%

United Kingdom
GDP
1.8%
31.4%
66.8%
1.1% Workforce
17.5% | 69%

Russia
BNP
24%
18.4%
67.6%
12.6% Workforce
18.4% | 69%

Japan
BNP
2%
33%
65%
6.8% Workforce
24.3% | 68.9%

D

Australia
GDP
4%
27%
60%
5.2% Workforce
13% | 4%

Brazil
GNP
13%
38%
49%
Workforce
31% | 42%
27%

Bangladesh
GDP
57%
17%
50%
Workforce
63.9% | 18%
16%

Kenya
GNP
27%
20%
53%
Workforce
77% | 16.6%
6%

← Coal export
← Oil export
● Large oil reserves
▲ Large coal reserves
■ Large gas reserves

Large trade deficit
Small trade deficit
Balance of trade
Large trade surplus
Small trade surplus

▲ THE LABOUR FORCE

The relative economic development of various countries can be seen by comparing the numbers of people employed in different types of work, and the contribution to the gross domestic product (GDP) made by each **[D]**. Developing countries such as Bangladesh have a high proportion of labour involved in agriculture, which is responsible for a comparatively high proportion of GDP. Nigeria is similar, but its extensive oil reserves account for a higher industrial contribution to GDP.

As countries make more use of natural resources, more of the population is employed in heavy industry, creating more wealth, while improvements in agriculture lead to increased efficiency, and a reduction in the numbers employed. The agricultural output tends to remain steady, so that its contribution as a percentage of GDP decreases. In the most developed nations the majority of the workforce is employed in the manufacture and service sectors.

The graphics in the illustration **[C]** show the labour forces of several countries. The bar at the bottom gives the percentage involved in the agricultural (brown), industrial (blue) and service (grey) sectors, while the pie chart shows the contribution that each of these sectors makes to the GDP of that country.

ON THE MOVE

Once the majority of humanity had settled down into permanent villages, towns and cities, they began to devise ways to travel between them to trade and treaty. It was quickly realized that whoever controlled trade routes or devised the quickest means of transport would be at an advantage. Just as today, communications were all-important.

At first, people could only move as far as they could walk in a day, at most 32km. Around 8000 years ago, as farming was becoming established, some domesticated animals were employed as a means of transport. This did not make travel much faster, but enabled more goods to be carried or pulled along on sleds.

The great transportation breakthrough was of course the wheel, which was invented about 5000 years ago somewhere in the eastern Mediterranean. The earliest known example of wheeled transport is an Egyptian chariot, built about 2000BC. Horsedrawn chariots formed a rapid transport communications network in all the great empires and kingdoms, where rulers needed to know what was going on all over their territory.

Chariots could go faster if they had straight roads to run along. The first road network was established c1122BC in China under the emperor Chou, but the most famous road system, traces of which still exist today, was established in the Roman Empire. In engineering terms, probably the most impressive road system was built by the Incas of Peru. Built entirely of dry stone, the 4800km system wound over the steep slopes of the western Andes. These roads were for messengers on horse or foot: the Incas never used the wheel for transport.

Ships and the sea

The development of sea travel parallels that of roads. Empires that needed good internal communications along roads also needed to reach trading partners quickly and efficiently by sea. The oar was developed around the same time and in the same part of the world as the wheel. At once a propellant and a steering device, the oar made it possible to control speed and direction.
The Phoenicians, a people from the eastern Mediterranean, combined oars with sail power in the galley, a long ship powered by a row of oars along each side. This eventually developed into the the Greek and Roman trireme, with three rows of oars on each side, which needed 200 rowers to power it.

Between the 14th and the 17th centuries ships and sea trading shaped the world. In 1300 northern European shipbuilders invented the rudder: before that, ships had been steered by a set of oars at the stern. In the mid-1400s, the Portuguese developed the three-masted ship, which at once increased sail-power, but kept the sails small enough to be easily handled. From the 15th to 17th centuries, these ships were used and developed by many nations, and oceans were criss-crossed by Portuguese, Dutch, Spanish and English ships claiming new colonies and discovering new trade routes.

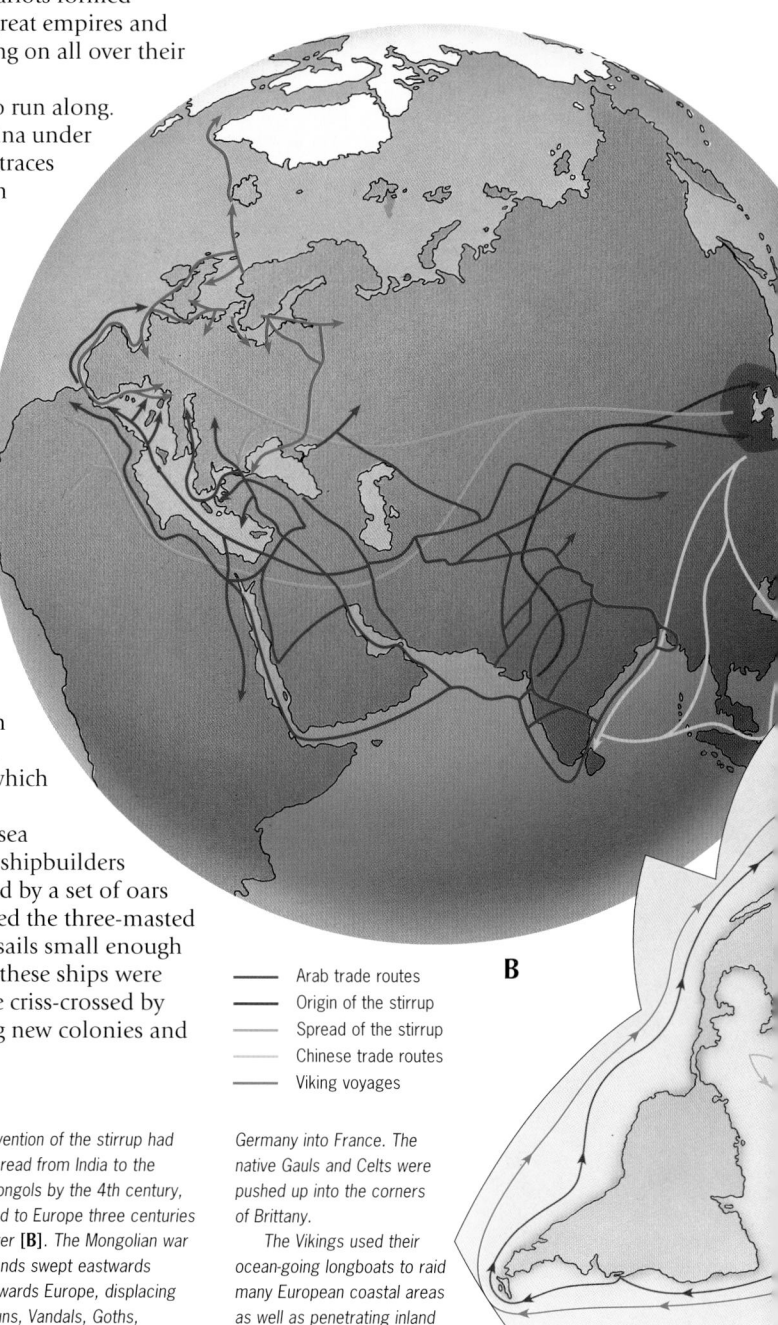

▲ **EARLY ROAD SYSTEMS**
In the first few centuries of the Christian era, the landmass of Eurasia was dominated by empires at its east and west extremes [A]. Transport was central to both these realms. In Europe, the Romans built an extensive network of roads which allowed troops, administrators, tax-collectors and traders to travel quickly from one end of the empire to the other.

Under the Han dynasty, China began extensive trade. As well as extensive sea trading routes, there was the old Silk Road linking oases across the deserts of central Asia, along which caravans carried China's silks and spices as far as the Greek and Roman worlds.

Roman roads
Roman Empire
Chinese Empire

Great Wall
Silk Road
Trade routes

Arab trade routes
Origin of the stirrup
Spread of the stirrup
Chinese trade routes
Viking voyages

▲ **THE DARK AGES**
The fall of the Roman Empire was a signal for mass movement across the known world. Arab traders opened trade routes that extended from Spain to China.

During the Dark Ages, both Europe and Asia were subject to raids by the Mongols, whose use of the stirrup gave them a mastery of warfare on horseback. The invention of the stirrup had spread from India to the Mongols by the 4th century, and to Europe three centuries later [B]. The Mongolian war bands swept eastwards towards Europe, displacing Huns, Vandals, Goths, Ostrogoths, Visigoths and Alans who moved into the western part of Europe, in turn displacing the Franks who moved from what is now Germany into France. The native Gauls and Celts were pushed up into the corners of Brittany.

The Vikings used their ocean-going longboats to raid many European coastal areas as well as penetrating inland along the great rivers. Some may have even reached the coast of North America.

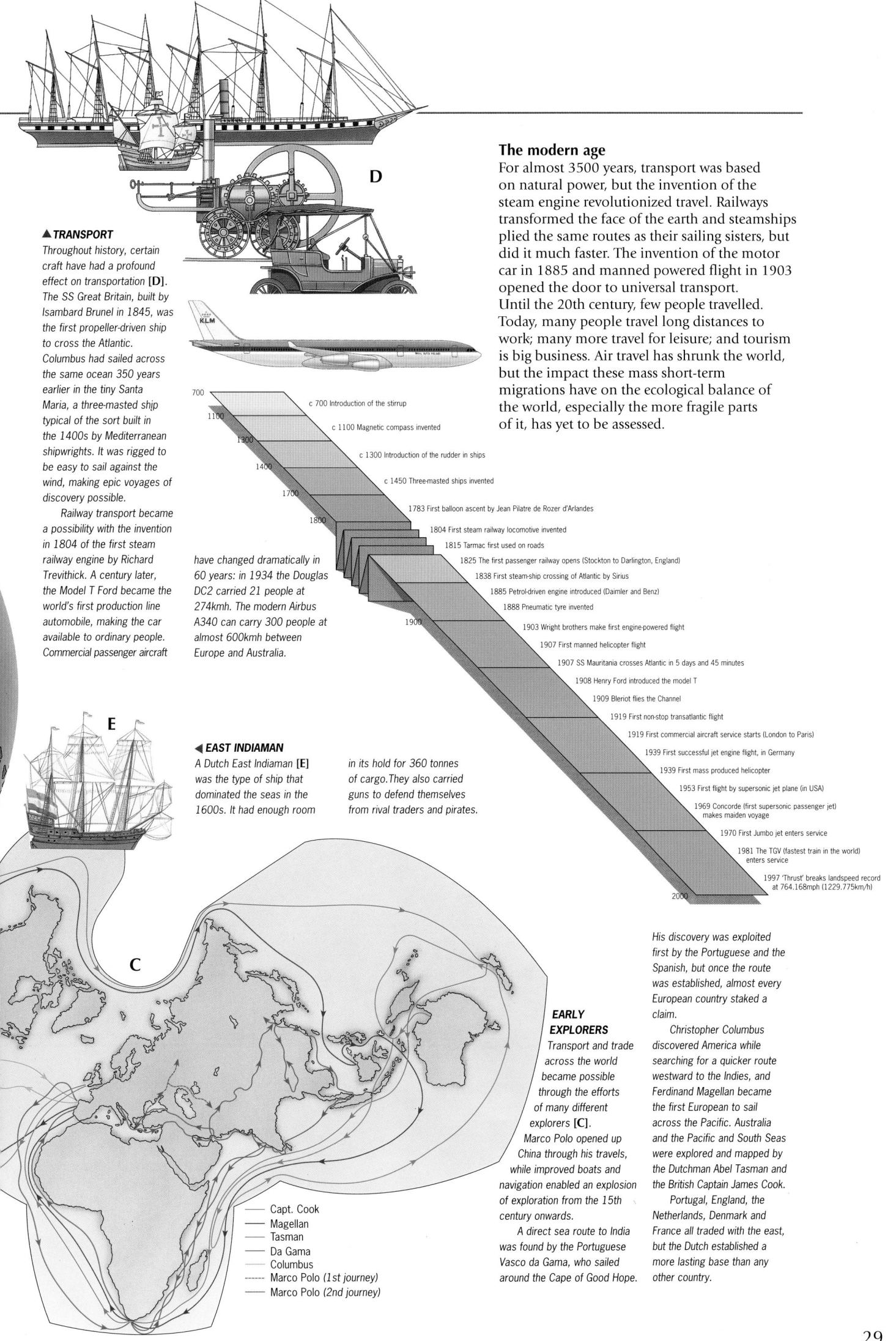

▲ TRANSPORT

Throughout history, certain craft have had a profound effect on transportation [**D**]. The SS Great Britain, built by Isambard Brunel in 1845, was the first propeller-driven ship to cross the Atlantic. Columbus had sailed across the same ocean 350 years earlier in the tiny Santa Maria, a three-masted ship typical of the sort built in the 1400s by Mediterranean shipwrights. It was rigged to be easy to sail against the wind, making epic voyages of discovery possible.

Railway transport became a possibility with the invention in 1804 of the first steam railway engine by Richard Trevithick. A century later, the Model T Ford became the world's first production line automobile, making the car available to ordinary people. Commercial passenger aircraft have changed dramatically in 60 years: in 1934 the Douglas DC2 carried 21 people at 274kmh. The modern Airbus A340 can carry 300 people at almost 600kmh between Europe and Australia.

The modern age

For almost 3500 years, transport was based on natural power, but the invention of the steam engine revolutionized travel. Railways transformed the face of the earth and steamships plied the same routes as their sailing sisters, but did it much faster. The invention of the motor car in 1885 and manned powered flight in 1903 opened the door to universal transport.

Until the 20th century, few people travelled. Today, many people travel long distances to work; many more travel for leisure; and tourism is big business. Air travel has shrunk the world, but the impact these mass short-term migrations have on the ecological balance of the world, especially the more fragile parts of it, has yet to be assessed.

c 700 Introduction of the stirrup
c 1100 Magnetic compass invented
c 1300 Introduction of the rudder in ships
c 1450 Three-masted ships invented
1783 First balloon ascent by Jean Pilatre de Rozer d'Arlandes
1804 First steam railway locomotive invented
1815 Tarmac first used on roads
1825 The first passenger railway opens (Stockton to Darlington, England)
1838 First steam-ship crossing of Atlantic by Sirius
1885 Petrol-driven engine introduced (Daimler and Benz)
1888 Pneumatic tyre invented
1903 Wright brothers make first engine-powered flight
1907 First manned helicopter flight
1907 SS Mauritania crosses Atlantic in 5 days and 45 minutes
1908 Henry Ford introduced the model T
1909 Bleriot flies the Channel
1919 First non-stop transatlantic flight
1919 First commercial aircraft service starts (London to Paris)
1939 First successful jet engine flight, in Germany
1939 First mass produced helicopter
1953 First flight by supersonic jet plane (in USA)
1969 Concorde (first supersonic passenger jet) makes maiden voyage
1970 First Jumbo jet enters service
1981 The TGV (fastest train in the world) enters service
1997 'Thrust' breaks landspeed record at 764.168mph (1229.775km/h)

◄ EAST INDIAMAN

A Dutch East Indiaman [**E**] was the type of ship that dominated the seas in the 1600s. It had enough room in its hold for 360 tonnes of cargo. They also carried guns to defend themselves from rival traders and pirates.

EARLY EXPLORERS

Transport and trade across the world became possible through the efforts of many different explorers [**C**].

Marco Polo opened up China through his travels, while improved boats and navigation enabled an explosion of exploration from the 15th century onwards.

A direct sea route to India was found by the Portuguese Vasco da Gama, who sailed around the Cape of Good Hope.

His discovery was exploited first by the Portuguese and the Spanish, but once the route was established, almost every European country staked a claim.

Christopher Columbus discovered America while searching for a quicker route westward to the Indies, and Ferdinand Magellan became the first European to sail across the Pacific. Australia and the Pacific and South Seas were explored and mapped by the Dutchman Abel Tasman and the British Captain James Cook.

Portugal, England, the Netherlands, Denmark and France all traded with the east, but the Dutch established a more lasting base than any other country.

— Capt. Cook
— Magellan
— Tasman
— Da Gama
— Columbus
----- Marco Polo (1st journey)
— Marco Polo (2nd journey)

CANADA BY SATELLITE

KEY TO MAP SYMBOLS

Political regions

CANADA   country

MONTANA   province or state

———————   international boundary

—·—·—·—·—   national boundary

——————————

Topographic features

3954
△
Mt. Robson   elevation above sea level (in metres)

ROCKY MOUNTAINS   physical feature

NEWFOUNDLAND   island

Cape Sable   cape, point

Cities, towns & capitals

☐ NEW YORK   over 1 million

○ Duluth   100 000-1 million

· Paulatuk   under 100 000

● Ottawa   country capital

○ Winnipeg   province or state capital

——————————

Hydrographic features

ATLANTIC OCEAN   ocean, sea

Hudson Bay   gulf, strait, bay

Lake Superior
St. Lawrence   lake, river

Scale 1 : 13 800 000

0   200   400   600 km
0 100 200 300 miles

A 65° 150° W 3 B 145° C 70° 140° D 135° E 130° F 2 125° G 120° H 115° J 110° K 105° L 100° M 95°

BEAUFORT SEA

BANKS ISLAND

Mackenzie Bay
Cape Kellett

ALASKA
Fairbanks

WHITE MOUNTAINS

4216
Mount Hayes

Inuvik

(U.S)

4996
Mt. Blackburn

Dawson

Sachs Harbour

Cape Bathurst

Cape Lambton

Franklin Bay

Paulatuk

VICTORIA ISLAND

Viscount Melville Sound

MELVILLE I.

BATHURST I.

CORNWALLIS I.

STEFANSSON I.

SOMERSET ISLAND

PRINCE OF WALES ISLAND

NORTHWEST

6050
Mt. Logan

YUKON TERRITORY

Whitehorse

Fort Franklin

Great Bear Lake

Amundsen Gulf

Prince Albert Sound

Coronation Gulf

Echo Bay

Bathurst Inlet

KING WILLIAM I.

Queen Maud Gulf

NUNA

Gulf of Alaska

Cross Sound

CHICHAGOF

Juneau

ALEXANDER ARCHIPELAGO

BARANOF I.

ADMIRALTY

KUPREANOF

PRINCE OF WALES I.

TERRITORIES

Watson Lake

Fort Simpson

Yellowknife

Reliance

Faber Lake

Lac la Martre

Great Slave Lake

Clinton-Golden Lake

Artillery Lake

Contwoyto Lake

Aberdeen Lake

Baker Lake

Dubawnt Lake

CANA

DALL I.

Dixon Entrance

QUEEN CHARLOTTE IS.

GRAHAM I.

MORESBY I.

Cape Saint James

Queen Charlotte Sound

Cape Knox

Hecate Strait

Prince Rupert

River Inlet

Fort Nelson

BRITISH COLUMBIA

Babine Lake

Williston Lake

Manning

Dawson Creek

Trout Lake

Bischo Lake

Hay River

CAMERON HILLS

CARIBOU MOUNTAINS

Buffalo Lake

Peace

Uranium City

Lake Athabasca

Selwyn Lake

Ennadai

Church

Wollaston Lake

Nueltin Lake

Cape Scott

VANCOUVER ISLAND

3994
Mt. Waddington

Prince George

Quesnel Lake

3954
Mt. Robson

ALBERTA

Lesser Slave Lake

Fort McMurray

Frobisher Lake

Cree Lake

Reindeer Lake

Lynn Lake

Missinipe

Lac la Ronge

Churchill Lake

Thompson

MANITOBA

Kamloops

VANCOUVER

Victoria

Cape Flattery

Strait of Juan de Fuca

3747
Mt. Columbia

Edmonton

Calgary

Athabasca

North Saskatchewan

SASKATCHEWAN

Prince Albert

Saskatoon

Cedar Lake

Grand Rapids

Lake Winnipeg

Island Lake

Bearskin Lake

SEATTLE

Tacoma

Olympia

WASHING-TON

Spokane

4392
Mt. Rainier

Lethbridge

Medicine Hat

Big Quill Lake

Lake Winnipegosis

Regina

Brandon

Lake Manitoba

Kenora

PORTLAND

Salem

Spring-field

Richland

Lewiston

Missoula

Great Falls

Missouri

Fort Peck Reservoir

Minot

Winnipeg

Lake of the Woods

OREGON

Boise

3859
Borah Peak

IDAHO

Helena

MONTANA

Billings

Lake Sakakawea

N. DAKOTA

Bismarck

Fargo

Grand Forks

MINNESOTA

Moorhead

Dulut

BLACK ROCK DESERT

4190
Grand Teton

Cloud Peak

Sheridan

Aberdeen

UNITED S

Superi

Reno

4202
Gannett Peak

WYOMING

BIGHORN MOUNTAINS

Rapid City

Casper

S. DAKOTA

MINNEAPOLIS

ST. PAUL

NEVADA

Carson City

Great Salt Lake

Sioux Falls

120° H 115° 40° J 110° K 105° L 100° M 95° N

© Helicon Publishing Ltd

32 **CANADA**

DEVON ISLAND

Lancaster Sound
Cape Sherard
Cape Liverpool
BYLOT I.
Cape Graham Moore

Baffin Bay

GREENLAND
(Denmark)

Arctic Circle

Ammassalik
(Angmagssalik)

QEQERTARSUAQ
(DISKO)

Cape Adair

Cape Christian

Denmark Strait

BAFFIN ISLAND

Clyde River

Cape Raper

Home Bay

CROWN PRINCE FREDERIK I.
Igloolik
KOCH I.
BRAY I.
ROWLEY I.
FOLEY I.
AIR FORCE I.
PENNY ICE CAP

1890
J.A.D. Jensens
Nunatakker

Nuuk
(Godthåb)

WALES I.
PRINCE CHARLES ISLAND
Netilling Lake

Cape Wilson

Nunap Isua
(Kap Farvel)

Foxe Basin

Amadjuak Lake

Kangerlussuaq
(Søndre Strømfjord)

Cumberland Sound

5

UT

VANSITTART I.
WHITE I.

Cape Queen

Iqaluit

Foxe Channel

Frobisher Bay

Cape Mercy

LEMIEUX ISLANDS

LABRADOR SEA

SOUTHAMPTON ISLAND
Cape Dorset
MILL I.
SALISBURY I.
NOTTINGHAM I.
CHARLES I.
Cap Wolstenholme

Cape Low
Evans Strait
COATS I.

Ross Welcome Sound

Hudson Strait

LOKS LAND
EDGELL I.
RESOLUTION I.

Gabriel Strait

Chesterfield Inlet
Fisher Strait

MANSEL I.
Ivujivik
SMITH I.

Lac Nantais

Cape Chidley
Cap Hopes Advance
AKPATOK I.

NEWFOUNDLAND

D A

Kangirsuk

Ungava Bay

Hebron

6

Hudson Bay

Inukjuak

Rivière aux Feuilles

Schefferville

SOUTH AULATSIVIK I.

Rigolet

LABRADOR
Lake Melville

Lac Minto

BELLE ISLE

Cape Bauld

Cape Tatnam

BELCHER ISLANDS
Kuujjuarapik

Smallwood Reservoir
Churchill

Strait of Belle Isle

FOGO I.
Cape Freels

Fort Severn

Cape Henrietta Maria

Réservoir Caniapiscau

Gander

NEWFOUNDLAND

7

Lake River

James Bay

TWIN IS.

Réservoir Manicouagan

Havre-St-Pierre

St. John's

Big Trout Lake

AKIMISKI I.

QUÉBEC

Sept-Îles

ÎLE D'ANTICOSTI

Détroit de Jacques-Cartier
Pointe de l'Est
Gulf of St. Lawrence

Corner Brook

Fortune Bay

ST-PIERRE-ET-MIQUELON (Fr.)

Placentia Bay

Fort Rupert
Lac Mistassini
Lac Albanel

Réservoir Pipmuacan

Détroit d'Honguedo
Cape Ray

Cabot Strait
Cape North

45°

ONTARIO

Ogoki

Lac Evans

ÎLES DE LA MADELEINE

SABLE I.

Lake Nipigon

Lac St-Jean

Jonquière

Baie des Chaleurs

P.E.I.
Charlotte-town

CAPE BRETON ISLAND

Timmins

Réservoir Gouin

Québec

NEW BRUNSWICK

PRINCE EDWARD

Strait of Canso

Thunder Bay

Val-d'Or

Fredericton

Halifax

ISLE ROYALE
MICHIPICOTEN I.

North Bay

MONTRÉAL

MAINE

Bay of Fundy

NOVA SCOTIA

8

Lake Superior

Sault Ste. Marie
Lake Nipissing
MANITOULIN I.

Ottawa

VER-MONT

Augusta

Gulf of Maine

Cape Sable

ATES

CONSIN

Appleton

Lake Winnebago

Lake Michigan

Lake Huron

TORONTO

Lake Ontario

Montpelier

NEW HAMP-SHIRE

NEW YORK

Concord

BOSTON

Cape Cod

ATLANTIC OCEAN

40°

MICHIGAN

Hamilton

Rochester

Albany

MASSA-CHUSETTS

PROVIDENCE

9

MILWAUKEE

Lansing

Flint

Niagara Falls

BUFFALO

Syracuse

Hartford

RHODE I.

Grand Rapids

DETROIT

Erie

Lake Erie

Jersey City

NEW YORK

CONN.

LONG I.

PENNSYLVANIA

NEWARK

Scale 1 : 6 500 000

| 0 | 100 | 200 | 300 km |

| 0 | 50 | 100 | 150 miles |

BANKS ISLAND

Sachs Harbour

Cape Kellett

Cape Lambton

Amundsen Gulf

NUNAVUT

MELVILLE HILLS

Echo Bay

Yellowknife

BEAUFORT SEA

Cape Bathurst

Franklin Bay

Paulatuk

Great Bear Lake

NORTHWEST TERRITORIES

Takit Aklin

Lac la Martre

Tuktoyaktuk

Mackenzie Bay

Tuk Saline Lakes

Fort Good Hope

Norman Wells

Fort Franklin

Mackenzie

Mackenzie

FRANKLIN MOUNTAINS

Fort Simpson

Inuvik

Fort McPherson

Mackenzie

RICHARDSON MTS.

MACKENZIE MOUNTAINS

Old Crow

70°

SELWYN MOUNTAINS

Watson Lake

Thomsbee

Faro

Ross River

Dawson

YUKON TERRITORY

PELLY MOUNTAINS

Yukon

150°W

Whitehorse

CASSIAR MOUNTAINS

R

O

Juneau

ALASKA (U.S.)

WHITE MOUNTAINS

Fairbanks

ADMIRALTY

CHICHAGOF

65°

Mt. McKinley 6194

Shnunt Rivers

Mt. Logan 6050

BARANOF

Cross Sound

ALEXANDER ARCHIPELAGO

Anchorage

Yakutat Bay

Gulf of Alaska

© Helicon Publishing Ltd

Scale 1 : 7 450 000

| 0 | 100 | 200 | 300 km |
| 0 | 50 | 100 | 150 miles |

Baffin Bay

Beaufort Sea

BANKS ISLAND

Cape Kellett
Sachs Harbour
Cape Lambton

Amundsen Gulf

MELVILLE HILLS

VICTORIA ISLAND

Fort Collinson

McClure Strait

Viscount Melville Sound

Prince Albert Sound

Coronation Gulf

Echo Bay

MELVILLE I.

BATHURST I.

CORNWALLIS I.

DEVON ISLAND

SOMERSET ISLAND

PRINCE OF WALES ISLAND

STEFANSSON I.

Ommanney Bay

McClintock Channel

Franklin Strait

Gulf of Boothia

Lancaster Sound

Cape Sherard

BYLOT I.

Cape Liverpool

Cape Graham Moore

Cape Adair

Cape Christian

Clyde River

Cape Raper

Houghton Head

BAFFIN ISLAND

KING WILLIAM I.

Queen Maud Gulf

Victoria Strait

Bathurst Inlet

Igloolik

CROWN PRINCE FREDERIK I.

MELVILLE PENINSULA

MANSEL I.

KOCH I.
BRAY I.
ROWLEY I.
AIR FORCE I.
FOLEY I.
PRINCE CHARLES ISLAND

Cape Wilson

VANSITTART I.
WHITE I.

Roes Welcome Sound

SOUTHAMPTON ISLAND

Cape Low

Fisher Strait

COATS I.

Evans Strait

Foxe Channel

Foxe Basin

Cape Queen

Hudson Strait

Cape Dorset

MILL I.
SALISBURY I.
NOTTINGHAM I.
CHARLES I.
Cap Wolstenholme
Ivujivik

Nottingham Lake

MOANSEL I.

SMITH I.

NUNAVUT

Baker Lake

Chesterfield Inlet

Dubawnt Lake

Ennadai

NORTHWEST TERRITORIES

Yellowknife

Great Slave Lake

Reliance

C A N A D A

© Helicon Publishing Ltd

HUDSON BAY

James Bay

Lake Superior

UNITED STATES

MANITOBA

SASKATCHEWAN

ONTARIO

MINNESOTA

N. DAKOTA

Inukjuak
Kuujjuarapik
BELCHER ISLANDS
NORTH BELCHER ISLANDS
Eastmain
Fort Rupert
TWIN IS.
AKIMISKI I.
Cape Henrietta Maria
Lake River
Attawapiskat
Fort Albany
Moosonee
Hearst
Kapuskasing
Cochrane
Iroquois Falls
Timmins
Kirkland Lake
Rouyn
North Bay
Lake Nipissing
Sudbury
Elliot Lake
MANITOULIN I.
Sault Ste. Marie
Wawa
MICHIPICOTEN I.
ISLE ROYALE
Thunder Bay
Longlac
Ogoki
Lake Nipigon
Sioux Lookout
Dryden
Kenora
Lake of the Woods
Superior
Duluth
Moorhead
Fargo
Grand Forks
Winnipeg
Portage la Prairie
Brandon
Minot
Bismarck
Lake Sakakawea
Fort Severn
Cape Tatnam
Churchill
Thompson
Bearskin Lake
Island Lake
Big Trout Lake
Grand Rapids
Lake Winnipeg
Lake Manitoba
Lake Winnipegosis
Cedar Lake
Flin Flon
Lynn Lake
Wollaston Lake
Missinipe
Lac la Ronge
Reindeer Lake
Stony Rapids
Buffalo Narrows
North Battleford
Prince Albert
Saskatoon
Moose Jaw
Regina
Swift Current
Lake Diefenbaker

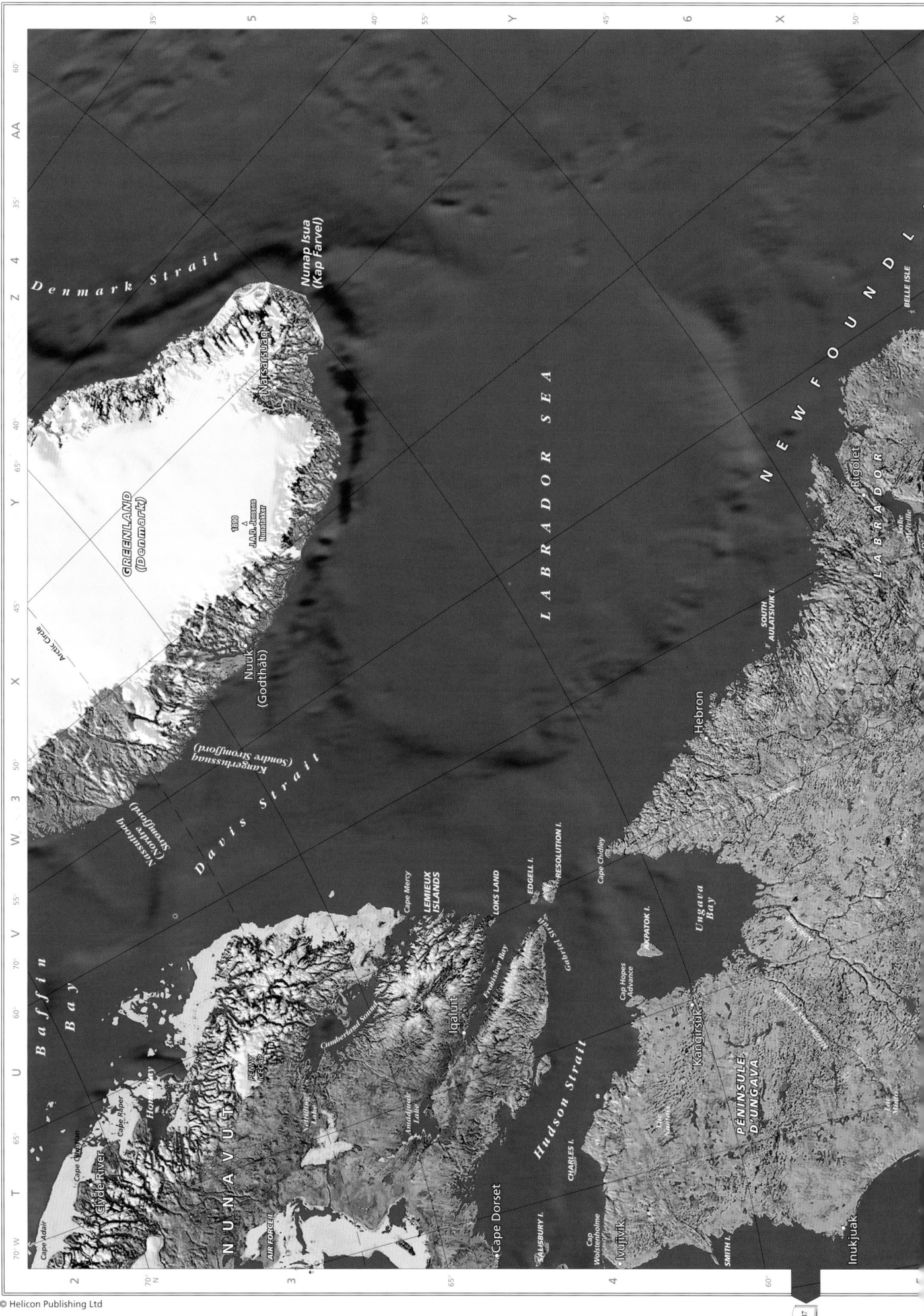

Scale 1 : 7 550 000

0   100   200   300 km

0   50   100   150 miles

Denmark Strait

**Nunap Isua
(Kap Farvel)**

Narsarsuaq

60°

35°

5

40°

55°

Y

45°

6

X

50°

AA

35°

Z

4

65°

40°

L A B R A D O R   S E A

N E W F O U N D L

BELLE ISLE

**GREENLAND
(Denmark)**

1890
J.A.D. Jensens
Nunatakker

Y

65°

45°

Rigolet
Lake
Melville

Nuuk
(Godthåb)

Kangerlussuaq
(Søndre Strømfjord)

X

50°

L A B R A D O R

Hebron

Arctic Circle

Nassuttuuq
(Nordre Strømfjord)

W

3

55°

SOUTH
AULATSIVIK I.

D a v i s   S t r a i t

Cape Mercy

**LEMIEUX
ISLANDS**

LOKS LAND

EDGELL I.

RESOLUTION I.

Cape Chidley

Ungava
Bay

V

70°

*B a f f i n
B a y*

Cumberland Sound

Frobisher Bay

Gabriel Strait

AKPATOK I.

Kangirsuk

U

60°

Hoare Bay

PENNY
ICECAP

Iqaluit

Cap Hopes
Advance

Kanglrsuk

**PÉNINSULE
D'UNGAVA**

Cape Raper

Cape Christian

Clyde River

Amadjuak
Lake

H u d s o n   S t r a i t

CHARLES I.

T

65°

Cape Adair

N U N A V U T

Nettilling
Lake

Cape Dorset

SALISBURY I.

Cap
Wolstenholme

SMITH I.

Inukjuak

2

70° N

AIR FORCE I.

3

65°

4

60°

Ivujivik

© Helicon Publishing Ltd

THE WORLD

KEY TO MAP SYMBOLS

Political regions

CANADA	country
ONTARIO	state or province
▬▬▬▬▬	international boundary (physical regional maps)
────────	international boundary (political continental maps)
────────	state or province boundary
─ ▬ ─ ▬ ─	undefined/disputed boundary or ceasefire/demarcation line

Communications

────────	motorway
────────	main road
────────	other road
─ ─ ─ ─ ─	track
────────	railway
✈	international airport

Hydrographic features

river, canal
seasonal river
Niagara Falls Kariba Dam	waterfall, dam
lake, seasonal lake
salt lake, seasonal salt lake
ice cap or glacier

Cities, towns & capitals

▣ **CHICAGO**	over 3 million
□ **HAMBURG**	1–3 million
○ **Bulawayo**	250 000–1 million
● Antofogasta	100 000–250 000
◌ Ajaccio	25 000–100 000
▪ Indian Springs	under 25 000
LONDON	country capital
Columbia	state or province capital
	urban area

Cultural features

⁂ Persepolis	ancient site or ruin
▪▪▪▪▪▪▪▪▪	ancient wall

Topographic features

▲ Mount Ziel 1510	elevation above sea level (in metres)
▾ 133	elevation of land below sea level (in metres)
⤳ Khyber Pass 1080	mountain pass (height in metres)

Each page also features a guide to relief colours

Equatorial Scale 1 : 112 000 000

0   1000   2000   3000   4000 km

0   1000   2000 miles

| A | 150° | B | 120° | C | 90° | D | 60° | E | 30° | F | 0° |

ARCTIC OCEAN

Ellesmere Island

GREENLAND
(Denmark)

Greenland
Sea

Beaufort Sea

Baffin Bay

Victoria
Island

Baffin Island

1

Nuuk
(Godthåb)

ICELAND

Norwegian
Sea

Arctic Circle

Yukon

ALASKA
(U.S.)

Mackenzie

Reykjavik

Anchorage

Hudson
Bay

UNITED
KINGDOM

DENMA

Bering
Sea

Gulf of
Alaska

CANADA

REPUBLIC OF
IRELAND

Dublin

NETHER-
LANDS

London

BEL

60°

ROCKY MOUNTAINS

Edmonton

Calgary   Winnipeg   Lake Superior

Paris

FRANCE

Vancouver

Lake
Huron

St. Lawrence

Québec

ANDORRA

MONACO

2

Seattle

Missouri

Lake
Michigan

Ottawa

Montréal

PORTUGAL

SPAIN

Denver

Chicago

Detroit

Toronto

Açores
(Portugal)

Lisboa

Madrid

UNITED STATES

New York

Tu

San Francisco

Kansas City

Philadelphia
Washington D.C.

Madeira
(Portugal)

Rabat

Alger

Los Angeles

Phoenix

Dallas

Atlanta

Bermuda
(U.K.)

ATLANTIC

Islas Canarias
(Spain)

MOROCCO

San Diego

Houston

Rio Grande

New Orleans

OCEAN

WESTERN
SAHARA
(Morocco)

ALGERIA

30°

Monterrey

Mississippi

Gulf of

THE
BAHAMAS

Tropic of Cancer

MEXICO   Mexico

Nouakchott

MAURITANIA

MALI

HAWAII
(U.S.)

Guadalajara

Ciudad
de México

La Habana
CUBA

DOMINICAN REP

PUERTO RICO (U.S.)

CAPE
VERDE

Dakar
THE GAMBIA

SEN

Niame

3

JAMAICA

HAITI

ST KITTS AND NEVIS
ANTIGUA & BARBUDA

Bamako
GUINEA-BISSAU

BURKINA
FASO

Guatemala
GUATEMALA

BELIZE
HONDURAS

DOMINICA
ST LUCIA

Caribbean Sea

GUINEA

NIC

EL SALVADOR

NICARAGUA

ST VINCENT &
THE GRENADINES

BARBADOS

SIERRA LEONE

CÔTE
D'IVOIRE

GHANA

Accra

BENIN

COSTA
RICA

San José

GRENADA

Caracas

TRINIDAD & TOBAGO

Monrovia

Yamous-
soukro

EQUAT. GUIN

PANAMA

Panamá

VENEZUELA

Georgetown
FRENCH
GUIANA (Fr.)

SÃO TOMÉ
& PRINCIPE

Bogotá

COLOMBIA

GUYANA

SURINAME

Quito

Islas Galápagos
(Ecuador)

ECUADOR

Iquitos

Amazon

Belém

Fortaleza

Equator

PACIFIC

Lima

Manaus

BRAZIL

Recife

0°

KIRIBATI

OCEAN

PERU

4

French
Polynesia

La Paz

BOLIVIA

Brasília

Salvador

Arequipa

Sucre

Belo Horizonte

Tropic of Capricorn

Paraguay

Rio de Janeiro

São Paulo

Asunción

Pitcairn Is.
(U.K.)

PARAGUAY

Curitiba
Porto Alegre

Santiago

Córdoba

URUGUAY

30°

CHILE

ARGENTINA

Buenos
Aires

Montevideo

5

Falkland
Islands
(U.K.)

South Georgia
(U.K.)

Punta
Arenas

South Sandwich
Islands
(U.K.)

60°

Antarctic Circle

Bellingshausen

6

Sea

Weddell Sea

Ross Sea

| A | 150° | B | 120° | C | 90° | D | 60° | E | 30° | F | 0° |

© Helicon Publishing Ltd

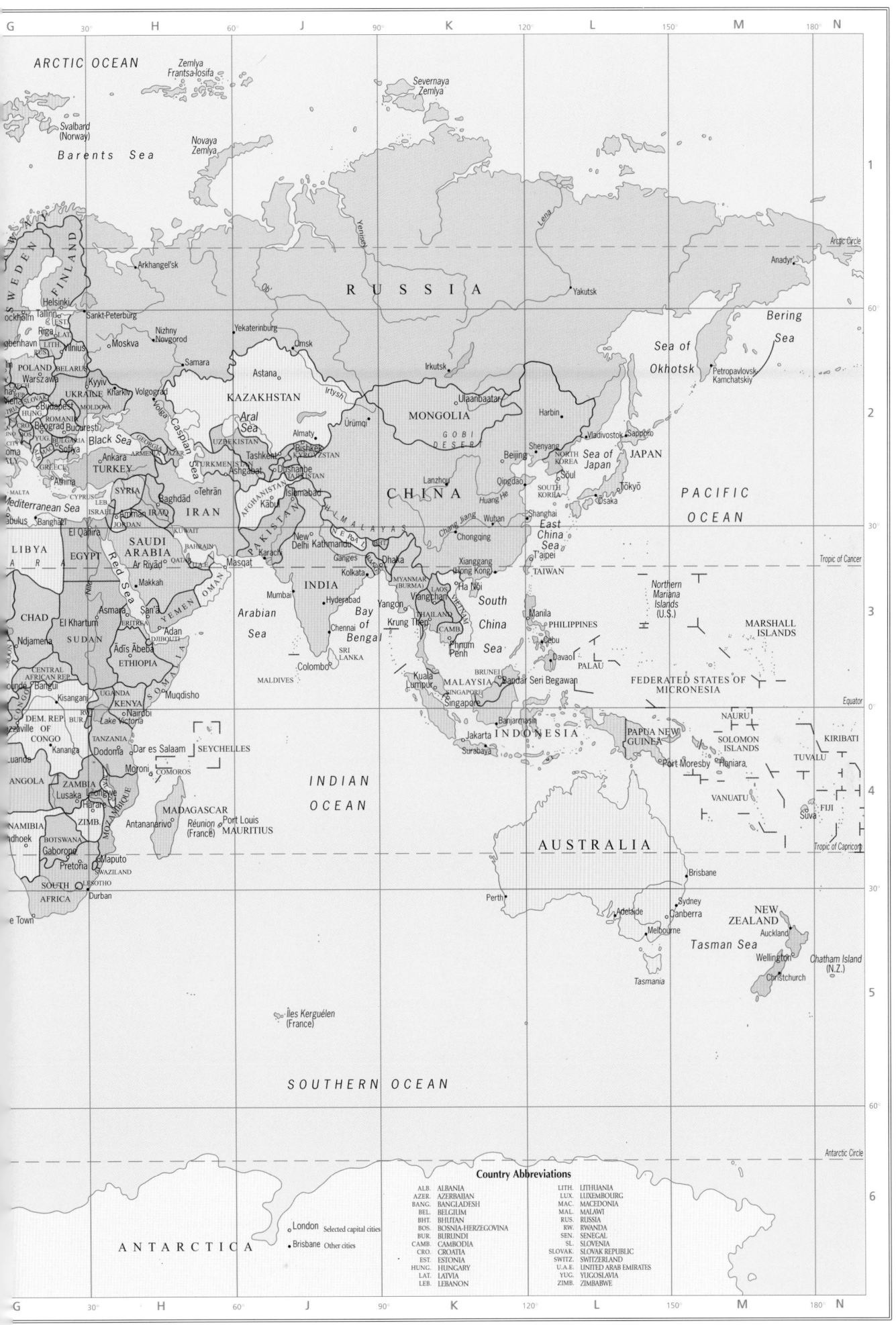

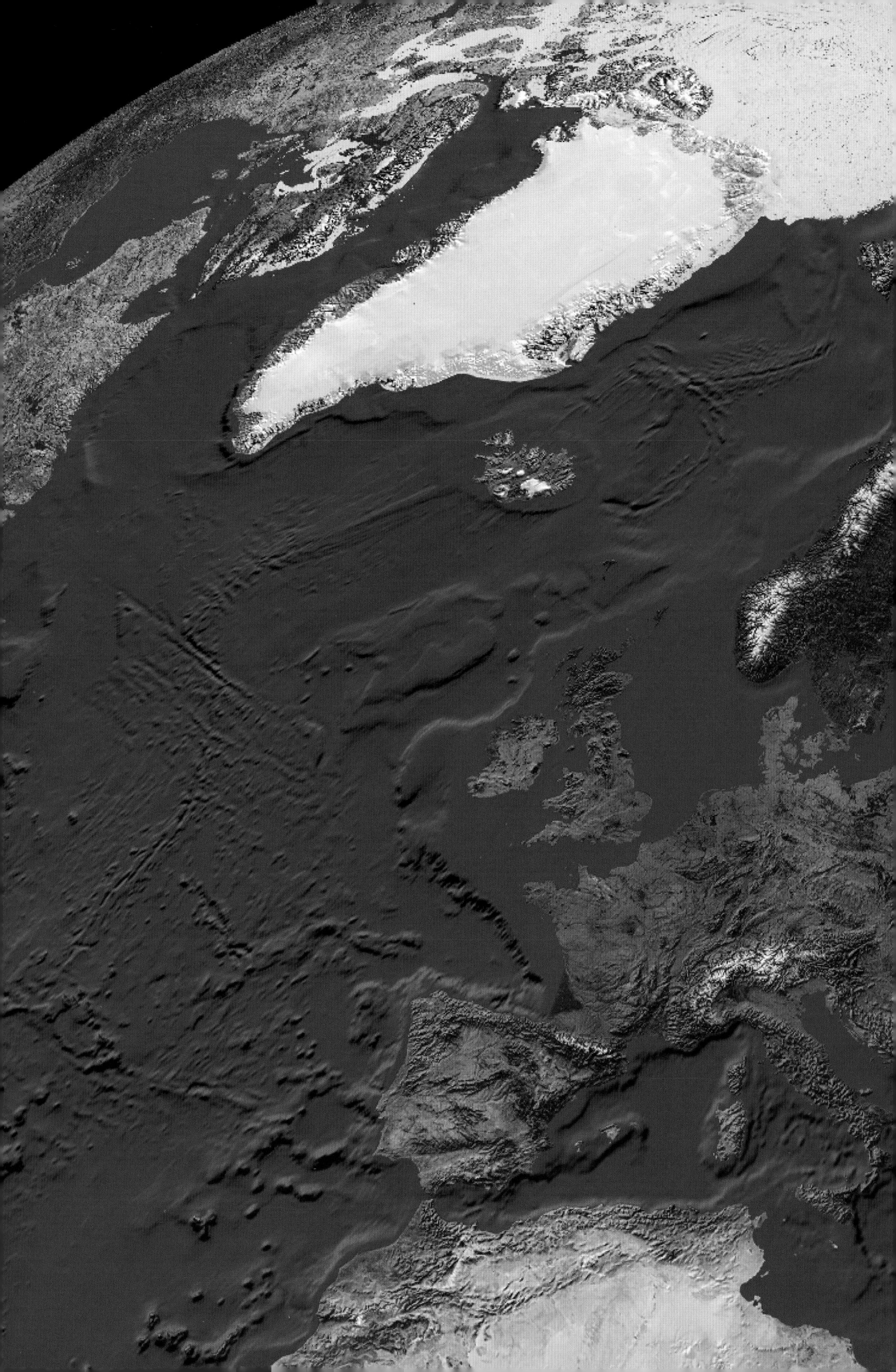

EUROPE

0   250   500   750 km
0 100 200 300 miles

60° N   A   1   30° W   B   20°   C   70° 10°   D   0°   E   10°   F   20°

Arctic Circle

Reykjavík ● **ICELAND**

Norwegian

Sea

Faeroes
(Denmark)

N O R W A Y   Tromsø

S W E D E N   *La*

Kiruna

Trondheim

Gulf of Bothnia

Rockall   Shetland Is.
(U.K.)   Bergen   Sundsvall   FI

Tampere

Outer
Hebrides   Orkney Is.   Stavanger   Oslo

SCOTLAND   Stockholm   Tallin

Glasgow   *North*   Göteborg   Gotland   *Vänern*   E

NORTHERN
IRELAND   Edinburgh   *Sea*   DENMARK   LA

REP. OF   Belfast   Århus   København   Gdańsk   RUSSIA   Rīga

IRELAND   UNITED   (Copenhagen)   Bornholm   Kaliningra   LITHU

DUBLIN   KINGDOM   HAMBURG   Kaunu

(BAILE ÁTHA CLIATH)   WALES   BIRMINGHAM   Hannover   Hrodna

Cardiff   ENGLAND   Amsterdam   BERLIN   WARSZAWA

Plymouth   's-Gravenhage   Elbe   (WARSAW)   L'viv

LONDON   (The Hague)   NETHER-   GERMANY   POLAND

English Channel   Bruxelles   LANDS   Bonn   Frankfurt   Odra (Oder)   Nistula

Channel   (Brussels)   BELGIUM   Rhine   PRAHA

Islands   Luxembourg   (PRAGUE)   CZECH REP.   L'viv

PARIS   LUXEMBOURG   MÜNCHEN   WIEN   SLOVAK REP.

Strasbourg   (MUNICH)   (VIENNA)   Bratislava

Bay   FRANCE   *Danube*   BUDAPEST   Cluj

of   Lyon   Vaduz   AUSTRIA   HUNGARY   Napoca

Biscay   Bordeaux   Bern   LIECHTENSTEIN   SLOVENIA   Zagreb   RO

Massif   SWITZERLAND   MILANO   Ljubljana   CROATIA

Central   4808   (MILAN)   SAN   BOSNIA-

Cabo Fisterra   Mt.   Genova   MARINO   HERZEGOVINA   BEOGRAD

Blanc   (Genoa)   Sarajevo   (BELGRADE)

Andorra   *Alps*   MONACO   ANDORRA   *Apennines*   YUGOSLAVIA   BU

Lisboa   la Vella   Rhône   Marseille   VATICAN   SOFIYA

(Lisbon)   PORTUGAL   *Pyrenees*   CITY   ROMA   *Adriatic Sea*   (SOFIA)

Tagus   MADRID   Corse   (ROME)   Tiranë   Skopje

Cabo de   Ebro   (Corsica)   (Tirana)   MACEDONIA

São Vicente   BARCELONA   (France)   Ajaccio   ITALY   ALBANIA

SPAIN   *Islas Baleares*   Sardegna   NAPOLI   Taranto

Valencia   (Balearic Islands)   (Sardinia)   (NAPLES)   Kerkyra

Gibraltar (U.K.)   Menorca   (Italy)   (Corfu)   GREEC

Strait of Gibraltar   Eivissa   Cagliari   Palermo   *Ionian*

Ceuta   Mallorca   Tyrrhenian   Sicilia   *Sea*   Athin

(Spain)   Sea   (Sicily)   Mte. Etna   (Athen

RABAT   Melilla   *M e d i t e r r a n e a n*   3340

(Spain)   Valletta

ALGER   Kri

(ALGIERS)   MALTA   (Cret

Tunis   *Sea*

Tarābulus   *Sea*

A F R I C A   (Tripoli)

Banghāzī

D   0°   E   10°   F   20°

© Helicon Publishing Ltd

ATLANTIC

OCEAN

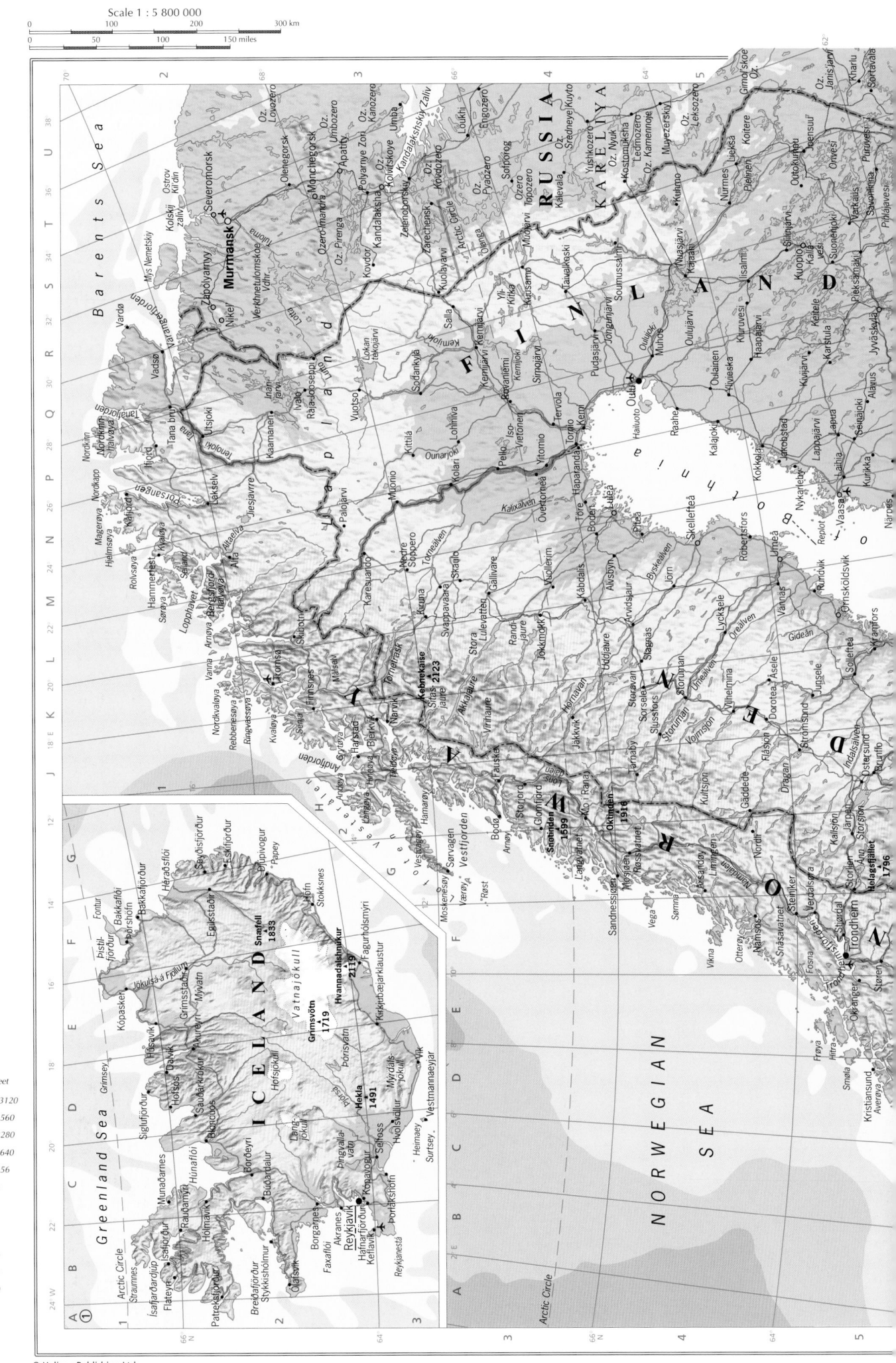

© Helicon Publishing Ltd

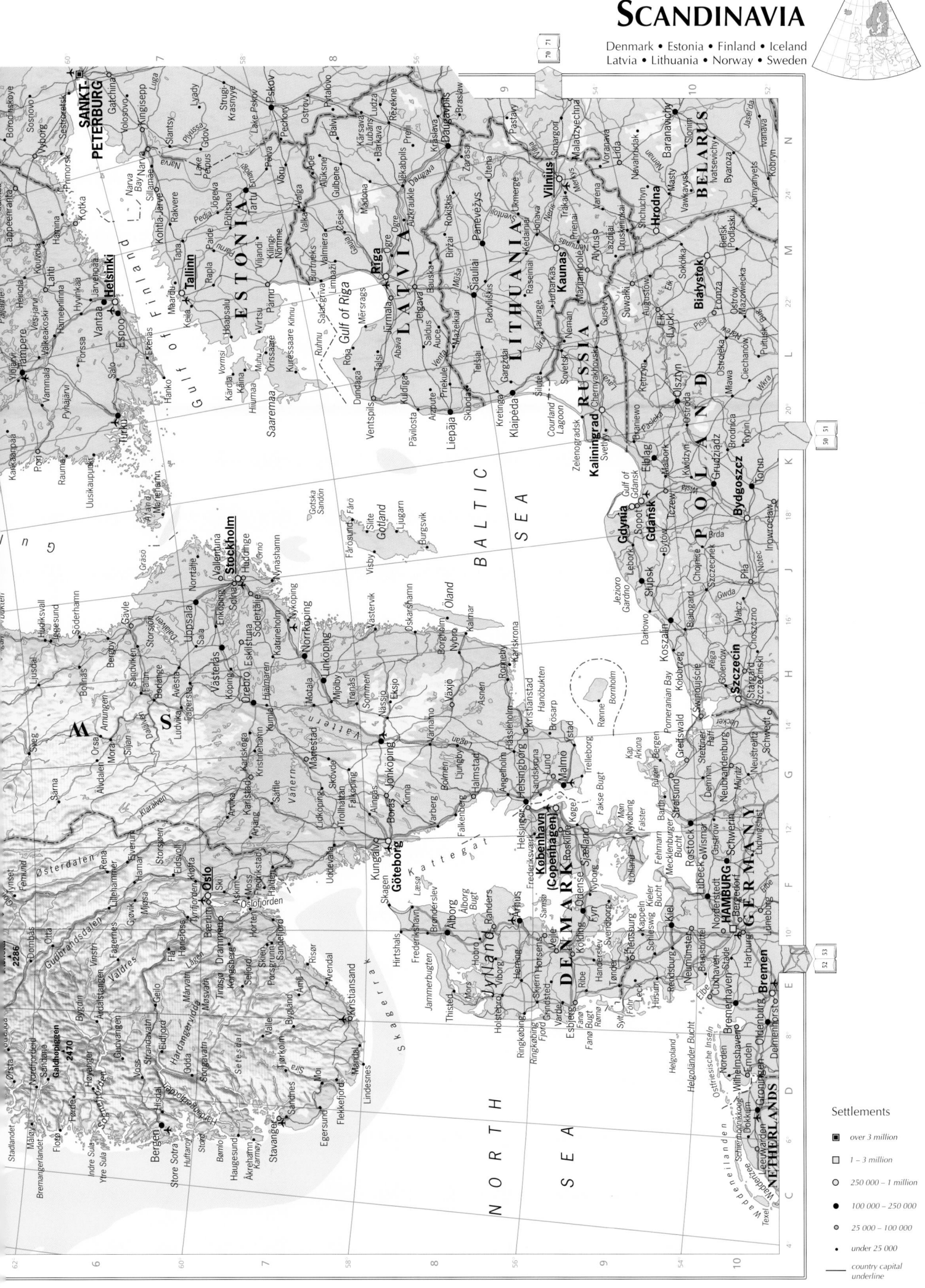

Settlements

- ■ over 3 million
- □ 1 – 3 million
- ○ 250 000 – 1 million
- ● 100 000 – 250 000
- ◉ 25 000 – 100 000
- • under 25 000
- ── country capital underline

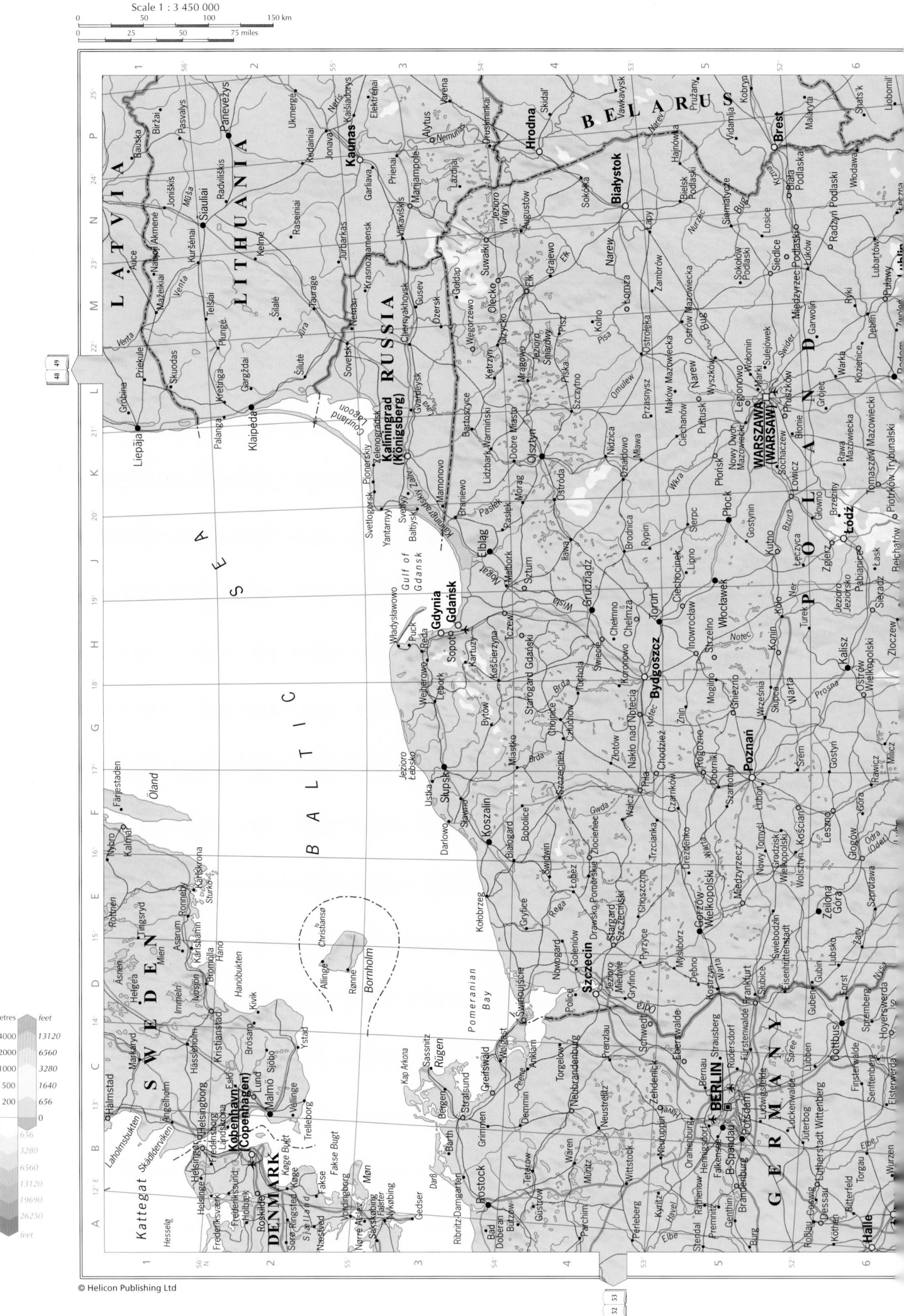

Scale 1 : 3 450 000

0   50   150 km
0 25 50 75 miles

© Helicon Publishing Ltd

metres   feet
4000   13120
2000   6560
1000   3280
500   1640
200   656
0   0
200   656
1000   3280
2000   6560
4000   13120
6000   19690
8000   26250
metres   feet

CENTRAL EUROPE

Czech Republic • Hungary • Poland • Slovak Republic

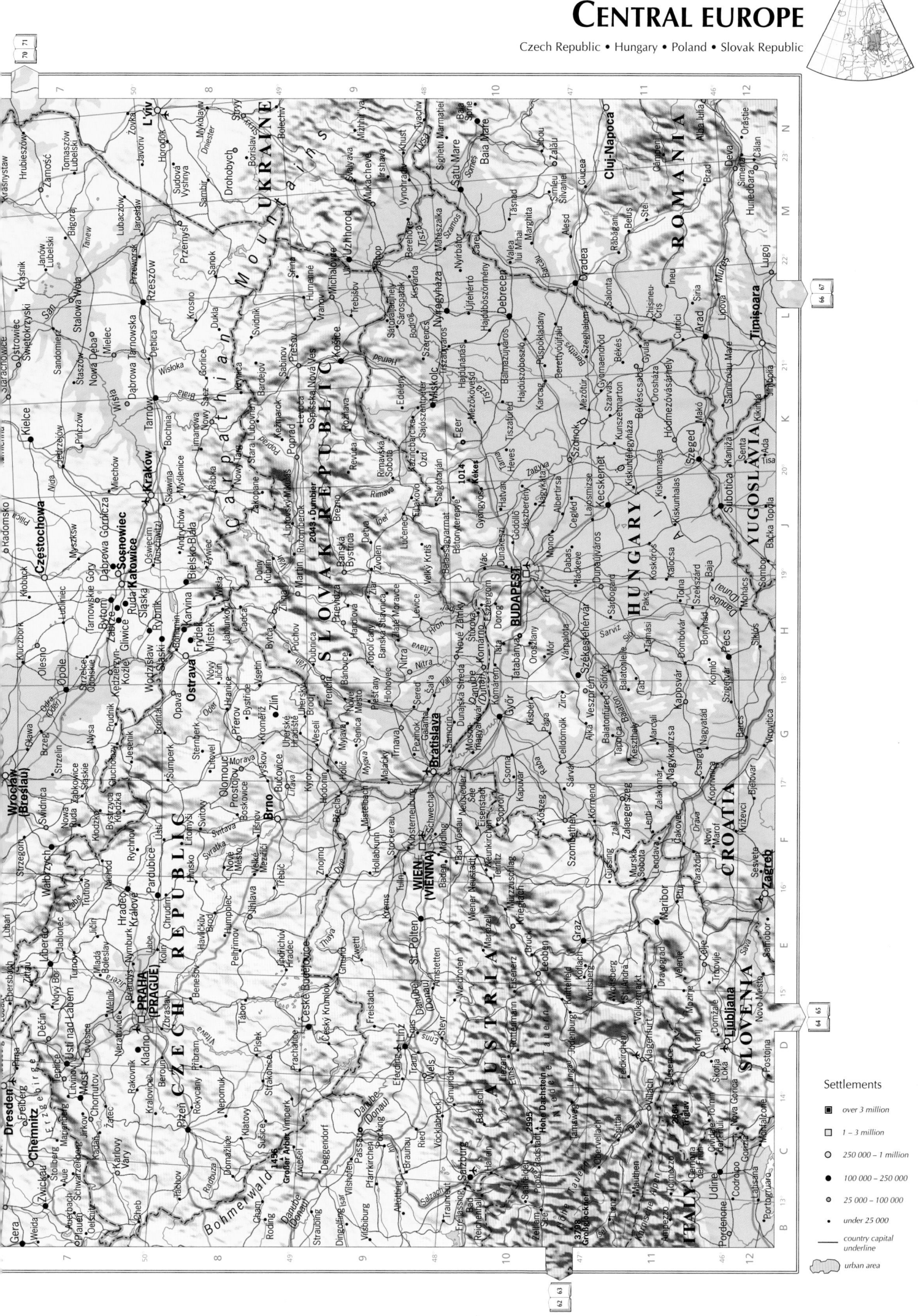

66 67

64 65

62 63

Settlements

- ◨ over 3 million
- ☐ 1 – 3 million
- ○ 250 000 – 1 million
- ● 100 000 – 250 000
- ◉ 25 000 – 100 000
- • under 25 000
- ─── country capital underline
- ⬡ urban area

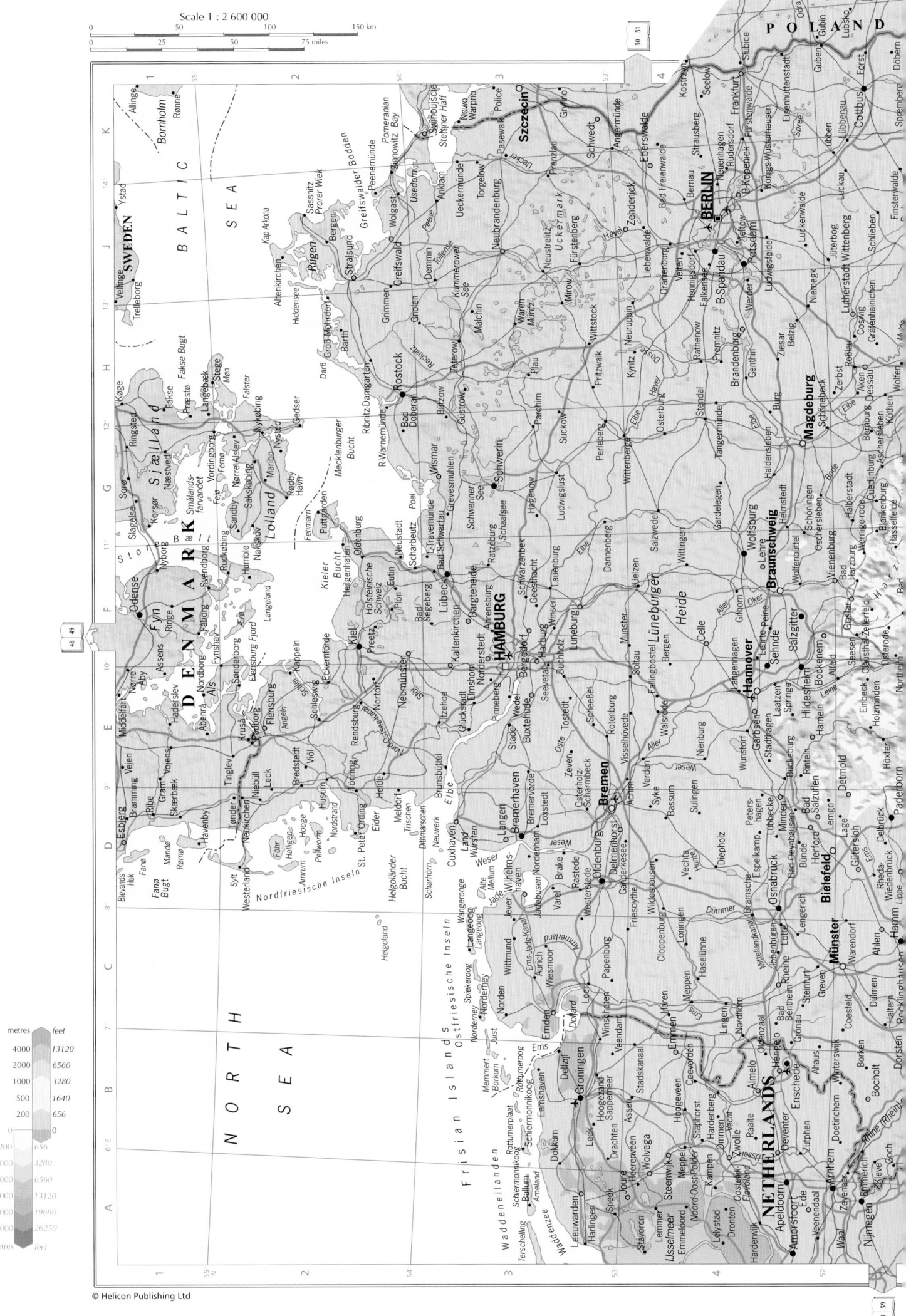

Scale 1 : 2 600 000

© Helicon Publishing Ltd

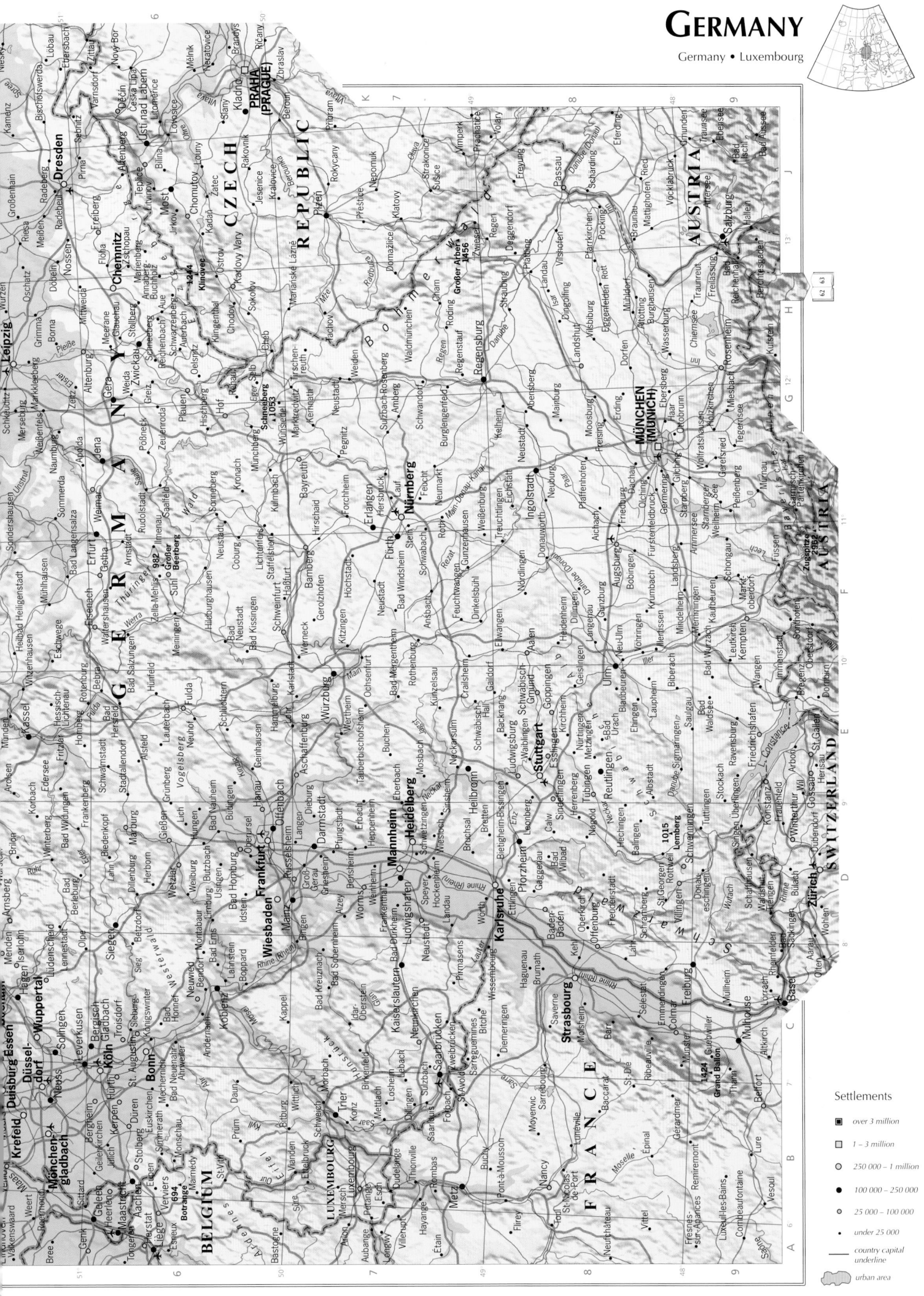

Settlements

■ over 3 million

□ 1 – 3 million

◎ 250 000 – 1 million

● 100 000 – 250 000

◌ 25 000 – 100 000

· under 25 000

— country capital
underline

urban area

Scale 1 : 2 300 000

© Helicon Publishing Ltd

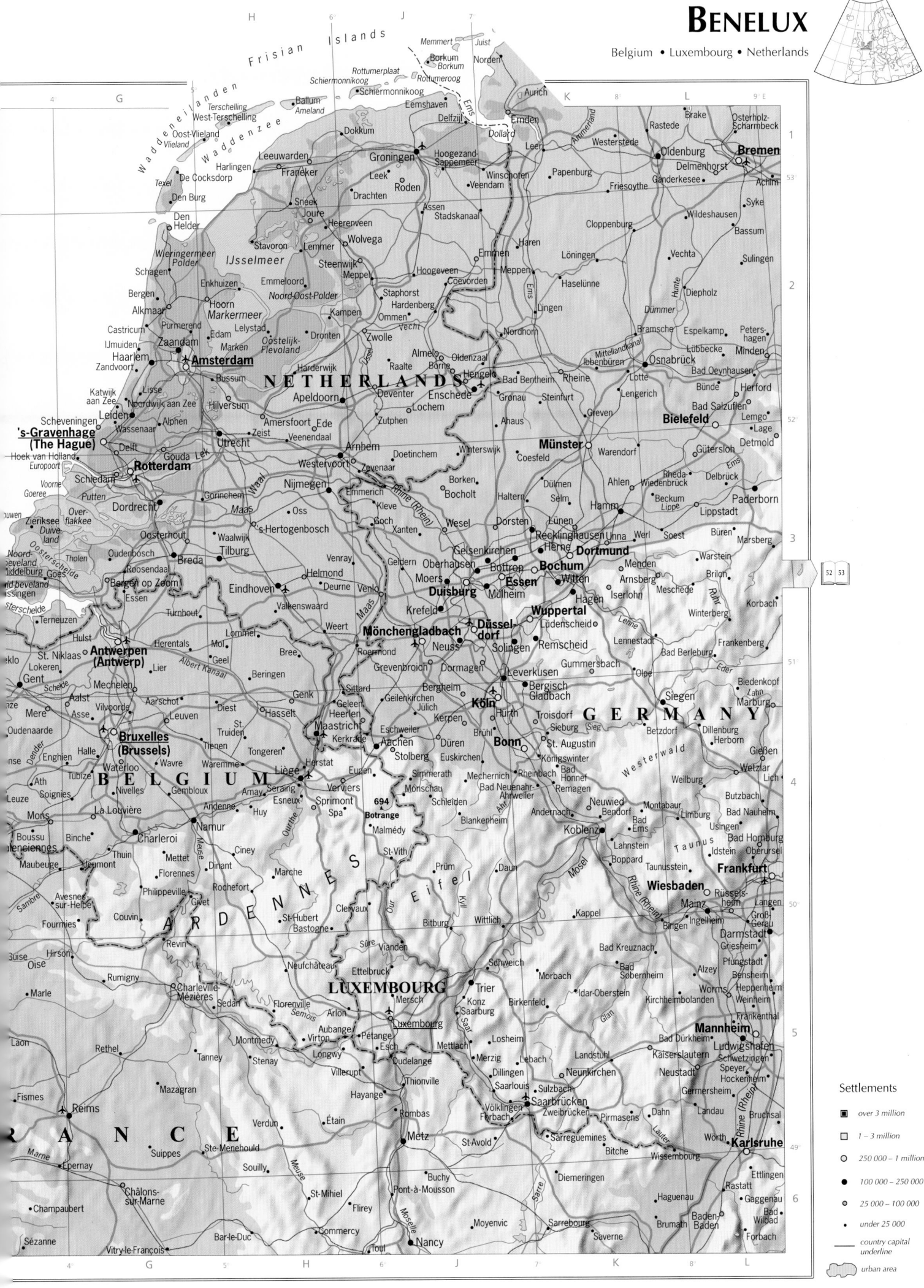

Frisian Islands

NETHERLANDS

BELGIUM

LUXEMBOURG

GERMANY

FRANCE

ARDENNES

IJsselmeer

Markermeer

Waddenzee

Waddeneilanden

Memmert
Juist
Borkum
Borkum
Rottumerplaat
Rottumeroog
Schiermonnikoog
Schiermonnikoog
Terschelling
West-Terschelling
Ballum
Ameland
Eemshaven
Oost-Vlieland
Vlieland
Texel
De Cocksdorp
Den Burg
Den Helder
Wieringermeer Polder
Schagen
Bergen
Alkmaar
Castricum
IJmuiden
Haarlem
Zandvoort
Katwijk aan Zee
Noordwijk aan Zee
Leiden
Wassenaar
Scheveningen
's-Gravenhage (The Hague)
Hoek van Holland
Europoort
Voorne
Goeree
Putten
Schiedam
Rotterdam
Delft
Gouda
Lek
Zierikzee
Duiveland
Goes
Middelburg
Vlissingen
Terneuzen
Hulst
St. Niklaas
Lokeren
Gent
Aalst
Mere
Oudenaarde
Enghien
Tubize
Ath
Soignies
Leuze
Mons
Boussu
Valenciennes
Maubeuge
Avesnes-sur-Helpe
Fourmies
Hirson
Guise
Oise
Marle
Laon
Fismes
Reims
Épernay
Champaubert
Sézanne
Châlons-sur-Marne
Vitry-le-François

Dokkum
Leeuwarden
Harlingen
Franeker
Leek
Roden
Groningen
Hoogezand-Sappemeer
Winschoten
Veendam
Drachten
Heerenveen
Sneek
Joure
Lemmer
Wolvega
Stavoren
Assen
Stadskanaal
Emmeloord
Noord-Oost-Polder
Kampen
Meppel
Staphorst
Hardenberg
Ommen
Zwolle
Hoogeveen
Coevorden
Emmen
Lelystad
Oostelijk-Flevoland
Dronten
Harderwijk
Raalte
Almelo
Borne
Hengelo
Oldenzaal
Apeldoorn
Deventer
Enschede
Lochem
Amersfoort
Ede
Veenendaal
Zeist
Arnhem
Westervoort
Zevenaar
Winterswijk
Doetinchem
Nijmegen
Emmerich
Kleve
Goch
Xanten
's-Hertogenbosch
Oss
Waalwijk
Tilburg
Oosterhout
Breda
Roosendaal
Bergen op Zoom
Essen
Turnhout
Eindhoven
Helmond
Deurne
Venray
Venlo
Geldern
Weert
Valkenswaard
Lommel
Mol
Geel
Bree
Herentals
Lier
Mechelen
Aarschot
Diest
Hasselt
Genk
Beringen
Sittard
Geleen
Geilenkirchen
Jülich
Maastricht
Kerkrade
Heerlen
Aachen
Eschweiler
Düren
Bruxelles (Brussels)
Waterloo
Nivelles
Wavre
Gembloux
Leuven
Tienen
Tongeren
Herstal
Liège
Seraing
Amay
Huy
Andenne
Namur
Ciney
La Louvière
Binche
Thuin
Jeumont
Charleroi
Mettet
Philippeville
Couvin
Revin
Dinant
Rochefort
Marche
St-Hubert
Bastogne
Neufchâteau
Vianden
Ettelbruck
Mersch
LUXEMBOURG
Luxembourg
Esch
Dudelange
Pétange
Aubange
Virton
Longwy
Villerupt
Thionville
Hayange
Montmédy
Rumigny
Mazagran
Stenay
Verdun
Étain
Metz
Nancy
Toul
Commercy
St-Mihiel
Pont-à-Mousson
Buchy
Souilly
Ste-Menehould
Bar-le-Duc
Flirey
Sedan
Charleville-Mézières
Florenville
Semois
Arlon
Tanney
Longwy

Emden
Norden
Aurich
Leer
Delfzijl
Dollard
Ems
Ammerland
Westerstede
Papenburg
Friesoythe
Cloppenburg
Löningen
Haren
Meppen
Haselünne
Lingen
Nordhorn
Lingen
Bad Bentheim
Gronau
Steinfurt
Ahaus
Coesfeld
Borken
Bocholt
Wesel
Dorsten
Haltern
Dülmen
Selm
Lünen
Recklinghausen
Gladbeck
Gelsenkirchen
Oberhausen
Bottrop
Moers
Duisburg
Mülheim
Essen
Bochum
Witten
Hagen
Krefeld
Mönchengladbach
Neuss
Düsseldorf
Solingen
Remscheid
Wuppertal
Lüdenscheid
Leverkusen
Köln
Bergisch Gladbach
Gummersbach
Olpe
Hürth
Brühl
Bonn
Siegburg
Troisdorf
St. Augustin
Königswinter
Bad Honnef
Remagen
Neuwied
Andernach
Koblenz
Lahnstein
Boppard
Mayen
Bad Neuenahr-Ahrweiler
Euskirchen
Bad Münstereifel
Rheinbach
Mechernich
Schleiden
Blankenheim
Daun
Prüm
St-Vith
Malmédy
Eupen
Verviers
Spa
Sprimont
Esneux
Ourthe
Amblève
Botrange 694
Monschau
Simmerath
Stolberg
Bitburg
Wittlich
Schweich
Trier
Konz
Saarburg
Birkenfeld
Idar-Oberstein
Morbach
Kappel
Bad Sobernheim
Bad Kreuznach
Mosel
Bad Ems
Limburg
Montabaur
Weilburg
Diez
Taunus
Taunusstein
Wiesbaden
Mainz
Bingen
Ingelheim
Rüsselsheim
Frankfurt
Langen
Groß-Gerau
Darmstadt
Griesheim
Pfungstadt
Alzey
Worms
Kirchheimbolanden
Bensheim
Heppenheim
Weinheim
Frankenthal
Ludwigshafen
Mannheim
Schwetzingen
Speyer
Hockenheim
Neustadt
Germersheim
Landau
Bruchsal
Karlsruhe
Wörth
Wissembourg
Haguenau
Brumath
Baden-Baden
Rastatt
Ettlingen
Gaggenau
Bad Wildbad
Forbach
Saverne
Sarrebourg
Moyenvic
Diemeringen
Bitche
Saarbrücken
Zweibrücken
Pirmasens
Dahn
Völklingen
Forbach
Saarlouis
Dillingen
Merzig
Sulzbach
Neunkirchen
Kaiserslautern
Landstuhl
Lebach
Losheim
Mettlach
Saarbrücken
Sarreguemines
St-Avold
Sarrebourg
Moyenvic
Lunéville
Oldenburg
Delmenhorst
Ganderkesee
Bremen
Achim
Syke
Bassum
Sulingen
Diepholz
Dümmer
Hunte
Vechta
Wildeshausen
Osterholz-Scharmbeck
Brake
Rastede
Peters-hagen
Espelkamp
Lübbecke
Minden
Bad Oeynhausen
Bünde
Herford
Bad Salzuflen
Lemgo
Lage
Detmold
Gütersloh
Rheda-Wiedenbrück
Delbrück
Paderborn
Lippstadt
Büren
Marsberg
Brilon
Winterberg
Bad Berleburg
Frankenberg
Korbach
Iserlohn
Meschede
Arnsberg
Menden
Werl
Soest
Unna
Hamm
Beckum
Lippe
Ahlen
Warendorf
Greven
Münster
Dülmen
Coesfeld
Bielefeld
Herford
Lotte
Ibbenbüren
Osnabrück
Bramsche
Bad Salzuflen
Lengerich
Rheine
Mittellandkanal
Albert Kanaal
Schelde
Dender
Maas
Waal
Rhine (Rhein)
Mosel
Saar
Eifel
Westerwald
Ardennes
Semois
Our
Sûre
Kyll
Nahe
Lauter
Murg
Sauer
Meuse
Aisne
Marne
Maas (Meuse)

Settlements
▪ over 3 million
□ 1 – 3 million
○ 250 000 – 1 million
● 100 000 – 250 000
◉ 25 000 – 100 000
· under 25 000
— country capital underline
urban area

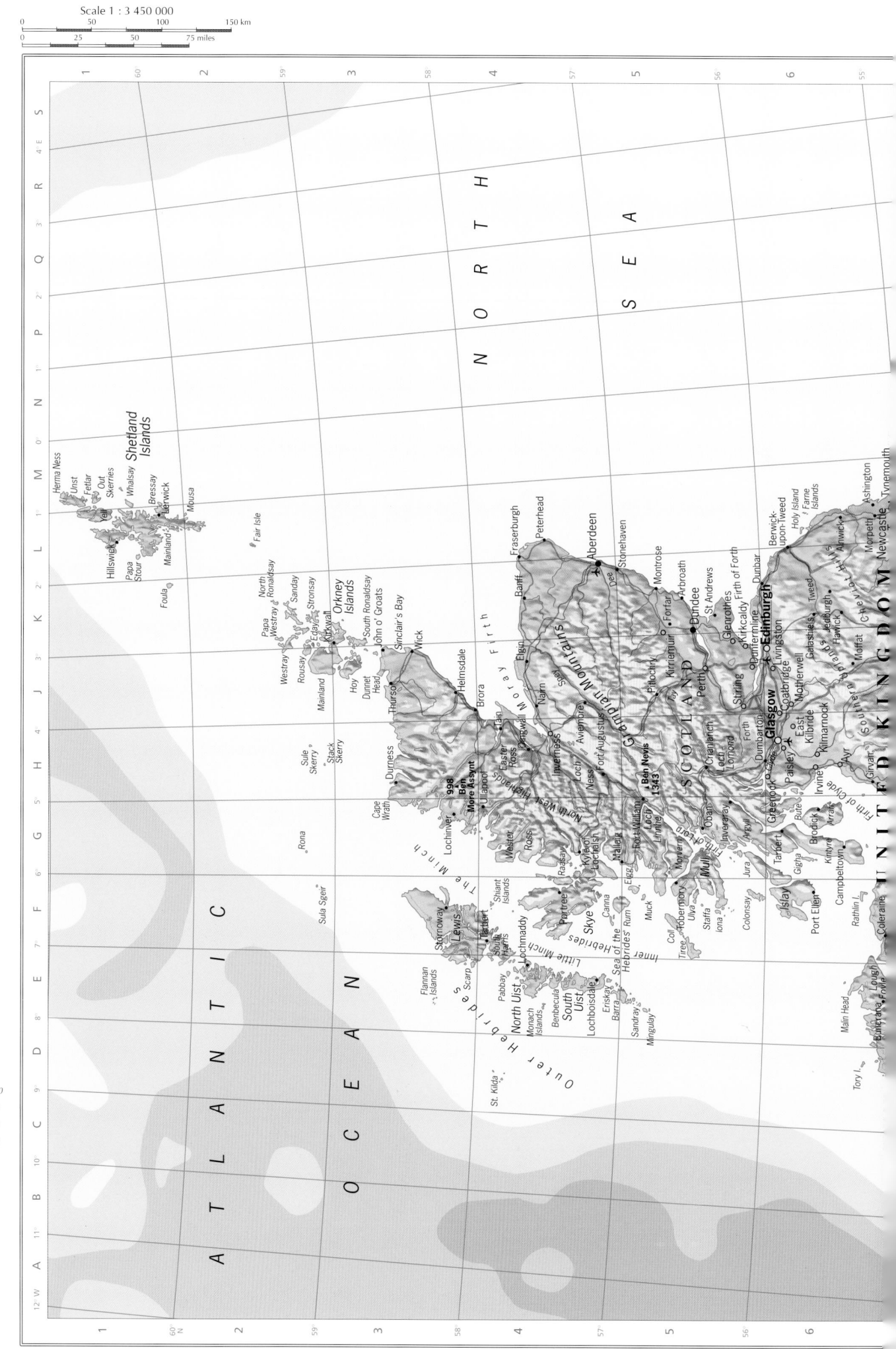

Scale 1 : 3 450 000

© Helicon Publishing Ltd

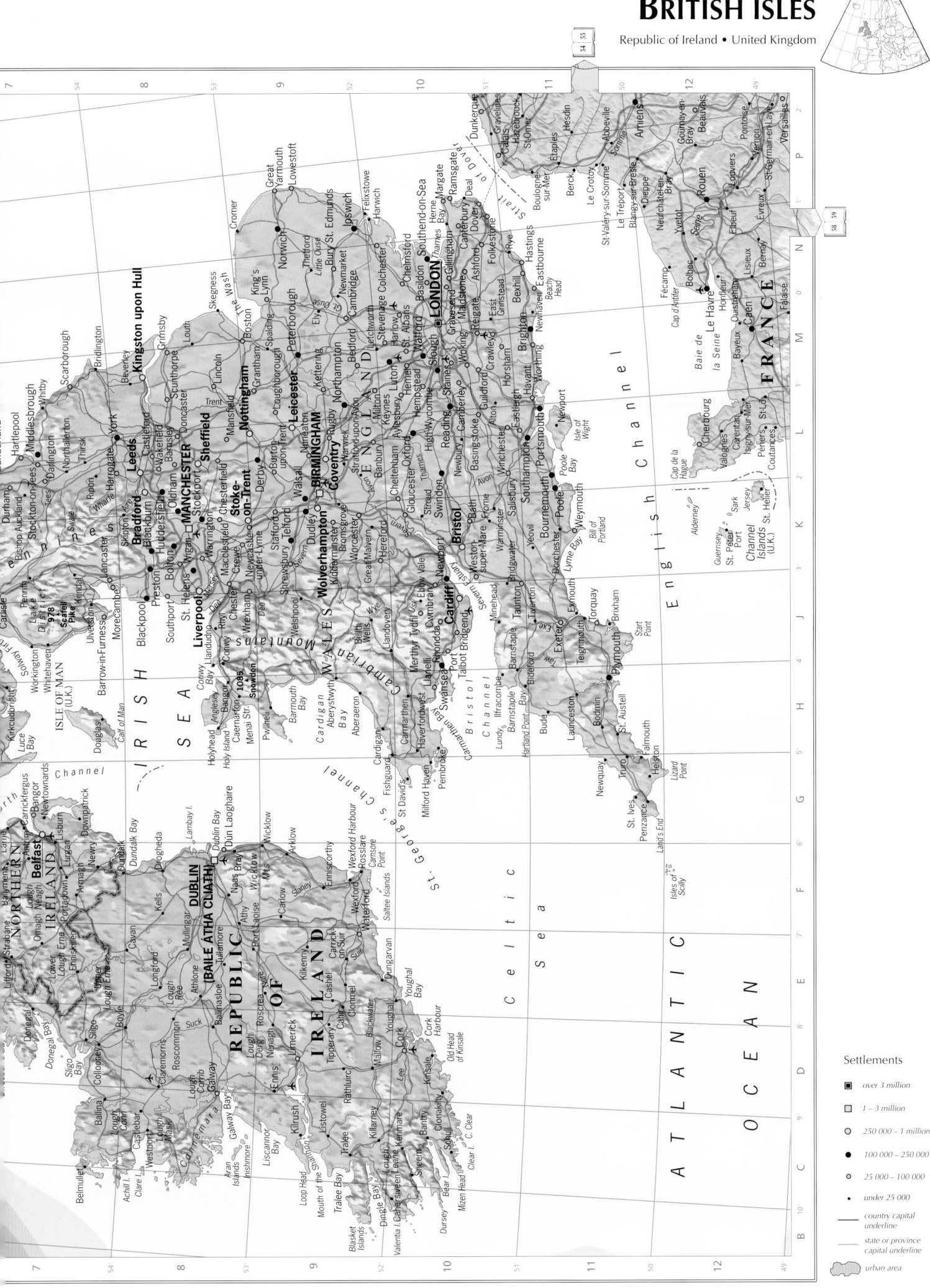

Settlements

■	over 3 million
□	1 – 3 million
◦	250 000 – 1 million
●	100 000 – 250 000
○	25 000 – 100 000
·	under 25 000
——	country capital underline
—	state or province capital underline
〰	urban area

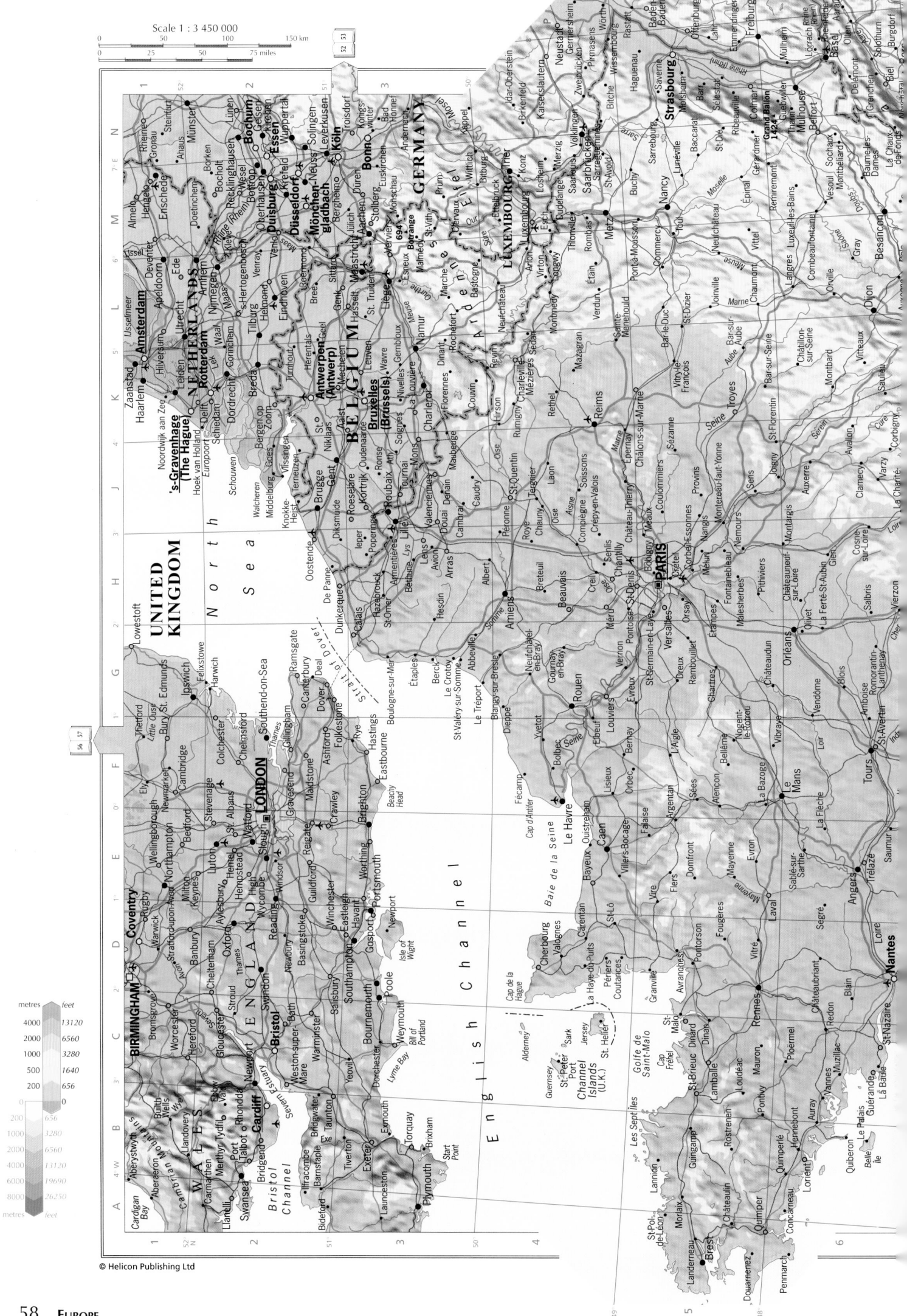

Scale 1 : 3 450 000

© Helicon Publishing Ltd

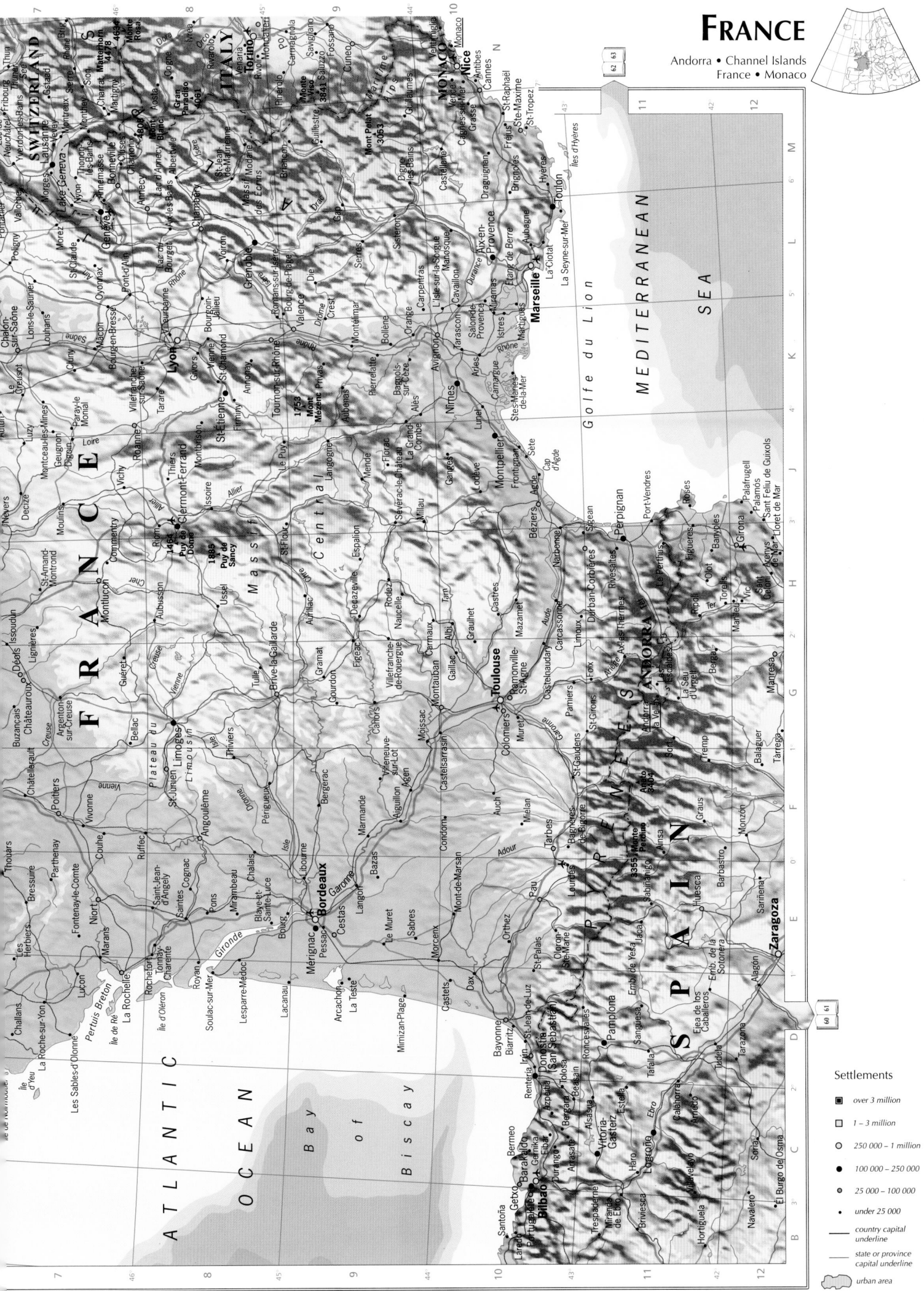

Settlements

■	over 3 million
□	1 – 3 million
○	250 000 – 1 million
●	100 000 – 250 000
◉	25 000 – 100 000
•	under 25 000
——	country capital underline
——	state or province capital underline
⬭	urban area

Scale 1 : 3 450 000

© Helicon Publishing Ltd

Settlements

■	over 3 million
□	1 – 3 million
◎	250 000 – 1 million
●	100 000 – 250 000
○	25 000 – 100 000
•	under 25 000
—	country capital underline
	urban area

Scale 1 : 2 600 000

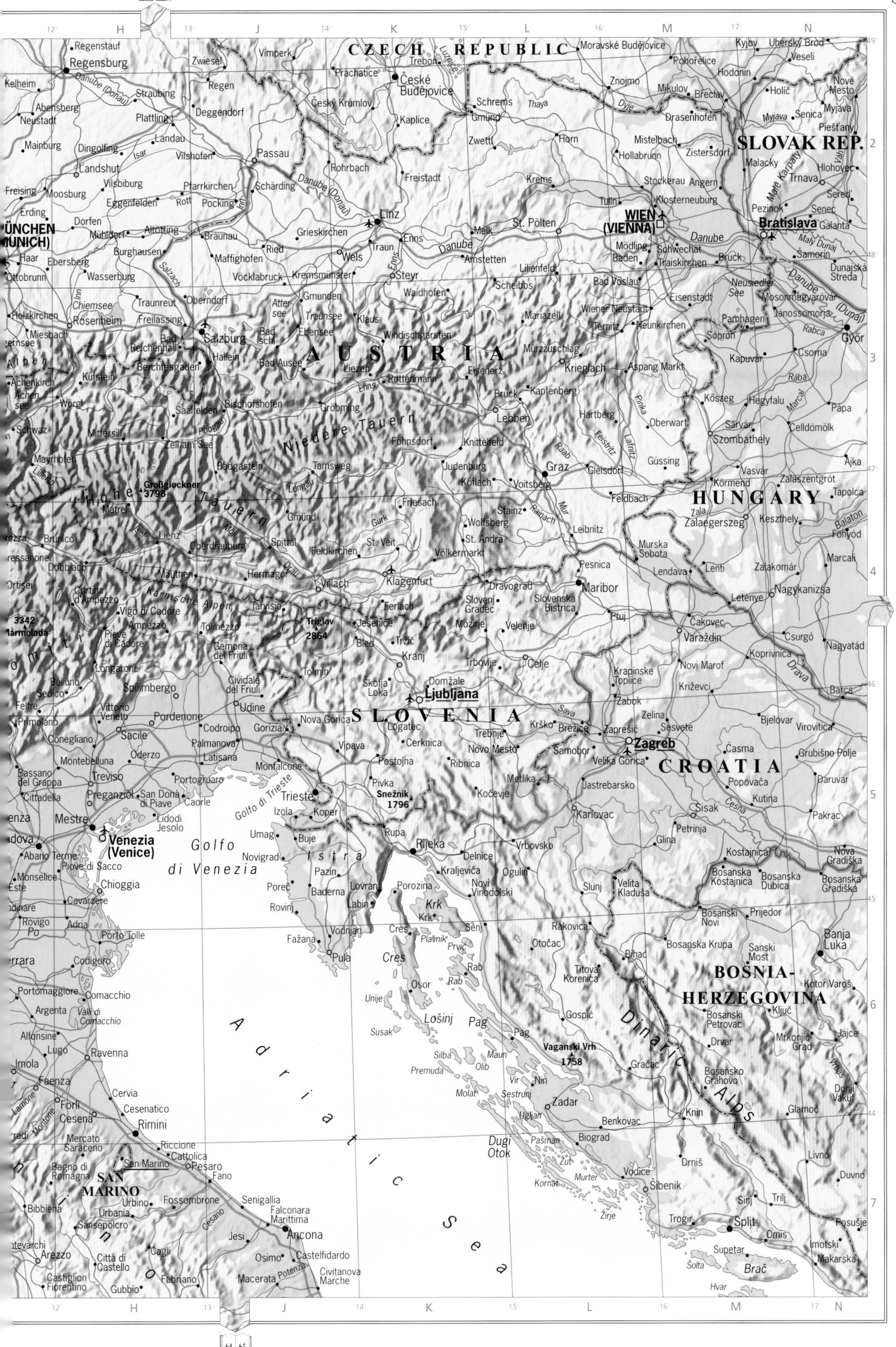

CZECH REPUBLIC

SLOVAK REP.

AUSTRIA

HUNGARY

SLOVENIA

CROATIA

BOSNIA-
HERZEGOVINA

SAN
MARINO

Regensburg
Regenstauf
Kelheim
Abensberg
Neustadt
Mainburg
Freising
Erding
Moosburg
Landshut
Vilsbiburg
Dorfen
Haar
Ottobrunn
(MUNICH)
MÜNCHEN
Holzkirchen
Miesbach
Rosenheim
Wasserburg
Traunreut
Chiemsee
Salzburg
Reichenhall
Bad
Berchtesgaden
Hallein
Kufstein
Wörgl
Schwaz
Mayrhofen
Zell am See
Mittersill
Lienz
Mátrei
Brúnico
Dobbiaco
Cortina
d'Ampezzo
Marmolada 3342
Grossglockner 3798
Hohe Tauern

Straubing
Deggendorf
Plattling
Landau
Vilshofen
Pocking
Passau
Schárding
Rohrbach
Freistadt
Linz
Traun
Wels
Steyr
Enns
Amstetten
Waidhofen
Scheibbs
Lilienfeld

České Budějovice
Český Krumlov
Kaplice
Gmünd
Zwettl
Horn
Krems
Melk
St. Pölten
WIEN (VIENNA)
Klosterneuburg
Mödling
Baden
Bad Vöslau
Wiener Neustadt
Neunkirchen

Moravské Budějovice
Pohořelice
Znojmo
Mikulov
Břeclav
Drasenhofen
Mistelbach
Hollabrunn
Zistersdorf
Stockerau
Schwechat
Eisenstadt
Neusiedler See
Sopron

SLOVENIA
Ljubljana
Kranj
Celje
Maribor
Klagenfurt
Villach
Graz

CROATIA
Zagreb
Rijeka
Karlovac

Venezia (Venice)
Golfo di Venezia
Trieste
Koper
Istra
Pula

Adriatic Sea

Triglav 2864
Snežnik 1796
Vaganski Vrh 1758
Dinaric Alps

Settlements

□ 1 – 3 million
○ 250 000 – 1 million
● 100 000 – 250 000
○ 25 000 – 100 000
• under 25 000
— country capital underline
urban area

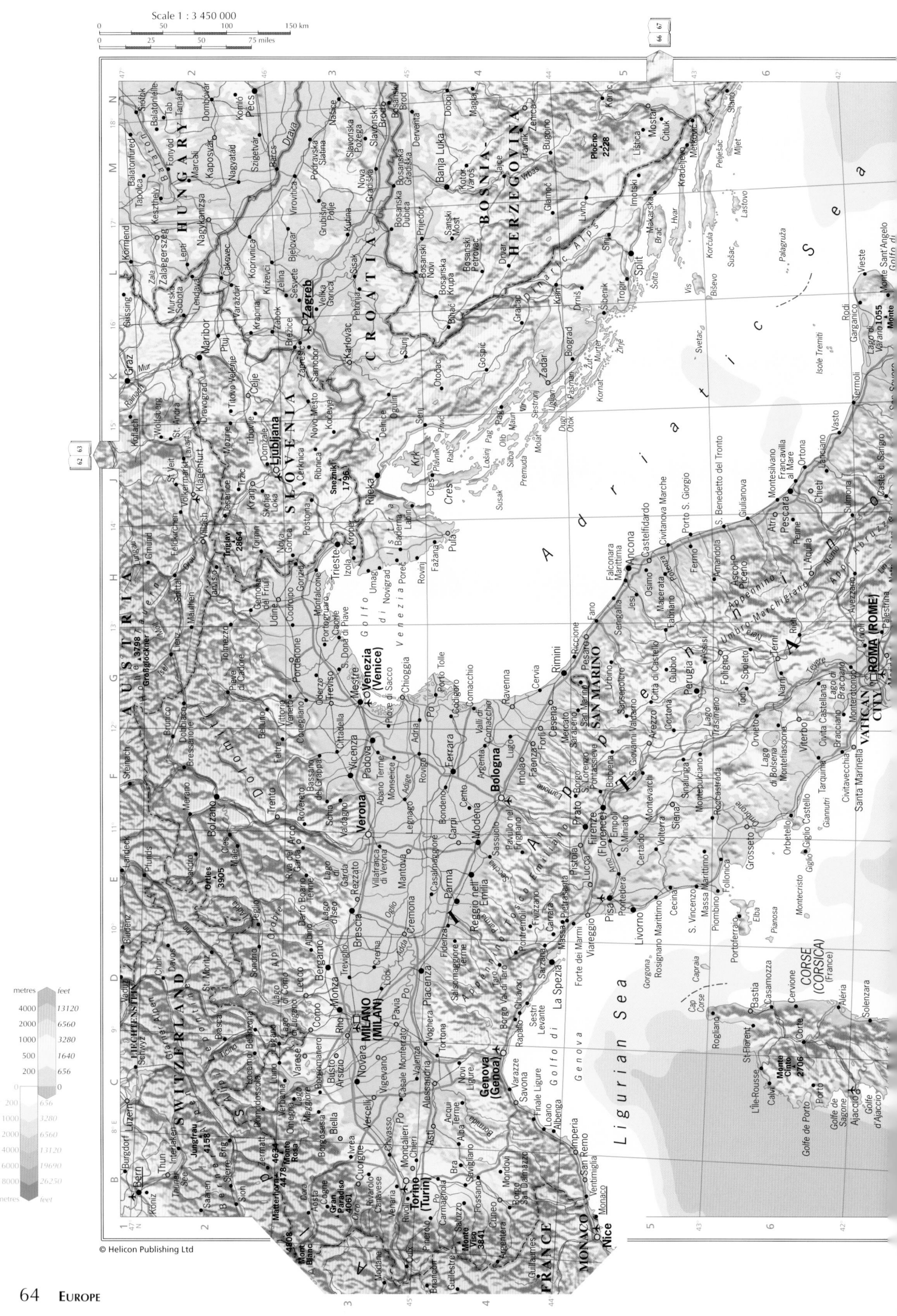

Scale 1 : 3 450 000

0   50   100   150 km
0   25   50   75 miles

© Helicon Publishing Ltd

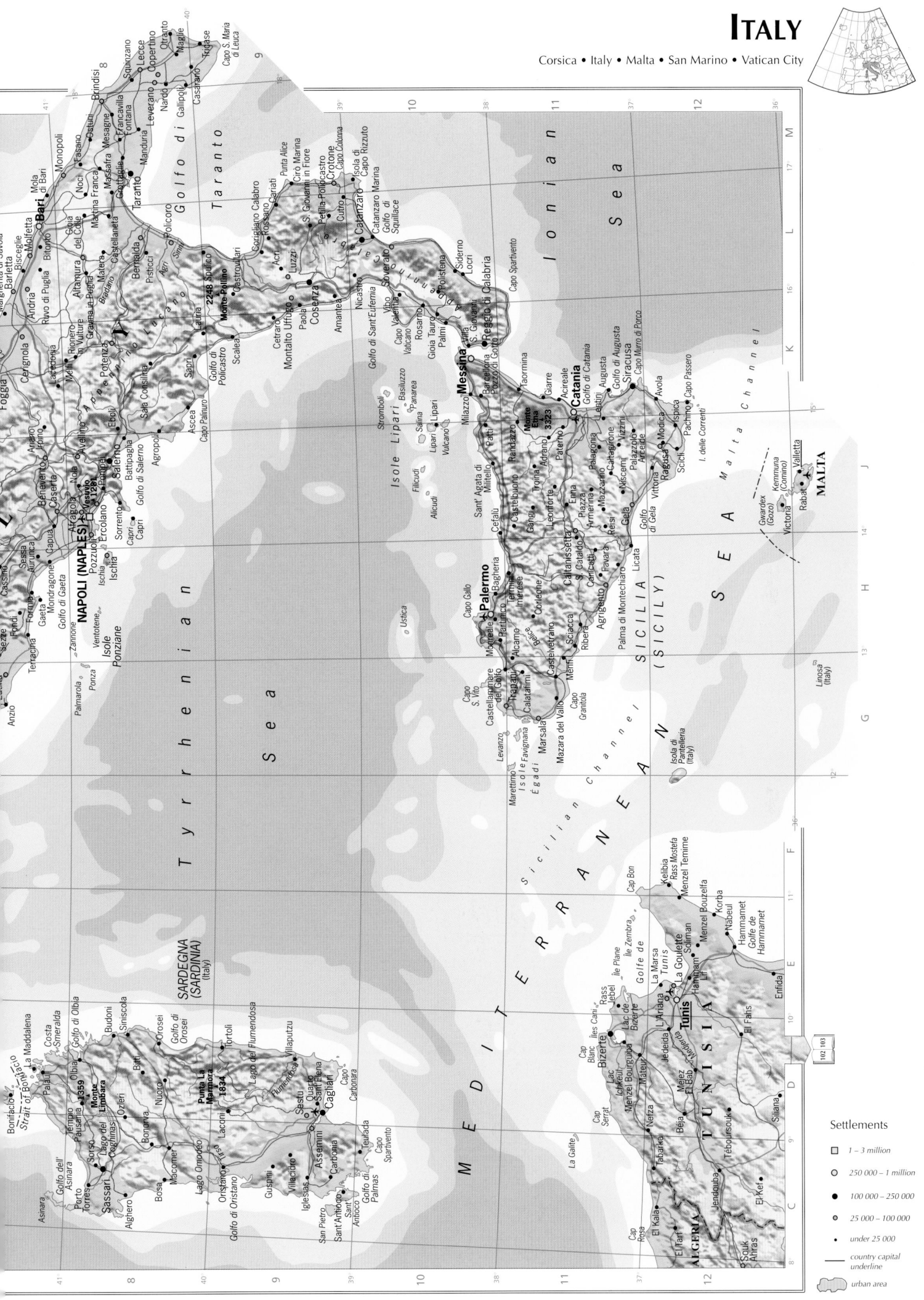

Settlements

☐	1 – 3 million
○	250 000 – 1 million
●	100 000 – 250 000
◉	25 000 – 100 000
·	under 25 000
——	country capital underline
⬭	urban area

Scale 1 : 3 450 000

UKRAINE

Uzhhorod

Svalyava
Mizhhir"ya
Mukacheve
Irshava

Berehove
Vynohradiv
Vásárosnamény
Mátészalka

Satu
Mare

Carei

Baia Mare

Khust
Tyachiv
Rakhiv

Sighetu
Marmației

Viseu
de Sus
Borșa

Borshchiv
Horodenka
Kolomyya
Kam"yanets'-
Podil's'kyy

Nadvirna
Prut

Chernivtsi

Storozhynets'
Verkhovyna
Hlyboka
Siret

Havrylivtsi
Briceni

Sokyryany

Mohyliv-
Podil's'kyy

Yampil'

Lipcani

Darabani

Edineț

Soroca

Drochia

Florești

Balta

Kodyma

Kotovs'k
Anan'yiv

Kryve
Ozero

Novoselivka

MOLDOVA

Ungheni
Străseni

Nisporeni

Chișinău Tiraspol

Grigoriopol'

Dubăsari

Orhei

Căușeni

ODESA
(ODESSA)

Illichivs'k

Ovidiopol'
Bilhorod-
Dnistrovs'kyy

UKRAINE

R O M A N I A

Baia
Sprie

Tășnad

Marghita

Simleu
Silvaniei

Zalău

Dej

Beclean

Bistrița

Gherla

Reghin

Gheorgheni

Bălan

Cluj-Napoca

Turda

Câmpia
Turzii

Luduș

Târgu
Mureș

Târnăveni

Aiud

Blaj

Mediaș

Agnita

Sighișoara

Sibiu

Codlea

Brașov

B U L G A R I A

SOFIJA
(SOFIA)

Pernik

Radomir

Kjustendil

Stanke
Dimitrov

Samokov

Kostenec

Pazardžik

Plovdiv

Stara Zagora

TURKEY

Edirne

Kırklareli

İSTANBUL

Kartal

GREECE

Settlements

■ over 3 million

□ 1 – 3 million

○ 250 000 – 1 million

● 100 000 – 250 000

◦ 25 000 – 100 000

· under 25 000

— country capital
underline

— state or province
capital underline

⬭ urban area

BLACK SEA

TURKEY

ANATOLIA

Settlements

■	over 3 million
□	1 – 3 million
○	250 000 – 1 million
●	100 000 – 250 000
◦	25 000 – 100 000
·	under 25 000
—	country capital underline
—	state or province capital underline
	urban area

92 93

Provadija
Devnja
Varna
Staro Orjahovo
Bjala
Ajtos
Nos Emine
Nesebâr
Pomorie
Karnobat
Burgas
Sozopol
Grudovo
Mičurin
Malko Târnovo
Resovo
İğneada
Kirklareli
Kiyiköy
Pinarhisar
Vize
Babaeski
Saray
Lüleburgaz
Çerkezköy
Hayrabolu
Muratli
Çorlu
Silivri
İnecik
Tekirdağ
Büyükçekmece
İSTANBUL
Sariyer
Beykoz
Şile
Ağva
İstanbul Boğazı (Bosporus)
Kartal
Pendik
Yeşilköy
Büyükada
Gebze
İzmit
Hendek
Düzce
Kumbağ
Marmara Adası
Yalova
Karamürsel
Sakarya
Bolu
Marmara Denizi (Sea of Marmara)
Kapıdağı Yarımadası
İmralı Adası
Gemlik Körfezi
Gemlik
İznik Gölü
İznik
Geyve
Mudurnu
Köroğlu Tepesi 2400
Köroğlu Dağları
Erdek
Bandırma
Mudanya
Bursa
Bilecik
Nallıhan
Beypazarı
Biga
Karacabey
Ulubat Gölü
İnegöl
Sakarya
Gönen
Mustafakemalpaşa
Çan
Susurluk
Bozüyük
Eskişehir
ANKARA
Elmadağ
Çubuk
Balıkesir
Dursunbey
Tavşanlı
Kaymaz
Polatlı
Bala
Burhaniye
Savaştepe
Bigadiç
Kütahya
Sivrihisar
Edremit
Ayvalık
Soma
Demirci
Simav
Gediz
Emirdağ
Yunak
Cihanbeyli
Tuz Gölü
Bergama
Kınık
Kırkağaç
Afyon
Çay
Bolvadin
Dikili
Akhisar
Saruhanlı
Gölmarmara
Uşak
Banaz
Sandıklı
Aliağa
Foça
Manisa
Salihli
Kula
Akşehir
Ilgın
Kadınhanı
Sarayönü
Menemen
Gediz
Karşıyaka
İZMIR
Turgutlu
Alaşehir
Dinar
Eğridir Gölü
Sarkıkaraağaç
Urla
Kemalpaşa
Seferihisar
Torbalı
Tire
Ödemiş
Sarayköy
Keçiborlu
Isparta
Eğridir
Beyşehir Gölü
Beyşehir
Konya
Selçuk
Germencik
Aydın
Nazilli
Açı Göl
Burdur
Çumra
Kuşadası
İncirliova
Ortaklar
Kocarlı
Çine
Denizli
2528 Eşler Dağ
Burdur Gölü
Bucak
Seydişehir
Söke
Çamiçigölü
Kale
Yenihisar
Yatağan
Boz Dağ 2419
Korkuteli
Kızılkaya
Akseki
Milas
Muğla
Körkuteli
Bodrum
Ören
Köyceğiz
Gölhisar
Serik
Manavgat
Kara Ada
Gökova Körfezi
Marmaris
Dalaman
3073
Elmalı
Kemer
Antalya
Datça
Fethiye
Kemer
Finike
Kumluca
Antalya Körfezi
Kalkan
Yardımcı Burnu

MEDITERRANEAN SEA

Scale 1 : 10 400 000

© Helicon Publishing Ltd

EUROPEAN RUSSIA

Belarus • European Russia • Ukraine

Settlements

- ■ over 3 million
- □ 1 – 3 million
- ○ 250 000 – 1 million
- ● 100 000 – 250 000
- ◦ 25 000 – 100 000
- • under 25 000
- ——— country capital underline
- ——— state or province capital underline

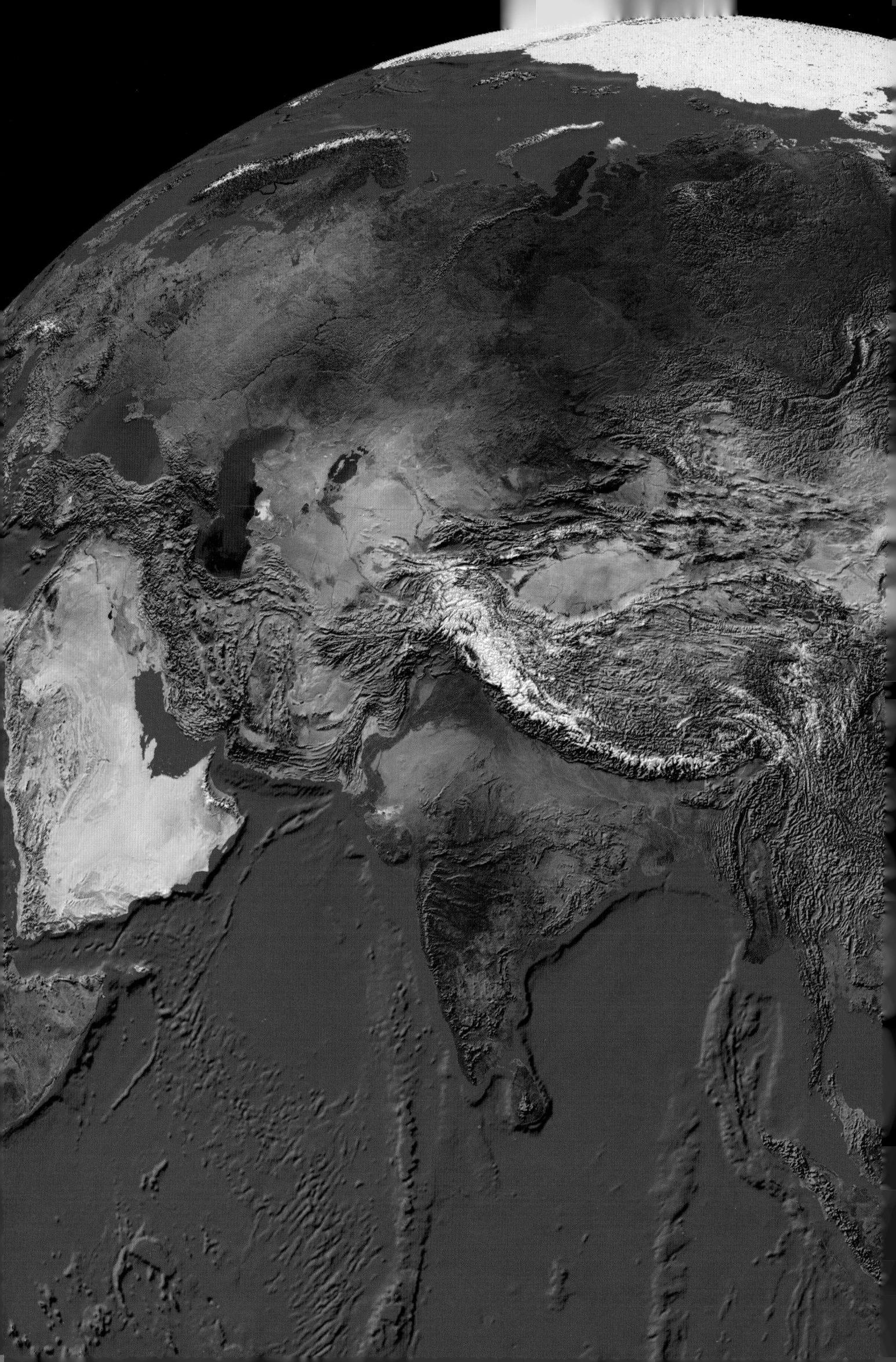

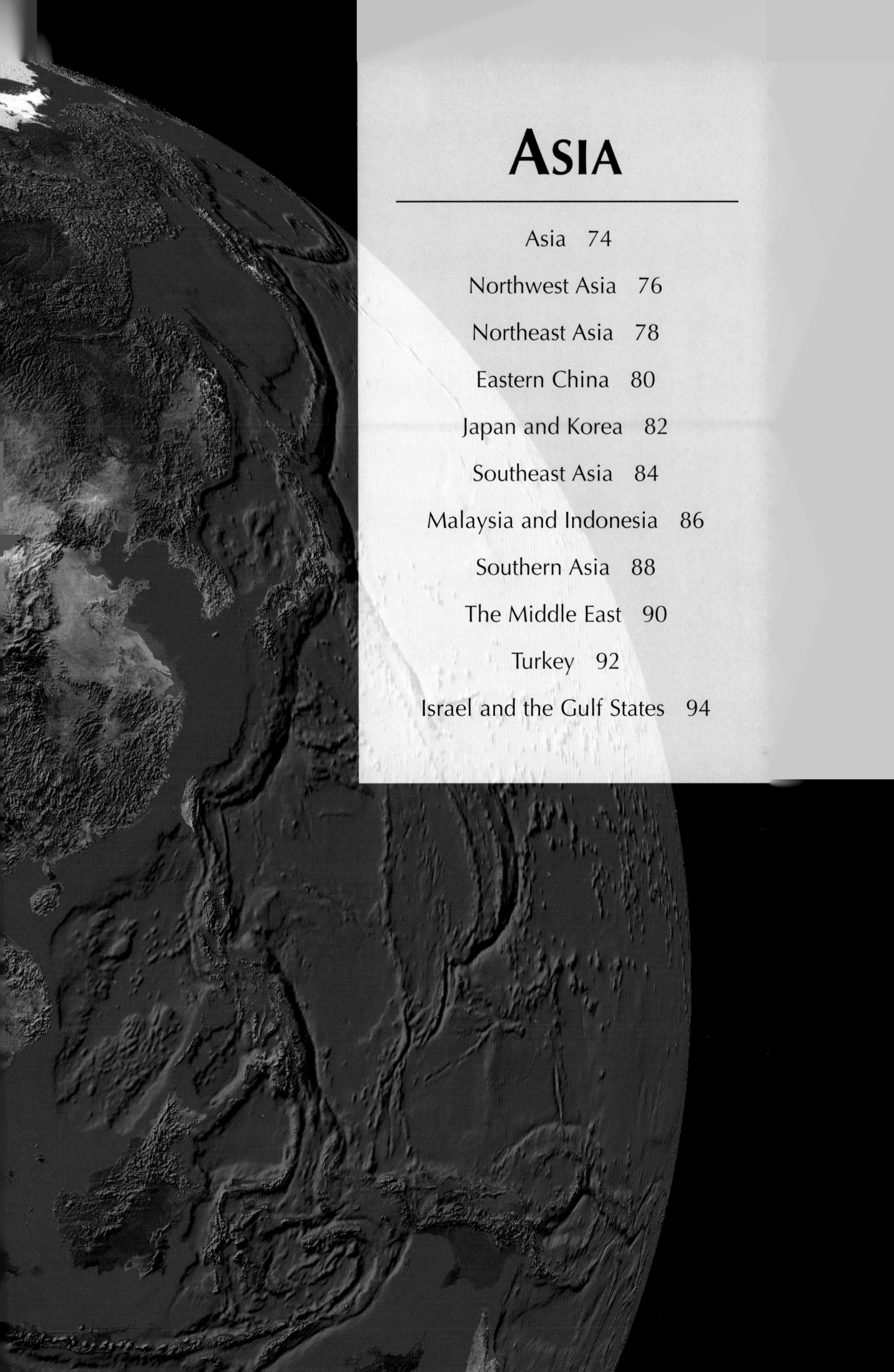

ASIA

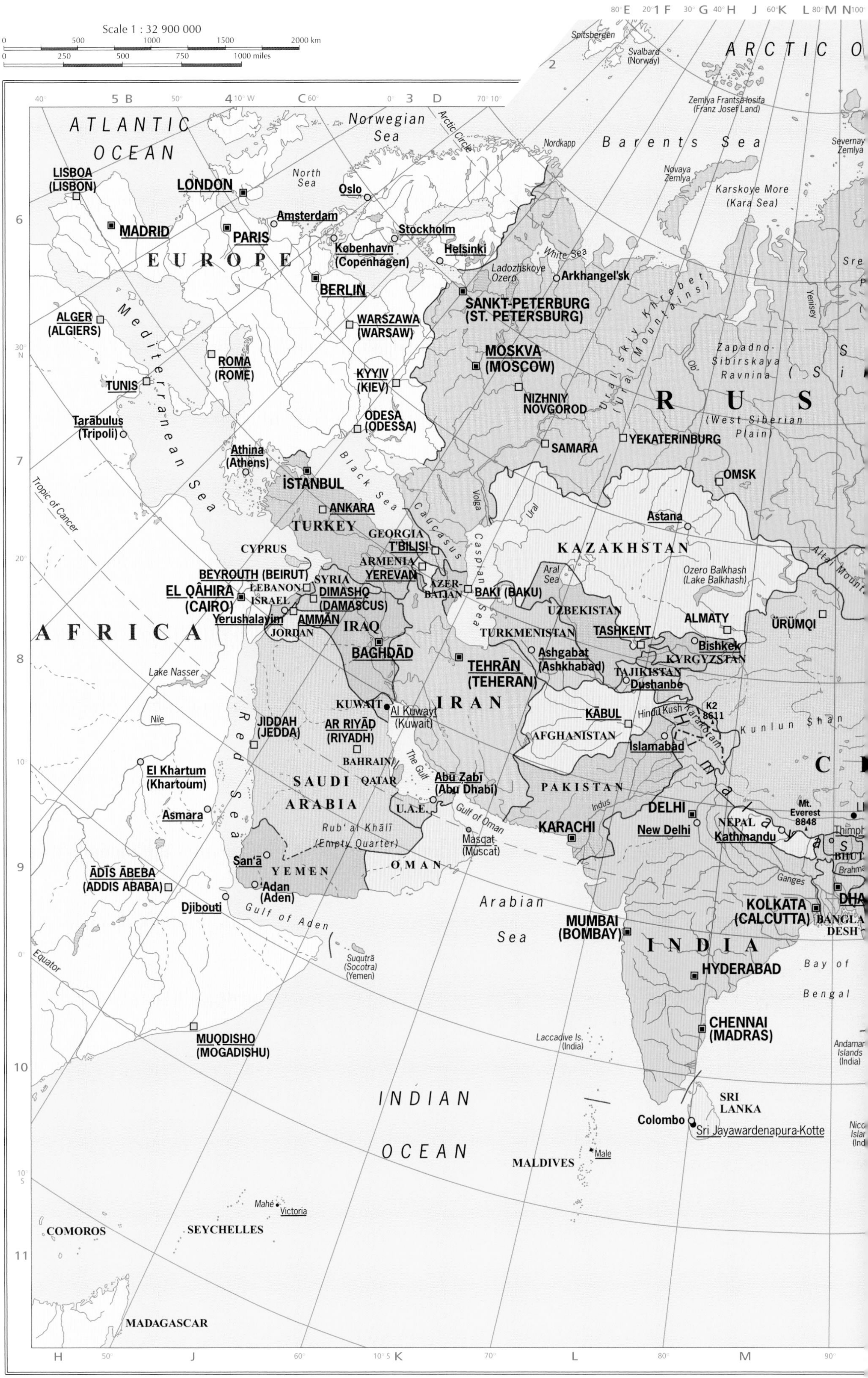

80°E 20°1F 30°G 40°H J 60°K L 80°M N100°

Spitsbergen

ARCTIC O

Svalbard
(Norway)

2

Zemlya Frantsa-Iosifa
(Franz Josef Land)

Severnay
Zemlya

Barents Sea

Nordkapp

Norwegian
Sea

ATLANTIC
OCEAN

Arctic Circle

Zemlya
Novaya

Karskoye More
(Kara Sea)

North
Sea

LISBOA
(LISBON)

LONDON

Oslo

Sre

MADRID

Amsterdam

PARIS

Kobenhavn
(Copenhagen)

Stockholm

Helsinki

White Sea

Ladozhskoye
Ozero

Arkhangel'sk

SANKT-PETERBURG
(ST. PETERSBURG)

Ural'skiy Khrebet (Ural Mountains)

Ob'

Yenisey

EUROPE

BERLIN

WARSZAWA
(WARSAW)

MOSKVA
(MOSCOW)

R U S

ALGER
(ALGIERS)

NIZHNIY
NOVGOROD

Zapadno-
Sibirskaya
Ravnina (S i

ROMA
(ROME)

KYYIV
(KIEV)

(West Siberian
Plain)

TUNIS

ODESA
(ODESSA)

SAMARA

YEKATERINBURG

Tarābulus
(Tripoli)

Tropic of Cancer

Mediterranean Sea

Athina
(Athens)

İSTANBUL

Black Sea

Caucasus

Volga

Ural

OMSK

Astana

ANKARA

GEORGIA

T'BILISI

KAZAKHSTAN

Altai Mount

TURKEY

CYPRUS

ARMENIA

YEREVAN

AZER-
BAIJAN

BAKİ (BAKU)

Caspian Sea

Aral
Sea

Ozero Balkhash
(Lake Balkhash)

BEYROUTH (BEIRUT)

SYRIA

DIMASHQ
(DAMASCUS)

UZBEKISTAN

ALMATY

ÜRÜMQI

AFRICA

EL QÂHIRA
(CAIRO)

LEBANON

ISRAEL

Yerushalayim

AMMAN

JORDAN

IRAQ

TURKMENISTAN

TASHKENT

Bishkek

KYRGYZSTAN

C

Lake Nasser

BAGHDĀD

TEHRĀN
(TEHERAN)

Ashgabat
(Ashkhabad)

TAJIKISTAN

Dushanbe

Nile

KUWAIT

Al Kuwayt
(Kuwait)

I R A N

KĀBUL

Hindu Kush

K2
8611

Karakoram

Kunlun Shan

Red Sea

JIDDAH
(JEDDA)

AR RIYĀD
(RIYADH)

AFGHANISTAN

Islamabad

BAHRAIN

El Khartum
(Khartoum)

SAUDI

QATAR

Abū Zabī
(Abu Dhabi)

PAKISTAN

Indus

DELHI

Mt.
Everest
8848

L

Asmara

ARABIA

U.A.E.

Gulf of Oman

KARACHI

New Delhi

NEPAL

Kathmandu

Thimph

BHUT

Brahma

Himalaya

S

Rub' al Khālī
(Empty Quarter)

Masqat
(Muscat)

ĀDĪS ĀBEBA
(ADDIS ABABA)

San'ā

YEMEN

OMAN

Ganges

KOLKATA
(CALCUTTA)

DHA

BANGLA
DESH

Djibouti

Adan
(Aden)

Gulf of Aden

Arabian
Sea

MUMBAI
(BOMBAY)

INDIA

Suqutrā
(Socotra)
(Yemen)

HYDERABAD

Bay of

Bengal

Equator

CHENNAI
(MADRAS)

Andaman
Islands
(India)

MUQDISHO
(MOGADISHU)

INDIAN

Laccadive Is.
(India)

SRI
LANKA

Nico
Islar
(Ind

OCEAN

Colombo

Sri Jayawardenapura-Kotte

MALDIVES

Male

Mahé

Victoria

COMOROS

SEYCHELLES

MADAGASCAR

40° 5 B 50° 4 10° W C 60° 0° 3 D 70° 10°

H 50° J 60° 10° S K 70° L M 90°

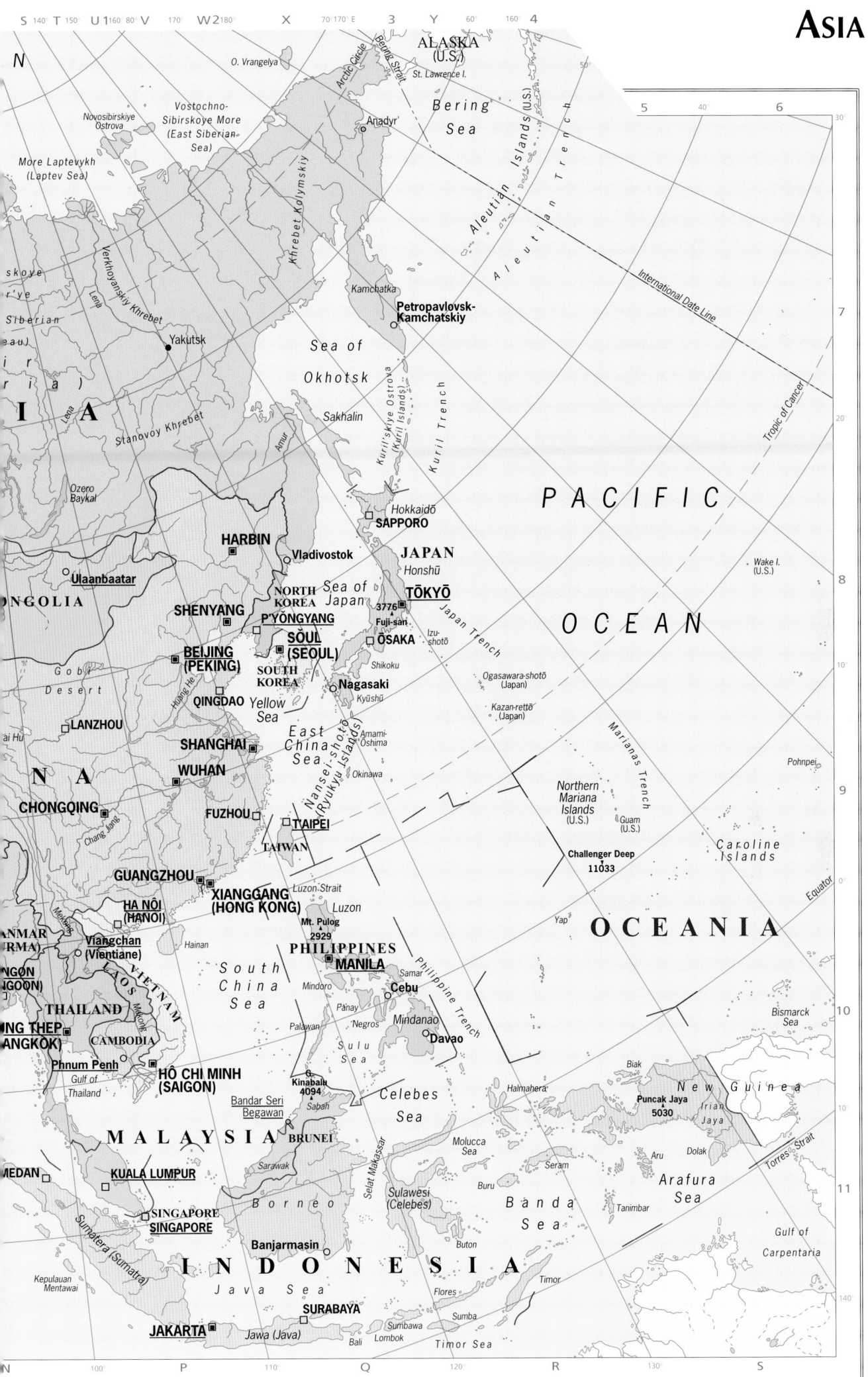

S 140° T 150° U 1160° 80° V 170° W 2180° X 70°170° E 3 Y 60° 160° 4

N

O. Vrangelya

ALASKA
(U.S.)

Arctic Circle

Bering Strait

St. Lawrence I.

5 40° 6

Novosibirskiye
Ostrova

Vostochno-
Sibirskoye More
(East Siberian
Sea)

Bering
Sea

Aleutian Islands (U.S.)

Aleutian Trench

7

More Laptevykh
(Laptev Sea)

Anadyr'

International Date Line

'ye

Siberian

eau)

ir
r i a)

AI A

Verkhoyanskiy Khrebet

Khrebet Kolymskiy

Lena

Kamchatka

Petropavlovsk-
Kamchatskiy

Tropic of Cancer

20°

Yakutsk

Sea of
Okhotsk

Stanovoy Khrebet

Amur

Lena

Sakhalin

Kuril Trench

Kuril'skiye Ostrova
(Kuril Islands)

Kuril Trench

PACIFIC

Ozero
Baykal

HARBIN

Vladivostok

Hokkaidō
SAPPORO

JAPAN
Honshū

OCEAN

Wake I.
(U.S.)

8

Ulaanbaatar

NORTH
KOREA

Sea of
Japan

3776
Fuji-san

TŌKYŌ

ONGOLIA

SHENYANG

P'YŎNGYANG

Japan Trench

SŎUL
(SEOUL)

ŌSAKA

Izu-
shotō

BEIJING
(PEKING)

SOUTH
KOREA

Shikoku

10°

Gobi

Huang He

QINGDAO

Nagasaki

Kyūshū

Ogasawara-shotō
(Japan)

Desert

LANZHOU

Yellow
Sea

Kazan-rettō
(Japan)

ai Hu

N A

SHANGHAI

East
China
Sea

Nansei-shotō
(Ryukyu Islands)

Amami-
Ōshima

9

WUHAN

Okinawa

Northern
Mariana
Islands
(U.S.)

Marianas Trench

Pohnpei

CHONGQING

Chang Jiang

FUZHOU

TAIPEI

Guam
(U.S.)

Caroline
Islands

TAIWAN

Challenger Deep
11033

GUANGZHOU

XIANGGANG
(HONG KONG)

Luzon Strait

Equator

0°

HA NÔI
(HANOI)

Luzon

Yap

OCEANIA

ANMAR
RMA)

Viangchan
(Vientiane)

Mt. Pulog
2929

Hainan

PHILIPPINES

Philippine Trench

NGØN
GOON)

VIETNAM

LAOS

South
China
Sea

MANILA

Samar

Bismarck
Sea

THAILAND

Mekong

Mindoro

Cebu

10°

Panay

CAMBODIA

NG THEP
ANGKÒK)

Palawan

Negros

Mindanao

Phnum Penh

HÔ CHI MINH
(SAIGON)

Gulf of
Thailand

Sulu
Sea

Davao

Biak

New Guinea

G.
Kinabalu
4094

Bandar Seri
Begawan

Halmahera

Puncak Jaya
5030

Irian
Jaya

MALAYSIA

Sabah

BRUNEI

Celebes
Sea

Molucca
Sea

Aru

Dolak

Torres Strait

MEDAN

KUALA LUMPUR

Sarawak

Selat Makassar

Seram

Arafura
Sea

10°

Borneo

Sulawesi
(Celebes)

Buru

Banda
Sea

Tanimbar

11

SINGAPORE
SINGAPORE

Sumatera (Sumatra)

Buton

Sulawesi
(Celebes)

Gulf of
Carpentaria

Kepulauan
Mentawai

I N D O N E S I A

Banjarmasin

Timor

140°

Java Sea

Flores

SURABAYA

Sumbawa

Sumba

JAKARTA

Jawa (Java)

Bali

Lombok

Timor Sea

N 100° P 110° Q 120° R 130° S

Scale 1 : 13 800 000

© Helicon Publishing Ltd

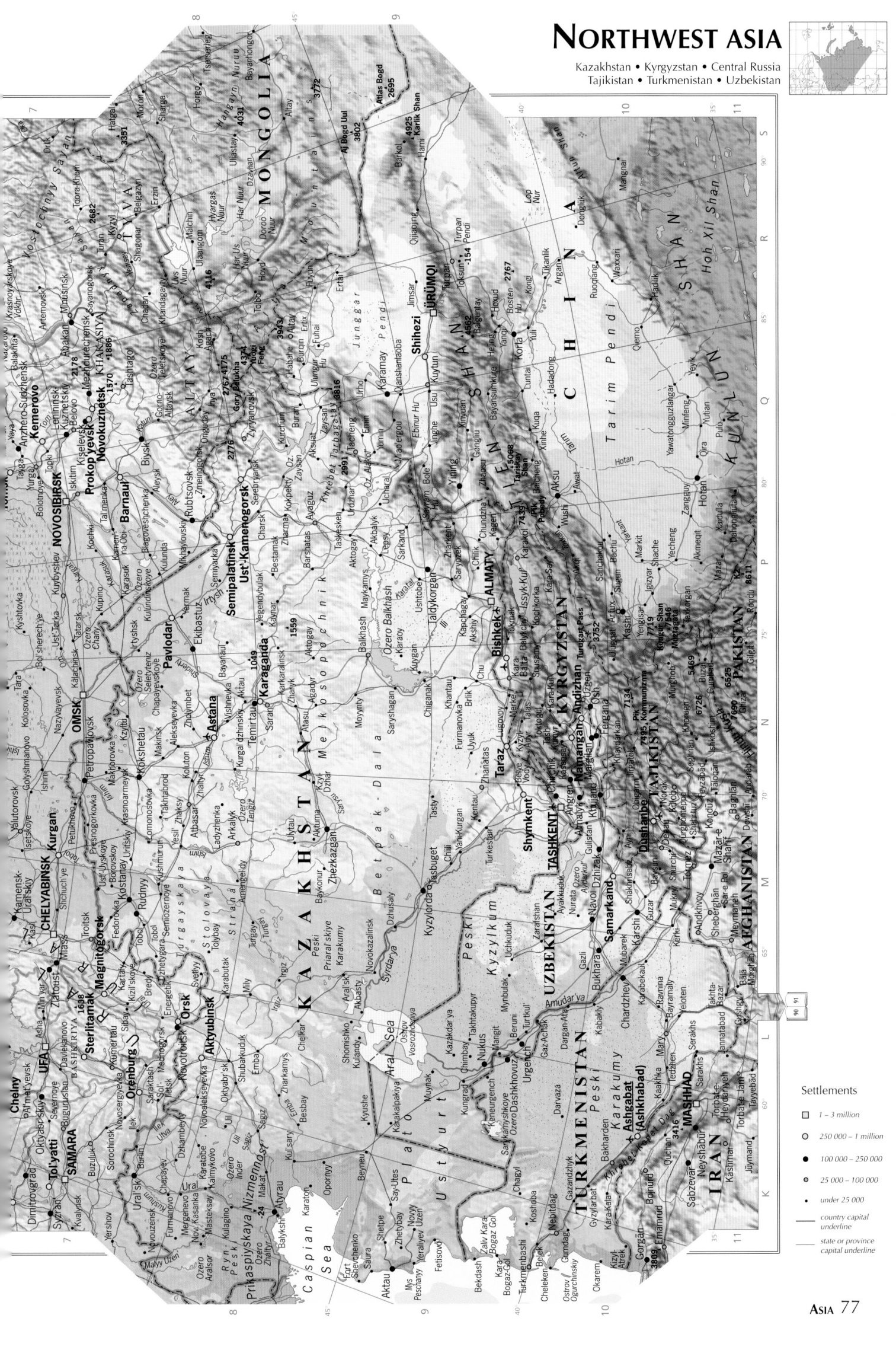

Kazakhstan • Kyrgyzstan • Central Russia
Tajikistan • Turkmenistan • Uzbekistan

Settlements

☐ 1 – 3 million

◎ 250 000 – 1 million

● 100 000 – 250 000

◉ 25 000 – 100 000

• under 25 000

— country capital
underline

— state or province
capital underline

© Helicon Publishing Ltd

Bering Strait
Arctic Circle

Seas and Oceans
- Chukchi Sea
- Vostochno-Sibirskoye More (East Siberian Sea)
- Bering Sea
- Sea of Okhotsk
- PACIFIC OCEAN

Map labels

140 Q 145 R 150 S 155 T 160 U 165 V 170 75 W 175° E X 180 Y2 175° W Z 170 70 AA 3

65° 165° W BB

Ostrov Vrangelya
Diomede Islands
Mys Dezhneva
King Island
Uelen
ALASKA (U.S.)
Enurmino
Lavrentiya
Vankarem
Val'karay
Uvargin
Polyarnyy
Chukotskiy Poluostrov
Provideniya
Gambell
St. Lawrence Island
Nunligram
Mys Shelagskiy
1810
Chukotskiy Khrebet
Egvekinot
Zaliv Kresta
Uel'kal
Pevek
Palyavaam
Ostrov Ayon
Chaunskaya Guba
Mal. Baranikha
Ust'-Chaun
Ugol'nyye Kopi
Anadyr
Anadyrskiy Zaliv
St. Matthew Island
Stanovaya
1775
Ambarchik
Vstrechnyy
Bilibino
1504
Anadyrskaya
Nizmennost'
Otrozhnyy
Beringovskiy
Mys Navarin
Cherskiy
Kolymskaye
Anyuysk
1651
Meynypil'gyno
Kolymskaya Nizmennost'
Omolon
'Chimchememel'
Markovo
Khatyrka
Ozero Ozhogino
Ozhogino
Belaya Gora
Sredenekolymsk
Druzhina
1465
Ayanka
Penzhina
2562
Gora Ledyanaya
Achayvayam
Bu-Khaybyt
Yukagirskoye Ploskogor'ye
Shcherbakove
Ust' Penzhino
Mikino
Tytkhoy
Olyutorskiy
Suordakh
Khonuu
Ozhogina
Yugo-Tala
Zyryanka
Ugol'naya Zyryanka
Dzhigudzhak
Gizhiga
Pakhachi
Mys Olyutorskiy
Tilichiki
Olyutorskiy Zaliv
Gora Pobeda 3147
Gizhiginskaya Guba
Korf
Adycha
Ust'-Nera
Artyk
1374
Dukat
Omsukchan
Nayakhan
Mys Govena
Khudzhakh
Seymchan
Ossora
Karaginskiy
Tomtor
Susuman
Debin
Orotukan
Strelka
Ostrov Karaginskiy Zaliv
Khrebet Cherskogo
Pik Aborigen 2586
Talaya
Ugulan
2959
Ust'-Omchug
Atka
Palana
Khrebet Suntar-Khayata
Zaliv Shelikhova
Yamsk
1385
Palatka
Magadan
Talon
Okurchan
Mys Tolstoy
Klyuchi
4750
Klyuchevskaya Sopka
Ust'-Kamchatsk
Nikol'skoye
Komandorskiye Ostrova
Aleutian Islands (U.S.)
Okhotsk
Ulya
Mys Alevina
Ust'-Khayryuzovo
Kamchatskiy Zaliv
Atlasove
Ostrov Beringa
Ostrov Mednyy
Attu Island
Buldir Island
Ayan
KAMCHATKA
Cape Wrangell
Agattu Island
Dzhugdzhur
Mys Enkan
Ust'-Sopochnoye
Mil'kovo
Kronotskiy Zaliv
3456
Yelizovo
Petropavlovsk-Kamchatskiy
Shantarskiye Ostrova
Mys Elizavety
Poluostrov Shmidta
Ostrov Bol. Shantar
Sakhalinskiy Zaliv
Okha
Oktyabr'skiy
Sea of Okhotsk
Litke
Mago
Bol. Vlas'evo
Takht
Nikolayevsk-na-Amure
Ozernovskiy
Amur
Bogorodskoye
Mys Lopatka
Imeni Poliny Osipenko
Lazarev
Nogliki
Ostrov Atlasova
Ostrov Shumshu
Sofiysk
De-Kastri
Severo-Kuril'sk
Berezovyy
Ostrov Paramushir
Komsomol'sk-na-Amure
1609
Aleksandrov-Sakhalinskiy
Ostrov Onekotan
Gurskoye
Smirnykh
Ostrov Shiashkotan
Proliv
Sakhalin
Shakhtërsk
Poronaysk
PACIFIC
Uglegorsk
Zaliv Terpeniya
Ostrov Rasshua
OCEAN
2078
Makarov
Mys Terpeniya
Sarapul'skoye
Vanino
Tomari
Ostrov Simushir
Khabarovsk
Nel'ma
Dolinsk
Kuril'skiye Ostrova (Kuril Islands)
Chekhov
Svetlaya
Yuzhno-Sakhalinsk
Korsakov
Ostrov Urup
Kholmsk
Zaliv Aniva
Mys Kril'on
Mys Aniva
Kuril'sk
Rebun-tō
La Pérouse Strait
Ostrov Iturup
Rishiri-tō
Wakkanai
Shiretoko-misaki
Monbetsu
Ostrov Kunashir
Asahikawa
Takikawa
Kitami
Habomai-shoto
Shikotan-tō
2290
Asahi-dake
Nemuro
Otaru
Obihiro
Kushiro
SAPPORO
Tomakomai
Hokkaidō
Hiroo
Oshamambe
Muroran
Okushiri-tō
Esan-misaki
Erimo-misaki
Hakodate
Mutsu
Tsugaru-kaikyō
JAPAN

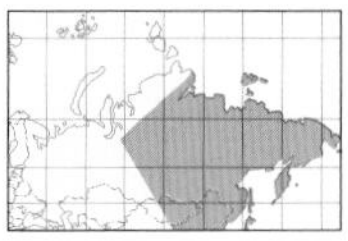

Settlements
- ■ over 3 million
- □ 1 – 3 million
- ◎ 250 000 – 1 million
- ● 100 000 – 250 000
- ○ 25 000 – 100 000
- • under 25 000
- ___ country capital underline
- ___ state or province capital underline

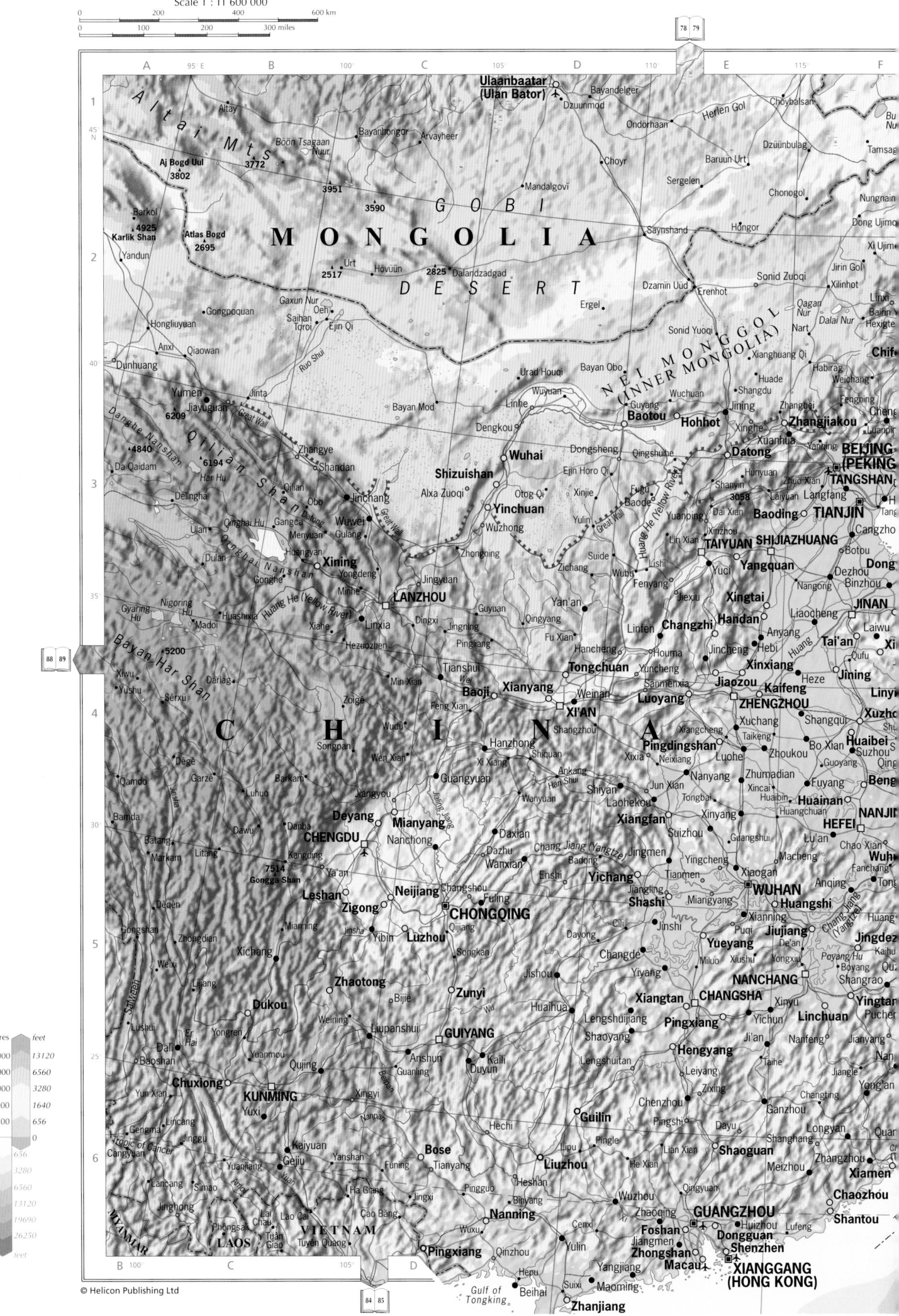

Scale 1 : 11 600 000

| 0 | 200 | 400 | 600 km |
| 0 | 100 | 200 | 300 miles |

A 95°E B 100° C 105° D 110° E 115° F

1

Altai Mts

Ulaanbaatar (Ulan Bator) Bayandelger Choybalsan
Aitay Dzuunmod Ondorhaan Herlen Gol Bu
Aj Bogd Uul Böön Tsagaan Bayanhongor Arvayheer Nr
3802 Nuur 3772 Choyr Baruun Urt Tamsag
3951 Mandalgovĭ Sergelen Chonogol Dzüunbulag Nungnain
3590 G O B I Saynshand Höngor Dong Ujimq
Barkol 4925 Atlas Bogd Dalandzadgad XI Ujim
Karlik Shan 2695 **M O N G O L I A** Dzamin Uüd Erenhot Sonid Zuoqi Jirin Gol
Yandun Urt Höyüün 2825 Ergel Xilinhot
Gaxun Nur Oeh 2517 D E S E R T Qagan Linx
Hongliuyuan Saihan Dzamin Uüd Sonid Yuoqi Nur Bairin Hexigte
Gongpoquan Toroi Ejin Qi N E I M O N G G O L Nart Dalai Nur
Anxi Qiaowan Ruo Shui Urad Houqi Bayan Obo (INNER MONGOLIA) Xianghuang Qi Habirag Chif
Dunhuang Bayan Mod Wuyuan Guyang Huade Shangdu Weichang Cheng
Yumen Jinta Great Wall Linhe Wuchuan Jining Zhangbei Fengning
6209 Jiayuguan Bayan Mod Dengkou **Baotou Hohhot** Xinghe Zhangjiakou
4840 6194 Zhangye Shandan Dongsheng Qingshuihe Xuanhua Yangao **BEIJING**
Da Qaidam Har Hu **Wuhai** Ejin Horo Qi Datong Hunyuan **(PEKING)**
Delingha Qilian Obo Jinchang **Shizuishan** Otog Qi Xinjie Fugu Shanyin Zhuo Xian **TANGSHAN**
Ulan Gangca Datong Wuwei Gulang **Yinchuan** Wuzhong Yulin Baode 3058 Dai Xian Langfang Tang
Qinghai Hu Menyuan Shandan Alxa Zuoqi Zhongning Suide Lishi Lin Xian Laiyuan **Baoding TIANJIN**
Huangyan **Xining** Yongdeng Minhe Jingyuan Zichang Wubu Fenyang Yuanping Xinzhou Cangzho
Dulan Qinghai Nanshan Gonghe **LANZHOU** Guyuan Yan'an Fu Xian Jiexiu **TAIYUAN SHIJIAZHUANG** Dong Dezhou
Gyaring Nigoring Huashixia Huang He (Yellow River) Linxia Dingxi Pingliang Qingyang Houma Yuci **Yangquan** Nangong Botou Binzhou
Hu Hu Madoi Xiahe Hezuozhen Jingning Hancheng Jincheng Hebi **Xingtai Handan** **JINAN** Laiwu
5200 Darlag Tianshui Min Xian Fu Xian Yuncheng Sanmenxia **Xinxiang** Anyang Liaocheng Xi
Xiwu Zoigê Baoji Xianyang Weinan **Jiaozuo** Heze Tai'an Qufu
Yushu Sêrxü Wei Feng Xian **XI'AN** Luoyang **Kaifeng** **Jining**
Bayan Har Shan Wudu Shangzhou **ZHENGZHOU** Shangqiu Linyi
Dêgê **C H I N A** Hanzhong Xi Xiang Shiquan Xixia Xuchang **Pingdingshan** Bo Xian **Xuzho**
Qamdo Garzê Barkam Songpan Wen Xian Ankang Han Shui Neixiang **Luohe** Zhoukou Guoyang **Huaibei** Suzhou Qing
Luhuo Jiangyou **Guangyuan** Shiyan Nanyang Zhumadian Fuyang Beng
Bamda Dawu Danba **Deyang Mianyang** Wanyuan Laohekou Xincai **Huainan NANJI**
Batang Markam Kangding **CHENGDU** Nanchong Daxian Jingmen Tianmen Xinyang Lu'an Chao Xian **HEFEI**
Dêqên 7514 Ya'an Leshan Dazhu Chang Jiang (Yangtze) Yingcheng Macheng Anqing Wuh
Gongshan Zhongdian Gongga Shan **Zigong** Neijiang Changshou **CHONGQING** Wanxian Enshi **Yichang** Xiaogan **WUHAN** Fanchang
Weixi Lijiang **Leshan** Fuling Badong **Shashi** Mianyang Xianning Huangshi Jingdez
Gengma Dukou Xichang Mianning Yibin Luzhou Qijiang Dayong Cili Jinshi Puqi **Jiujiang** Jngde
Dali Yongren Zhaotong Bijie Songkan Jishou Changde Yiyang Miluo Yongxiu **NANCHANG** Shangrao Qu
Lushui Er Zunyi Wu Hualua Yueyang De'an
Baoshan Hai Yuanmou Weining Liupanshui **GUIYANG** Huaihua Lengshuijiang Xiangtan **CHANGSHA** Xinyu Yingtan
Chuxiong Qujing Anshun Kaili Duyun Shaoyang **Pingxiang** Yichun **Linchuan** Pucher
Yun Xian **KUNMING** Guanling Lengshuitan Ji'an Nanfeng Jianyang Nan
Yuxi Xingyi Leiyang Taihe Jiangle
Cangyuan Lincang Jinggu Nanpan Hechi Pingshi Chenzhou Zixing Changting Yong'an
Kaiyuan Gejiu Yanshan **Guilin** Dayu Ganzhou Longyan Qua
Bose Lipu Pingle Lian Xian Shanghang Zhangzhou
Simao Tianyang Pingguo Heshan He Xian **Shaoguan** Meizhou **Xiamen**
Jinghong Lai Lao Cai Ha Giang Jingxi **Liuzhou** **Zhangzhou** Chaozhou
Menghai Chau Tuan Cao Bang Binyang Wuzhou Qingyuan **GUANGZHOU** Shantou
Giao **Nanning** Wuxu Yulin Zhaoqing **Foshan** Dongguan
VIETNAM Pingxiang Qinzhou **Macau** **Zhongshan** Shenzhen
LAOS Qinzhou Hepu Yangjiang Jiangmen **XIANGGANG**
Phongsali Tuyen Quang Beihai Suixi Maoming **(HONG KONG)**
Gulf of **Zhanjiang**
Tongking

2
3
4
5
25°
6

metres / feet
4000 / 13120
2000 / 6560
1000 / 3280
500 / 1640
200 / 656
0 / 0
200 / 656
1000 / 3280
2000 / 6560
4000 / 13120
6000 / 19690
8000 / 26250
metres / feet

Tropic of Cancer

MYANMAR

B 100° C 105° D E 110° F 115°

© Helicon Publishing Ltd

88 89

Da Hinggan Ling
Xiao Hinggan Ling
Zhangguangcai Ling
Sikhote Alin

Bei'an
Yichun Hegang
QIQIHAR
Jiamusi
Horqin Suihua
Youyi Anda Yilan
Qianqi Daqing Songhua Jixi Muling
Baicheng HARBIN Acheng Fangzheng Ozero Khanka
Dashizhai Zhaoyuan Shangzhi Spassk-Dal'niy
Tuquan Da'an Fuyue Sanchahe Mudanjiang Grodekovo
Jarud Qi Tongyu Yushu Wuchang Ning'an Ussuriysk
Jurhe Taipingchuan Shulan Dongjingcheng Rudnaya Pristan'
irin Zuoqi CHANGCHUN JILIN Naizishan Dunhua Yanji
Tongliao Shuangliao Huadian Antu Tumen Vladivostok Nakhodka
Ar Horqin Qi Kangping Liaoyuan Hailong Hunjiang Hoeryong Najin Mys Povorotnyy
Naiman Qi Zhangwu Faku Qingyuan Linjiang Ch'ongjin
Beipiao Tieling Hunjiang Myonggan
oyang Fuxin Hyesan
Jinxi SHENYANG FUSHUN Hyanren Kapsan Kimch'aek
Liaoyang Benxi Manp'o Kilchu
Jinzhou ANSHAN Kuandian Ch'osan Pukch'ong
Dawa Haicheng NORTH Hamhung
Yingkou Dandong Sinuiju KOREA Chongp'yong
Qinhuangdao Pakch'on Wonsan
Wafangdian Xinjin Kosong
Korea P'YONGYANG Songnim Sokch'o
Lushun DALIAN Bay Nampo Sariwon Kangnung
Miaodao Haeju Kaesong Tonghae
Qundao SOUL Ulchin
Yantai (SEOUL) Anyang
Weihai INCH'ON SOUTH Andong
Shandong Rongcheng Suwon KOREA P'ohang
Bandao Ch'ongju TAEJON TAEGU
Weifang YELLOW TAEJON Kunsan Tumen
QINGDAO SEA Ch'onju KOREA PUSAN
Jiaonan KWANGJU Sunch'on
Rizhao Mokp'o Cheju

SEA OF JAPAN

HOKKAIDO
Wakkanai
La Pérouse Strait
Rebun-to Esashi Shiretoko-misaki
Rishiri-to Monbetsu Ostrov Kunashir
Haboro Nayoro Abashiri Shikotan-to
Asahikawa 2290 Kitami Nemuro
Asahi-dake
Takikawa Obihiro
Otaru SAPPORO Hiroo
Oshamambe Tomakomai
Okushiri-to Mori Muroran Erimo-misaki
Esashi Esan-misaki
Matsumae Hakodate
Tsugaru-kaikyo Mutsu
Aomori Hachinohe
Hirosaki Odate
Noshiro Morioka
Akita Hanamaki
Ichinoseki Kamaishi
Sakata Furukawa Ishinomaki
Shinjo Sendai
Yamagata Fukushima
Niigata Koriyama
Ryotsu Iwaki
Sado-shima Utsunomiya
Joetsu Nagano Mito HONSHU
Suzu-misaki Maebashi Kashima
Nanao Matsumoto Kofu TOKYO
Toyama Fuji-san YOKOHAMA
Kanazawa 3776 Shizuoka
Fukui NAGOYA Shimoda
Tsuruoka Suzuka Izu-shoto
Oki-shoto Dogo Gifu Hamamatsu Miyake-jima
Yonago KYOTO Matsusaka
Tottori OSAKA Hachijo-jima
Izumo Chugoku-sanchi KOBE Matsusaka
Hamada Okayama Wakayama
Okayama Takamatsu
HIROSHIMA Tokushima
Hofu Matsuyama Shiono-misaki
KITA-KYUSHU Shimonoseki Kochi SHIKOKU Myojin
FUKUOKA Kurume Oita Nakamura Sumisu-jima
Sasebo Omuta Kumamoto
Goto-retto Yatsushiro KYUSHU
Fukue-jima Nagasaki Nobeoka Tori-shima
Akune Miyazaki Sofu-gan
Kagoshima Miyakonojo
Makurazaki Kanoya
Osumi-shoto Tanega-shima
Yaku-shima

JAPAN

YELLOW SEA

EAST CHINA SEA

PACIFIC OCEAN

Lianyungang
Guanyun
Baoying
Yancheng
Xinghua
Taizhou
Yangzhou Nantong
Zhenjiang Changzhou
Wuxi Changshu
Suzhou Jiaxing
NGZHOU Haining SHANGHAI
aoxing Yuyao
NINGBO
Fenghua Ninghai
Jinhua Linhai
Huangyan
Lishui Wenzhou
Rui'an
Fuding
Ningde

Nansei-shoto
(Ryukyu Islands)
Amami-Oshima
Naze

Nago Okinawa
Naha

Tropic of Cancer

ZHOU
Chilung
T'aoyuan T'AIPEI
Hsinchu 3884
Changhua T'aichung
Chiai 3950
ainan Yu Shan TAIWAN
Hsüeh Shan
Pingtung
AOHSIUNG
Oluanpi
Matsu (Taiwan)
Sakishima-shoto

Settlements

Symbol	Population
■	over 3 million
□	1 – 3 million
○	250 000 – 1 million
●	100 000 – 250 000
◦	25 000 – 100 000
·	under 25 000
—	country capital underline

Scale 1 : 5 800 000

© Helicon Publishing Ltd

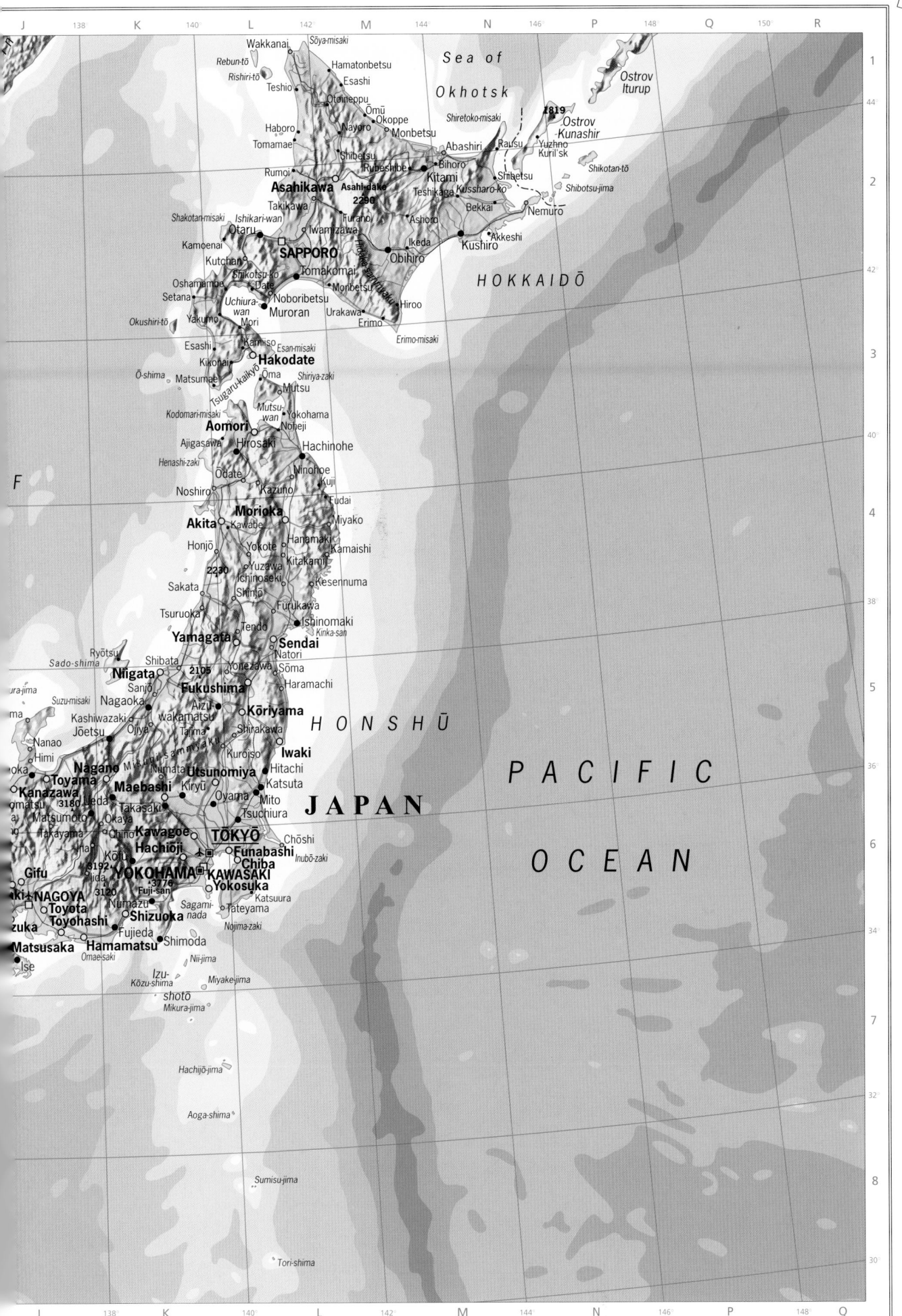

J 138° K 140° L 142° M 144° N 146° P 148° Q 150° R

Wakkanai
Rebun-tō
Rishiri-tō
Teshio
Hamatonbetsu
Esashi
Otoineppu
Ōmū
Okoppe
Nayoro
Monbetsu

Sea of
Okhotsk

Ostrov
Iturup

Haboro
Tomamae
Shibetsu
Rumoi
Ryubeshibe
Asahikawa
Takikawa
Asahi-dake
2290
Furano
Ashoro

Shiretoko-misaki
1819
Rausu
Abashiri
Bihoro
Kitami
Teshikaga
Kussharo-ko
Bekkai
Nemuro

Ostrov
Kunashir
Yuzhno
Kuril'sk
Shikotan-tō
Shibotsu-jima

Shakotan-misaki
Ishikari-wan
Iwamizawa
Otaru
Kamoenai
SAPPORO
Kutchan
Tomakomai
Shikotsu-ko
Shikotsu-ko
Date
Noboribetsu
Monbetsu
Setana
Oshamambe
Uchiura-wan
Muroran
Mori
Yakumo
Urakawa
Erimo

Ikeda
Obihiro
Kushiro
Akkeshi

HOKKAIDŌ

Hiroo
Erimo-misaki

Okushiri-tō
Ō-shima
Esashi
Kamiso
Kikonai
Hakodate
Matsumae
Esan-misaki
Ōma
Shiriya-zaki
Tsugaru-kaikyō
Mutsu

Kodomari-misaki
Mutsu-wan
Yokohama
Noheji
Aomori
Ajigasawa
Hirosaki
Hachinohe
Henashi-zaki
Ōdate
Ninohe
Noshiro
Kazuno
Kuji
Fudai
Miyako
Morioka
Akita
Kawabe
Honjō
Yokote
Hanamaki
Kamaishi
2230
Ichinoseki
Kitakami
Sakata
Shinjo
Kesennuma
Tsuruoka
Furukawa
Tendo
Ishinomaki
Kinka-san
Yamagata
Sendai
Ryōtsu
Natori
Sado-shima
Shibata
Yonezawa
Sōma
Niigata
2105
Haramachi
Sanjō
Fukushima
Suzu-misaki
Nagaoka
Aizu-
wakamatsu
Kashiwazaki
Ojiya
Tajima
Shirakawa
Jōetsu
Kōriyama
Nanao
Kuroiso
Iwaki
Himi
Numata
Hitachi
Nagano
Utsunomiya
Katsuta
Toyama
Kiryū
Mito
Kanazawa
Maebashi
Oyama
Tsuchiura
3180
Ueda
Takasaki
Matsumoto
Okaya
3192
Chino
Kawagoe
Chōshi
TŌKYŌ
Inubō-zaki
Takayama
Kōfu
Hachiōji
Funabashi
Iida
Fuji-san
Chiba
Gifu
3776
YOKOHAMA
KAWASAKI
3120
Fuji-san
Yokosuka
NAGOYA
Numazu
Katsuura
Toyota
Shizuoka
Sagami-nada
Tateyama
Matsusaka
Hamamatsu
Fujieda
Nojima-zaki
Toyohashi
Shimoda
Ise
Ōmae-saki
Izu-
Kōzu-shima
Miyakejima
shotō
Mikura-jima

HONSHŪ

JAPAN

PACIFIC

OCEAN

Hachijō-jima

Aoga-shima

Sumisu-jima

Tori-shima

1° 44°

2

42

3

F 40

4

38

5

36

6

34

7

32

8

30

J 138° K 140° L 142° M 144° N 146° P 148° Q

Settlements

■	over 3 million
□	1 – 3 million
○	250 000 – 1 million
●	100 000 – 250 000
◉	25 000 – 100 000
·	under 25 000
—	country capital underline

Scale 1 : 11 600 000

0   200   400   600 km
0   100   200   300 miles

95° E   B   100°   C   105°   D   110°

A

BHUTAN
Tashigang
Hāpoli
Pangin
Zayü
Dēqēn
Jishou
Huaihua
Zunyi
Wu

Barpeta
Itanagar
Dibrugarh
Tinsukia
Tāzungdant
Gongshan
Zhongdian
Xichang
Bijie
GUIYANG

1

Goalpara
Nagaon
Jorhat
Golaghat
Tabong
Weixi
Lijiang
Yongren
Dukou
Weining
Liupanshui
Anshun
Duyun
Kaili

INDIA
Guwahati
Dimapur
Kohima
Māingkwan
Myitkyina
Lushui
Dali
Yuanmou
Qujing
Guanling
Xingyi
CHI

Shillong
Imphal
Mogaung
Hopin
Baoshan
KUNMING
Guilin

25°N
Sylhet
Silchar
Chuxiong
Nanpan

Bhairab
Bazar
Aizawl
Tropic of Cancer
Agartala
Bhamo
Katha
Mong Yu
Lincang
Jingu
Gejiu
Yanshan
Funing
Heshan
Liuzho

Comilla
Feni
Karnafuli
Reservoir
Kalemyo
Mawlaik
Kanbalu
Mabein
Hsweni
Cangyuan
Yuanjiang
Lai
Chau
Cao Bằng
Pingguo
Binyang

2
Rangamati
Saiha
Haka
Chindwin
Mogok
Lashio
Mong Yai
Jinghong
Lancang
Simao
Phôngsali
Lao Cai
Tuyên Quang
Thai Nguyên
Pingxiang
Qinzhou
Hepu

CHITTAGONG
BANGLADESH
Monywa
Shwebo
Kyaukse
Mongkung
Kunhing
Kengtung
Muang
Sing
Muang
Namtha
Muang
Khoua
Sơn La
Việt Tri
HA NÔI
(HANOI)
Tiên Yen
Beihai
Nanning

Cox's
Bazar
Paletwa 3053
Mt. Victoria
Pakokku
Myingyan
Amarapura
MANDALAY
Taung-gyi
Muang Xai
Xam Nua
Môc Châu
Hon Gai
Zhanjiang

Teknaf
Chauk
Meiktila
Kunhing
Wan Hsa-la
MYANMAR
(BURMA)
Phôngsali
HAI PHONG
Xuw

20°
Sittwe
Magwe
Minbu
Sinbaungwe
Taungdwingyi
Salween
Chiang
Rai
Louangphrabang
Ban
Ban
Ninh Binh
Nam Dinh
Haikou
Dan Xian
Wenchai
Qionghai

Kyaukpyu
Ramree Island
Taungup
Pyè
Loikaw
Xianghoang
Thanh Hoa
Gulf of
Tongking
Dongfang
Hainan
Tongshi

Bay of
Bengal
Cheduba Island
Sandoway
Pyinmana
Toungoo
Mae Hong Sôn
Nan
Siri
Kit
Dam
LAOS
Viangchan
(Vientiane)
Nong Khai
Vinh
Ha Tinh
Sanya
Ling

3
Kyeintali
Zigon
Letpadan
Papun
Pasawng
Lampang
Chiang Mai
Uttaradit
Chiang
Khan
Loei
Udon Thani
Muang
Khammouan
Quang Tri
Huê

Bassein
Henzada
Insein
Thaton
Tak
Phitsanulok
Chum
Phae
Sakhon Nakhon
Muang
Phin
Da Nang
Hôi An

Myaungmya
Bogale
YANGON
(RANGOON)
Moulmein
Kawkareik
Nam Ping
Phichit
Khon Kaen
Mukdahan
Savannakhet
Khemmarat
Lam Chi
Cape
Negrais
Labutta
Ye
Mouths of
the Irrawaddy
Gulf of
Martaban
Nakhon
Sawan
Chaiyaphum
Roi Et
Ubon
Ratchathani
M. Khôngxédôn
Quang Ngai

15°
Preparis North Channel
Preparis Island
Sangkhla
Buri
Chai-nat
Nakhon
Ratchasima
Surin
Mae Nam Mun
Det Udom
Pakxé
Attapu
Kon
Tum

Preparis South Channel
Coco Island
Coco Channel
THAILAND
Ayutthaya
Sara Buri
KRUNG THEP
(BANGKOK)
Phumĭ Sâmraông
M. Không
Siĕmréab
Virôchey
Plây Cu
Qui Nhon

88 89
North Andaman
Andaman Islands
(India)
Middle Andaman
Rat Buri
Phet
Buri
Aranyaprathet
Sisôphôn
Bătdâmbâng
Tônlé Sap
Stœ̆ng Trêng
Buôn Mê
Thuôt
Tuy Hoa

Ritchie's
Archipelago
South Andaman
Port Blair
Bight
of
Bangkok
Pattaya
Rayong
CAMBODIA
Kâmpóng Cham
Da Lat
Ninh Hoa

Duncan Passage
Little Andaman
Andaman
Ban Hua Hin
Chánthaburi
Ko Chang
Kâmpóng Chhnǎng
Krông Kaôh Kông
Nha Trar
Cam Ranh
Bao Lôc
Phan Rang

Mergui
Prachuap Khiri Khan
Bang Saphan Yai
Phnum Penh
Chon Thanh
Tay Ninh
Biên Hoa
Phan Thiêt

10°
Ten Degree Channel
Mergui
Archipelago
Gulf
of
Thailand
Sihanoukville
Ko Kong
Kâmpôt
HÔ CHI MINH
(SAIGON)
Long Xuyên
My Tho
Vung Tau

Car Nicobar
Chumphon
Dao Phu Quôc
Rach Gia
Cân Tho
Mouths of
the Mekong

Kawthaung
Ranong
Ca Mau
Bac Liêu
Côn Son

Sea
Takua Pa
Nam Can
Nicobar Islands
(India)
Surat Thani
Ko Samui

Katchall
Nakhon Si Thammarat

Little
Nicobar
Great
Nicobar
Phuket
Krabi
Thung Song

5
Trang
Phatthalung
Thale
Luang
Songkhla
Hat Yai
Pattani
MALAY

metres   feet
4000   13120
2000   6560
1000   3280
500   1640
200   656
0   0

Satun
Langkawi
Kangar
Yala
Narathiwat
Kota Bharu
Sungei Patani
Alor Setar
Ban Betong
Kuala Kerai
Kuala Terengganu

George Town
Pinang
Gerik
G. Korbu
2182
Dungun
Kemasik

200   656
1000   3280
2000   6560
4000   13120
6000   19690
8000   26250

Taiping
Ipoh
Kuala Lipis
Malay
Laut
Panarik

metres   feet
Bireuen
Lhokseumawe
Langsa
Kuantan
Peninsula
Natuna Besar
Kepulauan
Natuna

INDIAN

Takengon
3145
Gunung Leuser
MEDAN
Bagun Datuk
Bentong
Temerloh
Subi Besar

6
OCEAN
SUMATERA
(SUMATRA)
Tebingtinggi
KUALA LUMPUR
Seremban
Jemaja
Kepulauan
Anambas
(Indonesia)

Sibigo
Sibolga
Pematangsiantar
Prapat
Danau Toba
Segamat
Mersing
Tanjung
Datu

Simeulue
Sinabang
Singkilbaru
Barus
Balige
Kotapinang
Dumai
Melaka
Muar
Kluang
Kuc

86 87
Nias
Gunungsitoli
Bagansiapiapi
Duri
Johor Bahru
SINGAPORE
Sambas
Sluas

INDONESIA
SINGAPORE
Strait of Malacca
Pemangkat

95° E   100°   C   105°   D   110°

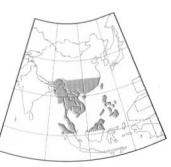

80 | 81

EAST CHINA SEA

JAPAN

Nago Okinawa
Okinawa
Naha

Tropic of Cancer

Nansei-shotō (Ryukyu Islands)

Sakishima-shotō

Xiangtan **CHANGSHA** Xinyu
Lianyuan **Linchuan** Pucheng **Wenzhou**
Lengshuijiang Yichun
Pingxiang Shangrao
oyang
Hengyang Ji'an Nanping Ningde Fuding
Taihe
Lengshuitan Zixing Changting **Yong'an**
Leiyang Chenzhou Ganzhou **FUZHOU** Matsu
A Putian (Taiwan) **Chilung**
Longyan Quanzhou **T'aoyüan** **T'AIPEI**
Shaoguan Zhangzhou Hsinchu Hsinchu
Lian Xian Meizhou **Xiamen** 3884
He Xian Qingyuan Chinmen Hsüeh Shan **T'aichung**
Wuzhou Huizhou **Chaozhou** (Taiwan)
GUANGZHOU Changhua Chiai **TAIWAN**
Zhaoqing **Dongguan** **Shantou** 3950
nxi Jiangmen **Foshan** **Shenzhen** T'ainan Yu Shan
Zhongshan **Macau** **XIANGGANG** **KAOHSIUNG** P'ingtung
oming Yangjiang **(HONG KONG)** Oluanpi T'aitung

Luzon Batan Islands
Strait Basco

Dongsha Qundao
(Pratas)
(China)

Balintang Channel

Babuyan Islands

Bangui Claveria San Vicente
Laoag Aparri
Kabugao Lal-Lo
Vigan Bangued Tuguegarao Palanan
Santa Cruz *Luzon*
San Fernando Bontoc Ilagan
Mt. Pulog Santiago
Baguio 2929
Alaminos Dagupan Casiguran
Lingayen San Carlos Baler
Tarlac Cabanatuan
Angeles Gapan
Olongapo **QUEZON CITY** Polillo Is.
MANILA Daet Pandan
Pasig San Pablo Calagua Is.
Nasugbu Calauag *Cantanduanes*
Batangas Lucena Lopez Naga
Boac Virac
Mamburao Calapan Pascual **Legaspi**
Mindoro 2488 Pinamalayan Sorsogon
Mount Baco Masbate Bulan Catarman
San Pedro Masbate Placer Allen *Samar*
Calamian Nabas Calbayog
Group Coron Kalibo Catbalogan
El Nido Roxas Bogo Borongan
Panay **Iloilo** *Cebu* Ormoc Tacloban
San Jose de Bago **Bacolod** *Leyte*
Buenavista Carcar **Cebu** Sogod Libjo
Roxas Talibon Maasin Dinagat
Palawan Cauayan *Bohol* Bais Surigao Dapa
Puerto Princesa *Negros* Tagbilaran Madrid
Quezon Dumaguete Butuan Tandag
PHILIPPINES Prosperidad
Brooke's Point Dipolog **Cagayan de Oro** Bislig
Bugsuk Manukan 2560 Iligan
Balabac Liloy Malaybalay Bislig
Kudat Sibuco Pagadian *Mindanao* Tagum
Langkon Cotabato **Davao**
Kota Belud 4094 Sandakan **Zamboanga** 2954 Mati
G. Kinabalu Ranau Isabela Tacurong **Mt. Apo**
Kota Kinabalu Jolo Palimbang Polomoloc Cape San Agustin
Beaufort **SABAH** Tungku *Pangutaran* *Group* **General Santos**
Langkon Jolo Glan
BRUNEI Lahad Datu Semporna Sarangani Is.
Bandar Seri Begawan Bongao *Sulu* *Archipelago*
Seria Tawitawi
BRUNEI Kalabakan
Gurung Mulu Tawau
2371
Bareo

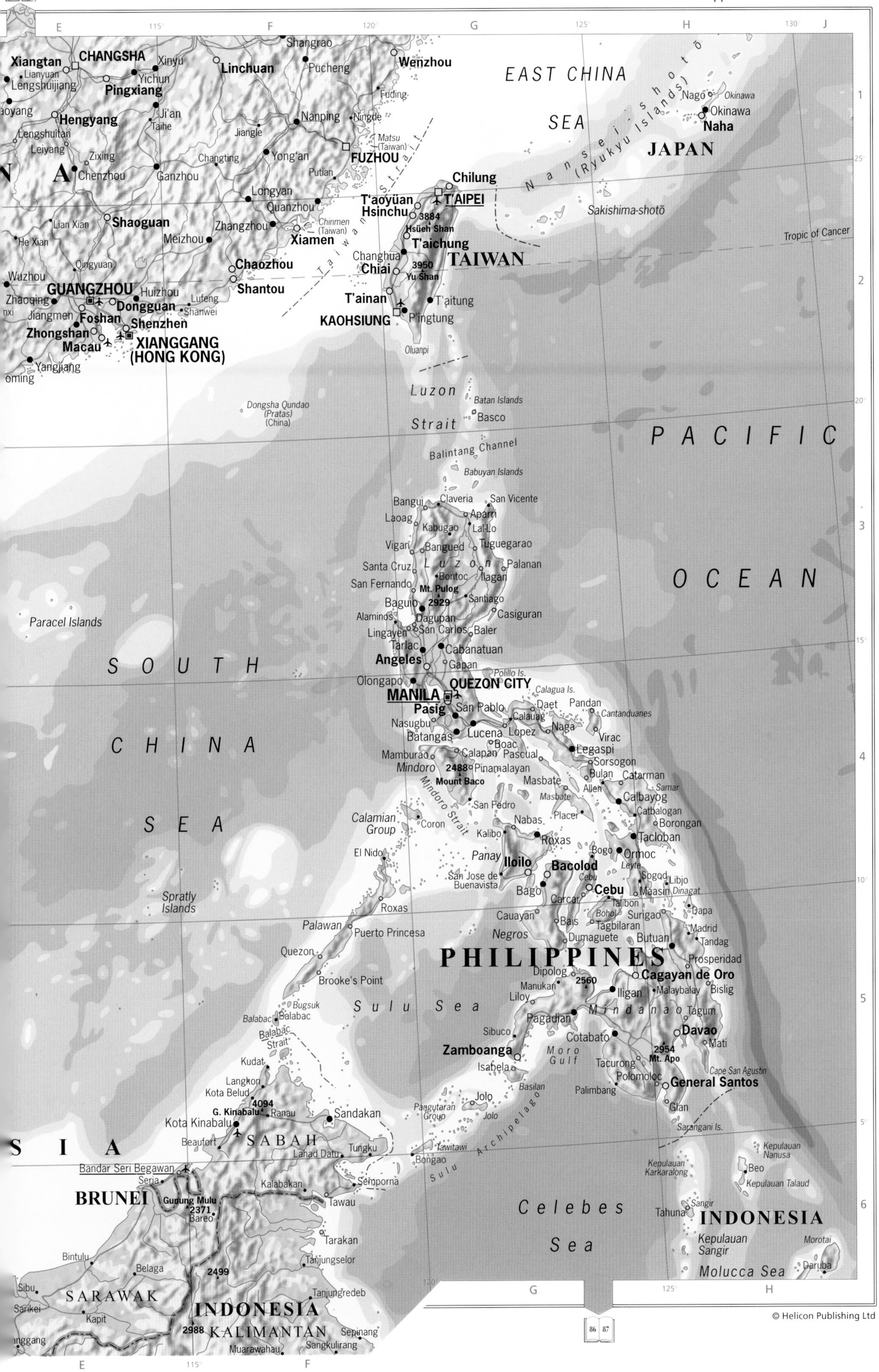

PACIFIC OCEAN

SOUTH CHINA SEA

Paracel Islands

Spratly Islands

Sulu Sea

Balabac
Strait

Moro Gulf

Celebes Sea

INDONESIA

Kepulauan
Nanusa

Kepulauan
Karkaralong Beo
Kepulauan Talaud

Sangir
Tahuna **INDONESIA**
Kepulauan
Sangir Morotai
Daruba
Molucca Sea

S I A
Bintulu Belaga
SARAWAK
Sibu 2499
Sarikei Kapit
ngga **INDONESIA**
2988 **KALIMANTAN**
Sepinang
Muarawahau Sangkulirang

Beaufort
Tarakan
Tanjungselor
Tanjungredeb

© Helicon Publishing Ltd

Settlements

■	*over 3 million*
□	*1 – 3 million*
○	*250 000 – 1 million*
●	*100 000 – 250 000*
○	*25 000 – 100 000*
•	*under 25 000*
——	*country capital underline*

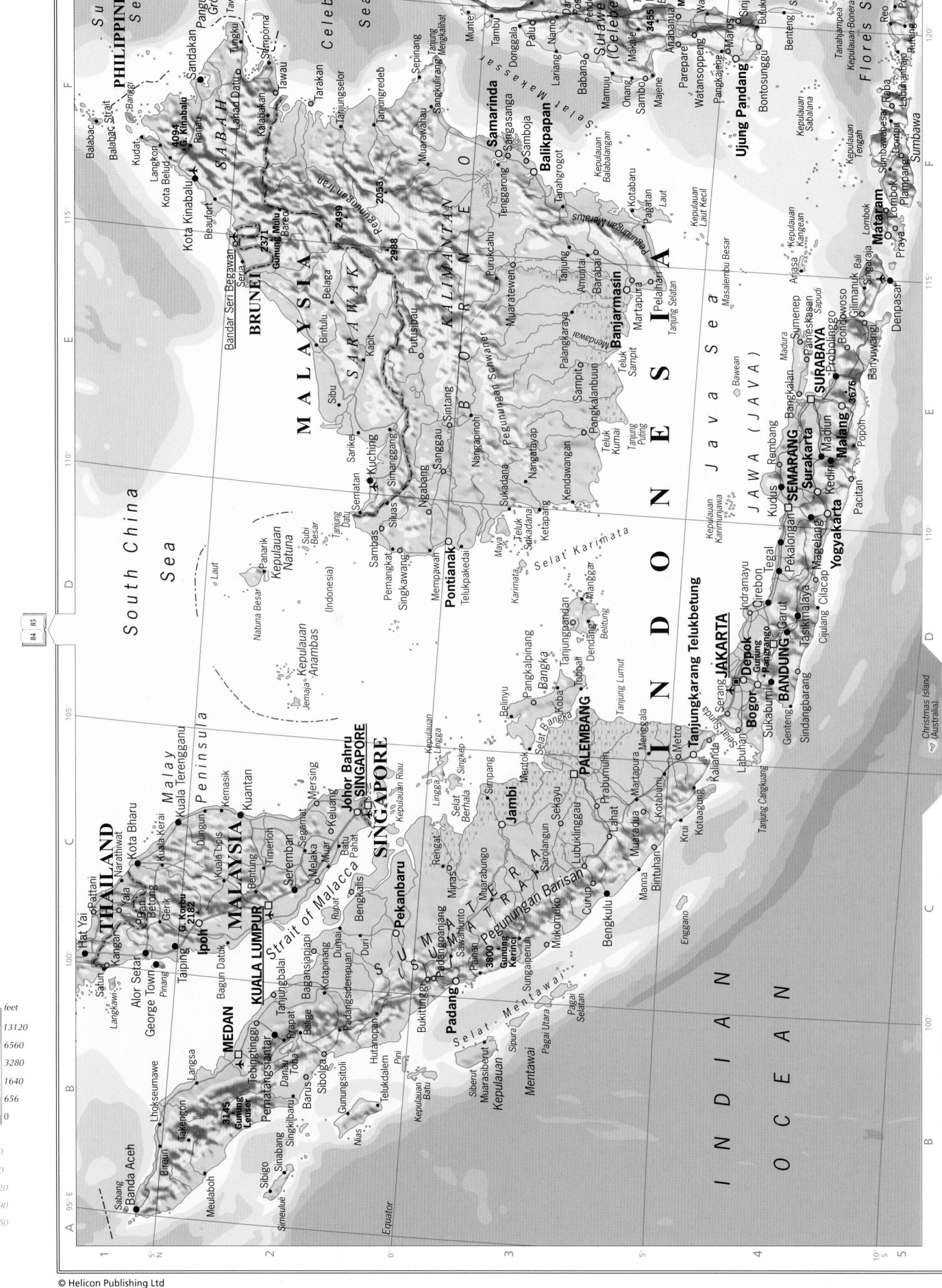

Scale 1 : 11 600 000

0   200   400   600 km

0   100   200   300 miles

metres		feet
4000		13120
2000		6560
1000		3280
500		1640
200		656
0		0
200		656
1000		3280
2000		6560
4000		13120
6000		19690
8000		26250
metres		feet

© Helicon Publishing Ltd

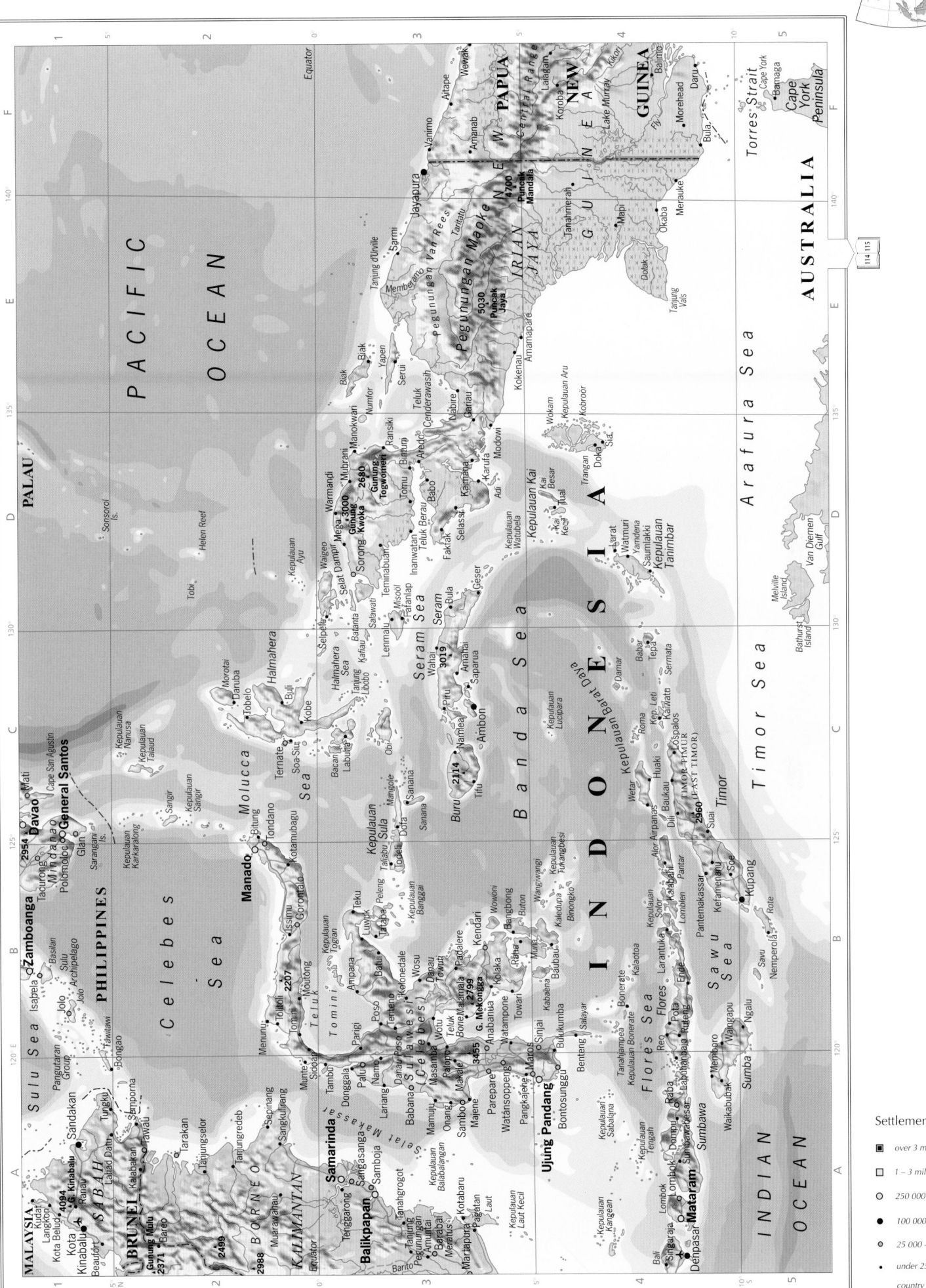

PACIFIC

OCEAN

PALAU

PHILIPPINES

Zamboanga
Davao
2954
Mindanao
General Santos
Cape San Agustin

MALAYSIA
Kota Kinabalu
G. Kinabalu 4094
Beaufort
SABAH
Sandakan
Tawau
BRUNEI
Gunung Tujuh 2371
2499
BORNEO
KALIMANTAN
2988
Balikpapan
Samarinda

Celebes
Sea

Manado
Gorontalo
Sulawesi
(Celebes)
2207
G. Mekongga 2799
3455
Ujung Pandang

Molucca
Sea

Halmahera
Ternate
Halmahera
Sea

INDONESIA

Selat Makassar

Flores Sea

Sawu
Sea

INDIAN
OCEAN

Denpasar
Mataram
Bali
Lombok
Sumbawa
Sumba
Flores
Timor
2960

NEW
PAPUA
GUINEA
IRIAN
JAYA
Central Range
Pegunungan Maoke
Puncak Mandala 4700
Puncak Jaya 5030
Jayapura

Pegunungan van Rees

Biak
Teluk
Cenderawasih

Manokwari
Gunung 3000
Gunung Kwoka 2680
Gunung Togwomeri
Sorong

AUSTRALIA

Arafura Sea

Timor Sea

Banda Sea

Seram Sea
Seram
3019

Buru
2114
Ambon

Kepulauan Kai
Kepulauan Tanimbar

Kepulauan Aru

Torres Strait
Cape York
Cape York
Peninsula

Settlements

- ◼ over 3 million
- ◻ 1 – 3 million
- ○ 250 000 – 1 million
- ● 100 000 – 250 000
- ◎ 25 000 – 100 000
- · under 25 000
- — country capital
  underline

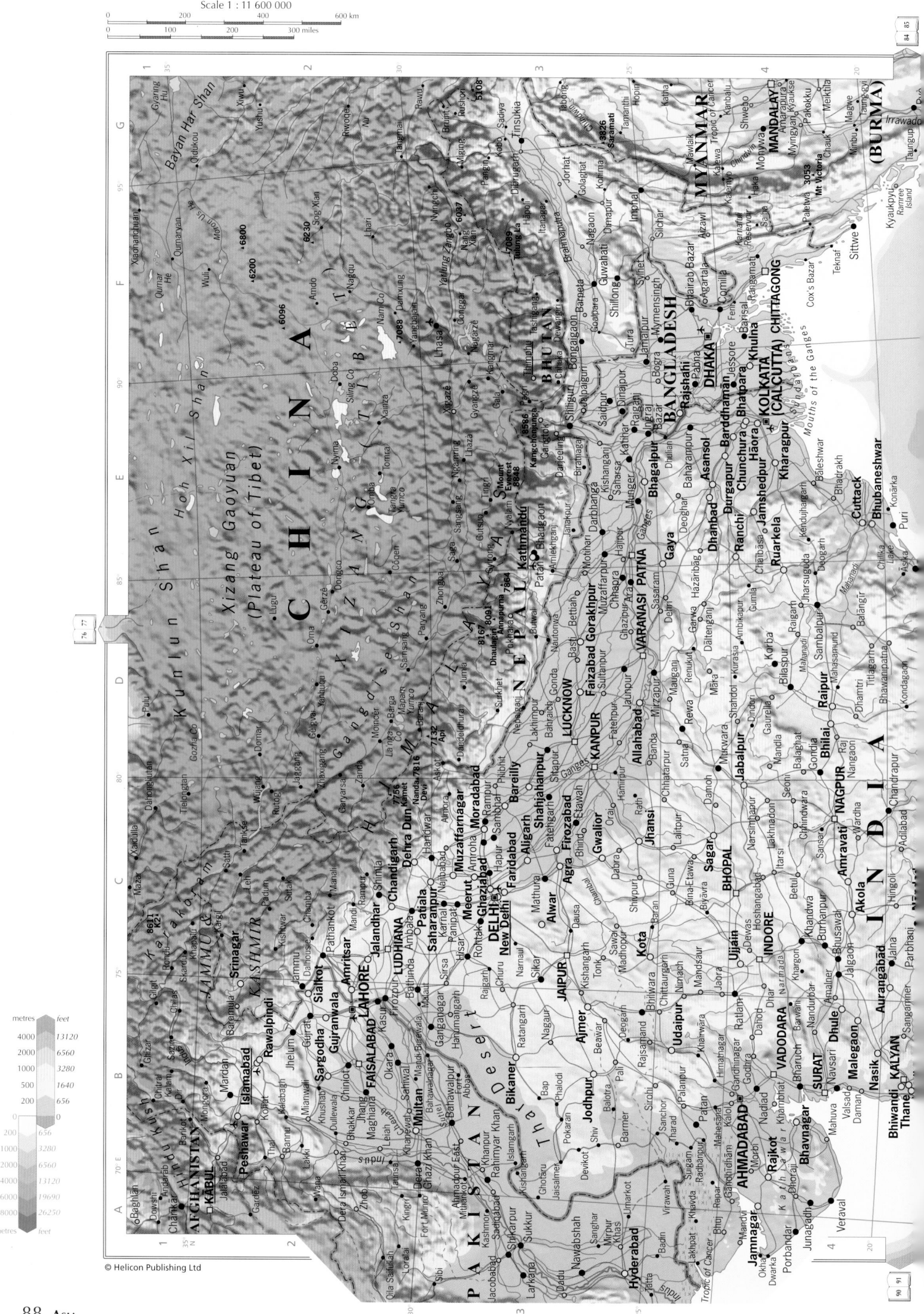

Scale 1 : 11 600 000

© Helicon Publishing Ltd

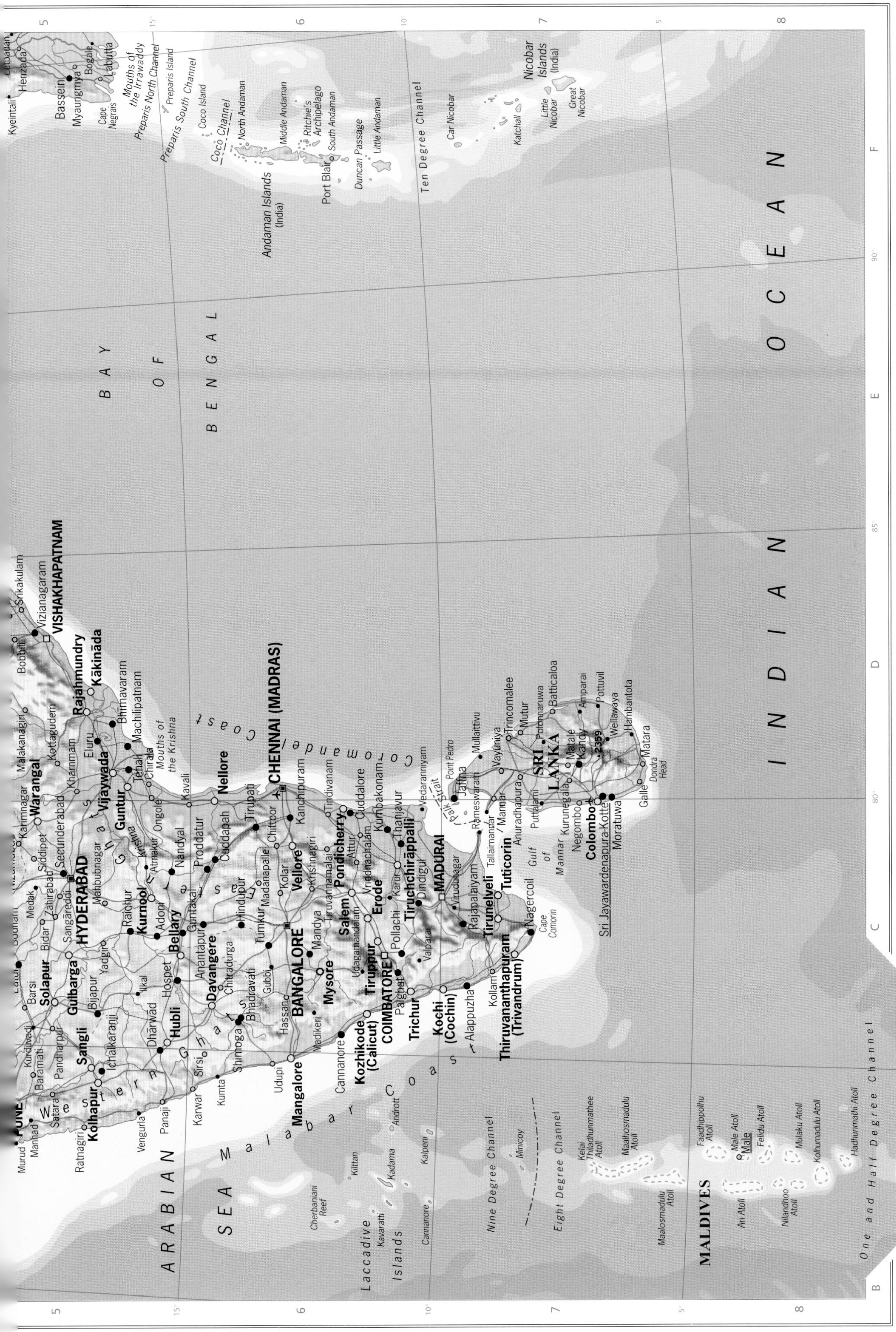

Bangladesh • Bhutan • Southern China
India • Maldives • Nepal • Sri Lanka

B A Y   O F   B E N G A L

Mouths of the Irrawaddy
Preparis North Channel
Preparis Island
Preparis South Channel
Coco Channel
North Andaman
Middle Andaman
Ritchie's Archipelago
South Andaman
Duncan Passage
Little Andaman
Ten Degree Channel

Andaman Islands (India)
Port Blair

Nicobar Islands (India)
Car Nicobar
Katchall
Little Nicobar
Great Nicobar

I N D I A N   O C E A N

Kyeintali
Henzada
Bassein
Myaungmya
Cape Negrais
Bogale
Labutta

Srikakulam
Vizianagaram
VISHAKHAPATNAM
Bobbili
Rajahmundry
Kākināda
Bhimavaram
Machilipatnam
Mouths of the Krishna
Eluru
Kottagudem
Khammam
Tenali
Vijayawada
Guntur
Ongole
Kavali
Nellore
CHENNAI (MADRAS)
Kanchipuram
Tirupati
Chittoor
Vellore
Tindivanam
Cuddalore
Pondicherry
Kumbakonam
Karaikal
Vedaranniyam
Thanjavur
Tiruchchirappalli
Karur
MADURAI
Dindigul
Virudunagar
Rajapalaiyam
Kollam
Tirunelveli
Tuticorin
Nagercoil
Cape Comorin

Warangal
Karimnagar
Siddipet
Secunderabad
HYDERABAD
Mahbubnagar
Nalgonda
Nandyal
Kurnool
Proddatur
Cuddapah
Anantapur
Gooty
Adoni
Bellary
Guntakal
Hindupur
Davangere
Chitradurga
Tumkur
BANGALORE
Mandya
Mysore
Salem
Erode
Pollachi
Tiruppur
COIMBATORE
Palghat
Trichur
Kochi (Cochin)
Alappuzha
Kollam
Thiruvananthapuram (Trivandrum)

PUNE
Barsi
Solapur
Gulbarga
Bidar
Sangli
Kolhapur
Ichalkaranji
Hubli
Dhārwād
Shimoga
Bhadravati
Hassan
Madikeri
Cannanore
Kozhikode (Calicut)
Mangalore
Udupi
Karwar
Panaji

A R A B I A N   S E A

Malabar Coast
Coromandel Coast
Western Ghats

Laccadive Islands
Cherbaniani Reef
Kiltan
Kadmat
Kavaratti
Andrott
Kalpeni
Minicoy

SRI LANKA
Point Pedro
Jaffna
Mullaittivu
Vavuniya
Trincomalee
Mutur
Batticaloa
Anuradhapura
Puttalam
Kurunegala
Matale
Kandy
2524
Negombo
Colombo
Sri Jayawardenapura-Kotte
Moratuwa
Galle
Matara
Dondra Head
Point Pedro
Talaimannar / Mannar
Mannar
Gulf of Mannar

MALDIVES
Maalosmadulu Atoll
Faadhippolhu Atoll
Male Atoll
Male
Felidu Atoll
Mulaku Atoll
Kolhumadulu Atoll
Ari Atoll
Nilandhoo Atoll
Hadhunmathi Atoll
Huvadu Atoll

Nine Degree Channel
Eight Degree Channel
One and Half Degree Channel
Equator

Settlements

■ over 3 million
□ 1 – 3 million
○ 250 000 – 1 million
● 100 000 – 250 000
◦ 25 000 – 100 000
· under 25 000
—— country capital underline

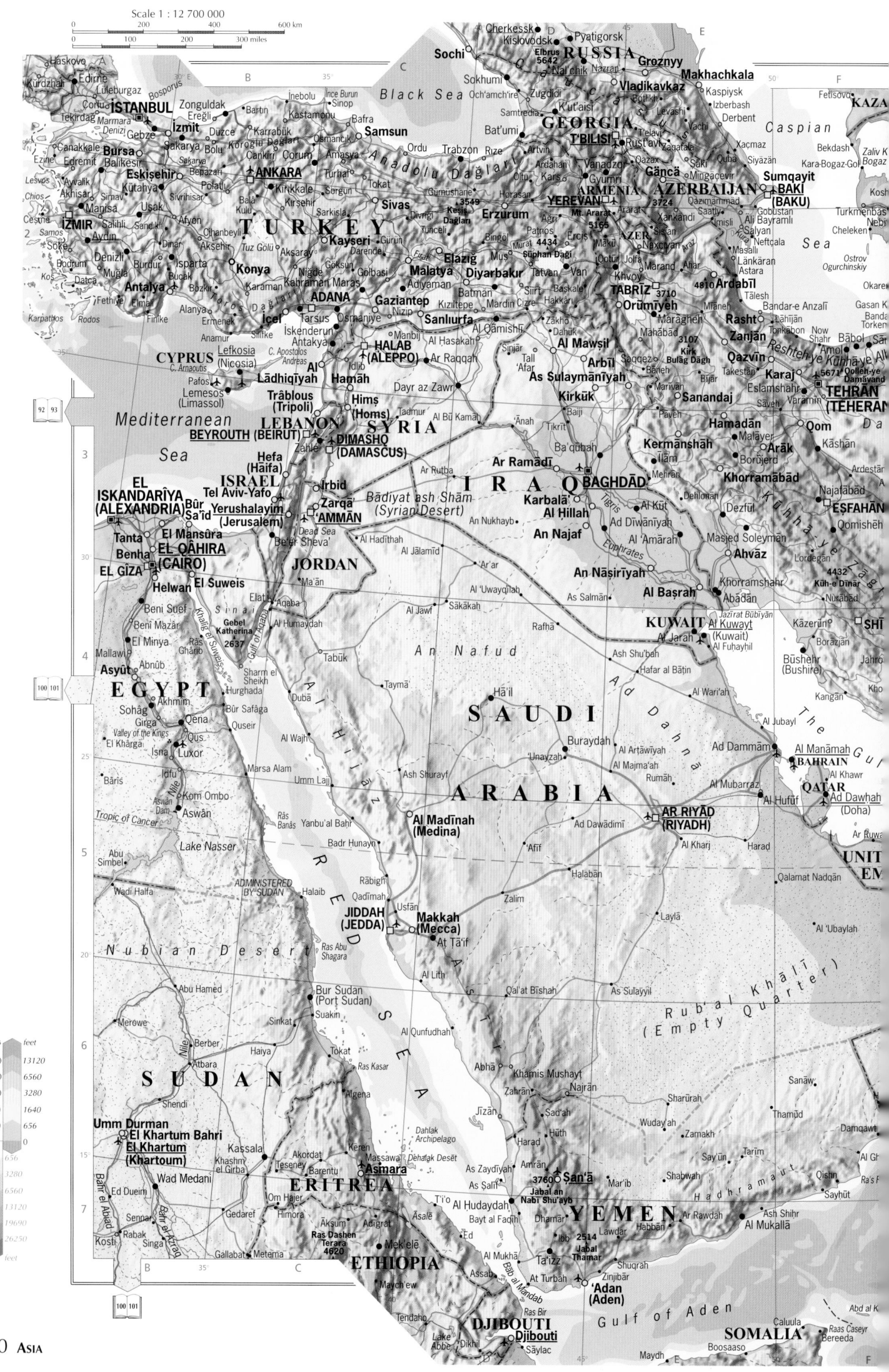

0   200   400   600 km
0   100   200   300 miles

Cherkessk   D   Pyatigorsk
Sochi   Kislovodsk   Elbrus   RUSSIA   Groznyy
Sokhumi   5642   Nal'chik   Nazran   Makhachkala
Och'amch'ire   Zugdidi   Vladikavkaz   Kaspiysk
Black Sea   Bat'umi   Samtredia   K'ut'aisi   Botlikh   Izberbash
İnebolu   Ordu   Rize   GEORGIA   T'elavi   Derbent
Ince Burun Sinop   Trabzon   Artvin   T'BILISI   Vachi   Xaçmaz   Caspian
İstanbul   Zonguldak   Bartın   Kastamonu   Bafra   Samsun   Ardahan   Oltu   Vanadzor   Qazax   Mingäçevir   Şäki   Quba   Siyäzän
Bosporus   Ereğli   Karabük   Çankırı   Çorum   Amasya   Turhal   Gümüşhane   Horasan   Kars   ARMENIA   Gäncä   AZERBAIJAN   Sumqayit

KAZA

THE MIDDLE EAST

Afghanistan • Iran • Iraq • Oman
Pakistan • Saudi Arabia • Syria • Yemen

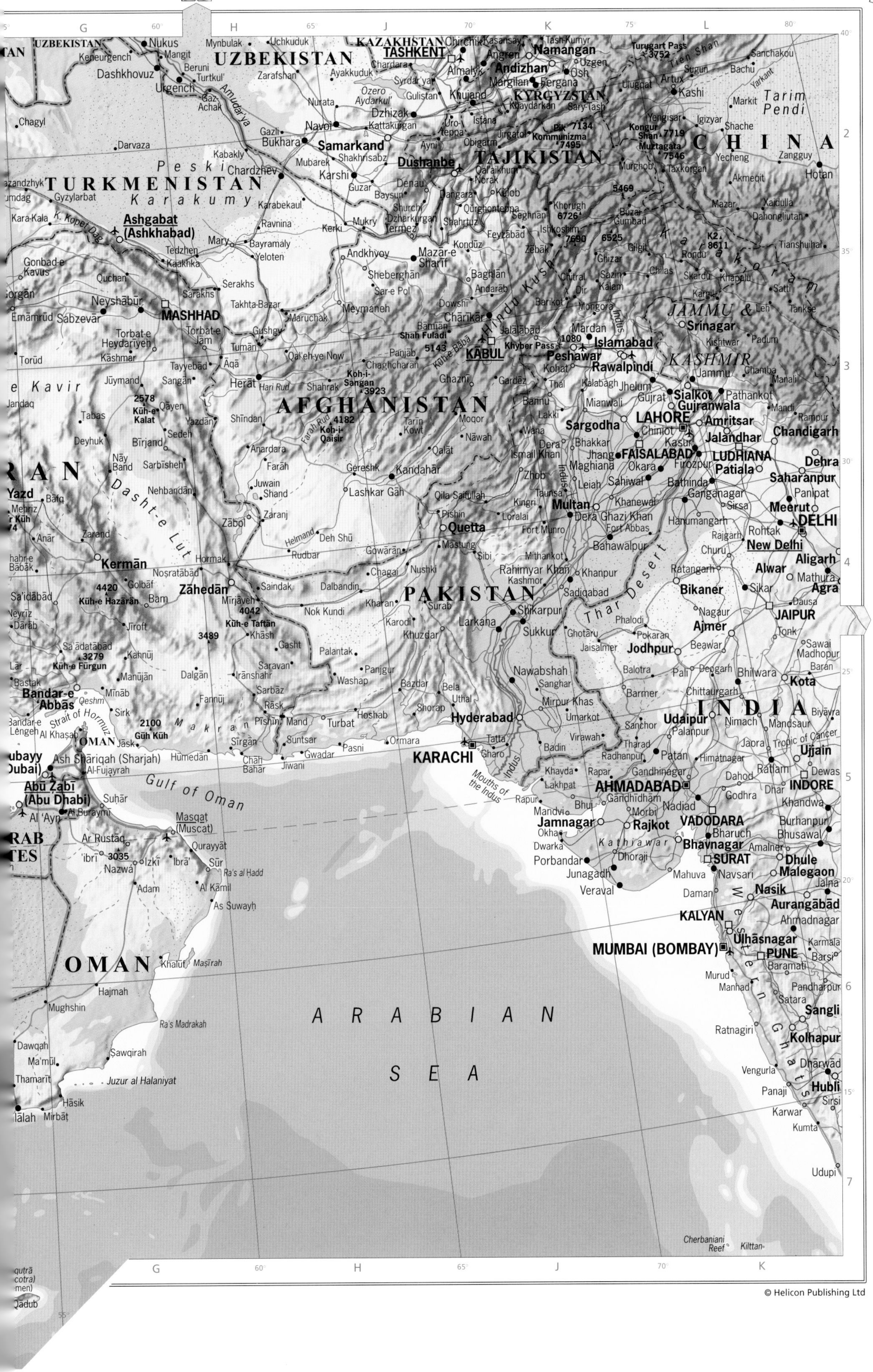

88 89

UZBEKISTAN

Nukus · Mangit
Keneurgench · Beruni
Dashkhovuz · Urgench · Turtkul'
Gaz-Achak · Zarafshan
Chagyl · Darvaza
Kara-Kala · Gyzylarbat
Gonbad-e Kavus

TURKMENISTAN
Karakumy
Peski

Ashgabat (Ashkhabad)

Mynbulak · Uchkuduk
KAZAKHSTAN
Chirchik · Kasansay
TASHKENT · Angren · Namangan
Ayakkuduk · Syrdar'ya · Almalyk · **Andizhan**
Chardara · Gulistan · Mārgilan · Fergana · Uzgen · Osh
Nurata · Ozero Aydarkul' · Khujand · **KYRGYZSTAN**
Navoi · Dzhizak · Uro-teppa · Jirgatol · Sary-Tash
Bukhara · Kattakurgan · **Samarkand** · Ayni · Obigarm · Pik 7134 Kommunizma
Kabakly · Shakhrisabz · **Dushanbe** · Denau · Norak · Kŭlob

TAJIKISTAN

Turugart Pass 3752
Angren · Uzgen
Kashi · Markit
Yengisar · 7719 Kongur Shan · Igizyar · Shache
Muztagata 7546 · Yecheng · Zangguy
Kongur · Rondu · Akmeqit · Hotan

CHINA
Tarim Pendi

Chardzhev · Karshi · Guzar · Baysun · Qürghonteppa
Kerki · Mukry · Termez · Shahrtŭz · Beghlan
Kondŭz · Feyzābād · Ishkoshim

Mary · Bayramaly · Ravnina
Tedzhen · Kāahka · Maruchak · Meymaneh
Serakhs · Takhta-Bazar · Gushgy · Sar-e Pol · Dowshi
Sarakhs · Tayyebād · Āqā · Maymaneh · Chārikār

MASHHAD
Neyshābūr · Torbat-e Heydāriyeh · Torbat-e Jām
Emāmrūd · Sabzevār · Tūmān · Qal'eh-ye Now
Torūd · Kāshmar · Herāt · Hari Rud · Shahrak · Koh-i-Baba 5143

AFGHANISTAN

Shah Fuladi
Bāmīān · Chaghcharān · Panjāb
Ghaznī · Gardez

2578 Kūh-e Kalat
Jūymand · Sangān · Sedeh · 4182 Koh-i-Qaisir · 3923 Sangan
Deyhuk · Bīrjand · Yazdān · Shindand · Anardara
Tabas · Qāyen · Farah · Tarin Kowt · Moqor
Nāy Band · Sarbīsheh · Juwain · Gereshk · Qalāt · Nāwah

e Kavir
Dasht-e Lut

Yazd · Mehrīz
· Anar
Bāfq
Nehbandān · Shand · Kandahār · Qila Safullah · Zhob
· Lashkar Gāh · Pishin · Loralai

hahr-e Bābak
Kermān · Zarand
4420 Kūh-e Hazārān · Golbaf · **Zāhedān** · Saindak · Dalbandin
Bam · Mirjāveh · 4042 · Kharan · Nushki
Sa'īdābād · Noṣratābād
Jīroft · 3489 Kūh-e Taftān · Khāsh · Nok Kundi · **Quetta**
· Kahnūj · Gasht · Karodi · Mastung · Sibi

Sa'ādatābād · 3279 Kūh-e Fürgun
Manūjān · Dalgān · Īrānshahr · Panjgur · Khuzdar
Lār · Fannūj · Sarbāz · Washap · Bazdar
Bandar-e **'Abbās** · Qeshm · Sirk · Mīnāb · 2100 Gūh Kūh · Rāsk · Bela · Uthal

PAKISTAN

Makran
Pishin · Mand · Turbat · Hoshab · Shorap
Sīrgān · Sūntsar · Pasni · Ormara
Chāh Bahar · Gwādar · Jiwani

Bandar-e Lengeh · Al Khaşab
OMAN · Jāsk · Hūmedān

Ḥubayy (Dubai)
Ash Shāriqah (Sharjah)
Abū Ẓabī (Abu Dhabi) · Suḥār
Al 'Ayn · Al Burayml · Ar Rustāq
RAB TES · 3035 · ibrī · Izkī · Ibrā' · **Masqaţ (Muscat)** · Qurayyāt
Nazwā · Adam · Ra's al Hadd
Sūr · Ra's al Hadd
Al Kāmil · As Suwayh

Gulf of Oman

OMAN
Khalūf · Maṣīrah
Mughshin
Hajmah
Dawqah · Ra's Madrakah
Ma'mūl · Shawqirah
Thamarīt · *Juzur al Halaniyat*
Hāsik · Mirbāt
lālah

ARABIAN SEA

Hindu Kush
5469 · 6726 · 7690 · 6525
Khorugh · Gilgit · K2 8611
Zēbāk · Gumbad · Chitral · Kalam · Skardu · Kargil
Ghizar · Dir · Mongora · Khapalu · Satti
Gilgit · Chilas · Kishtwar

JAMMU & KASHMIR
Srinagar · Leh · Padum · Tankse
Islamabad · Mardan · Jammu · Chamba · Manali
1080 Khyber Pass · **Peshawar** · **Rawalpindi** · Kishtwar · Padum
Kohat · Kalabagh · Jhelum · **Sialkot** · Pathankot · Mandi
Thal · Bannu · Mianwali · **Gujranwala** · **Jammu** · Rampur
Lakki · **LAHORE** · **Amritsar** · **Jalandhar** · **Chandigarh**
Dera Ismail Khan · **Sargodha** · Chiniot · Kasur · Dehra
Wana · Bhakkar · Jhang · **FAISALABAD** · **LUDHIANA** · Saharanpur
Maghiana · Okara · Firozpur · **Patiala** · Panipat
Leiah · Sahiwal · Bathinda · Ganganagar · Sirsa · **Meerut**
Kingri · Taunsa · Khanewal · Hanumangarh · Rohtak · **DELHI**
Dera Ghazi Khan · **Multan** · Churu · Rajgarh · **New Delhi**
Fort Munro · Kabirwala · Bahawalpur · **Alwar** · **Aligarh** · Mathura · **Agra**
Mithankot · Fort Abbas · Nagaur · Sikar · Dausa
Rahimyar Khan · Khanpur · Ratangarh · **Bikaner** · **JAIPUR**
Kashmor · Sadiqabad · Phalodi · **Ajmer** · Tonk · Sawai Madhopur
Shikarpur · Pokaran · **Jodhpur** · Beawar · Bārān
Larkāna · Sukkur · Ghotaru · Jaisalmer · **Kota**
Khuzdar · Ghotki · Balotra · Pali · Deggarh · **Bhilwara** · Biyāwar
Sanghar · Nawabshah · Barmer · Chittaurgarh
Khārān · Shorap · Uthal · Mirpur Khas · Sanchor · **Udaipur** · Nimach · Mandsaur

Thar Desert

INDIA

Tatta · Badin · Virawah · Tharad · **Palanpur** · Jaora · Tropic of Cancer
Hyderabad · Gharo · Umarkot · Radhanpur · **Ujjain**
KARACHI · Rapur · Khavda · Rapar · Himatnagar · Dewas
Mouths of the Indus · Lakhpat · Patan · Dahod · **INDORE**
Bhuj · Gāndhīdhām · Godhra · Dhar · Khandwa
AHMADABAD · Morbi · Nadiad · Burhanpur
Mandvi · **VADODARA** · Bhusawal
Jamnagar · **Rajkot** · Bharuch · Amalner
Okha · Dwarka · **Bhavnagar** · **SURAT** · **Dhule**
Kathiawar · Dhoraji · Navsari · **Malegaon**
Porbandar · Junagadh · Mahuva · Daman · **Nasik** · Jalna
Veraval · **Aurangābād**
KALYAN · Ahmadnagar
Ulhāsnagar · Karmala
MUMBAI (BOMBAY) · **PUNE** · Barsi
Murud · Baramati
Manhad · Pandharpur
Western Ghats · Satara · **Sangli**
Ratnagiri · Pandharpur
Vengurla · Baramati
Panaji · **Kolhapur** · **Dhārwād**
Hubli · Sirsi
Karwar · Kumta
Udupi

Cherbaniani Reef · Kilttan

ASIA 91

© Helicon Publishing Ltd

Settlements

▣	over 3 million
▢	1 – 3 million
◯	250 000 – 1 million
●	100 000 – 250 000
◉	25 000 – 100 000
·	under 25 000
—	country capital underline

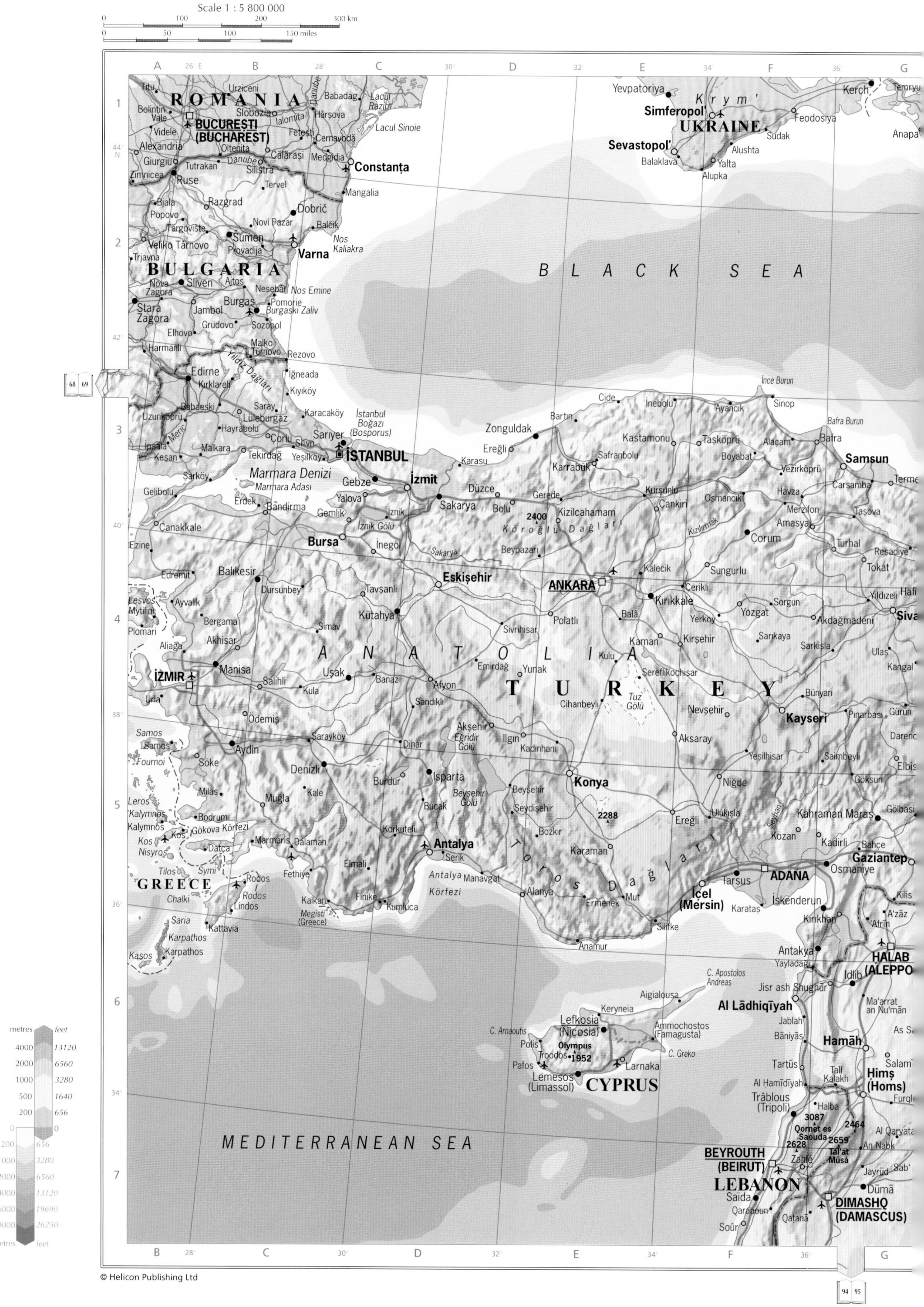

Scale 1 : 5 800 000

0   100   200   300 km
0   50   100   150 miles

A   26° E   B   28°   C   30°   D   32°   E   34°   F   36°   G

ROMANIA
Titu
Bolintin- Vale
Videle
□ BUCUREŞTI
(BUCHAREST)
Urziceni
Babadag
Lacul
Razim
Lacul Sinoie
Yevpatoriya
Krym'
Simferopol
UKRAINE
Kerch
Temryu
Alexandria
Giurgiu
Zimnicea
Olteniţa
Călăraşi
Medgidia
Fetesti
Cernavodă
Ialomiţa
Slobozia
Sevastopol'
Balaklava
Südak
Feodosiya
Anapa
Tutrakan
Silistra
Ruse
Danube
Constanţa
Yalta
Alupka
Alushta
Bjala
Popovo
Razgrad
Tărgovişte
Veliko Tărnovo
Trjavna
BULGARIA
Provadija
Šumen
Novi Pazar
Balčik
Dobrič
Varna
Mangalia
Nos Kaliakra

B L A C K   S E A

Nova
Zagora
Sliven
Ajtos
Nesebăr
Nos Emine
Stara
Zagora
Jambol
Burgas
Pomorie
Burgaski Zaliv
Elhovo
Grudovo
Sozopol
Harmanli
Malko
Tărnovo
Rezovo
Yıldız Dağları
Edirne
Kırklareli
İğneada
Kıyıköy
İnce Burun
Uzunköprü
Babaeski
Saray
Lüleburgaz
Karacaköy
Cide
İnebolu
Ayancık
Sinop
Bafra Burun
İpsala
Keşan
Hayrabolu
Çorlu
Silivri
Sarıyer
İstanbul
Boğazı
(Bosporus)
Zonguldak
Bartın
Kastamonu
Taşköprü
Alaçam
Bafra
Samsun
Malkara
Tekirdağ
Şarköy
Yeşilköy
□ **İSTANBUL**
Ereğli
Karasu
Safranbolu
Karabük
Boyabat
Vezirköprü
Çarşamba
Terme
Gelibolu
Marmara
Adası
Marmara Denizi
Gebze
İzmit
Düzce
Gerede
Kızılcahamam
Kurşunlu
Çankırı
Osmancık
Havza
Merzifon
Amasya
Taşova
Erdek
Bandırma
Gemlik
Yalova
İznik
İznik Gölü
Sakarya
Bolu
2400
Köroğlu Dağları
Kızılırmak
Çorum
Turhal
Reşadiye
Tokat
Ezine
Çanakkale
Bursa
İnegöl
Sakarya
Beypazarı
Kalecik
Sungurlu
Edremit
Balıkesir
Dursunbey
Tavşanlı
Eskişehir
□ **ANKARA**
Cerikli
Kırıkkale
Yıldızeli
Hafi
Lesvos
Mytilini
Ayvalık
Bergama
Akhisar
Simav
Kütahya
Sivrihisar
Polatlı
Balâ
Kırşehir
Yerköy
Yozgat
Sorgun
Akdağmadeni
Sarıkaya
Şarkışla
Ulaş
Siva
Kangal
Plomari
Aliağa
A N A T O L I A
Uşak
Banaz
Afyon
Emirdağ
Yunak
Kulu
T U R K E Y
Kaman
Şereflikoçhisar
Nevşehir
Bünyan
Gürün
Darende
İZMİR
□
Manisa
Salihli
Kula
Sandıklı
Akşehir
Eğridir
Gölü
Ilgın
Kadınhanı
Cihanbeyli
Tuz Gölü
Kayseri
Pınarbaşı
Urla
Samos
Samos
Fournoi
Ödemiş
Sarayköy
Dinar
Eğridir
Aksaray
Yeşilhisar
Şaimbeyli
Elbis
Leros
Kalymnos
Kalymnos
Aydın
Söke
Milas
Denizli
Burdur
Isparta
Beyşehir
Konya
Niğde
Göksun
Kos
Bodrum
Gökova Körfezi
Datça
Muğla
Kale
Bucak
Beyşehir
Gölü
Seydişehir
2288
Ereğli
Ulukışla
Kozan
Kahraman Maraş
Gölbaşı
Kadirli
Bahçe
Nisyros
Marmaris
Dalaman
Körkuteli
Bozkır
Karaman
Tarsus
□ **ADANA**
Gaziantep
Tilos
Symi
Fethiye
Elmalı
Antalya
Serik
Ermenek
Mut
İçel (Mersin)
İskenderun
Osmaniye
Kilis
GREECE
Rodos
Rodos
Kalkan
Finike
Kumluca
Antalya Körfezi
Manavgat
Alanya
Toros Dağları
Silifke
Karataş
Kırıkhan
A'zâz
Afrin
Chalki
Saria
Kattavia
Megisti (Greece)
Anamur
Antakya
Yayladağı
HALAB (ALEPPO)
İdlib
Kaşos
Karpathos
Karpathos
Lindos
C. Apostolos Andreas
Jisr ash Shughur
Ma'arrat
an Nu'mân
As Si
C. Arnaoutis
Keryneia
Aigialousa
Ammochostos
(Famagusta)
Al Lādhiqīyah
Jablah
Bāniyās
Hamāh
Polis
Lefkosia (Nicosia)
Troodos
Olympus
1952
C. Greko
Larnaka
Tartūs
Salam
Pafos
Lemesos (Limassol)
CYPRUS
Al Hamīdīyah
Tall Kalakh
Himş (Homs)
Furqlu
M E D I T E R R A N E A N   S E A
Trâblous
(Tripoli)
Halba
3087
Qornet es Saouda
2464
2659
Al Qaryata
An Nabk
2628
BEYROUTH (BEIRUT)
Zahlé
Tal'at Mūsá
Jayrūd
Sab'
LEBANON
Saida
Dūmā
□ **DIMASHQ (DAMASCUS)**
Şour
Qaraoun
Qatana

metres | feet
4000 | 13120
2000 | 6560
1000 | 3280
500 | 1640
200 | 656
0 | 0
200 | 656
1000 | 3280
2000 | 6560
4000 | 13120
6000 | 19690
8000 | 26250
metres | feet

© Helicon Publishing Ltd

B   28°   C   30°   D   32°   E   34°   F   36°   G

70 71

RUSSIA

Krasnodar
Krymsk
Novorossiysk
Gelendzhik
Tuapse
Sochi
Adler
Gagra
Gudaut'a
Sokhumi
Och'amch'ire
Zugdidi

Ust'-Labinsk
Armavir
Adygeysk
Labinsk
Belorechensk
Khadyzhensk
Maykop
Psebay

Svetlograd
Stavropol'
Nevinnomyssk

KALMYKIYA

Blagodarnyy
Budennovsk
Neftekumsk
Zelenokumsk
Mineral'nyye Vody

Yuzhno-Sukhokumsk
Kutan

Kizlyarskiy Zaliv
Os. Chechen'

CASPIAN

SEA

Cherkessk
Pyatigorsk
Kislovodsk
Prokhladnyy

KARACHAYEVO-CHERKESIYA
Karachayevsk
Teberda

KABARDINO-BALKARIYA
Nal'chik

5642 Elbrus
5203

SEVERNAYA
OSETIYA
5047 Kazbek

Vladikavkaz
Nazran

INGUSHETIYA
Urus Martan

CHECHNYA
Gudermes
Groznyy

Mozdok
Terek

Kargalinskaya
Babayurt

DAGESTAN
Khasavyurt

4494
4276 Dikloşmta

GEORGIA

Tqvarch'eli
Lajanurpekhi
Oni
Ts'khinvali

Sadon
Gori
Kaspi
Khashuri
Borjomi

Kargalinskaya
Gunib
Levashi
Kumukh

Kochubey

Makhachkala
Kaspiysk
Izberbash

Derbent

Agrakhanskiy
Poluostrov

Kraynovka
Kizlyar

K'ut'aisi
P'ot'i
Samtredia
Ozurget'i
Bat'umi
Hopa
Pazar

T'bilisi
Rust'avi
Akhalts'ikhe
Bolnisi
Akhalk'alak'i

T'elavi
Qvareli
Zaqatala
Qax
Dedoplis

Şäki
4466 Göra Bazardyuzi

4131

Qusar
Xaçmaz
Quba
Däväçi
Siyäzän

Gilazi

Sumqayıt
BAKI (BAKU)

Artvin
Yusufeli

Ardahan
Göle
Kars

Tashir
Alaverdi
Vanadzor
Dilijan

Qazax
Tovuz

AZERBAIJAN

Mingäçevir
Su Anbarı

Akhty
Qazax

Sämkir
Yevlax
Mingäçevir

Ismayıllı
Ağsu

Samaxı

Sanqaçal

Trabzon
Rize
3937

Anadolu Dağları

Ordu
Giresun

Gümüşhane
Bayburt

Olţu
Sarıkamış

Gyumri 4090
Ejmiadzin
ARMENIA
YEREVAN

Hrazdan
Sevana Lich
Vardenis

Gäncä
Bärdä

3724
Ağcabädi
Ağdam

Kür

Kürdämir
Saatlı
Salyan

Ali Bayramlı
Qazımämmäd

Biläsuvar
Calilabad
Masallı

Neftçala

Süşehri
Erzincan
Pulumur
Aşkale
Erzurum
Pasinler
Hörasan

Ağrı
Vedi
Ararat
Sısıan
Sähbuz
Goris
Horadız

Araz
Tazeh Kand

Lerik
Astara

Divriği
Kemaliye
Tunceli
Keban
Barajı
Palu

Karakoçan
Bingöl
Varto
Solhan
Muş

Patnos
Ercis
Muradiye

Mt. Ararat 5165

Doğubeyazıt

Mākū
Pareh
Qotūr

AZER.
Naxçıvan
3829
Culfa
Jolfa

Qazangöldag
Mincivan
Khodā Afarīn
Ävärsin

4810
Ardabīl

Agin
Elazığ
Maden
Fırat (Euphrates)
Malatya
Doğanşehir

Ergani
Silvan

4434 Süphan Dağı
Tatvan
Van Gölü
Bitlis
Gevaş

Van
Erçek
Başkale
Çatak

Marand
Khvoy
Tasūj
Salmās
Lūra Shirin

Ahar

Kirk Bulağ D. 3107

Tabrīz

3710 Kuh-e Sahand

Bastānābād
Sarāb

Hashtpar
Tälesh

Bandar-e Anzalī
Rasht

Kahta
Adıyaman
Bozova
Siverek
Viranşehir

Diyarbakır
Batman
Mardin
Kızıltepe
Nusaybin

Cizre
Şırnak
Zākho

Yüksekova
Hakkâri
Amādiyah

IRAN

Orūmīyeh
Bonāb
Haydarābād

Āzarān
Miāndowāb

Miāneh
Nik Pey

Abhar

Zanjān

Buhayrat al Asad
'Ayn 'Īsā
Manbij
Jarābulus
Akçakale
Al Qāmishlī
Al Hasakah
Tall 'Afar
Sinjār
Ash Shadādah

Dahūk
Zēbār

Rawānduz
Rānya

Saqqez
Bowkan
Mahābād

Bī700000
Sar Dasht
Baneh
Dīvāndarreh
Zāgheh-ye Bālā

Yangi Kand

Sanandaj
Qorveh

Ar Raqqah
Ar Ruşāfah
Dayr az Zawr
Mayādīn

Al Mawşil
Arbīl
Tall 'Uwaynāt

Ash Shargāt

Koi Sanjaq
Sar Dasht

Marīvān

Qorveh
Kāmyārān

SIRIA

As Sukhnah
Tadmur

Āl Bū Kamāl
Rāwah
Al Hadīthah
Anah
Ar Rutba
Khān al Baghdādī
Hīt
Euphrates

MESOPOTAMIA
'IRAQ

As Sulaymānīyah
Kirkūk
Tuz Khurmātū
Kifrī

Baiji
Tikrīt
Sāmarrā
Al Muqdādīyah
Ba'qūbah
Al Khālis

Halabja
Pāveh

BAGHDĀD
Ar Ramādī
Habbānīyah

Buhayrat ath Tharthār

Jalūlā

Bar al Milh

Sanandaj
Kermānshāh
Harsin

Eslāmābād e Gharb
Gilan Garb
Īlām
Mehrān

Karand
Gīlan Garb
Ravānsar

Kūhdasht
Mālavi
Dehlorān

Bādiyat ash Shām
(Syrian Desert)

Ar Rutba

90 91

100 101

Settlements

■ over 3 million
□ 1 – 3 million
◎ 250 000 – 1 million
● 100 000 – 250 000
○ 25 000 – 100 000
• under 25 000

— country capital underline
— state or province capital underline

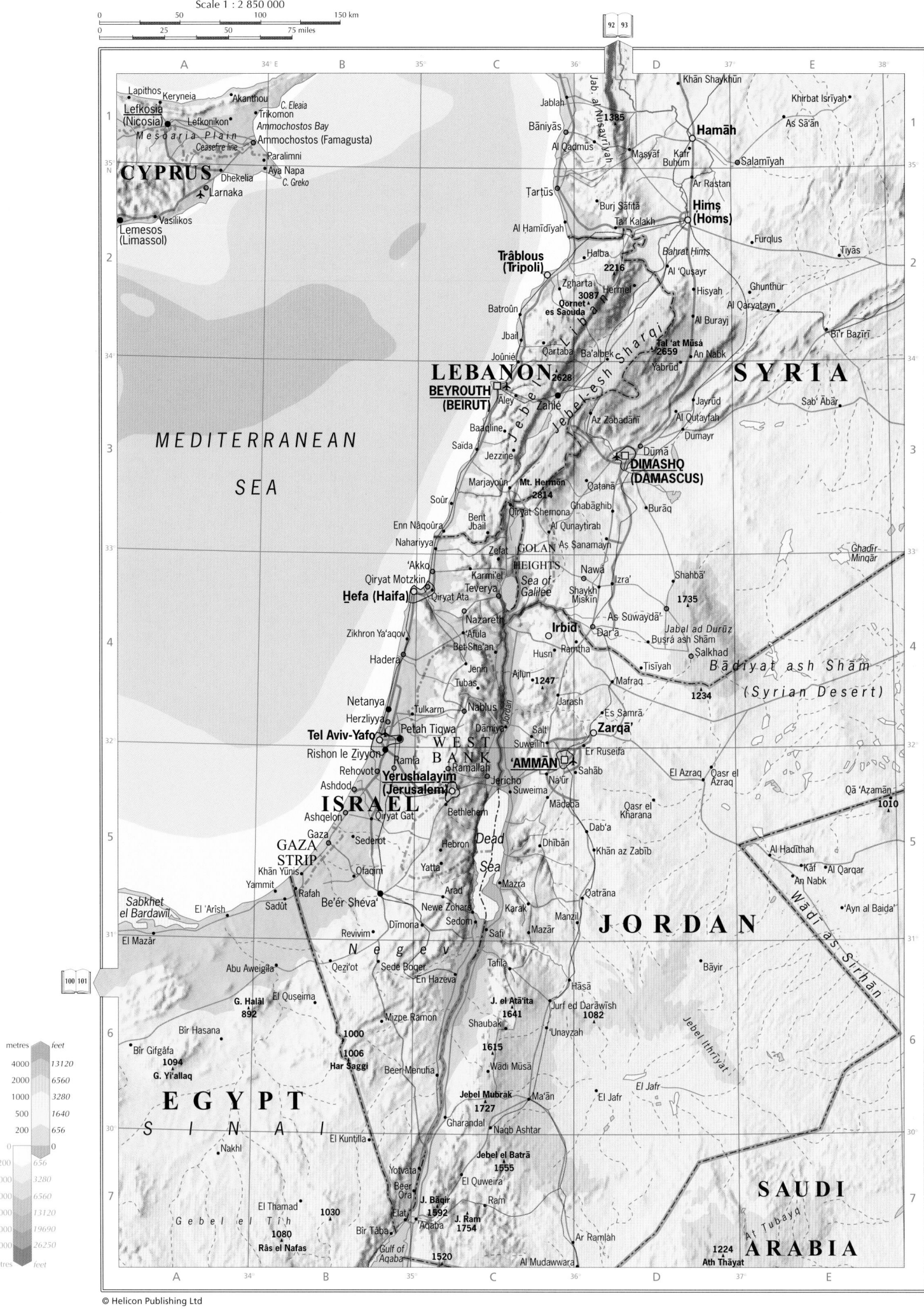

0   50   100   150 km

0   25   50   75 miles

92 | 93

CYPRUS

Lapithos • Keryneia
Lefkosia • • Akanthou
(Nicosia) • Lefkonikon • Trikomon   C. Eleaia
Mesoria Plain   Ammochostos Bay
Ceasefire line   Ammochostos (Famagusta)
Dhekelia • Aya Napa   • Paralimni   C. Greko
Larnaka

Vasilikos •
Lemesos
(Limassol)

MEDITERRANEAN

SEA

Khān Shaykhūn
Khirbat Isrīyah •
Jablah
Bāniyās   • As Sā'ān
• 1385   **Hamāh**
Al Qadmūs •   Masyāf • Kafr   • Salamīyah
Buhum
Ţarţūs •   Ar Rastan •
Burj Şāfitā •   **Himş**
Al Ḥamīdīyah •   Tall Kalakh •   **(Homs)**   Furqlus •
Halba •   Bahrat Himş   • Tiyās
Trâblous   2216 ▲   Al 'Qusayr •
(Tripoli)   Zgharta •   Ghunthūr •
3087 ▲   Hermel •   Hisyah •   Al Qaryatayn •
• Batroûn   Qornet   • Tal 'at Mūsá   • Bi'r Bazīrī
es Saouda   Ba'albek •   2659   An Nabk •
• Jbail   Qartaba •   Yabrūd •
Joûnié •   **LEBANON** 2628 ▲   Sab' Ābār •
BEYROUTH   Aley • Zahlé •   Jayrūd •
(BEIRUT)   Az Zabādānī •   **SYRIA**
Baaqline •   Al Qutayfah •
Saïda •   Dumayr •
Jezzine •   • Dūmā
Marjayoûn •   **DIMASHQ**
Soûr •   **Mt. Hermon** Qaţanā • **(DAMASCUS)**
Qiryat Shemona • 2814   Ghabāghib •
Bent   Al Qunayţirah • Burāq •
Jbail   Nawa •
Enn Nâqoûra •   Zefat •   **GOLAN** Aş Sanamayn •
Nahariyya •   **HEIGHTS** Izra' •   • Shahbā
'Akko •   Sea of   Shaykh • • As Suwaydā'   • 1735
Qiryat Motzkin •   Karmi'el • Teverya Galilee   Miskīn   Jabal ad Durūz
Hefa (Haifa) Qiryat Ata •   Nawa •
Qiryat Ata •   Nazareth •   **Irbid** Dar'ā •   Busrá ash Shām •
Zikhron Ya'aqov •   • Afula   Husn •   • Salkhad
Hadera •   Bet-She'an •   • Ramtha
Jenin •   Ajlun •   Tisīyah •   *Bādiyat ash Shām*
Tubas •   • 1247   Mafraq •   *(Syrian Desert)*
Netanya •   Nablus •   Jarash •   • 1234
Herzliyya •   Tulkarm • Dāmiya •   Es Samrā •
Petah Tiqwa •   **WEST**   Salt •   **Zarqā'**
Tel Aviv-Yafo •   **BANK**   Suweilih •   Er Ruseifa •
Rishon le Ziyyon •   Ramla •   **'AMMĀN**
Rehovot •   Ramallah •   El Azraq • Qasr el
Yerushalayim   Jericho •   Na'ur •   Azraq
(Jerusalem)   Suweima •   Qasr el
Ashdod •   Bethlehem •   Mādabā •   Kharana
ISRAEL   Dab'a •
Ashqelon • Qiryat Gat •   Hebron •   Dhībān •   • Khān az Zabīb
Gaza •   Dead   Al Hadīthah •
GAZA Sederot •   Yatta •   Sea   • Kāf • Al Qarqar
STRIP   • Arad   Mazra •   An Nabk •
Khān Yūnis •   Ofaqim •   Newe Zohar • Karak •   Qaţrāna •
Yammit •   Rafah •   Sedom •   Manzil •   'Ayn al Baida •
Sadūt •   Be'ér Shéva'   Safi •   Mazar •
El 'Arīsh •   Dīmona •   **JORDAN**
Sabkhet   Revivim •   Tafīla •   Bāyir •
el Bardawīl   El Mazâr •   *Negev*   Ḥāsā •
Abu Aweigîla •   Qezi'ot •   Sede Boger •   Jurf ed Darāwīsh •
En Hazeva •   **J. el Atā'ita** 1082   • 1641
G. Halâl Mizpe Ramon •   1641
892 El Quseima •   Shaubak •
• 1000   Unayzah •   El Jafr •
Bîr Hasana •   • 1006   1615 •
Bîr Gifgâfa •   **Har Saggi**   Wādi Mūsá •
1094   Beer Menuha •
G. Yi'allaq   **EGYPT**   Jebel Mubrak •
1727   Ma'ān •
SINAI   Gharandal •   • El Jafr
Nakhl •   • Naqb Ashtar
El Thamad •   Jebel el Batrā •
Jebel el Batrā
1555   **SAUDI**
Yotvata •
Gebel el Tîh   El Quweira •
1030   Beer   Ram •
El Thamad •   Ora   **J. Bāqir**   Ar Ramlāh •
1080   **Elat** 1592   **J. Ram**
Râs el Nafas   Bîr Tâba •   1754
1520   Gulf of   1224   **ARABIA**
Aqaba •   **Ath Thāyat**
Al Mudawwara •

© Helicon Publishing Ltd

Bahrain • Israel • Jordan • Kuwait
Lebanon • Qatar • United Arab Emirates

Scale 1 : 5 800 000

100   200   300 km
50   100   150 miles

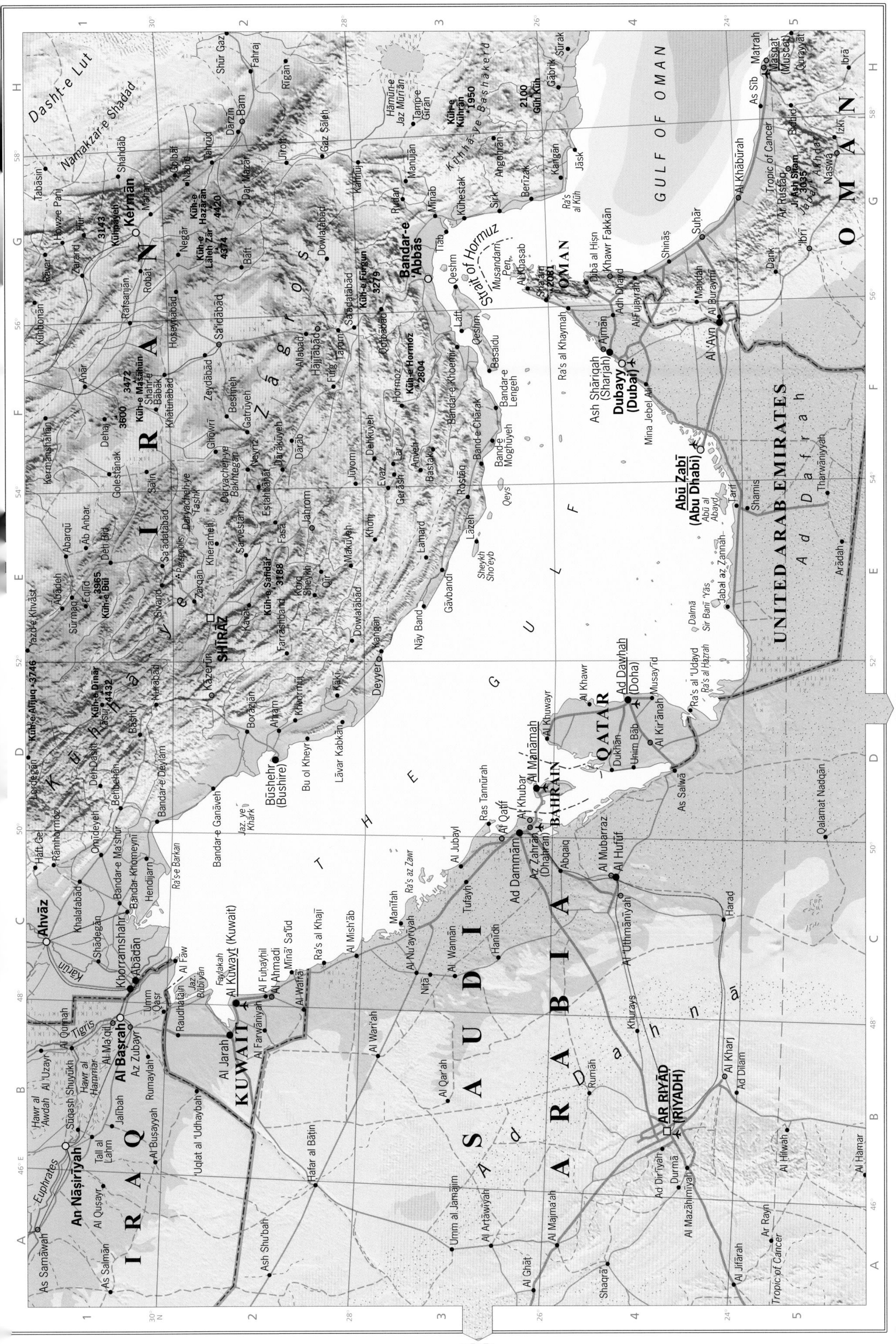

Countries and regions:

IRAN
IRAQ
SAUDI ARABIA
KUWAIT
OMAN
UNITED ARAB EMIRATES
QATAR
BAHRAIN

GULF OF OMAN
Strait of Hormuz
Musandam Pen.
Zagros
THE GULF
Ad Dafrah
Dasht-e Lut

Selected settlements:

Kermān, Bandar-e ʿAbbās, Shīrāz, Būshehr (Bushire), Ahvāz, Al Başrah, An Nāşirīyah, AL KUWAYT (Kuwait), Al Ahmadī, Al Jahrah, Ad Dammām (Dhahran), Al Khubar, AL MANĀMAH, BAHRAIN, AD DAWHAH (Doha), QATAR, Abū Zabī (ABU DHABI), Dubayy (Dubai), Ash Shāriqah (Sharjah), Ajmān, Al ʿAyn, Ra's al Khaymah, UNITED ARAB EMIRATES, Masqaţ (Muscat), AR RIYĀD (RIYADH)

Settlements

◻ 1 – 3 million
◯ 250 000 – 1 million
● 100 000 – 250 000
○ 25 000 – 100 000
• under 25 000

— country capital underline

urban area

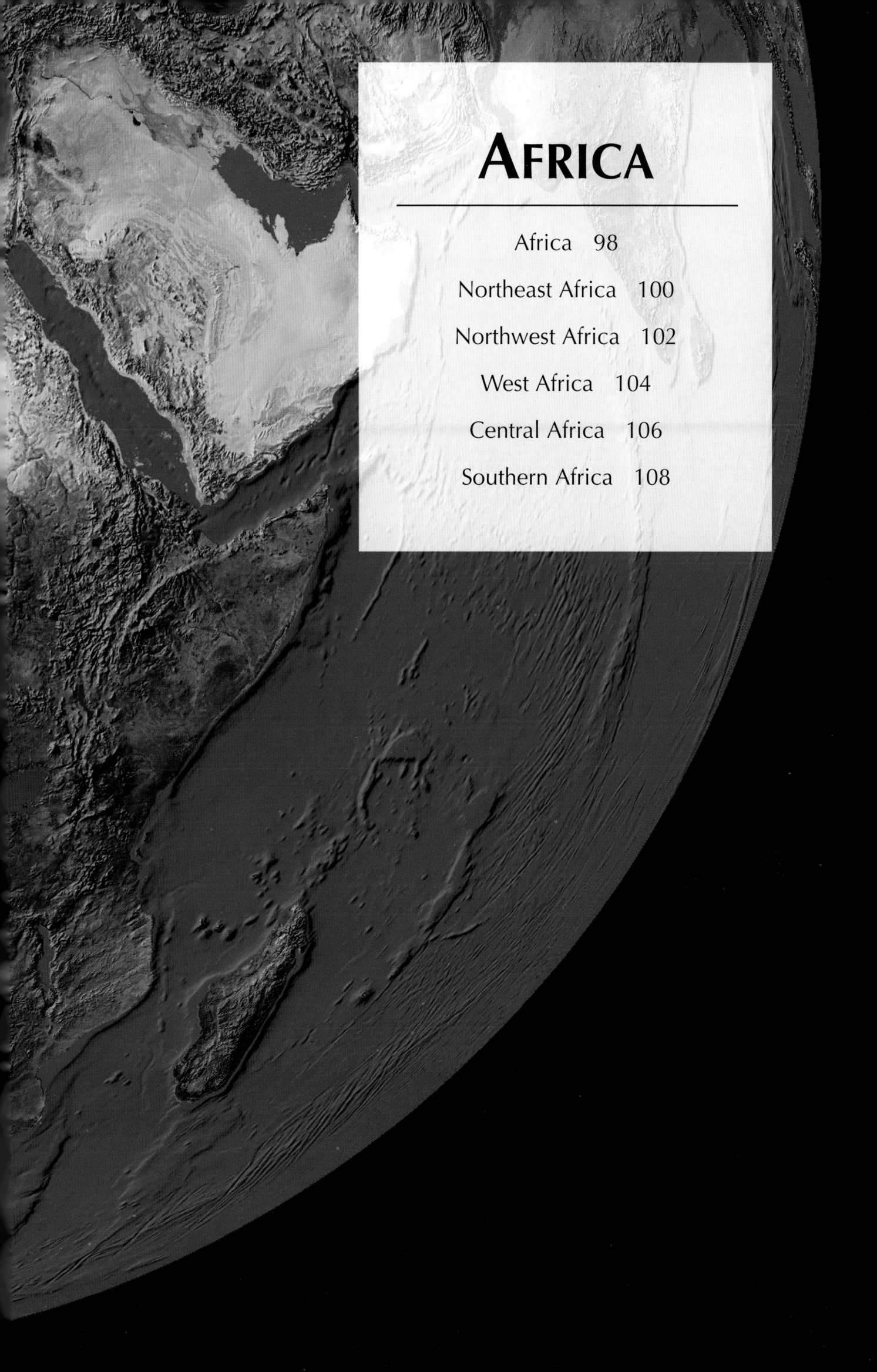

AFRICA

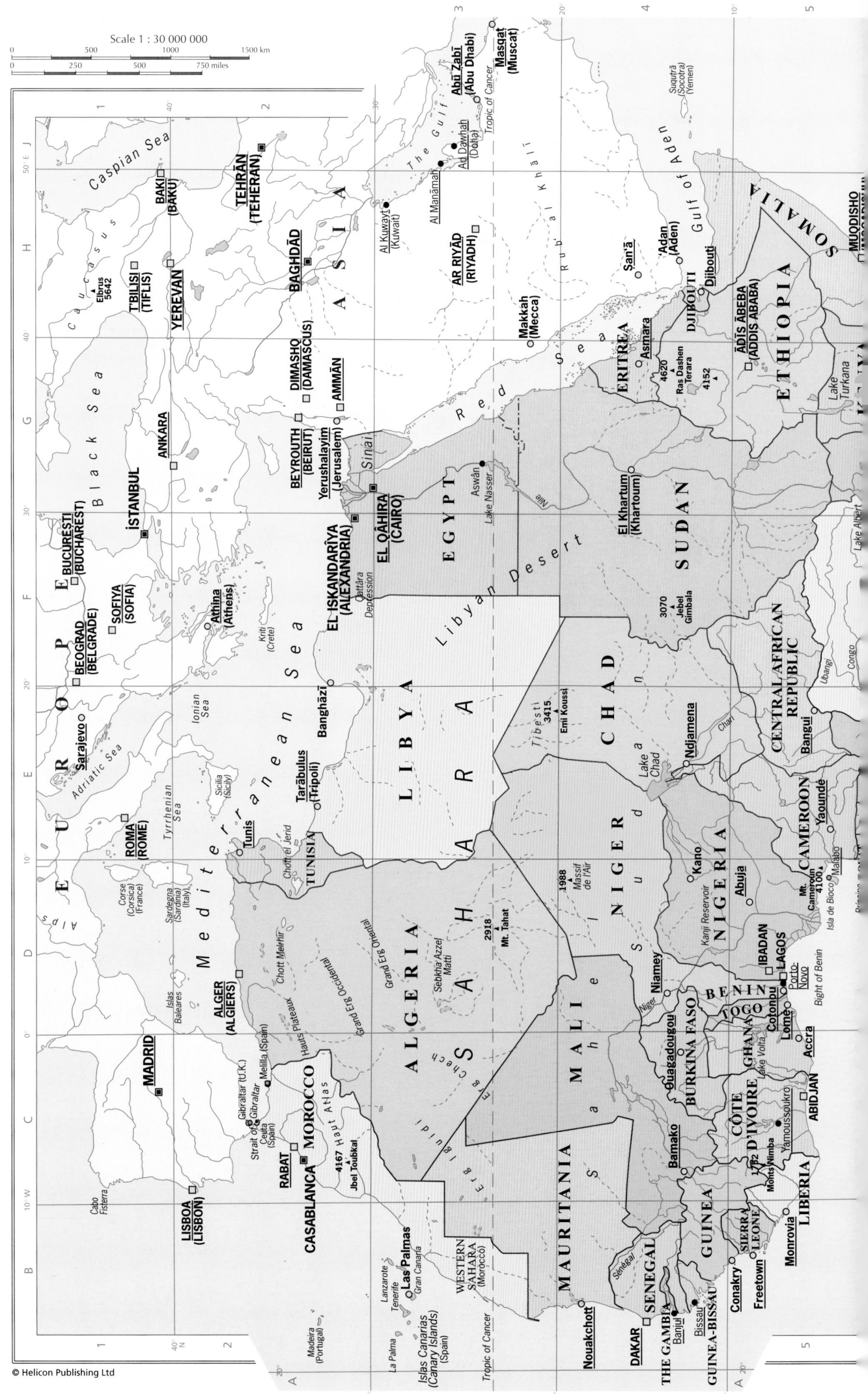

Scale 1 : 30 000 000

| 0 | 500 | 1000 | 1500 km |

| 0 | 250 | 500 | 750 miles |

© Helicon Publishing Ltd

ATLANTIC

OCEAN

INDIAN

OCEAN

SEYCHELLES

Seychelles Is.
Coëthy
Amirante Is.
Agalega Is.
(Mauritius)

Cosmoledo
Group
Glorieuses (France)
Tanjona
Bobaomby
ANTANANARIVO

COMOROS

Njazidja

Mayotte
(France)

MADAGASCAR

Tanjona
Vohimena

Tropic of Capricorn

Iles Crozet
(France)

Mozambique Channel

Juan de Nova
(France)

Prince Edward Island
(South Africa)

DAR ES SALAAM

Mombasa

Pemba I.

Zanzibar I.

NAIROBI

Mt. Kilimanjaro
5895

TANZANIA

Dodoma

MOZAMBIQUE

Lake Nyasa

MALAWI

Mt. Mulanje
3002

Beira

Lilongwe

Lake
Tanganyika

RWANDA
Kigali

BURUNDI
Bujumbura

Lake Kivu

Lago de
Cahora Bassa

HARARE

ZIMBABWE

Bulawayo

SWAZILAND
Mbabane

Maputo

Lobamba

DURBAN

Lake Mweru

Lubumbashi

Ndola

ZAMBIA

Lusaka

Lake
Kariba

Limpopo

Drakensberg

Port Elizabeth

Kananga

REPUBLIC

OF CONGO

Luapula

Zambezi

Okavango
Delta

Makgadikgadi

BOTSWANA

Kalahari
Desert

Gaborone

Pretoria
Johannesburg

LESOTHO
Maseru
3482

Bloemfontein
2430

SOUTH AFRICA

Cape Agulhas

KINSHASA

Kwango

ANGOLA

Cuanza

NAMIBIA

Etosha Pan

Windhoek

Brandberg
2574

Namib

Desert

Orange

St.
Helena
Bay

CAPE TOWN

Cape of Good Hope

Brazzaville

LUANDA

CABINDA
(Angola)

Annobón
(Pagalu)
(Equatorial Guinea)

Walvis Bay

Ascension
(U.K.)

St. Helena
(U.K.)

Tristan da Cunha
(U.K.)

Gough I.
(U.K.)

Tropic of Capricorn

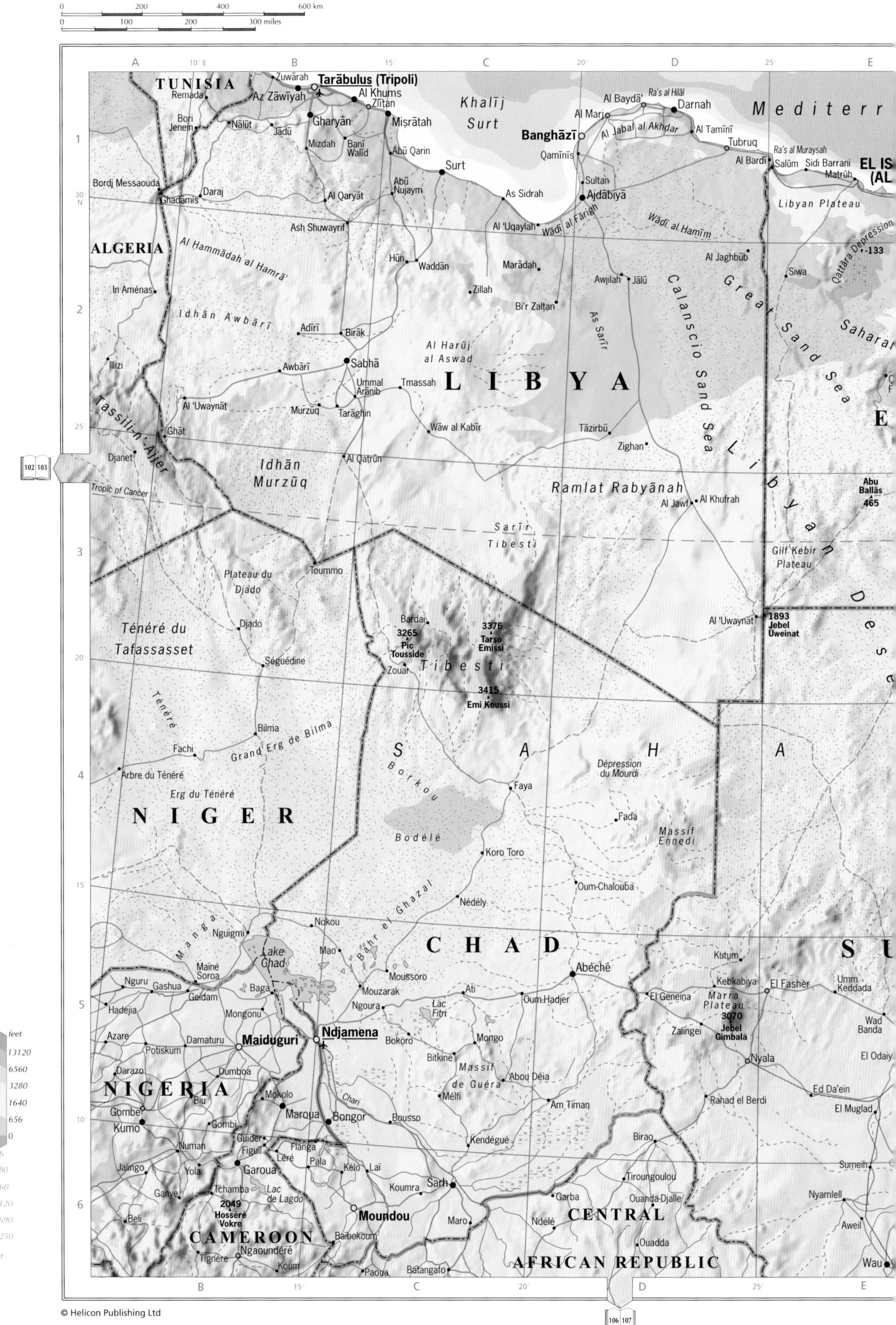

Scale 1 : 11 600 000

| 0 | 200 | 400 | 600 km |
| 0 | 100 | 200 | 300 miles |

TUNISIA
Remada
Bori Jenem
Nalut
Mizdah
Zuwārah
Az Zāwīyah
Gharyān
Jādū
Bani Walīd
Tarābulus (Tripoli)
Al Khums
Zlītan
Miṣrātah
Abū Qarin
Abū Nujaym
Surt

Khalīj Surt

Al Baydā
Al Marj
Ra's al Hilāl
Darnah
Mediterr
Banghāzī
Al Jabal al Akhdar
Al Tamīnī
Tubruq
Qamīnis
Ra's al Muraysah
Al Bardī
Salūm
Sidi Barrani
Matrūh
EL IS (AL

Bordj Messaouda
Ghadāmis
Daraj
Al Qaryāt
As Sidrah
Ajdābiyā
Sultan
ALGERIA
Al Hammādah al Hamrā'
Ash Shuwayrif
Al 'Uqaylah
Wādī al Fāriġh
Wādī al Hamīm
Libyan Plateau

In Aménas
Hūn
Waddān
Marādah
Bi'r Zaltān
Al Jaghbūb
Siwa
Qattāra Depression
-133

Idhān Awbārī
Adīrī
Birāk
Zillah
Awjilah
Jālū
As Sarīr
Calanscio Sand Sea
Great Sand Sea
Sahara

Illizi
Awbārī
Sabhā
Ummal Arānib
Tmassah
Al Harūj al Aswad
LIBYA

Al 'Uwaynāt
Murzūq
Tarāghin
Wāw al Kabīr
Tāzirbū
Zighan
E

Ghāt
Tassili-n-Ajjer
Djanet
Al Qaṭrūn
Idhān Murzūq
Ramlat Rabyānah
Al Jawf
Al Khufrah
Al 'Uwaynāt
Abu Ballās
465
Tropic of Cancer

Plateau du Djado
Toummo
Sarīr Tibesti
Gilf Kebir Plateau

Djado
Bardai
3265
Pic Tousside
3376
Tarso Emissi
Al 'Uwaynāt
1893
Jebel Uweinat
Ténéré du Tafassasset
Séguédine
Zouar
Tibesti

Bilma
3415
Emi Koussi
Libyan Desert

Fachi
Ténéré
Grand Erg de Bilma
S A H A R A
Dépression du Mourdi

Arbre du Ténéré
Erg du Ténéré
Faya
Massif Ennedi

N I G E R
Barkou
Fada
Bodélé
Koro Toro
Oum-Chalouba
Nédély
Kutum
Kebkabiya
El Fasher
Umm Keddada
Wad Banda

Nguigmi
Nokou
C H A D
Abéché
El Geneina
Marra Plateau
S U

Maïné Soroa
Mao
Moussoro
Atī
Oum-Hadjer
3070
Jebel Gimbāla
Nyala
El Odaiy

Nguru
Gashua
Geidam
Lake Chad
Baga
Mouzarak
Ngoura
Lac Fitri
Mongo
Zalingei

Hadejia
Mongonu
Ndjamena
Bokoro
Bitkine
Massif de Guéra
Abou Déia
Am Timan
Rahad el Berdi
Ed Da'ein
El Muglad

Azare
Damaturu
Maiduguri
Mélfi
Dumboa
Mongo

Darazo
Biu
Chari
Bousso
Kendégué
Birao

NIGERIA
Kumo
Gombe
Gombi
Mokolo
Maroua
Bongor
Tiroungoulou
Sumeih

Numan
Guider
Figuil
Flanga
Léré
Pala
Kélo
Laï
Garba
Ouanda-Djalle
Nyamlell

Jalingo
Yola
Tchamba
Garoua
Lac de Lagdo
Koumra
Sarh
CENTRAL

Beli
Ganye
2049
Hosséré Vokre
Moundou
Maro
Ndélé
Ouadda
Aweil

CAMEROON
Ngaoundéré
Tignère
Koum
Bāibokoum
Paoua
Bātangafo
AFRICAN REPUBLIC
Wau

metres	feet
4000	13120
2000	6560
1000	3280
500	1640
200	656
0	0
200	656
1000	3280
2000	6560
4000	13120
6000	19690
8000	26250
metres	feet

102 103

106 107

© Helicon Publishing Ltd

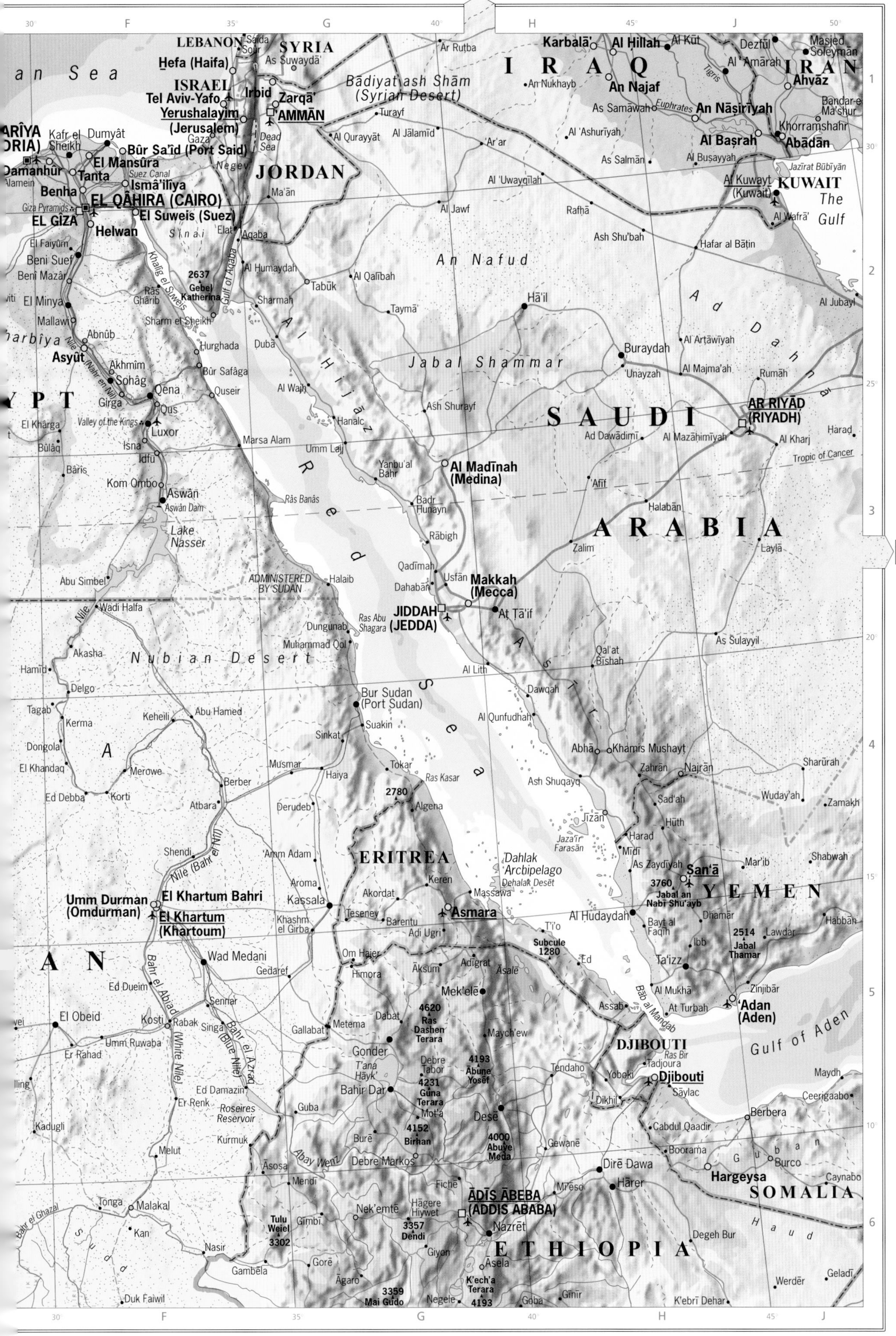

an Sea

LEBANON Saïda Soûr **SYRIA**
Hefa (Haifa) Irbid As Suwaydā'
ISRAEL Zarqā'
Tel Aviv-Yafo **AMMĀN**
Yerushalayim Gaza
(Jerusalem) Negev **JORDAN**
Dead Sea
Ma'ān

Bādiyat ash Shām
(Syrian Desert)

IRAQ
Ar Rutba **Karbalā'** **Al Hillah** Al Kūt Dezfūl
An Nukhayb **An Najaf** Al 'Amārah **IRAN**
Turayf Al Jālamīd As Samāwah An Nāṣirīyah **Ahvāz**
'Ar'ar As Ashurīyah **Al Baṣrah** **Abādān**
Al Qurayyāt As Salmān Al Busayyah Khorramshahr
Al 'Uwayqilah Jazīrat Būbīyān
Al Jawf Rafḥā **Al Kuwayt** **KUWAIT**
Ash Shu'bah (Kuwait) **The Gulf**
Hafar al Bāṭin Al Wafrā'

ÎARÎYA Kafr el Dumyât
DRIA) Sheikh **El Mansûra**
Damanhûr Tanta Ismâ'îliya
Alamein Benha **Bûr Sa'îd (Port Said)**
EL QÂHIRA (CAIRO) Suez Canal
Giza Pyramids **El Suweis (Suez)**
EL GÎZA Helwan Sinai
Elat 'Aqaba
El Faiyûm Al Humaydah
Beni Suef Al Qalībah
Beni Mazâr 2637 Al Jubayl
El Minya Gebel Ras Tabūk
Mallawi Katherina Ghârib Sharmah Taymā'
harbiya Abnûb Sharm et Sheikh Dubā
Asyût Âkhmîm Hurghada Al Wajh
Sohâg Bûr Safâga
Girga Qena Quseir Hanalc
Qus
El Khârga Valley of the Kings Ash Shurayf
Bûlâq Luxor Marsa Alam
Bâris Isna Umm Lajj
Idfu Yanbu'al Bahr
Kom Ombo **Al Madīnah**
Aswân **(Medina)**
Aswân Dam Râs Banâs Badr Hunayn
Lake Râbigh
Nasser

An Nafud

Hā'il
Jabal Shammar
Buraydah Al Artāwīyah
'Unayzah Al Majma'ah Ad Daḥnā
Ad Dawādimī Al Mazāhimīyah **AR RIYĀD**
Afīf **(RIYADH)** Al Kharj
Halabān Harad
Zalim Layla Tropic of Cancer

ARABIA
Ras Abu Qadīmah As Sulayyil
Shagara JIDDAH Usfān **Makkah**
Dahabān **(JEDDA)** **(Mecca)**
At Tā'if
Al Lith Qal'at Bishah
Al Qunfudhah Dawqah

Abu Simbel
ADMINISTERED
BY SUDAN Halaib
Wadi Halfa Dungunab
Nile Muhammad Qol

Nubian Desert
Akasha
Hamid Delgo
Tagab Abu Hamed
Kerma Keheili
Dongola Merowe
El Khandaq Berber
Ed Debba Korti Atbara
Shendi
'Amm Adam Aroma
Kassala
Umm Durman **El Khartum Bahri**
(Omdurman) **El Khartum**
(Khartoum) Khashm
el Girba
Wad Medani
AN Ed Dueim Gedaref
Sennar
El Obeid Er Rahad Rabak Singa
Kosti
Umm Ruwaba Ed Damazin
ei Er Renk Roseires
Kadugli Reservoir
Illing Melut
iii Kurmuk
Bahr el Ghazal
Tonga Malakal
Duk Faiwil

Red Sea

Bur Sudan
(Port Sudan)
Sinkat Suakin
Músmar
Haiya
2780 Tokar
Derudeb Ras Kasar
Algena

ERITREA
Keren
Akordat Massawa
Teseney
Barentu Adi Ugri
Asmara
Om Hajer Adigrat
Himora Aksum Āsalē
Metema
Gallabat
Gonder Dabat
T'ana Debre
Hāyk' Tabor Maych'ew
Bahir Dar 4231
Guna 4193
Terara Abune
Guba Mot'a Yosēf
Burē 4152
Āsosa Birhan 4000
Debre Markos Abuye
Mendi Meda
Debre Markos

Dahlak
Archipelago
Dahalak Desēt

Subcule
1280
Ed

Bāb al Mandab
Assab

**Āʿīzo
Al Hudaydah**
Bayt al
Faqīh Ibb
Ta'izz Jabal
2514 Thamar
Al Mukhā Lawdar
At Turbah **'Adan**
Zinjibār **(Aden)**
Ras Bir **Gulf of Aden**
Tadjoura
DJIBOUTI
Yoboki **Djibouti** Maydh
Dikhil Sāylac Berbera
Cabdul Qaadir Ceerigaabo
Gewanē Boorama

Ha'il

Halabān
Ad Dawādimī
Zahrān Najrān
Abhā **Khamis Mushayt** Sharūrah
Sad'ah Wuday'ah Zamakh
Jīzān Hūth
Jazā'ir Harad Midī As Zaydīyah **San'ā**
Farasān 3760
Jabal an
Nabi Shu'ayb
Mar'ib **YEMEN** Shabwah
Dhamār Habbān

SAUDI

SOMALIA
Burco
Caynabo
Hargeysa

Gonder
Gīmbī Nek'emtē Hāgere
Tulu Hiywet **ĀDĪS ĀBEBA**
Weiel Dendi **(ADDIS ABABA)**
3302 3357 Nazrēt
Dire Dawa Hārer M'reso
Degeh Bur
Mendi Gore Fiche Giyon Gīmir
Gambēla Āgaro Asela
Goba
3359 K'ech'a Werdēr
Mai Gudo Terara Geladī
Negēlē 4193 Goba K'ebrī Dehar

ETHIOPIA

Haud

Settlements

■ over 3 million

□ 1 – 3 million

○ 250 000 – 1 million

● 100 000 – 250 000

◎ 25 000 – 100 000

• under 25 000

___ country capital
underline

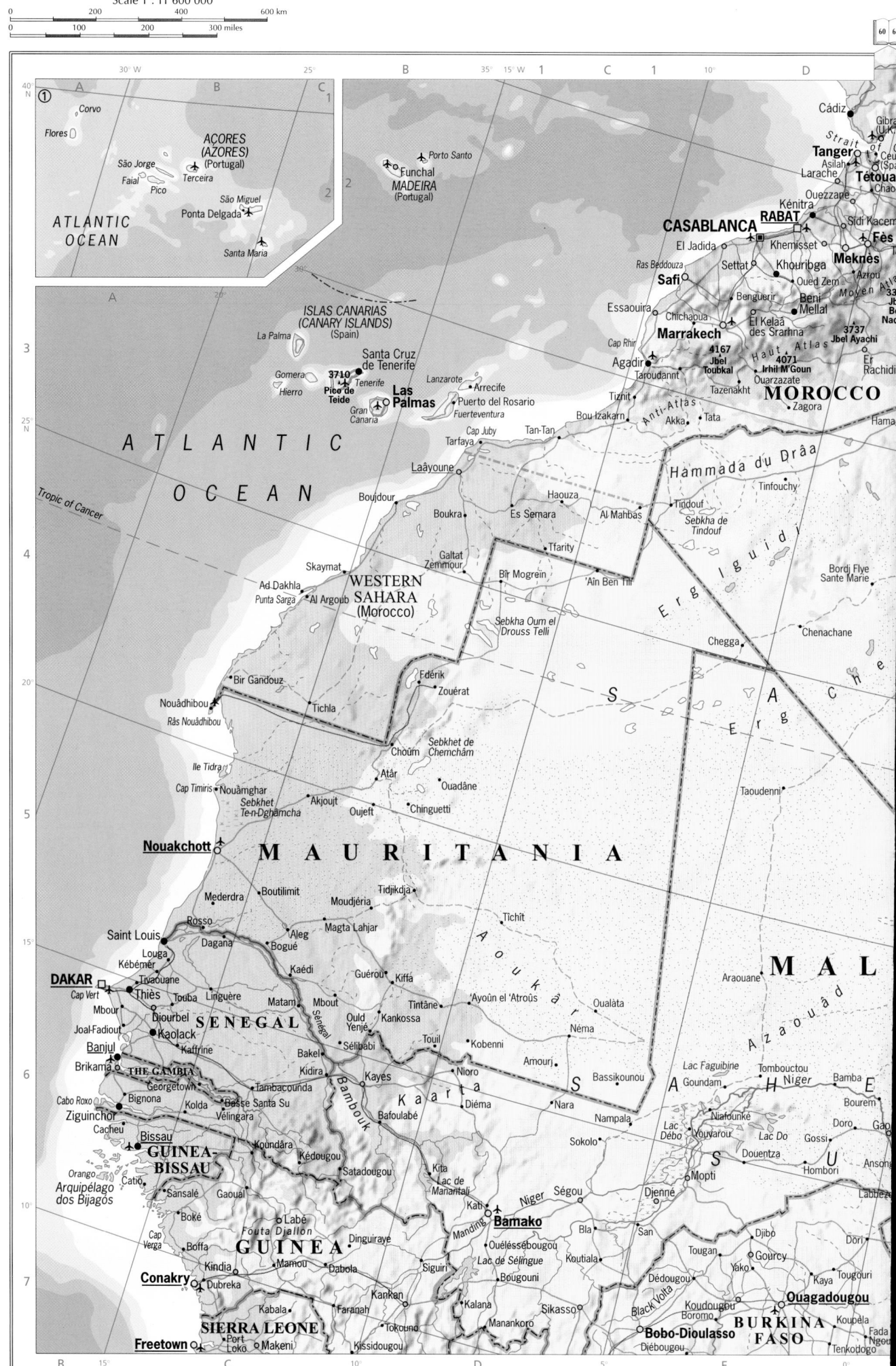

Scale 1 : 11 600 000

| 0 | 200 | 400 | 600 km |
| 0 | 100 | 200 | 300 miles |

① ACÔRES (AZORES) (Portugal)

Corvo
Flores
São Jorge
Faial   Pico
Terceira
São Miguel
Ponta Delgada
Santa Maria

ATLANTIC
OCEAN

MADEIRA (Portugal)
Porto Santo
Funchal

Cádiz
Gibraltar (U.K.)
Tanger
Larache
Asilah
Tétouan
Chaou
Kénitra
CASABLANCA   RABAT
El Jadida   Khemisset   Sidi Kacem
Safi   Settat   Khouribga   Meknès
Ras Beddouza   Benguerir   Oued Zem
Essaouira   Chichaoua   El Kelaâ   Beni Mellal
Cap Rhir   Marrakech   des Srarhna   Jbel Ayachi
Agadir   4167   Jbel   3737
Taroudannt   Jbel   Irhil M'Goun   4071
Tiznit   Toubkal   Ouarzazate   Er Rachidia
Bou Izakarn   Tazenakht   Zagora
Tan-Tan   Akka   Tata   MOROCCO
Cap Juby   Hamag
Tarfaya   Hammada du Drâa

ISLAS CANARIAS (CANARY ISLANDS) (Spain)
La Palma
Gomera   3710   Tenerife   Lanzarote
Hierro   Pico de Teide   Arrecife
Santa Cruz de Tenerife   Puerto del Rosario
Gran Canaria   Fuerteventura
Las Palmas

ATLANTIC

OCEAN

Tropic of Cancer

Laâyoune   Haouza   Tinfouchy
Boujdour   Al Mahbas   Tindouf
Boukra   Es Semara   Sebkha de Tindouf
Galtat Zemmour   Tfarity
Skaymat   Bîr Mogrein   'Aïn Ben Tili
Ad Dakhla   WESTERN   Bordj Flye Sante Marie
Punta Sarga   SAHARA
Al Argoub   (Morocco)   Sebkha Oum el Drouss Telli
Chegga   Chenachane
Fdérik
Bir Gandouz   Zouérat
Nouâdhibou   Tichla
Râs Nouâdhibou   Choûm   Sebkhet de Chemchâm
Ile Tidra   Atâr
Cap Timiris   Ouadâne   Taoudenni
Nouâmghar   Akjoujt
Sebkhet   Oujeft   Chinguetti
Te-n-Dghâmcha
Nouakchott   M A U R I T A N I A
Mederdra   Boutilimit   Tidjikdja
Rosso   Moudjéria
Saint Louis   Aleg   Magta Lahjar   Tîchît
Louga   Bogué
Dagana   Araouane   M A L
Kébémêr   Kaédi   Guérou   Kiffa
DAKAR   Tivaouane   Matam   'Ayoûn el 'Atroûs
Cap Vert   Thiès   Touba   Linguère   Mbout   Tintâne   Oualàta
Mbour   Diourbel   Ould   Kankossa   Néma
Joal-Fadiout   SENEGAL   Yenjé   Touil   Kobenni   Tombouctou
Kaolack   Kaffrine   Sélibabi   Amourj   Bassikounou   Goundam   Niger   Bamba
Banjul   Bakel   Kidira   Kayes   Nioro   Bourem
Brikama   THE GAMBIA   Diéma   Nara   Niafounké   Doro   Gao
Georgetown   Tambacounda   Kaarta   Nampala   Lac Faguibine   Gossi
Cabo Roxo   Bignona   Basse Santa Su   Bafoulabé   Sokolo   Lac Débo   Youvarou   Lac Do   Hombori   Anson
Ziguinchor   Kolda   Vélingara   Koundâra   Kédougou   Kita   Ségou   Mopti   Labbé
Cacheu   Lac de   Djenné
Bissau   Satadougou   Manantali   Kati   San
Orango   GUINEA-   BISSAU   Niger   Bamako   Bla   Djibo   Dori
Arquipélago dos Bijagós   Sansalé   Gaoual   Bougouni   Ouéléssébougou   Tougan   Gourcy
Boké   Labé   Koutiala   Yako   Tougouri
Cap Verga   Fouta Djallon   Dinguiraye   Manding   Lac de Sélingue   Dédougou   Kaya   Dôri
Boffa   GUINEA   Siguiri   Bougouni   Koudougou   Ouagadougou
Conakry   Kindia   Mamou   Dabola   Sikasso   Boromo   BURKINA
Dubreka   Kankan   Black Volta   Bobo-Dioulasso   FASO   Fada
SIERRA LEONE   Kabala   Faranah   Kalana   Manankoro   Diébougou   Tenkodogo
Freetown   Port Loko   Makeni   Tokounou   Koubéla
Kabala   Kissidougou

© Helicon Publishing Ltd

metres	feet
4000	13120
2000	6560
1000	3280
500	1640
200	656
0	0
200	656
1000	3280
2000	6560
4000	13120
6000	19690
8000	26250
metres	feet

MEDITERRANEAN SEA

SPAIN
Málaga
Almería

ITALY
Cosenza
Catanzaro
Palermo
Messina
Réggio di Calabria
Mte. Etna 3323
Catánia
Siracusa
SICILIA (SICILY)

SARDEGNA (SARDINIA) (Italy)
Cagliari

Isole Lipari

Pantelleria (Italy)
Lampedusa (Italy)
MALTA

Hoceima
Almería
Melilla (Spain)
Nador
Oran Mostaganem
Ghazaouet
Tiemcen
Oujda
Jerada
Taourirt
Sidi Bel Abbès
Mascara
Relizane
Saïda
Frenda
Tiaret
Djelfa

Ténès Khemis Miliana
ALGER (ALGIERS) Tizi Ouzou
Blida Bejaïa
Bouira Skikda
Ech Chélif
Bordj Bou Arréridj
Sétif
M'Sila
Bou Saâda
Chott el Hodna
Batna
Aïn Oussera

Bizerte
Annaba
Béja
Tunis Cap Bon
Nabeul
Hammam Lif
Golfe de Hammamet
Sousse
Kairouan
Ksour Essaf
Sfax
Îles Kerkenah
Golfe de Gabès
Gabès
Houmt Souk
Île de Jerba

Cap de Fer
Mila
Guelma
Jendouba
Constantine
Aïn Beïda
Kasserine
Tébessa
Khenchela

TUNISIA
Gafsa
Tozeur
Nefta
Chott el Jerid
Matmata
Medenine
Tataouine
Rass Ajdir

Messaad
Laghouat
Biskra
Négrine
Chott Melrhir
Djamâa
El Oued
Touggourt
Ghardaïa
Ouargla
Hassi Messaoud

Tarābulus (Tripoli)
Az Zāwiyah
Al Khums Zlītan
Tarhūnah
Gharyān
Mişrātah
Banī Walīd
Abū Qarin
Surt
As Sidrah
Khalīj Surt

Remada
Nālūt
Dehiba
Borj Jenein
Jādū
Mizdah
Abū Nujaym
Al Qaryāt
Ash Shuwayrif

Brézina
Aïn Sefra
Bénoud
Figuig
Bouârfa
Tendrara
Igli
Adrar

A L G E R I A

Grand Erg Occidental
Sebkha de Timimoun
Timimoun El Homr
El Goléa
Rebaa
Bordj Messaouda
Ghadāmis
Daraj
Al Hammādah al Hamrā

Sbaa
Adrar
Plateau du Tademait
Reggane
In Salah
Sebkha Mekerrhane
Sebkha Azzel Matti

Hassi Bel Guebbour
Ohanet
Bordj Omar Driss
In Aménas
In Amguid

L I B Y A
Birāk
Adīrī
Awbārī
Sabhā
Ummal Arānib
Murzūq
Tarāghin
Waw al Kabīr
Al Qaryāt
Hūn
Waddān
Zillah
Tmassah
Al Harūj al Aswad

Idhān Awbārī

Post Weygand
Meniet
In Ekker
Zaouatallaz
Djanet
Amguid
Illizi
Arak
Tassili-n'-Ajjer
Al 'Uwaynāt
Ghāt
Tin Alkoum

S A H A R A

Idhān Murzūq

Bordj Mokhtar
2918 Mont Tahat
2306 Mont Serkout
Tamanrasset
Hoggar

Sarīr
Tropic of Cancer
Tibesti

Tessalit
Tassili du Hoggar
Plateau du Djado
Toummo
Djado
Ténéré du Tafassasset

Adrar des Aguelhok
Ifôghas
In-Guezzam
Assamakka
Séguédine
Bardaï
3265 Pic Toussidé
3376 Tarso Emissi
Zouar
Tibesti

Kidal
Talak
1988 Adrar Tamgak
3415 Emi Koussi

M A L I
Arlit
Ténéré
Bilma

Ménaka
Andéramboukane
Vallée de Azaouagh
Massif de l'Aïr
2022 Monts Bagzane
Arbre du Ténéré
Fachi
Grand Erg de Bilma
Borkou
Faya

Tchin Tabaradene
Agadez
Falaise de Tiguidit
Erg du Ténéré
Bodélé

N I G E R
Tahoua
Aderbissinat

Bani-Bangou
Tillabéri
Bagaroua
Labé
Tanout
Gangara

Baléyara
Niamey
Dogondoutchi
Birnin Konni
Madaoua
Dakoro
Nguigmi
Nokou
Mao

Dosso
Sokoto
Maradi
Zinder
Lake Chad

Argungu
Sokoto
Katsina

NIGERIA

C H A D
Nédély
Bahr el Ghazal
Manga

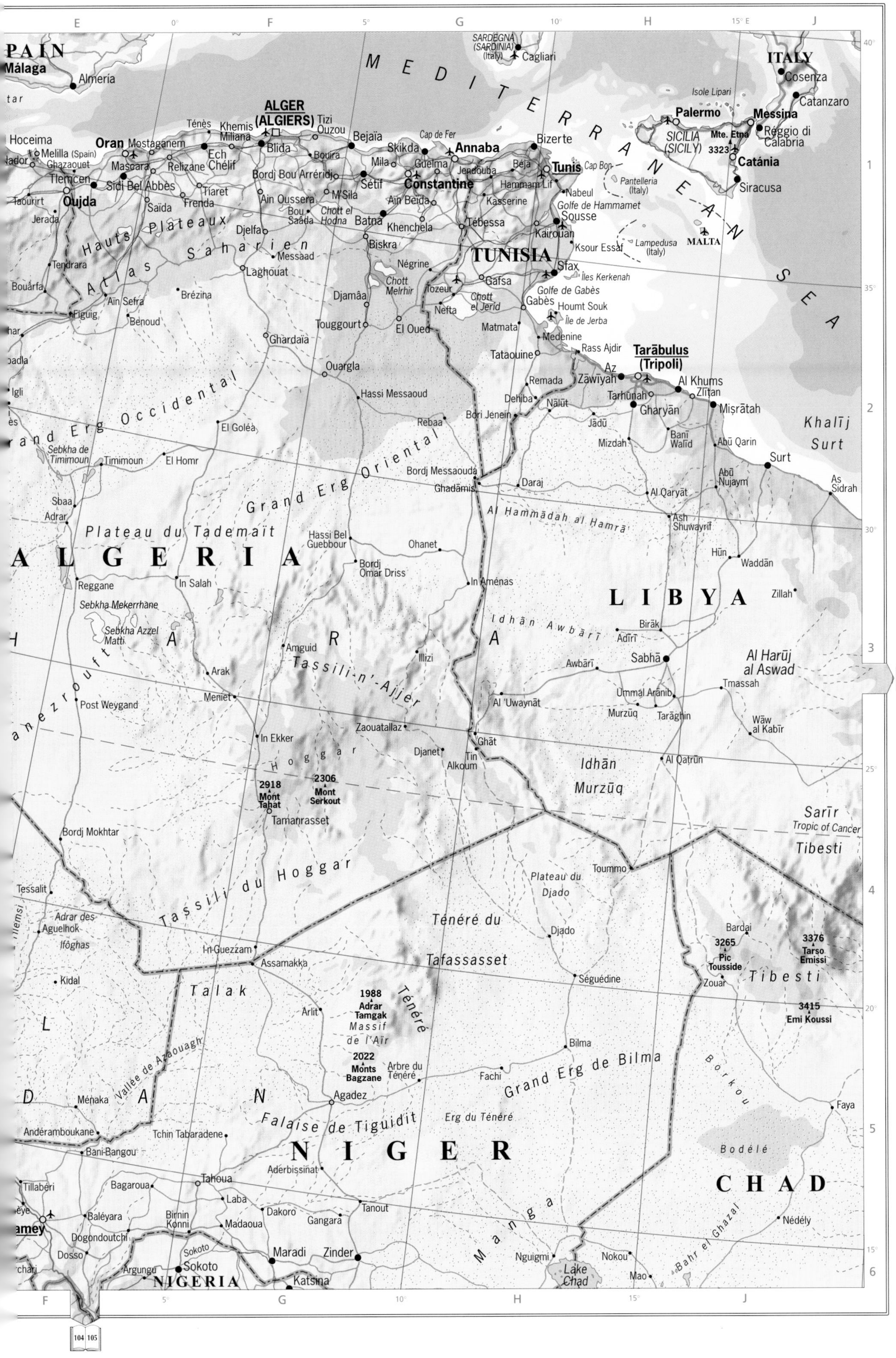

100 101
104 105

Settlements

■	over 3 million
☐	1 – 3 million
○	250 000 – 1 million
●	100 000 – 250 000
◦	25 000 – 100 000
•	under 25 000
—	country capital underline
—	state or province capital underline

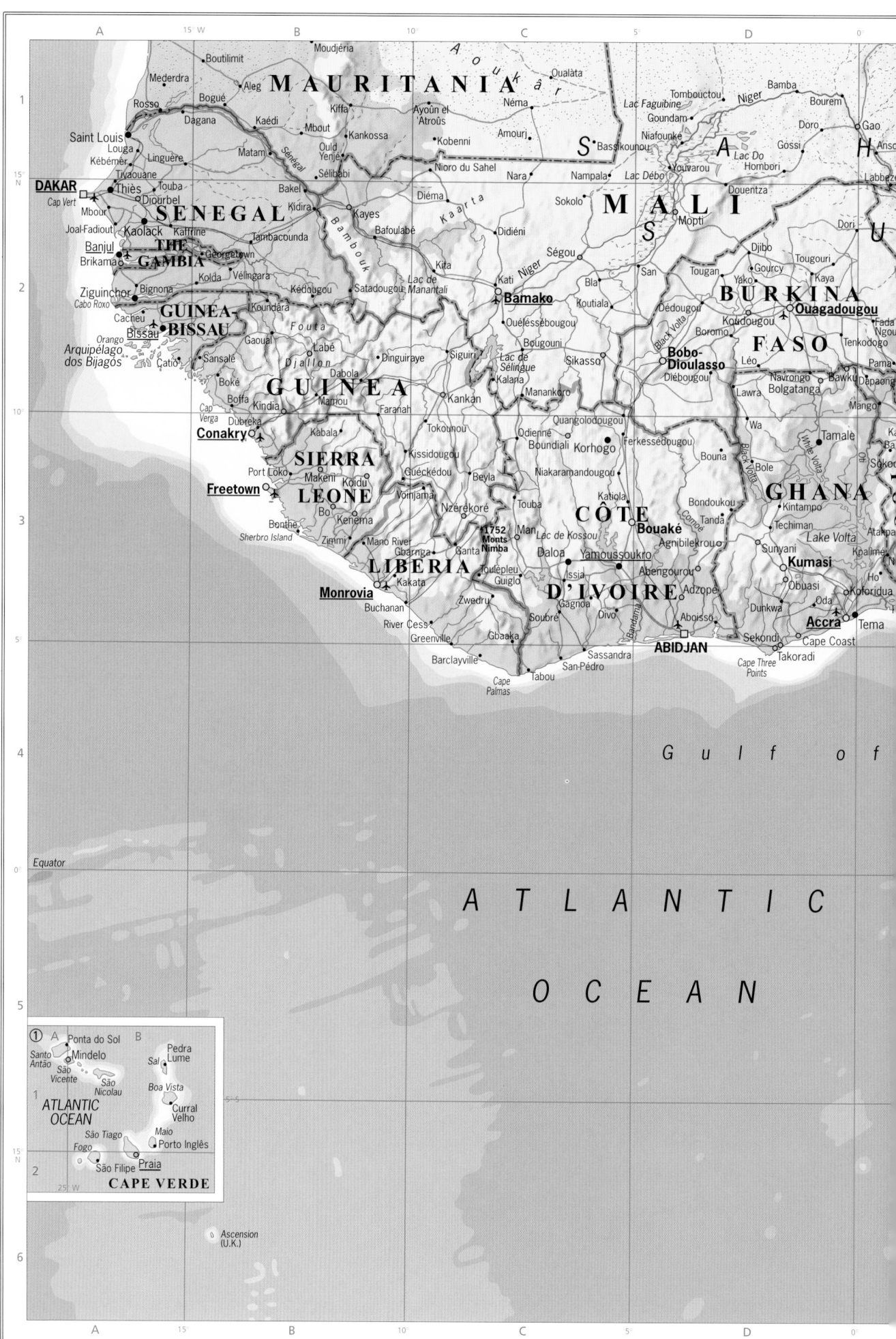

Scale 1 : 11 600 000

© Helicon Publishing Ltd

metres / feet

4000 / 13120
2000 / 6560
1000 / 3280
500 / 1640
200 / 656
0 / 0

200 / 656
1000 / 3280
2000 / 6560
4000 / 13120
6000 / 19690
8000 / 26250
metres / feet

CAPE VERDE

ATLANTIC OCEAN

Gulf of

ATLANTIC

OCEAN

Equator

WEST AFRICA

Benin • Burkina Faso • Cameroon • Cape Verde • Congo • Côte d'Ivoire • Equatorial Guinea • Gabon • The Gambia
Ghana • Guinea • Guinea-Bissau • Liberia • Nigeria • São Tomé & Príncipe • Senegal • Sierra Leone • Togo

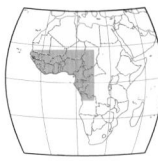

102 103

106 107

Settlements

■	*over 3 million*
□	*1 – 3 million*
◉	*250 000 – 1 million*
●	*100 000 – 250 000*
○	*25 000 – 100 000*
•	*under 25 000*
___	*country capital underline*
___	*state or province capital underline*

NIGER

Ménaka · dérambokane · Bani-Bangou · Tchin Tabaradene · AGades · *2022 Monts Bagzane* · *Arbre du Ténéré* · Faya

Vallée de Azaouagh · *Falaise de Tiguidit* · *Erg du Ténéré* · *Bodélé*

Ouallam · Tillabéri · Gothèye · Tahoua · Bagaroua · Laba · Dakoro · Gangará · Tanout · Nokou · Oum-Chalouba · Nédély

Niamey · Dogondoutchi · Birnin Konni · Madaoua · Maradi · Zinder · Nguigmi · Mao · *Lake Chad* · Moussoro · Ati · Oum-Hadjer

Dosso · Sokoto · Daura · Maïné Soroa · Diffa · Baga · Damasak · Ngoura · *Lac Fitri* · Mongo · Bitkine · Abéché

CHAD

Kandi · Argungu · Kaura Namoda · Katsina · Nguru · Geidam · Gashua · Mongonu · **Ndjamena** · Bokoro · *Massif du Guéra* · Abou Deïa · Am Timan

Gaya · Malanville · Birnin Kebbi · Gummi · Zuru · Funtua · Paki · **Kano** · Hadeja · Potiskum · Damaturu · Dikwa · Bousso · Mélfi · Kendégué

titingou · Jega · Birnin-Gwari · Azare · Biu · Mokolo · Chari · Maroua · Bongor · Dobá · Garba · Ndélé

BENIN · Kontagora · Tegina · Bauchi · Gombe · Deba Habe · Gombi · Guider · Figuil · Léré · Fianga · Laï · Kélo · Koumra · Sarh · Maro

Djougou · New Bussa · Minna · Jos · Pankshin · Numan · Benue · Yola · **Garoua** · Pala · *Lac de Lagdo* · **Moundou** · Dobá · Goré · Batangafo

Parakou · Kaiama · Bida · Kafanchan · Shendam · Jalingo · Ganye · Tchamba · Baïbokoum · Goré · Kaga Bandoro

NIGERIA · Kishi · Jebba · Lafiagi · Abuja · Akwanga · Lafia · Beli · Wukari · *2049 Hosséré Vokre* · Ngaoundéré · Koum · Bossangoa · **CENTRAL**

Savé · Shaki · **Ogbomosho** · **Ilorin** · Lokoja · Nassarawa · Makurdi · Tignère · Paoua · Bambari

bomey · Savalou · Iseyin · **Ede** · **Oshogbo** · **Ilesha** · Okene · Otukpo · Katsina Ala · Takum · Gembu · Banyo · *Lac de Mbakaou* · Garoua Boulaï · Bossembélé · **AFRICAN REPUBLIC**

Kétou · **IBADAN** · Ife · Akure · Idah · Ankpa · Tibati · Yoko · Carnot · Bozoum · Damara

Abeokuta · Shagamu · Ikire · Ondo · Owo · Auchi · **Enugu** · Nkambe · Banyo · Bouar · Baoro · Sibut

Mushin · Ikorodu · **Ijebu Ode** · Okitipupa · Awka · Abakaliki · Ikom · **Bamenda** · Foumban · **Bangui** · Bambari

Cotonou · Porto · **LAGOS** · Benin City · **Onitsha** · Afikpo · Ugep · Dschang · Bafoussam · Garoua Boulaï · Berbérati · Mbaïki · Zongo · Bosobolo · Mobaye

né · Novo · Sápele · Owerri · **Aba** · Calabar · Bangangté · Yoko · Bossembélé · Gamboula · Nola · Libenge · Mobayi-Mbongo

ght of Benin · Warri · Degema · Kumba · Mbanga · Bafia · *Sanaga* · Bertoua · Batouri · Damara · Dongo · Businga

Mouths of the Niger · **Port Harcourt** · *4100 Mont Cameroon* · Yabassi · **Yaoundé** · Abong Mbang · Gamboula · Nola · Impfondo · Makanza · Gemena

Malabo · Edéa · **Douala** · Eséka · Akonolinga · Yokadouma · Bomossa · Dongou · Imese · Kungu · Akula

Bight of Biafra · *Isla de Bioco* · Kribi · Mbalmayo · Dja · Bomassa · Epéna · Wenga · Bolomba

Guinea · **EQUATORIAL GUINEA** · Ebolowa · Sangmélima · Sembé · Ouésso · Congo · Bongandanga · Basankusu

Principe · Bata · Niefang · Oyem · *Ntem* · Mékambo · *Sangha* · Makoua · Mbandaka · Boende

SÃO TOMÉ AND PRÍNCIPE · *Cabo San Juan* · Cocobeach · Mitzic · Makokou · *Equator* · Busira · Bokatola · Lomela

São Tomé · *São Tomé* · **Libreville** · Kango · Ndjolé · Booué · Ewo · Owando · Obouya · *Lac Tumba* · Monkoto

Annobón (Pagalu) (Eq. Guinea) · *Cap Lopez* · Lambaréné · **CONGO** · Okoyo · Bolobo · Inongo

Port-Gentil · **GABON** · Lastoursville · Koulamoutou · Gamboma · Kutu · *Lac Mai-Ndombe*

Omboué · Fougamou · Moanda · Franceville · Djambala · Ngo · Kasai · Bandundu · Ilebo

Mouila · *Massif du Chaillu* · **DEMOCRATIC REPUBLIC OF CONGO** · Kwilu · Kikwit · Idiofa

Tchibanga · Moutamba · *Plateaux Batéké* · *Congo* · Bandundu · Kenge · Masi-Manimba

Mayumba · Loubomo · Kimongo · **Brazzaville** · Luozi · Mayamba · Gungu · Tshikapa

Pointe-Noire · Kimpese · **KINSHASA** · Mabanza-Ngungu · Inkisi-Kisantu · Popokabaka · Lukuni · Kahemba

CABINDA (Angola) · Boma · Matadi · Songololo · Maquela do Zombo · Chitato

Cabinda · *Ponta do Padrão* · M'banza Congo · Quimbele · Negage · Luremo · Cuilo

N'zeto · Negage · Cuango · Capenda Camulemba · Saurimo

Baía do Bengo · Caxito · **ANGOLA** · Lucala · Malanje

LUANDA

Scale 1 : 11 600 000

© Helicon Publishing Ltd

CENTRAL AFRICA

Angola • Burundi • Central African Republic • Democratic Republic of Congo
Djibouti • Ethiopia • Kenya • Rwanda • Somalia • Tanzania • Uganda

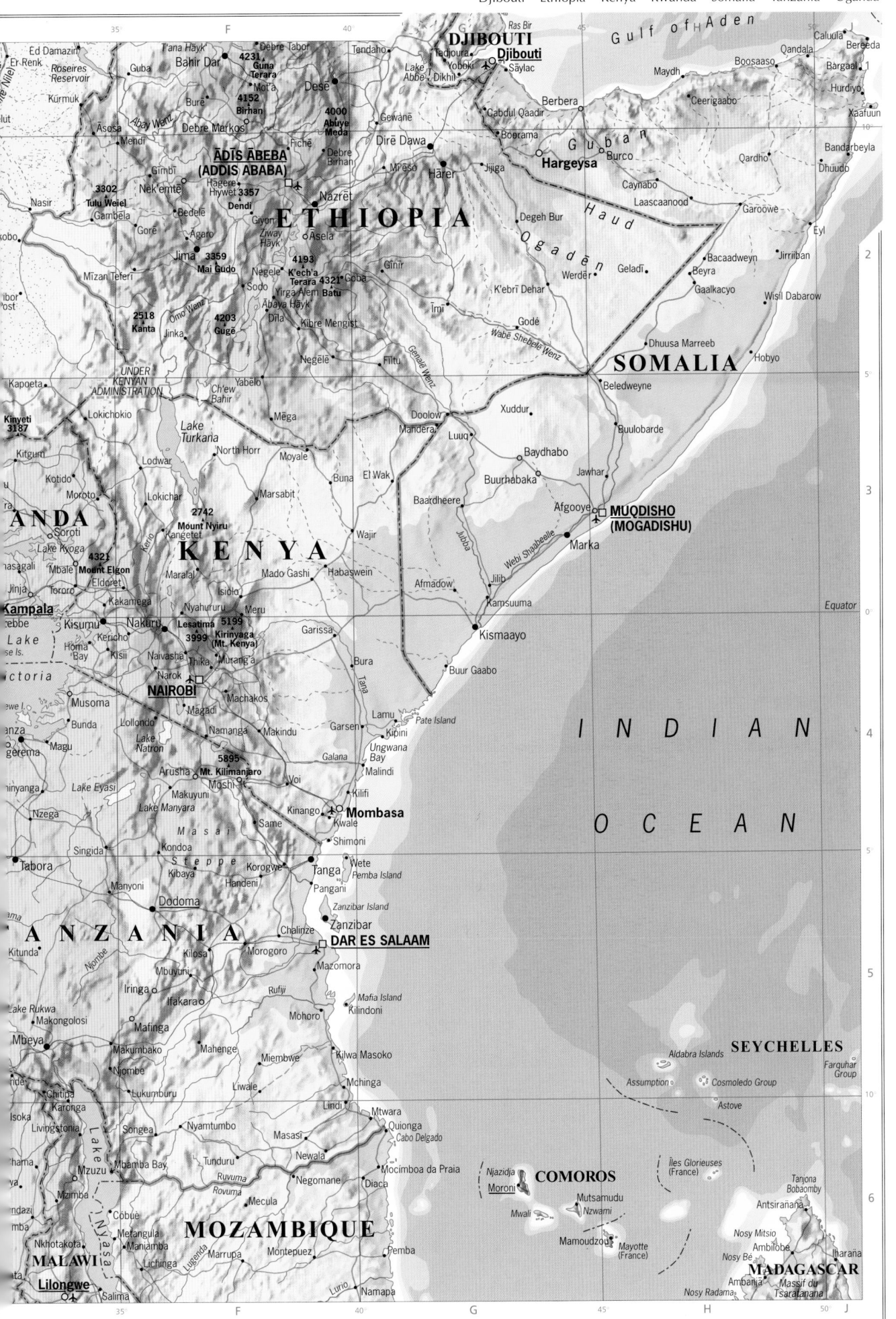

Settlements

■	over 3 million
□	1 – 3 million
○	250 000 – 1 million
●	100 000 – 250 000
○	25 000 – 100 000
•	under 25 000
—	country capital underline

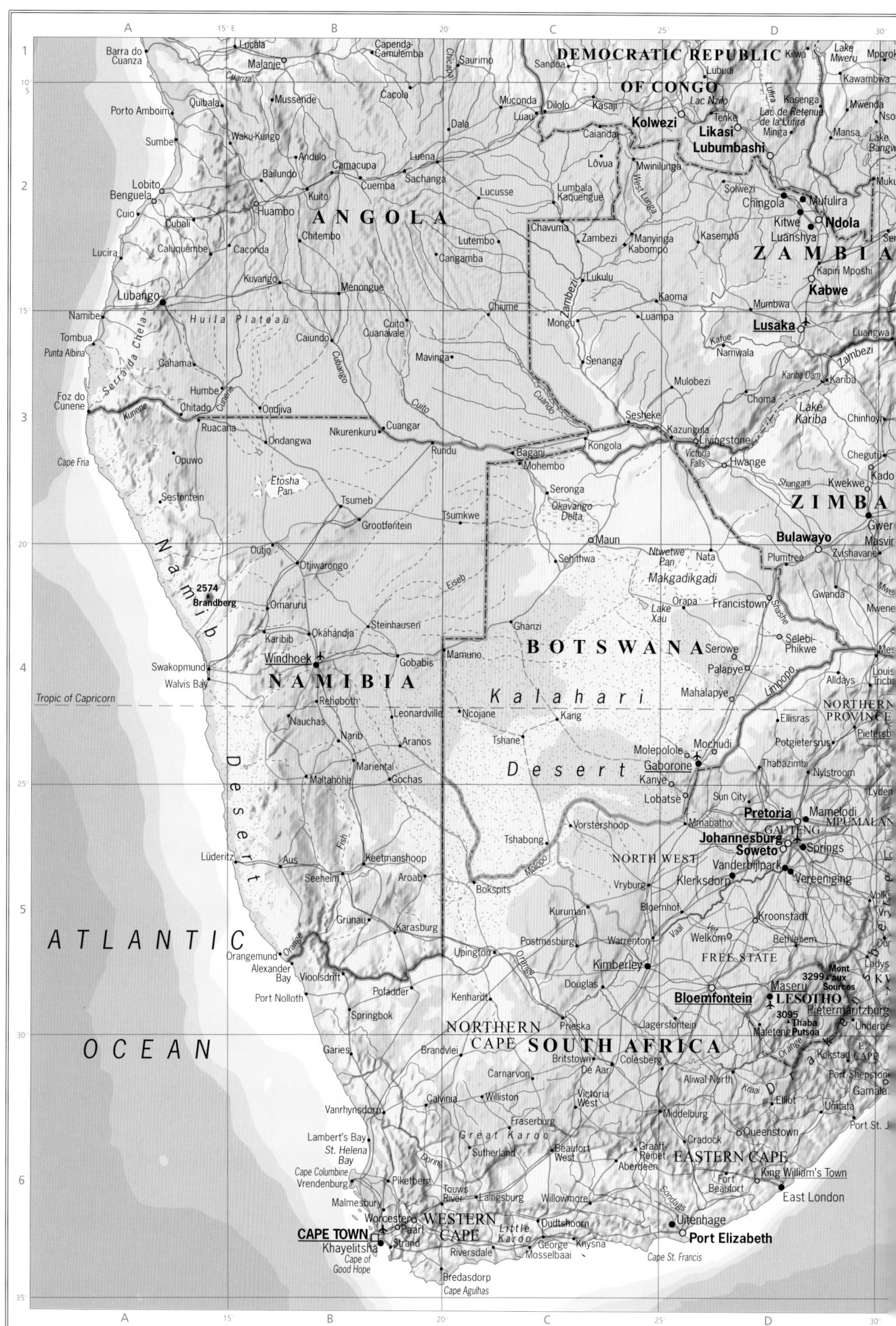

Scale 1 : 11 600 000

metres	feet
4000	13120
2000	6560
1000	3280
500	1640
200	656
	0
200	656
1000	3280
2000	6560
4000	13120
6000	19690
8000	26250
metres	feet

© Helicon Publishing Ltd

SOUTHERN AFRICA

Botswana • Comoros • Lesotho • Madagascar • Malawi • Mauritius
Mozambique • Namibia • Seychelles • South Africa • Swaziland • Zambia • Zimbabwe

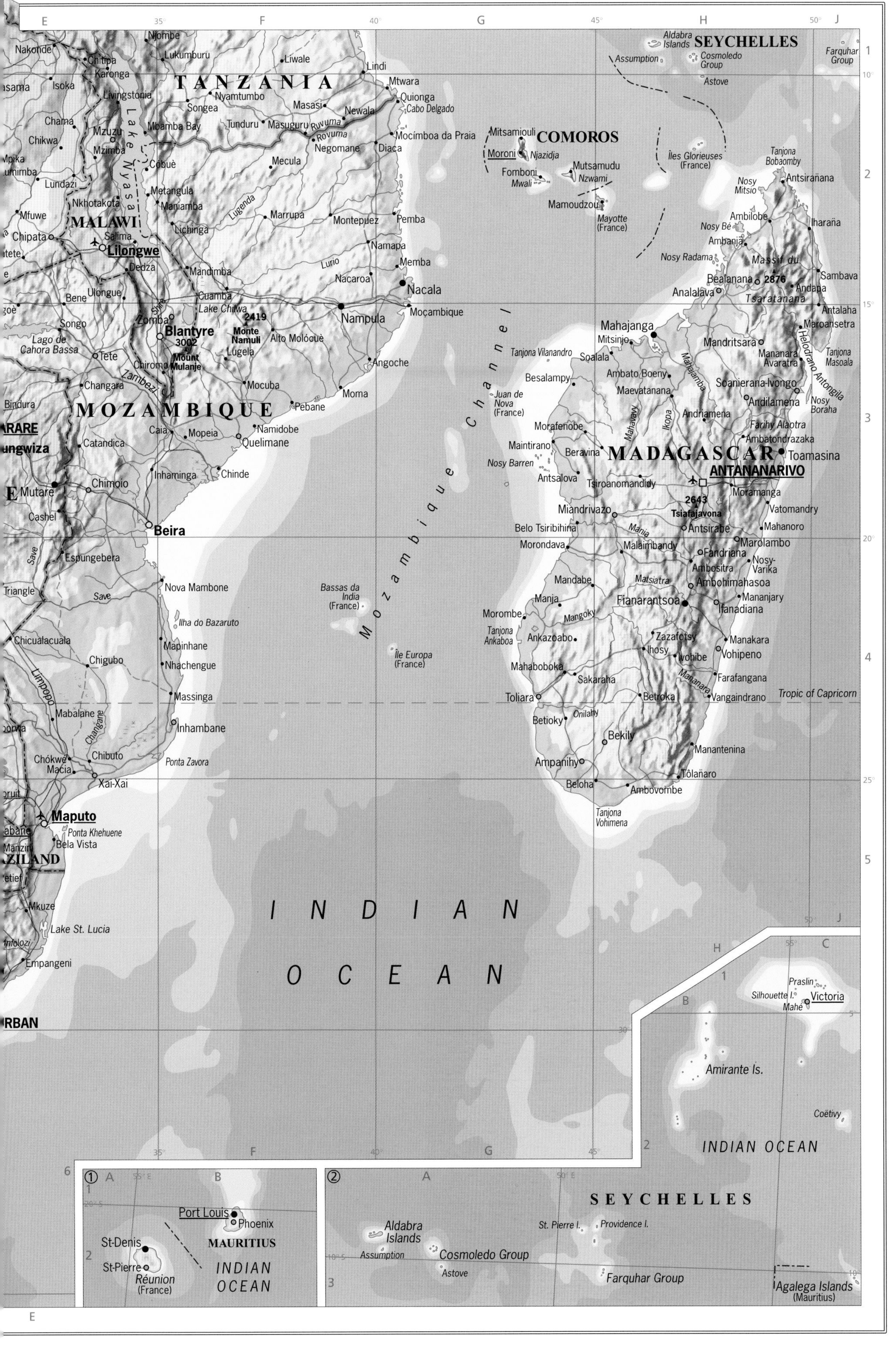

SEYCHELLES

Aldabra Islands
Assumption
Cosmoledo Group
Astove
Farquhar Group

TANZANIA

Nakonde
Chitipa
Karonga
Njombe
Lukumburu
Liwale
Lindi
Isoka
Livingstonia
Nyamtumbo
Mtwara
Chama
Mbamba Bay
Songea
Masasi
Newala
Quionga
Cabo Delgado
Chikwa
Mzuzu
Tunduru
Masuguru
Mocímboa da Praia
Mitsamiouli
COMOROS
Mpika
Mzimba
Cobuè
Negomane
Diaca
Moroni
Njazidja
Îles Glorieuses (France)
Tanjona Bobaompy
Antsirañana
Lundazi
Metangula
Rovuma
Mecula
Mutsamudu
Nzwani
Nosy Mitsio
Mfuwe
MALAWI
Maniamba
Marrupa
Montepuez
Pemba
Fomboni
Mwali
Mamoudzou
Mayotte (France)
Ambilobe
Nosy Bé
Iharaña
Chipata
Nkhotakota
Lichinga
Namapa
Ambanja
tete
Salima
Lilongwe
Mandimba
Nacaroa
Memba
Mayotte (France)
Nosy Radama
Massif du
Bealanana
2876
Sambava
Andapa
goe
Dedza
Lake Chilwa
Cuamba
Nampula
Moçambique
Analalava
Tsaratanana
Antalaha
Songo
Zomba
2419
Nacala
Mahajanga
Maroantsetra
Bene
Ulongue
Monte Namuli 3002
Alto Molócuè
Mitsinjo
Mandritsara
Mananara Avaratra
Tanjona Masoala
Lago de Cahora Bassa
Blantyre
Lugela
Tanjona Vilanandro
Soalala
Ambato Boeny
Maevatanana
Scanierana-Ivongo
Tete
Chiromo Mulanje
Mount Mulanje
Mocuba
Angoche
Besalampy
Andilamena
Nosy Boraha
Changara
Zambezi
Moma
Juan de Nova (France)
Morafenobe
Andriamena
Farihy Alaotra
MOZAMBIQUE
Caia
Mopeia
Namidobe
Quelimane
Maintirano
Beravina
Ambatondrazaka
Catandica
Pebane
MADAGASCAR
Toamasina
ungwiza
Inhaminga
Chinde
Nosy Barren
Antsalova
Tsiroanomandidy
ANTANANARIVO
Chimoio
Miandrivazo
Moramanga
Mutare
Belo Tsiribihina
2643
Tsiafajavona
Vatomandry
Cashel
Beira
Morondava
Antsirabe
Mahanoro
Espungebera
Malaimbandy
Marolambo
Nova Mambone
Mandabe
Matsiatra
Fandriana
Nosy-Varika
Triangle
Save
Bassas da India (France)
Ambositra
Ambohimahasoa
Chicualacuala
Ilha do Bazaruto
Manja
Fianarantsoa
Mananjary
Mapinhane
Île Europa (France)
Morombe
Mangoky
Ifanadiana
Chigubo
Nhachengue
Tanjona Ankaboa
Ankazoabo
Zazafotsy
Manakara
Massinga
Mahaboboka
Ihosy
Vohibe
Vohipeno
Mabalane
Inhambane
Sakaraha
Betroka
Farafangana
Chibuto
Ponta Zavora
Toliara
Onilahy
Vangaindrano
Chókwè Macia
Betioky
Bekily
Manantenina
Xai-Xai
Ampanihy
Maputo
Ponta Khehuene
Beloha
Ambovombe
Tôlañaro
Bela Vista
Tanjona Vohimena

Tropic of Capricorn

Mozambique Channel

INDIAN OCEAN

Mkuze
Lake St. Lucia
Empangeni

Inset ①

Port Louis
Phoenix
MAURITIUS
St-Denis
St-Pierre
Réunion (France)
INDIAN OCEAN

Inset ②

Aldabra Islands
Assumption
St. Pierre I.
Providence I.
Cosmoledo Group
Astove
Farquhar Group
SEYCHELLES

Praslin
Silhouette I.
Victoria
Mahé
Amirante Is.
Coëtivy
INDIAN OCEAN
Agalega Islands (Mauritius)

Settlements

- □ 1 – 3 million
- ◎ 250 000 – 1 million
- ● 100 000 – 250 000
- ◉ 25 000 – 100 000
- • under 25 000
- ___ country capital underline
- ___ state or province capital underline

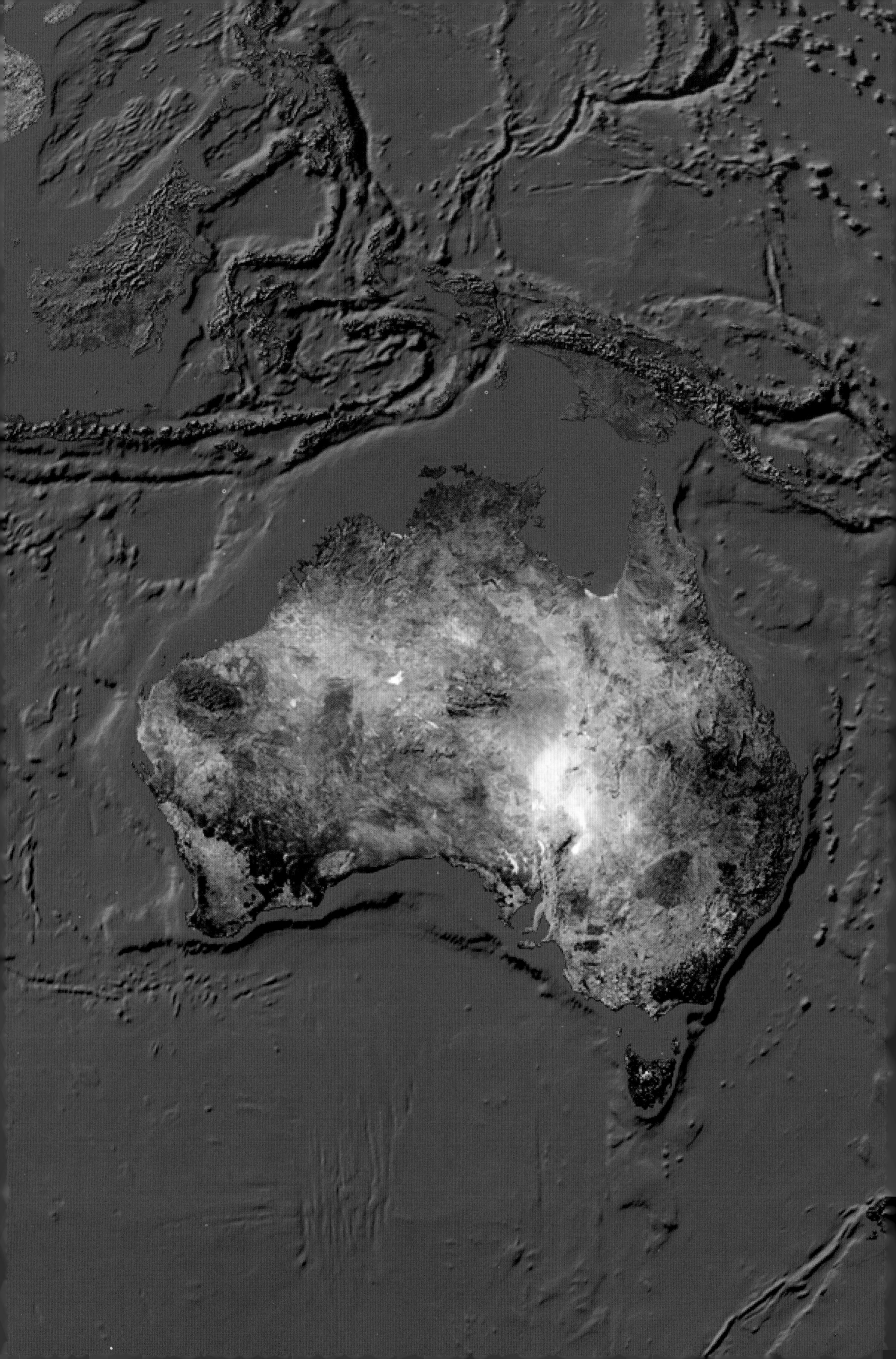

OCEANIA

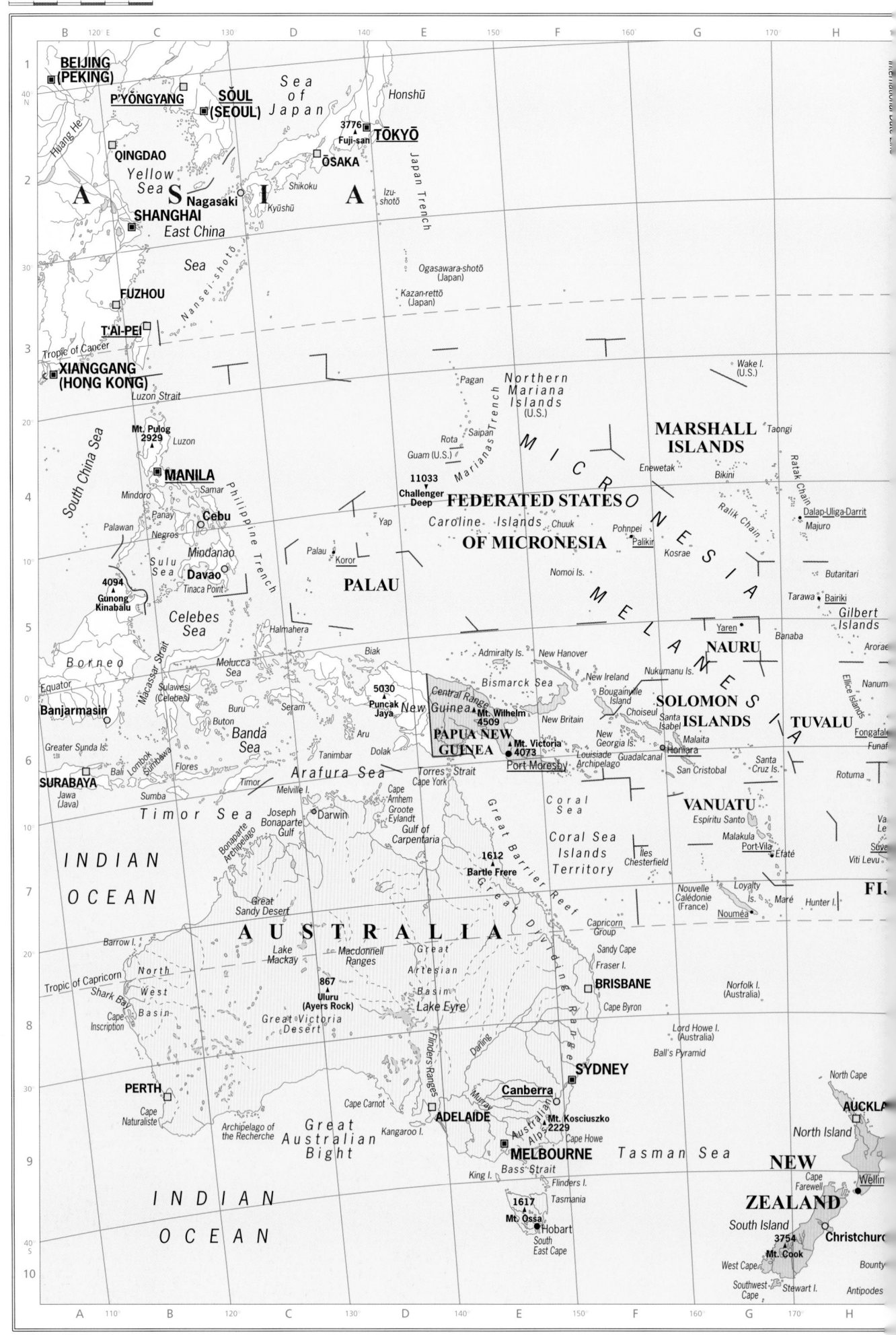

Scale 1 : 40 500 000

500   1000   1500 km

250   500   750 miles

B 120° E **C** 130° **D** 140° **E** 150° **F** 160° **G** 170° **H**

BEIJING (PEKING)

P'YŎNGYANG

Sea of Japan

Honshū

SŎUL (SEOUL)

3776 ▲ Fuji-san **TŌKYŌ**

QINGDAO

ŌSAKA

Yellow Sea

Shikoku

Izu-shotō

A S **I** A

SHANGHAI Nagasaki Kyūshū

East China

Japan Trench

Sea

Ogasawara-shotō (Japan)

FUZHOU

Kazan-rettō (Japan)

T'AI-PEI

Tropic of Cancer

Pagan

Northern Mariana Islands (U.S.)

Wake I. (U.S.)

XIANGGANG (HONG KONG)

Luzon Strait

Rota Saipan

Mt. Pulog ▲ 2929 Luzon

South China Sea

Guam (U.S.)

MARSHALL ISLANDS

Taongi

Enewetak

Bikini

Ratak Chain

11033 • Challenger Deep

FEDERATED STATES

MANILA

Samar

Mindoro

Yap

Caroline Islands

Chuuk

Dalap-Uliga-Darrit

Majuro

Cebu

Panay

Palau Koror

OF MICRONESIA

Pohnpei • Palikir

Ralik Chain

Negros

Mindanao

Kosrae

Sulu Sea

Davao

Nomoi Is.

Butaritari

4094 ▲ Gunong Kinabalu

Tinaca Point

PALAU

Tarawa • Bairiki

Gilbert Islands

Celebes Sea

Halmahera

Arorae

Borneo

Biak

Admiralty Is. New Hanover

NAURU

Banaba

Yaren

Equator

Molucca Sea

Buru Seram

5030 ▲ Puncak Jaya

Central Range

Bismarck Sea

New Ireland

Bougainville Island

SOLOMON

Ellice Islands

Nanum

Banjarmasin

Sulawesi (Celebes)

New Britain

Choiseul

Santa Isabel

ISLANDS

TUVALU

Buton

New Guinea

Mt. Wilhelm 4509

Malaita

Fongafale

Greater Sunda Is.

Bali Lombok

Tanimbar

PAPUA NEW

Mt. Victoria ▲ 4073

New Georgia Is.

• Honiara

Funafu

Aru Dolak

GUINEA

San Cristobal

Santa Cruz Is.

Rotuma

SURABAYA

Jawa (Java) Sumba

Flores

Timor

Arafura Sea

Torres Strait Cape York

Louisiade Archipelago

Guadalcanal

FI

Sumba

Melville I.

Cape Arnhem

Port Moresby

Coral Sea

VANUATU

Va— Le

Timor Sea

Joseph Bonaparte Gulf

• Darwin

Groote Eylandt

Gulf of Carpentaria

Coral Sea Islands Territory

Espíritu Santo

Viti Levu

Malakula Port-Vila • Éfaté

Sov—

INDIAN

Bonaparte Archipelago

Great Dividing Range

Îles Chesterfield

OCEAN

1612 ▲ Bartle Frere

Nouvelle Calédonie (France)

Loyalty Is. Maré

Hunter I.

Barrow I.

Great Sandy Desert

Nouméa

A **U** S **T** R **A** L **I** A

Tropic of Capricorn

North

Lake Mackay

Macdonnell Ranges

Great Artesian

Capricorn Group

Sandy Cape

Fraser I.

Shark Bay

West

Basin

867 ▲ Uluru (Ayers Rock)

Lake Eyre

BRISBANE

Norfolk I. (Australia)

Cape Naturaliste

Basin

Great Victoria Desert

Cape Byron

Cape Inscription

Lord Howe I. (Australia)

Ball's Pyramid

Darling

SYDNEY

North Cape

PERTH

Archipelago of the Recherche

Cape Carnot

Murray

Canberra

AUCKLA—

ADELAIDE

Kangaroo I.

Australian Alps

Mt. Kosciuszko 2229

Cape Howe

North Island

Great Australian Bight

King I.

MELBOURNE

Tasman Sea

NEW

Cape Farewell

Welli—

Bass Strait

Flinders I.

ZEALAND

INDIAN

1617 ▲ Mt. Ossa

Tasmania

South Island

3754 ▲ Mt. Cook

Christchur—

OCEAN

South East Cape

West Cape

Bounty

Southwest Cape

Stewart I.

Antipodes

A 110° **B** 120° **C** 130° **D** 140° **E** 150° **F** 160° **G** 170° **H**

© Helicon Publishing Ltd

PACIFIC

OCEAN

NORTH
AMERICA

LOS ANGELES

SAN DIEGO

Guadalupe
(Mexico)

Tropic of Cancer

Is. Revillagigedo
(Mexico)

ure I.
way Is.

Laysan I.

Hawaiian Islands

Necker I.

HAWAII
(U.S.)

Kauai
Oahu
Honolulu Maui

Hawaii

Johnston I.
(U.S.)

N. W. Christmas Island Ridge

Palmyra I.
(U.S.)

Tabuaeran

Kiritimati

Line Islands

Howland (U.S.)
Baker (U.S.)

Jarvis
(U.S.)

Malden I.

Equator

Phoenix Islands

Birnie
Rawaki

KIRIBATI

Orona *Manra*

Starbuck I.

P O L Y N E S I A

Atafu *Tokelau*
Nukunonu *(New Zealand)*

Tongareva

Marquesas Islands

et
na
ce)

Swains I.

Danger Is.
Nassau

Vostok I.

Caroline I.

Nuku Hiva

Manihiki

Flint I.

Hiva Oa

SAMOA *American*
Samoa

Savaii *Apia*
Tutuila

Suvorov I.

Îles de
Désappointement

orn Is.
rance)

Upolu

Rose I.

Motu One

Îles Palliser

Pukapuka

Tafahi

Cook Islands

Arch.

Raroia

TONGA

Niue *Palmerston I.*
(New Zealand)

Aitutaki

de la Société *Tahiti*

Hao

Archipel des Tuamotu

alofa

Rarotonga

French
Polynesia

Îles Duc de
Gloucester

Ata

Tonga Trench

Mangaia

Îles
Maria

Rurutu

Groupe Actéon

Horizon Depth
10882

Tubuai

Mururoa

Morane

Gambier
Is.

Tubuai Islands

Raevavae

Mangareva

Oeno

Tropic of Capricorn

Trench

Rapa
Marotiri

Henderson I.

Pitcairn Is.
(U.K.)

Ducie I.

Easter I.
(Chile)

madec Islands
ew Zealand)

Kermadec Trench

South West

Pacific

Basin

n Is.
ealand)

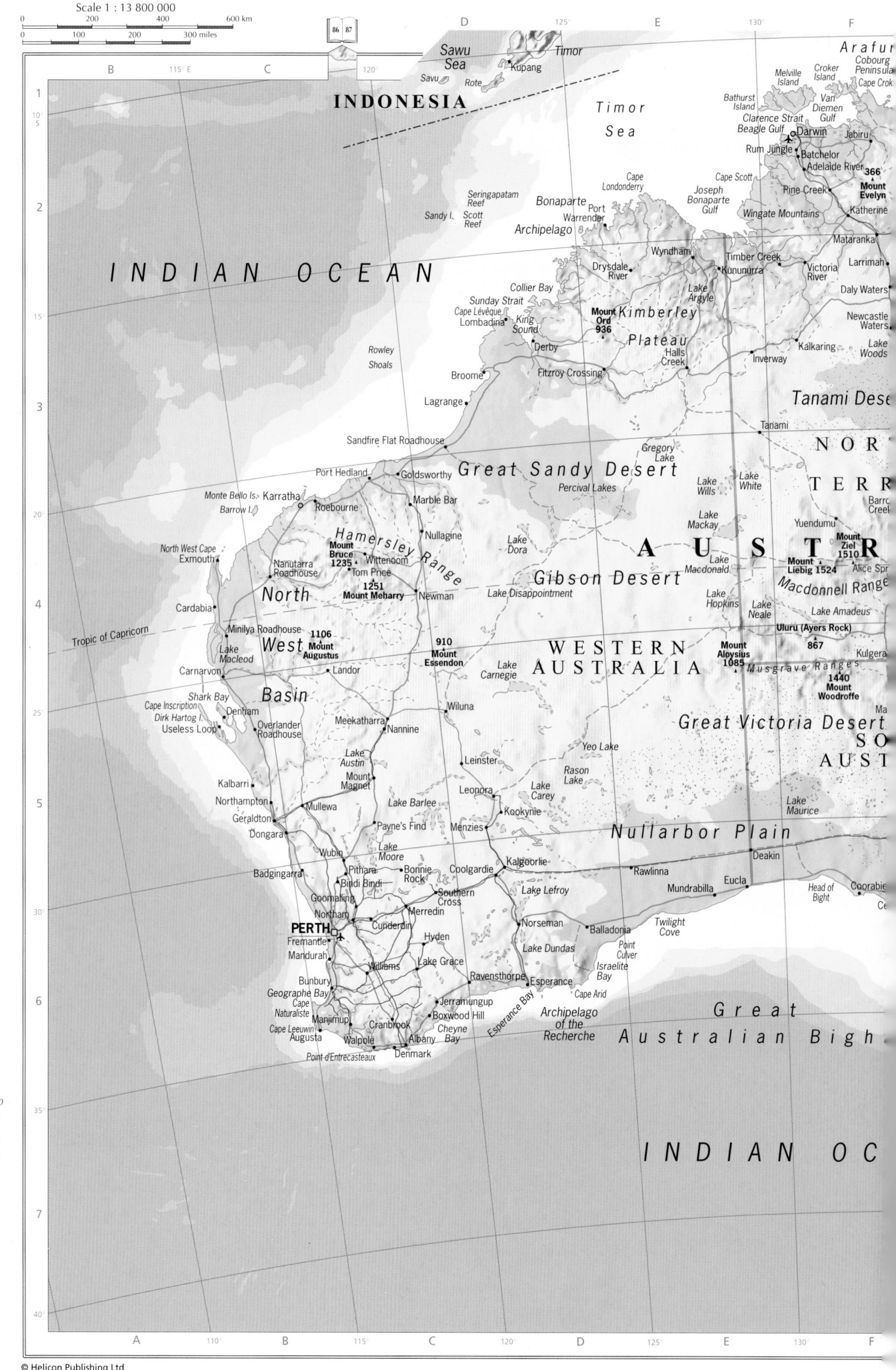

Scale 1 : 13 800 000

INDONESIA

INDIAN OCEAN

© Helicon Publishing Ltd

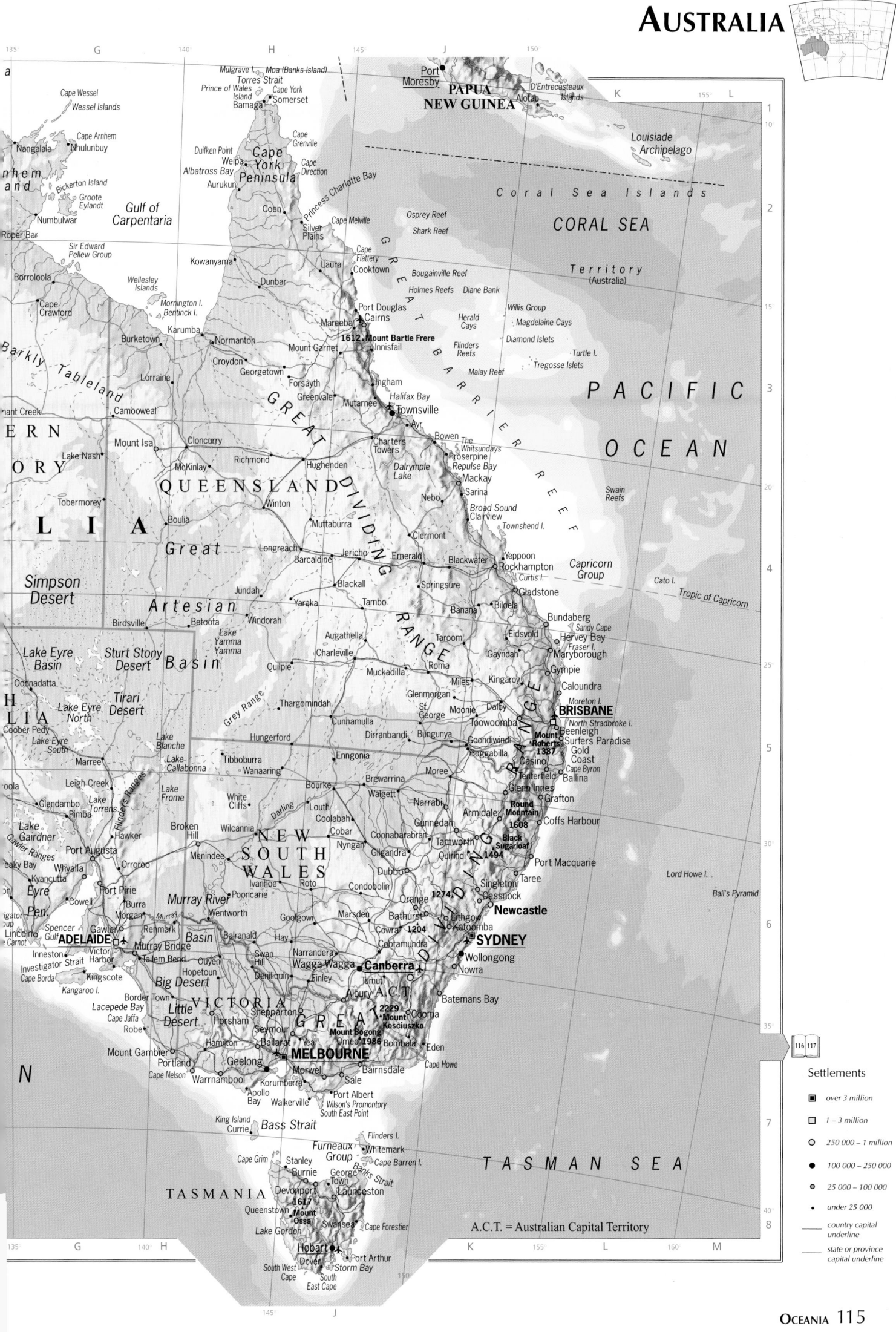

Cape Wessel
Wessel Islands

Nangalala Nhulunbuy
Cape Arnhem

anhem
and

Numbulwar

Roper Bar

Borroloola

Cape
Crawford

Bickerton Island
Groote
Eylandt

Sir Edward
Pellew Group

Gulf of
Carpentaria

Wellesley
Islands

Mornington I.
Bentinck I.

ERN
ORY

Mount Isa

Lake Nash

Tobermorey

Camooweal

L I A

QUEENSLAND

Simpson
Desert

Great

Artesian

Birdsville

Betoota

Windorah

Basin

Lake Eyre
Basin

Sturt Stony
Desert

Tirari
Desert

Oodnadatta

H
LIA

Coober Pedy

Lake Eyre
North

Lake Eyre
South

Marree

Lake
Blanche

Lake
Callabonna

Grey Range

Thargomindah

Mulgrave I. Moa (Banks Island)
Torres Strait
Prince of Wales
Island Cape York
Bamaga Somerset

Duifken Point
Weipa *Cape*
Albatross Bay *York*
Aurukun *Peninsula* Cape
Direction

Cape
Greville

Princess Charlotte Bay

Coen

Silver
Plains

Cape Melville

Laura

Cooktown

Cape
Flattery

Port Douglas
Mareeba Cairns
1612 Mount Bartle Frere
Innisfail

Mount Garnet

Kowanyama

Dunbar

Normanton

Croydon

Georgetown

Forsayth

Greenvale

Mutarnee
Halifax Bay

Ingham

Townsville

Ayr

Bowen The
Whitsundays

Charters
Towers Proserpine
Repulse Bay

Dalrymple
Lake Mackay

Sarina

Nebo

Broad Sound
Clairview

Townshend I.

Yeppoon

Capricorn
Group

Rockhampton
Curtis I.

Gladstone

Bundaberg

Sandy Cape
Hervey Bay Fraser I.
Maryborough

Gympie

Caloundra

Moreton I.

BRISBANE
North Stradbroke I.
Beenleigh
Surfers Paradise
Gold
Coast

Cape Byron
Ballina

McKinlay

Richmond

Cloncurry

Hughenden

Winton

Muttaburra

Boulia

Longreach

Barcaldine

Jericho

Emerald

Blackwater

Clermont

Springsure

CORAL SEA

Osprey Reef

Shark Reef

Bougainville Reef

Holmes Reefs Diane Bank

Herald
Cays

Willis Group

Magdelaine Cays

Diamond Islets

Flinders
Reefs

Malay Reef

Tregosse Islets

Turtle I.

Territory
(Australia)

PACIFIC

OCEAN

Swain
Reefs

Cato I.

Tropic of Capricorn

Blackall

Yaraka

Tambo

Augathella

Charleville

Quilpie

Muckadilla
Roma

Glenmorgan

Miles

St.
George Moonie
Dalby
Toowoomba

Kingaroy

Gayndah

Eidsvold

Taroom

Banana

Biloela

Windorah

Cunnamulla

Dirranbandi Bungunya

Goondiwindi

Boggabilla

Casino

Tenterfield

Mount
Roberts
1387

Glen Innies

Hungerford

Tibboburra

Wanaaring

Enngonia

Brewarrina

Moree

Narrabri

Grafton

Coffs Harbour

Round
Mountain
1608

NEW
SOUTH
WALES

Bourke

Louth
Coolabah

Cobar

Walgett

Gunnedah

Coonabarabran

Armidale

Black
Sugarloaf
1494

Tamworth

Quirindi

Port Macquarie

White
Cliffs

Wilcannia

Nyngan

Gilgandra

Taree

Broken
Hill Menindee

Ivanhoe

Cobar

Dubbo

Condobolin

Orange **1274**
Bathurst Lithgow
Katoomba

Singleton
Cessnock

Newcastle

Lord Howe I.

Ball's Pyramid

Roto

Marsden

Cowra **1204**
Cootamundra

SYDNEY

Wollongong

Nowra

Murray River

Balranald

Hay

Narrandera
Wagga Wagga

Canberra

Batemans Bay

Basin

Wentworth

Pooncarie

Goolgowi

Swan
Hill Deniliquin Finley

Albury **A.C.T.**

2229
Mount
Kosciuszko Cooma

Bombala

Eden

VICTORIA

Shepparton

Seymour

GREAT

Mount Bogong
Omeo **1986**

Little
Desert

Horsham

Ballarat
Yea

Hamilton

MELBOURNE

Bairnsdale

Sale

Cape Howe

Mount Gambier

Portland

Geelong

Warrnambool

Korumburra
Morwell

Apollo
Bay Walkerville
Port Albert
Wilson's Promontory
South East Point

King Island
Currie

Bass Strait

Flinders I.

Whitemark

Cape Barren I.

TASMAN SEA

Furneaux
Group

Cape Grim Stanley
Burnie George
Town Banks Strait

TASMANIA

Devonport Launceston

Queenstown **1617**
Mount
Ossa Swansea

Lake Gordon Cape Forestier

A.C.T. = Australian Capital Territory

Hobart
Dover Port Arthur
South West Storm Bay
Cape South
East Cape

Settlements

■ over 3 million

□ 1 – 3 million

◎ 250 000 – 1 million

● 100 000 – 250 000

◉ 25 000 – 100 000

· under 25 000

—— country capital
underline

—— state or province
capital underline

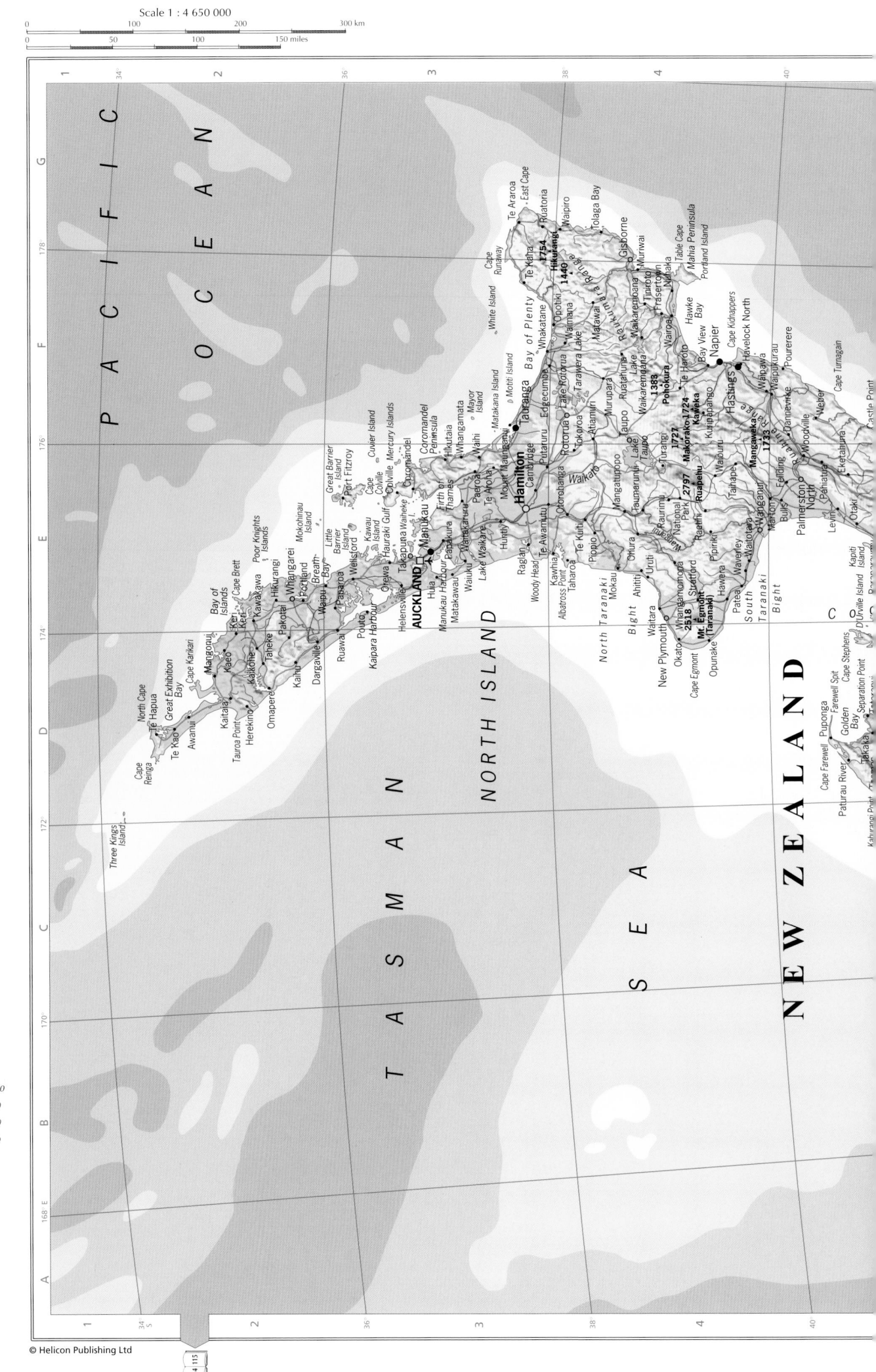

Scale 1 : 4 650 000

© Helicon Publishing Ltd

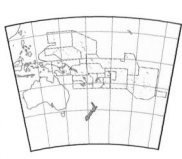
Map labels

Chatham Islands inset (1)
Chatham Islands (New Zealand)
The Sisters
Hanson Bay
Chatham I.
Petre Bay
Waitangi **287**
Pitt Strait
Pitt I.
Pyramid I.
Western Reef
PACIFIC OCEAN

Antipodes Islands inset (3)
Antipodes Islands (New Zealand) **366**
PACIFIC OCEAN

Auckland / Campbell inset (2)
Auckland Islands (New Zealand) **668**
South West Cape
Campbell Island (New Zealand) **569**
PACIFIC OCEAN

Main map

PACIFIC OCEAN

Flat Point
Cape Palliser
Ngawihi
Wellington **983** Mt. Ross
Seddon
Cape Campbell
Ward
Blenheim
Kekerengu
Clarence
Kaikoura
Parnassus
Cheviot
Waiau
Waipara
Rangiora
Oxford
Sheffield
Christchurch
Pegasus Bay
Banks Peninsula
Lyttelton
Akaroa
Leeston
Rolleston
Mount Hutt
Canterbury Plains
Ashburton
Geraldine
Temuka
Timaru
Studholme Junction
Waimate
Pukeuri Junction
Oamaru
Herbert
Hampden
Palmerston
Otago Peninsula
Cape Saunders
Dunedin
Mosgiel
Milton
Clarks Junction
Balclutha
Nugget Point
Kaitangata
Owaka
Papatowai
Waikawa

Richmond
Mt. Richmond **1760**
Twins **1811**
Mt. Owen
Howard Junction
Saint Arnaud
Murchison
2085 Tapuaenuku
2174 Dillon Cone
2338 Mt. Travers
Inangahua
Murchison **2400**
Reefton **1532**
Springs Junction
Maruia
Hanmer Springs
Waiau
Culverden
Scargill
Waikari

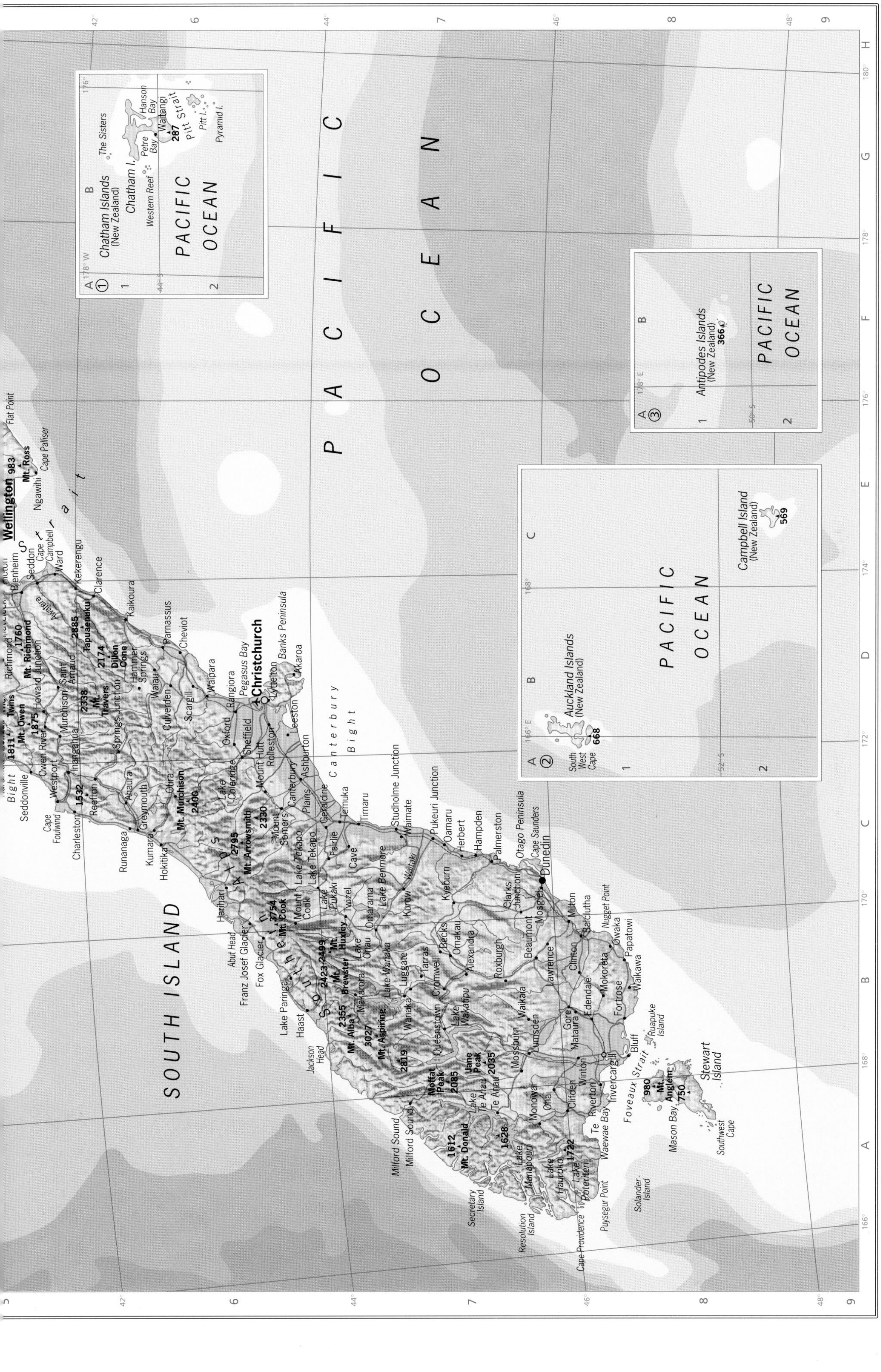

Cape Foulwind
Westport
Seddonville
Owen River
Charleston
Cape Foulwind
Runanga
Greymouth
Kumara
Hokitika
Ross
Lake Coleridge
Mount Somers
Mt. Arrowsmith **2795**
Mount Hutt
2330
Lake Tekapo
Lake Pukaki
Fairlie
Cave
Lake Benmore
Waitaki
Kurow
Kyeburn
Clyde
Alexandra
Clarks Junction

Harihari
Franz Josef Glacier
Fox Glacier
Abut Head
Mt. Cook **3754**
2423 **2499**
Mt. Brewster Huxley
Lake Ohau
Omarama
Becks
Omakau
Roxburgh
Beaumont
Lawrence
Edendale
Mokoreta
Fortrose

Lake Paringa
Haast
Jackson Head
Mt. Alba **2355**
3027 Mt. Aspiring
Lake Wanaka
Wanaka
Lake Hawea
Hawea
Tarras
Cromwell
Luggate
Lake Wakatipu
Queenstown
Lake Wanaka

Milford Sound
Milford Sound
2819
Moffat Peak **2085**
Jane Peak **2035**
Lake Te Anau
Te Anau
Kingston
Mossburn
Lumsden
Waikaia
Riversdale
Gore
Mataura
Wyndham

Secretary Island
Resolution Island
1612
Mt. Donald
Lake Manapouri
Manapouri
1628
1732
Lake Monowai
Lake Hauroko
Lake Poteriteri
Cape Providence
Puysegur Point
Solander Island
Monowai
Ohai
Clifden
Tuatapere
Te Waewae Bay
Waewae Bay
Riverton
Winton
Invercargill
Bluff
Foveaux Strait
Ruapuke Island
980 **Mt. Anglem** **750**
Mason Bay
Stewart Island
Southwest Cape

SOUTH ISLAND
Southern Alps
Tasman Bay
Golden Bay

Canterbury Bight

Settlements legend

□ 1 – 3 million
◎ 250 000 – 1 million
● 100 000 – 250 000
◦ 25 000 – 100 000
• under 25 000
— country capital underline

OCEANIA 117

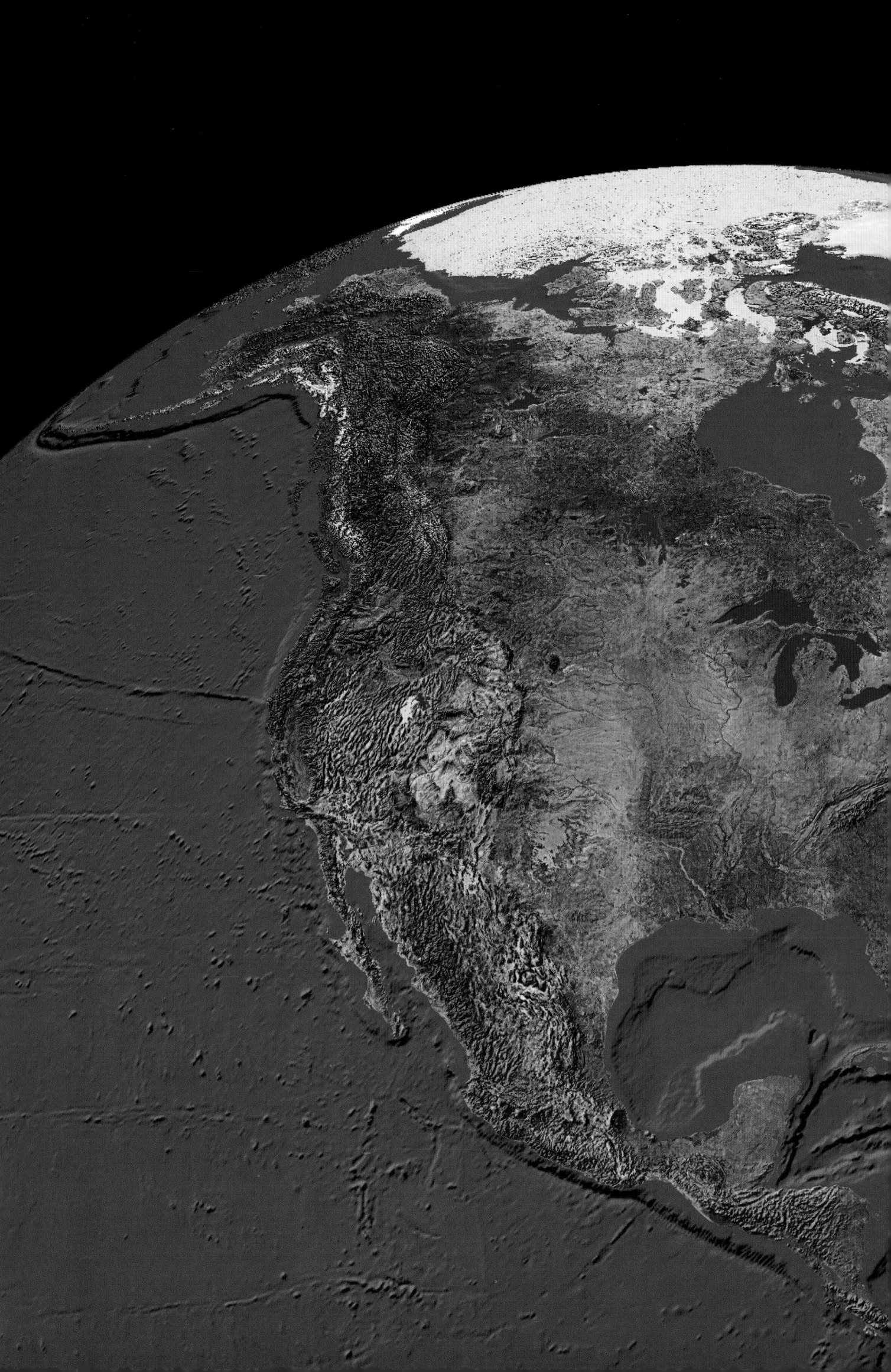

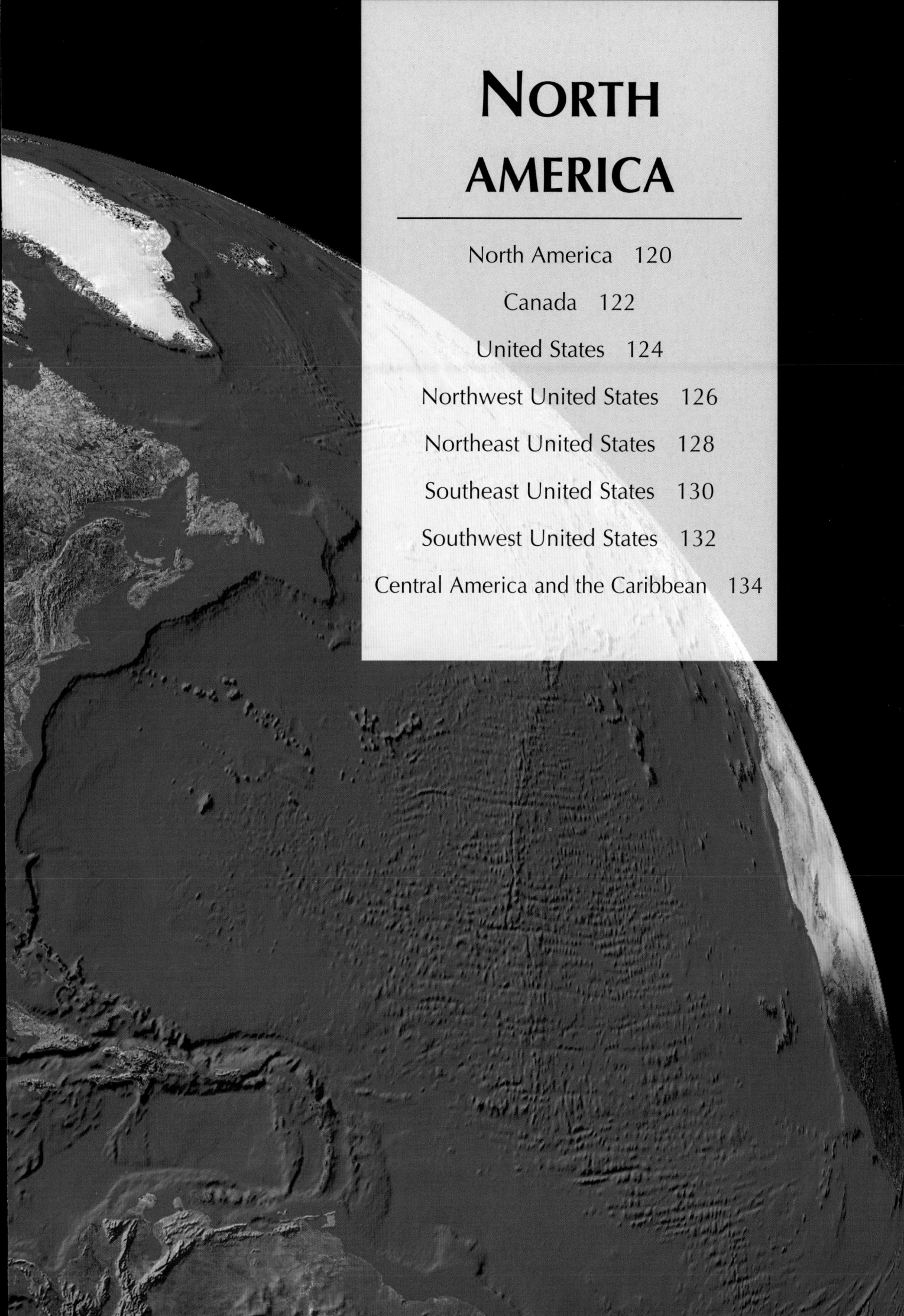

NORTH AMERICA

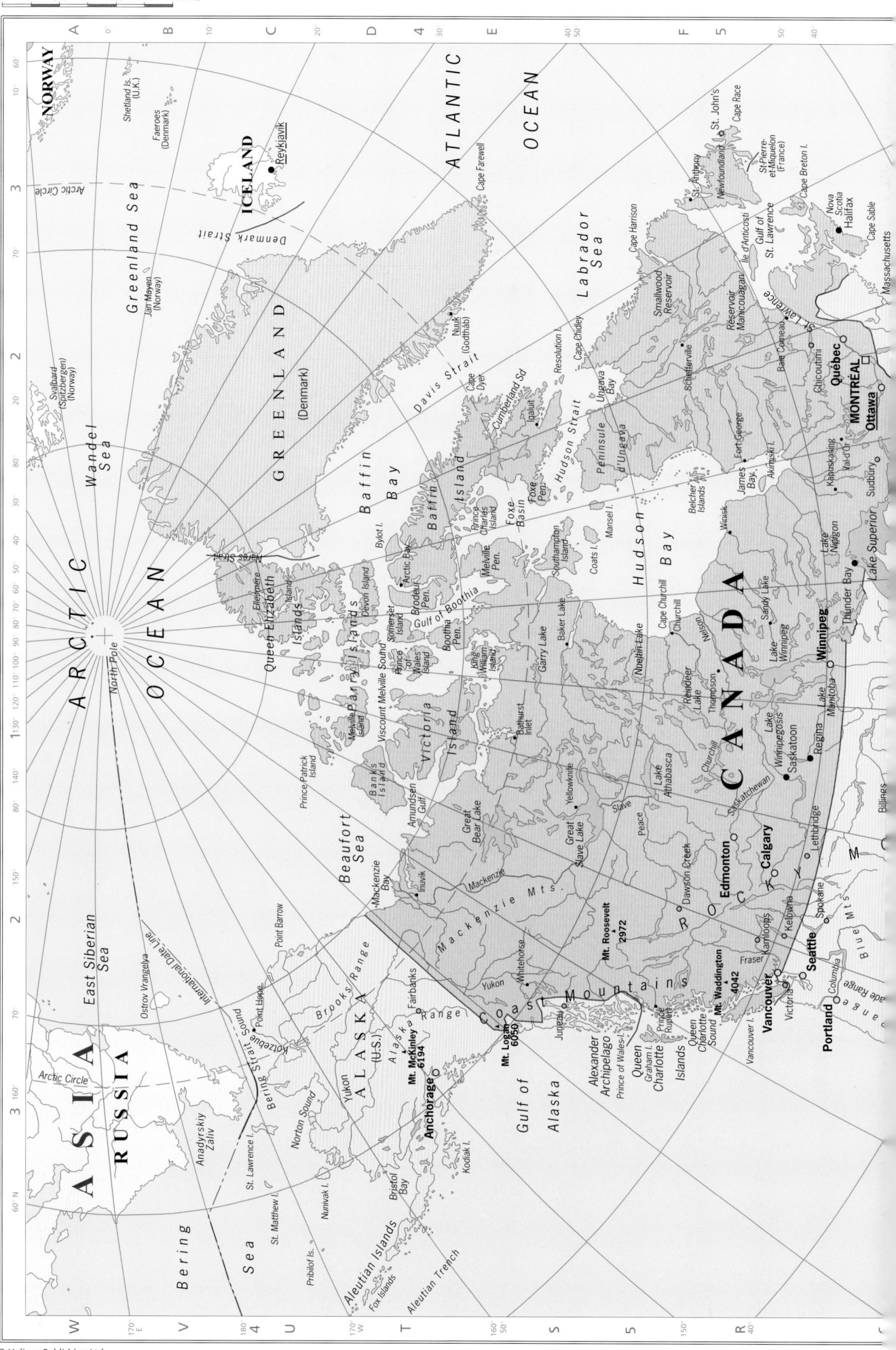

Scale 1 : 34 700 000

© Helicon Publishing Ltd

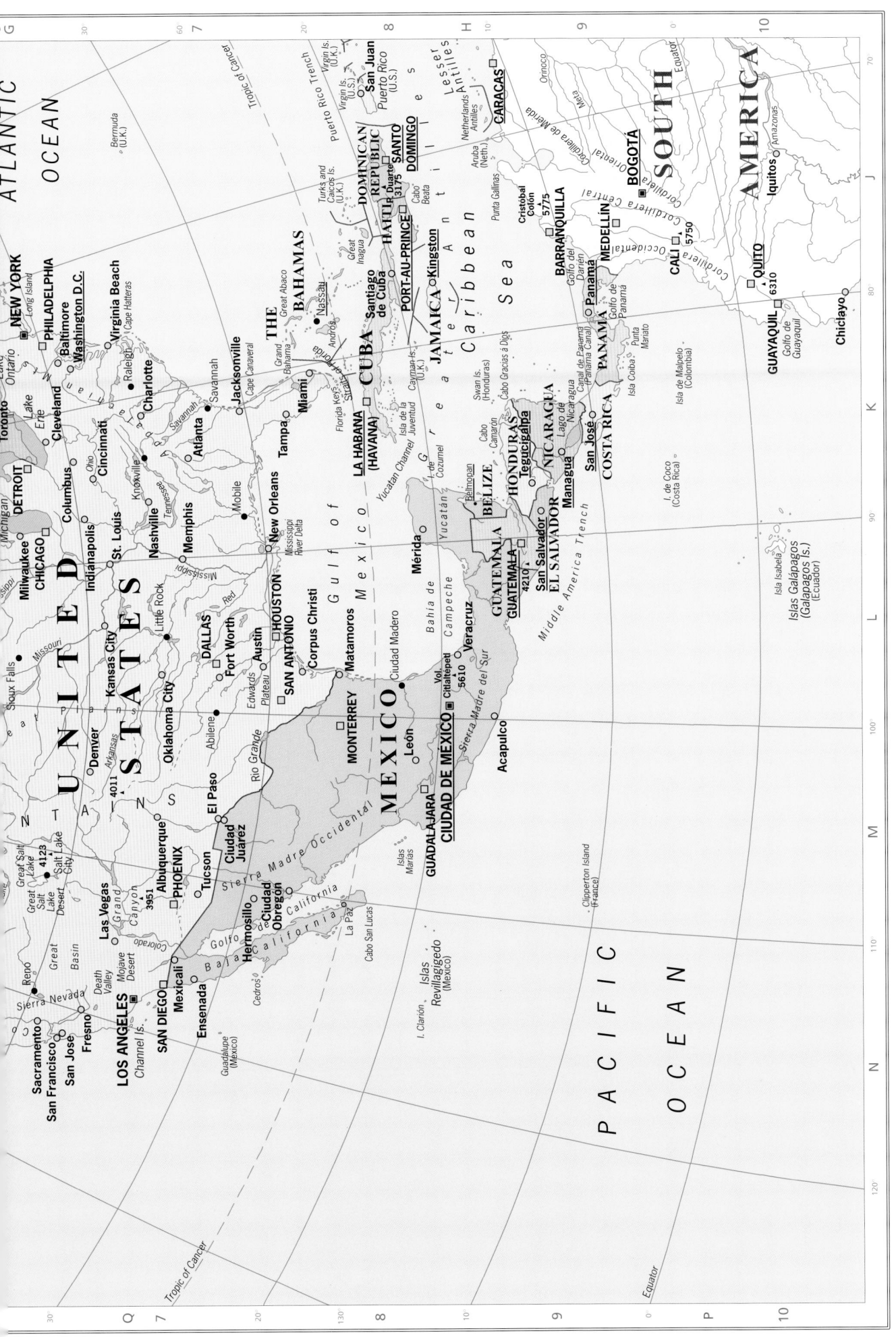

ATLANTIC OCEAN

Bermuda (U.K.)

NEW YORK
PHILADELPHIA
Baltimore
Washington D.C.
Virginia Beach
Cape Hatteras

Toronto
Lake Ontario
Cleveland
Lake Erie
Columbus
Cincinnati
Knoxville
Raleigh
Charlotte
Jacksonville
Savannah
Atlanta
DETROIT
Lake Michigan
Milwaukee
CHICAGO
Indianapolis
St. Louis
Nashville
Memphis
Mobile
New Orleans
Tampa
Miami
Cape Canaveral

THE BAHAMAS
Grand Bahama
Great Abaco
Nassau
Andros
Great Exuma
Grand Turk

Turks and Caicos Is. (U.K.)

Puerto Rico Trench

Virgin Is. (U.K.)
Virgin Is. (U.S.)
San Juan
Puerto Rico (U.S.)

Lesser Antilles

Netherlands Antilles
Aruba (Neth.)

CARACAS
Orinoco

SOUTH AMERICA

Cordillera de Mérida

BOGOTÁ
Iquitos
Amazonas

DOMINICAN REPUBLIC
SANTO DOMINGO
Duarte 3175
Cabo Beata

HAITI
PORT-AU-PRINCE
Kingston
JAMAICA
Cayman Is. (U.K.)
Santiago de Cuba

CUBA
LA HABANA (HAVANA)
Isla de la Juventud
Florida Keys
Straits of Florida

Cristóbal Colón 5775

Punta Gallinas

BARRANQUILLA
MEDELLÍN
Golfo del Darién
Panamá
Golfo de Panamá
PANAMÁ

CALI 5750

Quito 6310

GUAYAQUIL
Golfo de Guayaquil
Chiclayo

Cordillera Central
Cordillera Oriental

Cordillera Occidental

Caribbean Sea

Swan Is. (Honduras)
Cabo Gracias á Dios

Isla de Malpelo (Colombia)
Isla Coiba
Punta Mariato

Canal de Panamá (Panama Canal)

I. de Coco (Costa Rica)

Yucatán Channel
Isla de Cozumel
Belmopan
BELIZE
HONDURAS
Tegucigalpa
Cabo Camarón
NICARAGUA
Lago de Nicaragua
Managua
COSTA RICA
San José
GUATEMALA
GUATEMALA 4210
San Salvador
EL SALVADOR

Middle America Trench

Mérida
Bahía de Campeche
Yucatán

UNITED STATES

Sioux Falls
Missouri
Kansas City
Little Rock
Oklahoma City
Abilene
DALLAS
Fort Worth
Austin
SAN ANTONIO
HOUSTON
Corpus Christi
Matamoros
Veracruz
Ciudad Madero
MONTERREY
León
GUADALAJARA
CIUDAD DE MÉXICO
Vol. Citlaltépetl 5610
Acapulco

MÉXICO

Denver
4011
Arkansas
Red
Edwards Plateau
Rio Grande
El Paso
Ciudad Juárez
Albuquerque
PHOENIX 3951
Tucson
Las Vegas
Grand Canyon
Salt Lake City
Great Salt Lake 4123
Great Salt Lake Desert
Mojave Desert
Colorado
Death Valley
Sierra Nevada
Reno
Sacramento
San Francisco
San Jose
Fresno
LOS ANGELES
Channel Is.
SAN DIEGO
Mexicali
Ensenada
Hermosillo
Ciudad Obregón
Sierra Madre Occidental
La Paz
Cabo San Lucas
Baja California
Golfo de California
Cedros
Guadalupe (México)

Islas Marías
Islas Revillagigedo (México)
I. Clarión

Sierra Madre del Sur

Clipperton Island (France)

Islas Galápagos (Galápagos Is.) (Ecuador)
Isla Isabela

PACIFIC OCEAN

Tropic of Cancer

Equator

ROCKY MOUNTAINS

Great Plains

Great Basin

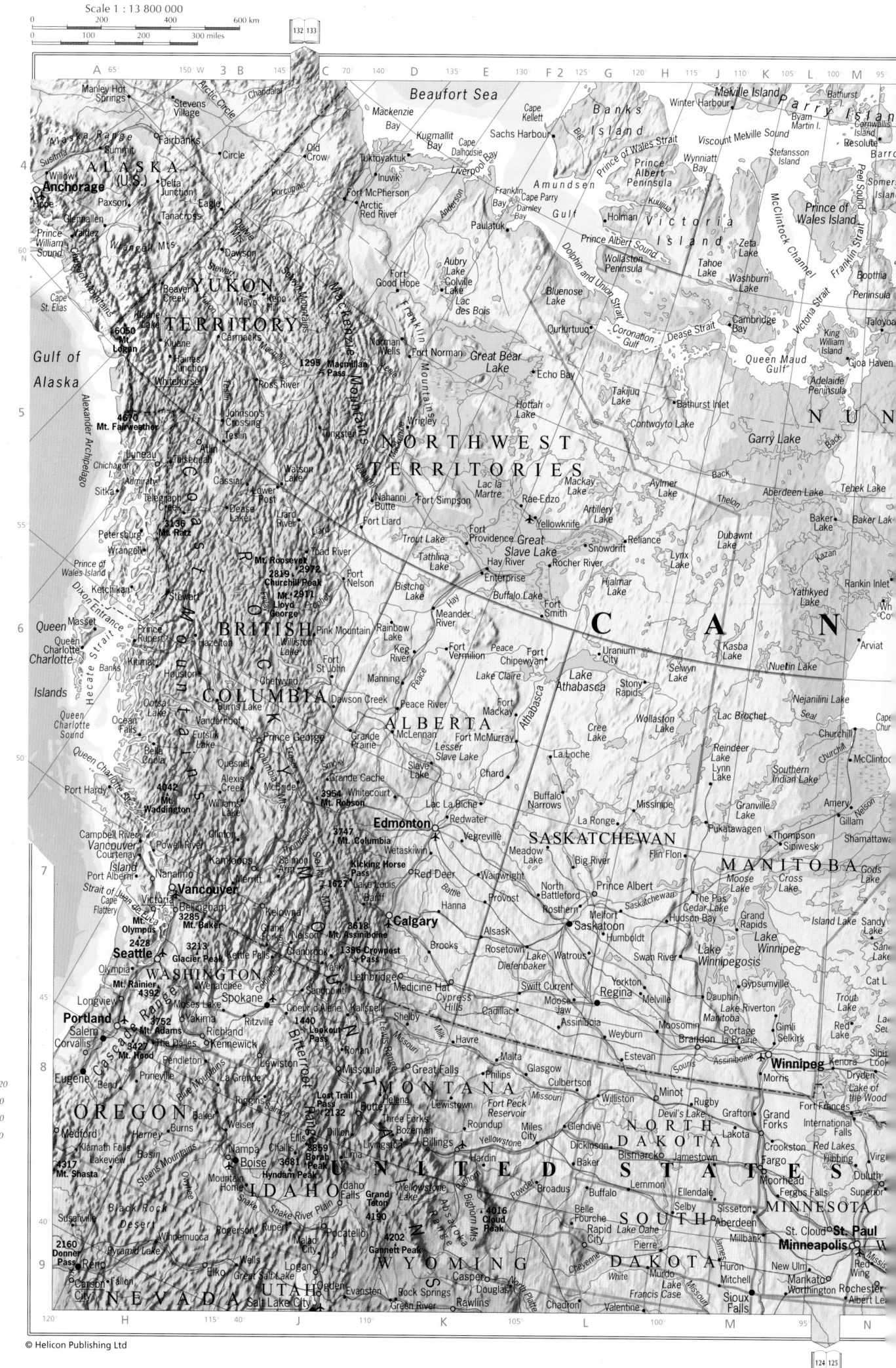

Scale 1 : 13 800 000

200   400   600 km
100   200   300 miles

A 65°   150° W   3 B   145°   C 70°   140°   D   135°   E   130°   F 2   125°   G   120°   H   115°   J   110°   K   105°   L   100°   M   95°

Beaufort Sea

Manley Hot Springs
Stevens Village
Fairbanks
Summit
Circle
Old Crow
Chandalar

Banks Island

Melville Island
Byam Martin I.
Winter Harbour
Bathurst
Resolute
Barro

ALASKA (U.S.)
Anchorage
Hope
Glennallen
Valdez
Paxson
Delta Junction
Eagle
Tanacross

Mackenzie Bay
Kugmallit Bay
Tuktoyaktuk
Inuvik
Fort McPherson
Arctic Red River

Cape Kellett
Sachs Harbour
Cape Dalhousie
Liverpool Bay

Prince of Wales Strait
Viscount Melville Sound
Stefansson Island

Prince Albert Peninsula
Franklin Bay
Cape Parry
Darnley Bay
Paulatuk

Amundsen Gulf

Holman

Prince of Wales Island
Somer
Islan

Wrangell Mts.
Prince William Sound
Cape St. Elias

YUKON
TERRITORY
Dawson
Mayo
Keno Hill

Victoria Island

McClintock Channel
Zeta Lake
Tahoe Lake
Cambridge Bay
Washburn Lake

Boothia Peninsula

Gulf of Alaska

Beaver Creek
6050 Mt. Logan
Kluane
Haines Junction
Whitehorse
Carmacks
Ross River
1295 Macmillan Pass

Mackenzie Mountains

Fort Good Hope
Norman Wells
Fort Norman

Aubry Lake
Colville Lake
Lac des Bois

Great Bear Lake
Echo Bay

Dolphin and Union Strait
Wollaston Peninsula
Bluenose Lake
Coronation Gulf
Qurlurtuuq

Dease Strait

King William Island
Gjoa Haven

Adelaide Peninsula

Queen Maud Gulf

N U N

4670 Mt. Fairweather
Atlin
Chichagof I.
Juneau
Tulsequah
Admiralty I.
Sitka

Teslin
Johnson's Crossing
Watson Lake

NORTHWEST
TERRITORIES

Hottah Lake
Wrigley

Takijuq Lake

Contwoyto Lake

Garry Lake

Bathurst Inlet

Back

3136 Mt. Ratz
Telegraph Creek
Cassiar
Dease Lake
Lower Post
Liard River

Nahanni Butte
Fort Simpson
Fort Liard

Lac la Martre
Rae-Edzo
Yellowknife

Mackay Lake
Artillery Lake

Aylmer Lake
Thelon
Reliance

Aberdeen Lake
Tehek Lake

Baker Lak

Petersburg
Wrangell
Prince of Wales Island
Ketchikan

Mt. Roosevelt
2819 2972
Churchill Peak
Mt. 2971
Lloyd George
Toad River
Liard

Trout Lake
Fort Providence
Great Slave Lake
Hay River
Enterprise

Snowdrift
Rocher River

Dubawnt Lake
Lynx Lake

Selwyn Lake

Kasba Lake
Nuetin Lake

Rankin Inlet

Arviat

Wh
Co

Queen Charlotte
Masset
Queen Charlotte
Islands

Prince Rupert
Kitimat
Hazelton

Pink Mountain
Fort St. John

Rainbow Lake
Keg River

Meander River
Fort Vermilion

Peace

Fort Chipewyan

Hay

Fort Smith

Uranium City

Bistcho Lake

Lake Claire

Stony Rapids

Wollaston Lake

Lac Brochet

Seal

Nejanilini Lake

Cape
Chur

BRITISH
COLUMBIA

Houston
Ootsa Lake

Williston Lake

Chetwynd

Dawson Creek

Manning

Peace River

Fort Mackay

Lake Athabasca

Reindeer Lake

Churchill

Hecate Strait

Bella Coola
Ocean Falls

Eutsuk Lake

Prince George

Grande Prairie

McLennan
Lesser Slave Lake

Fort McMurray

La Loche

Cree Lake

Lynn Lake

Southern Indian Lake

Granville Lake
Amery

Gillam

Nelson

Queen Charlotte Sound

Port Hardy

4042 Mt. Waddington

Williams Lake

Alexis Creek

Quesnel

McBride

3954 Mt. Robson

Whitecourt

Lac La Biche

Chard

Buffalo Narrows

Missinipe

La Ronge

Pukatawagen

Thompson
Sipiwesk

Shamattawa

Campbell River
Courtenay
Vancouver Island
Port Alberni
Nanaimo

Powell River

Clinton

Kamloops

3747 Mt. Columbia
Edmonton
Wetaskiwin
Vegreville

Redwater

SASKATCHEWAN

Meadow Lake

Big River

Flin Flon

Moose Lake

Cross Lake

MANITOBA

Gods Lake

Vancouver
Victoria
Bellingham

Merritt
Salmon Arm

Kicking Horse Pass
1627

Red Deer

Battle

Wainwright

North Battleford

Prince Albert

Melfort

The Pas
Cedar Lake

Grand Rapids

Island Lake

Sandy

Sam

Mt. Olympus 3285
Mt. Baker

Glacier Peak 3213
2428
Seattle
Olympia

Kelowna

Grand Forks

Nelson

3618 Mt. Assiniboine
Calgary

1396 Crowsnest Pass

Cranbrook

Banff
Lake Louise

Brooks

Alsask

Rosetown

Saskatoon
Humboldt

Watrous

Hudson Bay
Swan River

Yorkton

Dauphin

Lake Winnipeg

Lake
Winnipegosis

Cat L

Trout Lake

WASHINGTON
Mt. Rainier 4392
Longview

Wenatchee
Moses Lake
Spokane

Kettle Falls

Yahk

Lethbridge

Medicine Hat
Cypress Hills

Cadillac

Rosetown

Lake Diefenbaker

Moose Jaw

Regina

Assiniboia

Weyburn

Swift Current

Melville

Moosomin

Brandon
La Prairie

Gimli
Selkirk

Portage

Red
La

Winnipeg

Kenora

Siou

Portland
Salem
Corvallis
Eugene

3752 Mt. Adams
Yakima
Richland
Kennewick
The Dalles
5427 Mt. Hood

Pendleton

La Grande

Ritzville

Coeur d'Alene
Kalispell

Sandpoint

Lewiston

Shelby

Havre

Malta

Glasgow

Estevan

Souris

Assiniboine

Minot

Devil's Lake

Grafton

Grand Forks

International Falls

Lake of the Wood

Dryden

Winnipeg

Morris

OREGON

Medford
Klamath Falls
Lakeview

Bend
Prineville
Burns

Baker
Weiser

Riggins

1440 Lookout Pass

Lost Trail Pass 2132

Butte

Missoula

Helena

Three Forks
Bozeman

MONTANA

Lewistown

Fort Peck Reservoir

Roundup

Billings

Philips

Culbertson

Williston

Glendive

Miles City

Dickinson

Baker

Lemmon

NORTH
DAKOTA

Jamestown

Bismarck

Lakota

Crookston

Fargo

Red Lakes

Hibbing

Moorhead

Fergus Falls

Duluth

Superior

Virg

4317 Mt. Shasta

Susanville

Black Rock Desert

Winnemucca

Nampa
Boise
Mountain Home

3681 Hyndam Peak

IDAHO

Challis
5859 Borah Peak

Lima

Dillon

Yellowstone Lake

Livingston

Hardin

Yellowstone

Bighorn Mts.

Powder

4016 Cloud Peak

Broadus

Belle Fourche

Buffalo

SOUTH

Ellendale

Selby

Aberdeen

Sisseton

MINNESOTA

St. Cloud
Minneapolis
St. Paul

New Ulm

Mankato

Red Wing

2160 Donner Pass
Reno
Carson City
Fallon

Pyramid Lake

Rogerson
Rupert

Malad City

Pocatello

Snake River Plain

4190 Grand Teton

4202 Gannett Peak

Casper

Douglas

Rapid City
Lake Oahe

Pierre

WYOMING

New Platte

Cheyenne

DAKOTA

White

Lake Francis Case

Murdo

Valentine

Chadron

Huron

Mitchell

Sioux Falls

Worthington

Rochester

Albert Le

Mississ

NEVADA

Susanville

Elko

Wells

Great Salt Lake

Logan

Ogden

Salt Lake City

UTAH

Evanston

Green River

Rock Springs

Rawlins

120°   H   115°   40°   J   110°   K   105°   L   100°   N

© Helicon Publishing Ltd

124 125

metres / feet
4000 / 13120
2000 / 6560
1000 / 3280
500 / 1640
200 / 656
0 / 0
200 / 656
1000 / 3280
2000 / 6560
4000 / 13120
6000 / 19690
8000 / 26250
metres / feet

GREENLAND
(Denmark)

Upernavik
Kangersuatsiaq (Prøven)
Illorsuit
Nuussuaq
Uummannaq (Ûmânaq)
Qeqertarsuaq (Disko)
Ilulissat (Jakobshavn)
Qeqertarsuup Tunua (Disko Bugt)
Kangaatsiaq
Sisimiut (Holsteinsborg)
Maniitsoq (Sukkertoppen)
Napasoq
Nuuk (Godthåb)
Kangerluarsoruseq (Færingehavn)
Qeqertarsuatsiaat (Fiskenæsset)
Paamiut (Frederikshåb)
Ivittuut
Nanortalik
Nunarsuit

Ammassalik (Angmagssalik)
Gyldenløves Fjord
Kong Frederick VI Kyst
Kangeq (Kap Cort Adelaer)
Kangerlussuatsiaq (Lindenow Fjord)
Nunap Isua (Kap Farvel)

Arctic Circle

Baffin Bay

Lancaster Sound
Bylot Island
Arctic Bay
Borden Peninsula
Pond Inlet
Buchan Gulf
Scott Inlet
Cape Christian
Clyde River
Home Bay
Broughton Island
Cape Dyer
Cumberland Peninsula
Pangnirtung
Cumberland Sound
Cape Mercy

Baffin Island

Davis Strait

LABRADOR SEA

ATLANTIC OCEAN

Igloolik
Hall Beach
Rowley I.
Air Force I.
Prince Charles Island
Amadjuak Lake
Hall Peninsula
Lemieux Islands
Iqaluit
Frobisher Bay
Loks Land
Lake Harbour
Resolution Island

Repulse Bay
Cape Dominion
Bowman Bay
Cape Dorchester
Foxe Peninsula
Igaluit
Salisbury I.
Nottingham I.
Cap de Nouvelle-France
Cape Chidley
Port Burwell

Foxe Basin

Foxe Channel

Hudson Strait

1729

Quaqtaq
Akpatok Island

Ivujivik
Salluit
Kangiqsujuaq

Péninsule D'Ungava

Ungava Bay

Akulivik
Kangirsuk
Kangiqsualujjuaq
Hebron
Cod Island
Nutak
Nain

NEWFOUNDLAND

Puvurnituq
Lac Payne
Kuujjuaq
Hopedale
Cape Harrison
Groswater Bay
Rigolet
Cartwright

Inukjuak
Lac Minto
Lac à l'Eau Claire

HUDSON BAY

Lake Melville
Cape Harrison

Fort Severn
Winisk
Cape Henrietta Maria
King George Is.
Sleeper Is.
Belcher Islands
Long I.
Lac Bienville
Schefferville
Smallwood Reservoir
Churchill Falls
Churchill
Labrador

Port Hope Simpson
Battle Harbour
Belle Isle
Cape Bauld
St. Anthony
Roddickton
White Bay
Notre Dame Bay
Fogo I.
Bonavista Bay
Gander
St. John's

Big Trout Lake
Winisk Lake
Attawapiskat
Akimiski Island
Ekwan
Charlton
Eastmain

James Bay

Rés. de La Grande 4
Rés. de La Grande 3
Rés. de La Grande 2
Réservoir Opinaca
Fort George

QUÉBEC

Monts Otish
1021

Réservoir Caniapiscau
Labrador City
Wabush
Ashuanipi
Ashuanipi Lake
Natashquan

Deer Lake
Newfoundland
Long Range Mts.
St-Augustin
Petit Mécatina
Grand Falls

Fort Rupert
Moosonee
Fort Hope
Albany
Missinaibi
Coral
Rupert
L. Mistassini
Baie-du-Poste
Chibougamau
Eastmain
Chute des Passes
Réservoir Pipmuacan

Stephenville
Harbour Breton
Fortune Bay
Grand Bank
Channel-Port aux Basques
St-Pierre et-Miquelon (France)

ONTARIO

Armstrong
Nakina
Longlac
Geraldton
Nipigon
Hearst
Kapuskasing
Cochrane
Amos
Val-d'Or
Senneterre
Rouyn
Miquelon
Réservoir Gouin
Lac St-Jean
Jonquière
Baie St. Paul
Chicoutimi
Les Escoumins
Rimouski
Matane
Péninsule de Gaspé
Sept-Îles
Port-Menier
Île d'Anticosti
St. Lawrence
Gulf of St. Lawrence
Îles de la Madeleine
Cape Ray
Cape Breton Island
Sydney

Lake Nipigon
Thunder Bay
Isle Royale
Copper Harbor
Keweenaw Pen.
Marathon
Wawa
Chapleau
Foleyet
Timmins
Kirkland Lake
Cobalt
Lake Abitibi
La Tuque
Mont-Laurier
Trois Rivières
Sherbrooke
Québec
Lévis
Montmagny
Sorel
Granby
Jackman

PRINCE EDWARD ISLAND
Charlottetown
Northumberland Strait
Port Hawkesbury
New Glasgow
Sable I.

Edmundston
NEW BRUNSWICK
Moncton
Fredericton
St. John
Bay of Fundy
Amherst
Truro
Dartmouth
Halifax
NOVA SCOTIA
Bridgewater
Liverpool
Shelburne
Cape Sable
Yarmouth

Thunder Bay
Sault Ste. Marie
Blind River
Sudbury
Pembroke
Ottawa
Smiths Falls
Ottawa
Cornwall
MONTRÉAL
Mt. Wash.
Washington
1917

Presque Isle
Houlton
MAINE
St. Stephen
St. John

Lake Superior
Isle Royale
Marquette
Manistique
Escanaba
Ironwood
Iron Mountain
Rhinelander
MICHIGAN

Parry Sound
North Bay
Manitoulin I.
Tobermory
Huntsville
Orillia
Kingston
Peterborough
Oshawa

Ogdensburg
Montpelier
Plattsburgh
Burlington
1629
NEW HAMPSHIRE
Augusta
Lewiston
Portland
Concord
Portsmouth
VERMONT

Lake Huron
Georgian Bay
Owen Sound
Barrie
Collingwood
Toronto
Kitchener
Rochester
Syracuse
Utica
Albany
Watertown
Massachusetts Bay
Cape Cod

MILWAUKEE
Wausau
Appleton
Oshkosh
Sheboygan
Green Bay
Traverse City
Mt. Pleasant
Bay City
Saginaw
Flint
Grand Rapids
Lansing
Ann Arbor
DETROIT
Windsor
Lake St. Clair
Chatham
Sarnia
London
Hamilton
St. Catharines
Buffalo
Binghamton
Jamestown
Meadville
NEW YORK
Catskill Mts.
1295
Springfield
Hartford
MASS.
CONN.
New Haven
Bridgeport
RHODE ISLAND
Boston
Worcester
Providence
New Bedford

Scranton
Paterson
PENNSYLVANIA
Erie
Lake Erie
Newark
NEW YORK
Long I.

Settlements

■	over 3 million
□	1 – 3 million
○	250 000 – 1 million
●	100 000 – 250 000
◎	25 000 – 100 000
•	under 25 000
——	country capital underline
——	state or province capital underline

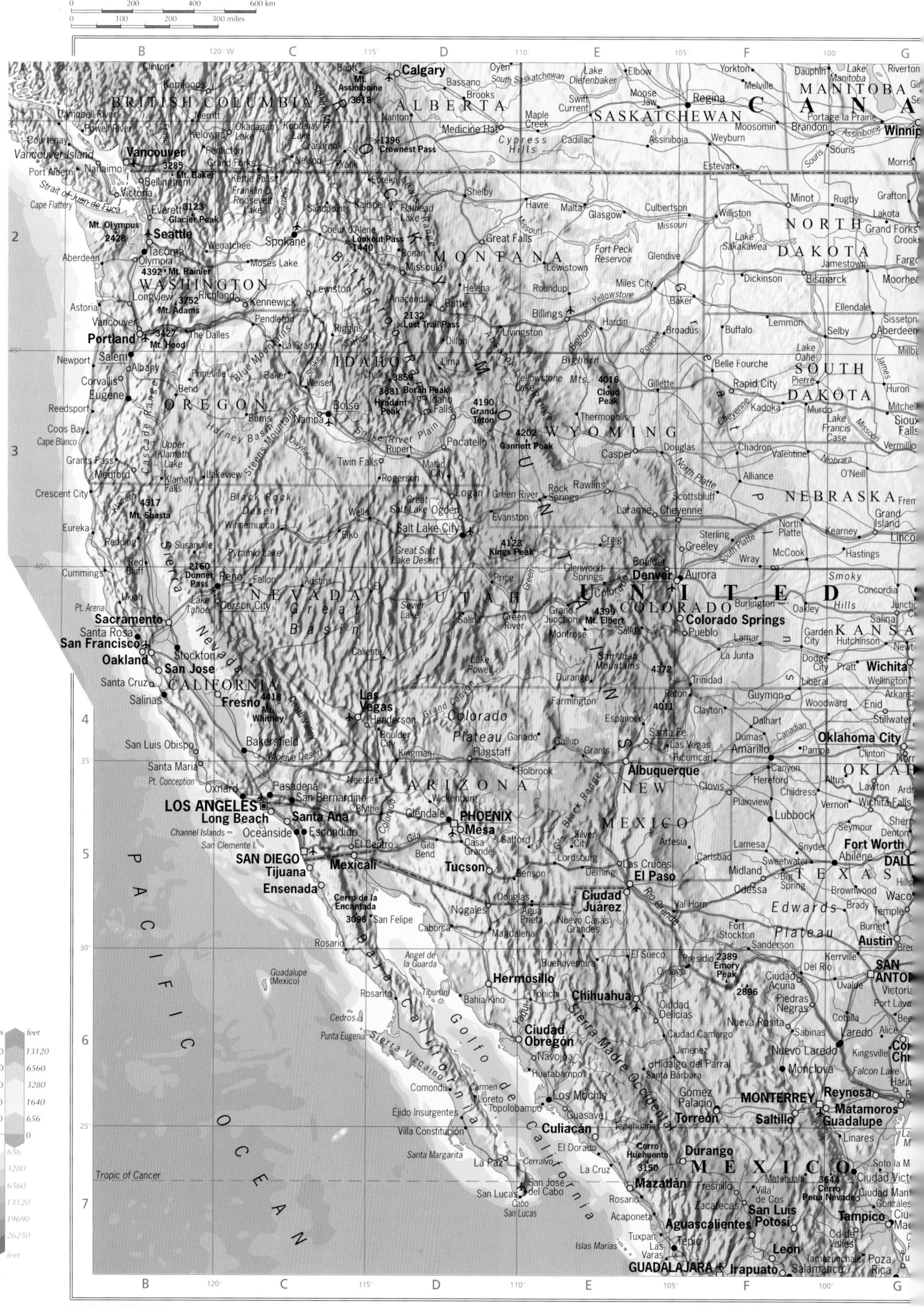

Scale 1 : 15 500 000

© Helicon Publishing Ltd

123

CANADA

ONTARIO — QUÉBEC

L. Mistassini · Lac Evans · Chibougamau · Chute des Passes · Baie-du-Poste · Miquelon · Senneterre · Réservoir Gouin · Dolbeau · Pipmuacan · Chicoutimi · Rivière-du-Loup · Edmundston

Trout Lake · Lac St. Joseph · Nakina · Missinabi · Coral · Longlac · Geraldton · Hearst · Kapuskasing · Cochrane · Amos · Rouyn · Val-d'Or · La Tuque · Réservoir Cabonga · Baie St. Paul · Presque Isle · Houlton

Kenora · Sioux Lookout · Dryden · Lake of the Woods · Fort Frances · Upsala · Nipigon · Marathon · Timmins · Foleyet · Kirkland Lake · Lake Abitibi · Mont-Laurier · Québec · Lévis · Fredericton · St. Stephen

International Falls · Red Lakes · Silver Bay · Thunder Bay · Isle Royale · Copper Harbor · Keweenaw Pen. · Sault Ste. Marie · Sudbury · North Bay · Pembroke · Ottawa · Cornwall · MONTRÉAL · Granby · Sherbrooke · Drummondville · Trois Rivières · Jackman

MINNESOTA · Hibbing · Virginia · Duluth · Superior · Ironwood · Apostle Is. · Marquette · Manistique · Escanaba · Iron Mountain · Blind River · Tobermory · Parry Sound · Huntsville · Smiths Falls · Plattsburgh · Burlington · Montpelier · MAINE · Augusta

Benson · St. Cloud · Minneapolis · St. Paul · WISCONSIN · Eau Claire · Wausau · Green Bay · Traverse City · Mount Pleasant · Bay City · Saginaw · Owen Sound · Barrie · Orillia · Peterborough · Kingston · Watertown · VERMONT · 1629 · NEW HAMPSHIRE · Concord · Lewiston · Portland

Mankato · Albert Lea · Rochester · La Crosse · Madison · Oshkosh · Sheboygan · Portage · Milwaukee · Racine · Michigan · Lansing · Flint · Sarnia · Toronto · Hamilton · Lake Ontario · St. Catharines · Rochester · Syracuse · Utica · Albany · Springfield · MASS. · Worcester · Boston · Nashua · Lowell · Providence

Cedar Falls · IOWA · Cedar Rapids · Dubuque · Rockford · Waukegan · Kalamazoo · Ann Arbor · Windsor · DETROIT · London · Chatham · Erie · Jamestown · Brighamton · NEW YORK · Catskill Mts. · 1295 · Hartford · CONN. · New Haven · R.I. · New Bedford · C. Cod

Waterloo · Ames · Des Moines · Iowa City · Davenport · Clinton · Aurora · CHICAGO · Joliet · Gary · South Bend · Fort Wayne · Lima · Toledo · Cleveland · Akron · Youngstown · PENNSYLVANIA · Meadville · Scranton · Altoona · Allentown · Paterson · NEW YORK · Newark · NEW JERSEY

Omaha · Council Bluffs · Maryville · Macon · ILLINOIS · Peoria · Bloomington · INDIANA · Decatur · OHIO · Columbus · Dayton · Pittsburgh · Wheeling · Harrisburg · Trenton · PHILADELPHIA

STATES · Topeka · Kansas City · Independence · MISSOURI · St. Louis · East St. Louis · Springfield · Terre Haute · Columbus · Indianapolis · Cincinnati · Hamilton · Parkersburg · Clarksburg · MARYLAND · Washington D.C. · Baltimore · Annapolis · DELAWARE · Cambridge · Salisbury

Jefferson City · St. Louis · Mt. Vernon · Vincennes · Louisville · Frankfort · Lexington · Covington · Portsmouth · Ashland · Charleston · WEST VIRGINIA · Alexandria · Charlottesville · VIRGINIA

Nevada · Rolla · Cape Girardeau · Marion · KENTUCKY · Owensboro · Bowling Green · Beckley · Bluefield · Roanoke · Richmond · Petersburg · Norfolk · Virginia Beach · Chesapeake

Springfield · Poplar Bluff · Sikeston · Paducah · Clarksville · Kingsport · Winston-Salem · Durham · Raleigh · Greenville · Pamlico Sound · Cape Hatteras

Tulsa · Fayetteville · Jonesboro · Jackson · Nashville · Morristown · Oak Ridge · Knoxville · Greensboro · Greenville

Eufaula Lake · Russellville · Searcy · Memphis · TENNESSEE · Chattanooga · Murphy · NORTH CAROLINA · Charlotte · Fayetteville · Goldsboro · Wilmington

Hot Springs · Little Rock · ARKANSAS · Corinth · Tupelo · Decatur · Huntsville · Dalton · Gainesville · Rome · Spartanburg · Rock Hill · Jacksonville

Arkadelphia · Hope · Pine Bluff · Dumas · Clarksdale · MISSISSIPPI · Grenada · Birmingham · Anniston · Atlanta · Columbia · SOUTH CAROLINA · Florence · Myrtle Beach · Cape Fear

Texarkana · El Dorado · Greenville · Tuscaloosa · Bessemer · Auburn · La Grange · Macon · Charleston · Summerville

Longview · Monroe · Tallulah · Meridian · Demopolis · Montgomery · Columbus · GEORGIA · Vidalia · Hilton Head Island

Shreveport · Winnfield · Jackson · Brookhaven · ALABAMA · Troy · Albany · Cordele · Tifton · Jesup · Savannah · Brunswick

Palestine · Natchitoches · Natchez · Laurel · Hattiesburg · Dothan · Bainbridge · Waycross

Lufkin · Alexandria · McComb · Mobile · Evergreen · Valdosta

LOUISIANA · Beaumont · Lafayette · Baton Rouge · Biloxi · Crestview · Marianna · Panama City · Tallahassee · Lake City · Jacksonville

HOUSTON · Port Arthur · Galveston Bay · Marsh I. · Houma · Venice · Cape San Blas · Apalachee Bay · Gainesville · St. Augustine

New Orleans · Mississippi River Delta · Leesburg · Ocala · Daytona Beach

Freeport · Corda Island · Progreso · Cancún · Mérida · CUBA · Orlando · Cape Canaveral · Tampa · St. Petersburg · Melbourne · Fort Pierce · FLORIDA · Port Charlotte · West Palm Beach · Freeport City · Fort Myers · Naples · Fort Lauderdale · Hollywood · Miami · Key Largo · Bimini Is. · Key West · Straits of Florida

Gulf of Mexico

ATLANTIC OCEAN

THE BAHAMAS · Nassau · New Providence · Eleuthera · Andros · Great Bahama Bank · San Salvador · Rum Cay · Exuma Sound · Cat I. · Tropic of Cancer

LA HABANA (HAVANA) · Matanzas · Pinar del Rio · Guane · Golfo de Batabanó · Isla de la Juventud · Cienfuegos · Santa Clara · Santa la Grande · 1156 · Sancti Spiritus · Ciego de Ávila · Camagüey · Holguín · San Juan · Victoria de las Tunas · Crooked I. · Mayaguana · Acklins I. · Little Inagua · Great Inagua · Turks and Caicos Is. (U.K.) · Caicos Is. · Turks Is.

Appalachian Mountains · Mississippi · Lake Superior · Lake Michigan · Lake Huron · Georgian Bay · Lake Erie · Lake Ontario

Settlements

- ◼ over 3 million
- ◻ 1 – 3 million
- ◯ 250 000 – 1 million
- ● 100 000 – 250 000
- ◍ 25 000 – 100 000
- · under 25 000
- —— country capital underline
- —— state or province capital underline

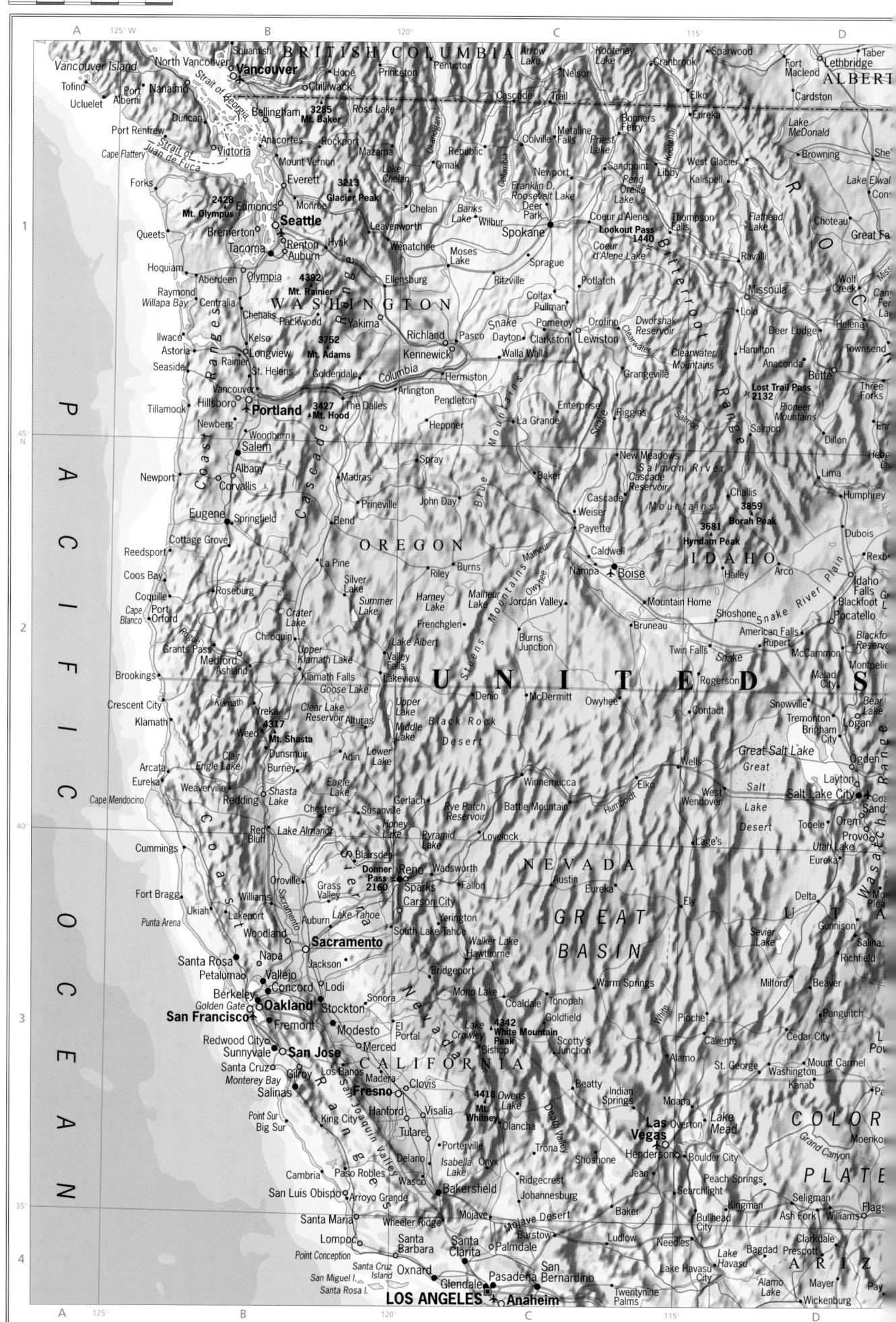

Scale 1 : 7 200 000

© Helicon Publishing Ltd

Northwest United States

Colorado • Idaho • Montana • Nebraska • Nevada
North Dakota • Oregon • South Dakota • Utah • Washington • Wyoming

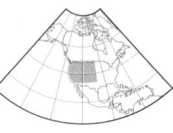

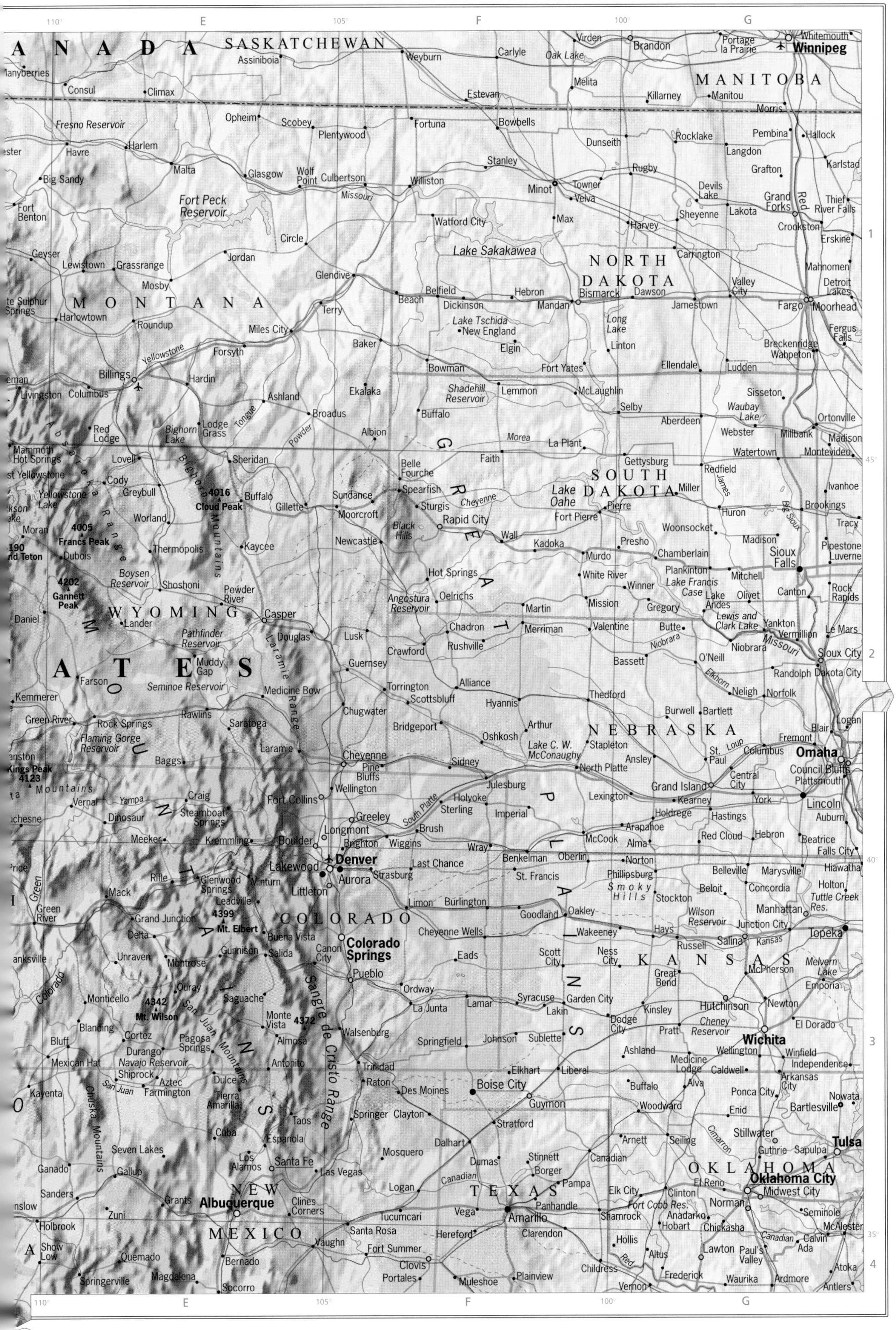

Settlements

▣	over 3 million
□	1 – 3 million
○	250 000 – 1 million
●	100 000 – 250 000
⊙	25 000 – 100 000
•	under 25 000
———	country capital underline
———	state or province capital underline

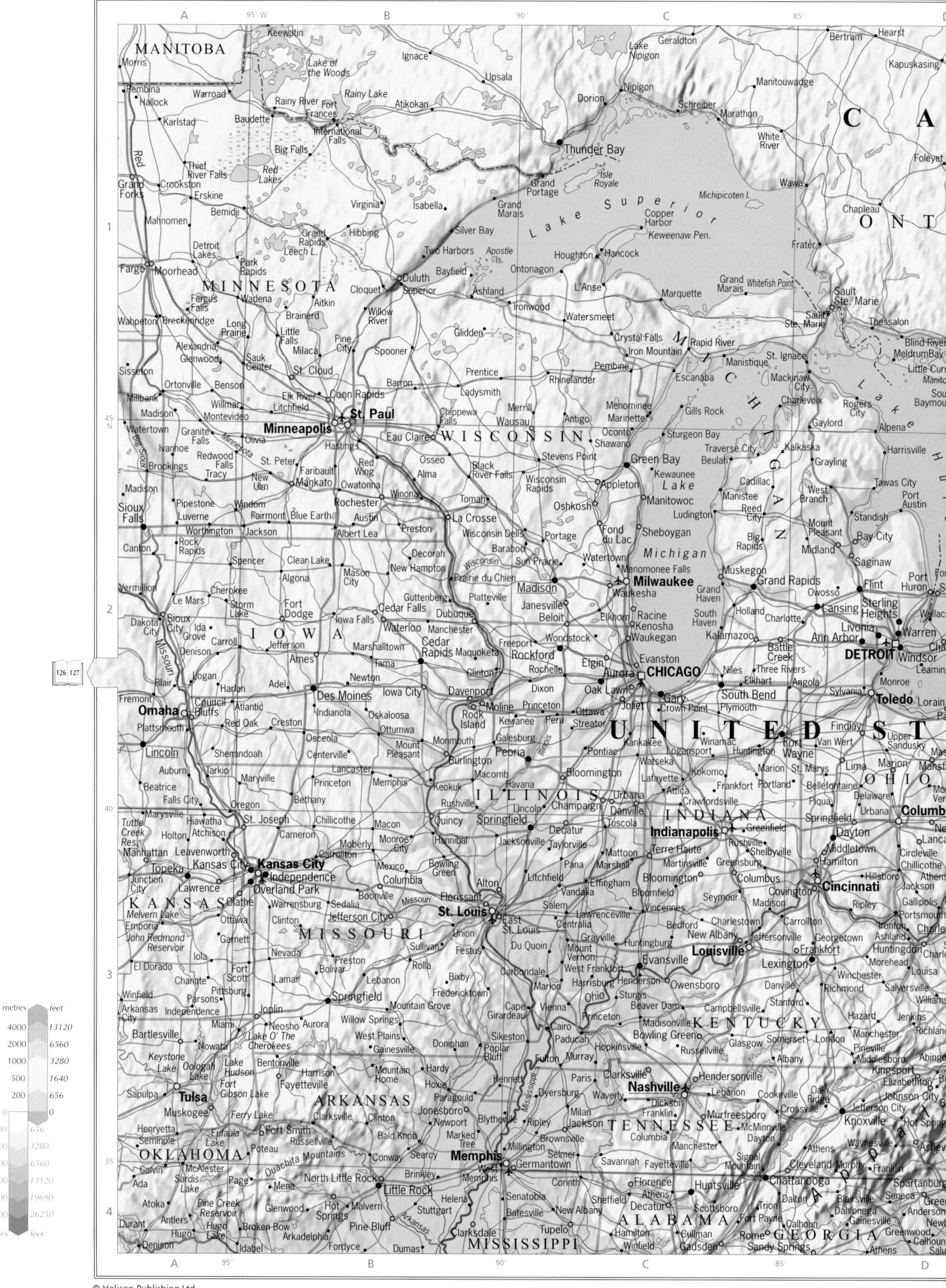

© Helicon Publishing Ltd

Connecticut • Delaware • District of Columbia • Illinois • Indiana • Iowa • Maine • Maryland • Massachusetts • Michigan
Minnesota • New Hampshire • New Jersey • New York • Ohio • Pennsylvania • Rhode Island • Vermont • West Virginia • Wisconsin

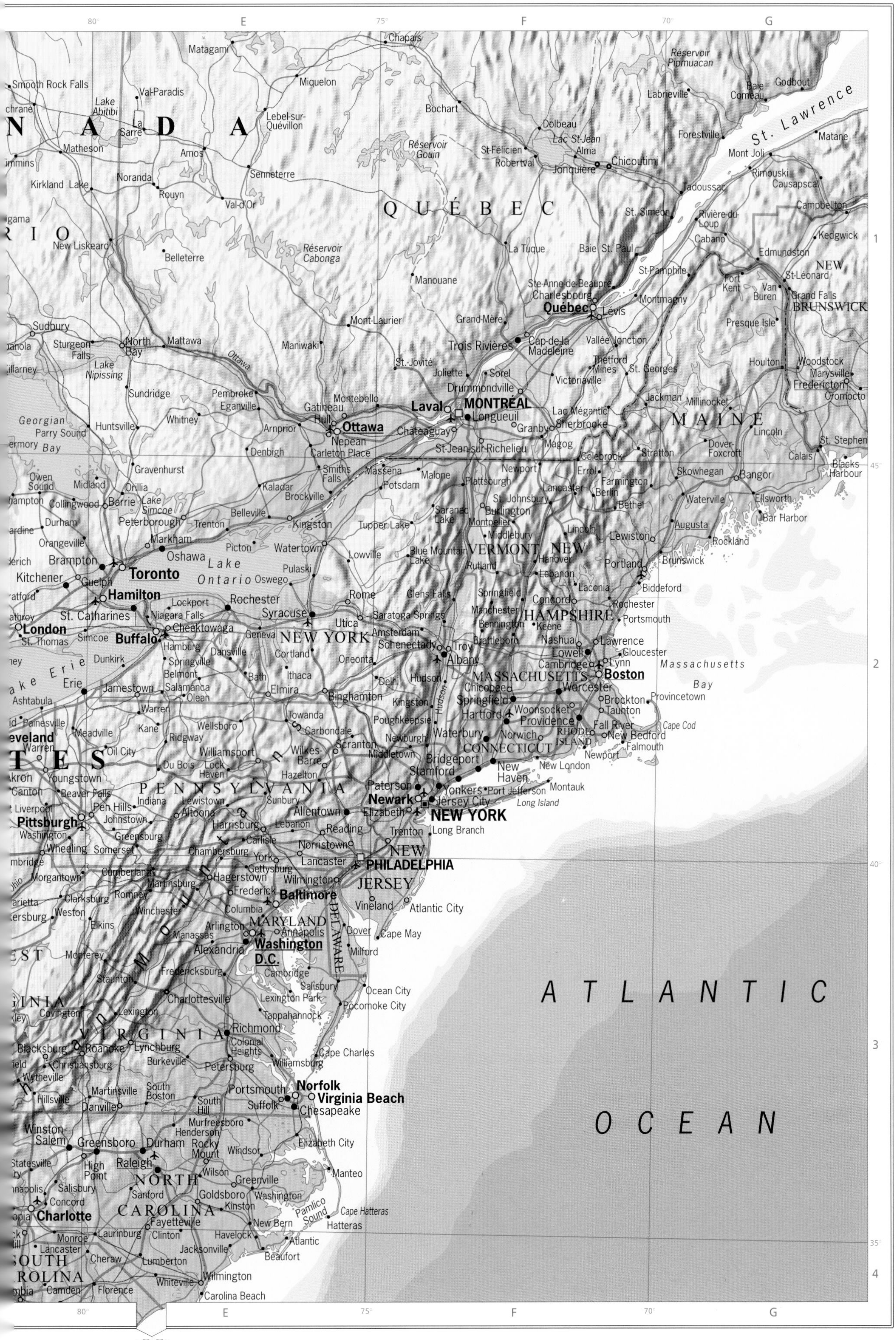

CANADA

QUÉBEC

MAINE

St. Lawrence

NEW BRUNSWICK

Réservoir Pipmuacan

Réservoir Goun

Réservoir Cabonga

Lake Abitibi

Lake Nipissing

Georgian Bay

Parry Sound

Lake Ontario

Lake Erie

VERMONT

NEW HAMPSHIRE

MASSACHUSETTS

Massachusetts Bay

Cape Cod

RHODE ISLAND

CONNECTICUT

Long Island

NEW YORK

PENNSYLVANIA

NEW JERSEY

DELAWARE

MARYLAND

Washington D.C.

WEST VIRGINIA

VIRGINIA

ALLEGHENY MOUNTAINS

NORTH CAROLINA

SOUTH CAROLINA

Pamlico Sound

ATLANTIC OCEAN

Smooth Rock Falls • Matagami • Miguelon • Chapais • Bochart • Godbout • Baie Comeau • Labrieville
Val-Paradis • Lebel-sur-Quévillon • Dolbeau • Lac St-Jean • Alma • Forestville • Matane
Matheson • Amos • Senneterre • St-Félicien • Robertval • Chicoutimi • Jonquière • Mont Joli • Rimouski • Causapscal
Noranda • Rouyn • Val-d'Or • St. Siméon • Rivière-du-Loup • Campbellton • Kedgwick
Kirkland Lake • Belleterre • Manouane • Cabano • Edmundston • Port Kent • Van Buren • Grand Falls
New Liskeard • Mont-Laurier • La Tuque • Baie St. Paul • St-Pamphile • Presque Isle • Woodstock
Sudbury • Maniwaki • Grand-Mère • Québec • Lévis • Montmagny • Houlton • Marysville • Fredericton • Oromocto
Sturgeon Falls • North Bay • Mattawa • Montebello • Trois Rivières • Cap-de-la-Madeleine • St. Georges • Jackman • Millinocket • Lincoln • St. Stephen
Sundridge • Whitney • Pembroke • Eganville • Gatineau • Hull • Laval • MONTRÉAL • Longueuil • Sherbrooke • Lac Mégantic • Stratton • Dover-Foxcroft • Calais
Huntsville • Arnprior • Ottawa • Nepean • Granby • Magog • Colebrook • Errol • Skowhegan • Bangor • Blacks Harbour
Gravenhurst • Denbigh • Smiths Falls • Massena • Malone • Plattsburgh • Newport • Berlin • Farmington • Waterville • Ellsworth
Owen Sound • Midland • Orillia • Kaladar • Brockville • Potsdam • St. Johnsbury • Montpelier • Bethel • Augusta • Bar Harbor
Collingwood • Barrie • Belleville • Kingston • Tupper Lake • Saranac Lake • Burlington • Middlebury • Lewiston • Rockland
Durham • Peterborough • Trenton • Picton • Watertown • Lowville • Blue Mountain • Rutland • Hanover • Portland • Brunswick
Orangeville • Markham • Oshawa • Pulaski • Oswego • Glens Falls • Springfield • Lebanon • Laconia • Biddeford
Toronto • Hamilton • Lockport • Rochester • Rome • Saratoga Springs • Manchester • Concord • Rochester • Portsmouth
St. Catharines • Niagara Falls • Syracuse • Amsterdam • Bennington • Keene • Nashua • Lawrence • Gloucester
London • Buffalo • Cheektowaga • Geneva • Utica • Schenectady • Troy • Albany • Brattleboro • Lowell • Lynn
Simcoe • Hamburg • Dansville • Cortland • Oneonta • Delhi • Hudson • Chicopee • Worcester • Provincetown
Dunkirk • Springville • Belmont • Bath • Ithaca • Binghamton • Kingston • Springfield • Hartford • Brockton • Taunton
Erie • Jamestown • Salamanca • Olean • Elmira • Poughkeepsie • Waterbury • Norwich • Providence • Fall River • New Bedford
Ashtabula • Warren • Kane • Ridgway • Towanda • Carbondale • Middletown • Bridgeport • New Haven • Newport • Falmouth
Painesville • Meadville • Oil City • Du Bois • Williamsport • Wilkes-Barre • Scranton • Newburgh • Stamford • New London • Montauk
Cleveland • Warren • Youngstown • Indiana • Lewistown • Lock Haven • Hazleton • Paterson • Yonkers • Port Jefferson
Akron • Canton • Beaver Falls • Altoona • Sunbury • Allentown • Newark • Jersey City • Long Branch
Pittsburgh • Johnstown • Greensburg • Harrisburg • Lebanon • Reading • Elizabeth • NEW YORK
Washington • Somerset • Chambersburg • Carlisle • Norristown • Trenton • Long Branch
Wheeling • Morgantown • Cumberland • York • Lancaster • PHILADELPHIA
Marietta • Clarksburg • Weston • Martinsburg • Hagerstown • Gettysburg • Wilmington • Vineland • Atlantic City
Parkersburg • Elkins • Romney • Frederick • Columbia • Baltimore • Dover • Cape May
Monterey • Winchester • Arlington • Annapolis • Milford
Staunton • Manassas • Alexandria • Washington D.C. • Cambridge
Fredericksburg • Salisbury • Ocean City
Charlottesville • Lexington Park • Pocomoke City
Lexington • Tappahannock
Covington • Richmond • Colonial Heights • Williamsburg • Cape Charles
Blacksburg • Roanoke • Lynchburg • Burkeville • Petersburg • Cape Charles
Christiansburg • Wytheville • South Boston • Portsmouth • Norfolk • Virginia Beach
Hillsville • Martinsville • South Hill • Suffolk • Chesapeake
Danville • Murfreesboro • Henderson • Windsor • Elizabeth City
Winston-Salem • Greensboro • Durham • Rocky Mount • Manteo
Statesville • High Point • Raleigh • Wilson • Washington
Salisbury • Concord • Sanford • Goldsboro • Kinston • New Bern • Cape Hatteras
Charlotte • Fayetteville • Greenville • Havelock • Hatteras
Monroe • Laurinburg • Clinton • Atlantic • Beaufort
Lancaster • Cheraw • Lumberton • Jacksonville
Camden • Whiteville • Wilmington • Carolina Beach
Columbia • Florence

Settlements

- ■ over 3 million
- □ 1 – 3 million
- ○ 250 000 – 1 million
- ● 100 000 – 250 000
- ◉ 25 000 – 100 000
- • under 25 000
- ___ country capital underline
- ___ state or province capital underline

130 131

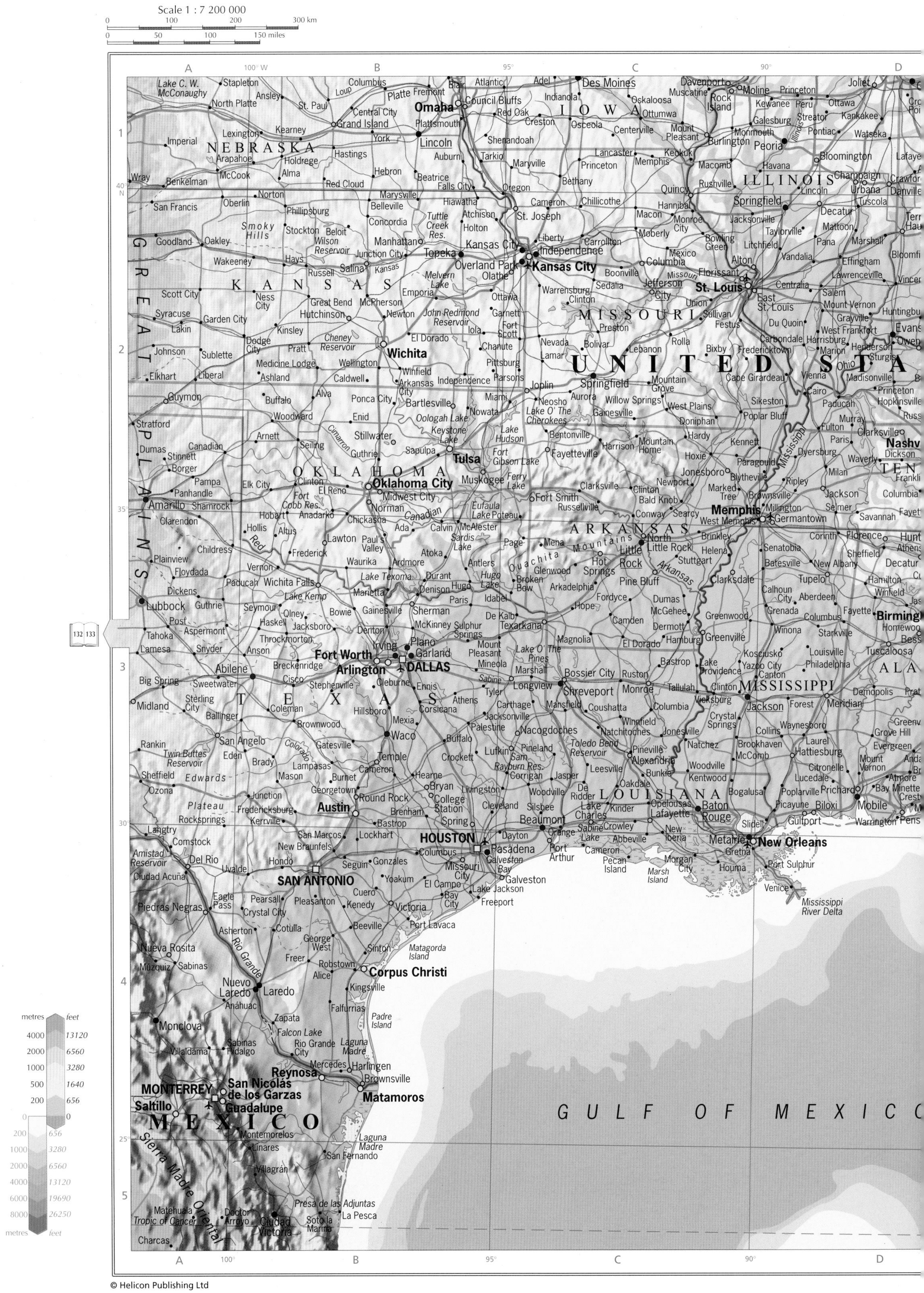

Scale 1 : 7 200 000

0   100   200   300 km
0   50   100   150 miles

© Helicon Publishing Ltd

GULF OF MEXICO

NEBRASKA · KANSAS · OKLAHOMA · TEXAS · MEXICO · IOWA · ILLINOIS · MISSOURI · UNITED STATES · ARKANSAS · LOUISIANA · MISSISSIPPI · TENNESSEE · OHIO · ALABAMA

GREAT PLAINS

metres / feet
4000 13120
2000 6560
1000 3280
500 1640
200 656
0 0
200 656
1000 3280
2000 6560
4000 13120
6000 19690
8000 26250
metres / feet

132 133

SOUTHEAST UNITED STATES

Alabama • Arkansas • The Bahamas • Florida • Georgia • Kentucky • Louisiana
Mississippi • Missouri • North Carolina • South Carolina • Tennessee • Texas • Virginia

128 129

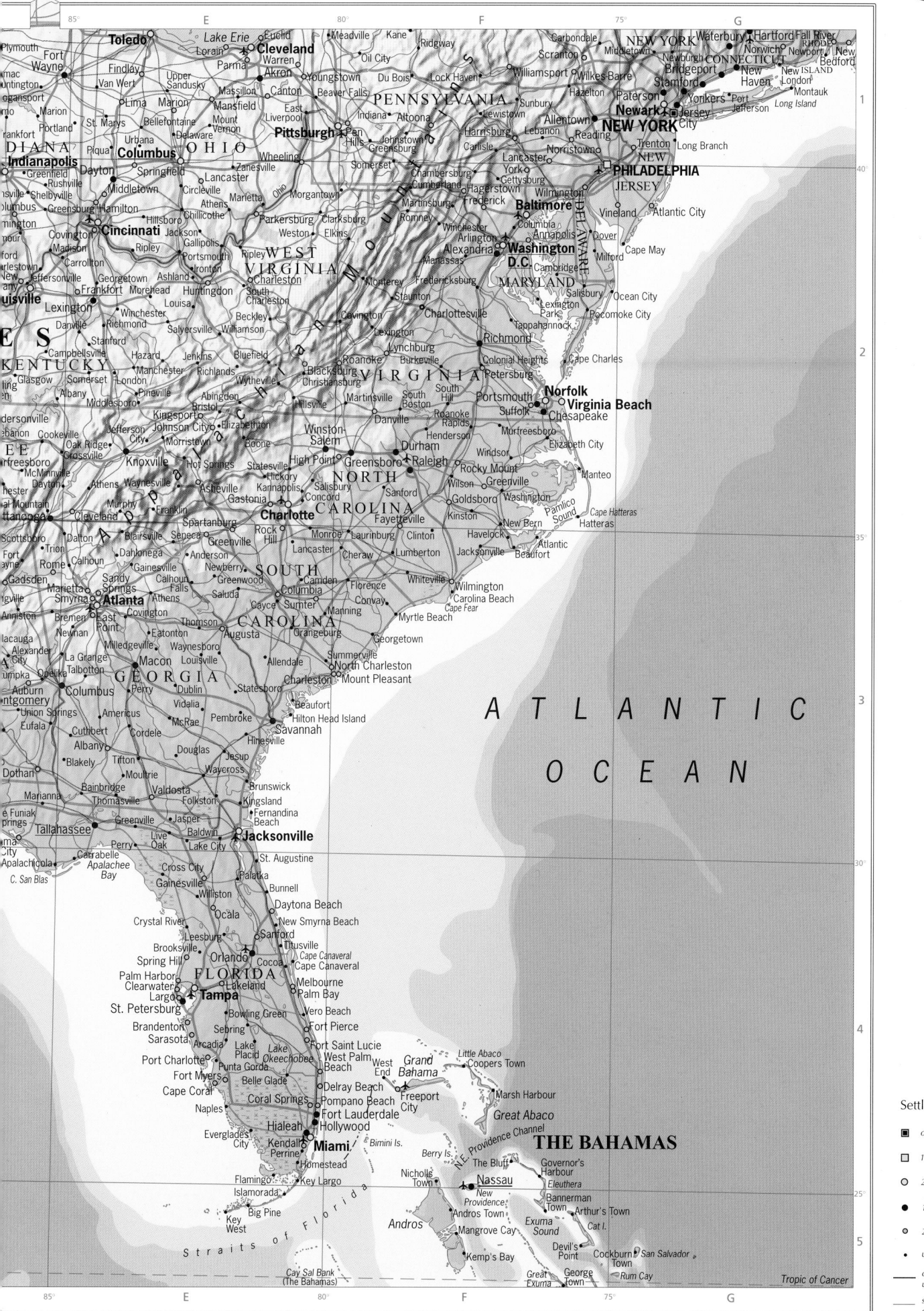

Settlements

- ■ over 3 million
- □ 1 – 3 million
- ○ 250 000 – 1 million
- ● 100 000 – 250 000
- ○ 25 000 – 100 000
- • under 25 000
- — country capital underline
- — state or province capital underline

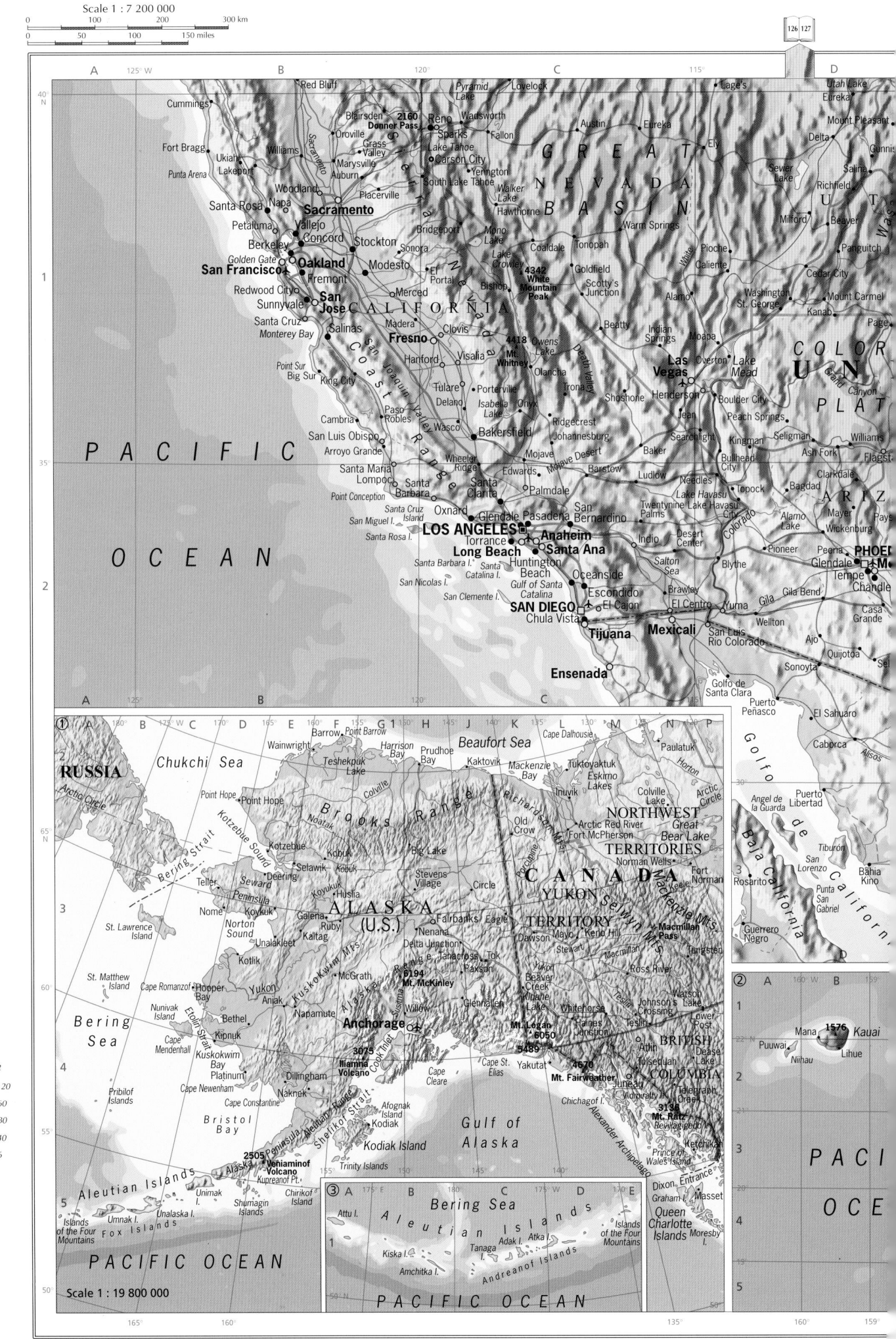

Scale 1 : 7 200 000

© Helicon Publishing Ltd

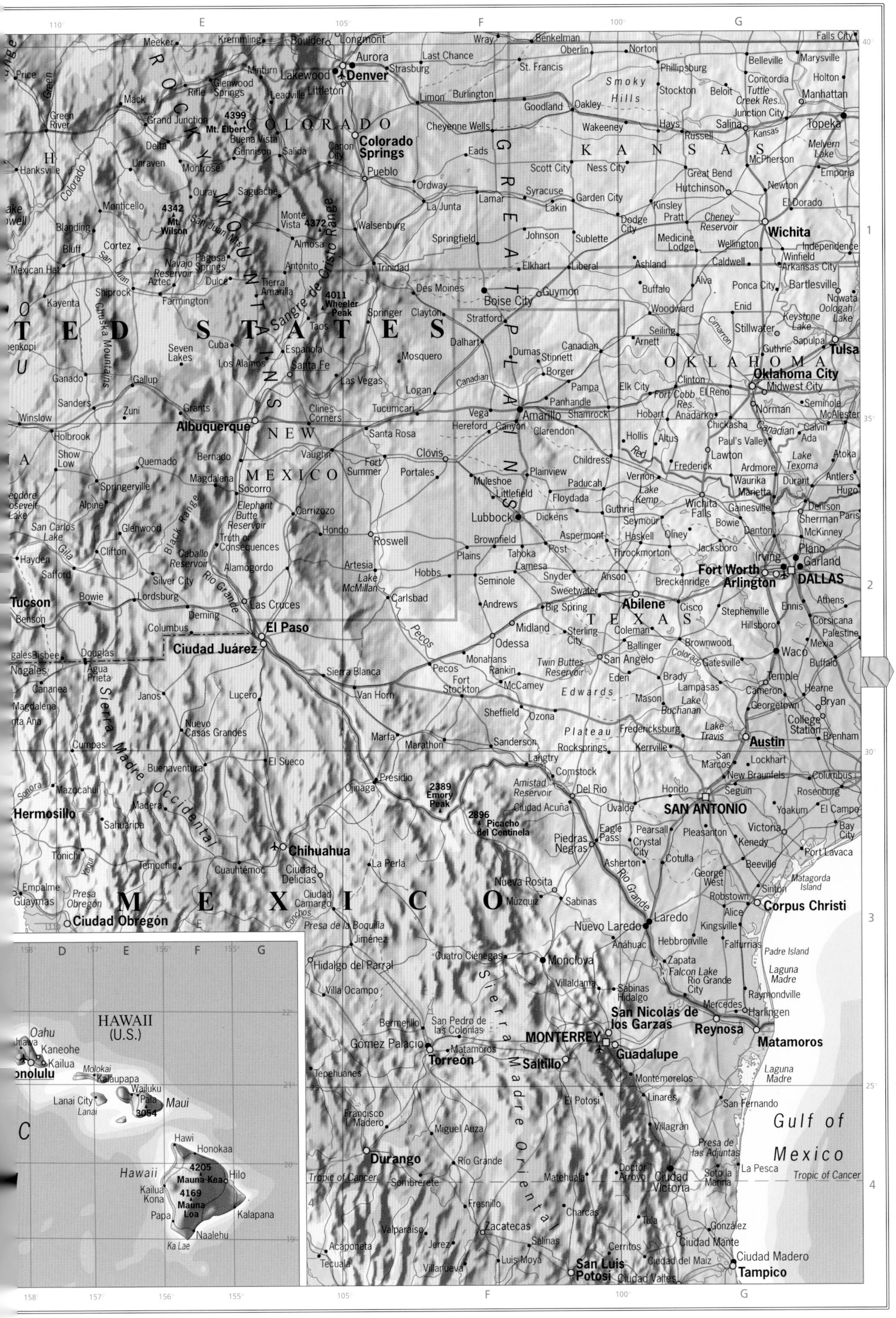

Settlements

- ▣ over 3 million
- ▢ 1 – 3 million
- ◯ 250 000 – 1 million
- ● 100 000 – 250 000
- ◦ 25 000 – 100 000
- · under 25 000
- ⎯⎯ country capital underline
- ⎯⎯ state or province capital underline

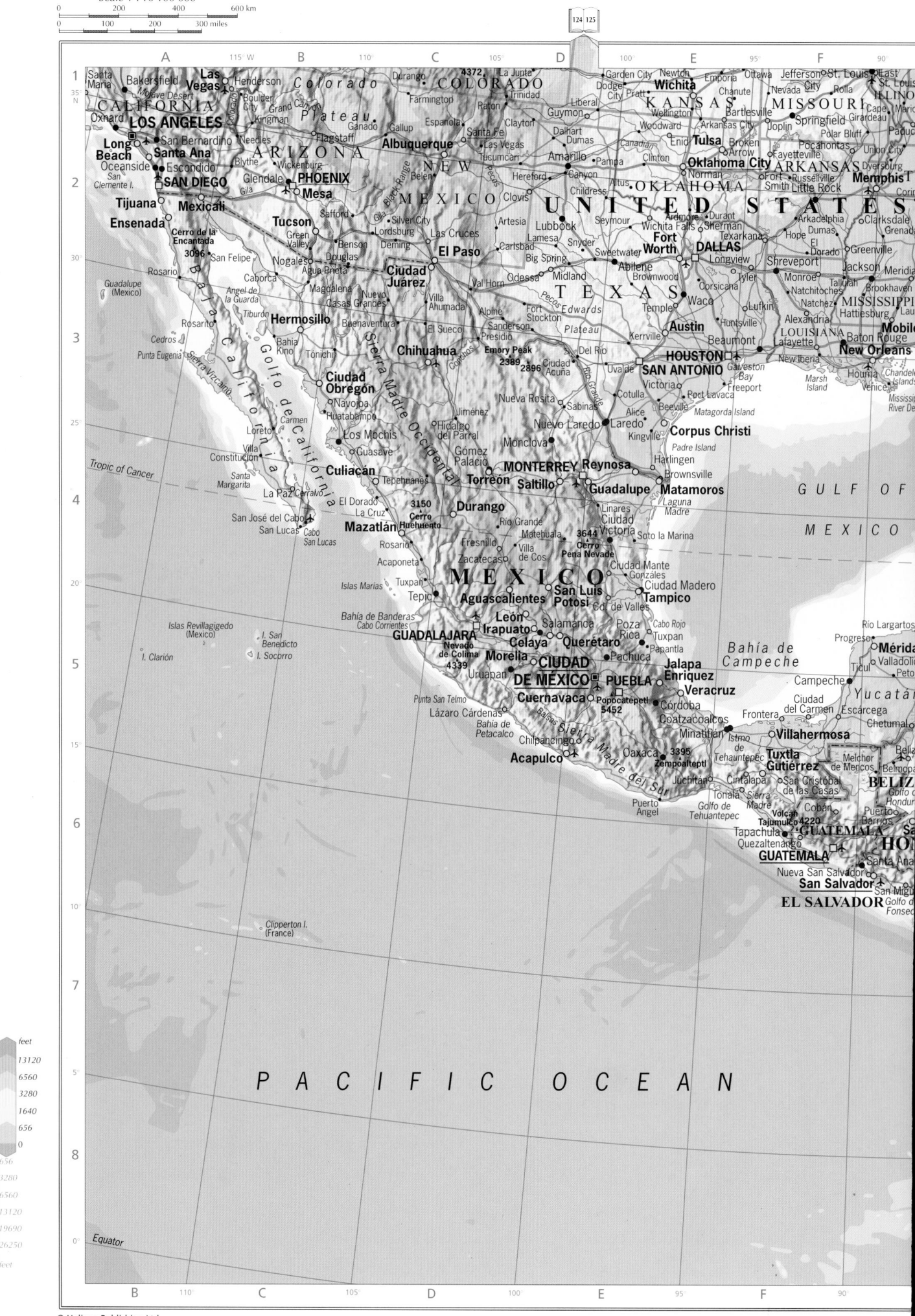

Scale 1 : 16 100 000

124 125

G 85° H 80° J 75° K 70° L 65° M 60° N

Vincennes
Louisville Ohio Ashland
Frankfort Lexington Charleston MARYLAND
Evansboro Beckley Salisbury
KENTUCKY WEST Petersburg
Clarksville VIRGINIA Bluefield Richmond
Kingsport VIRGINIA Norfolk 1
Nashville Knoxville Winston- Durham Raleigh Virginia Beach
Chattanooga Oak Ridge Salem
TENNESSEE Charlotte NORTH Cape Hatteras
Huntsville Gainesville Spartanburg Rock Hill CAROLINA
Decatur Rome SOUTH Wilmington Cape Lookout
Birmingham Columbia CAROLINA Onslow 2
ALABAMA La Grange GEORGIA Bay
Bessemer Auburn Macon Charleston Cape Fear
Tuscaloosa Columbus Hilton Head Island Long
Montgomery Albany Jesup Savannah Bay

Troy
Evergreen Tifton Brunswick
Dothan Bainbridge Waycross
Crestview Valdosta ATLANTIC 3
Panama Tallahassee Lake City Jacksonville
City FLORIDA St. Augustine OCEAN
Cape Apalachee Daytona Beach Bermuda (U.K.)
San Blas Bay Ocala Hamilton 30°
Leesburg Orlando Cape Canaveral
Tampa Melbourne
Clearwater Fort Pierce
St. Petersburg
Port Charlotte Freeport Little Abaco
Fort Myers Fort Grand Marsh Harbour 25° 4
Naples Lauderdale Bahama Great Abaco
Hollywood Bimini
Miami Is. THE
Key West Nassau BAHAMAS Eleuthera
Straits of Florida New Tropic of Cancer
Providence Cat I. San Salvador
LA HABANA Matanzas Andros
(HAVANA) Sagua Great Exuma Rum Cay
Pinar del Río Güines la Grande Santa Clara Exuma Sound Long Crooked I.
Guane Golfo de 1156 Sancti Spíritus Arch. de Mayaguana
Isla de la Cienfuegos San Ciego Camagüey Acklins I. Turks and Caicos Is. (U.K.)
Cabo Juventud Juan de Ávila Camagüey Little Inagua Caicos Is. 20°
Catoche CUBA Holguín Turks Is.
Cancún Victoria de las Tunas Great DOMINICAN Leeward Islands 5
Isla de Bayamo Inagua REPUBLIC Virgin Anguilla
Cozumel Manzanillo Guantánamo Cap- Hispaniola Islands (U.K.) St. Maarten (Netherlands)
Cayman Islands Cabo Cruz Haïtien Santiago (U.K.) St. Barthélemy (France)
(U.K.) Santiago HAITI 3175 La Vega San Juan Saba ANTIGUA
Montego de Cuba Pico La Romana 1838 (Neth. AND BARBUDA
Bay Île de la Duarte Caguas Antilles) Antigua
JAMAICA Gonâve PORT-AU-PRINCE Maya- Ponce ST. KITTS Montserrat Guadeloupe (France)
Kingston Jacmel güez Puerto AND Marie Galante 15°
Swan Islands Windward Passage Cabo Rico NEVIS (U.K.) DOMINICA
(Honduras) Beata (U.S.) Virgin Roseau
Islas Mona Passage Islands Basse-Terre Martinique (France)
de Greater Antilles (U.S.)
la Bahía Fort-de-France ST. LUCIA
Cabo Camarón Castries
Pedro Sula Laguna de CARIBBEAN SEA BARBADOS 6
HONDURAS Caratasca ST. VINCENT & Bridgetown
Tegucigalpa Cabo Gracias a Dios THE GRENADINES Kingstown
Coco Cayos Miskitos GRENADA 10°
NICARAGUA Puerto Cabezas St. George's Tobago
Managua Isla de Providencia (Colombia) Netherlands TRINIDAD AND
Antilles TOBAGO
Rama Willemstad Güiria Port of Spain
Rivas Bluefields Isla de San Andrés (Colombia) Aruba Isla de Carúpano
Lago de (Neth.) Islas Los Margarita Porlamar Trinidad
Canada Nicaragua Punta Gallinas Roques Cumaná Maturín
Santa Elena Península de Ríohacha San Juan de Boca
nta Elena Cabo Guajira Santa Marta los Cayos La Grande
Puntarenas San Juan BARRANQUILLA P. Cristóbal Golfo de Coro CARACAS Tortuga Barcelona Delta del Orinoco 5°
Limón Golfo de los Colón 5775 Venezuela MARACAIBO Maracay Petare (Orinoco Delta)
San José Mosquitos Cartagena Cabimas Los Teques El Tigre Ciudad
COSTA Chirripó Canal de Panamá Valledupar Barquisimeto Valencia San Juan de Guayana
RICA 3820 Colón (Panama Canal) Golfo del Monteria Valera Acarigua los Morros Ciudad Bolívar 7
San José PANAMA Darién Sincelejo El Banco Mérida Guanare El Baúl Calabozo El Callao
Volcán 3475 Panamá La Caucasia Ocaña Barinas Achaguas San Fernando El Dorado
Barú David Chitré Palma Turbo Cúcuta San Cristóbal de Apure Maripa La Paragua
Golfo de Peninsula Golfo de Monteria Pamplona VENEZUELA Cerro Yavi
Chiriquí de Azuero Panamá Cúcuta Puerto 2441 0°
Isla Punta 4083 Bucaramanga Apure Carreño La Gran
Coiba Mariato Bello 5493 Puerto Puerto Ayacucho Sabana
Golfo de MEDELLÍN Nuevo Cerro
Cupica La Dorada Tunja BOGOTÁ Meta Marahuaca
Quibdó Manizales Sogamoso Orocué 2579
Isla de Coco Nuquí Pereira Ibagué Villavicencio Puerto RORAIMA
(Costa Rica) Cabo Corrientes Armenia 4560 Inírida Serra
Buenaventura Palmira San José La Esmeralda Parima
Isla de Malpelo Tumaco Patia CALI de Ocuné Inírida
(Colombia) 5750 Neiva Guaviare Orinoco
Popayán Mesa de San Carlos 8
4685 Yambi Cerro
COLOMBIA Calamar Marahuaca
Isla Gorgona Miraflores Mitú Pico da BRAZIL
Tumaco Neblina
Pasto Florencia 3014
AMAZONAS Cucuí
Equator 0°

H 80° J 75° K 70° L 65° M

140 141

Settlements

□ over 3 million
□ 1 – 3 million
○ 250 000 – 1 million
● 100 000 – 250 000
◉ 25 000 – 100 000
• under 25 000
— country capital underline
— state or province capital underline

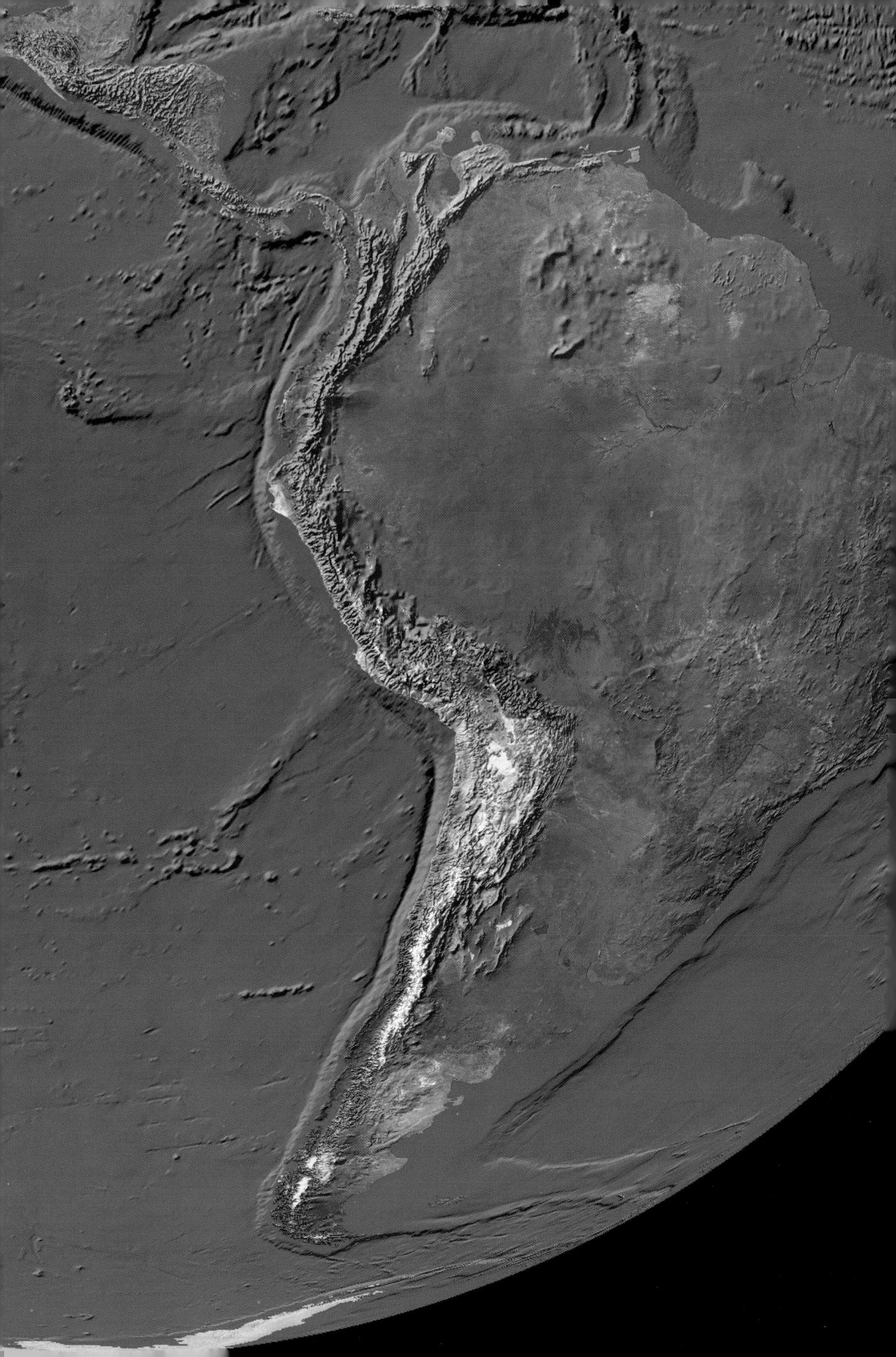

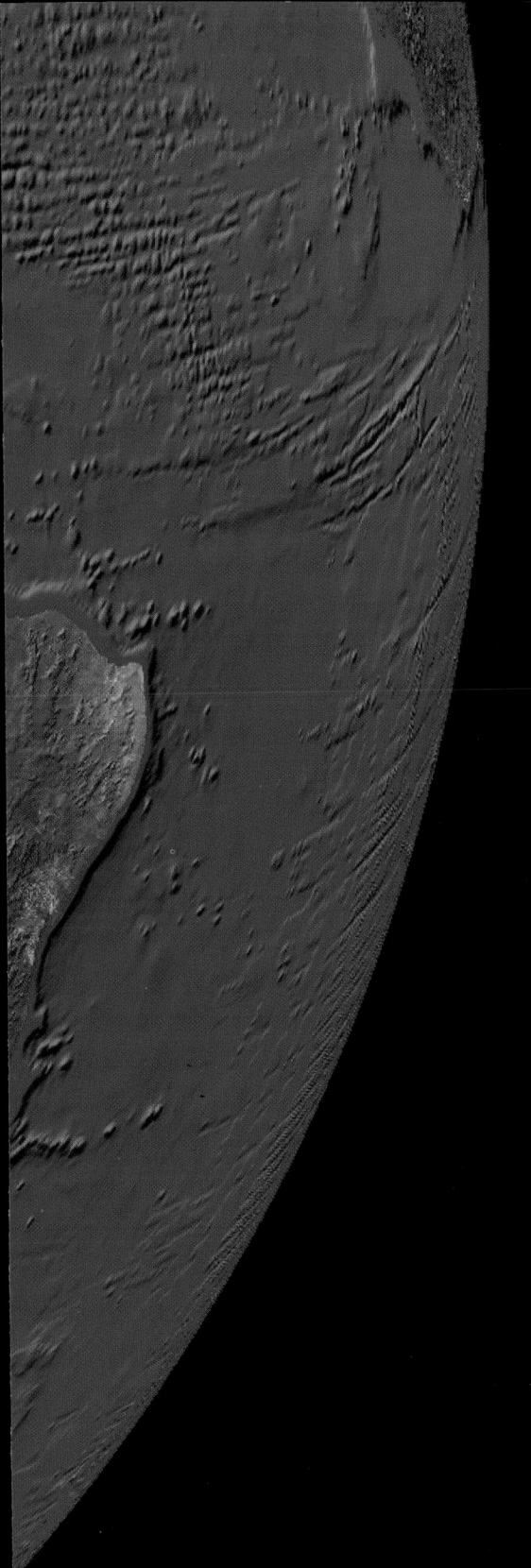

SOUTH AMERICA

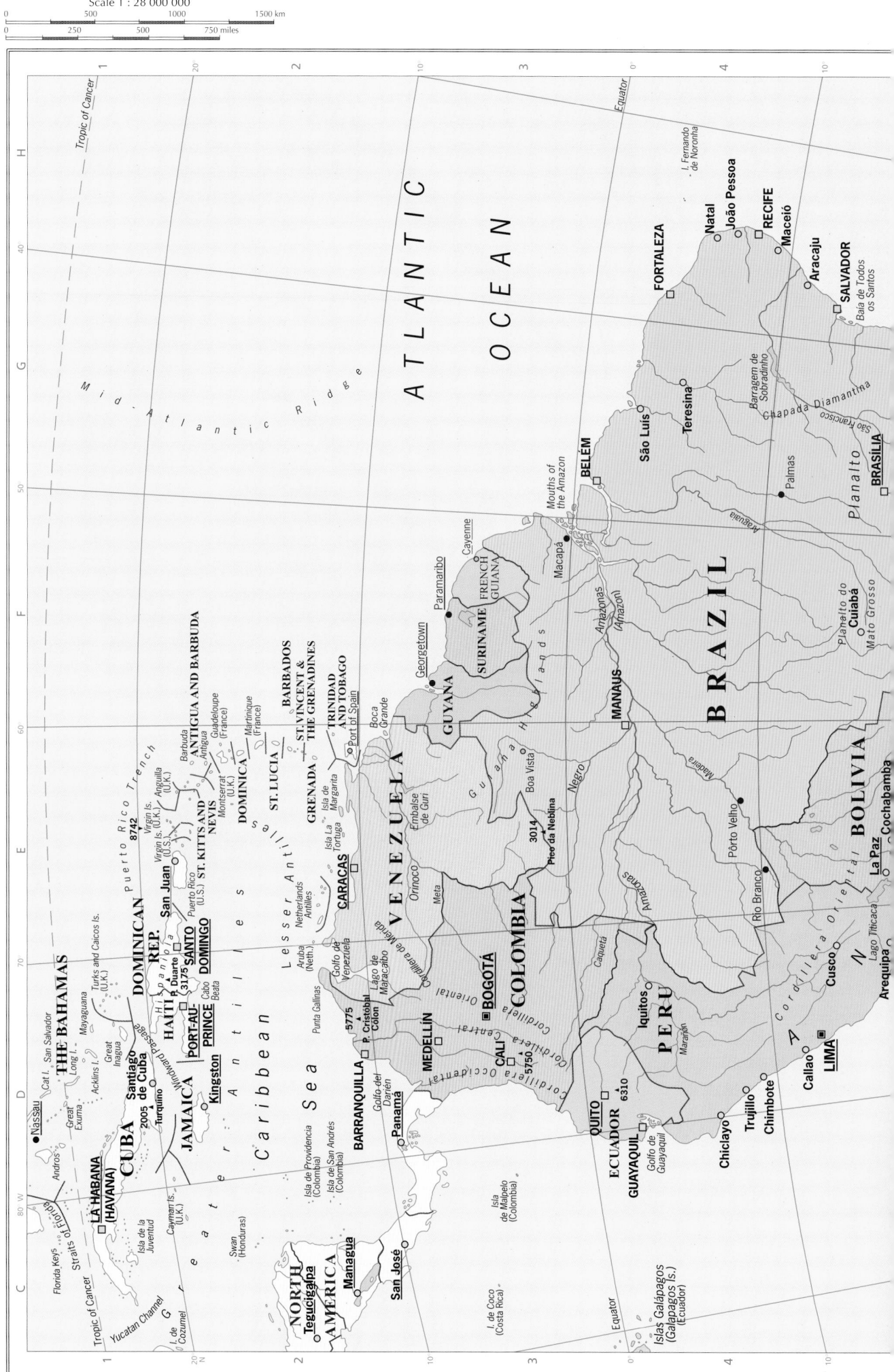

Scale 1 : 28 000 000

0   500   1000   1500 km
0   250   500   750 miles

© Helicon Publishing Ltd

PACIFIC OCEAN

ATLANTIC OCEAN

SCOTIA SEA

ARGENTINA

PARAGUAY

URUGUAY

CHILE

BELO HORIZONTE
Campo Grande
SÃO PAULO
Ribeirão Prêto
Niterói
RIO DE JANEIRO
Vitória
Santos
CURITIBA
Florianópolis
PORTO ALEGRE
Rio Grande
Lagoa dos Patos
Asunción
Resistencia
San Miguel de Tucuman
Santa Fé
Rosario
CÓRDOBA
Mendoza
Aconcagua 6960
Ojos del Salado 6908
Valparaíso
SANTIAGO
Talcahuano
Valdivia
MONTEVIDEO
La Plata
BUENOS AIRES
Embalse del Rio Negro
Laguna Mar Chiquita
Bahía Blanca
Neuquén
Golfo San Matías
Comodoro Rivadavia
Golfo de San Jorge
Río Gallegos
Bahía Grande
Punta Arenas
Isla Grande de Tierra del Fuego
Isla de los Estados
Cabo de Hornos (Cape Horn)
Archipiélago de los Chonos
Isla de Chiloé
Archipiélago de la Reina Adelaida

Paraguay
Paraná
Serra de
Sierra de Catalasteo
Pampas
Patagonia

Chile Trench
Nazca Ri...
Lago de Poopó
Tarija
Central
Occidental

Islas de los Desventurados (Chile)
Islas Juan Fernández (Chile)

Drake Passage

Falkland Is. (U.K.)
Stanley
East Falkland
West Falkland
Scotia Ridge
South Georgia (U.K.)
Shag Rocks (U.K.)
South Orkney Is. (U.K.)
South Shetland Is. (U.K.)
South Sandwich Is. (U.K.)
South Sandwich Trench
Meteor Depth 8325
Traversay Is.
Candlemas I.
Saunders I.
Montague I.

Ilha da Trindade (Brazil)
Ilhas Martin Vaz (Brazil)
Tropic of Capricorn
Tropic of Capricorn

Rio de la Plata

Scale 1 : 16 100 000

CARIBBEAN SEA
Lesser Antilles

NICARAGUA

COSTA
RICA
San José
Chirripó
3820

Volcán Barú
3475

PANAMA

Panamá

COLOMBIA

VENEZUELA

MARACAIBO

CARACAS

ECUADOR

QUITO

GUAYAQUIL

PERU

LIMA
Callao

BOLIVIA

La Paz

CHILE

PACIFIC

OCEAN

ARGENTINA

① A   90° W   B
I. Culpepper   Islas Galápagos
                (Galapagos Islands)
1 I. Wenman   (Ecuador)
        Isla
        Pinta
            Isla Marchena
  Equator
        Isla San Salvador
  Isla   Isla Santa Cruz
  Fernandina   Isla
                    San Cristóbal
2 Isla Isabela
        Isla Santa   Isla
        María   Española

metres   feet
4000   13120
2000   6560
1000   3280
 500   1640
 200   656
   0   0
 200   656
1000   3280
2000   6560
4000   13120
6000   19690
8000   26250
metres   feet

© Helicon Publishing Ltd

Settlements

- ■ *over 3 million*
- □ *1 – 3 million*
- ○ *250 000 – 1 million*
- ● *100 000 – 250 000*
- ◦ *25 000 – 100 000*
- · *under 25 000*
- —— *country capital underline*
- —— *state or province capital underline*

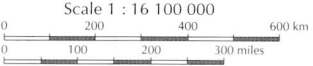

PERU
Nazca Nudo Coropuna, 6425 Puno
Lomas Arequipa Juli Lago Titicaca Montero El Cerro San José de Chiquitos
Atico Guaqui La Paz Cochabamba Santa Cruz
Camana Corocoro Oruro Totora Samaipata Robore
Mollendo Ilo Nevado Poopó Samaipata Bañados
Tacna Sajama Challapata BOLIVIA del Izozog
Arica 6542 Sucre Lagunillas
Cuya Rio Potosí Boyuibe Bahía
Mulatos Villa Fortín Coronel Cha
Salar de Uyuni Montes Eugenio Garay
Iquique Uyuni Tupiza Tarija La Esmeralda Bore
Quillagua Volcán Villazón Mariscal
Tocopilla San La Quiaca Orán Tartagal Estigar
María Elena Pedro Chuquicamata Tartagal Embarcación Filadélfia
Punta Angamos 6159 Calama Los Blancos Teuco PA
Baquedano San Salvador San Pedro Las Lomitas
Antofagasta San Antonio de Jujuy Esteros
Los Vientos Volcán de los Cobres Salta Monte
Santa Catalina Llullaillaco 6723 6720 Nevados Quemado Castelli
Taltal 6440 de Cachi Metán Campo Gallo Presidencia
Punta Ballena Volcán Tafi Viejo Sáenz Pe
Antofalla San Miguel La Banda Quimili Resister
Chañaral Ojos del de Tucumán Santiago del Estero General
Salado Paso de San Francisco La Banda Añatuya
Caldera 6908 4722 Andalgalá Catamarca Recongu
Copiapó 6872 Cerro Tinogasta Frias Ceres San Cris
Bonete Recreo Salinas
Huasco Majicana La Rioja Grandes Morteros
Cabo Bascuñán 6250 Dean Rafaela San
Cruz del Eje Funes San Francisco
La Serena Rivadavia 6332 San José Chepes CÓRDOBA Las Varillas
Coquimbo Cerro de Jáchal Cerro Champaqui Villa
Punta Lengua de Vaca Las Tortolas 2880 Rosario
Ovalle San Juan Rio Cuarto San Nicol
Combarbalá Cerro Paso de la San Luis de los Arroy
Mercedario Cumbre Mendoza La Toma Pergami
6770 3832 Mercedes Justo
Cerro Aconcagua 6960 Cerro Tupungato Daract Labouldye
Viña del Mar 6800 Huinca Renancó 9 de Juli
Valparaíso SANTIAGO Beazley San
San Antonio San Bernardo Villa Huidobro Realicó Pehuajó
Rancagua San Rafael Pico
Pichilemu San Fernando General Alvear General Pico Catriló
Curicó Telén Coronel
Talca 3810 Santa Santa Rosa Suárez
Linares 2500 Cerro Isabel
Cauquenes 4709 Nevado General Acha Rivera Cerro
San Carlos Volcán Tres
Tomé Domuyo ARGENTINA Picos
Talcahuano Chillán Puelén Bahía
Concepción Los Angeles Puelches Blanca
Punta Lavapié Angol Neuquén Rio Colorado Pedro
Lebu 1884 Rio Negro Luro
Victoria Paso de Gen. Roca San Antonio
Temuco Hachado Oeste Vied
Volcán Sierra Colorada
Valdivia Lanin Golfo
Punta Galera 3740 Valcheta San Matías
Osorno Maquinchao Sierra Grande Puerto Punta
Ingeniero Madryn Penins
Puerto Montt San Carlos Jacobacci Telsen Valdés
Maullín de Bariloche Gastre Trelew
Ancud Minchinmávida Paso de Chubut Rawson
Isla de 2470 Indios
Chiloé 2300 Las Plumas
Volcán José de San Martín Camarones
Corcovado Cabo dos Bahías
Golfo de Corcovado Nueva Comodoro Rivadavia
Isla Guafo Lubecka Golfo de
Archipiélago Puerto Aisén Colonia San Jorge
Las Heras
de los Coihaique Deseado Cabo Tres Puntas
Paso Deseado
Río Mayo Punta Medanosa
Chonos Chile Chico Perito
4058 Moreno Las Horquetas
Cerro 3700 Gobernador
San Valentin Cerro Gregores San Julián
Golfo San Lorenzo Chico
de Penas Cabo San Francisco de P
Isla Tres Lagos Puerto Santa Cruz
Campana Lago Bahía
Isla 3600 Santa Cruz Grande
Wellington Cerro Argentino Oy Río Gallegos
Muralión
Puerto Natales El Turbio Punta Dungeness
Río Verde
Archipiélago de Isla Isla Grande
la Reina Adelaida Riesco de
Isla Río Grande
Punta Arenas Tierra del Fuego
Isla Desolación Cabo
Isla Santa Inés San Diego
Isla 2469
Clarence Cerro Isla
Isla Londonderry Yogan Navarino Islas Wolla
Isla Hoste Cabo de Hor
(Cape Hor)

PACIFIC
OCEAN

Islas de los Desventurados
(Chile)
San Félix San Ambrosio

Tropic of Capricorn

Nazca Ridge

Peru-Ch

Isla
Robinson Crusoe
Islas Juan Fernández
(Chile)
Isla
Alejandro Selkirk

metres feet
4000 13120
2000 6560
1000 3280
500 1640
200 656
0
200 656
1000 3280
2000 6560
4000 13120
6000 19690
8000 26250
metres feet

Drake Passage

© Helicon Publishing Ltd

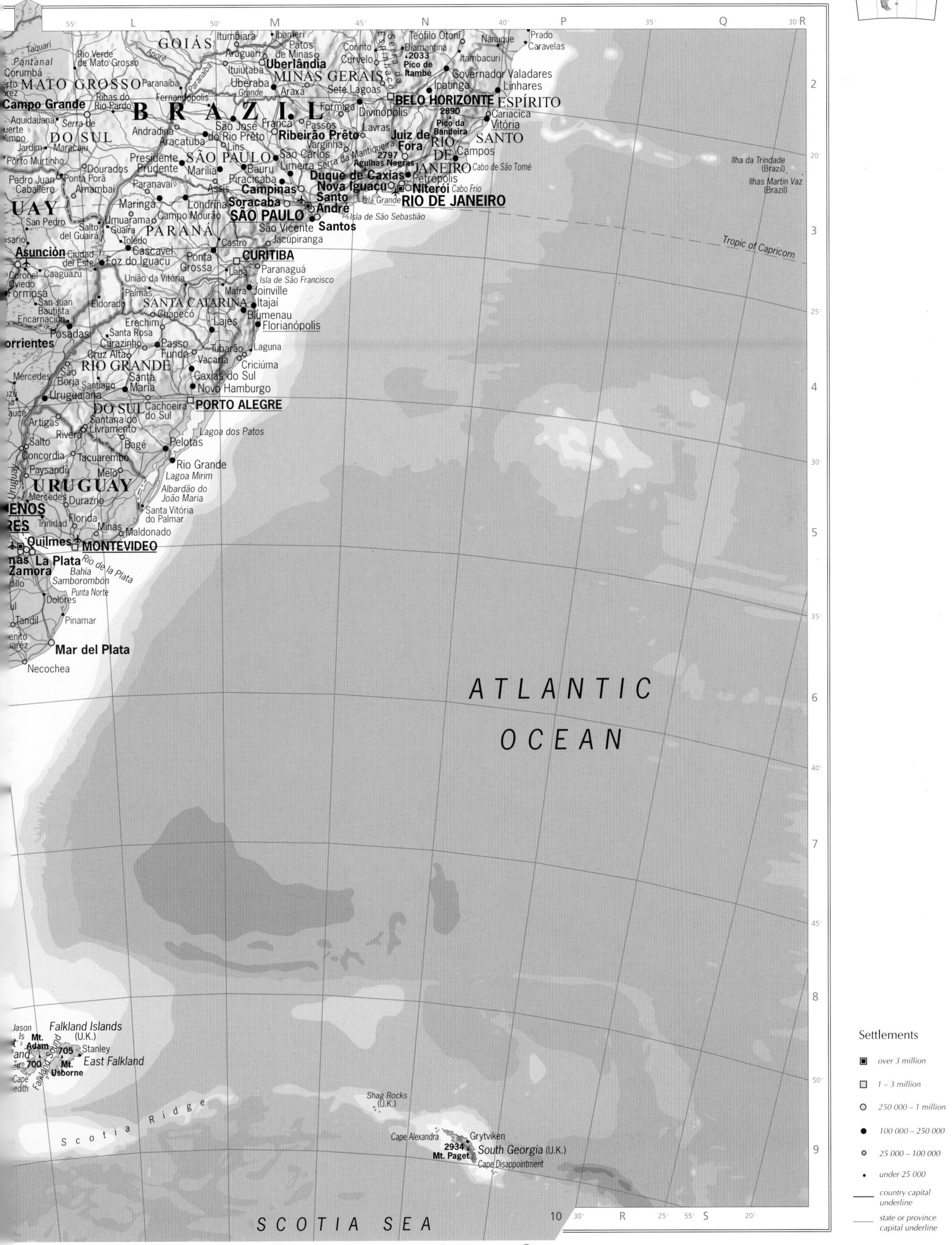

SOUTHERN SOUTH AMERICA

Argentina • Chile • Falkland Islands • Paraguay • Uruguay

L 50° M 45° N 40° P 35° Q 30° R

GOIÁS
Taquari
Pántanal
Corumbá
Corumbá
rto Grande
Campo Grande
MATO GROSSO
DO SUL
Aquidauana
Rio Verde
de Mato Grosso
Apore
Ituiutaba
Araguari
Ibameri
Ipameri
Itumbiara
Patos
de Minas
Corinto
Curvelo
Diamantina
Teófilo Otoni
Naruque
Prado
Caravelas
Uberlândia
MINAS GERAIS
2033
Pico de
Itambé
Itambacuri
Governador Valadares
Linhares
Uberaba
Araxá
Sete Lagoas
Ipatinga
Ribas do
Rio Pardo
Paranaíba
Fernandópolis
Andradina
Formiga
BELO HORIZONTE
2890
Pico da
Bandeira
ESPÍRITO
Cariacica
Vitória
SANTO
uerte
Maracaju
Jardim
Porto Murtinho
Dourados
Presidente
Prudente
São José
do Rio Prêto
Franca
Lins
Passos
Lavras
Ribeirão Prêto
Varginha
2797
Agulhas Negras
Juiz de
Fora
RIO DE
JANEIRO
Campos
Cabo de São Tomé
Pedro Juan
Amambaí
Ponta Porã
SÃO PAULO
Marília
Bauru
São Carlos
Limeira
Serra da Mantiqueira
Petrópolis
Cabo Frio
UAY
Paranavaí
Assis
Campinas
Piracicaba
Duque de Caxias
Nova Iguaçu
Niterói
San Pedro
Maringá
Campo Mourão
Londrina
Soracaba
Santo
André
Santos
RIO DE JANEIRO
rio
Salto
del Guairá
Guaíra
Umuarama
SÃO PAULO
São Vicente
Isla Grande
Isla de São Sebastião
Asunción
PARANÁ
Toledo
Castro
Jacupiranga
Ciudad
del Este
Foz do Iguaçu
Cascavel
Ponta
Grossa
Lapa
CURITIBA
Paranaguá
Isla de São Francisco
Tropic of Capricorn
Coronel
Caaguazu
Oviedo
União da Vitória
Palmas
Mafra
Joinville
Formosa
Eldorado
Itajaí
Blumenau
San Juan
Bautista
Carazinho
SANTA CATARINA
Chapecó
Lajes
Florianópolis
Encarnación
Posadas
Erechim
Santa Rosa
orrientes
Cruz Alta
Passo
Fundo
Tubarão
Vacaria
Laguna
Criciúma
Mércedes
São
Borja
Santiago
RIO GRANDE
Santa
Maria
Caxias do Sul
Novo Hamburgo
izu
auce
Uruguaiana
DO SUL
Cachoeira
do Sul
PORTO ALEGRE
Artigas
Santana do
Livramento
Lagoa dos Patos
Rivera
Salto
Bagé
Pelotas
Concordia
Tacuarembó
Melo
Rio Grande
Paysandú
Lagoa Mirim
Albardão do
João Maria
URUGUAY
Mércedes
Durazno
Santa Vitória
do Palmar
ENOS
RES
Trinidad
Florida
Minas
Maldonado
Quilmes
MONTEVIDEO
nas
La Plata
Rio de la Plata
Zamora
Bahía
Samborombón
Punta Norte
dillo
Dolores
ul
Tandil
Pinamar
enito
iarez
Mar del Plata
Necochea

ATLANTIC

OCEAN

Ilha da Trindade
(Brazil)

Ilhas Martin Vaz
(Brazil)

Jason
Is
Mt.
Adam
Falkland Islands
(U.K.)
705
Stanley
and
700
Mt.
Usborne
East Falkland
Cape
edith

Scotia Ridge

Shag Rocks
(U.K.)

Cape Alexandra
Grytviken
2934
Mt. Paget
South Georgia (U.K.)
Cape Disappointment

SCOTIA SEA

30° R 25° S 20°

J 60° K 55° L 50° M 45° N 40° P 35° Q

Settlements

■	over 3 million
□	1 – 3 million
⊙	250 000 – 1 million
●	100 000 – 250 000
○	25 000 – 100 000
·	under 25 000
—	country capital underline
—	state or province capital underline

POLAR REGIONS

Scale 1 : 50 700 000

0   500   1000   1500 km
0   250   500   750 miles

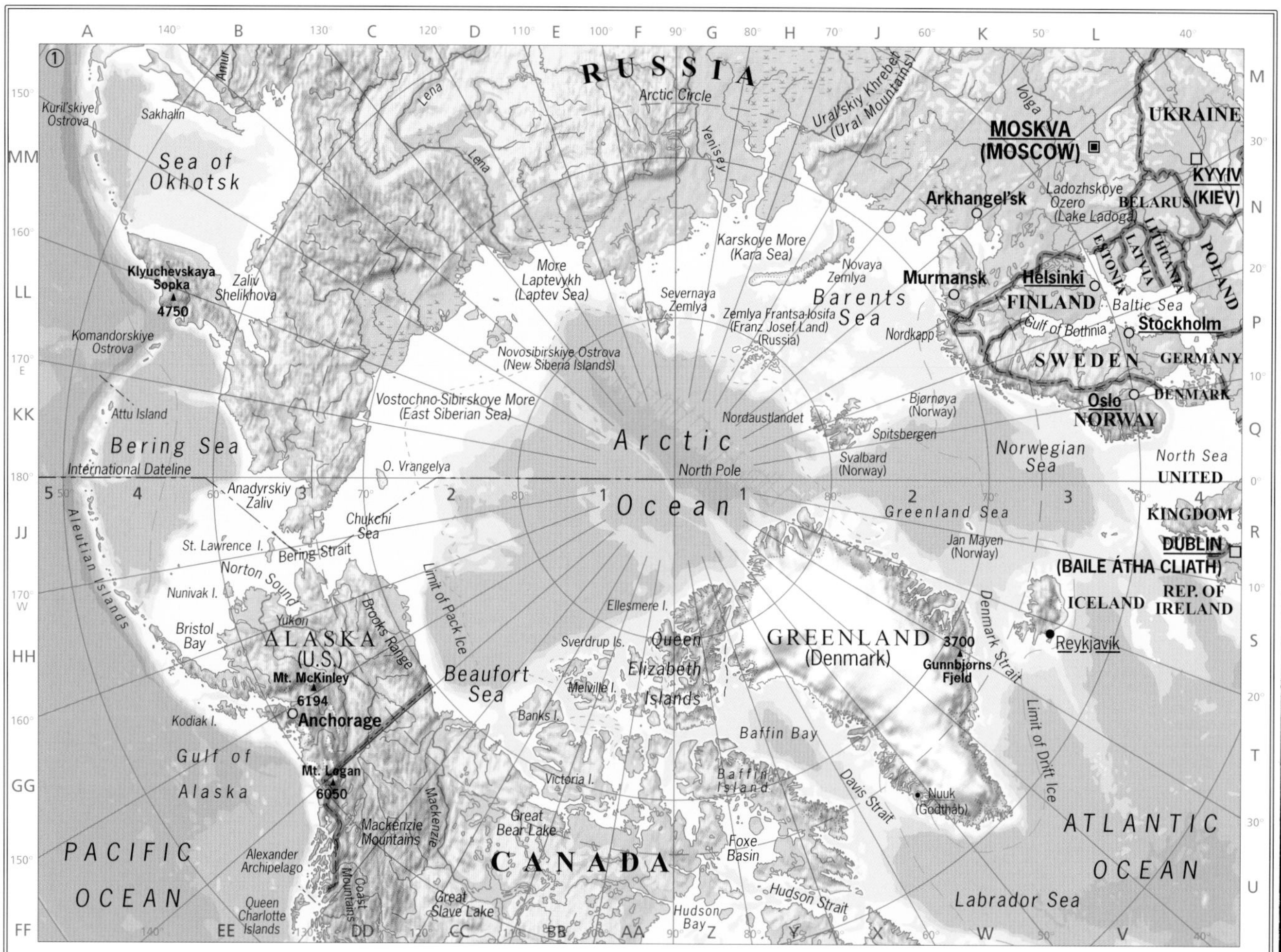

① Map 1 (Arctic)

A 140° B 130° C 120° D 110° E 100° F 90° G 80° H 70° J 60° K 50° L 40° M

RUSSIA
Arctic Circle

Kuril'skiye
Ostrova
Sakhalin
Amur
Lena
Yenisey
Ural'skiy Khrebet
(Ural Mountains)
Volga

MOSKVA
(MOSCOW)
UKRAINE

Sea of
Okhotsk
Lena
Karskoye More
(Kara Sea)
Arkhangel'sk
KYYIV
(KIEV)
BELARUS

Klyuchevskaya
Sopka
4750
Zaliv
Shelikhova
More
Laptevykh
(Laptev Sea)
Severnaya
Zemlya
Novaya
Zemlya
Zemlya Frantsa-Iosifa
(Franz Josef Land)
(Russia)
Barents
Sea
Murmansk
Nordkapp
Helsinki
FINLAND
Stockholm
Baltic Sea
LITHUANIA
LATVIA
ESTONIA
POLAND

Komandorskiye
Ostrova
Novosibirskiye Ostrova
(New Siberia Islands)
SWEDEN
GERMANY

Attu Island
Vostochno-Sibirskoye More
(East Siberian Sea)
Nordaustlandet
Bjørnøya
(Norway)
Spitsbergen
Svalbard
(Norway)
Oslo
NORWAY
DENMARK

Bering Sea
International Dateline
Arctic
North Pole
Norwegian
Sea
North Sea
UNITED

5 50 4 60 3 70 2 80 1 1 2 3 4

Chukchi
Sea
Ocean
Greenland Sea
KINGDOM

Anadyrskiy
Zaliv
Jan Mayen
(Norway)
DUBLIN
(BAILE ÁTHA CLIATH)

St. Lawrence I.
Bering Strait
ICELAND
REP. OF
IRELAND

Nunivak I.
Norton Sound
Ellesmere I.
Denmark Strait
Reykjavik

Bristol
Bay
Yukon
Brooks Range
Limit of Pack Ice
Sverdrup Is.
Queen
GREENLAND
(Denmark)
3700
Gunnbjørns
Fjeld

ALASKA
(U.S.)
Mt. McKinley
6194
Anchorage
Beaufort
Sea
Melville I.
Elizabeth
Islands
Limit of Drift Ice

Kodiak I.
Banks I.
Baffin Bay

Mt. Logan
6050
Mackenzie
Victoria I.
Baffin
Island
Davis Strait
Nuuk
(Godthåb)
ATLANTIC

Gulf of
Alaska
Mackenzie
Mountains
Great
Bear Lake
OCEAN

PACIFIC
Alexander
Archipelago
CANADA
Foxe
Basin

OCEAN
Coast
Mountains
Great
Slave Lake
Great
Slave Lake
Hudson Strait
Labrador Sea

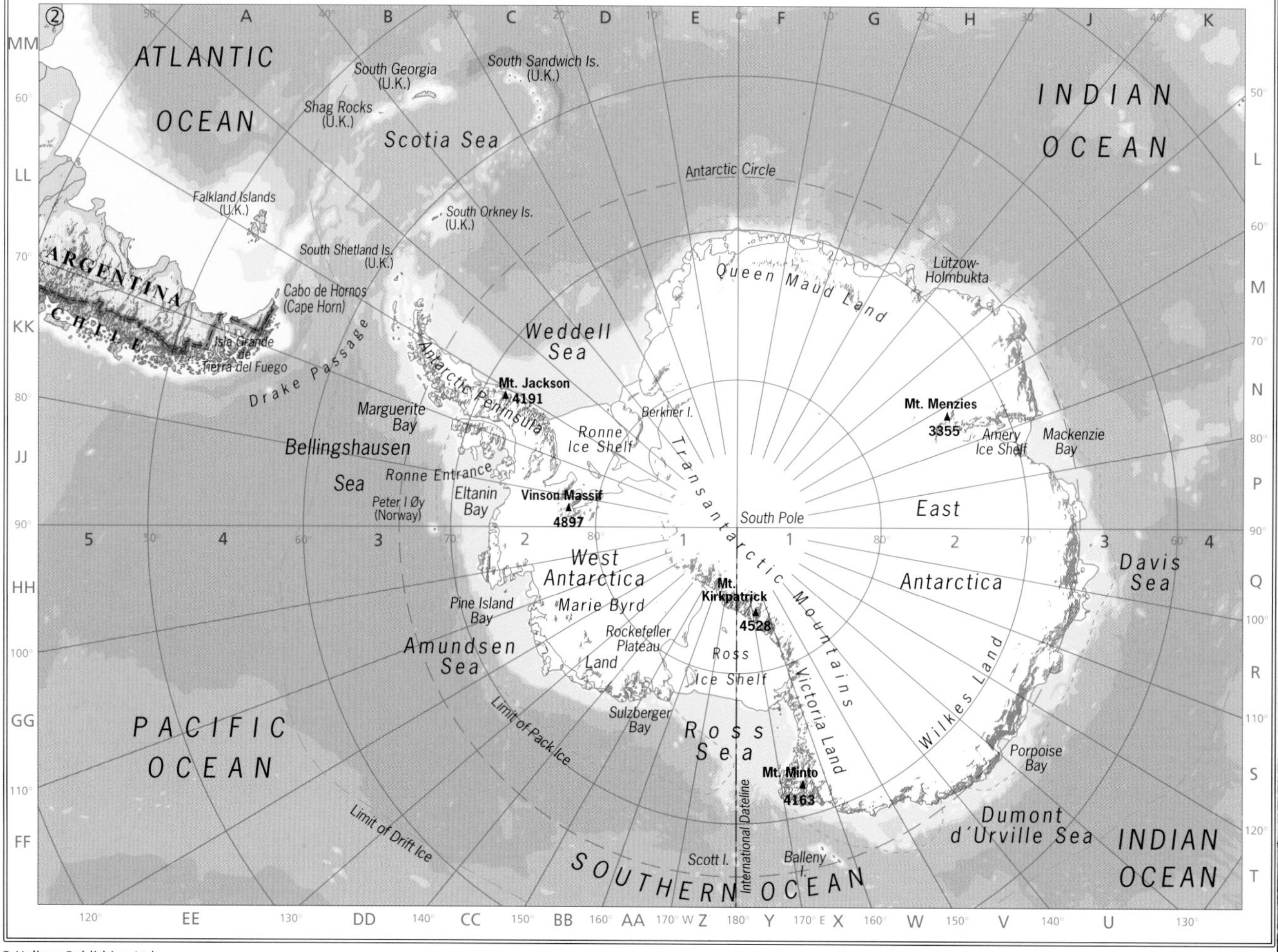

Queen
Charlotte
Islands
Hudson
Bay

FF EE 140° DD 130° CC 120° BB AA 100° Z 90° Y 80° X 70° W 60° V 50° 40°

② Map 2 (Antarctic)

A B C D E F G H J K

ATLANTIC
OCEAN
60°
South Georgia
(U.K.)
South Sandwich Is.
(U.K.)
INDIAN
OCEAN
50°

Shag Rocks
(U.K.)
Scotia Sea
Antarctic Circle

Falkland Islands
(U.K.)
South Orkney Is.
(U.K.)
60°
Lützow-
Holmbukta

ARGENTINA
South Shetland Is.
(U.K.)
Queen Maud Land
70°

Cabo de Hornos
(Cape Horn)
Weddell
Sea
Mt. Menzies
3355
Amery
Ice Shelf
Mackenzie
Bay

CHILE
Isla Grande de
Tierra del Fuego
Drake Passage
Antarctic Peninsula
Mt. Jackson
4191
Berkner I.
Transantarctic Mountains
80°

Marguerite
Bay
Ronne
Ice Shelf
East

Bellingshausen
Ronne Entrance
Eltanin
Bay
Vinson Massif
4897
South Pole
Antarctica
Davis
Sea

Sea
Peter I Øy
(Norway)
West
Antarctica
Mt.
Kirkpatrick
4528
90°
100°

HH
Pine Island
Bay
Marie Byrd
Rockefeller
Plateau
Ross
Victoria Land
Wilkes Land
Porpoise
Bay

Amundsen
Sea
Land
Ross
Ice Shelf
100°

PACIFIC
OCEAN
Sulzberger
Bay
Ross
Sea
Mt. Minto
4163
110°

Limit of Pack Ice
Dumont
d'Urville Sea
INDIAN
OCEAN

Limit of Drift Ice
Scott I.
Balleny
Is.
International Dateline

SOUTHERN OCEAN

120° EE 130° DD 140° CC 150° BB 160° AA 170°W Z 180° Y 170°E X 160° W 150° V 140° U 130°

Settlements

- ■ over 3 million
- ☐ 1 – 3 million
- ○ 250 000 – 1 million
- ● 100 000 – 250 000
- —— country capital underline

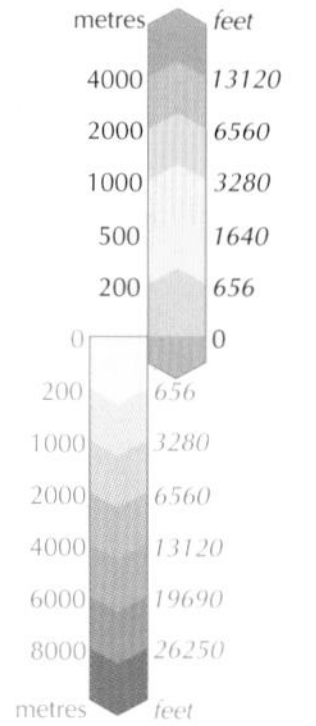

metres	feet
4000	13120
2000	6560
1000	3280
500	1640
200	656
0	0
200	656
1000	3280
2000	6560
4000	13120
6000	19690
8000	26250
metres	feet

© Helicon Publishing Ltd

Nations of the World

THIS IS AN ALPHABETICAL LISTING of all the 192 sovereign nations of the world. A map page reference is included for each country. The statistics used are the latest available at the time of going to press. Place names are given in English where a popular form exists and otherwise are shown in their local form.

There is a list of useful web site links for each country denoted by the following symbol:

Sites for each country are listed below with the web address and a brief description on the site content. Certain sites cover many or all of the countries of the world. These are indicated by the abbreviations alongside the web site symbol. An explanation of these abbreviations together with the details of each site are given opposite:

■ **CIA**

World Factbook 2000

http://www.odci.gov/cia/publications/factbook/

Official Central Intelligence Agency Web site for The World Factbook. This site offers detailed and accurate statistics for all the countries of the world, including sections on geography, population, government, and economy. Although the site contains few graphics, a map of each country and an image of its flag are also included.

■ **LC**

Library of Congress: Country Studies

http://lcweb2.loc.gov/frd/cs/

Online version of a series of books published by the Federal Research Division of the US Library of Congress. Studies of over 100 countries are featured, covering such subjects as geography, economy, and government. There are also informative articles on each country's historical and social background, together with maps and timelines.

■ **AN**

Arabnet

http://www.arab.net/

Features detailed country data on all the major Arab nations, including sections on history, government, business, and culture. The site contains the latest Arab-related news worldwide, as well as a collection of articles written by leading journalists and editors from the Middle East. Although the site lacks graphics, this is compensated for by the large amount of information available.

■ **LP**

Lonely Planet Online

http://www.lonelyplanet.com/

From the makers of the Lonely Planet series comes a comprehensive resource for travellers. The 'World guide' section offers detailed

information on each country, with pages for attractions, health risks, and visa requirements. There is also regularly updated news, as well as a bulletin board for travellers to share advice.

■ **RG**

Rough Guides to Travel

http://travel.roughguides.com/

Well-designed resource from the makers of the Rough Guide travel series. The 'Travel talk' section allows users to share advice on travelling the world, with sections including 'First-time travel', and 'Travel partners'. The site features regular articles on selected destinations around the world, and the opportunity to sign up for weekly travel updates.

■ **WTG**

World Travel Guide

http://www.wtgonline.com/navigate/world.asp

Informative travel guide to the countries of the world. There are sections on history and government for every featured country, as well as advice aimed more specifically at the traveller. It will keep you up-to-date on visa and currency requirements, accommodation options, travel, and highlights not to be missed.

■ **NA**

New Africa

http://www.newafrica.com/

Extensive resource that features detailed information on each country in Africa, with subjects including health, economy, and population. The site also features the latest news events affecting Africa, as well as information on investment opportunities. Although the site's emphasis is primarily on statistical data, it also provides a useful insight into the continent's national parks and tourist attractions, as well as a travel guide for each country.

AFGHANISTAN
Map page 90

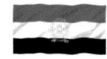

National name Dowlat-e Eslāmi-ye Afghānestān/Islamic State of Afghanistan

Area 652,225 sq km/ 251,825 sq mi

Capital Kābul

Major towns/cities Kandahār, Herāt, Mazār-e Sharīf, Jalālābād, Konduz, Qal'eh-ye Now

Physical features mountainous in centre and northeast (Hindu Kush mountain range; Khyber and Salang passes, Wakhan salient, and Panjshir Valley), plains in north and southwest, Amu Darya (Oxus) River, Helmand River, Lake Saberi

Currency afgháni

GNP per capita (PPP) (US$) 800 (1999 est)

Resources natural gas, coal, iron ore, barytes, lapis lazuli, salt, talc, copper, chrome, gold, silver, asbestos, small petroleum reserves

Population 22,720,000 (2000 est)

Population density (per sq km) 34 (1999 est)

Language Pashto, Dari (both official), Uzbek, Turkmen, Balochi, Pashai

Religion Muslim (84% Sunni, 15% Shiite), other 1%

Time difference GMT+4.5

 ■ CIA ■ LP ■ WTG

ALBANIA
Map page 68

National name Republika e Shqipërisë/Republic of Albania

Area 28,748 sq km/11,099 sq mi

Capital Tirana

Major towns/cities Durrës, Shkodër, Elbasan, Vlorë, Korçë

Major ports Durrës

Physical features mainly mountainous, with rivers flowing east–west, and a narrow coastal plain

Currency lek

GNP per capita (PPP) (US$) 2,892 (1999)

Resources chromite (one of world's largest producers), copper, coal, nickel, petroleum and natural gas

Population 3,113,000 (2000 est)

Population density (per sq km) 108 (1999 est)

Language Albanian (official), Greek

Religion Muslim, Albanian Orthodox, Roman Catholic

Time difference GMT +1

 ■ CIA ■ LC ■ LP ■ WTG

■ **Albanian World Wide Web Page**

http://www.albanian.com/main/

Facts, pictures, and maps help you explore Albania and the Albanian-populated regions of the Balkans. Historical, cultural, and travel information is provided, along with a small English–Albanian dictionary. A 'virtual tour' enables you to click on a map and visit places in Albania to find out about their history and tourist attractions.

■ **Tirana**

http://www.albania.co.uk/cityguide/tirana.html

Good introduction to the Albanian capital. There are descriptions of the city, its history, public buildings, and cultural and artistic institutions. There are a number of photographs to accompany the descriptions.

ALGERIA
Map page 102

National name Al-Jumhuriyyat al-Jaza'iriyya ad-Dimuqratiyya ash-Sha'biyya/Democratic People's Republic of Algeria

Area 2,381,741 sq km/ 919,590 sq mi

Capital Algiers (Arabic al-Jaza'ir)

Major towns/cities Oran, Annaba, Blida, Sétif, Constantine

Major ports Oran (Ouahran), Annaba (Bône)

Physical features coastal plains backed by mountains in north, Sahara desert in south; Atlas mountains, Barbary Coast, Chott Melrhir depression, Hoggar mountains

Currency Algerian dinar

GNP per capita (PPP) (US$) 4,753 (1999)

Resources natural gas and petroleum, iron ore, phosphates, lead, zinc, mercury, silver, salt, antimony, copper

Population 31,471,000 (2000 est)

Population density (per sq km) 13 (1999 est)

Language Arabic (official), Berber, French

Religion Sunni Muslim (state religion) 99%, Christian and Jewish 1%

Time difference GMT +/–0

 ■ CIA ■ LC ■ AN ■ LP ■ NA ■ WTG

■ **Algeria**

http://i-cias.com/m.s/algeria/index.htm

Colourful travelling guide to Algeria and some of its major cities. It includes sections on 'Getting there', 'Visas and passports', 'Climate', 'Health', 'What to buy', as well as a long, illustrated list of places to go.

ANDORRA
Map page 60

National name Principat d'Andorra/ Principality of Andorra

Area 468 sq km/181 sq mi

Capital Andorra la Vella

Major towns/cities Les Escaldes

Physical features mountainous, with narrow valleys; the eastern Pyrenees, Valira River

Currency French franc and Spanish peseta

GNP per capita (PPP) (US$) 18,000 (1996 est)

Resources iron, lead, aluminium, hydroelectric power

Population 78,000 (2000 est)

Population density (per sq km) 146 (1999 est)

Language Catalan (official), Spanish, French

Religion Roman Catholic (92%)

www. ■ CIA ■ LP ■ WTG

ANGOLA

Map page 98

National name República de Angolo/Republic of Angola
Area 1,246,700 sq km/ 481,350 sq mi
Capital Luanda (and chief port)
Major towns/cities Lobito, Benguela, Huambo, Lubango, Malanje, Namibe, Kuito
Major ports Huambo, Lubango, Malanje
Physical features narrow coastal plain rises to vast interior plateau with rainforest in northwest; desert in south; Cuanza, Cuito, Cubango, and Cunene rivers
Currency kwanza
GNP per capita (PPP) (US$) 632 (1999)
Resources petroleum, diamonds, granite, iron ore, marble, salt, phosphates, manganese, copper
Population 12,878,000 (2000 est)
Population density (per sq km) 10 (1999 est)
Language Portuguese (official), Bantu, other native dialects
Religion Roman Catholic 38%, Protestant 15%, animist 47%
Time difference GMT +1

 www. ■ CIA ■ LC ■ LP ■ NA ■ WTG

■ **Angola**
http://www.angola.org/
Angola's official Web site has a noticeable pro-government stance, but is well worth looking up for travel information; notes on the country's economy, geography, population, and history; and a virtual tour of Angola's historic buildings.

ANTIGUA AND BARBUDA

Map page 134

Area 440 sq km/169 sq mi (Antigua 280 sq km/108 sq mi, Barbuda 161 sq km/62 sq mi, plus Redonda 1 sq km/0.4 sq mi)
Capital St. John's (on Antigua) (and chief port)
Major towns/cities Codrington (on Barbuda)
Physical features low-lying tropical islands of limestone and coral with some higher volcanic outcrops; no rivers and low rainfall result in frequent droughts and deforestation. Antigua is the largest of the Leeward Islands; Redonda is an uninhabited island of volcanic rock rising to 305 m/1,000 ft
Currency East Caribbean dollar
GNP per capita (PPP) (US$) 8,959 (1999 est)
Population 68,000 (2000 est)
Population density (per sq km) 246 (1999 est)
Language English (official), local dialects
Religion Christian (mostly Anglican)
Time difference GMT –4

 www. ■ CIA ■ LP ■ RG ■ WTG

■ **Official Guide to Antigua and Barbuda**
http://www.interknowledge.com/antigua-barbuda/
Official Web site of Antigua and Barbuda's Department of Tourism aimed, naturally enough, at the prospective tourist, with sections on travel tips, activities, and accommodation.

ARGENTINA

Map page 142

National name República Argentina/Argentine Republic
Area 2,780,400 sq km/1,073,518 sq mi
Capital Buenos Aires
Major towns/cities Rosario, Córdoba, San Miguel de Tucumán, Mendoza, Santa Fé, La Plata
Major ports La Plata and Bahía Blanca

Physical features mountains in west, forest and savannah in north, pampas (treeless plains) in east-central area, Patagonian plateau in south; rivers Colorado, Salado, Paraná, Uruguay, Río de La Plata estuary; Andes mountains, with Aconcagua the highest peak in western hemisphere; Iguaçu Falls

Territories disputed claim to the Falkland Islands (Islas Malvinas), and part of Antarctica
Currency peso (= 10,000 australs, which it replaced in 1992)
GNP per capita (PPP) (US$) 11,324 (1999)
Resources coal, crude oil, natural gas, iron ore, lead ore, zinc ore, tin, gold, silver, uranium ore, marble, borates, granite
Population 37,032,000 (2000 est)
Population density (per sq km) 13 (1999 est)
Language Spanish (official) (95%), Italian (3%), English, German, French
Religion predominantly Roman Catholic (state-supported), 2% protestant, 2% Jewish
Time difference GMT –3

 www. ■ CIA ■ LP ■ WTG

■ **Introduction to Argentina**
http://www.interknowledge.com/argentina/index.html
Lively, illustrated guide to the six major regions which make up this country, and sections on such things as 'History & culture', 'Calendar of events', and 'Travel tips'.

■ **Buenos Aires, Argentina**
http://travel.lycos.com/Destinations/South_America/Argentina/Buenos_Aires/
Profile of Argentina's multi-ethnic capital, Buenos Aires. There is a general introduction to the city's main features, and four sections – 'Visitors' guide', 'Culture and history', 'News and weather', and 'Entertainment' – with links to photographs, and to further useful information in English and Spanish about the city and the country.

■ **Tierra del Fuego, Argentina**
http://www.tierradelfuego.org.ar/
General introduction to the 'land of fire', Tierra del Fuego, and its capital Ushuaia. This official site also includes photographs, and information on the activities available in the surrounding area, such as fishing and skiing.

ARMENIA

Map page 92

National name Hayastani Hanrapetoutioun/Republic of Armenia
Area 29,800 sq km/11,505 sq mi
Capital Yerevan
Major towns/cities Gyumri (formerly Leninakan), Vanadzor (formerly Kirovakan), Hrazdan, Aboyvan
Physical features mainly mountainous (including Mount Ararat), wooded
Currency dram (replaced Russian rouble in 1993)
GNP per capita (PPP) (US$) 2,210 (1999)
Resources copper, zinc, molybdenum, iron, silver, marble, granite
Population 3,520,000 (2000 est)
Population density (per sq km) 118 (1999 est)
Language Armenian (official)
Religion Armenian Orthodox
Time difference GMT +4

 www. ■ CIA ■ LC ■ LP ■ WTG

■ **Armenian Land and Culture Organization**
http://www.lcousa.org/
Armenian international organization intent on preserving their monuments and history. As well as providing an Armenian perspective on the history, culture, and sovereignty of this region of Azerbaijan, this site gives information about the organization's campaigns and how the organization operates.

AUSTRALIA

Map page 114

National name Commonwealth of Australia
Area 7,682,850 sq km/ 2,966,136 sq mi
Capital Canberra
Major towns/cities Adelaide, Alice Springs, Brisbane, Darwin, Melbourne, Perth, Sydney, Hobart, Newcastle, Wollongong
Physical features Ayers Rock; Arnhem Land; Gulf of Carpentaria; Cape York Peninsula; Great Australian Bight; Great Sandy Desert; Gibson Desert; Great Victoria Desert; Simpson Desert; the Great Barrier Reef; Great Dividing Range and Australian Alps in the east (Mount Kosciusko, 2,229 m/7,136 ft, Australia's highest peak). The fertile southeast region is watered by the Darling, Lachlan, Murrumbridgee, and Murray rivers. Lake Eyre basin and Nullarbor Plain in the south
Territories Norfolk Island, Christmas Island, Cocos (Keeling) Islands, Ashmore and Cartier Islands, Coral Sea Islands, Heard Island and McDonald Islands, Australian Antarctic Territory
Currency Australian dollar
GNP per capita (PPP) (US$) 22,448 (1999)
Resources coal, iron ore (world's third-largest producer), bauxite, copper, zinc (world's second-largest producer), nickel (world's fifth-largest producer), uranium, gold, diamonds
Population 18,886,000 (2000 est)
Population density (per sq km) 2 (1999 est)
Language English (official), Aboriginal languages
Religion Anglican 26%, Roman Catholic 26%, other Christian 24%
Time difference GMT +8/10

 www. ■ CIA ■ LP ■ RG ■ WTG

■ **Sydney Interactive Visitors Guide**
http://www.visitorsguide.aust.com/~tourism/sydney/index.html
Interactive guide to Sydney, Australia. The guide features the 'museums, art galleries, history, maps, attractions, tours, festivals, hotels, and fine dining for both visitors and residents of Sydney.'

■ **Melbourne City Search**
http://www.melbourne.vic.gov.au//
Searchable source of information on Australia's second city. Primarily designed for residents, this site is updated on a daily basis with news of local events, community groups, local government, cultural life, sport, and weather. For visitors there is information on accommodation and tourist attractions.

■ **Great Barrier Reef Marine Park Authority**
http://www.gbrmpa.gov.au/
Comprehensive official information on all aspects of the Great Barrier Reef and efforts to preserve this World Heritage Area. The online edition of the authority's quarterly Reef Research gives detail of current related scientific work.

■ **Destination Queensland**
http://www.qttc.com.au/
Large source of well-organized official tourist information on Australia's fastest growing state. The attractions of all regions of the vast state are described and easily accessible. Practical information is provided together with links to further sources. There is extensive information on the state's commitment to ecotourism and environmental protection.

■ **Tasmania – Discover Your Natural State**
http://www.tourism.tas.gov.au/nu_index.html
Official guide to Australia's island state. The quiet charms of 'Tassie' and local pride in its heritage, culture, and cuisine are evoked by informative text and a series of photographs. The history of the state is presented by means of quotes from famous visitors. All the regions of the state are covered.

■ **Australian Capital Territory**
http://www.act.gov.au/
Official guide to Australia's federal territory. There is information on government services, business life, local amenities, and the environment. This site also includes a guide to tourist attractions in Canberra and elsewhere in the territory.

AUSTRIA

Map page 62

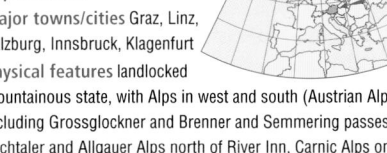

National name Republik Österreich/
Republic of Austria
Area 83,859 sq km/32,367 sq mi
Capital Vienna
Major towns/cities Graz, Linz,
Salzburg, Innsbruck, Klagenfurt
Physical features landlocked
mountainous state, with Alps in west and south (Austrian Alps,
including Grossglockner and Brenner and Semmering passes,
Lechtaler and Allgauer Alps north of River Inn, Carnic Alps on
Italian border) and low relief in east where most of the population
is concentrated; River Danube
Currency schilling
GNP per capita (PPP) (US$) 23,808 (1999)
Resources lignite, iron, kaolin, gypsum, talcum, magnesite, lead,
zinc, forests
Population 8,211,000 (2000 est)
Population density (per sq km) 98 (1999 est)
Language German (official)
Religion Roman Catholic 78%, Protestant 5%
Time difference GMT +1

 ▪ CIA ▪ LC ▪ LP ▪ RG ▪ WTG

▪ Vienna
http://www.info-austria.net
Guide to Vienna. Aimed at the tourist, this site details what to do
before you go, and what to do when you get there. History,
geography, and travel information, as well as features on festivals,
make up the majority of the remaining information on this site,
but there are also details of local transport and a list of useful
telephone numbers.

▪ Information from Austria
http://www.austria.gv.at/e/
Easily navigable official guide to Austria from the office of the
Chancellor. There is comprehensive information on Austrian
foreign policy, as well as education, electoral, parliamentary, and
social security systems. There is regularly updated news and
foreign ministry press releases. This is an essential first stop for
anybody wanting to know about Austria.

▪ City of Graz
http://www.gcongress.com/graz.htm
Informative guide to Austria's second city. An aerial photo on the
home page leads to comprehensive information on history,
museums, business, and the city's universities. There is also
practical information on hotels, restaurants, and transport.

▪ Innsbruck, Austria
http://travel.lycos.com/Destinations/Europe/Austria/Innsbruck/
Guide to the Tirolean capital. There is a good description of this
city and its attractions. There are also links to a number of local
institutions and the media.

AZERBAIJAN

Map page 92

National name Azärbaycan
Respublikasi/Republic of Azerbaijan
Area 86,600 sq km/33,436 sq mi
Capital Baku
Major towns/cities Gäncä,
Sumqayit, Naxçivan, Xankändi,
Mingäçevir
Physical features Caspian Sea with rich oil reserves; the
country ranges from semidesert to the Caucasus Mountains
Currency manat (replaced Russian rouble in 1993)
GNP per capita (PPP) (US$) 2,322 (1999)
Resources petroleum, natural gas, iron ore, aluminium, copper,
barytes, cobalt, precious metals, limestone, salt
Population 7,734,000 (2000 est)
Population density (per sq km) 89 (1999 est)
Language Azeri (official), Russian
Religion Shiite Muslim 68%, Sunni Muslim 27%, Russian
Orthodox 3%, Armenian Orthodox 2%
Time difference GMT +4

 ▪ CIA ▪ LC ▪ LP ▪ WTG

THE BAHAMAS

Map page 134

National name Commonwealth of
the Bahamas
Area 13,880 sq km/5,383 sq mi
Capital Nassau (on New
Providence island)
Major towns/cities Freeport (on Grand
Bahama)
Physical features comprises 700 tropical coral islands and
about 1,000 cays; the Exumas are a narrow spine of 365 islands;
only 30 of the desert islands are inhabited; Blue Holes of Andros,
the world's longest and deepest submarine caves
Currency Bahamian dollar
GNP per capita (PPP) (US$) 13,955 (1999 est)
Resources aragonite (extracted from seabed), chalk, salt
Population 307,000 (2000 est)
Population density (per sq km) 22 (1999 est)
Language English (official), Creole
Religion Christian 94% (Baptist 32%, Roman Catholic 19%,
Anglican 20%, other Protestant 23%)
Time difference GMT –5

 ▪ CIA ▪ LP ▪ WTG

▪ Bahamas Online
http://www.bahamas-on-line.com/
One-stop information service for anyone planning to visit the
Bahamas, with sections on such topics as Bahamian history,
shops and services, places to stay, and things to do.

BAHRAIN
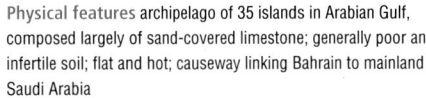
Map page 95

National name Dawlat
al-Bahrayn/State of Bahrain
Area 688 sq km/266 sq mi
Capital Al Manāmah (on Bahrain
island)
Major towns/cities Sitra, Al
Muharraq, Jidd Ḥafş, Madinat 'Īsá
Physical features archipelago of 35 islands in Arabian Gulf,
composed largely of sand-covered limestone; generally poor and
infertile soil; flat and hot; causeway linking Bahrain to mainland
Saudi Arabia
Currency Bahraini dinar
GNP per capita (PPP) (US$) 11,527 (1999 est)
Resources petroleum and natural gas
Population 617,000 (2000 est)
Population density (per sq km) 882 (1999 est)
Language Arabic (official), Farsi, English, Urdu
Religion 85% Muslim (Shiite 60%, Sunni 40%), Christian; Islam
is the state religion
Time difference GMT +3

 ▪ CIA ▪ LC ▪ AN ▪ LP ▪ WTG

BANGLADESH

Map page 88

National name Gana Prajatantri
Bangladesh/People's Republic of
Bangladesh
Area 144,000 sq km/55,598 sq mi
Capital Dhaka
Major towns/cities Rajshahi,
Khulna, Chittagong, Sylhet,
Rangpur, Narayanganj
Major ports Chittagong, Khulna
Physical features flat delta of rivers Ganges (Padma) and
Brahmaputra (Jamuna), the largest estuarine delta in the world;
annual rainfall of 2,540 mm/100 in; some 75% of the land is less
than 3 m/10 ft above sea level; hilly in extreme southeast and
northeast
Currency taka
GNP per capita (PPP) (US$) 1,475 (1999)
Resources natural gas, coal, limestone, china clay, glass sand

Population 129,155,000 (2000 est)
Population density (per sq km) 881 (1999 est)
Language Bengali (official), English
Religion Muslim 88%, Hindu 11%; Islam is the state religion
Time difference GMT +6

 ▪ CIA ▪ LC ▪ LP ▪ WTG

▪ Bangladesh
http://www.bangladesh.net/
Online guide to Bangladesh. The site includes information on all
aspects of life and culture in Bangladesh, including the
architecture and history of the country.

BARBADOS

Map page 134

Area 430 sq km/166 sq mi
Capital Bridgetown
Major towns/cities
Speightstown, Holetown, Oistins
Physical features most easterly
island of the West Indies; surrounded by coral reefs; subject to
hurricanes June–November; highest point Mount Hillaby 340 m/
1,115 ft
Currency Barbados dollar
GNP per capita (PPP) (US$) 12,260 (1998)
Resources petroleum and natural gas
Population 270,000 (2000 est)
Population density (per sq km) 625 (1999 est)
Language English (official), Bajan (a Barbadian English dialect)
Religion 40% Anglican, 8% Pentecostal, 6% Methodist, 4%
Roman Catholic
Time difference GMT –4

 ▪ CIA ▪ LP ▪ RG ▪ WTG

▪ Barbados – Isle of Dreams
http://www.barbados.org/
Here are facts and figures about Barbados, weather reports, an
illustrated history and chronology, a feature on Barbados rum,
and links to associated sites.

BELARUS

Map page 70

National name Respublika Belarus/
Republic of Belarus
Area 207,600 sq km/80,154 sq mi
Capital Minsk (Belorussian Mensk)
Major towns/cities Homyel',
Vitsyebsk, Mahilyow, Babruysk,
Hrodna, Brest
Physical features more than 25% forested; rivers Dvina,
Dnieper and its tributaries, including the Pripet and Beresina; the
Pripet Marshes in the east; mild and damp climate
Currency Belarus rouble, or zaichik
GNP per capita (PPP) (US$) 6,518 (1999)
Resources petroleum, natural gas, peat, salt, coal, lignite
Population 10,236,000 (2000 est)
Population density (per sq km) 50 (1999 est)
Language Belorussian (official), Russian, Polish
Religion 80% Eastern Orthodox; Baptist, Roman Catholic
Muslim, and Jewish minorities
Time difference GMT +2

 ▪ CIA ▪ LC ▪ LP ▪ WTG

▪ Minsk in Your Pocket Home Page
http://www.inyourpocket.com/Belarus/Minsk_home.shtml
Guide to everything you ever wanted to know about this
Belarusian capital city. This is an electronic form of a published
guide book and includes sections on such topics as language,
media, what to see, getting there, and where to stay.

BELGIUM
Map page 54

National name Royaume de Belgique
(French), Koninkrijk België (Flemish)/
Kingdom of Belgium
Area 30,510 sq km/11,779 sq mi
Capital Brussels
Major towns/cities Antwerp,
Ghent, Liège, Charleroi, Brugge,
Mons, Namur, Louvain
Major ports Antwerp, Oostende, Zeebrugge
Physical features fertile coastal plain in northwest, central
rolling hills rise eastwards, hills and forest in southeast; Ardennes
Forest; rivers Schelde and Meuse
Currency Belgian franc
GNP per capita (PPP) (US$) 24,200 (1999)
Resources coal, coke, natural gas, iron
Population 10,161,000 (2000 est)
Population density (per sq km) 333 (1999 est)
Language Flemish (a Dutch dialect, known as Vlaams; official)
(spoken by 56%, mainly in Flanders, in the north), French
(especially the dialect Walloon; official) (spoken by 32%, mainly
in Wallonia, in the south), German (0.6%; mainly near the eastern
border)
Religion Roman Catholic 75%, various Protestant
denominations
Time difference GMT +1

 ■ CIA ■ LP ■ RG ■ WTG

■ **Antwerp**
http://users.pandora.be/eric.kumiko/
General introduction to the city, including history, art, and culture,
with links to more specific sites.

■ **Things to see in Brussels**
http://pespmc1.vub.ac.be/BRUSSEL.html
Guide to places of interest to visit in this city, from medieval
houses to futuristic buildings, provided by the Free University of
Brussels.

■ **Belgium: Overview**
http://pespmc1.vub.ac.be/Belgcul.html
General information about Belgium, its cities and regions, plus a
special focus on its culture, with features on 'typically Belgian
things', such as the Belgian character and Hergé's Tintin.

■ **Tourist Office for Flanders**
http://www.toervl.be/en/intra_0_en.shtml
Good official source of information on the history, geography, and
culture of the Dutch-speaking region of Belgium. There are
sections on gastronomy, accommodation, attractions, festivals
and celebrations, in addition to profiles of the main cities and
towns of Flanders.

■ **Belgian Federal Government Online**
http://belgium.fgov.be/pa/ena_frame.htm
Official Belgium site that includes a history of the country and its
organs of state. Visitors can read governmental press releases
and find a wealth of information in the databases of the 'Federal
information service', from photographs of the Belgian royal
family, to electoral results for the last decade.

BELIZE
Map page 134

Area 22,963 sq km/8,866 sq mi
Capital Belmopan
Major towns/cities Belize,
Dangriga, Orange Walk, Corozal,
San Ignacio
Major ports Belize, Dangriga, Punta Gorda
Physical features tropical swampy coastal plain, Maya
Mountains in south; over 90% forested
Currency Belize dollar
GNP per capita (PPP) (US$) 4,492 (1999)
Population 241,000 (2000 est)
Population density (per sq km) 10 (1999 est)
Language English (official), Spanish (widely spoken), Creole
dialects
Religion Roman Catholic 62%, Protestant 30%
Time difference GMT –6

 ■ CIA ■ LC ■ LP ■ WTG

■ **Belize Online Tourism and Investment Guide**
http://www.belize.com/
Designed to attract tourists and commerce to the country, with
information grouped under headings such as culture, music,
ancient treasures, and news and information.

BENIN
Map page 104

National name République du
Bénin/Republic of Benin
Area 112,622 sq km/
43,483 sq mi
Capital Porto-Novo (official),
Cotonou (de facto)
Major towns/cities Abomey,
Natitingou, Parakou, Kandi, Ouidah, Djougou, Bohicon, Cotonou
Major ports Cotonou
Physical features flat to undulating terrain; hot and humid in
south; semiarid in north; coastal lagoons with fishing villages on
stilts; Niger River in northeast
Currency franc CFA
GNP per capita (PPP) (US$) 886 (1999)
Resources petroleum, limestone, marble
Population 6,097,000 (2000 est)
Population density (per sq km) 53 (1999 est)
Language French (official), Fon (47%), Yoruba (9%) (both in the
south), six major tribal languages in the north
Religion animist 70%, Muslim 15%, Christian 15%
Time difference GMT +1

 ■ CIA ■ LP ■ NA ■ WTG

BHUTAN
Map page 88

National name Druk-yul/Kingdom of
Bhutan
Area 47,500 sq km/18,147 sq mi
Capital Thimphu
Major towns/cities Paro,
Punakha, Mongar, Phuntsholing,
Tashigang
Physical features occupies southern slopes of the Himalayas;
Gangkar Punsum (7,529 m/24,700 ft) is one of the world's
highest unclimbed peaks; cut by valleys formed by tributaries of
the Brahmaputra; thick forests in south
Currency ngultrum, although the Indian rupee is also accepted
GNP per capita (PPP) (US$) 1,496 (1999 est)
Resources limestone, gypsum, coal, slate, dolomite, lead, talc,
copper
Population 2,124,000 (2000 est)
Population density (per sq km) 44 (1999 est)
Language Dzongkha (a Tibetan dialect; official), Tibetan,
Sharchop, Bumthap, Nepali, English
Religion 70% Mahayana Buddhist (state religion), 25% Hindu
Time difference GMT +6

 ■ CIA ■ LC ■ LP ■ WTG

BOLIVIA
Map page 140

National name República de
Bolivia/Republic of Bolivia
Area 1,098,581 sq km/
424,162 sq mi
Capital La Paz (seat of
government), Sucre (legal capital
and seat of the judiciary)
Major towns/cities Santa Cruz,
Cochabamba, Oruro, El Alto, Potosí,
Tarija
Physical features high plateau (Altiplano) between mountain
ridges (cordilleras); forest and lowlands (llano) in east; Andes;

lakes Titicaca (the world's highest navigable lake, 3,800 m/
12,500 ft) and Poopó
Currency boliviano
GNP per capita (PPP) (US$) 2,193 (1999)
Resources petroleum, natural gas, tin (world's fifth-largest
producer), zinc, silver, gold, lead, antimony, tungsten, copper
Population 8,329,000 (2000 est)
Population density (per sq km) 7 (1999 est)
Language Spanish (official) (4%), Aymara, Quechua
Religion Roman Catholic 90% (state-recognized)
Time difference GMT –4

 ■ CIA ■ LC ■ LP ■ WTG

■ **Bolivia Web**
http://www.boliviaweb.com/
Whether it's Bolivian history, music and arts, tourism, or sport,
this site should have the answer. There are plenty of photographs,
music to listen to, and links to Bolivian newspapers and radio
stations. Most of it is in English, but some information is only
available in Spanish.

■ **La Paz, Bolivia**
http://travel.lycos.com/Destinations/South_America/Bolivia/
La_Paz/
Profile of La Paz, Bolivia, the highest capital city in the world.
There is a general introduction to the city's main features, and
four sections – 'Visitors' guide', 'Culture and history', 'News and
weather', and 'Entertainment and photos' – with links to
photographs, and to useful information in English and Spanish
about both the city and the country.

■ **Potosí, Bolivia**
http://travel.lycos.com/Destinations/South_America/Bolivia/Potosi/
Profile of Potosí, Bolivia, once one of South America's wealthiest
cities. There is a general introduction to its main features, and
four sections – 'Visitors' guide', 'Culture and history', 'News and
weather', and 'Entertainment and photos' – with links to
photographs, and to further useful information in English and
Spanish about both the city and the country.

BOSNIA-HERZEGOVINA
Map page 66

National name Bosna i Hercegovina/
Bosnia-Herzegovina
Area 51,129 sq km/19,740 sq mi
Capital Sarajevo
Major towns/cities Banja
Luka, Mostar, Prijedor, Tuzla,
Zenica, Bihac, Gorazde
Physical features barren, mountainous country, part of the
Dinaric Alps; limestone gorges; 20 km/12 mi of coastline with no
harbour
Currency dinar
GNP per capita (PPP) (US$) 450 (1996 est)
Resources copper, lead, zinc, iron ore, coal, bauxite, manganese
Population 3,972,Q00 (2000 est)
Population density (per sq km) 75 (1999 est)
Language Serbian, Croat, Bosnian
Religion 40% Muslim, 31% Serbian Orthodox, 15% Roman
Catholic
Time difference GMT +1

 ■ CIA ■ LP ■ WTG

■ **Bosnia Home Page**
http://www.cco.caltech.edu/~bosnia/bosnia.html
Political and social news about this troubled country, with photo-
essays, a timeline of the conflict, maps of ethnic occupation and
military front lines, features on its culture and daily life, and links
to other Bosnian sites.

BOTSWANA
Map page 108

National name Republic of
Botswana
Area 582,000 sq km/
224,710 sq mi
Capital Gaborone
Major towns/cities Mahalapye,
Serowe, Francistown,

Selebi-Phikwe, Molepolole, Maun

Physical features Kalahari Desert in southwest (70–80% of national territory is desert), plains (Makgadikgadi salt pans) in east, fertile lands and Okavango Delta in north

Currency franc CFA

GNP per capita (PPP) (US$) 6,032 (1999)

Resources diamonds (world's third-largest producer), copper-nickel ore, coal, soda ash, gold, cobalt, salt, plutonium, asbestos, chromite, iron, silver, manganese, talc, uranium

Population 1,622,000 (2000 est)

Population density (per sq km) 3 (1999 est)

Language English (official), Setswana (national)

Religion Christian 50%, animist 50%

Time difference GMT +2

 www. ■ CIA ■ LP ■ NA ■ WTG

BRAZIL
Map page 138

National name República Federativa do Brasil/Federative Republic of Brazil

Area 8,511,965 sq km/ 3,286,469 sq mi

Capital Brasília

Major towns/cities São Paulo, Belo Horizonte, Nova Iguaçu, Rio de Janeiro, Belém, Recife, Porto Alegre, Salvador, Curitiba, Manaus, Fortaleza

Major ports Rio de Janeiro, Belém, Recife, Porto Alegre, Salvador

Physical features the densely forested Amazon basin covers the northern half of the country with a network of rivers; south is fertile; enormous energy resources, both hydroelectric (Itaipú Reservoir on the Paraná, and Tucuruí on the Tocantins) and nuclear (uranium ores); mostly tropical climate

Currency real

GNP per capita (PPP) (US$) 6,317 (1999)

Resources iron ore (world's second-largest producer), tin (world's fourth-largest producer), aluminium (world's fourth-largest producer), gold, phosphates, platinum, bauxite, uranium, manganese, coal, copper, petroleum, natural gas, hydroelectric power, forests

Population 170,115,000 (2000 est)

Population density (per sq km) 20 (1999 est)

Language Portuguese (official), Spanish, English, French, 120 Indian languages

Religion Roman Catholic 70%; Indian faiths

Time difference GMT –2/5

 www. ■ CIA ■ LC ■ LP ■ RG ■ WTG

■ **Brasilia's Home Page**
http://www.geocities.com/TheTropics/3416/
Good introduction to the Brazilian capital. There is a history of the construction of the city, a description of its attractions, and a frank listing of its problems. There are a large number of photos.

■ **Belem, Brazil**
http://www.belem.com/
Profile of Brazil's port city of Belém. There is a general introduction to its main features, and four sections – 'visitors' guide', 'culture and history', 'news and weather', and 'entertainment and photos' – with links to photographs, and to further useful information in English and Portuguese about both the city and the country.

■ **Rio de Janeiro, Brazil**
http://www.if.ufrj.br/general/tourist.html
Profile of the colourful Brazilian city of Rio de Janeiro. There is a general introduction to the its main features, and four sections – 'visitors' guide', 'culture and history', 'news and weather', and 'entertainment' – with links to photographs, and to further useful information in English and Portuguese about both the city and the country.

■ **São Paolo, Brazil**
http://www.spguia.com.br/Ingles/indexi.html
Profile of São Paolo, Brazil's largest city. There is useful information on areas such as accommodation, transport, and cultural events.

BRUNEI
Map page 86

National name Negara Brunei Darussalam/State of Brunei

Area 5,765 sq km/2,225 sq mi

Capital Bandar Seri Begawan (and chief port)

Major towns/cities Seria, Kuala Belait

Physical features flat coastal plain with hilly lowland in west and mountains in east (Mount Pagon 1,850 m/6,070 ft); 75% of the area is forested; the Limbang valley splits Brunei in two, and its cession to Sarawak in 1890 is disputed by Brunei; tropical climate; Temburong, Tutong, and Belait rivers

Currency Bruneian dollar, although the Singapore dollar is also accepted

GNP per capita (PPP) (US$) 24,824 (1999 est)

Resources petroleum, natural gas

Population 328,000 (2000 est)

Population density (per sq km) 56 (1999 est)

Language Malay (official), Chinese (Hokkien), English

Religion Muslim 66%, Buddhist 14%, Christian 10%

Time difference GMT +8

 www. ■ CIA ■ LP ■ RG ■ WTG

BULGARIA
Map page 66

National name Republika Bulgaria/ Republic of Bulgaria

Area 110,912 sq km/42,823 sq mi

Capital Sofia

Major towns/cities Plovdiv, Varna, Ruse, Burgas, Stara Zagora, Pleven

Major ports Burgas, Varna

Physical features lowland plains in north and southeast separated by mountains (Balkan and Rhodope) that cover three-quarters of the country; River Danube in north

Currency lev

GNP per capita (PPP) (US$) 4,914 (1999)

Resources coal, iron ore, manganese, lead, zinc, petroleum

Population 8,225,000 (2000 est)

Population density (per sq km) 75 (1999 est)

Language Bulgarian (official), Turkish

Religion Eastern Orthodox Christian, Muslim, Jewish, Roman Catholic, Protestant

Time difference GMT +2

 www. ■ CIA ■ LC ■ LP ■ RG ■ WTG

■ **All About Bulgaria**
http://www.cs.columbia.edu/~radev/bulginfo.html
Links to more than 700 Bulgarian-related sites, answers to 'Frequently Asked Questions', and an archive of 200 poems make this an impressive page.

■ **Welcome to Sofia**
http://www.sofia.com:8080/realindex.html
Large source of information on past and present life in the Bulgarian capital. The contents include shopping, sightseeing, a good history, a guide to cultural events, accommodation, restaurants, media, and sports. There is also a map and many photographs of the city.

■ **Welcome to Plovdiv!**
http://www.plovdiv.org/
Guide to the second-largest Bulgarian city. A good history of the city and guide to its attractions are illustrated with photographs. There is also information on famous residents, as well as cultural and commercial events.

BURKINA FASO
Map page 104

Area 274,122 sq km/105,838 sq mi

Capital Ouagadougou

Major towns/cities Bobo-Dioulasso, Koudougou, Banfora, Ouahigouya, Tenkodogo

Physical features landlocked plateau with hills in west and southeast; headwaters of the River Volta; semiarid in north, forest and farmland in south; linked by rail to Abidjan in Côte d'Ivoire, Burkina Faso's only outlet to the sea

Currency franc CFA

GNP per capita (PPP) (US$) 898 (1999 est)

Resources manganese, zinc, limestone, phosphates, diamonds, gold, antimony, marble, silver, lead

Population 11,937,000 (2000 est)

Population density (per sq km) 42 (1999 est)

Language French (official), 50 Sudanic languages (90%)

Religion animist 40%, Sunni Muslim 50%, Christian (mainly Roman Catholic) 10%

Time difference GMT+/–0

 www. ■ CIA ■ LP ■ NA ■ WTG

BURUNDI
Map page 106

National name Republika y'Uburundi/République du Burundi/ Republic of Burundi

Area 27,834 sq km/10,746 sq mi

Capital Bujumbura

Major towns/cities Gitega, Bururi, Ngozi, Muyinga, Ruyigi, Kayanaza

Physical features landlocked grassy highland straddling watershed of Nile and Congo; Lake Tanganyika, Great Rift Valley

Currency Burundi franc

GNP per capita (PPP) (US$) 553 (1999 est)

Resources nickel, gold, tungsten, phosphates, vanadium, uranium, peat, petroleum deposits have been detected

Population 6,695,000 (2000 est)

Population density (per sq km) 236 (1999 est)

Language Kirundi, French (both official), Kiswahili

Religion Roman Catholic 62%, Pentecostalist 5%, Anglican 1%, Muslim 1%, animist

Time difference GMT +2

 www. ■ CIA ■ LP ■ WTG

CAMBODIA
Map page 84

National name Preah Réaché'anachâkr Kâmpuchéa/ Kingdom of Cambodia

Area 181,035 sq km/69,897 sq mi

Capital Phnum Penh

Major towns/cities Bâtdâmbâng, Kâmpóng Cham, Siëmréab, Prey Vêng

Major ports Kâmpóng Cham

Physical features mostly flat, forested plains with mountains in southwest and north; Mekong River runs north–south; Lake Tonle Sap

Currency Cambodian riel

GNP per capita (PPP) (US$) 1,286 (1999 est)

Resources phosphates, iron ore, gemstones, bauxite, silicon, manganese

Population 11,168,000 (2000 est)

Population density (per sq km) 66 (1999 est)

Language Khmer (official), French

Religion Theravada Buddhist 95%, Muslim, Roman Catholic

Time difference GMT +7

 www. ■ CIA ■ LC ■ LP ■ WTG

■ **Cambodia Mega Attraction – Angkor**
http://www.asiatour.com/cambodia/e-04angk/ec-ang10.htm
Guide to Cambodia's most impressive attraction. Good photographs accompany a history of the vast complex and details of Angkor Thom, Angkor Wat, and other sites.

CAMEROON

Map page 104

National name République du Cameroun/Republic of Cameroon
Area 475,440 sq km/ 183,567 sq mi
Capital Yaoundé
Major towns/cities Garoua, Douala, Nkongsamba, Maroua, Bamenda, Bafoussam, Ngaoundéré
Major ports Douala
Physical features desert in far north in the Lake Chad basin, mountains in west, dry savannah plateau in the intermediate area, and dense tropical rainforest in south; Mount Cameroon 4,070 m/ 13,358 ft, an active volcano on the coast, west of the Adamawa Mountains
Currency franc CFA
GNP per capita (PPP) (US$) 1,444 (1999)
Resources petroleum, natural gas, tin ore, limestone, bauxite, iron ore, uranium, gold
Population 15,085,000 (2000 est)
Population density (per sq km) 31 (1999 est)
Language French, English (both official; often spoken in pidgin), Sudanic languages (in the north), Bantu languages (elsewhere); there has been some discontent with the emphasis on French – there are 163 indigenous peoples with their own African languages
Religion animist 50%, Christian 33%, Muslim 16%
Time difference GMT +1

 ▪ CIA ▪ LP ▪ NA ▪ WTG

▪ Home Page of the Republic of Cameroon
http://www.compufix.demon.co.uk/camweb/
Factual data about the country of Cameroon, plus links to a number of associated sites. This site includes a map, an audio clip of the national anthem, and a brief text-only section on tourism in this African country.

CANADA

Map page 122

Area 9,970,610 sq km/3,849,652 sq mi
Capital Ottawa
Major towns/cities Toronto, Montréal, Vancouver, Edmonton, Calgary, Winnipeg, Québec, Hamilton, Saskatoon, Halifax, London, Kitchener, Mississauga, Laval, Surrey
Physical features mountains in west, with low-lying plains in interior and rolling hills in east; St. Lawrence Seaway, Mackenzie River; Great Lakes; Arctic Archipelago; Rocky Mountains; Great Plains or Prairies; Canadian Shield; Niagara Falls; climate varies from temperate in south to arctic in north; 45% of country forested
Currency Canadian dollar
GNP per capita (PPP) (US$) 23,725 (1999)
Resources petroleum, natural gas, coal, copper (world's third-largest producer), nickel (world's second-largest producer), lead (world's fifth-largest producer), zinc (world's largest producer), iron, gold, uranium, timber
Population 31,147,000 (2000 est)
Population density (per sq km) 3 (1999 est)
Language English (60%), French (24%) (both official), American Indian languages, Inuktitut (Inuit)
Religion Roman Catholic 45%, various Protestant denominations
Time difference GMT –3.5/9

 ▪ CIA ▪ LP ▪ RG ▪ WTG

▪ Oh Canada!
http://www.ualberta.ca/~bleeck/canada/
Aims to define, by means of selected annotated links, what it is to be Canadian. It includes information on Canadian history, the constitution, national anthem, and more.

▪ Montreal
http://www.tourism-montreal.org/
Both historical and contemporary information on Montreal. Visitors can choose from a general presentation of the city and its

development, tourist information, specialized overviews of arts, architecture, and business in the city.

▪ Toronto Star City Search
http://www.starcitysearch.com/
Huge source of information on Canada's largest city. Primarily designed for residents, this site is constantly updated with news of local events, community groups, local government, cultural life, sport, and weather. For visitors there is information on accommodation and tourist attractions. There is also a good search engine.

▪ Welcome to Whitehorse Online
http://www.city.whitehorse.yk.ca/
Official guide to Canada's most westerly city. There are details of local government services, business activities, and community groups. Information for visitors includes local attractions, suggested drives and hikes, and a guide to the Klondike Bathtub Race and other events.

▪ Québec History at a Glance
http://www.tourisme.gouv.qc.ca/anglais/menu_a/histoire_a.html
Introduction to the history, culture, and economy of Quebec. It is accompanied by photos of the province and a video. This is part of the official site of the Quebec government which contains a wealth of information on the provincial government, economic opportunities, tourist information, and local news stories.

▪ Government of Canada
http://infocan.gc.ca/index_e.html
A wealth of information about this country, including numerous fact sheets, a discussion of 'Flag etiquette', and photographs and biographies of Canadian prime ministers between 1867 and 1994. There is also an overview of the government structure, as well as downloadable files containing the full contents of a wide range of laws and acts.

CAPE VERDE

Map page 104

National name República de Cabo Verde/Republic of Cape Verde
Area 4,033 sq km/1,557 sq mi
Capital Praia
Major towns/cities Mindelo, Santa Maria
Major ports Mindelo
Physical features archipelago of ten volcanic islands 565 km/ 350 mi west of Senegal; the windward (Barlavento) group includes Santo Antão, São Vicente, Santa Luzia, São Nicolau, Sal, and Boa Vista; the leeward (Sotovento) group comprises Maio, São Tiago, Fogo, and Brava; all but Santa Luzia are inhabited
Currency Cape Verde escudo
GNP per capita (PPP) (US$) 3,497 (1999 est)
Resources salt, pozzolana (volcanic rock), limestone, basalt, kaolin
Population 428,000 (2000 est)
Population density (per sq km) 104 (1999 est)
Language Portuguese (official), Creole
Religion Roman Catholic 93%, Protestant (Nazarene Church)
Time difference GMT –1

 ▪ CIA ▪ LP ▪ NA ▪ WTG

▪ Republic of Cape Verde Home Page
http://www.umassd.edu/SpecialPrograms/caboverde/capeverdean
.html
Information about Cape Verde – its islands, geography and environment, history, culture, and news, plus food aid updates and a 'Did you know...?' section.

CENTRAL AFRICAN REPUBLIC

Map page 106

National name République Centrafricaine/Central African Republic
Area 622,436 sq km/ 240,322 sq mi
Capital Bangui
Major towns/cities Berbérati, Bouar, Bambari, Bossangoa, Carnot, Kaga Bandoro

Physical features landlocked flat plateau, with rivers flowing north and south, and hills in northeast and southwest; dry in north, rainforest in southwest; mostly wooded; Kotto and Mbali river falls; the Oubangui River rises 6 m/20 ft at Bangui during the wet season (June–November)
Currency franc CFA
GNP per capita (PPP) (US$) 1,131 (1999 est)
Resources gem diamonds and industrial diamonds, gold, uranium, iron ore, manganese, copper
Population 3,615,000 (2000 est)
Population density (per sq km) 6 (1999 est)
Language French (official), Sangho (national), Arabic, Hunsa, Swahili
Religion Protestant 25%, Roman Catholic 25%, animist 24%, Muslim 15%
Time difference GMT +1

 ▪ CIA ▪ LP ▪ NA ▪ WTG

CHAD

Map page 100

National name République du Tchad/Republic of Chad
Area 1,284,000 sq km/ 495,752 sq mi
Capital Ndjamena (formerly Fort Lamy)
Major towns/cities Sarh, Moundou, Abéché, Bongor, Doba, Kélo, Koumra
Physical features landlocked state with mountains (Tibetsi) and part of Sahara Desert in north; moist savannah in south; rivers in south flow northwest to Lake Chad
Currency franc CFA
GNP per capita (PPP) (US$) 816 (1999 est)
Resources petroleum, tungsten, tin ore, bauxite, iron ore, gold, uranium, limestone, kaolin, titanium
Population 7,651,000 (2000 est)
Population density (per sq km) 6 (1999 est)
Language French, Arabic (both official), over 100 African languages
Religion Muslim 50%, Christian 25%, animist 25%
Time difference GMT +1

 ▪ CIA ▪ LC ▪ LP ▪ NA ▪ WTG

CHILE

Map page 142

National name República de Chile/Republic of Chile
Area 756,950 sq km/ 292,258 sq mi
Capital Santiago
Major towns/cities Concepción, Viña del Mar, Valparaíso, Talcahuano, Puente Alto, Temuco, Antofagasta
Major ports Valparaíso, Antofagasta, Arica, Iquique, Punta Arenas
Physical features Andes mountains along eastern border, Atacama Desert in north, fertile central valley, grazing land and forest in south
Territories Easter Island, Juan Fernández Islands, part of Tierra del Fuego, claim to part of Antarctica
Currency Chilean peso
GNP per capita (PPP) (US$) 8,370 (1999)
Resources copper (world's largest producer), gold, silver, iron ore, molybdenum, cobalt, iodine, saltpetre, coal, natural gas, petroleum, hydroelectric power
Population 15,211,000 (2000 est)
Population density (per sq km) 20 (1999 est)
Language Spanish (official)
Religion Roman Catholic 80%, Protestant 13%, atheist and nonreligious 6%
Time difference GMT –4

 ▪ CIA ▪ LC ▪ LP ▪ WTG

Santiago
http://sunsite.dcc.uchile.cl/chile/turismo/santiago.html
Comprehensive introduction to Chile's capital city, Santiago. The page includes information about historical landmarks, cultural and artistic life, its natural environment, shopping, restaurants, conference centres, and its suburbs, as well as general information about population, climate, language, and transport. There is also a list of useful addresses in the city.

Snapshot of Chile
http://www.gobiernodechile.cl/nuestro_pais/snapshot.htm
This government site, aiming to promote Chile for both investment and tourism purposes, contains a range of detailed information including a thorough explanation of the governmental structure and social policy, and information for visitors.

CHINA

Map page 74

National name Zhonghua Renmin Gongheguo (Zhongguo)/People's Republic of China
Area 9,572,900 sq km/ 3,696,000 sq mi
Capital Beijing (or Peking)
Major towns/cities Shanghai, Hong Kong, Chongqing, Tianjin, Guangzhou (English Canton), Shenyang (formerly Mukden), Wuhan, Nanjing, Harbin, Chengdu, Xi'an
Major ports Tianjin, Shanghai, Hong Kong, Qingdao, Guangzhou
Physical features two-thirds of China is mountains or desert (north and west); the low-lying east is irrigated by rivers Huang He (Yellow River), Chang Jiang (Yangtze-Kiang), Xi Jiang (Si Kiang)
Territories Paracel Islands
Currency yuan
GNP per capita (PPP) (US$) 3,291 (1999)
Resources coal, graphite, tungsten, molybdenum, antimony, tin (world's largest producer), lead (world's fifth-largest producer), mercury, bauxite, phosphate rock, iron ore (world's largest producer), diamonds, gold, manganese, zinc (world's third-largest producer), petroleum, natural gas, fish
Population 1,277,558,000 (2000 est)
Population density (per sq km) 133 (1999 est)
Language Chinese (dialects include Mandarin (official), Yue (Cantonese), Wu (Shanghaiese), Minbai, Minnah, Xiang, Gan, and Hakka)
Religion Taoist, Confucianist, and Buddhist; Muslim 2–3%; Christian about 1% (divided between the 'patriotic' church established in 1958 and the 'loyal' church subject to Rome); Protestant 3 million
Time difference GMT +8

 ■ CIA ■ LC ■ LP ■ RG ■ WTG

Beijing Pages
http://www.flashpaper.com/beijing/
Everything about the Chinese capital, from its location and population to its culture, economy, and government. The site also includes detailed tourism links as well as information about industrial development in the city.

China Today
http://www.chinatoday.com/
Complete guide to China, including culture and ethnology, art and entertainment, education, political organizations, and travel. There is also a section on current events and a basic introduction to this country.

Discover Hong Kong
http://www.discoverhongkong.com/eng/gateway/index.jhtml
Jumping-off point for sources of political, social, and cultural news about Hong Kong. This site is directed at the tourist and includes practical information on such topics as sightseeing, shopping, transportation, where to stay, and local culture, as well as a more practical hotel and restaurant guide.

Tibet in the 20th Century
http://www.tibetinfo.net/tibet-file/chronol.htm
Brief chronology of significant events in Tibet's history over the past century – 1902–90 – prepared by the Tibet Information Network, an independent organization based in the UK and the USA. Click on links at the bottom of the page to access news updates, reports, and basic information.

Inner Mongolia Overview
http://www.bupt.edu.cn/regnet/english/inmon.html
All about Inner Mongolia – its population, climate, education, economy, agriculture, industry, transportation, and cities. The page is illustrated with a few colour photographs, and there are links to others showing features and national customs.

Shanghai
http://www.sh.com/attracti/attracti.htm
Guide to Shanghai. History, geography, and travel information as well as features on festivals make up the majority of the tourist-oriented information on this site, in addition to local transport information and a list of useful telephone numbers.

COLOMBIA

Map page 140

National name República de Colombia/Republic of Colombia
Area 1,141,748 sq km/ 440,828 sq mi
Capital Bogotá
Major towns/cities Medellín, Cali, Barranquilla, Cartagena, Bucaramanga, Cúcuta, Ibagué
Major ports Barranquilla, Cartagena, Buenaventura
Physical features the Andes mountains run north–south; flat coastland in west and plains (llanos) in east; Magdalena River runs north to Caribbean Sea; includes islands of Providencia, San Andrés, and Mapelo; almost half the country is forested
Currency Colombian peso
GNP per capita (PPP) (US$) 5,709 (1999 est)
Resources petroleum, natural gas, coal, nickel, emeralds (accounts for about half of world production), gold, manganese, copper, lead, mercury, platinum, limestone, phosphates
Population 42,321,000 (2000 est)
Population density (per sq km) 36 (1999 est)
Language Spanish (official) (95%)
Religion Roman Catholic
Time difference GMT –5

 ■ CIA ■ LC ■ LP ■ WTG

Colombia
http://www.ddg.com/LIS/aurelia/colombi.htm
General resource on Colombia, with plenty of information on topics such as history, geography, the economy, and politics. There are also two maps to accompany the text.

Bogotá, Colombia
http://travel.lycos.com/Destinations/South_America/Colombia/Bogota/
Page devoted to Colombia's largest city Bogotá. There is a general introduction to the city's attractions, and four sections – 'Visitor's guide', 'Culture and history', 'News and weather', and 'Entertainment' – each with links to further useful information in both English and Spanish about both the city and the country.

Medellín, Colombia
http://travel.lycos.com/Destinations/South_America/Colombia/Medellin/
Page devoted to the Colombian city of Medellín, a busy industrial and commercial centre. There is a general introduction to the city's attractions, and four sections – 'Visitors' guide', 'Culture and history', 'News and weather', and 'Entertainment' – each with links to further useful information in English and Spanish about both the city and the country.

COMOROS

Map page 108

National name Jumhuriyyat al-Qumur al-Itthadiyah al-Islamiyah (Arabic), République fédérale islamique des Comores (French)/ Federal Islamic Republic of the Comoros
Area 1,862 sq km/718 sq mi
Capital Moroni
Major towns/cities Mutsamudu, Domoni, Fomboni, Mitsamiouli

Physical features comprises the volcanic islands of Njazídja, Nzwani, and Mwali (formerly Grande Comore, Anjouan, Moheli); at northern end of Mozambique Channel in Indian Ocean between Madagascar and coast of Africa
Currency Comorian franc
GNP per capita (PPP) (US$) 1,360 (1999 est)
Population 694,000 (2000 est)
Population density (per sq km) 363 (1999 est)
Language Arabic, French (both official), Comorian (a Swahili and Arabic dialect), Makua
Religion Muslim; Islam is the state religion
Time difference GMT +3

 ■ CIA ■ LC ■ AN ■ LP ■ WTG

CONGO, DEMOCRATIC REPUBLIC OF

Map page 106

National name République Démocratique du Congo/ Democratic Republic of Congo
Area 2,344,900 sq km/ 905,366 sq mi
Capital Kinshasa
Major towns/cities Lubumbashi, Kananga, Mbuji-Mayi, Kisangani, Kolwezi, Likasi, Boma
Major ports Matadi, Kalemie
Physical features Congo River basin has tropical rainforest (second-largest remaining in world) and savannah; mountains in east and west; lakes Tanganyika, Albert, Edward; Ruwenzori Range
Currency congolese franc
GNP per capita (PPP) (US$) 731 (1999 est)
Resources petroleum, copper, cobalt (65% of world's reserves), manganese, zinc, tin, uranium, silver, gold, diamonds (one of the world's largest producers of industrial diamonds)
Population 51,654,000 (2000 est)
Population density (per sq km) 21 (1999 est)
Language French (official), Swahili, Lingala, Kikongo, Tshiluba (all national languages), over 200 other languages
Religion Roman Catholic 41%, Protestant 32%, Kimbanguist 13%, animist 10%, Muslim 1–5%
Time difference GMT +1/2

 ■ CIA ■ LC ■ LP ■ NA ■ WTG

CONGO

Map page 104

National name République du Congo/Republic of Congo
Area 342,000 sq km/ 132,046 sq mi
Capital Brazzaville
Major towns/cities Pointe-Noire, Nkayi, Loubomo, Bouenza, Mossendjo, Ouésso, Owando
Major ports Pointe-Noire
Physical features narrow coastal plain rises to central plateau, then falls into northern basin; Congo River on the border with the Democratic Republic of Congo; half the country is rainforest
Currency franc CFA
GNP per capita (PPP) (US$) 897 (1999)
Resources petroleum, natural gas, lead, zinc, gold, copper, phosphate, iron ore, potash, bauxite
Population 2,943,000 (2000 est)
Population density (per sq km) 8 (1999 est)
Language French (official), Kongo, Monokutuba and Lingala (both patois), and other dialects
Religion Christian 50%, animist 48%, Muslim 2%
Time difference GMT +1

 ■ CIA ■ LP ■ NA ■ WTG

COSTA RICA

Map page 134

National name República de Costa Rica/Republic of Costa Rica
Area 51,100 sq km/19,729 sq mi
Capital San José
Major towns/cities Alajuela, Cartago, Limón, Puntarenas, San Isidro, Desamparados
Major ports Limón, Puntarenas
Physical features high central plateau and tropical coasts; Costa Rica was once entirely forested, containing an estimated 5% of the Earth's flora and fauna
Currency colón
GNP per capita (PPP) (US$) 5,770 (1999 est)
Resources gold, salt, hydro power
Population 4,023,000 (2000 est)
Population density (per sq km) 77 (1999 est)
Language Spanish (official)
Religion Roman Catholic 95% (state religion)
Time difference GMT –6

 ■ CIA ■ LP ■ WTG

■ **Costa Rica: Facts**
http://www.centralamerica.com/
Costa Rica for tourists. The site provides a summary of Costa Rican history, geography, and politics, as well as information about the activities you can enjoy in the country.

■ **Costa Rica TravelWeb**
http://www.crica.com/info/info_intro.html
Information for the traveller and prospective business investor, with details of Costa Rica's government and political parties, healthcare and medical system, plus an overview of its history and culture.

CÔTE D'IVOIRE

Map page 104

National name République de la Côte d'Ivoire/Republic of the Ivory Coast
Area 322,463 sq km/124,502 sq mi
Capital Yamoussoukro
Major towns/cities Abidjan, Bouaké, Daloa, Man, Korhogo, Gagnoa
Major ports Abidjan, San Pedro
Physical features tropical rainforest (diminishing as exploited) in south; savannah and low mountains in north; coastal plain; Vridi canal, Kossou dam, Monts du Toura
Currency franc CFA
GNP per capita (PPP) (US$) 1,546 (1999)
Resources petroleum, natural gas, diamonds, gold, nickel, reserves of manganese, iron ore, bauxite
Population 14,786,000 (2000 est)
Population density (per sq km) 45 (1999 est)
Language French (official), over 60 ethnic languages
Religion animist 17%, Muslim 39% (mainly in north), Christian 26% (mainly Roman Catholic in south)
Time difference GMT +/–0

 ■ CIA ■ LC ■ LP ■ NA ■ WTG

■ **Côte d'Ivoire**
http://www.newafrica.com/profiles/profile.asp?CountryID=17
Informative guide to Côte d'Ivoire that is concerned more with hard facts than information for tourists. The site is divided into a number of sections, such as 'Culture', 'Government', and 'Travel Facts', each offering a large number of facts and statistics about this African country.

CROATIA

Map page 66

National name Republika Hrvatska/Republic of Croatia
Area 56,538 sq km/21,829 sq mi
Capital Zagreb
Major towns/cities Osijek, Split, Dubrovnik, Rijeka, Zadar, Pula

---

Major ports chief port: Rijeka (Fiume); other ports: Zadar, Šibenik, Split, Dubrovnik
Physical features Adriatic coastline with large islands; very mountainous, with part of the Karst region and the Julian and Styrian Alps; some marshland
Currency kuna
GNP per capita (PPP) (US$) 6,915 (1999)
Resources petroleum, natural gas, coal, lignite, bauxite, iron ore, salt
Population 4,473,000 (2000 est)
Population density (per sq km) 79 (1999 est)
Language Croat (official), Serbian
Religion Roman Catholic (Croats) 76.5%; Orthodox Christian (Serbs) 11%, Protestant 1.4%, Muslim 1.2%
Time difference GMT +1

 ■ CIA ■ LP ■ RG ■ WTG

■ **Facts about Croatia**
http://www.hr/index_en.shtml
Presentation of Croatia with a variety of focuses on history, culture and media, financial aspects, political issues and government structure, sections on educational institutions, social and health care, a science fact-sheet, and gastronomic guidance. An extra bonus of the site is its extensive list of Web links on contemporary Croatia, including Web sites of ministries, educational and cultural organizations and networks, tourist associations, and media enterprises.

■ **Government of the Republic of Croatia**
http://www.vlada.hr/eindex.html
Full information about the Croatian government, including biographies and pictures of all the political leaders, documents including the Croatian constitution, and links to other related sites.

■ **Celebrating 17 Centuries of the City of Split**
http://www.st.carnet.hr/split/
Good source of information on this Croatian port. There are many photos of the city and descriptions of Diocletian's palace and other noted buildings. This site was prepared to mark the 1,700th anniversary of the founding of the city.

■ **Welcome to Zagreb**
http://www.tel.fer.hr/hrvatska/HRgradovi/Zagreb/Zagreb.html
Guide to the Croatian capital that includes a description and outline of Zagreb's history. This site also includes maps, photos, a Webcam trained on the city centre, and a restaurant guide.

CUBA

Map page 134

National name República de Cuba/Republic of Cuba
Area 110,860 sq km/42,803 sq mi
Capital Havana
Major towns/cities Santiago de Cuba, Camagüey, Holguín, Guantánamo, Santa Clara, Bayamo, Cienfuegos
Physical features comprises Cuba and smaller islands including Isle of Youth; low hills; Sierra Maestra mountains in southeast; Cuba has 3,380 km/2,100 mi of coastline, with deep bays, sandy beaches, coral islands and reefs
Currency Cuban peso
GNP per capita (PPP) (US$) N/A
Resources iron ore, copper, chromite, gold, manganese, nickel, cobalt, silver, salt
Population 11,201,000 (2000 est)
Population density (per sq km) 101 (1999 est)
Language Spanish (official)
Religion Roman Catholic; also Episcopalians and Methodists
Time difference GMT –5

 ■ CIA ■ LP ■ RG ■ WTG

■ **CubaWeb**
http://www.cubaweb.com/
Business library, with background information about Cuba for the prospective business investor, and a culture library, covering Cuban history, art, music, literature, food, sport, and collections of photographs.

CYPRUS

Map page 68

National name Kipriakí Dimokratía/Greek Republic of Cyprus (south); Kibris Cumhuriyeti/Turkish Republic of Northern Cyprus (north)
Area 9,251 sq km/3,571 sq mi (3,335 sq km/1,287 sq mi is Turkish-occupied)
Capital Nicosia (divided between Greek and Turkish Cypriots)
Major towns/cities Limassol, Larnaka, Pafos, Lefkosia, Famagusta
Major ports Limassol, Larnaka, and Pafos (Greek); Keryneia and Famagusta (Turkish)
Physical features central plain between two east–west mountain ranges
Currency Cyprus pound and Turkish lira
GNP per capita (PPP) (US$) 18,395 (1999 est)
Resources copper precipitates, beutonite, umber and other ochres
Population 786,000 (2000 est)
Population density (per sq km) 84 (1999 est)
Language Greek, Turkish (both official), English
Religion Greek Orthodox 78%, Sunni Muslim 18%, Maronite, Armenian Apostolic
Time difference GMT +2

 ■ CIA ■ LC ■ LP ■ WTG

■ **Cyprus**
http://www.stwing.upenn.edu/~durduran/cyprus2.shtml
Devoted to Cyprus – its news, geography, and culture. Included are picture galleries, Cypriot jokes, and guides to Cypriot and Turkish Cypriot dances.

■ **Republic of Cyprus**
http://www.pio.gov.cy/
This official Web site contains detailed information about the Cyprus government system (including a full copy of the Cypriot constitution), Cypriot international relations, and documents relating to the 'Cyprus issue'. This site also includes a history of the island and the culture of the people.

CZECH REPUBLIC
Map page 50

National name Ceská Republika/Czech Republic
Area 78,864 sq km/30,449 sq mi
Capital Prague
Major towns/cities Brno, Ostrava, Olomouc, Liberec, Plzen, Hradec Králové, České Budějovice
Physical features mountainous; rivers: Morava, Labe (Elbe), Vltava (Moldau)
Currency koruna (based on the Czechoslovak koruna)
GNP per capita (PPP) (US$) 12,289 (1999)
Resources coal, lignite
Population 10,244,000 (2000 est)
Population density (per sq km) 130 (1999 est)
Language Czech (official), Slovak
Religion Roman Catholic 39%, atheist 30%, Protestant 5%, Orthodox 3%
Time difference GMT +1

 ■ CIA ■ LC ■ LP ■ RG ■ WTG

■ **Czech Info Centre**
http://www.muselik.com/czech/
Updated daily and aimed primarily at the traveller. However, this site also has information on how to trace a Czech ancestor, traditional recipes, and Czech fonts to download.

■ **Czech Republic**
http://www.czech.cz/
Root page for the official Czech Republic site, with information on history, geography, and politics. It contains a daily news section, photographs, and Czech music, as well as practical information for tourists.

DENMARK
Map page 48

National name Kongeriget Danmark/Kingdom of Denmark
Area 43,075 sq km/16,631 sq mi
Capital Copenhagen
Major towns/cities Århus, Odense, Ålborg, Esbjerg, Randers, Kolding, Horsens
Major ports Århus, Odense, Ålborg, Esbjerg
Physical features comprises the Jutland peninsula and about 500 islands (100 inhabited) including Bornholm in the Baltic Sea; the land is flat and cultivated; sand dunes and lagoons on the west coast and long inlets on the east; the main island is Sjæland (Zealand), where most of Copenhagen is located (the rest is on the island of Amager)
Territories the dependencies of Faroe Islands and Greenland
Currency Danish krone
GNP per capita (PPP) (US$) 24,280 (1999)
Resources crude petroleum, natural gas, salt, limestone
Population 5,293,000 (2000 est)
Population density (per sq km) 123 (1999 est)
Language Danish (official), German
Religion Evangelical Lutheran 87% (national church), other Protestant and Roman Catholic 3%
Time difference GMT +1

www. ▪ CIA ▪ LP ▪ RG ▪ WTG

▪ **Aarhus Webben**
http://www.aarhuswebben.dk/index.uk.html
Guide to the Danish city of Aarhus. There is information on the city's culture, entertainment, restaurants, and hotels. A street map is also provided and there are links to local Web sites.

▪ **Copenhagen, Denmark**
http://travel.excite.com/show/?loc=13648
Comprehensive guide around Copenhagen that offers all the essential facts plus useful directions concerning hotels, eating out, transportation, and sightseeing. Its travel tools include searchable maps, message boards and a 'Yellow pages' section on things to see and do. The site also features selected links to useful pages on all aspects of life in Copenhagen.

▪ **Greenland Guide**
http://www.greenland-guide.dk/
Official guide to Greenland. The site is highly informative about all regions of the country and is filled with practical information. There are also links to several other sites on Greenland.

▪ **Faroe Islands Tourist Board**
http://www.tourist.fo/
Comprehensive official source of information on the Faroe Islands. There are sections on the Faroese language, geography, history, economy, tourism, and current political controversies in this autonomous region of Norway.

DJIBOUTI
Map page 100

National name Jumhouriyya Djibouti/Republic of Djibouti
Area 23,200 sq km/8,957 sq mi
Capital Djibouti (and chief port)
Major towns/cities Tadjoura, Obock, Dikhil, Ali-Sabieh
Physical features mountains divide an inland plateau from a coastal plain; hot and arid
Currency Djibouti franc
GNP per capita (PPP) (US$) 1,200 (1999 est)
Population 638,000 (2000 est)
Population density (per sq km) 27 (1999 est)
Language French (official), Issa (Somali), Afar, Arabic
Religion Sunni Muslim
Time difference GMT +3

www. ▪ CIA ▪ AN ▪ LP ▪ NA ▪ WTG

DOMINICA
Map page 134

National name Commonwealth of Dominica
Area 751 sq km/290 sq mi
Capital Roseau
Major towns/cities Portsmouth, Marigot, Mahaut, Atkinson, Grand Bay
Major ports Roseau, Portsmouth, Berekua, Marigot
Physical features second-largest of the Windward Islands, mountainous central ridge with tropical rainforest
Currency East Caribbean dollar, although the pound sterling and French franc are also accepted
GNP per capita (PPP) (US$) 4,825 (1999)
Resources pumice, limestone, clay
Population 71,000 (2000 est)
Population density (per sq km) 100 (1999 est)
Language English (official), a Dominican patois (which reflects earlier periods of French rule)
Religion Roman Catholic 80%
Time difference GMT –4

www. ▪ CIA ▪ LP ▪ WTG

DOMINICAN REPUBLIC
Map page 134

National name República Dominicana/Dominican Republic
Area 48,442 sq km/18,703 sq mi
Capital Santo Domingo
Major towns/cities Santiago, La Romana, San Pedro de Macoris, La Vega, San Juan, San Cristóbal
Physical features comprises eastern two-thirds of island of Hispaniola; central mountain range with fertile valleys; Pico Duarte 3,174 m/10,417 ft, highest point in Caribbean islands
Currency Dominican Republic peso
GNP per capita (PPP) (US$) 4,653 (1999 est)
Resources ferro-nickel, gold, silver
Population 8,495,000 (2000 est)
Population density (per sq km) 173 (1999 est)
Language Spanish (official)
Religion Roman Catholic
Time difference GMT –4

www. ▪ CIA ▪ LC ▪ LP ▪ WTG

▪ **Dominican Republic on the Internet**
http://www.latinworld.com/caribe/rdominicana/index.html
Resources about the Dominican Republic – its news, culture, government, sport, travel opportunities, and economy, plus links to other sites. Please note that some of the information is only available in Spanish.

ECUADOR
Map page 140

National name República del Ecuador/Republic of Ecuador
Area 270,670 sq km/104,505 sq mi
Capital Quito
Major towns/cities Guayaquil, Cuenca, Machala, Portoviejo, Manta, Ambato, Santo Domingo
Major ports Guayaquil
Physical features coastal plain rises sharply to Andes Mountains, which are divided into a series of cultivated valleys; flat, low-lying rainforest in the east; Galapagos Islands; Cotopaxi, the world's highest active volcano. Ecuador is crossed by the Equator, from which it derives its name
Currency sucre
GNP per capita (PPP) (US$) 2,605 (1999)
Resources petroleum, natural gas, gold, silver, copper, zinc, antimony, iron, uranium, lead, coal
Population 12,646,000 (2000 est)

Population density (per sq km) 46 (1999 est)
Language Spanish (official), Quechua, Jivaro, other indigenous languages
Religion Roman Catholic
Time difference GMT –5

www. ▪ CIA ▪ LC ▪ LP ▪ WTG

▪ **Guayaquil, Ecuador**
http://travel.lycos.com/Destinations/South_America/Ecuador/Guayaquil/
Profile of the city of Guayaquil, Ecuador's busiest port. There is a general introduction to the city's main features, and four sections – 'Visitors' guide', 'Culture and history', 'News and weather', and 'Entertainment' – each with links to photographs, and further information in English and Spanish about both the city and the country.

▪ **Quito, Ecuador**
http://travel.lycos.com/Destinations/South_America/Ecuador/Quito/
Profile of the Ecuadorian capital, the beautiful city of Quito. There is a general introduction to the city's attractions, and four sections – 'Visitors' guide', 'Culture and history', 'News and weather', and 'Entertainment' – each with links to further useful information in English and Spanish about both the city and the country.

EGYPT
Map page 100

National name Jumhuriyyat Misr al-'Arabiyya/Arab Republic of Egypt
Area 1,001,450 sq km/386,659 sq mi
Capital Cairo
Major towns/cities El Giza, Shubrâ el Kheima, Alexandria, Port Said, El-Mahalla el-Koubra, El Mansûra, Suez
Major ports Alexandria, Port Said, Suez, Dumyât, Shubra Al Khayma
Physical features mostly desert; hills in east; fertile land along Nile valley and delta; cultivated and settled area is about 35,500 sq km/13,700 sq mi; Aswan High Dam and Lake Nasser; Sinai
Currency Egyptian pound
GNP per capita (PPP) (US$) 3,303 (1999)
Resources petroleum, natural gas, phosphates, manganese, uranium, coal, iron ore, gold
Population 68,470,000 (2000 est)
Population density (per sq km) 67 (1999 est)
Language Arabic (official), Coptic (derived from ancient Egyptian), English, French
Religion Sunni Muslim 90%, Coptic Christian and other Christian 6%
Time difference GMT +2

www. ▪ CIA ▪ LC ▪ AN ▪ LP ▪ NA ▪ WTG

▪ **Cairo, the Jewel of the Orient**
http://ce.eng.usf.edu/pharos/cairo/
Comprehensive guide to the city's history with a gallery of maps and pictures. It includes detailed information for visitors – places to visit (both ancient and modern), where to stay, where to eat, and details of transportation.

▪ **Alexandria, Egypt**
http://ce.eng.usf.edu/pharos/alexandria/
Information about the Egyptian city of Alexandria including an historical guide, a visitor guide, a picture gallery, maps, and links to related Web sites.

▪ **Aswan**
http://touregypt.net/aswan/
Tourist guide to this relatively undiscovered Egyptian resort. It contains practical information including maps, weather forecasts, and hotel listings. Perhaps unsurprisingly, the bulk of the site is devoted to the museums and monuments, for which there is plenty of historical information. Part of a collection of guides to all major and less popular destinations in Egypt.

EL SALVADOR

Map page 134

National name República de El Salvador/Republic of El Salvador
Area 21,393 sq km/8,259 sq mi
Capital San Salvador
Major towns/cities Santa Ana, San Miguel, Nueva San Salvador, Apopa, Delgado
Physical features narrow coastal plain, rising to mountains in north with central plateau
Currency US dollar (replaced Salvadorean colón in 2001)
GNP per capita (PPP) (US$) 4,048 (1999 est)
Resources salt, limestone, gypsum
Population 6,276,000 (2000 est)
Population density (per sq km) 288 (1999 est)
Language Spanish (official), Nahuatl
Religion about 75% Roman Catholic, Protestant
Time difference GMT –6

 www. ▪ CIA ▪ LC ▪ LP ▪ WTG

EQUATORIAL GUINEA

Map page 104

National name República de Guinea Ecuatorial/Republic of Equatorial Guinea
Area 28,051 sq km/10,830 sq mi
Capital Malabo
Major towns/cities Bata, Mongomo, Ela Nguema, Mbini, Campo Yaunde, Los Angeles
Physical features comprises mainland Río Muni, plus the small islands of Corisco, Elobey Grande and Elobey Chico, and Bioko (formerly Fernando Po) together with Annobón (formerly Pagalu); nearly half the land is forested; volcanic mountains on Bioko
Currency franc CFA
GNP per capita (PPP) (US$) 3,545 (1999 est)
Resources petroleum, natural gas, gold, uranium, iron ore, tantalum, manganese
Population 453,000 (2000 est)
Population density (per sq km) 16 (1999 est)
Language Spanish (official), pidgin English, a Portuguese patois (on Annobón, whose people were formerly slaves of the Portuguese), Fang and other African patois (on Río Muni)
Religion Roman Catholic, Protestant, animist
Time difference GMT +1

 www. ▪ CIA ▪ LP ▪ NA ▪ WTG

ERITREA
Map page 100

National name Hagere Eretra al-Dawla al-Iritra/State of Eritrea
Area 125,000 sq km/48,262 sq mi
Capital Asmara
Major towns/cities Assab, Keren, Massawa, Adi Ugri, Ed
Major ports Assab, Massawa
Physical features coastline along the Red Sea 1,000 km/620 mi; narrow coastal plain that rises to an inland plateau; Dahlak Islands
Currency Ethiopian nakfa
GNP per capita (PPP) (US$) 1,012 (1999 est)
Resources gold, silver, copper, zinc, sulphur, nickel, chrome, potash, basalt, limestone, marble, sand, silicates
Population 3,850,000 (2000 est)
Population density (per sq km) 30 (1999 est)
Language Tigre, Tigrinya, Arabic, English, Afar, Amharic, Kunama, Italian
Religion mainly Sunni Muslim and Coptic Christian, some Roman Catholic, Protestant, and animist
Time difference GMT +3

 www. ▪ CIA ▪ LP ▪ NA ▪ WTG

ESTONIA

Map page 48

National name Eesti Vabariik/Republic of Estonia
Area 45,000 sq km/17,374 sq mi
Capital Tallinn
Major towns/cities Tartu, Narva, Kohtla-Järve, Pärnu
Physical features lakes and marshes in a partly forested plain; 774 km/481 mi of coastline; mild climate; Lake Peipus and Narva River forming boundary with Russian Federation; Baltic islands, the largest of which is Saaremaa
Currency kroon
GNP per capita (PPP) (US$) 7,826 (1999)
Resources oilshale, peat, phosphorite ore, superphosphates
Population 1,396,000 (2000 est)
Population density (per sq km) 31 (1999 est)
Language Estonian (official), Russian
Religion Eastern Orthodox, Evangelical Lutheran, Russian Orthodox, Muslim, Judaism
Time difference GMT +2

 www. ▪ CIA ▪ LC ▪ LP ▪ RG ▪ WTG

▪ **Estonia Country Guide**
http://www.ciesin.ee/ESTCG/
General information and news about Estonia, plus sections on its history, political system, economy, and culture. There is, however, little information of direct use to people wishing to visit the country, except for pages on upcoming events and public transport.

▪ **Tallinn**
http://www.tallinn.ee/english/index.html
Good official guide to the Estonian capital. There is good coverage of the city's rich history, culture, economy, educational and scientific institutions, and transport services. In addition there is a demographic profile of its inhabitants.

ETHIOPIA

Map page 98

National name Ya'Ityopya Federalawi Dimokrasiyawi Repeblik/Federal Democratic Republic of Ethiopia
Area 1,096,900 sq km/423,513 sq mi
Capital Addis Ababa
Major towns/cities Dirē Dawa, Harar, Nazrēt, Desē, Gonder, Mek'ele, Bahir Dar
Physical features a high plateau with central mountain range divided by Rift Valley; plains in east; source of Blue Nile River; Danakil and Ogaden deserts
Currency Ethiopian birr
GNP per capita (PPP) (US$) 599 (1999)
Resources gold, salt, platinum, copper, potash. Reserves of petroleum have not been exploited
Population 62,565,000 (2000 est)
Population density (per sq km) 56 (1999 est)
Language Amharic (official), Arabic, Tigrinya, Orominga, about 100 other local languages
Religion Muslim 45%, Ethiopian Orthodox Church (which has had its own patriarch since 1976) 35%, animist 12%, other Christian 8%
Time difference GMT +3

 www. ▪ CIA ▪ LC ▪ LP ▪ NA ▪ WTG

▪ **Ethiopia, Land of Zion**
http://www.webstories.co.nz/focus/etiopia/
Fascinating guide to Ethiopia. Divided into three sections – 'Past', 'Land', and 'People' – the site offers a series of illustrated articles, covering topics such as Ethiopian wildlife, Rastafarians, and Haile Selassie.

FIJI

Map page 112

National name Matanitu Ko Viti/Republic of the Fiji Islands
Area 18,333 sq km/7,078 sq mi
Capital Suva
Major towns/cities Lautoka, Nadi, Ba, Labasa, Nausori
Major ports Lautoka, Levuka
Physical features comprises about 844 Melanesian and Polynesian islands and islets (about 100 inhabited), the largest being Viti Levu (10,429 sq km/4,028 sq mi) and Vanua Levu (5,556 sq km/2,146 sq mi); mountainous, volcanic, with tropical rainforest and grasslands; almost all islands surrounded by coral reefs; high volcanic peaks
Currency Fiji dollar
GNP per capita (PPP) (US$) 4,536 (1999)
Resources gold, silver, copper
Population 817,000 (2000 est)
Population density (per sq km) 44 (1999 est)
Language English (official), Fijian, Hindi
Religion Methodist 37%, Hindu 38%, Muslim 8%, Roman Catholic 8%, Sikh
Time difference GMT +12

 **www.** ▪ CIA ▪ LP ▪ WTG

▪ **Fiji Online Home Page**
http://www.fiji-online.com.fj
Official Fiji Island Home Page. Visitors will find all the basic facts about the islands, as well as tourism, trade, and finance sections. The site also offers listings of educational institutions, non-profit organizations, and commercial agencies.

FINLAND

Map page 48

National name Suomen Tasavalta (Finnish)/Republiken Finland (Swedish)/Republic of Finland
Area 338,145 sq km/130,557 sq mi
Capital Helsinki (Swedish Helsingfors)
Major towns/cities Tampere, Turku, Espoo, Vantaa, Oulu
Major ports Turku, Oulu
Physical features most of the country is forest, with low hills and about 60,000 lakes; one-third is within the Arctic Circle; archipelago in south includes Åland Islands; Helsinki is the most northerly national capital on the European continent. At the 70th parallel there is constant daylight for 73 days in summer and 51 days of uninterrupted night in winter.
Currency markka
GNP per capita (PPP) (US$) 21,209 (1999)
Resources copper ore, lead ore, gold, zinc ore, silver, peat, hydro power, forests
Population 5,176,000 (2000 est)
Population density (per sq km) 15 (1999 est)
Language Finnish (93%), Swedish (6%) (both official), Saami (Lapp), Russian
Religion Evangelical Lutheran 87%, Greek Orthodox 1%
Time difference GMT +2

 www. ▪ CIA ▪ LC ▪ LP ▪ RG ▪ WTG

▪ **Virtual Finland**
http://virtual.finland.fi/finfo/english/finnmap.html
Set of maps of Finland which include road, rail, and weather, as well as historical maps. There is also an 'active' map which will take you to pages of information about individual towns, cities, and sites of interest.

▪ **City of Oulu**
http://www.ouka.fi/oulu_ee.html
Large and well-presented trilingual source of information on the largest city in the north of Finland. This site includes history, cultural heritage, local government services and local democracy, local community news, the environment, economy, and employment and investment opportunities. There are a number of photos and an impressive series of links to local institutions and companies.

Welcome to Tampere

http://www.tampere.fi/elke/mato/english/

Information on this Finnish city which is Scandinavia's largest inland community. There is a history of Tampere, description of places of interest, guide to museums, and information on restaurants and accommodation. A number of photos of Tampere are included, which can be sent as electronic 'postcards' across the Internet.

FRANCE
Map page 58

National name République Française/ French Republic
Area (including Corsica) 543,965 sq km/210,024 sq mi
Capital Paris
Major towns/cities Lyon, Lille, Bordeaux, Toulouse, Nantes, Marseille, Nice, Strasbourg, Montpellier, Rennes, Le Havre
Major ports Marseille, Nice, Le Havre
Physical features rivers Seine, Loire, Garonne, Rhône; mountain ranges Alps, Massif Central, Pyrenees, Jura, Vosges, Cévennes; Auvergne mountain region; Mont Blanc (4,810 m/ 15,781 ft); Ardennes forest; Riviera; caves of Dordogne with relics of early humans; the island of Corsica
Territories Guadeloupe, French Guiana, Martinique, Réunion, St. Pierre and Miquelon, Southern and Antarctic Territories, New Caledonia, French Polynesia, Wallis and Futuna, Mayotte, Bassas da India, Clipperton Island, Europa Island, Glorioso Islands, Juan de Nova Island, Tromelin Island
Currency franc
GNP per capita (PPP) (US$) 21,897 (1999)
Resources coal, petroleum, natural gas, iron ore, copper, zinc, bauxite
Population 59,080,000 (2000 est)
Population density (per sq km) 108 (1999 est)
Language French (official; regional languages include Basque, Breton, Catalan, Corsican, and Provençal)
Religion Roman Catholic, about 90%; also Muslim, Protestant, and Jewish minorities
Time difference GMT +1

 ▪ CIA ▪ LP ▪ RG ▪ WTG

France
http://www.france.diplomatie.fr/france/index.gb.html
Multilingual resource (French, English, Spanish, and German) on this European country produced by the French Foreign Affairs office. It includes an introduction to the country, history, geography, education, science, and culture. All of these are presented in the form of quite in-depth essays. There is also a section on contemporary news and a source of practical information for visitors.

FranceWay
http://www.franceway.com/
Overview of French culture and heritage, with features on such topics as the French regions and French cuisine and wines, and information for travellers.

Paris Pages
http://www.paris.org/
Essential reference tool for every wanderer around Paris, as it is crammed with information on every aspect of Parisian life. Among its many attractions, the site has features on the culture of the city as well as masses of tourist information.

Tahiti
http://tahiti.com/
Huge source of well-presented information on Tahiti and other islands in French Polynesia. Polynesian history and culture are sympathetically explained. There is also a host of practical information and suggestions for visitors.

New Caledonia Tourism
http://www.new-caledonia-tourism.nc/
Guide to the French Pacific territory. There is a good introduction to local history and Melanesian culture. Visitors are provided with practical information about attractions, transport, and accommodation.

Touring Guide of Provence
http://www.provenceweb.fr/e/provpil.htm
Comprehensive guide to the six départements comprising the region of Provence. There are details of the history and attractions of all the cities in the region. The site also includes maps and information on accommodation and restaurants.

Bretagne – History and Tradition
http://www.brittany-bretagne.com/level1.cfm?level1=pat
Huge source of information on the history, culture, and heritage of Brittany. There is a history of the region from Neolithic times to the modern day. In addition, this site has information on Brittany's maritime heritage and profiles of famous Bretons.

Strasbourg Online
http://www.strasbourg.com/index.html
Well-presented guide to the seat of the European parliament. There are sections on art, history, culture, business, Alsatian wine and cuisine, and famous residents. This site includes a map of the city, practical information for visitors, and a large number of links to sources of further information in both English and French.

GABON
Map page 104

National name République Gabonaise/Gabonese Republic
Area 267,667 sq km/ 103,346 sq mi
Capital Libreville
Major towns/cities Port-Gentil, Franceville (or Masuku), Lambaréné, Oyem, Mouila
Major ports Port-Gentil and Owendo
Physical features virtually the whole country is tropical rainforest; narrow coastal plain rising to hilly interior with savannah in east and south; Ogooué River flows north–west
Currency franc CFA
GNP per capita (PPP) (US$) 5,325 (1999)
Resources petroleum, natural gas, manganese (one of world's foremost producers and exporters), iron ore, uranium, gold, niobium, talc, phosphates
Population 1,226,000 (2000 est)
Population density (per sq km) 4 (1999 est)
Language French (official), Fang (in the north), Bantu languages, and other local dialects
Religion Christian 60% (mostly Roman Catholic), animist about 4%, Muslim 1%
Time difference GMT +1

 ▪ CIA ▪ LP ▪ NA ▪ WTG

THE GAMBIA
Map page 104

National name Republic of the Gambia
Area 10,402 sq km/4,016 sq mi
Capital Banjul
Major towns/cities Brikama, Bakau, Farafenni, Gunjur, Basse
Physical features consists of narrow strip of land along the River Gambia; river flanked by low hills
Currency dalasi
GNP per capita (PPP) (US$) 1,492 (1999)
Resources ilmenite, zircon, rutile, petroleum (well discovered, but not exploited)
Population 1,305,000 (2000 est)
Population density (per sq km) 122 (1999 est)
Language English (official), Mandinka, Fula, Wolof, other indigenous dialects
Religion Muslim 85%, with animist and Christian minorities
Time difference GMT +/–0

 ▪ CIA ▪ LP ▪ RG ▪ WTG

Republic of The Gambia
http://www.gambia.com/
Official Web site of The Gambia, with information about the country's history, geography, government, investment opportunities, and economic development, plus a guide for travellers.

GEORGIA
Map page 92

National name Sak'art'velo/Georgia
Area 69,700 sq km/26,911 sq mi
Capital T'bilisi
Major towns/cities K'ut'aisi, Rust'avi, Bat'umi, Zugdidi, Gori
Physical features largely mountainous with a variety of landscape from the subtropical Black Sea shores to the ice and snow of the crest line of the Caucasus; chief rivers are Kura and Rioni
Currency lari
GNP per capita (PPP) (US$) 3,606 (1999)
Resources coal, manganese, barytes, clay, petroleum and natural gas deposits, iron and other ores, gold, agate, marble, alabaster, arsenic, tungsten, mercury
Population 4,968,000 (2000 est)
Population density (per sq km) 72 (1999 est)
Language Georgian (official), Russian, Abkazian, Armenian, Azeri
Religion Georgian Orthodox, also Muslim
Time difference GMT +3

 ▪ CIA ▪ LC ▪ LP ▪ WTG

Sakartvelo – former Republic of Georgia
http://www.sakartvelo.com/indexOLD.html
Substantial source of data about Georgia – with maps, statistics, images, audio clips, and information about such topics as its history, architecture, and folklore.

Tbilisi – The Warm Heart of Georgia
http://www.parliament.ge/~nino/tbilisi/tbilisi.html
Good introduction to the Georgian capital. The history and cultural traditions of the city are presented with the help of good photographs. This site also contains information on cultural and educational institutions in the city.

GERMANY
Map page 52

National name Bundesrepublik Deutschland/Federal Republic of Germany
Area 357,041 sq km/ 137,853 sq mi
Capital Berlin
Major towns/cities Koln, Hamburg, Munich, Essen, Frankfurt am Main, Dortmund, Stuttgart, Düsseldorf, Leipzig, Dresden, Hannover
Major ports Hamburg, Kiel, Bremerhaven, Rostock
Physical features flat in north, mountainous in south with Alps; rivers Rhine, Weser, Elbe flow north, Danube flows southeast, Oder and Neisse flow north along Polish frontier; many lakes, including Müritz; Black Forest, Harz Mountains, Erzgebirge (Ore Mountains), Bavarian Alps, Fichtelgebirge, Thüringer Forest
Currency Deutschmark
GNP per capita (PPP) (US$) 22,404 (1999)
Resources lignite, hard coal, potash salts, crude oil, natural gas, iron ore, copper, timber, nickel, uranium
Population 82,220,000 (2000 est)
Population density (per sq km) 230 (1999 est)
Language German (official)
Religion Protestant (mainly Lutheran) 38%, Roman Catholic 34%
Time difference GMT +1

 ▪ CIA ▪ LC ▪ LP ▪ RG ▪ WTG

Munich
http://www.munich-tourist.de/english/englisch/cityinformation/munich-cityinformation-introduction.htm
Overview of the city of Munich, including arts and entertainment facilities, news, weather, places of interest to visit, and travel information.

Bavaria Online
http://www.bavaria.com/
Multilingual site on this area of Germany that includes sections on culture, travel, business, entertainment, and shopping. The site is filled with images and short essays on related subjects like architecture and the Oktoberfest.

Berlin

http://userpage.chemie.fu-berlin.de/adressen/berlin.html

City guide to Berlin. Aimed at the tourist, this site details what to do before you go and what to do when you get there. History, geography, and travel information, as well as features on festivals, make up the majority of the remaining information on this site, as well as details of local transport and a list of useful telephone numbers. There are also some images of Berlin, and maps of the city area.

Frankfurt am Main

http://expedia.msn.com/wg/Europe/Germany/P14119.asp

Good source of information on Germany's financial capital. There are sections providing an overview of the city's history, culture, tourist attractions, and economic base. There are also a number of photographs.

Bundesregierung Deutschland

http://194.94.238.74/tatsachen_ueber_deutschland/englisch/

Lots of factual information about Germany including its history, people, political system, education, and culture. Choose to read the information in German or English. Navigate around the site by using the 'tree' structure, on the left-hand side. The site is also available to view in German, for extra reading comprehension.

GermNews

http://www.mathematik.uni-ulm.de/germnews/

Latest news from Germany. This text-based site presents all the latest happenings from a German perspective and also has an archive dating back to 1993. The articles are clear and concise and provide good German reading practice. There is also an English version to help out if the German gets too difficult.

Germany

http://eng.bundesregierung.de/frameset/index.jsp

Well-presented official introduction to Germany from the Press and Information Office of the Federal Government. There are thorough overviews of Germany's geography, history, political and judicial system, economy, culture, education, and science. The site also offers links to online versions of information magazines, to federal institutions, and to leading political parties. This is a good first stop for those wanting information about Germany.

GHANA
Map page 104

National name Republic of Ghana
Area 238,540 sq km/92,100 sq mi
Capital Accra
Major towns/cities Kumasi, Tamale, Tema, Sekondi, Takoradi, Cape Coast, Koforidua, Bolgatanga, Obuasi
Major ports Sekondi, Tema
Physical features mostly tropical lowland plains; bisected by River Volta
Currency cedi
GNP per capita (PPP) (US$) 1,793 (1999 est)
Resources diamonds, gold, manganese, bauxite
Population 20,212,000 (2000 est)
Population density (per sq km) 83 (1999 est)
Language English (official), Ga, other African languages
Religion Christian 40%, animist 32%, Muslim 16%
Time difference GMT +/–0

 ▪ CIA ▪ LC ▪ LP ▪ RG ▪ WTG

Republic of Ghana Home Page

http://www.ghana.com/republic/index.html

Introduction to Ghana, with background notes on its geography, regions, and culture, plus maps of the country, links to newspapers, and tourist information.

GREECE
Map page 68

National name Elliniki Dimokratia/Hellenic Republic
Area 131,957 sq km/50,948 sq mi
Capital Athens
Major towns/cities
Thessaloniki, Peiraias, Patra,

Iraklion, Larisa, Peristerio, Kallithéa
Major ports Peiraias, Thessaloniki, Patra, Iraklion
Physical features mountainous (Mount Olympus); a large number of islands, notably Crete, Corfu, and Rhodes, and Cyclades and Ionian Islands
Currency drachma
GNP per capita (PPP) (US$) 14,595 (1999)
Resources bauxite, nickel, iron pyrites, magnetite, asbestos, marble, salt, chromite, lignite
Population 10,645,000 (2000 est)
Population density (per sq km) 81 (1999 est)
Language Greek (official)
Religion Greek Orthodox, over 96%; about 1% Muslim
Time difference GMT +2

 ▪ CIA ▪ LP ▪ RG ▪ WTG

Ancient City of Athens

http://www.indiana.edu/~kglowack/athens/

Photographic archive of the archaeological and architectural remains of ancient Athens, Greece. As the site says, 'It is intended primarily as a resource for students of classical art & archaeology, civilization, languages, and history'. However, there is much here of interest for the general browser.

Corfu, Greece

http://travel.lycos.com/Destinations/Europe/Greece/Corfu/

Large source of information on the northernmost of Greece's Ionian Islands. All aspects of the island's history, archaeology, and culture are covered here. There is a map and details of accommodation, places of interest, and local transport.

Internet Guide to Greece

http://www.gogreece.com/

Annotated links to Greek-related resources, under headings such as arts and entertainment, culture, music, food, business and finance, news, and travel information.

Cultural Map of Hellas

http://www.culture.gr/2/21/maps/hellas.html

'Clickable' map allowing you to browse around contemporary Greece and discover detailed information about the different museums, archaeological sites, and monuments in each region.

Rhodes

http://rhodes.helios.gr/

Guide to the largest of Greece's Dodecanese islands. There is a good overall description. Details of the history and attractions of the towns on the island are supported by photographs. There is a wealth of practical information on transport, accommodation, and wining and dining.

About Peloponnese – Introduction

http://www.vacation.net.gr/p/pelopon.html

Comprehensive guide to Greece's Peloponnese region. Landscape, history, and attractions are described for all parts of this mountainous peninsula. There is also a map of the region.

GRENADA
Map page 134

Area (including the southern Grenadine Islands, notably Carriacou and Petit Martinique) 344 sq km/ 133 sq mi
Capital St. George's
Major towns/cities Grenville, Sauteurs, Victoria, Gouyave
Physical features southernmost of the Windward Islands; mountainous; Grand-Anse beach; Annandale Falls; the Great Pool volcanic crater
Currency East Caribbean dollar
GNP per capita (PPP) (US$) 5,847 (1999)
Population 94,000 (2000 est)
Population density (per sq km) 286 (1999 est)
Language English (official), some French-African patois
Religion Roman Catholic 53%, Anglican about 14%, Seventh Day Adventist, Pentecostal, Methodist
Time difference GMT –4

 ▪ CIA ▪ LP ▪ WTG

GUATEMALA
Map page 134

National name República de Guatemala/Republic of Guatemala
Area 108,889 sq km/42,042 sq mi
Capital Guatemala
Major towns/cities Quezaltenango, Escuintla, Puerto Barrios (naval base), Chinautla
Physical features mountainous; narrow coastal plains; limestone tropical plateau in north; frequent earthquakes
Currency quetzal
GNP per capita (PPP) (US$) 3,517 (1999 est)
Resources petroleum, antimony, gold, silver, nickel, lead, iron, tungsten
Population 11,385,000 (2000 est)
Population density (per sq km) 102 (1999 est)
Language Spanish (official), 22 Mayan languages (45%)
Religion Roman Catholic 70%, Protestant 10%, traditional Mayan
Time difference GMT –6

 ▪ CIA ▪ LP ▪ WTG

About Guatemala

http://www.tradepoint.org.gt/travelguate.html

Lively window onto Guatemala. The site includes extensive sections on the country's ancient history, colonial times, and modern period. Visitors are also treated to a helpful introduction to the people of contemporary Guatemala with colourful visual material, suggestions for fun and adventure, and a short presentation on the country's flora and fauna.

GUINEA
Map page 104

National name République de Guinée/Republic of Guinea
Area 245,857 sq km/94,925 sq mi
Capital Conakry
Major towns/cities Labé, Nzérékoré, Kankan, Kindia, Mamou, Siguiri
Physical features flat coastal plain with mountainous interior; sources of rivers Niger, Gambia, and Senegal; forest in southeast; Fouta Djallon, area of sandstone plateaux, cut by deep valleys
Currency Guinean franc
GNP per capita (PPP) (US$) 1,761 (1999)
Resources bauxite (world's top exporter of bauxite and second-largest producer of bauxite ore), alumina, diamonds, gold, granite, iron ore, uranium, nickel, cobalt, platinum
Population 7,430,000 (2000 est)
Population density (per sq km) 30 (1999 est)
Language French (official), Susu, Pular (Fulfude), Malinke, and other African languages
Religion Muslim 85%, Christian 6%, animist
Time difference GMT +/–0

 ▪ CIA ▪ LP ▪ NA ▪ WTG

GUINEA-BISSAU
Map page 104

National name República da Guiné-Bissau/Republic of Guinea-Bissau
Area 36,125 sq km/13,947 sq mi
Capital Bissau (and chief port)
Major towns/cities Bafatá, Bissorã, Bolama, Gabú, Bubaque, Cacheu, Catió, Farim
Physical features flat coastal plain rising to savannah in east
Currency Guinean peso
GNP per capita (PPP) (US$) 595 (1999)
Resources bauxite, phosphate, petroleum (largely unexploited)
Population 1,213,000 (2000 est)

Population density (per sq km) 33 (1999 est)

Language Portuguese (official), Crioulo (a Cape Verdean dialect of Portuguese), African languages

Religion animist 58%, Muslim 40%, Christian 5% (mainly Roman Catholic)

Time difference GMT +/–0

 www. ■ CIA ■ LP ■ NA ■ WTG

GUYANA

Map page 140

National name Cooperative Republic of Guyana

Area 214,969 sq km/82,999 sq mi

Capital Georgetown (and chief port)

Major towns/cities Linden, New Amsterdam, Bartica, Corriverton

Major ports New Amsterdam

Physical features coastal plain rises into rolling highlands with savannah in south; mostly tropical rainforest; Mount Roraima; Kaietur National Park, including Kaietur Falls on the Potaro (tributary of Essequibo) 250 m/821 ft

Currency Guyanese dollar

GNP per capita (PPP) (US$) 3,242 (1999 est)

Resources gold, diamonds, bauxite, copper, tungsten, iron, nickel, quartz, molybdenum

Population 861,000 (2000 est)

Population density (per sq km) 4 (1999 est)

Language English (official), Hindi, American Indian languages

Religion Christian 57%, Hindu 34%, Sunni Muslim 9%

Time difference GMT –3

 www. ■ CIA ■ LC ■ LP ■ WTG

■ Georgetown, Guyana

http://travel.lycos.com/Destinations/South_America/Guyana/Georgetown/

Profile of Guyana's attractive capital, Georgetown. There is a general introduction to the city's main features, and four sections – 'Visitors' guide', 'Culture and history', 'News and weather', and 'Entertainment' – each with links to further useful information about both the city and the country.

■ Guyana Online Tourist Guide

http://www.turq.com/guyana/

Colourful guide to the South American country Guyana. Aimed at the tourist, the site features illustrated pages describing the country's many attractions, as well as information on climate, language, and accommodation. A map of Guyana is also included.

HAITI

Map page 134

National name République d'Haïti/Republic of Haiti

Area 27,750 sq km/10,714 sq mi

Capital Port-au-Prince

Major towns/cities Cap-Haïtien, Gonaïves, Les Cayes, St. Marc, Carrefour, Delmas

Physical features mainly mountainous and tropical; occupies western third of Hispaniola Island in Caribbean Sea

Currency gourde

GNP per capita (PPP) (US$) 1,407 (1999 est)

Resources marble, limestone, calcareous clay, unexploited copper and gold deposits

Population 8,222,000 (2000 est)

Population density (per sq km) 291 (1999 est)

Language French (20%), Creole (both official)

Religion Christian 95% (of which 70% are Roman Catholic), voodoo 4%

Time difference GMT –5

 www. ■ CIA ■ LC ■ LP ■ WTG

■ Haiti Guide

http://www.haitiguide.com/

Detailed guide to Haiti. The site is divided into a number of

---

sections, including 'Geography', 'People', and 'Economy', each offering a number of facts and statistics on the country.

HONDURAS

Map page 134

National name República de Honduras/Republic of Honduras

Area 112,100 sq km/43,281 sq mi

Capital Tegucigalpa

Major towns/cities San Pedro Sula, La Ceiba, El Progreso, Choluteca, Juticalpa, Danlí

Major ports La Ceiba

Physical features narrow tropical coastal plain with mountainous interior, Bay Islands, Caribbean reefs

Currency lempira

GNP per capita (PPP) (US$) 2,254 (1999 est)

Resources lead, zinc, silver, gold, tin, iron, copper, antimony

Population 6,485,000 (2000 est)

Population density (per sq km) 56 (1999 est)

Language Spanish (official), English, American Indian languages

Religion Roman Catholic 97%

Time difference GMT –6

 www. ■ CIA ■ LC ■ LP ■ WTG

■ Honduras.Net

http://www.honduras.net/

Honduran culture, history, and tourist information Web site. Featuring descriptions of the Honduran constitution, a brief history, news, and local recipes, this page has something for everyone interested in this Central American country.

HUNGARY

Map page 50

National name Magyar Köztársaság/Republic of Hungary

Area 93,032 sq km/35,919 sq mi

Capital Budapest

Major towns/cities Miskolc, Debrecen, Szeged, Pécs, Győr, Nyíregyháza, Székesfehérvár, Kecskemét

Physical features Great Hungarian Plain covers eastern half of country; Bakony Forest, Lake Balaton, and Transdanubian Highlands in the west; rivers Danube, Tisza, and Raba; more than 500 thermal springs

Currency forint

GNP per capita (PPP) (US$) 10,479 (1999)

Resources lignite, brown coal, natural gas, petroleum, bauxite, hard coal

Population 10,036,000 (2000 est)

Population density (per sq km) 108 (1999 est)

Language Hungarian (official)

Religion Roman Catholic 65%, Calvinist 20%, other Christian denominations, Jewish, atheist

Time difference GMT +1

www. ■ CIA ■ LC ■ LP ■ RG ■ WTG

■ Budapest: A Little Tour

http://www.fsz.bme.hu/hungary/budapest/budapest.html

Comprehensive guide to the city, including its history, detailed information on places of interest, transport, and entertainment. The site contains a gallery of maps and pictures, and some audio clips of Hungarian music.

■ Győr

http://www.arrabonet.gyor.hu/gyor/index-eng.html

Good guide to the Hungarian city. A guided tour of the town is accompanied by a series of photographs. There is a description of the sensitive and extensive post-1945 restoration of the city centre.

■ Hungarian Home Page

http://www.fsz.bme.hu/hungary/homepage.html

Masses of information about Hungary, including a virtual tour of Budapest, Hungarian–English and English–Hungarian dictionaries, and recipes for dishes from goulash to Transylvanian layered cabbage.

ICELAND

Map page 48

National name Lýðveldið Ísland/Republic of Iceland

Area 103,000 sq km/39,768 sq mi

Capital Reykjavík

Major towns/cities Akureyri, Kópavogur, Hafnarfjördur, Keflavík, Vestmannaeyjar

Physical features warmed by the Gulf Stream; glaciers and lava fields cover 75% of the country; active volcanoes (Hekla was once thought the gateway to Hell), geysers, hot springs, and new islands created offshore (Surtsey in 1963); subterranean hot water heats 85% of Iceland's homes; Sidujokull glacier moving at 100 metres a day

Currency krona

GNP per capita (PPP) (US$) 26,283 (1999)

Resources aluminium, diatomite, hydroelectric and thermal power, fish

Population 281,000 (2000 est)

Population density (per sq km) 3 (1999 est)

Language Icelandic (official)

Religion Evangelical Lutheran about 90%, other Protestant and Roman Catholic about 4%

Time difference GMT +/–0

 www. ■ CIA ■ LP ■ WTG

■ Iceland

http://www.iceland.org/

Official introduction to Iceland. There is easily accessible information on business, education, history, culture, and language. A tourist guide is supported by photos and a video clip. The site also includes a weather report, regularly updated Icelandic news, and an interactive map.

■ Reykjavik – Next Door to Nature

http://tourist.reykjavik.is/

Well-arranged bilingual source of information on the Icelandic capital. The needs of tourists and investors are well provided for, including sections on the history, accommodation, transport, cultural events, and entertainment. There are also a number of photographs.

INDIA

Map page 88

National name Bharat (Hindi)/India; Bharatiya Janarajya (unofficial)/Republic of India

Area 3,166,829 sq km/1,222,713 sq mi

Capital New Delhi

Major towns/cities Mumbai (formerly Bombay), Kolkata (formerly Calcutta), Chennai (formerly Madras), Bangalore, Hyderabad, Ahmadabad, Kanpur, Pune, Nagpur, Bhopal, Jaipur, Lucknow, Surat

Major ports Kolkata, Mumbai, Chennai

Physical features Himalayas on northern border; plains around rivers Ganges, Indus, Brahmaputra; Deccan peninsula south of the Narmada River forms plateau between Western and Eastern Ghats mountain ranges; desert in west; Andaman and Nicobar Islands, Lakshadweep (Laccadive Islands)

Currency rupee

GNP per capita (PPP) (US$) 2,149 (1999 est)

Resources coal, iron ore, copper ore, bauxite, chromite, gold, manganese ore, zinc, lead, limestone, crude oil, natural gas, diamonds

Population 1,013,662,000 (2000 est)

Population density (per sq km) 315 (1999 est)

Language Hindi, English, Assamese, Bengali, Gujarati, Kannada, Kashmiri, Konkani, Malayalam, Manipuri, Marathi, Nepali, Oriya, Punjabi, Sanskrit, Sindhi, Tamil, Telugu, Urdu (all official), more than 1,650 dialects

Religion Hindu 80%, Sunni Muslim 10%, Christian 2.5%, Sikh 2%, Buddhist, Jewish

Time difference GMT +5.5

 www. ■ CIA ■ LC ■ LP ■ RG ■ WTG

AgraOnline
http://www.agraonline.com/
Complete guide to the Indian city of Agra aimed at both tourists and residents alike. For the tourist, there is detailed information about the ways to travel to Agra and also where to stay once you get there. There are also notes on the places to visit, where to go shopping, and the best places to eat out. In a developing section for the resident, there are details of handicrafts and emporiums and also other trade information.

Goa
http://travel.indiamart.com/goa/
A useful background aimed mainly at tourists on India's premier holiday resort, which has information on attractions, excursions, shopping, and dining, in addition to a brief historical account of the island.

Government of India
http://www.indiagov.org/
Introduction to the politics, history, culture, and society of India. Additional links to relevant sites on the Web are provided. This site is run by the official tourist board and includes descriptions of all the major states, as well as more general background under such headings as 'News', 'Culture', 'Economy', and 'Sport'.

Bombay: The Gateway of India
http://www.fhraindia.com/home/cities/mumbai.htm
General outline of the city of Bombay (from 1995 known as Mumbai), including a detailed history section, important institutions, and pictures of landmarks. The introduction claims that the city's squalid reputation is outweighed by its charisma and its safety as a base from which to explore.

Calcutta
http://www.nd.edu/~kmukhopa/cal300/calcutta/
Detailed tour of the city of Kolkata (formerly Calcutta), including its people, architecture, economy, and history. There is also an overview of the museums, libraries, and other cultural institutions that can be found in this city.

Rajasthan
http://www.rajasthandiary.com/
Rajasthani traditions and spirit are captured at this site, with pictures and information on each of its major cities – Jaipur, Jodhpur, Udaipur, and Jaisalmer. You can also find out about cuisine, travel, accommodation, and historical landmarks.

INDONESIA
Map page 86

National name Republik Indonesia/ Republic of Indonesia
Area 1,904,569 sq km/ 735,354 sq mi
Capital Jakarta
Major towns/cities Surabaya, Bandung, Medan, Semarang, Palembang, Tangerang, Tanjungkarang-Telukbetung, Ujung Pandang, Malang
Major ports Surabaya, Semarang (Java), Ujung Pandang (Sulawesi)
Physical features comprises 13,677 tropical islands (over 6,000 of them are inhabited): the Greater Sundas (including Java, Madura, Sumatra, Sulawesi, and Kalimantan (part of Borneo)), the Lesser Sunda Islands/Nusa Tenggara (including Bali, Lombok, Sumbawa, Flores, Sumba, Alor, Lomblen, Timor, Roti, and Savu), Maluku/Moluccas (over 1,000 islands including Ambon, Ternate, Tidore, Tanimbar, and Halmahera), and Irian Jaya (part of New Guinea); over half the country is tropical rainforest; it has the largest expanse of peatlands in the tropics
Currency rupiah
GNP per capita (PPP) (US$) 2,439 (1999)
Resources petroleum (principal producer of petroleum in the Far East), natural gas, bauxite, nickel (world's third-largest producer), copper, tin (world's second-largest producer), gold, coal, forests
Population 212,107,000 (2000 est)
Population density (per sq km) 110 (1999 est)
Language Bahasa Indonesia (closely related to Malay; official), Javanese, Dutch, over 550 regional languages and dialects
Religion Muslim 87%, Protestant 6%, Roman Catholic 3%, Hindu 2% and Buddhist 1% (the continued spread of Christianity, together with an Islamic revival, have led to greater religious tensions)
Time difference GMT +7/9

 ▪ CIA ▪ LC ▪ LP ▪ RG ▪ WTG

Indonesian Home Page
http://www.uni-stuttgart.de/indonesia/
List of resources relating to Indonesia and its people, with daily news updates, maps, and travel information. The site also contains some general information on this archipelago and regularly updated links to related Indonesian Web sites.

Bali
http://werple.mira.net.au/~wreid/bali_p1a.html
Guide to the Indonesian holiday destination of Bali. Aimed at the tourist, this site details what to do before you go, and what to do when you get there. There are also details of the area's history and geography, as well as features on festivals, and some useful travel information. The site also includes many images of Bali, and maps of the area.

IRAN
Map page 90

National name Jomhûrî-ye Eslâmi-ye Îrân/Islamic Republic of Iran
Area 1,648,000 sq km/ 636,292 sq mi
Capital Teheran
Major towns/cities Eşfahān, Mashhad, Tabrīz, Shīrāz, Ahvāz, Kermānshāh, Qom, Karaj
Major ports Abādān
Physical features plateau surrounded by mountains, including Elburz and Zagros; Lake Rezayeh; Dasht-e-Kavir desert; occupies islands of Abu Musa, Greater Tunb and Lesser Tunb in the Gulf
Currency rial
GNP per capita (PPP) (US$) 5,163 (1999)
Resources petroleum, natural gas, coal, magnetite, gypsum, iron ore, copper, chromite, salt, bauxite, decorative stone
Population 67,702,000 (2000 est)
Population density (per sq km) 41 (1999 est)
Language Farsi (official), Kurdish, Turkish, Arabic, English, French
Religion Shiite Muslim (official) 91%, Sunni Muslim 8%; Zoroastrian, Christian, Jewish, and Baha'i comprise about 1%
Time difference GMT +3.5

 ▪ CIA ▪ LC ▪ LP ▪ WTG

Iran Watch
http://www.harborwatchpub.com/iran/
Reference works about Iran and the country's leaders, government, economy, and culture. The main focus of the current site is 'Iranians in the news' – brief biographies of key Iranians including their career and political tendencies.

Iranian Cultural and Information Centre
http://tehran.stanford.edu/
First official Web site of Iran, comprising a wealth of information on Iranian culture and contemporary life. Amongst its attractions are included extensive presentations on literature of and about Iran, the Iranian past, cultural events, and travel opportunities. It also offers an impressive photo gallery with images of Iran and Persian art.

IRAQ
Map page 90

National name al-Jumhuriyya al'Iraqiyya/Republic of Iraq
Area 434,924 sq km/ 167,924 sq mi
Capital Baghdād
Major towns/cities Al Mawşil, Al Başrah, Kirkūk, Al Ḥillah, An Najaf, An Nāşirīyah, Arbīl
Major ports Al Başrah
Physical features mountains in north, desert in west; wide valley of rivers Tigris and Euphrates running northwest-southeast; canal linking Baghdād and The Gulf opened in 1992
Currency Iraqi dinar
GNP per capita (PPP) (US$) N/A
Resources petroleum, natural gas, sulphur, phosphates

Population 23,115,000 (2000 est)
Population density (per sq km) 52 (1999 est)
Language Arabic (80%) (official), Kurdish (15%), Assyrian, Armenian
Religion Shiite Muslim 60%, Sunni Muslim 37%, Christian 3%
Time difference GMT +3

 ▪ CIA ▪ LC ▪ AN ▪ LP ▪ WTG

IRELAND, REPUBLIC OF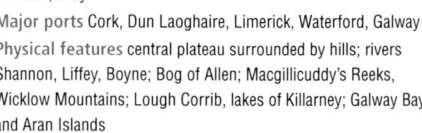
Map page 56

National name Poblacht Na hÉireann/ Republic of Ireland
Area 70,282 sq km/ 27,135 sq mi
Capital Dublin
Major towns/cities Cork, Limerick, Galway, Waterford, Dundalk, Bray
Major ports Cork, Dun Laoghaire, Limerick, Waterford, Galway
Physical features central plateau surrounded by hills; rivers Shannon, Liffey, Boyne; Bog of Allen; Macgillicuddy's Reeks, Wicklow Mountains; Lough Corrib, lakes of Killarney; Galway Bay and Aran Islands
Currency Irish pound, or punt Eireannach
GNP per capita (PPP) (US$) 19,180 (1999)
Resources lead, zinc, peat, limestone, gypsum, petroleum, natural gas, copper, silver
Population 3,730,000 (2000 est)
Population density (per sq km) 53 (1999 est)
Language Irish Gaelic, English (both official)
Religion Roman Catholic 92%, Church of Ireland, other Protestant denominations 3%
Time difference GMT +/–0

 ▪ CIA ▪ LP ▪ RG ▪ WTG

Complete Guide to Ireland
http://members.tripod.com/~AndrewGallagher/ireland/
Guide to the geography, history, and politics of Ireland. The site can be viewed with or without frames and also includes sections on sport, tourism, culture, and the Celts.

Cork Guide Online
http://www.cork-guide.ie/corkcity.htm
Good source of information on Ireland's third-largest city. A description of the city, its heritage, and attractions is accompanied by some fine photographs. There is also information on accommodation, entertainment, transport, and restaurants

Complete Guide to Galway
http://www.wombat.ie/galwayguide/
Thorough and well-arranged source of information on this western Irish county. The needs of residents, tourists, and investors are fully met with sections on attractions, transport, entertainment, accommodation, things to do with children, community groups, and local government services. In addition to a good summary of Galway's history, there are online versions of several detailed history books of the county.

Kerry Insight
http://www.kerry-insight.com/
Guide to the Irish county. This site includes sections on fishing, sports, entertainment, accommodation, places of historical interest, events and festivals, an extensive commercial directory, community organizations, guides to towns in the county, maps, and a weather report.

Government of Ireland
http://www.irlgov.ie/gov.htm
Complete guide to all the departments of the Irish government, including contact details. The 'Department of the taoiseach' includes a virtual tour of the parliament building, complete with the history of the position of taoiseach, or prime minister.

ISRAEL
Map page 94

National name Medinat Israel/State of Israel
Area 20,800 sq km/8,030 sq mi (as at 1949 armistice)
Capital Jerusalem (not recognized by the United Nations)

Major towns/cities Tel Aviv-Yafo, Haifa, Bat-Yam, Holon, Ramat Gan, Petah Tiqwa, Rishon le Ziyyon, Be'ér Sheva'

Major ports Tel Aviv-Yafo, Haifa, 'Akko (formerly Acre), Elat

Physical features coastal plain of Sharon between Haifa and Tel Aviv noted since ancient times for its fertility; central mountains of Galilee, Samaria, and Judea; Dead Sea, Lake Tiberias, and River Jordan Rift Valley along the east are below sea level; Negev Desert in the south; Israel occupies Golan Heights, West Bank, East Jerusalem, and Gaza Strip (the last was awarded limited autonomy, with West Bank town of Jericho, in 1993)

Currency shekel

GNP per capita (PPP) (US$) 16,867 (1999)

Resources potash, bromides, magnesium, sulphur, copper ore, gold, salt, petroleum, natural gas

Population 6,217,000 (2000 est)

Population density (per sq km) 293 (1999 est)

Language Hebrew, Arabic (both official), English, Yiddish, other European and west Asian languages

Religion Israel is a secular state, but the predominant faith is Judaism 80%; also Sunni Muslim (about 15%), Christian, and Druze

Time difference GMT +2

 ■ CIA ■ LC ■ LP ■ WTG

■ Haifa

http://www.infotour.co.il/TourismArea/21001.html

Official site for Haifa and Israel. The top-level page has a historical overview and tourist information as well as a wonderfully illustrated section with practical and historical information for either visiting or learning about Israel's nature reserves and national parks. From this page a related site on Haifa Municipality can be accessed that provides further information on history, the local economy, culture, tourism, and investment opportunities.

■ Bethlehem University

http://www.bethlehem.edu/

History of the town, guide to churches and religious institutions. This is site is part of the Web site of Bethlehem University.

■ Applied Resource Institute – Jerusalem

http://www.arij.org/

Comprehensive Palestinian source of up-to-date information on geography, climate, water, agriculture, land use, and settlement activities in the West Bank. This site is indispensable for understanding the Israeli-Palestinian conflict over natural resources.

ITALY

Map page 64

National name Repubblica Italiana/ Italian Republic

Area 301,300 sq km/ 116,331 sq mi

Capital Rome

Major towns/cities Milan, Naples, Turin, Palermo, Genoa, Bologna, Florence

Major ports Naples, Genoa, Palermo, Bari, Catania, Trieste

Physical features mountainous (Maritime Alps, Dolomites, Apennines) with narrow coastal lowlands; continental Europe's only active volcanoes: Vesuvius, Etna, Stromboli; rivers Po, Adige, Arno, Tiber, Rubicon; islands of Sicily, Sardinia, Elba, Capri, Ischia, Lipari, Pantelleria; lakes Como, Maggiore, Garda

Currency lira

GNP per capita (PPP) (US$) 20,751 (1999)

Resources lignite, lead, zinc, mercury, potash, sulphur, fluorspar, bauxite, marble, petroleum, natural gas, fish

Population 57,298,000 (2000 est)

Population density (per sq km) 190 (1999 est)

Language Italian (official), German and Ladin (in the north), French (in the Valle d'Aosta region), Greek and Albanian (in the south)

Religion Roman Catholic 98% (state religion)

Time difference GMT +1

 ■ CIA ■ LP ■ RG ■ WTG

■ Windows on Italy – History

http://www.mi.cnr.it/WOI/

Packed with information about the history and culture of Italy's regions and towns. This index leads to pages of information dealing with every major period from prehistoric times to the present day.

■ History of Venice

http://www.doge.it/storia/storiai.htm

From the first inhabitants to the present day, this is a look at the origins and historical development of the Italian city of Venice. It includes numerous pictures and photographs of the city, and a map of the surrounding area.

■ History of Sardinia

http://www.crs4.it/~luigi/SARDEGNA/sardegna.html

Illustrated history of Sardinia from prehistoric times to the modern age. There are many pictures of historical artefacts and their locations, as well as explanatory maps of the island.

■ Florence and Tuscany

http://es.rice.edu/ES/humsoc/Galileo/Student_Work/Florence96/

Web site run by Rice University on Renaissance Florence and Tuscany. The site includes a tour of Florence, details of Florentine music, the Medici family, Florentine architecture, and details of modern life in the city and region.

■ Sicilia

http://www.mi.cnr.it/WOI/deagosti/regions/sicilia.html#Sicilia

Well-arranged profile of the largest Mediterranean island. There is information on geography, landscape, flora and fauna, population, Sicilian dialects, the island's autonomous status, cultural heritage, and the economy. This site includes a map of the island and suggestions for tourists. There are also descriptions of the sights and history of Palermo, Catania, and other Sicilian cities.

■ Rome, Italy

http://www.geocities.com/Athens/Forum/2680/

Huge source of information on 'the eternal city'. An offbeat introduction to the 'home of popes and pickpockets' leads to detailed information on the history, monuments, and modern attractions of the Italian capital. There is a weather report, links to local media, and access to a large number of guides to Rome.

■ Milan, Italy

http://www.smau.it/magellano/english/ciaomi99/

Good source of information on Italy's second-largest city. There is extensive coverage of history, attractions, accommodation, culture, entertainment, and commercial services. There are links to the latest financial information, the weather, an entertainment guide, and the trilingual site of the local football team, A C Milan.

JAMAICA

Map page 134

Area 10,957 sq km/4,230 sq mi

Capital Kingston

Major towns/cities Montego Bay, Spanish Town, Portmore, May Pen

Physical features mountainous tropical island; Blue Mountains (so called because of the haze over them)

Currency Jamaican dollar

GNP per capita (PPP) (US$) 3,276 (1999)

Resources bauxite (one of world's major producers), marble, gypsum, silica, clay

Population 2,583,000 (2000 est)

Population density (per sq km) 234 (1999 est)

Language English (official), Jamaican Creole

Religion Protestant 70%, Rastafarian

Time difference GMT –5

 ■ CIA ■ LP ■ RG ■ WTG

■ JamaicaTravel.com

http://www.jamaicatravel.com/

Official site of the Jamaica Tourist Board. A colourful site, this guide covers everything the visitor needs to know, such as where to stay, what to do, and what to see. There is also a calendar to keep you abreast of events in Jamaica, and a visitor's forum to share questions and advice with other visitors.

JAPAN

Map page 82

National name Nihon-koku/State of Japan

Area 377,535 sq km/145,766 sq mi

Capital Tōkyō

Major towns/cities Yokohama, Ōsaka, Nagoya, Fukuoka, Kita-Kyūshū, Kyōto, Sapporo, Kobe, Kawasaki, Hiroshima

Major ports Ōsaka, Nagoya, Yokohama, Kobe

Physical features mountainous, volcanic (Mount Fuji, volcanic Mount Aso, Japan Alps); comprises over 1,000 islands, the largest of which are Hokkaido, Honshu, Kyushu, and Shikoku

Currency yen

GNP per capita (PPP) (US$) 24,041 (1999)

Resources coal, iron, zinc, copper, natural gas, fish

Population 126,714,000 (2000 est)

Population density (per sq km) 335 (1999 est)

Language Japanese (official), Ainu

Religion Shinto, Buddhist (often combined), Christian (less than 1%)

Time difference GMT +9

 ■ CIA ■ LC ■ LP ■ RG ■ WTG

■ Japan Information Network

http://www.jinjapan.org/index.html

Searchable set of links to resources about Japan – its regions, society, culture, current events, and other aspects of Japanese life.

■ Tokyo

http://www.pandemic.com/tokyo/

City guide to the Japanese capital Tokyo. There are also details of the city's history, geography, and features on festivals. The section on tourist information is supplemented with maps and photographs and contains a list of useful phone numbers.

■ Kyoto Information

http://www.joho-kyoto.or.jp/Joho-KyotoHome/Infor/Infor/INFOR.html

Good guide to the Japanese port. An overview of Kyoto's 1,200 year history is supported with ample photos. In addition to a guide to the city's traditional crafts and industries, there is information on the contemporary business scene. Details of local attractions are also given at this site.

JORDAN

Map page 90

National name Al-Mamlaka al-Urduniyya al-Hashemiyyah/ Hashemite Kingdom of Jordan

Area 89,206 sq km/34,442 sq mi (excluding the West Bank 5,879 sq km/2,269 sq mi)

Capital Ammān

Major towns/cities Zarqā', Irbid, Ma'ān

Major ports Aqaba

Physical features desert plateau in east; Rift Valley separates east and west banks of River Jordan

Currency Jordanian dinar

GNP per capita (PPP) (US$) 3,542 (1999)

Resources phosphates, potash, shale

Population 6,669,000 (2000 est)

Population density (per sq km) 73 (1999 est)

Language Arabic (official), English

Religion over 90% Sunni Muslim (official religion), small communities of Christians and Shiite Muslims

Time difference GMT +2

 ■ CIA ■ LC ■ AN ■ LP ■ WTG

■ Hashemite Kingdom of Jordan

http://www.websofjordan.com.jo/

Unofficial site, with links to documents about Jordan's politics, history and culture, economy, tourism, and education opportunities.

■ Pictures of Jordan

http://www.geocities.com/TheTropics/Cabana/2973/Jordan.html

Impressive collection of photographs from Jordan. This site includes photographs of some of Jordan's most interesting places such as Petra, Mount Nebo, Wadi Rum, The Dead Sea, and Aquaba, as well as an 'Impressions' section.

KAZAKHSTAN

Map page 76

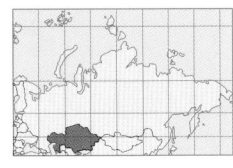

National name Kazak Respublikasy/Republic of Kazakhstan
Area 2,717,300 sq km/ 1,049,150 sq mi
Capital Astana (formerly Akmola)
Major towns/cities Qaraghandy, Pavlodar, Semey, Petropavl, Shymkent
Physical features Caspian and Aral seas, Lake Balkhash; Steppe region; natural gas and oil deposits in the Caspian Sea
Currency tenge
GNP per capita (PPP) (US$) 4,408 (1999)
Resources petroleum, natural gas, coal, bauxite, chromium, copper, iron ore, lead, titanium, magnesium, tungsten, molybdenum, gold, silver, manganese
Population 16,223,000 (2000 est)
Population density (per sq km) 6 (1999 est)
Language Kazakh (related to Turkish; official), Russian
Religion Sunni Muslim 50–60%, Russian Orthodox 30–35%
Time difference GMT +6

 ▪ CIA ▪ LC ▪ LP ▪ WTG

KENYA

Map page 106

National name Jamhuri ya Kenya/ Republic of Kenya
Area 582,600 sq km/ 224,941 sq mi
Capital Nairobi
Major towns/cities Mombasa, Kisumu, Nakuru, Eldoret, Nyeri
Major ports Mombasa
Physical features mountains and highlands in west and centre; coastal plain in south; arid interior and tropical coast; semi-desert in north; Great Rift Valley, Mount Kenya, Lake Nakuru (salt lake with world's largest colony of flamingos), Lake Turkana (Rudolf)
Currency Kenyan shilling
GNP per capita (PPP) (US$) 975 (1999)
Resources soda ash, fluorspar, salt, limestone, rubies, gold, vermiculite, diatonite, garnets
Population 30,080,000 (2000 est)
Population density (per sq km) 51 (1999 est)
Language English, Kiswahili (both official), many local dialects
Religion Roman Catholic 28%, Protestant 8%, Muslim 6%, traditional tribal religions
Time difference GMT +3

 ▪ CIA ▪ LP ▪ RG ▪ NA ▪ WTG

▪ **Kenyaweb**
http://www.kenyaweb.com/
Social, cultural, and political information about Kenya. This site includes travel-oriented information about this African country, including sections on safaris, national parks, key facts, and even a bus route guide.

KIRIBATI

Map page 112

National name Ribaberikan Kiribati/Republic of Kiribati
Area 717 sq km/277 sq mi
Capital Bairiki (on Tarawa atoll)
Major towns/cities principal islands are the Gilbert Islands, the Phoenix Islands, the Line Islands, Banaba
Major ports Bairiki, Betio (on Tarawa)
Physical features comprises 33 Pacific coral islands: the

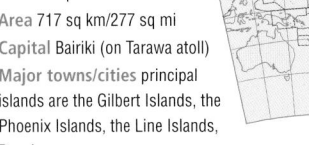

Kiribati (Gilbert), Rawaki (Phoenix), Banaba (Ocean Island), and three of the Line Islands including Kiritimati (Christmas Island); island groups crossed by Equator and International Date Line
Currency Australian dollar
GNP per capita (PPP) (US$) 3,186 (1999)
Resources phosphate, salt
Population 83,000 (2000 est)
Population density (per sq km) 107 (1999 est)
Language English (official), Gilbertese
Religion Roman Catholic, Protestant (Congregationalist)
Time difference GMT –10/–11

 ▪ CIA ▪ LP ▪ WTG

KUWAIT

Map page 95

National name Dowlat al-Kuwayt/ State of Kuwait
Area 17,819 sq km/6,879 sq mi
Capital Kuwait (and chief port)
Major towns/cities as-Salimiya, Ḥawallī, Al Farwānīyah, Abraq Kheetan, Al Jahrah, Al Aḥmadī, Al Fuḥayḥil
Physical features hot desert; islands of Faylakah, Bubiyan, and Warbah at northeast corner of Arabian Peninsula
Currency Kuwaiti dinar
GNP per capita (PPP) (US$) 24,270 (1997)
Resources petroleum, natural gas, mineral water
Population 1,972,000 (2000 est)
Population density (per sq km) 106 (1999 est)
Language Arabic (78%) (official), English, Kurdish (10%), Farsi (4%)
Religion Sunni Muslim 45%, Shiite Muslim 40%; Christian, Hindu, and Parsi about 5%
Time difference GMT +3

 ▪ CIA ▪ LC ▪ AN ▪ LP ▪ WTG

KYRGYZSTAN

Map page 76

National name Kyrgyz Respublikasy/Kyrgyz Republic
Area 198,500 sq km/76,640 sq mi
Capital Bishkek (formerly Frunze)
Major towns/cities Osh, Karakol, Kyzyl-Kiya, Tokmak, Djalal-Abad
Physical features mountainous, an extension of the Tien Shan range
Currency som
GNP per capita (PPP) (US$) 2,223 (1999)
Resources petroleum, natural gas, coal, gold, tin, mercury, antimony, zinc, tungsten, uranium
Population 4,699,000 (2000 est)
Population density (per sq km) 24 (1999 est)
Language Kyrgyz (a Turkic language; official), Russian
Religion Sunni Muslim 70%, Russian Orthodox 20%
• Time difference GMT +5

 ▪ CIA ▪ LC ▪ LP ▪ WTG

▪ **Destination Kyrgyzstan**
http://www.peacecorps.gov/wws/guides/kyrgyzstan/
Peace Corps guide, for schoolchildren, to this tiny Central Asian state. There are classroom activities divided by age group and teachers' notes, as well as plentiful maps, illustrations, and guides to other Internet resources.

LAOS

Map page 84

National name Sathalanalat Praxathipatai Paxaxôn Lao/ Democratic People's Republic of Laos

Area 236,790 sq km/ 91,424 sq mi
Capital Vientiane
Major towns/cities Louangphrabang (the former royal capital), Pakxé, Savannakhet
Physical features landlocked state with high mountains in east; Mekong River in west; rainforest covers nearly 60% of land
Currency new kip
GNP per capita (PPP) (US$) 1,726 (1999)
Resources coal, tin, gypsum, baryte, lead, zinc, nickel, potash, iron ore; small quantities of gold, silver, precious stones
Population 5,433,000 (2000 est)
Population density (per sq km) 22 (1999 est)
Language Lao (official), French, English, ethnic languages
Religion Theravada Buddhist 85%, animist beliefs among mountain dwellers
Time difference GMT +7

 ▪ CIA ▪ LC ▪ LP ▪ WTG

▪ **Laos – The Internet Travel Guide**
http://www.pmgeiser.ch/laos/
Written by a traveller for travellers, this is a useful resource for anyone visiting Laos in Southeast Asia. The guide is divided into a number of sections, offering advice on 'Climate', 'Events', 'Border crossing', and so on. A large part of the guide is devoted to the country's numerous attractions, ranging from the Ho Chi Minh trail to the Plain of Jars.

LATVIA

Map page 48

National name Latvijas Republika/ Republic of Latvia
Area 63,700 sq km/24,594 sq mi
Capital Rīga
Major towns/cities Daugavpils, Liepāja, Jūrmala, Jelgava, Ventspils
Major ports Ventspils, Liepāja
Physical features wooded lowland (highest point 312 m/ 1,024 ft), marshes, lakes; 472 km/293 mi of coastline; mild climate
Currency lat
GNP per capita (PPP) (US$) 5,938 (1999)
Resources peat, gypsum, dolomite, limestone, amber, gravel, sand
Population 2,357,000 (2000 est)
Population density (per sq km) 38 (1999 est)
Language Latvian (official)
Religion Lutheran, Roman Catholic, Russian Orthodox
Time difference GMT +2

 ▪ CIA ▪ LC ▪ LP ▪ RG ▪ WTG

▪ **LatviaNet**
http://www.tvnet.lv/en/
Bilingual guide to this Eastern European country, including an overview of the Baltic region, as well as plenty of country-specific information on such topics as the environment, communications, government, tourism, and society.

▪ **Riga in Your Pocket Home Page**
http://www.inyourpocket.com/Latvia/Riga_home.shtml
Guide to everything you ever wanted to know about this Baltic capital city. This is an electronic form of a published guide book and includes sections on such topics as language, media, what to see, getting there, and where to stay.

LEBANON

Map page 94

National name Jumhouria al-Lubnaniya/Republic of Lebanon
Area 10,452 sq km/4,035 sq mi
Capital Beirut (and chief port)
Major towns/cities Tripoli, Zahlé, Baabda, Ba'albek, Jezzine
Major ports Tripoli, Soûr, Saïda, Joûnié
Physical features narrow coastal plain; fertile Bekka valley

running north–south between Lebanon and Anti-Lebanon mountain ranges

Currency Lebanese pound

GNP per capita (PPP) (US$) 4,129 (1999)

Resources there are no commercially viable mineral deposits; small reserves of lignite and iron ore

Population 3,282,000 (2000 est)

Population density (per sq km) 310 (1999 est)

Language Arabic (official), French, Armenian, English

Religion Muslim 70% (Shiite 35%, Sunni 23%, Druze 7%, other 5%); Christian 30% (mainly Maronite 19%), Druze 3%; other Christian denominations including Greek Orthodox, Armenian, and Roman Catholic

Time difference GMT +2

 ■ CIA ■ LC ■ AN ■ LP ■ WTG

LESOTHO
Map page 108

National name Mmuso oa Lesotho/ Kingdom of Lesotho

Area 30,355 sq km/11,720 sq mi

Capital Maseru

Major towns/cities Qacha's Nek, Teyateyaneng, Mafeteng, Hlotse, Roma, Quthing

Physical features mountainous with plateaux, forming part of South Africa's chief watershed

Currency loti

GNP per capita (PPP) (US$) 2,058 (1999)

Resources diamonds, uranium, lead, iron ore; believed to have petroleum deposits

Population 2,153,000 (2000 est)

Population density (per sq km) 69 (1999 est)

Language English (official), Sesotho, Zulu, Xhosa

Religion Protestant 42%, Roman Catholic 38%, indigenous beliefs

Time difference GMT +2

 ■ CIA ■ LP ■ RG ■ NA ■ WTG

■ Lesotho Page
http://www.sas.upenn.edu/African_Studies/Country_Specific/ Lesotho.html

Concise set of resources, including a map, US travel advisories, a database of its languages, and links to further sources of information.

LIBERIA
Map page 104

National name Republic of Liberia

Area 111,370 sq km/42,999 sq mi

Capital Monrovia (and chief port)

Major towns/cities Bensonville, Gbarnga, Voinjama, Buchanan

Major ports Buchanan, Greenville

Physical features forested highlands; swampy tropical coast where six rivers enter the sea

Currency Liberian dollar

GNP per capita (PPP) (US$) N/A

Resources iron ore, diamonds, gold, barytes, kyanite

Population 3,154,000 (2000 est)

Population density (per sq km) 26 (1999 est)

Language English (official), over 20 Niger-Congo languages

Religion animist 70%, Sunni Muslim 20%, Christian 10%

Time difference GMT +/–0

 ■ CIA ■ LP ■ NA ■ WTG

LIBYA
Map page 100

National name Al-Jamahiriyya al-'Arabiyya al-Libiyya ash-Sha'biyya al-Ishtirakiyya al-'Uzma/Great Libyan Arab

---

Socialist People's State of the Masses

Area 1,759,540 sq km/ 679,358 sq mi

Capital Tripoli

Major towns/cities Banghāzī, Mişrātah, Az Zāwīyah, Tubruq, Ajdābiyā, Darnah

Major ports Banghāzī, Mişrāta, Az Zāwīyah, Tubruq, Ajdābiyā, Darnah

Physical features flat to undulating plains with plateaux and depressions stretch southwards from the Mediterranean coast to an extremely dry desert interior

Currency Libyan dinar

GNP per capita (PPP) (US$) N/A

Resources petroleum, natural gas, iron ore, potassium, magnesium, sulphur, gypsum

Population 5,605,000 (2000 est)

Population density (per sq km) 3 (1999 est)

Language Arabic (official), Italian, English

Religion Sunni Muslim 97%

Time difference GMT +1

 ■ CIA ■ LC ■ AN ■ LP ■ NA ■ WTG

LIECHTENSTEIN
Map page 62

National name Fürstentum Liechtenstein/Principality of Liechtenstein

Area 160 sq km/62 sq mi

Capital Vaduz

Major towns/cities Balzers, Schaan, Eschen

Physical features landlocked Alpine; includes part of Rhine Valley in west

Currency Swiss franc

GNP per capita (PPP) (US$) 24,000 (1998 est)

Resources hydro power

Population 33,000 (2000 est)

Population density (per sq km) 199 (1999 est)

Language German (official), an Alemannic dialect

Religion Roman Catholic 80%, Protestant 7%

Time difference GMT +1

 ■ CIA ■ LP ■ WTG

■ Liechtenstein National Tourist Guide
http://www.news.li/

Official guide to the tiny principality. There is comprehensive information on history, attractions, sporting and recreational pursuits, entertainment, accommodation, and transport. There is a commercial directory, a listing of events, and a guide for philatelists.

LITHUANIA
Map page 48

National name Lietuvos Respublika/ Republic of Lithuania

Area 65,200 sq km/25,173 sq mi

Capital Vilnius

Major towns/cities Kaunas, Klaipėda, Šiauliai, Panevėžys

Physical features central lowlands with gentle hills in west and higher terrain in southeast; 25% forested; some 3,000 small lakes, marshes, and complex sandy coastline; River Nenumas

Currency litas

GNP per capita (PPP) (US$) 6,093 (1999)

Resources small deposits of petroleum, natural gas, peat, limestone, gravel, clay, sand

Population 3,670,000 (2000 est)

Population density (per sq km) 56 (1999 est)

Language Lithuanian (official)

Religion predominantly Roman Catholic; Evangelical Lutheran, also Russian Orthodox, Evangelical Reformist, and Baptist

---

Time difference GMT +2

 ■ CIA ■ LC ■ LP ■ RG ■ WTG

■ Vilnius in Your Pocket Home Page
http://www.inyourpocket.com/Lithuania/Vilnius_home.shtml

Guide to everything you ever wanted to know about this Baltic capital city. This is an electronic form of a published guide book and includes sections on such topics as language, media, what to see, getting there, and where to stay.

LUXEMBOURG
Map page 54

National name Grand-Duché de Luxembourg/Grand Duchy of Luxembourg

Area 2,586 sq km/998 sq mi

Capital Luxembourg

Major towns/cities Esch, Differdange, Dudelange, Pétange

Physical features on the River Moselle; part of the Ardennes (Oesling) forest in north

Currency Luxembourg franc

GNP per capita (PPP) (US$) 38,247 (1999)

Resources iron ore

Population 431,000 (2000 est)

Population density (per sq km) 165 (1999 est)

Language Letzeburgisch (a German-Moselle-Frankish dialect; official), English

Religion Roman Catholic about 95%, Protestant and Jewish 4%

Time difference GMT +1

 ■ CIA ■ LP ■ RG ■ WTG

■ Luxembourg Tourist Office in London
http://www.luxembourg.co.uk/

Detailed guide to Luxembourg that is aimed primarily at the tourist. The site comprises a number of articles, covering topics such as the country's museums, activities, and culture. Also featured is a directory of hotels, guesthouses, and youth hostels.

MACEDONIA
Map page 68

National name Republika Makedonija/Republic of Macedonia (official internal name); Poranesna Jugoslovenska Republika Makedonija/Former Yugoslav Republic of Macedonia (official international name)

Area 25,700 sq km/9,922 sq mi

Capital Skopje

Major towns/cities Bitola, Prilep, Kumanovo, Tetovo

Physical features mountainous; rivers: Struma, Vardar; lakes: Ohrid, Prespa, Scutari; partly Mediterranean climate with hot summers

Currency Macedonian denar

GNP per capita (PPP) (US$) 4,339 (1999)

Resources coal, iron, zinc, chromium, manganese, lead, copper, nickel, silver, gold

Population 2,024,000 (2000 est)

Population density (per sq km) 78 (1999 est)

Language Macedonian (related to Bulgarian; official), Albanian

Religion Christian, mainly Orthodox 67%; Muslim 30%

Time difference GMT +1

 ■ CIA ■ LP ■ WTG

■ Macedonia – Frequently Asked Questions
http://faq.rmacedonia.org/

Large source of well-presented information on the Balkan state. There is comprehensive information about the Macedonian language, literary heritage, history, cuisine, arts, economy, sports, and religion. This site also has regularly updated news of internal and external affairs.

■ Skopje, Republic of Macedonia
http://www.skopje.com.mk/angliski/prva.asp

Guide to the Macedonian capital. The economic basis and cultural life of Skopje are described prior to a summary of the city's long history. There are also a number of photographs.

MADAGASCAR
Map page 108

National name Repoblikan'i Madagasikara/République de Madagascar/Republic of Madagascar
Area 587,041 sq km/ 226,656 sq mi
Capital Antananarivo
Major towns/cities Antsirabe, Mahajanga, Fianarantsoa, Toamasina, Ambatondrazaka
Major ports Toamasina, Antsiranana, Mahajanga
Physical features temperate central highlands; humid valleys and tropical coastal plains; arid in south
Currency Malagasy franc
GNP per capita (PPP) (US$) 766 (1999)
Resources graphite, chromite, mica, titanium ore, small quantities of precious stones, bauxite and coal deposits, petroleum reserves
Population 15,942,000 (2000 est)
Population density (per sq km) 26 (1999 est)
Language Malagasy, French (both official), local dialects
Religion over 50% traditional beliefs, Roman Catholic, Protestant about 40%, Muslim 7%
Time difference GMT +3

www. ■ CIA ■ LC ■ LP ■ NA ■ WTG

■ **Madagascar**
http://www.geocities.com/SoHo/Atrium/5431/mad/Index.html
Virtual tour of the island of Madagascar that is aimed at the independent traveller. The tour consists of a series of photographs that follow a trail across the island. There is also a map of the island, as well as an article and fact sheet on Madagascar.

MALAWI
Map page 108

National name Republic of Malawi
Area 118,484 sq km/45,735 sq mi
Capital Lilongwe
Major towns/cities Blantyre, Mzuzu, Zomba
Physical features landlocked narrow plateau with rolling plains; mountainous west of Lake Nyasa
Currency Malawi kwacha
GNP per capita (PPP) (US$) 581 (1999)
Resources marble, coal, gemstones, bauxite and graphite deposits, reserves of phosphates, uranium, glass sands, asbestos, vermiculite
Population 10,925,000 (2000 est)
Population density (per sq km) 90 (1999 est)
Language English, Chichewa (both official), other Bantu languages
Religion Protestant 50%, Roman Catholic 20%, Muslim 2%, animist
Time difference GMT +2

www. ■ CIA ■ LP ■ NA ■ WTG

■ **Malawi – The Warm Heart of Africa**
http://members.tripod.com/~malawi/
Well-illustrated guide to Malawi. Aimed at the traveller, this site offers advice on the country's attractions and accommodation. Visitors can also learn a few words of Chichewa and sample some of the country's music.

MALAYSIA
Map page 86

National name Persekutuan Tanah Malaysia/Federation of Malaysia
Area 329,759 sq km/127,319 sq mi

Capital Kuala Lumpur
Major towns/cities Johor Bahru, Ipoh, George Town (on Penang island), Kuala Terengganu, Kuala Bahru, Petaling Jaya, Kelang, Kuching (on Sarawak), Kota Kinabalu (on Sabah)
Major ports Kelang
Physical features comprises peninsular Malaysia (the nine Malay states – Johore, Kedah, Kelantan, Negri Sembilan, Pahang, Perak, Perlis, Selangor, Terengganu – plus Malacca and Penang); states of Sabah and Sarawak on the island of Borneo; and the federal territory of Kuala Lumpur; 75% tropical rainforest; central mountain range; Mount Kinabalu, the highest peak in southeast Asia, is in Sabah; swamps in east; Niah caves (Sarawak)
Currency ringgit
GNP per capita (PPP) (US$) 7,963 (1999)
Resources tin, bauxite, copper, iron ore, petroleum, natural gas, forests
Population 22,244,000 (2000 est)
Population density (per sq km) 66 (1999 est)
Language Bahasa Malaysia (Malay; official), English, Chinese, Tamil, Iban, many local dialects
Religion Muslim (official) about 53%, Buddhist 19%, Hindu, Christian, local beliefs
Time difference GMT +8

www. ■ CIA ■ LP ■ RG ■ WTG

■ **Malaysia Home Page**
http://www.sesrtcic.org/members/mly/mlyhome.shtml
Information about Malaysian history, events, education, economy, politics, tourism, and laws, as well as hyperlinks to other relevant sites.

MALDIVES
Map page 88

National name Divehi Raajjeyge Jumhuriyya/Republic of the Maldives
Area 298 sq km/115 sq mi
Capital Malé
Physical features comprises 1,196 coral islands, grouped into 12 clusters of atolls, largely flat, none bigger than 13 sq km/5 sq mi, average elevation 1.8 m/6 ft; 203 are inhabited
Currency rufiya
GNP per capita (PPP) (US$) 3,545 (1999)
Resources coral (mining was banned as a measure against the encroachment of the sea)
Population 286,000 (2000 est)
Population density (per sq km) 933 (1999 est)
Language Divehi (a Sinhalese dialect; official), English, Arabic
Religion Sunni Muslim
Time difference GMT +5

www. ■ CIA ■ LP ■ WTG

■ **Visit Maldives**
http://www.visitmaldives.com/intro.html
Well-designed guide to the Maldives from their Ministry of Tourism. The site features a 'Travel advisor', offering practical information on health and resorts. There is also a photo gallery, as well as sections devoted to sailing and diving in the Maldives.

MALI
Map page 102

National name République du Mali/ Republic of Mali
Area 1,240,142 sq km/ 478,818 sq mi
Capital Bamako
Major towns/cities Mopti, Kayes, Ségou, Tombouctou, Sikasso
Physical features landlocked state with River Niger and savannah in south; part of the Sahara in north; hills in northeast; Senegal River and its branches irrigate the southwest

Currency franc CFA
GNP per capita (PPP) (US$) 693 (1999)
Resources iron ore, uranium, diamonds, bauxite, manganese, copper, lithium, gold
Population 11,234,000 (2000 est)
Population density (per sq km) 9 (1999 est)
Language French (official), Bambara, other African languages
Religion Sunni Muslim 80%, animist, Christian
Time difference GMT +/–0

www. ■ CIA ■ LP ■ NA ■ WTG

MALTA
Map page 64

National name Repubblika ta'Malta/ Republic of Malta
Area 320 sq km/124 sq mi
Capital Valletta (and chief port)
Major towns/cities Rabat, Birkirkara, Qormi, Sliema
Major ports Marsaxlokk, Valletta
Physical features includes islands of Gozo 67 sq km/26 sq mi and Comino 3 sq km/1 sq mi
Currency Maltese lira
GNP per capita (PPP) (US$) 15,066 (1999 est)
Resources stone, sand; offshore petroleum reserves were under exploration 1988–95
Population 389,000 (2000 est)
Population density (per sq km) 1,206 (1999 est)
Language Maltese, English (both official)
Religion Roman Catholic 98%
Time difference GMT +1

www. ■ CIA ■ LP ■ WTG

■ **Official Web Site of the Maltese Government**
http://www.magnet.mt/
Good source of official information on the Mediterranean island state. There are sections on the complex history, culture, government services, and the economy. The needs of tourists are also well catered for with a host of practical information.

MARSHALL ISLANDS
Map page 112

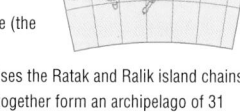

National name Majol/Republic of the Marshall Islands
Area 181 sq km/70 sq mi
Capital Dalap-Uliga-Darrit (on Majuro atoll)
Major towns/cities Ebeye (the only other town)
Physical features comprises the Ratak and Ralik island chains in the West Pacific, which together form an archipelago of 31 coral atolls, 5 islands, and 1,152 islets
Currency US dollar
GNP per capita (PPP) (US$) 1,860 (1999 est)
Resources phosphates
Population 64,000 (2000 est)
Population density (per sq km) 343 (1999 est)
Language Marshallese, English (both official)
Religion Christian (mainly Protestant) and Baha'i
Time difference GMT +12

www. ■ CIA ■ LP

■ **Internet Guide to the Republic of the Marshall Islands**
http://www.rmiembassyus.org/
Comprehensive official guide to the Micronesian state. The history, culture, cuisine, economy, government services, and democratic system of the Marshall Islands are fully explained with the help of maps and photos. RMI concerns about global warming, from a state whose highest elevation is a mere six metres, are set out.

MAURITANIA

Map page 102

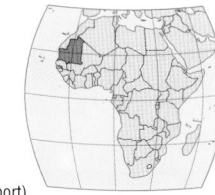

National name Al-Jumhuriyya al-Islamiyya al-Mawritaniyya/ République Islamique Arabe et Africaine de Mauritanie/Islamic Republic of Mauritania

Area 1,030,700 sq km/ 397,953 sq mi

Capital Nouakchott (and chief port)

Major towns/cities Nouâdhibou, Kaédi, Zouérat, Kiffa, Rosso, Atâr

Major ports Nouâdhibou

Physical features valley of River Senegal in south; remainder arid and flat

Currency ouguiya

GNP per capita (PPP) (US$) 1,522 (1999 est)

Resources copper, gold, iron ore, gypsum, phosphates, sulphur, peat

Population 2,670,000 (2000 est)

Population density (per sq km) 3 (1999 est)

Language Hasaniya Arabic (official), Pulaar, Soninke, Wolof (all national languages), French (particularly in the south)

Religion Sunni Muslim (state religion)

Time difference GMT +/–0

 CIA LC AN LP NA WTG

MAURITIUS

Map page 108

National name Republic of Mauritius

Area 1,865 sq km/720 sq mi

Capital Port Louis (and chief port)

Major towns/cities Beau Bassin, Rose Hill, Curepipe, Quatre Bornes, Vacoas-Phoenix

Physical features mountainous, volcanic island surrounded by coral reefs; the island of Rodrigues is part of Mauritius; there are several small island dependencies

Currency Mauritian rupee

GNP per capita (PPP) (US$) 8,652 (1999)

Population 1,158,000 (2000 est)

Population density (per sq km) 616 (1999 est)

Language English (official), French, Creole (36%), Bhojpuri (32%), other Indian languages

Religion Hindu over 50%, Christian (mainly Roman Catholic) about 30%, Muslim 17%

Time difference GMT +4

 CIA LC LP WTG

MEXICO
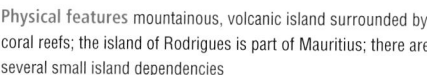
Map page 134

National name Estados Unidos Mexicanos/United States of Mexico

Area 1,958,201 sq km/ 756,061 sq mi

Capital Mexico City

Major towns/cities Guadalajara, Monterrey, Puebla, Ciudad Juárez, Tijuana

Major ports 49 ocean ports

Physical features partly arid central highlands; Sierra Madre mountain ranges east and west; tropical coastal plains; volcanoes, including Popocatepetl; Rio Grande

Currency Mexican peso

GNP per capita (PPP) (US$) 7,719 (1999)

Resources petroleum, natural gas, zinc, salt, silver, copper, coal, mercury, manganese, phosphates, uranium, strontium sulphide

Population 98,881,000 (2000 est)

Population density (per sq km) 50 (1999 est)

Language Spanish (official), Nahuatl, Maya, Zapoteco, Mixteco, Otomi

Religion Roman Catholic about 90%

Time difference GMT –6/8

 CIA LC LP RG WTG

Amigo! Mexico Online

http://www.mexonline.com/

Although a membership-based service, this page also offers lots of free information for the casual browser – with sections on activities, arts and culture, pre-Columbian history, and help for prospective travellers.

Mexico

http://www.trace-sc.com/index1.htm

Wide variety of fully-searchable information on Mexico. It includes pages about the ancient Aztec culture, including examples of some historical documents. On a more contemporary note, there is a current news section, as well as information on places for the tourist to visit.

Acapulco Today

http://accessmexico.com/acapulco/

Cornucopia of images, maps, news, and general information on this Mexican seaside resort – its culture, nightlife, food, and events. This site also includes details of local archaeological digs and an exploration of the Mayan world, with many links to other Mexican sites.

MICRONESIA, FEDERATED STATES OF

Map page 112

National name Federated States of Micronesia (FSM)

Area 700 sq km/270 sq mi

Capital Palikir (in Pohnpei island state)

Major towns/cities Kolonia (in Pohnpei), Weno (in Truk), Lelu (in Kosrae)

Physical features an archipelago of 607 equatorial, volcanic islands in the West Pacific

Currency US dollar

GNP per capita (PPP) (US$) 3,860 (1999 est)

Population 119,000 (2000 est)

Population density (per sq km) 165 (1999 est)

Language English (official), eight officially recognized local languages (including Trukese, Pohnpeian, Yapese, and Kosrean), a number of other dialects

Religion Christianity (mainly Roman Catholic in Yap state, Protestant elsewhere)

Time difference GMT +10 (Chuuk and Yap); +11 (Kosrae and Pohnpei)

 CIA LP WTG

Welcome to the Federated States of Micronesia

http://www.fsmgov.org/

Official site of the four Pacific islands comprising the Federated States of Micronesia. The contents include a good history, information on culture, language, natural resources, and government structures. The tourist attractions of the four states of Micronesia are listed, together with practical information for visitors.

MOLDOVA

Map page 66

National name Republica Moldova/ Republic of Moldova

Area 33,700 sq km/13,011 sq mi

Capital Chişinău (Russian Kishinev)

Major towns/cities Tiraspol, Bălţi, Tighina

Physical features hilly land lying largely between the rivers Prut and Dniester; northern Moldova comprises the level plain of the Bălţi Steppe and uplands; the climate is warm and moderately continental

Currency leu

GNP per capita (PPP) (US$) 2,358 (1999)

Resources lignite, phosphorites, gypsum, building materials; petroleum and natural gas deposits discovered in the early 1990s were not yet exploited in 1996

Population 4,380,000 (2000 est)

Population density (per sq km) 130 (1999 est)

Language Moldovan (official), Russian, Gaganz (a Turkish dialect)

Religion Eastern Orthodox 98.5%; remainder Jewish

Time difference GMT +2

 CIA LC LP WTG

Chisinau, Moldova

http://www.beebware.com/directory/Regional/Europe/Moldova/ Localities/Chisinau/

Good introduction to the Moldovan capital. There is a description of the city, its economy, and history. Among the useful links are
• those to the Moldovan government site and one describing the revival of the Jewish community in Chisinau.

MONACO

Map page 58

National name Principauté de Monaco/ Principality of Monaco

Area 1.95 sq km/0.75 sq mi

Physical features steep and rugged; surrounded landwards by French territory; being expanded by filling in the sea

Currency French franc

GNP per capita (PPP) (US$) 27,000 (1999 est)

Population 34,000 (2000 est)

Population density (per sq km) 16,074 (1999 est)

Language French (official), Monégasgne (a mixture of the French Provençal and Italian Ligurian dialects), Italian

Religion Roman Catholic about 90%

Time difference GMT +1

 CIA LP WTG

Monaco Online

http://www.monaco.mc

Colourful site on the Principality of Monaco. There are sections on all major aspects of life in the principality including the history of Monaco, the Grand Prix, financial advice, a business directory, the annual television festival, and a panorama of impressive shots of the cliffs and shores of Monaco.

MONGOLIA

Map page 78

National name Mongol Uls/ State of Mongolia

Area 1,565,000 sq km/ 604,246 sq mi

Capital Ulaanbaatar

Major towns/cities Darhan, Choybalsan, Erdenet

Physical features high plateau with desert and steppe (grasslands); Altai Mountains in southwest; salt lakes; part of Gobi desert in southeast; contains both the world's southernmost permafrost and northernmost desert

Currency tugrik

GNP per capita (PPP) (US$) 1,496 (1999)

Resources copper, nickel, zinc, molybdenum, phosphorites, tungsten, tin, fluorospar, gold, lead; reserves of petroleum discovered in 1994

Population 2,662,000 (2000 est)

Population density (per sq km) 2 (1999 est)

Language Khalkha Mongolian (official), Kazakh (in the province of Bagan-Ölgiy), Chinese, Russian, Turkic languages

Religion there is no state religion, but traditional lamaism (Mahayana Buddhism) is gaining new strength; the Sunni Muslim Kazakhs of Western Mongolia have also begun the renewal of their religious life, and Christian missionary activity has increased

Time difference GMT +8

 CIA LC LP WTG

Mongolia Page

http://www.ozemail.com.au/~mongolei/ENGLISH/engindex.html

Account of the geography, history, politics, and culture of Mongolia. It includes an overview of the country's art, music, and festivals, and a collection of images. This site also has information on travel and even some useful contacts in this country.

MOROCCO
Map page 102

National name Al-Mamlaka al-Maghribyya/Kingdom of Morocco
Area 458,730 sq km/ 177,115 sq mi (excluding Western Sahara)
Capital Rabat
Major towns/cities Casablanca, Marrakech, Fès, Oujda, Kénitra, Tétouan, Meknès
Major ports Casablanca, Tanger, Agadir
Physical features mountain ranges, including the Atlas Mountains northeast–southwest; fertile coastal plains in west
Currency dirham
GNP per capita (PPP) (US$) 3,190 (1999)
Resources phosphate rock and phosphoric acid, coal, iron ore, barytes, lead, copper, manganese, zinc, petroleum, natural gas, fish
Population 28,351,000 (2000 est)
Population density (per sq km) 61 (1999 est)
Language Arabic (75%) (official), Berber dialects (25%), French, Spanish
Religion Sunni Muslim; Christian and Jewish minorities
Time difference GMT +/–0

 ▪ CIA ▪ AN ▪ LP ▪ RG ▪ WTG

▪ **Kingdom of Morocco**
http://www.mincom.gov.ma/
Morocco's official bilingual window on the World Wide Web. It offers articles on Moroccan identity, lifestyle, and culture, overviews of the different regions of the country, a fauna and flora section, a financial and investment guide, and information on the government.

MOZAMBIQUE
Map page 108

National name República de Moçambique/Republic of Mozambique
Area 799,380 sq km/ 308,640 sq mi
Capital Maputo (and chief port)
Major towns/cities Beira, Nampula, Nacala, Chimoio
Major ports Beira, Nacala, Quelimane
Physical features mostly flat tropical lowland; mountains in west; rivers Zambezi and Limpopo
Currency metical
GNP per capita (PPP) (US$) 797 (1999 est)
Resources coal, salt, bauxite, graphite; reserves of iron ore, gold, precious and semi-precious stones, marble, natural gas (all largely unexploited in 1996)
Population 19,680,000 (2000 est)
Population density (per sq km) 24 (1999 est)
Language Portuguese (official), 16 African languages
Religion animist 48%, Muslim 20%, Roman Catholic 16%, Protestant 16%
Time difference GMT +2

 ▪ CIA ▪ LP ▪ NA ▪ WTG

▪ **Mozambique Home Page**
http://www.mozambique.mz/eindex.htm
Informative guide to Mozambique available in both English and Portuguese. The site consists of a number of sections, such as 'Government', 'Environment', 'Tourism', each of which contains a number of articles. The tourist guide is well worth a visit, and offers a useful insight into Mozambique's provinces and attractions.

MYANMAR (BURMA)
Map page 84

National name Pyedawngsu Myanma Naingngan/Union of Myanmar
Area 676,577 sq km/ 261,226 sq mi
Capital Yangon (formerly Rangoon) (and chief port)
Major towns/cities Mandalay, Moulmein, Bago, Bassein, Taung-gyi, Sittwe,
Physical features over half is rainforest; rivers Irrawaddy and Chindwin in central lowlands ringed by mountains in north, west, and east
Currency kyat
GNP per capita (PPP) (US$) 1,200 (1999 est)
Resources natural gas, petroleum, zinc, tin, copper, tungsten, coal, lead, gems, silver, gold
Population 45,611,000 (2000 est)
Population density (per sq km) 70 (1999 est)
Language Burmese (official), English, tribal dialects
Religion Hinayana Buddhist 89%, Christian 5%, Muslim 4%, animist 1.5%
Time difference GMT +6.5

 ▪ CIA ▪ LP ▪ WTG

▪ **Shan People of Burma**
http://pw2.netcom.com/~burma/tai/pride.html
Pages devoted to the history, language, culture, and present situation of the Shan, or Tai, people of Burma. There is also a link to the Panglong Agreement that led to Burma's independence in 1948.

NAMIBIA
Map page 108

National name Republic of Namibia
Area 824,300 sq km/318,262 sq mi
Capital Windhoek
Major towns/cities Swakopmund, Rehoboth, Rundu
Major ports Walvis Bay
Physical features mainly desert (Namib and Kalahari); Orange River; Caprivi Strip links Namibia to Zambezi River; includes the enclave of Walvis Bay (area 1,120 sq km/432 sq mi)
Currency Namibian dollar
GNP per capita (PPP) (US$) 5,369 (1999 est)
Resources uranium, copper, lead, zinc, silver, tin, gold, salt, semi-precious stones, diamonds (one of the world's leading producers of gem diamonds), hydrocarbons, lithium, manganese, tungsten, cadmium, vanadium
Population 1,726,000 (2000 est)
Population density (per sq km) 2 (1999 est)
Language English (official), Afrikaans, German, Ovambo (51%), Nama (12%), Kavango (10%), other indigenous languages
Religion about 90% Christian (Lutheran, Roman Catholic, Dutch Reformed Church, Anglican)
Time difference GMT +1

 ▪ CIA ▪ LP ▪ NA ▪ WTG

▪ **Namibia Online Travel Guide**
http://www.southafrica-travel.net/namibia/enamib.htm
Colourful and informative guide to Namibia. Not only are there descriptions of the country's history and government, but the site also covers Namibia's climate and vegetation as well as its many popular attractions.

NAURU
Map page 112

National name Republic of Nauru
Area 21 sq km/8.1 sq mi
Capital Yaren District (seat of government)
Physical features tropical coral

island in southwest Pacific; plateau encircled by coral cliffs and sandy beaches
Currency Australian dollar
GNP per capita (PPP) (US$) 11,800 (1994 est)
Resources phosphates
Population 12,000 (2000 est)
Population density (per sq km) 524 (1999 est)
Language Nauruan, English (both official)
Religion majority Protestant, Roman Catholic
Time difference GMT +12

 ▪ CIA ▪ LP ▪ WTG

▪ **Nauru**
http://www.tbc.gov.bc.ca/cwgames/country/Nauru/nauru.html
Official guide to Nauru sponsored by the Commonwealth. The site provides information on the geography, history, culture, economy, government, and judicial system of this phosphate-rich island.

NEPAL

Map page 88

National name Nepál Adhirajya/ Kingdom of Nepal
Area 147,181 sq km/56,826 sq mi
Capital Kathmandu
Major towns/cities Biratnagar, Lalitpur, Bhadgaon, Pokhara, Birganj, Dharan Bazar
Physical features descends from the Himalayas in the north through foothills to the River Ganges plain in the south; Mount Everest, Mount Kanchenjunga
Currency Nepalese rupee
GNP per capita (PPP) (US$) 1,219 (1999)
Resources lignite, talcum, magnesite, limestone, copper, cobalt
Population 23,930,000 (2000 est)
Population density (per sq km) 159 (1999 est)
Language Nepali (official), Tibetan, numerous local languages
Religion Hindu 90%; Buddhist 5%, Muslim 3%, Christian
Time difference GMT +5.5

 ▪ CIA ▪ LC ▪ LP ▪ RG ▪ WTG

NETHERLANDS
Map page 54

National name Koninkrijk der Nederlanden/Kingdom of the Netherlands
Area 41,863 sq km/16,163 sq mi
Capital Amsterdam (official), The Hague (legislative and judicial)
Major towns/cities Rotterdam, Utrecht, Eindhoven, Groningen, Tilburg, Maastricht, Apeldoorn, Nijmegen, Breda
Major ports Rotterdam
Physical features flat coastal lowland; rivers Rhine, Schelde, Maas; Frisian Islands
Territories Aruba, Netherlands Antilles (Caribbean)
Currency guilder
GNP per capita (PPP) (US$) 23,052 (1999)
Resources petroleum, natural gas
Population 15,786,000 (1999 est)
Population density (per sq km) 376 (1999 est)
Language Dutch (official)
Religion atheist 39%, Roman Catholic 31%, Dutch Reformed Church 14%, Calvinist 8%
Time difference GMT +1

 ▪ CIA ▪ LP ▪ RG ▪ WTG

▪ **Amsterdam Channel Home Page**
http://www.channels.nl/adam.html
Provides an innovative 'tour' through Amsterdam through a wealth of images of the city – select the direction you wish to follow next and a view of that area is called up. There are links to details of some sites and a street map is also available.

▪ **Directorate IJsselmeer Region**
http://www.waterland.net/rdij/indexen.html

Well-presented official information from the Dutch Ministry of Works on 'the wet heart of the Netherlands'. There is a good history of the IJsselmeer polders and the scheme to tame the Zuider Zee. The operation of the complex water management scheme is fully explained. Several environmental aspects of the scheme are also covered.

■ **General Information on the Netherlands**
http://www.netherlands-embassy.org/
Well-organized official introduction to Holland from the Dutch embassy in Washington DC. The easily accessed sections include information on the country's history, economy, industry, defence, political structure, social policy, tourism, health, education, environment, and the media. There are a large number of useful links making this site a starting point for finding further information on Holland.

NEW ZEALAND

Map page 116

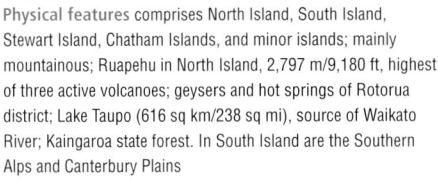

National name Aotearoa/ New Zealand
Area 268,680 sq km/ 103,737 sq mi
Capital Wellington
Major towns/cities Auckland, Hamilton, Christchurch, Manukau
Major ports Auckland, Wellington
Physical features comprises North Island, South Island, Stewart Island, Chatham Islands, and minor islands; mainly mountainous; Ruapehu in North Island, 2,797 m/9,180 ft, highest of three active volcanoes; geysers and hot springs of Rotorua district; Lake Taupo (616 sq km/238 sq mi), source of Waikato River; Kaingaroa state forest. In South Island are the Southern Alps and Canterbury Plains
Territories Tokelau (three atolls transferred in 1926 from former Gilbert and Ellice Islands colony); Niue Island (one of the Cook Islands, separately administered from 1903: chief town Alafi); Cook Islands are internally self-governing but share common citizenship with New Zealand; Ross Dependency in Antarctica
Currency New Zealand dollar
GNP per capita (PPP) (US$) 16,566 (1999)
Resources coal, clay, limestone, dolomite, natural gas, hydroelectric power, pumice, iron ore, gold, forests
Population 3,862,000 (2000 est)
Population density (per sq km) 14 (1999 est)
Language English (official), Maori
Religion Christian (Anglican 18%, Roman Catholic 14%, Presbyterian 13%)
Time difference GMT +12

www. ■ CIA ■ LP ■ WTG

■ **New Zealand on the Web**
http://nz.com/
Aimed at the prospective visitor, this site includes a virtual tour of New Zealand, a guidebook, and background information on its history and culture. There is also some information about trade and commerce.

■ **Welcome to Paradise – the Cook Islands**
http://www.ck/index.html
Very thorough guide to the Cook Islands in English and French. The many pages are packed with information on the geography, culture, economy, and government of the fifteen far-flung islands. The differing needs of tourists and investors are both met by this well-organized site.

■ **Hamilton – Heart of the Mighty Waikato**
http://www.chemistry.co.nz/waikato.htm
Well-arranged guide to the city of Hamilton and the Waikato region. The attractions, economy, and lifestyle of New Zealand's productive agricultural region are set out. There is also a history and practical information for visitors.

■ **Bay of Plenty**
http://www.bayofplenty.co.nz/
Guide to the towns, beaches, and other natural attractions of this New Zealand region. There is practical information for visitors and a suggested itinerary. There are also a number of links to other sites about towns and places around the inlet.

■ **NZHistory.net.nz**
http://www.nzhistory.net.nz/index.html
Site for anyone interested in the recent history of New Zealand, with illustrated extracts from history books and biographies

spanning the 19th and 20th centuries, and exhibitions on military, social, and government history. There are also links to other relevant sites and a discussion group.

NICARAGUA

Map page 134

National name República de Nicaragua/Republic of Nicaragua
Area 127,849 sq km/49,362 sq mi
Capital Managua
Major towns/cities León, Chinandega, Masaya, Granada, Estelí
Major ports Corinto, Puerto Cabezas, El Bluff
Physical features narrow Pacific coastal plain separated from broad Atlantic coastal plain by volcanic mountains and lakes Managua and Nicaragua; one of the world's most active earthquake regions
Currency cordoba
GNP per capita (PPP) (US$) 2,154 (1999)
Resources gold, silver, copper, lead, antimony, zinc, iron, limestone, gypsum, marble, bentonite
Population 5,074,000 (2000 est)
Population density (per sq km) 39 (1999 est)
Language Spanish (official), English, American Indian languages
Religion Roman Catholic 95%
Time difference GMT –6

www. ■ CIA ■ LC ■ LP ■ WTG

■ **Experience Nicaragua**
http://library.thinkquest.org/17749/
Well-designed and in-depth resource for the study of Nicaragua. The site is divided into three main sections – 'History', 'Economy', and 'Culture' – with numerous articles and graphics in each. Travel advice is also included, as well as a number of video and audio clips that offer a sample of Nicaraguan society and culture.

NIGER

Map page 102

National name République du Niger/Republic of Niger
Area 1,186,408 sq km/ 458,072 sq mi
Capital Niamey
Major towns/cities Zinder, Maradi, Tahoua, Agadez, Birnin Konni, Arlit
Physical features desert plains between hills in north and savannah in south; River Niger in southwest, Lake Chad in southeast
Currency franc CFA
GNP per capita (PPP) (US$) 727 (1999)
Resources uranium (one of world's leading producers), phosphates, gypsum, coal, cassiterite, tin, salt, gold; deposits of other minerals (including petroleum, iron ore, copper, lead, diamonds, and tungsten) have been confirmed
Population 10,730,000 (2000 est)
Population density (per sq km) 9 (1999 est)
Language French (official), Hausa (70%), Djerma, other ethnic languages
Religion Sunni Muslim 95%; also Christian, and traditional animist beliefs
Time difference GMT +1

www. ■ CIA ■ LP ■ NA ■ WTG

■ **Margaret Rehm's Niger Page**
http://www.davison.k12.mi.us/academic/rehm1.htm
Photographic panorama of Niger with photos taken by a volunteer from the Peace Corps. The site is divided into four categories, related to agriculture, village life, livestock, and water.

NIGERIA

Map page 104

National name Federal Republic of Nigeria
Area 923,773 sq km/356,668 sq mi

Capital Abuja
Major towns/cities Ibadan, Lagos, Ogbomosho, Kano, Oshogbo, Ilorin, Abeokuta, Zaria, Port Harcourt
Major ports Lagos, Port Harcourt, Warri, Calabar
Physical features arid savannah in north; tropical rainforest in south, with mangrove swamps along coast; River Niger forms wide delta; mountains in southeast
Currency naira
GNP per capita (PPP) (US$) 744 (1999)
Resources petroleum, natural gas, coal, tin, iron ore, uranium, limestone, marble, forest
Population 111,506,000 (2000 est)
Population density (per sq km) 118 (1999 est)
Language English, French (both official), Hausa, Ibo, Yoruba
Religion Sunni Muslim 50% (in north), Christian 35% (in south), local religions 15%
Time difference GMT +1

www. ■ CIA ■ LC ■ LP ■ NA ■ LP

NORTH KOREA

Map page 82

National name Chosun Minchu-chui Inmin Konghwa-guk/Democratic People's Republic of Korea
Area 120,538 sq km/ 46,539 sq mi
Capital P'yŏngyang
Major towns/cities Hamhŭng, Ch'ŏngjin, Namp'o, Wŏnsan, Sinŭiji
Physical features wide coastal plain in west rising to mountains cut by deep valleys in interior
Currency won
GNP per capita (PPP) (US$) 950 (1999 est)
Resources coal, iron, lead, copper, zinc, tin, silver, gold, magnesite (has 40–50% of world's deposits of magnesite)
Population 24,039,000 (2000 est)
Population density (per sq km) 197 (1999 est)
Language Korean (official)
Religion Buddhist (predominant religion), Chondoist, Christian, traditional beliefs
Time difference GMT +9

www. ■ CIA ■ LC ■ LP ■ WTG

■ **Korea Central News Agency**
http://www.kcna.co.jp/
Site of the Korea Central News Agency. This online propaganda from the North Korean regime provides a fascinating insight into the outlook of one of the world's most isolated regimes.

NORWAY

Map page 48

National name Kongeriket Norge/ Kingdom of Norway
Area 387,000 sq km/149,420 sq mi (including Svalbard and Jan Mayen)
Capital Oslo
Major towns/cities Bergen, Trondheim, Stavanger, Kristiansand, Drammen
Physical features mountainous with fertile valleys and deeply indented coast; forests cover 25%; extends north of Arctic Circle
Territories dependencies in the Arctic (Svalbard and Jan Mayen) and in Antarctica (Bouvet and Peter I Island, and Queen Maud Land)
Currency Norwegian krone
GNP per capita (PPP) (US$) 26,522 (1999)
Resources petroleum, natural gas, iron ore, iron pyrites, copper, lead, zinc, forests
Population 4,465,000 (2000 est)
Population density (per sq km) 14 (1999 est)
Language Norwegian (official), Saami (Lapp), Finnish

Religion Evangelical Lutheran (endowed by state) 88%; other Protestant and Roman Catholic 4%

Time difference GMT +1

 ■ CIA ■ LP ■ RG ■ WTG

■ Welcome to Bergen – The Gateway to the Fjords of Norway
http://www.uib.no/Bergen/reiseliv/tourist/index.html

Well-arranged guide to the Norwegian city. This site includes a history, a guide to local attractions, and information about cultural life. There are also details of how to visit nearby fjords.

■ Stavanger
http://www.stavanger-web.com/

Good introduction to the Norwegian seaport. There are over 1,800 links to sites about Stavanger, including information on history, accommodation, transport, cultural events, and entertainment.

■ Official Documentation and Information from Norway
http://odin.dep.no/odin/engelsk/index-b-n-a.html

Well-presented official introduction to all aspects of Norwegian life. There are sections on geography, economy, foreign policy, the political system, the royal family, culture, education, health, sport, and Norway's position within the European Union. Assistance is provided for those wishing to trace their Norwegian ancestry. The site is frequently updated with official Foreign Ministry information and news articles on Norwegian life.

■ Tromsø, Norway
http://www.destinasjontromso.no/eng_default.htm

Information on the northern Norwegian 'gateway to the Arctic'. An introduction to the city includes a weather report. A large number of photos are included of Tromso in all seasons including the midnight sun and northern lights.

OMAN
Map page 90

National name Saltanat `Uman/ Sultanate of Oman

Area 272,000 sq km/ 105,019 sq mi

Capital Muscat

Major towns/cities Sallālah, Ibrī, Suḥār, Al Buraymī, Nazwá, Sūr, Maṭraḥ

Physical features mountains to the north and south of a high arid plateau; fertile coastal strip; Jebel Akhdar highlands; Kuria Muria Islands

Currency Omani rial

GNP per capita (PPP) (US$) 8,690 (1997)

Resources petroleum, natural gas, copper, chromite, gold, salt, marble, gypsum, limestone

Population 2,542,000 (2000 est)

Population density (per sq km) 9 (1999 est)

Language Arabic (official), English, Urdu, other Indian languages

Religion Muslim 75% (predominantly Ibadhi Muslim), about 25% Hindu

Time difference GMT +4

 ■ CIA ■ LC ■ AN ■ LP ■ WTG

■ Oman Infoworld
http://Home.InfoRamp.Net/~emous/oman/about.htm

Variety of information on Oman. The site includes a useful fact sheet and a brief overview of the history of the country, sections on its art and architecture, heritage, traditions and customs, fashion and crafts, and sports pages, a presentation of the economic structure including pages on industry, trading, finance, banking, and transport, and a separate tourist information page.

PAKISTAN
Map page 90

National name Islami Jamhuriyya e Pakistan/Islamic Republic of Pakistan

Area 803,940 sq km/ 310,321 sq mi

Capital Islamabad

Major towns/cities Lahore,

Rawalpindi, Faisalabad, Karachi, Hyderabad, Multan, Peshawar, Gujranwala, Quetta

Major ports Karachi

Physical features fertile Indus plain in east, Baluchistan plateau in west, mountains in north and northwest; the 'five rivers' (Indus, Jhelum, Chenab, Ravi, and Sutlej) feed the world's largest irrigation system; K2 mountain; Khyber Pass

Currency Pakistan rupee

GNP per capita (PPP) (US$) 1,757 (1999)

Resources iron ore, natural gas, limestone, rock salt, gypsum, silica, coal, petroleum, graphite, copper, manganese, chromite

Population 156,483,000 (2000 est)

Population density (per sq km) 189 (1999 est)

Language Urdu (official), English, Punjabi, Sindhi, Pashto, Baluchi, other local dialects

Religion Sunni Muslim 90%, Shiite Muslim 5%; also Hindu, Christian, Parsee, Buddhist

Time difference GMT +5

 ■ CIA ■ LC ■ LP ■ WTG

PALAU
Map page 112

National name Belu'u era Belau/Republic of Palau

Area 508 sq km/196 sq mi

Capital Koror (on Koror island)

Physical features more than 350 (mostly uninhabited) islands, islets, and atolls in the west Pacific; warm, humid climate, susceptible to typhoons

Currency US dollar

GNP per capita (PPP) (US$) N/A

Population 19,000 (2000 est)

Population density (per sq km) 39 (1999 est)

Language Palauan, English (both official in most states)

Religion Christian, principally Roman Catholic; Modekngei (indigenous religion)

Time difference GMT +9

 ■ CIA ■ LP ■ WTG

■ Welcome to Palau
http://visit-palau.com/

Guide to the Pacific state. Information on local history and Palaun culture is supported by good photographs. There is practical information for tourists and for those interested in fishing and diving.

PANAMA
Map page 134

National name República de Panamá/Republic of Panama

Area 77,100 sq km/29,768 sq mi

Capital Panamá

Major towns/cities San Miguelito, Colón, David, La Chorrera, Santiago, Chitré, Changuinola

Major ports Colón, Cristóbal, Balboa

Physical features coastal plains and mountainous interior; tropical rainforest in east and northwest; Archipelago de las Perlas in Gulf of Panama; Panama Canal

Currency balboa

GNP per capita (PPP) (US$) 5,016 (1999)

Resources limestone, clay, salt; deposits of coal, copper, and molybdenum have been discovered

Population 2,856,000 (2000 est)

Population density (per sq km) 36 (1999 est)

Language Spanish (official), English

Religion Roman Catholic 93%

Time difference GMT –5

 ■ CIA ■ LC ■ LP ■ WTG

■ Welcome to the Panama Canal
http://www.pancanal.com/

Good source of information on the organization, operation, and

history of the Panama Canal from its operating authority. Photographs and diagrams help explain the workings of the canal and its system of locks.

PAPUA NEW GUINEA
Map page 112

National name Gau Hedinarai ai Papua-Matamata Guinea/ Independent State of Papua New Guinea

Area 462,840 sq km/178,702 sq mi

Capital Port Moresby (on East New Guinea)

Major towns/cities Lae, Madang, Arawa, Wewak, Goroka, Rabaul

Major ports Port Moresby, Rabaul

Physical features mountainous; swamps and plains; monsoon climate; tropical islands of New Ireland, New Britain, and Bougainville; Admiralty Islands, D'Entrecasteaux Islands, and Louisiade Archipelago; active volcanoes Vulcan and Tavurvur

Currency kina

GNP per capita (PPP) (US$) 2,263 (1999 est)

Resources copper, gold, silver; deposits of chromite, cobalt, nickel, quartz; substantial reserves of petroleum and natural gas (petroleum production began in 1992)

Population 4,807,000 (2000 est)

Population density (per sq km) 10 (1999 est)

Language English (official), pidgin English, over 700 local languages

Religion Christian 97%, of which 3% Roman Catholic; local pantheistic beliefs

Time difference GMT +10

 ■ CIA ■ LP ■ WTG

■ Papua New Guinea Information Site
http://www.niugini.com/

Guide to Papua New Guinea. The ethnic and linguistic diversity of the country and its complex history are well presented. A 'clickable' map accesses information on each of the country's twenty provinces.

PARAGUAY
Map page 142

National name República del Paraguay/Republic of Paraguay

Area 406,752 sq km/ 157,046 sq mi

Capital Asunción (and chief port)

Major towns/cities Ciudad del Este, Pedro Juan Caballero, San Lorenzo, Fernando de la Mora, Lambare, Luque, Capiatá

Major ports Concepción

Physical features low marshy plain and marshlands; divided by Paraguay River; Paraná River forms southeast boundary

Currency guaraní

GNP per capita (PPP) (US$) 4,193 (1999 est)

Resources gypsum, kaolin, limestone, salt; deposits (not commercially exploited) of bauxite, iron ore, copper, manganese, uranium; deposits of natural gas discovered in 1994; exploration for petroleum deposits ongoing mid-1990s

Population 5,496,000 (2000 est)

Population density (per sq km) 13 (1999 est)

Language Spanish (official), Guaraní (an indigenous Indian language)

Religion Roman Catholic (official religion) 85%; Mennonite, Anglican

Time difference GMT –3/4

 ■ CIA ■ LC ■ LP ■ WTG

■ Asuncion, Paraguay
http://travel.lycos.com/Destinations/South_America/Paraguay/Asuncion/

Profile of Asunción, capital of Paraguay. There is a general introduction to its main features, and four sections – 'Visitors' guide', 'Culture and history', 'News and weather', and

'Entertainment' – with links to photographs, and to further useful information in English and Spanish about the city and the country.

PERU

Map page 140

National name República del Perú/Republic of Peru
Area 1,285,200 sq km/ 496,216 sq mi
Capital Lima
Major towns/cities Arequipa, Iquitos, Chiclayo, Trujillo, Huancayo, Piura, Chimbote
Major ports Callao, Chimbote, Salaverry
Physical features Andes mountains running northwest–southeast cover 27% of Peru, separating Amazon river-basin jungle in northeast from coastal plain in west; desert along coast north–south (Atacama Desert); Lake Titicaca
Currency nuevo sol
GNP per capita (PPP) (US$) 4,387 (1999)
Resources lead, copper, iron, silver, zinc (world's fourth-largest producer), petroleum
Population 25,662,000 (2000 est)
Population density (per sq km) 20 (1999 est)
Language Spanish, Quechua (both official), Aymara, many indigenous dialects
Religion Roman Catholic (state religion) 95%
Time difference GMT –5

 ▪ CIA ▪ LC ▪ LP ▪ WTG

▪ **Peru Home Page**
http://www.rcp.net.pe/peru/peru_ingles.html
Basic information about Peru, including links to audio clips of Peruvian music and a section on ecotourism.

▪ **Arequipa, Peru**
http://travel.lycos.com/Destinations/South_America/Peru/Arequipa/
Profile of the 'white city' of Arequipa in southern Peru. There is a general introduction to the city's main features, and four sections – 'Visitors' guide', 'Culture and history', 'News and weather', and 'Entertainment' – each with links to further useful information in English and Spanish about both the city and the country.

▪ **Cuzco, Peru**
http://travel.lycos.com/Destinations/South_America/Peru/Cuzco/
Page devoted to the ancient Peruvian city of Cuzco. There is a general introduction to the city's main features, and four sections – 'Visitors' guide', 'Culture and history', 'News and weather', and 'Entertainment' – each with links to further useful information in English and Spanish about both the city and the country.

▪ **Lima, Peru**
http://travel.lycos.com/Destinations/South_America/Peru/Lima/
Profile of the historic city of Lima, capital of Peru. There is a general introduction to the city's main features, and four sections – 'Visitors' guide', 'Culture and history', 'News and weather', and 'Entertainment' – each with links to further useful information in English and Spanish about both the city and the country.

PHILIPPINES

Map page 84

National name Republika Ñg Pilipinas/Republic of the Philippines
Area 300,000 sq km/115,830 sq mi
Capital Manila (on Luzon island) (and chief port)
Major towns/cities Quezon City, Davao, Caloocan, Cebu, Bacolod, Cagayan de Oro, Iloilo
Major ports Cebu, Davao (on Mindanao), Iloilo, Zamboanga (on Mindanao)
Physical features comprises over 7,000 islands; volcanic mountain ranges traverse main chain north–south; 50% still forested. The largest islands are Luzon 108,172 sq km/ 41,754 sq mi and Mindanao 94,227 sq km/36,372 sq mi; others include Samar, Negros, Palawan, Panay, Mindoro, Leyte, Cebu, and the Sulu group; Pinatubo volcano (1,759 m/5,770 ft); Mindanao has active volcano Apo (2,954 m/9,690 ft) and mountainous rainforest

Currency peso
GNP per capita (PPP) (US$) 3,815 (1999)
Resources copper ore, gold, silver, chromium, nickel, coal, crude petroleum, natural gas, forests
Population 75,967,000 (2000 est)
Population density (per sq km) 248 (1999 est)
Language Filipino, English (both official), Spanish, Cebuano, Ilocano, more than 70 other indigenous languages
Religion Christian 94%, mainly Roman Catholic (84%), Protestant; Muslim 4%, local religions
Time difference GMT +8

 ▪ CIA ▪ LC ▪ LP ▪ WTG

▪ **Philippine History**
http://www.tribo.org/history.html
Well organized source of information about Philippine history, with sections on such topics as the islands' ancient past, the colonial period, the Spanish and US occupations, and the Philippine republic.

▪ **Kalayaan – A Celebration of the 100 Glorious Years of Philippine Independence**
http://www.abs-cbn.com/centennial/index.html
Information on the celebrations surrounding the centennial of Philippine independence. The Web site includes information on events taking place during the celebrations and in particular the Mythical Island exhibition site. Two further areas of the Web site which are still under construction describe heroes of the Philippines and provide images of the country.

POLAND

Map page 50

National name Rzeczpospolita Polska/ Republic of Poland
Area 312,683 sq km/120,726 sq mi
Capital Warsaw
Major towns/cities Łódź, Kraków, Wroclaw, Poznan, Gdansk, Szczecin, Katowice, Bydgoszcz, Lublin
Major ports Gdansk (Danzig), Szczecin (Stettin), Gdynia (Gdingen)
Physical features part of the great plain of Europe; Vistula, Oder, and Neisse rivers; Sudeten, Tatra, and Carpathian mountains on southern frontier
Currency zloty
GNP per capita (PPP) (US$) 7,894 (1999)
Resources coal (world's fifth-largest producer), copper, sulphur, silver, petroleum and natural gas reserves
Population 38,765,000 (2000 est)
Population density (per sq km) 124 (1999 est)
Language Polish (official)
Religion Roman Catholic 95%
Time difference GMT +1

 ▪ CIA ▪ LC ▪ LP ▪ RG ▪ WTG

▪ **Welcome to Warsaw**
http://www.geocities.com/Heartland/9413/warszawa.html
General guide to the city of Warsaw, its university, its weather, and additional information about other sights and attractions in Poland.

▪ **Cracow**
http://www.krakow.pl/en/
Official guide to the Polish World Heritage city. There are sections on the government structure, local economy, cultural life, and local attractions. There is practical information for visitors.

▪ **Polish National Tourist Office**
http://www.polandtour.org/
Well-designed guide to Poland that is available in English, French, and German. Choose from five different sections – 'About Poland', 'Travel information', 'Regions and cities', 'Recreation and sports', and 'Culture and arts' – each of which offers a number of in-depth articles about the country.

PORTUGAL

Map page 60

National name República Portuguesa/Republic of Portugal
Area 92,000 sq km/35,521 sq mi (including the Azores and Madeira)
Capital Lisbon
Major towns/cities Porto, Coimbra, Amadora, Setúbal, Funchal, Braga, Vila Nova de Gaia
Major ports Porto, Setúbal
Physical features mountainous in the north (Serra da Estrêla mountains); plains in the south; rivers Minho, Douro, Tagus (Tejo), Guadiana
Currency escudo
GNP per capita (PPP) (US$) 15,147 (1999)
Resources limestone, granite, marble, iron, tungsten, copper, pyrites, gold, uranium, coal, forests
Population 9,875,000 (2000 est)
Population density (per sq km) 107 (1999 est)
Language Portuguese (official)
Religion Roman Catholic 97%
Time difference GMT +/–0

 ▪ CIA ▪ LC ▪ LP ▪ RG ▪ WTG

▪ **Lisbon**
http://www.EUnet.pt/Lisboa/i/lisboa.html
Bilingual site with information about the 'city of the seven hills' including its history, a town map, and information on museums, restaurants, bars, and hotels. It also includes plenty of pictures and some audio clips from Portuguese artists.

▪ **Porto, Portugal**
http://travel.lycos.com/Destinations/Europe/Portugal/Porto/
Good source of practical, historical, and cultural information on Portugal's second city. The attractions of the city are well-presented. There is also information on the celebrated 'vinho do Porto' – port – which takes it name from the city.

▪ **Welcome to the Algarve**
http://www.nexus-pt/algarve.htm
Comprehensive source of information on the region of southern Portugal. A 'clickable' map gives access to information on the history, culture, and facilities of all the communities of the Algarve. There is a weather report and links to local newspapers, as well as more practical information for tourists and residents.

▪ **Madeira Web**
http://www.madeira-web.com/PagesUK/index.html
Guide to the Portuguese island group. There are sections on history, culture, food, and government services, in addition to practical information for visitors to Madeira and Porto Santo. There is also a bibliography giving links to further sources of information.

▪ **Portugal's National Tourism Service**
http://www.portugal-live.net/
Travel guide dedicated to those planning a holiday or business trip to Portugal. The site features a directory of hotels and resorts, together with information on the country's attractions and a number of maps to help you locate them! The site is kept up to date, especially the useful sections on current events and weather.

QATAR

Map page 95

National name Dawlat Qatar/ State of Qatar
Area 11,400 sq km/4,401 sq mi
Capital Doha (and chief port)
Major towns/cities Dukhān, ad Dawhah, ar-Rayyan, Umm Salal, Musay'īd, aš-Šahniyah
Physical features mostly flat desert with salt flats in south
Currency Qatari riyal
GNP per capita (PPP) (US$) N/A
Resources petroleum, natural gas, water resources
Population 599,000 (2000 est)
Population density (per sq km) 52 (1999 est)
Language Arabic (official), English
Religion Sunni Muslim 95%
Time difference GMT +3

www. ▪ CIA ▪ LC ▪ AN ▪ LP ▪ WTG

ROMANIA

Map page 66

National name România/Romania
Area 237,500 sq km/91,698 sq mi
Capital Bucharest
Major towns/cities Brasov, Timisoara, Cluj-Napoca, Iaşi, Constanta, Galati, Craiova
Major ports Galati, Constanta, Brǎila
Physical features mountains surrounding a plateau, with river plains in south and east. Carpathian Mountains, Transylvanian Alps; River Danube; Black Sea coast; mineral springs
Currency leu
GNP per capita (PPP) (US$) 5,647 (1999)
Resources brown coal, hard coal, iron ore, salt, bauxite, copper, lead, zinc, methane gas, petroleum (reserves expected to be exhausted by mid- to late 1990s)
Population 22,327,000 (2000 est)
Population density (per sq km) 94 (1999 est)
Language Romanian (official), Hungarian, German
Religion Romanian Orthodox 87%; Roman Catholic and Uniate 5%, Reformed/Lutheran 3%, Unitarian 1%
Time difference GMT +2

www. ▪ CIA ▪ LC ▪ LP ▪ RG ▪ WTG

▪ Virtual Romania
http://internettrash.com/users/adrian/vromania.html
Canadian-based page with a large interactive map, links to news sources, and essays on aspects of Romanian history and culture.

▪ Romania & Constitutional Monarchy
http://www.geocities.com/CapitolHill/Lobby/8957/
Historical information, facts, and stories about Romania. The history of the Romanian Monarchy and, in particular, His Majesty, King Michael I, are described here. The Web site features interviews with the king and many photographs of members of the Romanian royal family.

▪ Bucharest Online – Your Complete Guide to the Capital of Romania
http://bucharest.com/bol/
Well-presented guide to the Romanian capital. Descriptions of the city and its history are accompanied by photographs. There is also transport and commercial information. This site also includes a search engine.

▪ Cluj-Napoca
http://travel.lycos.com/destinations/location.asp?pid=334499
Good guide to the Transylvanian capital. There is a description and history of the city in addition to information on museums, accommodation, and entertainment. There are a large number of useful links to other sources of information.

RUSSIA

Map page 74

National name Rossiiskaya Federatsiya/Russian Federation
Area 17,075,400 sq km/6,592,811 sq mi
Capital Moscow
Major towns/cities St. Petersburg, Nizhniy Novgorod, Samara, Yekaterinburg, Novosibirsk, Chelyabinsk, Kazan, Omsk, Perm', Ufa
Physical features fertile Black Earth district; extensive forests; the Ural Mountains with large mineral resources; Lake Baikal, world's deepest lake
Currency rouble
GNP per capita (PPP) (US$) 6,339 (1999)
Resources petroleum, natural gas, coal, peat, copper (world's fourth-largest producer), iron ore, lead, aluminium, phosphate rock, nickel, manganese, gold, diamonds, platinum, zinc, tin
Population 146,934,000 (2000 est)
Population density (per sq km) 9 (1999 est)
Language Russian (official) and many East Slavic, Altaic, Uralic, Caucasian languages
Religion traditionally Russian Orthodox; significant Muslim and Buddhist communities
Time difference GMT +2–12

www. ▪ CIA ▪ LC ▪ LP ▪ RG ▪ WTG

▪ Saint Petersburg, Russia
http://www.geocities.com/TheTropics/Shores/6751/
Introduction to the city of St Petersburg, including a walking tour and a map, a guide to the city's museums, a history, and a regularly updated 'What's new' section.

▪ Russia Alive!
http://www.alincom.com/russ/index.htm
Guide to the new Russia, with links to related sites and a virtual tour of Moscow.

▪ SovInform Bureau
http://www.siber.com/sib/index.html
Dedicated to all things Russian, including information about Russian art, culture, humour, politics, communication and technology, travel, and visas. Advice and tools are also offered which enable you to 'Russify' your PC.

▪ Russia Today
http://www.russiatoday.com/
Extensive general information magazine on Russia. As well as daily press reviews and business news, the site provides sections on the government, the constitution, and coverage of hot current issues. Russia Today has a reputation for being on top of the news and getting its readers involved: it even offered them a chance to select the next Russian president in a mock election. A must for everyone wanting to make sense of the bewildering developments in the region.

▪ Exploring Moscow
http://www.interknowledge.com/russia/moscow01.htm
Walk about Moscow with stops at the Kremlin, Red Square, Lenin's Mausoleum, St Basil's cathedral, old Moscow, and other highlights of the Russian capital. The site also offers separate sections on fine art and theatrical life in the city, a calendar of events, and advice on accommodation.

▪ Kalingrad in Your Pocket Home Page
http://www.inyourpocket.com/Kaliningrad/index.shtml
Guide to everything you ever wanted to know about this Russian enclave. This is an electronic form of a published guide book and includes sections on such topics as language, media, what to see, getting there, and where to stay.

▪ Novgorod the Great
http://www.adm.nov.ru/web.nsf/pages/englishhome
Good guide to the culture and history of the Russian World Heritage city. There are descriptions and photos of the many historical buildings in Novgorod. This site includes sections on Novgorodian artistic and musical traditions.

RWANDA

Map page 106

National name Republika y'u Rwanda/Republic of Rwanda
Area 26,338 sq km/10,169 sq mi
Capital Kigali
Major towns/cities Butare, Ruhengeri, Gisenyi, Kibungo, Cyangugu
Physical features high savannah and hills, with volcanic mountains in northwest; part of lake Kivu; highest peak Mount Karisimbi 4,507 m/14,792 ft; Kagera River (whose headwaters are the source of the Nile)
Currency Rwandan franc
GNP per capita (PPP) (US$) 690 (1998)
Resources cassiterite (a tin-bearing ore), wolframite (a tungsten-bearing ore), natural gas, gold, columbo-tantalite, beryl
Population 7,733,000 (2000 est)
Population density (per sq km) 275 (1999 est)
Language Kinyarwanda, French (both official), Kiswahili
Religion about 50% animist; about 40% Christian, mainly Roman Catholic; 9% Muslim
Time difference GMT +2

www. ▪ CIA ▪ LP ▪ NA ▪ WTG

ST. KITTS AND NEVIS

Map page 134

National name Federation of St. Christopher and St. Nevis
Area 262 sq km/101 sq mi (St. Kitts 168 sq km/65 sq mi, Nevis 93 sq km/36 sq mi)
Capital Basseterre (on St. Kitts) (and chief port)
Major towns/cities Charlestown (Nevis), Newcastle, Sandy Point Town, Dieppe Bay Town
Physical features both islands are volcanic; fertile plains on coast; black beaches
Currency East Caribbean dollar
GNP per capita (PPP) (US$) 9,801 (1999)
Population 38,000 (2000 est)
Population density (per sq km) 160 (1999 est)
Language English (official)
Religion Anglican 36%, Methodist 32%, other Protestant 8%, Roman Catholic 10%
Time difference GMT –4

www. ▪ CIA ▪ LP ▪ WTG

▪ St Kitts and Nevis Government
http://www.stkittsnevis.net/index.html
The 'How we are governed' section provides a detailed explanation of the structure of this twin-island nation. There is also regularly updated information about the hurricanes that may affect the islands, as well as a biography of the 'Hero of the nation', Robert L Bradshaw, who was instrumental in securing their independence.

ST. LUCIA

Map page 134

Area 617 sq km/238 sq mi
Capital Castries
Major towns/cities Soufrière, Vieux Fort, Choiseul, Gros Islet
Major ports Vieux-Fort
Physical features mountainous island with fertile valleys; mainly tropical forest; volcanic peaks; Gros and Petit Pitons
Currency East Caribbean dollar
GNP per capita (PPP) (US$) 5,022 (1999)
Resources geothermal energy
Population 154,000 (2000 est)
Population density (per sq km) 252 (1999 est)
Language English (official), French patois
Religion Roman Catholic 85%; Anglican, Protestant
Time difference GMT –4

www. ▪ CIA ▪ LP ▪ RG ▪ WTG

▪ St Lucia Travel Guide
http://www.stluciaguide.com/
Guide offering information on and reservations for accommodation and car rental in the Caribbean island of St Lucia. The site also includes advice on the country's many attractions, which include the national rainforest, sulphur springs, and scuba-diving.

ST. VINCENT AND THE GRENADINES
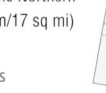
Map page 134

Area 388 sq km/150 sq mi (including islets of the Northern Grenadines 43 sq km/17 sq mi)
Capital Kingstown
Major towns/cities Georgetown, Châteaubelair, Dovers
Physical features volcanic mountains, thickly forested; La Soufrière volcano
Currency East Caribbean dollar
GNP per capita (PPP) (US$) 4,667 (1999)
Population 114,000 (2000 est)

Population density (per sq km) 355 (1999 est)

Language English (official), French patois

Religion Anglican, Methodist, Roman Catholic

Time difference GMT –4

 www. ■ CIA ■ LP ■ WTG

■ **St Vincent and the Grenadines – Jewels of the Caribbean**
http://www.svgtourism.com/
From the Department of Tourism, this guide offers detailed information on St Vincent and the Grenadines. It includes advice on travel information and accommodation, as well as sections on the islands' attractions, sports, and current events. Be sure to visit the site's photo album, which highlights the beauty of the islands.

SAMOA
Map page 112

National name 'O la Malo Tu To'atasi o Samoa/Independent State of Samoa

Area 2,830 sq km/1,092 sq mi

Capital Apia (on Upolu island) (and chief port)

Major towns/cities Lalomanu, Tuasivi, Falealupo, Falelatai, Taga

Physical features comprises South Pacific islands of Savai'i and Upolu, with two smaller tropical islands and uninhabited islets; mountain ranges on main islands; coral reefs; over half forested

Currency tala, or Samoan dollar

GNP per capita (PPP) (US$) 3,915 (1999)

Population 180,000 (2000 est)

Population density (per sq km) 63 (1999 est)

Language English, Samoan (both official)

Religion Congregationalist; also Roman Catholic, Methodist

Time difference GMT –11

 www. ■ CIA ■ LP ■ WTG

SAN MARINO
Map page 64

National name Serenissima Repubblica di San Marino/Most Serene Republic of San Marino

Area 61 sq km/24 sq mi

Capital San Marino

Major towns/cities Serravalle, Faetano, Fiorentino, Borgo Maggiore, Domagnano

Physical features the slope of Mount Titano

Currency Italian lira

GNP per capita (PPP) (US$) 20,000 (1997 est)

Resources limestone and other building stone

Population 27,000 (2000 est)

Population density (per sq km) 417 (1999 est)

Language Italian (official)

Religion Roman Catholic 95%

Time difference GMT +1

 www. ■ CIA ■ WTG

■ **Welcome to the Republic of San Marino**
http://inthenet.sm/rsm/intro.htm
Good official guide to the world's smallest and oldest nation state. The history of San Marino is interestingly presented. There is a wealth of practical information on attractions, accommodation, and restaurants, as well as coverage of all aspects of political, economic, and cultural life. The pride of the 25,000 Sammarinese shines through this well-organized site.

SÃO TOMÉ AND PRÍNCIPE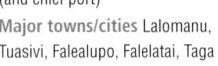
Map page 104

National name República Democrática de São Tomé e Príncipe/Democratic Republic of São Tomé and Príncipe

Area 1,000 sq km/386 sq mi

Capital São Tomé

Major towns/cities Santo António, Sant Ana, Porto Alegre, Neves, Santo Amaro

Physical features comprises two main islands and several smaller ones, all volcanic; thickly forested and fertile

Currency dobra

GNP per capita (PPP) (US$) 1,335 (1999)

Population 147,000 (2000 est)

Population density (per sq km) 161 (1999 est)

Language Portuguese (official), Fang (a Bantu language), Lungwa São Tomé (a Portuguese Creole)

Religion Roman Catholic 80%, animist

Time difference GMT +/–0

 www. ■ CIA ■ LP ■ NA ■ WTG

SAUDI ARABIA
Map page 90

National name Al-Mamlaka al-'Arabiyya as-Sa'udiyya/Kingdom of Saudi Arabia

Area 2,200,518 sq km/ 849,620 sq mi

Capital Riyadh

Major towns/cities Jedda, Mecca, Medina, Ad Dammām, Tabūk, Buraydah

Major ports Jedda, Ad Dammām, Jīzān, Yanbu

Physical features features desert, sloping to The Gulf from a height of 2,750 m/9,000 ft in the west

Currency riyal

GNP per capita (PPP) (US$) 10,472 (1999 est)

Resources petroleum, natural gas, iron ore, limestone, gypsum, marble, clay, salt, gold, uranium, copper, fish

Population 21,607,000 (2000 est)

Population density (per sq km) 9 (1999 est)

Language Arabic (official), English

Religion Sunni Muslim 85%; there is a Shiite minority

Time difference GMT +3

 www. ■ CIA ■ LC ■ AN ■ LP ■ WTG

■ **All Saudi**
http://www.all-saudi.com/en
A dedicated search engine for all things related to Saudi Arabia, with maps, recipes, a travel guide, and useful Arabic phrases.

SENEGAL
Map page 104

National name République du Sénégal/Republic of Senegal

Area 196,200 sq km/75,752 sq mi

Capital Dakar (and chief port)

Major towns/cities Thiès, Kaolack, Saint-Louis, Ziguinchor, Diourbel, Mbour

Physical features plains rising to hills in southeast; swamp and tropical forest in southwest; River Senegal; The Gambia forms an enclave within Senegal

Currency franc CFA

GNP per capita (PPP) (US$) 1,341 (1999)

Resources calcium phosphates, aluminium phosphates, salt, natural gas; offshore deposits of petroleum to be developed

Population 9,481,000 (2000 est)

Population density (per sq km) 47 (1999 est)

Language French (official), Wolof, other ethnic languages

Religion mainly Sunni Muslim; Christian 4%, animist 1%

Time difference GMT +/–0

 www. ■ CIA ■ LP ■ NA ■ WTG

SEYCHELLES
Map page 108

National name Republic of Seychelles

Area 453 sq km/174 sq mi

Capital Victoria (on Mahé island) (and chief port)

Major towns/cities Cascade, Anse Boileau, Takamaka

Physical features comprises two distinct island groups: one, the Granitic group, concentrated, the other, the Outer or Coralline group, widely scattered; totals over 100 islands and islets

Currency Seychelles rupee

GNP per capita (PPP) (US$) 10,381 (1999)

Resources guano; natural gas and metal deposits were being explored mid-1990s

Population 77,000 (2000 est)

Population density (per sq km) 174 (1999 est)

Language Creole (an Asian, African, European mixture) (95%), English, French (all official)

Religion Roman Catholic 90%

Time difference GMT +4

 www. ■ CIA ■ LC ■ LP ■ NA ■ WTG

■ **Seychelles Super Site**
http://www.sey.net/
Immodestly-named guide to the Seychelles that lives up to its title. The site contains a wealth of information about the islands, including sections on 'Accommodation', 'What to see & do', and 'Activities'. The 'Travellers' information' section is particularly useful for locating advice about visas, money, and health.

SIERRA LEONE
Map page 104

National name Republic of Sierra Leone

Area 71,740 sq km/27,698 sq mi

Capital Freetown

Major towns/cities Koidu, Bo, Kenema, Makeni

Major ports Bonthe

Physical features mountains in east; hills and forest; coastal mangrove swamps

Currency leone

GNP per capita (PPP) (US$) 414 (1999)

Resources gold, diamonds, bauxite, rutile (titanium dioxide)

Population 4,854,000 (2000 est)

Population density (per sq km) 66 (1999 est)

Language English (official), Krio (a Creole language), Mende, Limba, Temne

Religion animist 45%, Muslim 44%, Protestant 8%, Roman Catholic 3%

Time difference GMT +/–0

 www. ■ CIA ■ LP ■ NA ■ WTG

SINGAPORE
Map page 86

National name Repablik Singapura/Republic of Singapore

Area 622 sq km/240 sq mi

Capital Singapore

Physical features comprises Singapore Island, low and flat, and 57 small islands; Singapore Island is joined to the mainland by causeway across Strait of Johore

Currency Singapore dollar

GNP per capita (PPP) (US$) 27,024 (1999)

Resources granite

Population 3,567,000 (2000 est)

Population density (per sq km) 5,662 (1999 est)

Language Malay, Mandarin Chinese, Tamil, English (all official), other Indian languages, Chinese dialects

Religion Buddhist, Taoist, Muslim, Hindu, Christian

Time difference GMT +8

 ■ CIA ■ LC ■ LP ■ RG ■ WTG

■ Singapore
http://www.stb.com.sg/

Guide to Singapore. History, geography, and travel information, as well as features on festivals, make up the majority of the tourist- and business-oriented information on this site. However, there is also a useful 'Tourist news' features with regularly updated information on events in and around Singapore.

■ Singapore – The People
http://www.sg/flavour/people.html

Comprehensive page devoted to the people of Singapore, their origins, religion, and customs. Scroll through the information, or click on headings, to find out about early immigration; birth, marriage and death; language and literacy; religions; and numerous local festivals.

■ Singapore Government
http://www.gov.sg/

Official Web site of the Singapore government that includes an overview of the government departments, and a section dedicated to recent government campaigns. There is also the opportunity to send the government your comments and suggestions.

SLOVAK REPUBLIC
Map page 50

National name Slovenská Republika/ Slovak Republic

Area 49,035 sq km/18,932 sq mi

Capital Bratislava

Major towns/cities Košice, Nitra, Prešov, Banská Bystrica, Zilina, Trnava, Martin

Physical features Western range of Carpathian Mountains, including Tatra and Beskids in north; Danube plain in south; numerous lakes and mineral springs

Currency Slovak koruna (based on Czechoslovak koruna)

GNP per capita (PPP) (US$) 9,811 (1999)

Resources brown coal, lignite, copper, zinc, lead, iron ore, magnesite

Population 5,387,000 (2000 est)

Population density (per sq km) 110 (1999 est)

Language Slovak (official), Hungarian, Czech, other ethnic languages

Religion Roman Catholic (over 50%), Lutheran, Reformist, Orthodox, atheist 10%

Time difference GMT +1

 ■ CIA ■ LP ■ RG ■ WTG

■ Slovakia Document Store
http://slovakia.eunet.sk/

Collection of resources in Slovak and English, including a traveller's guide and information about the country's geography, natural resources, history, culture, and religion.

SLOVENIA
Map page 62

National name Republika Slovenija/ Republic of Slovenia

Area 20,251 sq km/7,818 sq mi

Capital Ljubljana

Major towns/cities Maribor, Kranj, Celje, Velenje, Koper, Novo Mesto

Major ports Koper

Physical features mountainous; Sava and Drava rivers

Currency tolar

GNP per capita (PPP) (US$) 15,062 (1999)

Resources coal, lead, zinc; small reserves/deposits of natural gas, petroleum, salt, uranium

Population 1,986,000 (2000 est)

Population density (per sq km) 98 (1999 est)

Language Slovene (related to Serbo-Croat; official), Hungarian, Italian

Religion Roman Catholic 70%; Eastern Orthodox, Lutheran, Muslim

Time difference GMT +1

 ■ CIA ■ LP ■ RG ■ WTG

■ Slovenia – Country Information
http://www.matkurja.com/eng/country-info/

Index of pages covering Slovenia. There is information about history, culture, food and drink, and places to visit, as well as Slovenia's economy and government.

■ Ljubljana
http://www.ijs.si/slo/ljubljana/

Well-presented guide to the Slovenian capital. A 'clickable' map highlights points of interest in the city. There is history and a large number of photographs in addition to practical information for visitors.

SOLOMON ISLANDS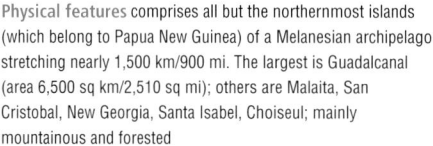
Map page 112

Area 27,600 sq km/ 10,656 sq mi

Capital Honiara (on Guadalcanal island) (and chief port)

Major towns/cities Gizo, Auki, Kirakira, Buala

Major ports Yandina

Physical features comprises all but the northernmost islands (which belong to Papua New Guinea) of a Melanesian archipelago stretching nearly 1,500 km/900 mi. The largest is Guadalcanal (area 6,500 sq km/2,510 sq mi); others are Malaita, San Cristobal, New Georgia, Santa Isabel, Choiseul; mainly mountainous and forested

Currency Solomon Island dollar

GNP per capita (PPP) (US$) 1,793 (1999)

Resources bauxite, phosphates, gold, silver, copper, lead, zinc, cobalt, asbestos, nickel

Population 444,000 (2000 est)

Population density (per sq km) 16 (1999 est)

Language English (official), pidgin English, more than 80 Melanesian dialects (85%), Papuan and Polynesian languages

Religion more than 80% Christian; Anglican 34%, Roman Catholic 19%, South Sea Evangelical, other Protestant, animist 5%

Time difference GMT +11

 ■ CIA ■ LP ■ WTG

■ Solomon Islands – Pearl of the Pacific
http://www.solomons.com/

Good source of information on the far-flung islands, atolls, and reefs comprising the state of the Solomon Islands. The contents include a good history, map, and information on the culture, investment opportunities, and government structures. There is also practical information for tourists.

SOMALIA
Map page 106

National name Jamhuuriyadda Soomaaliya/Republic of Somalia

Area 637,700 sq km/ 246,215 sq mi

Capital Mogadishu (and chief port)

Major towns/cities Hargeysa, Berbera, Kismaayo, Marka

Major ports Berbera, Marka, Kismaayo

Physical features mainly flat, with hills in north

Currency Somali shilling

GNP per capita (PPP) (US$) 600 (1999 est)

Resources chromium, coal, salt, tin, zinc, copper, gypsum, manganese, iron ore, uranium, gold, silver; deposits of petroleum and natural gas have been discovered but remain unexploited

Population 10,097,000 (2000 est)

Population density (per sq km) 15 (1999 est)

Language Somali, Arabic (both official), Italian, English

Religion Sunni Muslim; small Christian community, mainly Roman Catholic

Time difference GMT +3

 ■ CIA ■ LC ■ AN ■ LP ■ NA ■ WTG

SOUTH AFRICA
Map page 108

National name Republiek van Suid-Afrika/Republic of South Africa

Area 1,222,081 sq km/ 471,845 sq mi

Capital Cape Town (legislative), Pretoria (administrative), Bloemfontein (judicial)

Major towns/cities Johannesburg, Durban, Port Elizabeth, Vereeniging, Pietermaritzburg, Kimberley, Soweto, Tembisa

Major ports Cape Town, Durban, Port Elizabeth, East London

Physical features southern end of large plateau, fringed by mountains and lowland coastal margin; Drakensberg Mountains, Table Mountain; Limpopo and Orange rivers

Territories Marion Island and Prince Edward Island in the Antarctic

Currency rand

GNP per capita (PPP) (US$) 8,318 (1999)

Resources gold (world's largest producer), coal, platinum, iron ore, diamonds, chromium, manganese, limestone, asbestos, fluorspar, uranium, copper, lead, zinc, petroleum, natural gas

Population 40,377,000 (2000 est)

Population density (per sq km) 33 (1999 est)

Language English, Afrikaans, Xhosa, Zulu, Sesotho (all official), other African languages

Religion Dutch Reformed Church and other Christian denominations 77%, Hindu 2%, Muslim 1%

Time difference GMT +2

 ■ CIA ■ LC ■ LP ■ RG ■ NA ■ WTG

■ South Africa.com – News & Information
http://www.southafrica.com/

South African site with general information about, and maps of, the country and links to over ten different newspapers, related organizations, and the South African yellow pages. You can also get hourly weather reports from various weather stations across the country. There are also links back to large sections on 'Travel & tourism', 'Business & finance', and 'Society & culture'.

■ Cape Town
http://www.toptentravel.com/capetown.html

City guide to Cape Town, South Africa. Aimed at the tourist, this site details what to do before you go, and what to do when you get there. History, geography, and travel information, as well as features on festivals, make up the majority of the remaining information on this site, but there are also details of local transport and a list of useful telephone numbers. It also includes images of Cape Town, and maps of the city area.

SOUTH KOREA
Map page 82

National name Daehan Minguk/ Republic of Korea

Area 98,799 sq km/38,146 sq mi

Capital Seoul

Major towns/cities Pusan, Taegu, Inch'ŏn, Kwangju, Taejŏn, Songnam

Major ports Pusan, Inch'ŏn

Physical features southern end of a mountainous peninsula separating the Sea of Japan from the Yellow Sea

Currency won

GNP per capita (PPP) (US$) 14,637 (1999)

Resources coal, iron ore, tungsten, gold, molybdenum, graphite, fluorite, natural gas, hydroelectric power, fish

Population 46,844,000 (2000 est)

Population density (per sq km) 473 (1999 est)

Language Korean (official)

Religion Buddhist 48%, Confucian 3%, Christian 47%, mainly

Protestant; Chund Kyo (peculiar to Korea, combining elements of Shaman, Buddhist, and Christian doctrines)

Time difference GMT +9

 ■ CIA ■ LC ■ LP ■ WTG

■ **Welcome to Pusan**

http://pusanweb.com/

Comprehensive guide to Korea's main port. There is useful information on Pusan's history, culture, cuisine, transport, and facilities for visitors.

SPAIN
Map page 60

National name España/Spain

Area 504,750 sq km/194,883 sq mi (including the Balearic and Canary islands)

Capital Madrid

Major towns/cities Barcelona, Valencia, Zaragoza, Sevilla, Málaga, Bilbao, Las Palmas (on Gran Canarias island), Murcia, Palma (on Mallorca)

Major ports Barcelona, Valencia, Cartagena, Málaga, Cádiz, Vigo, Santander, Bilbao

Physical features central plateau with mountain ranges, lowlands in south; rivers Ebro, Douro, Tagus, Guadiana, Guadalquivir; Iberian Plateau (Meseta); Pyrenees, Cantabrian Mountains, Andalusian Mountains, Sierra Nevada

Territories Balearic and Canary Islands; in North Africa: Ceuta, Melilla, Alhucemas, Chafarinas Islands, Peñón de Vélez

Currency peseta

GNP per capita (PPP) (US$) 16,730 (1999)

Resources coal, lignite, anthracite, copper, iron, zinc, uranium, potassium salts

Population 39,630,000 (2000 est)

Population density (per sq km) 79 (1999 est)

Language Spanish (Castilian; official), Basque, Catalan, Galician

Religion Roman Catholic 98%

Time difference GMT +1

 ■ CIA ■ LC ■ LP ■ RG ■ WTG

■ **Barcelona, Spain**

http://travel.lycos.com/Destinations/Europe/Spain/Barcelona/

Guide to the Catalan capital. Information on the history, culture, traditions, churches, museums, architectural sites, cafes, transport system, and restaurants of Barcelona is well-presented. There is also a weather report, maps, and links to local media.

■ **Bilbao, Spain**

http://www.bizkaia.net/bizkaia/English/General_information/Routes_and_places/I1VILLA.HTM

Good source of information on the northern Spanish city. This site includes a history of Bilbao, an introduction to Basque culture, details of local attractions, and information on transport and other government services. There is also practical information for visitors, a map, a weather report, and links to local newspapers.

■ **Seville, Spain**

http://www.sol.com/

Substantial source of information on the Andalusian capital. The history, culture, and cuisine of Seville are well-presented. There is a wealth of practical information about accommodation, restaurants, the Alcazar and other local attractions, the famous fiesta, and cultural events.

■ **Costa del Sol, Spain**

http://travel.lycos.com/Destinations/Europe/Spain/Costa_del_Sol/

Comprehensive source of information on the 300 km long Spanish coastal region. There is information on all the main resorts as well as the history and culture of the region. The needs of tourists, residents, and investors are all catered for. This site also includes a weather report and links to local media.

■ **Balearic Islands, Spain**

http://travel.lycos.com/Destinations/Europe/Spain/Balearic_Islands/

Source of information on all of the Balearic Islands. The history, culture, and political status of this Mediterranean island chain are well-presented and there is a wealth of practical information for visitors and residents. This site also includes a weather report and links to local media and other sources of local information.

■ **Turespaña**

http://www.tourspain.es/

Official site of the Spanish National Tourist Office, available in English, Spanish, French, and German. The site features articles on the country's cities and islands, arts and culture, and landscapes and beaches. There is also an accommodation directory containing listings of hotels, apartments, and campsites.

SRI LANKA
Map page 88

National name Sri Lanka Prajatantrika Samajavadi Janarajaya/Democratic Socialist Republic of Sri Lanka

Area 65,610 sq km/25,332 sq mi

Capital Sri Jayewardenapura Kotte

Major towns/cities Colombo, Kandy, Dehiwala-Mount Lavinia, Moratuwa, Jaffna, Galle

Major ports Colombo, Jaffna, Galle, Negombo, Trincomalee

Physical features flat in north and around coast; hills and mountains in south and central interior

Currency Sri Lankan rupee

GNP per capita (PPP) (US$) 3,056 (1999)

Resources gemstones, graphite, iron ore, monazite, rutile, uranium, iemenite sands, limestone, salt, clay

Population 18,827,000 (2000 est)

Population density (per sq km) 284 (1999 est)

Language Sinhala, Tamil (both official), English

Religion Buddhist 69%, Hindu 15%, Muslim 8%, Christian 8%

Time difference GMT +5.5

 ■ CIA ■ LC ■ LP ■ WTG

■ **Sri Lanka Info Page**

http://www.lacnet.org/srilanka/

Host of links grouped under headings such as news, issues, culture, nature, food and cooking, and travel and tourism.

SUDAN
Map page 100

National name Al-Jumhuryyat es-Sudan/Republic of Sudan

Area 2,505,800 sq km/967,489 sq mi

Capital Khartoum

Major towns/cities Omdurman, Port Sudan, Juba, Wad Medani, El Obeid, Kassala, Gedaref, Nyala

Major ports Port Sudan

Physical features fertile Nile valley separates Libyan Desert in west from high rocky Nubian Desert in east

Currency Sudanese dinar

GNP per capita (PPP) (US$) 1,298 (1999)

Resources petroleum, marble, mica, chromite, gypsum, gold, graphite, sulphur, iron, manganese, zinc, fluorspar, talc, limestone, dolomite, pumice

Population 29,490,000 (2000 est)

Population density (per sq km) 12 (1999 est)

Language Arabic (51%) (official), 100 local languages

Religion Sunni Muslim 70%; also animist 25%, and Christian 5%

Time difference GMT +2

 ■ CIA ■ LC ■ AN ■ LP ■ NA ■ WTG

SURINAME
Map page 140

National name Republiek Suriname/Republic of Suriname

Area 163,820 sq km/63,250 sq mi

Capital Paramaribo

Major towns/cities Nieuw Nickerie, Moengo, Brokopondo, Nieuw Amsterdam, Albina, Groningen

Physical features hilly and forested, with flat and narrow coastal plain; Suriname River

Currency Suriname guilder

GNP per capita (PPP) (US$) 3,820 (1998 est)

Resources petroleum, bauxite (one of the world's leading producers), iron ore, copper, manganese, nickel, platinum, gold, kaolin

Population 417,000 (2000 est)

Population density (per sq km) 3 (1999 est)

Language Dutch (official), Spanish, Sranan (Creole), English, Hindi, Javanese, Chinese, various tribal languages

Religion Christian 47%, Hindu 28%, Muslim 20%

Time difference GMT –3.5

 ■ CIA ■ LP ■ WTG

■ **Paramaribo, Suriname**

http://travel.lycos.com/Destinations/South_America/Suriname/Paramaribo/

Profile of Surinam's historic capital, Paramaribo. There is a general introduction to the city's main features, and four sections – 'Visitors' guide', 'Culture and history', 'News and weather', and 'Entertainment' – each with links to further information in English and Dutch about both the city and the country.

SWAZILAND
Map page 108

National name Umbuso wakaNgwane/Kingdom of Swaziland

Area 17,400 sq km/6,718 sq mi

Capital Mbabane, Lobamba

Major towns/cities Manzini, Big Bend, Mhlume, Nhlangano

Physical features central valley; mountains in west (Highveld); plateau in east (Lowveld and Lubombo plateau)

Currency lilangeni

GNP per capita (PPP) (US$) 4,200 (1999)

Resources coal, asbestos, diamonds, gold, tin, kaolin, iron ore, talc, pyrophyllite, silica

Population 1,008,000 (2000 est)

Population density (per sq km) 56 (1999 est)

Language Swazi, English (both official)

Religion about 60% Christian, animist

Time difference GMT +2

 ■ CIA ■ LP ■ RG ■ NA ■ WTG

■ **Swaziland Internet**

http://www.directory.sz/internet/

Searchable guide to aspects of life in Swaziland today. Type in a word in the search box, or click on links to find out about the country's information technology, food and agriculture, religious organizations, tourism and leisure, and government and diplomatic institutions.

SWEDEN
Map page 48

National name Konungariket Sverige/Kingdom of Sweden

Area 450,000 sq km/173,745 sq mi

Capital Stockholm

Major towns/cities Göteborg, Malmö, Uppsala, Norrköping, Västerås, Linköping, Örebro, Helsingborg

Major ports Helsingborg, Malmö, Göteborg, Stockholm

Physical features mountains in west; plains in south; thickly forested; more than 20,000 islands off the Stockholm coast; lakes, including Vänern, Vättern, Mälaren, and Hjälmaren

Currency Swedish krona

GNP per capita (PPP) (US$) 20,824 (1999)

Resources iron ore, uranium, copper, lead, zinc, silver, hydroelectric power, forests

Population 8,910,000 (2000 est)

Population density (per sq km) 20 (1999 est)

Language Swedish (official), Finnish, Saami (Lapp)

Religion Evangelical Lutheran, Church of Sweden (established national church) 90%; Muslim, Jewish

Time difference GMT +1

 ▪ CIA ▪ LP ▪ RG ▪ WTG

▪ Stockholm
http://travel.excite.com/show/?loc=2693

Guide to the city of Stockholm. This site includes local news and weather, as well as details of places to visit, hotels, transportation, and maps of the area.

▪ Sweden – Provincial Information
http://www.sverigeturism.se/smorgasbord/

Guide to all 27 regions of Sweden from an active map on the home page. Each region contains sections of useful tourist information, such as 'History', 'Culture', 'Events and festivities', 'Family', and 'Major cities'. There is also a separate section called 'Swedish image gallery'.

▪ Visby – World Heritage City
http://www.ovpm.org/ville.asp?v=88

Information about the capital of Gotland and World Heritage site. There is a history of the Hanseatic League city and a description of its sights. There is also a link to information about UNESCO's criteria for World Heritage status.

▪ Göteborg Tourist Information
http://centralen.gp.se/tourist/

Good guide to the Swedish port city. This site includes a description, and detailed guides to attractions, history, restaurants, and accommodation. There is also a useful search engine.

SWITZERLAND
Map page 62

National name Schweizerische Eidgenossenschaft (German)/ Confédération Suisse (French)/ Confederazione Svizzera (Italian)/ Confederaziun Svizra (Romansch)/Swiss Confederation

Area 41,300 sq km/15,945 sq mi

Capital Bern

Major towns/cities Zürich, Geneva, Basel, Lausanne, Luzern, St. Gallen, Winterthur

Major ports river port Basel (on the Rhine)

Physical features most mountainous country in Europe (Alps and Jura mountains); highest peak Dufourspitze 4,634 m/15,203 ft in Apennines

Currency Swiss franc

GNP per capita (PPP) (US$) 27,486 (1999)

Resources salt, hydroelectric power, forest

Population 7,386,000 (2000 est)

Population density (per sq km) 178 (1999 est)

Language German (65%), French (18%), Italian (10%), Romansch (1%) (all official)

Religion Roman Catholic 46%, Protestant 40%

Time difference GMT +1

 ▪ CIA ▪ LP ▪ RG ▪ WTG

▪ Geneva
http://www.geneva-guide.ch/

An attractive 'alternative guide' to Geneva, affording an unusual glimpse of this Swiss city by means of four virtual tours of its streets. The site contains sections on local history as well as maps and guides to accommodation, local customs, language, and currency. There are also links to information on the country's other major cities.

▪ Basel Online
http://www.bsonline.ch/english/index.cfm

Large source of information on the Swiss city. There are sections on the history, culture, traditions, museums, nightlife, transport system, accommodation, and cuisine of the city. There are also a number of photos and links to regularly updated information on local events.

▪ Welcome to Berne
http://www.berntourismus.ch/

Large source of well-arranged official information on the Swiss federal capital. There are sections on the city's history, attractions, accommodation, as well as some lesser known facts.

This site also offers maps, a guide to the local cuisine, and a listing of restaurants.

SYRIA
Map page 90

National name al-Jumhuriyya al-Arabiyya as-Suriyya/Syrian Arab Republic

Area 185,200 sq km/71,505 sq mi

Capital Damascus

Major towns/cities Aleppo, Homs, Al Lādhiqīyah, Hamāh, Ar Raqqah, Dayr az Zawr

Major ports Al Lādhiqīyah

Physical features mountains alternate with fertile plains and desert areas; Euphrates River

Currency Syrian pound

GNP per capita (PPP) (US$) 2,761 (1999)

Resources petroleum, natural gas, iron ore, phosphates, salt, gypsum, sodium chloride, bitumen

Population 16,125,000 (2000 est)

Population density (per sq km) 85 (1999 est)

Language Arabic (89%) (official), Kurdish (6%), Armenian (3%), French, English, Aramaic, Circassian

Religion Sunni Muslim 74%; other Islamic sects 16%, Christian 10%

Time difference GMT +2

 ▪ CIA ▪ LC ▪ AN ▪ LP ▪ WTG

▪ Cafe Syria
http://www.cafe-syria.com/

Portal dedicated to promoting all things to do with Syria. Included here is descriptions of all major cities, facts and information for the tourist, and an overview of the history and government of the country.

TAIWAN
Map page 104

National name Chung-hua Min-kuo/Republic of China

Area 36,179 sq km/13,968 sq mi

Capital T'aipei

Major towns/cities Kaohsiung, T'aichung, T'ainan, Panch'iao, Chungho, Sanch'ung

Major ports Kaohsiung, Chilung

Physical features island (formerly Formosa) off People's Republic of China; mountainous, with lowlands in west; Penghu (Pescadores), Jinmen (Quemoy), Mazu (Matsu) islands

Currency New Taiwan dollar

GNP per capita (PPP) (US$) 18,950 (1998 est)

Resources coal, copper, marble, dolomite; small reserves of petroleum and natural gas

Population 22,113,000 (1999 est)

Population density (per sq km) 685 (1999 est)

Language Chinese (dialects include Mandarin (official), Min, and Hakka)

Religion officially atheist; Buddhist 23%, Taoist 18%, I-Kuan Tao 4%, Christian 3%, Confucian and other 3%

Time difference GMT +8

 ▪ CIA ▪ LP ▪ WTG

▪ Visitor's Guide to Taiwan
http://peacock.tnjc.edu.tw/ADD/TOUR/main.html

Detailed guide to Taiwan. The site includes sections on the major attractions of Taiwan, including Lion's Head Mountain, black sand beaches, and 'Aborigine country'. There are also a selection of articles on Taiwan's culture, sports, and wildlife.

TAJIKISTAN
Map page 100

National name Jumhurii Tojikston/Republic of Tajikistan

Area 143,100 sq km/55,250 sq mi

Capital Dushanbe

Major towns/cities Khŭjand, Qūrghonteppa, Külob, Ŭroteppa, Kofarnihon

Physical features mountainous, more than half of its territory lying above 3,000 m/10,000 ft; huge mountain glaciers, which are the source of many rapid rivers

Currency Tajik rouble

GNP per capita (PPP) (US$) 981 (1999)

Resources coal, aluminium, lead, zinc, iron, tin, uranium, radium, arsenic, bismuth, gold, mica, asbestos, lapis lazuli; small reserves of petroleum and natural gas

Population 6,188,000 (2000 est)

Population density (per sq km) 43 (1999 est)

Language Tajik (related to Farsi; official), Russian

Religion Sunni Muslim; small Russian Orthodox and Jewish communities

Time difference GMT +5

 ▪ CIA ▪ LC ▪ LP ▪ WTG

TANZANIA
Map page 106

National name Jamhuri ya Muungano wa Tanzania/United Republic of Tanzania

Area 945,000 sq km/364,864 sq mi

Capital Dodoma (official), Dar es Salaam (administrative)

Major towns/cities Zanzibar, Mwanza, Mbeya, Tanga, Morogoro

Major ports Dar es Salaam

Physical features central plateau; lakes in north and west; coastal plains; lakes Victoria, Tanganyika, and Nyasa; half the country is forested; comprises islands of Zanzibar and Pemba; Mount Kilimanjaro, 5,895 m/19,340 ft, the highest peak in Africa; Olduvai Gorge; Ngorongoro Crater, 14.5 km/9 mi across, 762 m/2,500 ft deep

Currency Tanzanian shilling

GNP per capita (PPP) (US$) 478 (1999)

Resources diamonds, other gemstones, gold, salt, phosphates, coal, gypsum, tin, kaolin (exploration for petroleum in progress)

Population 33,517,000 (2000 est)

Population density (per sq km) 35 (1999 est)

Language Kiswahili, English (both official), Arabic (in Zanzibar), many local languages

Religion Muslim, Christian, traditional religions

Time difference GMT +3

 ▪ CIA ▪ LP ▪ NA ▪ WTG

▪ Tanzania
http://www.tanzania-online.gov.uk/tourism/tourism.html

Official Web site of the Tanzania High Commission in London, England. The site features articles on Tanzania's national parks, game reserves, and mountains, and also includes more general information on visa requirements, currency, and the best time of year to visit.

THAILAND
Map page 84

National name Ratcha Anachak Thai/Kingdom of Thailand

Area 513,115 sq km/198,113 sq mi

Capital Bangkok (and chief port)

Major towns/cities Chiang Mai, Hat Yai, Khon Kaen, Songkhla, Nakhon Ratchasima, Nonthaburi, Udon Thani

Major ports Nakhon Sawan

Physical features mountainous, semi-arid plateau in northeast, fertile central region, tropical isthmus in south; rivers Chao Phraya, Mekong, and Salween

Currency baht

GNP per capita (PPP) (US$) 5,599 (1999)

Resources tin ore, lignite, gypsum, antimony, manganese, copper, tungsten, lead, gold, zinc, silver, rubies, sapphires, natural gas, petroleum, fish

Population 61,399,000 (2000 est)

Population density (per sq km) 119 (1999 est)

Language Thai, Chinese (both official), English, Lao, Malay, Khmer

Religion Buddhist 95%; Muslim 5%

Time difference GMT +7

 ▪ CIA ▪ LC ▪ LP ▪ RG ▪ WTG

▪ Bangkok

http://www.bu.ac.th/thailand/bangkok.html

Aspects of life in this thriving Thai city, described by some as the Venice of the East. This site, run by Bangkok University, is equally appropriate for the business traveller and the tourist, with maps, photographs, accommodation and embassy details, in addition to cultural background and culinary information.

▪ Thailand Information

http://www.bu.ac.th/thailand/thailand.html

Cultural background and tourist information combine with beautiful photographs to make this site the best starting point for a virtual tour of the 'Land of Smiles'. From Thai boxing to road distances, this Bangkok University run site has a whole range of facts about the country.

TOGO
Map page 104

National name République Togolaise/Togolese Republic

Area 56,800 sq km/21,930 sq mi

Capital Lomé

Major towns/cities Sokodé, Kpalimé, Kara, Atakpamé, Bassar, Tsévié

Physical features two savannah plains, divided by range of hills northeast–southwest; coastal lagoons and marsh; Mono Tableland, Oti Plateau, Oti River

Currency franc CFA

GNP per capita (PPP) (US$) 1,346 (1999 est)

Resources phosphates, limestone, marble, deposits of iron ore, manganese, chromite, peat; exploration for petroleum and uranium was under way in the early 1990s

Population 4,629,000 (2000 est)

Population density (per sq km) 79 (1999 est)

Language French (official), Ewe, Kabre, Gurma, other local languages

Religion animist about 50%, Catholic and Protestant 35%, Muslim 15%

Time difference GMT +/–0

 ▪ CIA ▪ LP ▪ NA ▪ WTG

TONGA
Map page 112

National name Pule'anga Fakatu'i 'o Tonga/Kingdom of Tonga

Area 750 sq km/290 sq mi

Capital Nuku'alofa (on Tongatapu island)

Major towns/cities Neiafu, Vaini

Physical features three groups of islands in southwest Pacific, mostly coral formations, but actively volcanic in west; of the 170 islands in the Tonga group, 36 are inhabited

Currency pa'anga, or Tongan dollar

GNP per capita (PPP) (US$) 4,281 (1999)

Population 99,000 (2000 est)

Population density (per sq km) 131 (1999 est)

Language Tongan (official), English

Religion mainly Free Wesleyan Church; Roman Catholic, Anglican

Time difference GMT +13

 ▪ CIA ▪ LP ▪ WTG

▪ Welcome to the Royal Kingdom of Tonga

http://www.vacations.tvb.gov.to/

Well-presented official guide to the Polynesian monarchy. There is a map, history, and guide to local culture and investment opportunities. The needs of tourists are met with practical information on attractions and accommodation. This site also includes an audio welcome message from Tonga's Crown Prince.

TRINIDAD AND TOBAGO
Map page 134

National name Republic of Trinidad and Tobago

Area 5,130 sq km/1,980 sq mi (Trinidad 4,828 sq km/1,864 sq mi and Tobago 300 sq km/115 sq mi)

Capital Port of Spain (and chief port)

Major towns/cities San Fernando, Arima, Point Fortin

Major ports Scarborough

Physical features comprises two main islands and some smaller ones in Caribbean Sea; coastal swamps and hills east–west

Currency Trinidad and Tobago dollar

GNP per capita (PPP) (US$) 7,262 (1999)

Resources petroleum, natural gas, asphalt (world's largest deposits of natural asphalt)

Population 1,295,000 (2000 est)

Population density (per sq km) 251 (1999 est)

Language English (official), Hindi, French, Spanish

Religion Roman Catholic 33%, Hindu 25%, Anglican 15%, Muslim 6%, Presbyterian 4%

Time difference GMT –4

 ▪ CIA ▪ LP ▪ RG ▪ WTG

▪ Welcome to Trinidad and Tobago!

http://www.visittnt.com/

Official Web site of Trinidad and Tobago tourism. This site provides information on the 'cool, serene, and green' country, divided into four main sections: 'General information', 'How to get here?', 'Where to stay?', and 'What to do here?'. Particularly worth a visit is the section on the annual carnival, which includes photographs and audio clips from previous years.

TUNISIA
Map page 102

National name Al-Jumhuriyya at-Tunisiyya/Tunisian Republic

Area 164,150 sq km/63,378 sq mi

Capital Tunis (and chief port)

Major towns/cities Sfax, L'Ariana, Bizerte, Gabès, Sousse, Kairouan

Major ports Sfax, Sousse, Bizerte

Physical features arable and forested land in north graduates towards desert in south; fertile island of Jerba, linked to mainland by causeway (identified with island of lotus-eaters); Shott el Jerid salt lakes

Currency Tunisian dinar

GNP per capita (PPP) (US$) 5,478 (1999)

Resources petroleum, natural gas, phosphates, iron, zinc, lead, aluminium fluoride, fluorspar, sea salt

Population 9,586,000 (2000 est)

Population density (per sq km) 58 (1999 est est)

Language Arabic (official), French

Religion Sunni Muslim (state religion); Jewish and Christian minorities

Time difference GMT +1

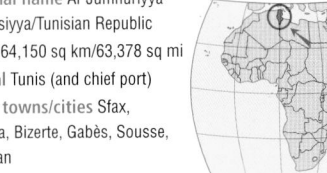 ▪ CIA ▪ AN ▪ LP ▪ NA ▪ WTG

TURKEY
Map page 92

National name Türkiye Cumhuriyeti/Republic of Turkey

Area 779,500 sq km/300,964 sq mi

Capital Ankara

Major towns/cities İstanbul, İzmir, Adana, Bursa, Gaziantep, Konya, Mersin, Antalya, Diyarbakduringr

Major ports İstanbul and İzmir

Physical features central plateau surrounded by mountains, partly in Europe (Thrace) and partly in Asia (Anatolia); Bosporus and Dardanelles; Mount Ararat (highest peak Great Ararat, 5,137 m/16,854 ft); Taurus Mountains in southwest (highest peak Kaldi Dag, 3,734 m/12,255 ft); sources of rivers Euphrates and Tigris in east

Currency Turkish lira

GNP per capita (PPP) (US$) 6,126 (1999)

Resources chromium, copper, mercury, antimony, borax, coal, petroleum, natural gas, iron ore, salt

Population 66,591,000 (2000 est)

Population density (per sq km) 84 (1999 est)

Language Turkish (official), Kurdish, Arabic

Religion Sunni Muslim 99%; Orthodox, Armenian churches

Time difference GMT +3

 ▪ CIA ▪ LC ▪ LP ▪ RG ▪ WTG

▪ Time Out Guide to Istanbul

http://www.ddg.com/ISTANBUL/

Virtual tour of Istanbul including a description of all the important sites, a library of pictures, and both 2D and 3D maps of the city.

▪ Discover Turkey

http://www.turkishnews.com/DiscoverTurkey/

Collection of pages on Turkey, its culture, and people. There is a country map, as well as sections on tourism, business, poetry, politics, and even carpets.

▪ Turkey

http://www.turkey.org/start.html

Guide to Turkey and Turkish culture, with links to the country's history as well as a detailed biography of Turkish leader Mustafa Kemal Ataturk.

▪ Pamukkale

http://www.exploreturkey.com/pamukkal.htm

Good guide to the history of Turkey's 'Holy City' and the current attractions of Pamukkale. Information on recent archaeological discoveries is presented here and there are also good pictures of the ruins and the spectacular geological formations in the area.

▪ Ankara

http://www.hitit.co.uk/regions/Ankara/About.html

Tourist guide to the Turkish capital. The history of the city is summarized and its public buildings, institutions, and attractions described. There is also a section outlining places of interest outside the capital.

▪ Izmir

http://www.turkey.org/tourism/izmir/izmir.htm

Good guide to Turkey's third biggest city – 'the pearl of the Aegean'. There is an outline of the city's history and heritage, and a guide to hotels, museums, and other places of interest. Information on nearby recreational areas is supported by photographs.

▪ NatureKey Online Travel Magazine

http://www.naturekey.com/

Devoted, not to the towns and cities of Turkey, but to the country's natural areas. The monthly issues of this online magazine include regular features such as 'news' and links to related outdoor pursuits sites. It also contains an image gallery, a 'clickable' map of Turkey's regions, and features on specific areas written by both visitors and local inhabitants.

TURKMENISTAN
Map page 76

National name Türkmenistan/Turkmenistan

Area 488,100 sq km/188,455 sq mi

Capital Ashkhabad

Major towns/cities Chardzhev, Mary, Nebitdag, Dashkhovuz, Turkmenbashi

Major ports Turkmenbashi

Physical features about 90% of land is desert including the

Kara Kum 'Black Sands' desert (area 310,800 sq km/120,000 sq mi)

Currency manat

GNP per capita (PPP) (US$) 3,099 (1999)

Resources petroleum, natural gas, coal, sulphur, magnesium, iodine-bromine, sodium sulphate and different types of salt

Population 4,459,000 (2000 est)

Population density (per sq km) 9 (1999 est)

Language Turkmen (a Turkic language; official), Russian, Uzbek, other regional languages

Religion Sunni Muslim

Time difference GMT +5

 ■ CIA ■ LC ■ LP ■ WTG

TUVALU
Map page 112

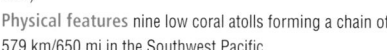

National name Fakavae Aliki-Malo i Tuvalu/ Constitutional Monarchy of Tuvalu

Area 25 sq km/9.6 sq mi

Capital Fongafale (on Funafuti atoll)

Physical features nine low coral atolls forming a chain of 579 km/650 mi in the Southwest Pacific

Currency Australian dollar

GNP per capita (PPP) (US$) 970 (1998 est)

Population 12,000 (2000 est)

Population density (per sq km) 423 (1999 est)

Language Tuvaluan, English (both official), a Gilbertese dialect (on Nui)

Religion Protestant 96% (Church of Tuvalu)

Time difference GMT +12

 ■ CIA ■ LP ■ WTG

■ **Tuvalu Travel Guide**

http://www.pi-travel.co.nz/tuvalu/index.html

Travel guide to the islands of Tuvalu, one of the world's smallest and most isolated countries. The guide is divided into a number of sections, offering information on the country's attractions, a directory of accommodation, and practical advice on topics such as entry requirements and health risks.

UGANDA
Map page 106

National name Republic of Uganda

Area 236,600 sq km/ 91,351 sq mi

Capital Kampala

Major towns/cities Jinja, Mbale, Entebbe, Masaka, Mbarara, Soroti

Physical features plateau with mountains in west (Ruwenzori Range, with Mount Margherita, 5,110 m/16,765 ft); forest and grassland; 18% is lakes, rivers, and wetlands (Owen Falls on White Nile where it leaves Lake Victoria; Lake Albert in west); arid in northwest

Currency Ugandan new shilling

GNP per capita (PPP) (US$) 1,136 (1999 est)

Resources copper, apatite, limestone; believed to possess the world's second-largest deposit of gold (hitherto unexploited); also reserves of magnetite, tin, tungsten, beryllium, bismuth, asbestos, graphite

Population 21,778,000 (2000 est)

Population density (per sq km) 89

Language English (official), Kiswahili, other Bantu and Nilotic languages

Religion Christian 65%, animist 20%, Muslim 15%

Time difference GMT +3

 ■ CIA ■ LC ■ LP ■ NA ■ WTG

UKRAINE
Map page 70

National name Ukrayina/ Ukraine

Area 603,700 sq km/ 233,088 sq mi

Capital Kiev

Major towns/cities Kharkiv, Donets'k, Dnipropetrovs'k, L'viv, Kryyyy Rih, Zaporizhzhya, Odessa

Physical features Russian plain; Carpathian and Crimean Mountains; rivers: Dnieper (with the Dnieper dam 1932), Donetz, Bug

Currency hryvna

GNP per capita (PPP) (US$) 3,142 (1999)

Resources coal, iron ore (world's fifth-largest producer), crude oil, natural gas, salt, chemicals, brown coal, alabaster, gypsum

Population 50,456,000 (2000 est)

Population density (per sq km) 84 (1999 est)

Language Ukrainian (a Slavonic language; official), Russian (also official in Crimea), other regional languages

Religion traditionally Ukrainian Orthodox; also Ukrainian Catholic; small Protestant, Jewish, and Muslim communities

Time difference GMT +2

 ■ CIA ■ LP ■ WTG

■ **EuroScope: Ukraine**

http://pages.prodigy.net/euroscope/guidetoc.html

Tourist guide to Ukraine. This in-depth site features profiles of Ukraine's major towns and cities, with information on hotels and restaurants in each. Make sure you visit the photo galleries, which offer an insight into Hutsul folk art and Ukrainian Jewry.

■ **Kiev, Ukraine**

http://travel.lycos.com/Destinations/Europe/Ukraine/Kiev/

Large source of information on the Ukrainian capital. There are descriptions of the city, its history, attractions, entertainment, and cultural events. There are also links to a number of sources of information on Ukraine.

■ **Odessa Web**

http://www.odessit.com/tours/tours/english/overview.htm

Guide to this Ukrainian seaport. Dealing with both the old and the new, this site has sections on the history and cultural traditions and also the night life. There are also a number of photographs of notable buildings.

UNITED ARAB EMIRATES
Map page 95

National name Dawlat Imarat al-'Arabiyya al Muttahida/State of the Arab Emirates (UAE)

Area 83,657 sq km/32,299 sq mi

Capital Abu Dhabi

Major towns/cities Dubai, Sharjah, Ra's al Khaymah, Ajmān, Al 'Ayn

Major ports Dubai

Physical features desert and flat coastal plain; mountains in east

Currency UAE dirham

GNP per capita (PPP) (US$) 18,825 (1999 est)

Resources petroleum and natural gas

Population 2,441,000 (2000 est)

Population density (per sq km) 29 (1999 est)

Language Arabic (official), Farsi, Hindi, Urdu, English

Religion Muslim 96% (of which 80% Sunni); Christian, Hindu

Time difference GMT +4

 ■ CIA ■ LC ■ AN ■ LP ■ WTG

■ **Tourism – United Arab Emirates**

http://www.ecssr.ac.ae/tourism.html

Guide to the tourist attractions of the United Arab Emirates, with basic practical information for visitors. It is largely text-based but has some good images of local wildlife.

■ **Ras al Khaimah**

http://www.uaeforever.com/RasAlKhaimah/

Guide to the most traditional of the United Arab Emirates. There is a good description of the history and attractions of the small

strategically placed emirate. There are also good photos of Ras al Khaimah and its leader.

■ **Abu Dhabi**

http://www.uaeforever.com/AbuDhabi/

Well-presented guide to the largest and richest of the United Arab Emirates. There is a good description of the history, cultural heritage, attractions, and local economy. There are a number of good photos of Abu Dhabi and its ruler, the UAE president.

■ **Dubai**

http://www.uaeforever.com/Dubai/

Well-presented guide to the second-largest of the United Arab Emirates. There is a good description of the history of the trading entrepot, the role of the Makhtoum family, as well as details of it's cultural heritage, attractions, and the local economy. There are a number of good photos of Dubai and its ruler.

UNITED KINGDOM
Map page 56

National name United Kingdom of Great Britain and Northern Ireland (UK)

Area 244,100 sq km/94,247 sq mi

Capital London

Major towns/cities Birmingham, Glasgow, Leeds, Sheffield, Liverpool, Manchester, Edinburgh, Bradford, Bristol, Coventry, Belfast, Cardiff

Major ports London, Grimsby, Southampton, Liverpool

Physical features became separated from European continent in about 6000 BC; rolling landscape, increasingly mountainous towards the north, with Grampian Mountains in Scotland, Pennines in northern England, Cambrian Mountains in Wales; rivers include Thames, Severn, and Spey

Territories Anguilla, Bermuda, British Antarctic Territory, British Indian Ocean Territory, British Virgin Islands, Cayman Islands, Falkland Islands, Gibraltar, Montserrat, Pitcairn Islands, St. Helena and Dependencies (Ascension, Tristan da Cunha), South Georgia, South Sandwich Islands, Turks and Caicos Islands; the Channel Islands and the Isle of Man are not part of the UK but are direct dependencies of the crown

Currency pound sterling

GNP per capita (PPP) (US$) 20,883 (1999)

Resources coal, limestone, crude petroleum, natural gas, tin, iron, salt, sand and gravel

Population 58,830,000 (2000 est)

Population density (per sq km) 240 (1999 est)

Language English (official), Welsh (also official in Wales), Gaelic

Religion about 46% Church of England (established church); other Protestant denominations, Roman Catholic, Muslim, Jewish, Hindu, Sikh

Time difference GMT +/–0

 ■ CIA ■ LP ■ RG ■ WTG

■ **Gateway to Scotland**

http://www.geo.ed.ac.uk/home/scotland/scotland.html

Guide to all things Scottish, including an 'active map', a guide to the major cities, and information on the language, as well as sections on famous residents and history.

■ **UK Travel Guide**

http://www.uktravel.com/index.html

Essential resource for anyone planning to travel in the UK. It includes an A–Z of practical information from accommodation to the weather. The site also includes a 'clickable' map with features on towns and cities as well as several images.

■ **Lake District National Park Authority**

http://www.lake-district.gov.uk/index.htm

Official guide to the attractions of Britain's largest national park. There are sections on geology, history, conservation activities, and exhibitions in the Park's visitor's centre. There is a daily weather report for keen walkers. There are also some fabulous photographs of Lakeland beauty spots.

■ **Cardiff, Capital City of Wales**

http://www.cardiff.gov.uk/

Official guide to the Welsh capital. Local government functions are fully explained and investment opportunities outlined. There are many photos of the city and a listing of local amenities and historic sites.

■ **States of Jersey**

http://www.jersey.gov.uk/

Official information about the largest of the Channel Islands. This well organized site caters for the needs of residents and visitors. There is good coverage of the history and cultural heritage of Jersey. Information for visitors is first-rate with details of local attractions, events, and even the weather.

■ **LondonNet – The Net Magazine Guide to London**
http://www.londonnet.co.uk/
Informative guide to London, suitable for both tourists and residents alike. There are notes on accommodation in London, covering hotels, apartments, and even places for the 'cost conscious'. Other areas covered here include the museums to visit, the best ways to travel, and the pick of the London nightlife. In addition, there are also notes on the places to shop and eat.

■ **Northern Ireland Tourist Board**
http://www.ni-tourism.com/index.asp
This site covers the needs of anyone planning to visit Northern Ireland, from accommodation to events and attractions. It also features a virtual tour covering history, activities, food and drink, and places to stay.

UNITED STATES OF AMERICA

Map page 124

National name United States of America (USA)
Area 9,372,615 sq km/ 3,618,766 sq mi
Capital Washington D.C.
Major towns/cities New York, Los Angeles, Chicago, Philadelphia, Detroit, San Francisco, Dallas, San Diego, San Antonio, Houston, Boston, Phoenix, Indianapolis, Honolulu, San José
Physical features topography and vegetation from tropical (Hawaii) to arctic (Alaska); mountain ranges parallel with east and west coasts; the Rocky Mountains separate rivers emptying into the Pacific from those flowing into the Gulf of Mexico; Great Lakes in north; rivers include Hudson, Mississippi, Missouri, Colorado, Columbia, Snake, Rio Grande, Ohio
Territories the commonwealths of Puerto Rico and Northern Marianas; Guam, the US Virgin Islands, American Samoa, Wake Island, Midway Islands, Johnston Atoll, Baker Island, Howland Island, Jarvis Island, Kingman Reef, Navassa Island, Palmyra Island
Currency US dollar
GNP per capita (PPP) (US$) 30,600 (1999)
Resources coal, copper (world's second-largest producer), iron, bauxite, mercury, silver, gold, nickel, zinc (world's fifth-largest producer), tungsten, uranium, phosphate, petroleum, natural gas, timber
Population 278,357,000 (2000 est)
Population density (per sq km) 29 (1999 est)
Language English, Spanish
Religion Protestant 58%; Roman Catholic 28%; atheist 10%; Jewish 2%; other 4% (1998)
Time difference GMT –5–11

 ■ CIA ■ LP ■ RG ■ WTG

■ **Best of Hawaii**
http://www.bestofhawaii.com/
Jumping-off point for visitors seeking information about the best of Hawaii. This site includes a wealth of information aimed at the tourist – including maps, food, weather, accommodation, and even an online version of the Hawaiian phone directory.

■ **Grand Canyon**
http://www.kaibab.org/
Visitors to this site will find an outline of the geological and human history tracing the gradual conquest of the Canyon, and a spectacular photo gallery with close-ups and panoramas. There are also details of recommended hikes and trails, and you can discover valuable tips on hiking and backpacking.

■ **New York**
http://newyork.citysearch.com/
Impressive, user-friendly guide to New York City, filled with practical information. There are interesting feature articles and constant updates on what's on in the Big Apple. If the pace of life gets too hectic, the search engine can even provide a comprehensive listing of mind and body healing centres.

■ **Washington DC**
http://www.washington.org/
Site of the Washington DC Convention and Visitors' Association. This is a helpful guide filled with practical information for tourists and details of the attractions in the Washington area. There is also a useful set of maps.

■ **Niagara Falls Convention and Visitors Bureau**
http://www.nfcvb.com/
Official guide to the Niagara area in the state of New York. In addition to interesting facts about the falls, there is extensive information on local tours, transport, accommodation, places to eat, local festivals, and events.

■ **Prehistory of Alaska**
http://www.nps.gov/akso/akarc/
Alaska's prehistory divided into five sections: 'early prehistory', 'tundra and Arctic Alaska', 'southeast Alaska', 'southwest Alaska and Pacific coast', and 'interior Alaska'. there are also links to Alaska's 15 national parks and preserves – click on the acronym to access a general description of each park's cultural resources.

URUGUAY

Map page 142

National name República Oriental del Uruguay/Eastern Republic of Uruguay
Area 176,200 sq km/68,030 sq mi
Capital Montevideo
Major towns/cities Salto, Paysandú, Las Piedras, Rivera, Tacuarembó
Physical features grassy plains (pampas) and low hills; rivers Negro, Uruguay, Río de la Plata
Currency Uruguayan peso
GNP per capita (PPP) (US$) 8,280 (1999)
Resources small-scale extraction of building materials, industrial minerals, semi-precious stones; gold deposits are being developed
Population 3,337,000 (2000 est)
Population density (per sq km) 19 (1999 est)
Language Spanish (official), Brazilero (a mixture of Spanish and Portuguese)
Religion mainly Roman Catholic
Time difference GMT –3

 ■ CIA ■ LP ■ WTG

■ **Uruguay – General Information**
http://www.embassy.org/uruguay/
Comprehensive information about Uruguay. There are links to a profile of the country detailing its main features, as well as to its history, geography and climate, culture, cuisine, and wine. The site includes a map and a list of new Uruguay telephone numbers.

UZBEKISTAN

Map page 76

National name Özbekiston Respublikasi/Republic of Uzbekistan
Area 447,400 sq km/ 172,741 sq mi
Capital Tashkent
Major towns/cities Samarkand, Bukhara, Namangan, Andijon, Nukus, Karshi
Physical features oases in deserts; rivers: Amu Darya, Syr Darya; Fergana Valley; rich in mineral deposits
Currency som
GNP per capita (PPP) (US$) 2,092 (1999)
Resources petroleum, natural gas, coal, gold (world's seventh-largest producer), silver, uranium (world's fourth-largest producer), copper, lead, zinc, tungsten
Population 24,318,000 (2000 est)
Population density (per sq km) 54 (1999 est)
Language Uzbek (a Turkic language; official), Russian, Tajik
Religion predominantly Sunni Muslim; small Wahhabi, Sufi, and Orthodox Christian communities
Time difference GMT +5

 ■ CIA ■ LC ■ LP ■ WTG

VANUATU

Map page 112

National name Ripablik blong Vanuatu/République de Vanuatu/Republic of Vanuatu
Area 14,800 sq km/5,714 sq mi
Capital Port-Vila (on Efate island) (and chief port)
Major towns/cities Luganville (on Espíritu Santo)
Physical features comprises around 70 inhabited islands, including Espíritu Santo, Malekula, and Efate; densely forested, mountainous; three active volcanoes; cyclones on average twice a year
Currency vatu
GNP per capita (PPP) (US$) 2,771 (1999 est)
Resources manganese; gold, copper, and large deposits of petroleum have been discovered but have hitherto remained unexploited
Population 190,000 (2000 est)
Population density (per sq km) 13 (1999 est)
Language Bislama (82%), English, French (all official)
Religion Christian 80%, animist about 8%
Time difference GMT +11

 ■ CIA ■ LP ■ WTG

■ **Vanuatu Online**
http://www.vanuatu.net.vu/VanuatuOnlineDirectory.html
Source of information on the Melanesian state. There is a history of the islands, information on government services, the local economy, and attractions. This is in addition to practical information for tourists which includes a special section for philatelists.

■ **Port-Vila, Vanuatu**
http://travel.lycos.com/Destinations/Australia_and_Pacific/Vanuatu/Port_Vila/
Guide to the capital of Vanuatu. There is coverage of local attractions, culture, and history. The site also has practical information for visitors and those planning to reside in the city, and the text is improved by the inclusion of several photographs of Port-Vila.

VATICAN CITY

Map page 64

National name Stato della Città del Vaticano/Vatican City State
Area 0.4 sq km/0.2 sq mi
Physical features forms an enclave in the heart of Rome, Italy
Currency Vatican City lira and Italian lira
GNP per capita (PPP) see Italy
Population 1,000 (2000 est)
Population density (per sq km) 2,500 (2000 est)
Language Latin (official), Italian
Religion Roman Catholic
Time difference GMT +1

 ■ CIA ■ LP ■ WTG

■ **Holy See (Vatican City)**
http://www.vatican.va/
Multilingual, searchable page, with recent news reports and press releases from the Vatican Information Service. As well as the latest news from the Vatican City State, it also includes information about the Vatican museums and their plans for celebrating the year 2000.

VENEZUELA

Map page 140

National name República de Venezuela/Republic of Venezuela
Area 912,100 sq km/352,161 sq mi
Capital Caracas

Major towns/cities Maracaibo, Maracay, Barquisimeto, Valencia, Ciudad Guayana, Petare

Major ports Maracaibo

Physical features Andes Mountains and Lake Maracaibo in northwest; central plains (llanos); delta of River Orinoco in east; Guiana Highlands in southeast

Currency bolívar

GNP per capita (PPP) (US$) 5,268 (1999)

Resources petroleum, natural gas, aluminium, iron ore, coal, diamonds, gold, zinc, copper, silver, lead, phosphates, manganese, titanium

Population 24,170,000 (2000 est)

Population density (per sq km) 26 (1999 est)

Language Spanish (official), Indian languages (2%)

Religion Roman Catholic 92%

Time difference GMT –4

 ■ CIA ■ LC ■ LP ■ WTG

■ **Fodor's Trip Planner – Caracas**

http://www.fodors.com/ptpshort.cgi?Caracas

Create your own personal mini-guide to the Venezuelan capital with this handy on-line tourist guide. By choosing price ranges of accommodation and restaurants, and selecting options such as transport, currency and languages, a detailed pamphlet can be quickly compiled. If you select the language option, a link will appear to a site that provides useful phrases.

■ **Venezuela Yours**

http://www.venezuelatuya.com/eng.htm

Guide to Venezuela that is available in six languages, including English. The site features profiles of a number of the country's attractions, including the Andes, Caracas, and La Gran Sabana. There is also a selection of beautifully-illustrated articles on Venezuela's history and wildlife.

Vietnam
Map page 84

National name Công-hòa xâ-hôi chu-nghia Viêt Nam/Socialist Republic of Vietnam

Area 329,600 sq km/127,258 sq mi

Capital Hanoi

Major towns/cities Ho Chi Minh (formerly Saigon), Hai Phong, Da Näng, Cân Tho, Nha Trang, Biên Hoa, Huê

Major ports Ho Chi Minh (formerly Saigon), Da Näng, Hai Phong

Physical features Red River and Mekong deltas, centre of cultivation and population; tropical rainforest; mountainous in north and northwest

Currency dong

GNP per capita (PPP) (US$) 1,755 (1999)

Resources petroleum, coal, tin, zinc, iron, antimony, chromium, phosphate, apatite, bauxite

Population 79,832,000 (2000 est)

Population density (per sq km) 237 (1999 est)

Language Vietnamese (official), French, English, Khmer, Chinese, local languages

Religion mainly Buddhist; Christian, mainly Roman Catholic (8–10%); Taoist, Confucian, Hos Hoa, and Cao Dai sects

Time difference GMT +7

 ■ CIA ■ LC ■ LP ■ WTG

■ **Administrative Structure Of Vietnam**

http://www.batin.com.vn/vninfo/asv.htm

Fascinating insight into Vietnamese government and politics: at times it almost feels as if you are privy to state secrets! There are few multimedia frills on this site, but the colourful propaganda easily makes up for that.

■ **Vietnam Pictures**

http://sunsite.unc.edu/vietnam/

Multimedia archive of Vietnam, including photographs, audio clips, video footage, and text articles covering many aspects of Vietnamese life. The many hypertext links included on this page can take you on a virtual tour of this Southeast Asian country.

Yemen
Map page 90

National name Al-Jumhuriyya al Yamaniyya/Republic of Yemen

Area 531,900 sq km/205,366 sq mi

Capital Şan'ā

Major towns/cities Aden, Ta'izz, Al Mukallā, Al Ḥudaydah, Ibb, Dhamār

Major ports Aden

Physical features hot, moist coastal plain, rising to plateau and desert

Currency riyal

GNP per capita (PPP) (US$) 688 (1999)

Resources petroleum, natural gas, gypsum, salt; deposits of copper, gold, lead, zinc, molybdenum

Population 18,112,000 (2000 est)

Population density (per sq km) 33 (1999 est)

Language Arabic (official)

Religion Sunni Muslim 63%, Shiite Muslim 37%

Time difference GMT +3

 ■ CIA ■ AN ■ LP ■ WTG

■ **Yemen**

http://www.al-bab.com/yemen/

Impressive source of comprehensive information on Yemen. There is coverage of history, culture, archaeology, tourism, economics, the political scene, international relations, and the local media. A large number of photographs include some stunning satellite images.

Yugoslavia
Map page 66

National name Savezna Republika Jugoslavija/Federal Republic of Yugoslavia

Area 58,300 sq km/22,509 sq mi

Capital Belgrade

Major towns/cities Priština, Novi Sad, Niš, Kragujevac, Podgorica (formerly Titograd), Subotica

Physical features federation of republics of Serbia and Montenegro and two former autonomous provinces, Kosovo and Vojvodina

Currency new Yugoslav dinar

GNP per capita (PPP) (US$) 5,880 (1997 est)

Resources petroleum, natural gas, coal, copper ore, bauxite, iron ore, lead, zinc

Population 10,640,000 (2000 est)

Population density (per sq km) 182 (1999 est)

Language Serbo-Croat (official), Albanian (in Kosovo)

Religion Serbian and Montenegrin Orthodox; Muslim in southern Serbia

Time difference GMT +1

 ■ CIA ■ LC ■ LP ■ WTG

Zambia
Map page 108

National name Republic of Zambia

Area 752,600 sq km/290,578 sq mi

Capital Lusaka

Major towns/cities Kitwe, Ndola, Kabwe, Mufulira, Chingola, Luanshya, Livingstone

Physical features forested plateau cut through by rivers; Zambezi River, Victoria Falls, Kariba Dam

Currency Zambian kwacha

GNP per capita (PPP) (US$) 686 (1999)

Resources copper (world's fourth-largest producer), cobalt, zinc, lead, coal, gold, emeralds, amethysts and other gemstones, limestone, selenium

Population 9,169,000 (2000 est)

Population density (per sq km) 12 (1999 est)

Language English (official), Bantu languages

Religion about 64% Christian, animist, Hindu, Muslim

Time difference GMT +2

 ■ CIA ■ LP ■ NA ■ WTG

■ **Travel Guide to Zambia**

http://www.africa-insites.com/zambia/travel/Default.htm

Comprehensive, illustrated guide to travelling in Zambia. There is information on the country's cities, towns, and game reserves, as well as a series of articles on the safaris and other adventure holidays possible in Zambia, which include surfing on the Zambezi beneath Victoria Falls, house-boating on Lake Kariba, and white-water rafting.

Zimbabwe
Map page 108

National name Republic of Zimbabwe

Area 390,300 sq km/150,694 sq mi

Capital Harare

Major towns/cities Bulawayo, Gweru, Kwekwe, Mutare, Kadoma, Chitungwiza

Physical features high plateau with central high veld and mountains in east; rivers Zambezi, Limpopo; Victoria Falls

Currency Zimbabwe dollar

GNP per capita (PPP) (US$) 2,470 (1999)

Resources gold, nickel, asbestos, coal, chromium, copper, silver, emeralds, lithium, tin, iron ore, cobalt

Population 11,669,000 (2000 est)

Population density (per sq km) 30 (1999 est)

Language English, Shona, Ndebele (all official)

Religion 50% follow a syncretic (part Christian, part indigenous beliefs) type of religion, Christian 25%, animist 24%, small Muslim minority

Time difference GMT +2

■ CIA ■ LP ■ NA ■ WTG

INDEX

HOW TO USE THE INDEX

This is an alphabetically arranged index of the places and features that can be found on the maps in this atlas. Each name is generally indexed to the largest scale map on which it appears. If that map covers a double page, the name will always be indexed by the left-hand page number.

Names composed of two or more words are alphabetized as if they were one word.

All names appear in full in the index, except for 'St.' and 'Ste.', which, although abbreviated, are indexed as though spelled in full.

Where two or more places have the same name, they can be distinguished from each other by the country or province name that immediately follows the entry. These names are indexed in the alphabetical order of the country or province.

Alternative names, such as English translations, can also be found in the index and are cross-referenced to the map form by the '=' sign. In these cases the names also appear in brackets on the maps.

Settlements are indexed to the position of the symbol; all other features are indexed to the position of the name on the map.

Abbreviations and symbols used in this index are explained in the list opposite.

FINDING A NAME ON THE MAP

Each index entry contains the name, followed by a symbol indicating the feature type (for example, settlement, river), a page reference and a grid reference:

Name	Owosso	● 128	D2
	Owyhee	● 126	C2
	Owyhee	⚊ 126	C2
Symbol	Oxford, New Zealand	● 116	D6
	Oxford, United Kingdom	● 38	G4
	Oxnard	● 132	C2
Page reference	Oxford	● **38**	J4
	Oyama	● 82	K5
	Oyapock	⚊ 140	G3
Grid reference	Oyem	● 104 — G4

The grid reference locates a place or feature within a rectangle formed by the network of lines of longitude and latitude. A name can be found by referring to the red letters and numbers placed around the maps. First find the letter, which appears along the top and bottom of the map, and then the number, down the sides. The name will be found within the rectangle uniquely defined by that letter and number. A number in brackets preceding the grid reference indicates that the name is to be found within an inset map.

ABBREVIATIONS

Ak.	Alaska	N.D.	North Dakota
Al.	Alabama	Nebr.	Nebraska
Ariz.	Arizona	Nev.	Nevada
Ark.	Arkansas	Nfld.	Newfoundland
B.C.	British Columbia	N.H.	New Hampshire
Calif.	California	N. Ire.	Northern Ireland
Colo.	Colorado	N.J.	New Jersey
Conn.	Connecticut	N. Mex.	New Mexico
Del.	Delaware	N.W.T.	Northwest Territories
Dem. Rep. of Congo		N.Y.	New York
Democratic Republic of Congo		Oh.	Ohio
Eng.	England	Okla.	Oklahoma
Fla.	Florida	Ont.	Ontario
Ga.	Georgia	Oreg.	Oregon
Ia.	Iowa	Orkney Is.	Orkney Islands
Id.	Idaho	Pa.	Pennsylvania
Ill.	Illinois	R.G.S.	Rio Grande do Sul
Ind.	Indiana	R.I.	Rhode Island
Kans.	Kansas	S.C.	South Carolina
Ky.	Kentucky	Scot.	Scotland
La.	Louisiana	S.D.	South Dakota
Man.	Manitoba	Shetland Is.	Shetland Islands
Mass.	Massachusetts	Tenn.	Tennessee
Md.	Maryland	Tex.	Texas
Me.	Maine	Ut.	Utah
M.G.	Mato Grosso	Va.	Virginia
Mich.	Michigan	Vt.	Vermont
Minn.	Minnesota	Wash.	Washington
Miss.	Mississippi	Wis.	Wisconsin
Mo.	Missouri	W. Va.	West Virginia
Mont.	Montana	Wyo.	Wyoming
N.B.	New Brunswick	Y.T.	Yukon Territory
N.C.	North Carolina		

SYMBOLS

☒ Continent name	◢ Lake, salt lake
Ⓐ Country name	◥ Gulf, strait, bay
ⓐ State or province name	◤ Sea, ocean
■ Country capital	▷ Cape, point
◳ State or province capital	Island or island group, rocky or coral reef
● Settlement	✳ Place of interest
▲ Mountain, volcano, peak	▲ National park or other protected area
▲ Mountain range	
Physical region or feature	Historical or cultural region
⚊ River, canal	

GLOSSARY

This is an alphabetically arranged glossary of the geographical terms used on the maps and in this index. The first column shows the map form, the second the language of origin and the third the English translation.

A

açude	Portuguese	reservoir
adası	Turkish	island
akra	Greek	peninsula
alpen	German	mountains
alpes	French	mountains
alpi	Italian	mountains
älven	Swedish	river
archipiélago	Spanish	archipelago
arquipélago	Portuguese	archipelago

B

bab	Arabic	strait
bahía	Spanish	bay
bahir, bahr	Arabic	bay, lake, river
baía	Portuguese	bay
baie	French	bay
baja	Spanish	lower
bandar	Arabic, Somalian, Malay, Persian	harbour, port
baraji	Turkish	dam
barragem	Portuguese	reservoir
ben	Gaelic	mountain
Berg(e)	German	mountain(s)
boğazı	Turkish	strait
Bucht	German	bay
buḥayrat	Arabic	lake
burnu, burun	Turkish	cape

C

cabo	Spanish	cape
canal	French, Spanish	canal, channel
canale	Italian	canal, channel
cerro	Spanish	mountain
chott	Arabic	marsh, salt lake
co	Tibetan	lake
collines	French	hills
cordillera	Spanish	range

D

dağ(ı)	Turkish	mountain
dağlar(ı)	Turkish	mountains
danau	Indonesian	lake
daryacheh	Persian	lake
dasht	Persian	desert
djebel	Arabic	mountain(s)
-do	Korean	island

E

embalse	Spanish	reservoir
erg	Arabic	sandy desert
estrecho	Spanish	strait

F

feng	Chinese	mountain
-fjördur	Icelandic	fjord
-flói	Icelandic	bay

G

Gebirge	German	range
golfe	French	bay, gulf
golfo	Italian, Portuguese, Spanish	bay, gulf
göl, gölü	Turkish	lake
gora	Russian	mountain
gory	Russian	mountains
gunong	Malay	mountain
gunung	Indonesian	mountain

H

hai	Chinese	lake, sea
hāmūn	Persian	lake, marsh
hawr	Arabic	lake
hu	Chinese	lake, reservoir

I

île(s)	French	island(s)
ilha(s)	Portuguese	island(s)
isla(s)	Spanish	island(s)

J

jabal	Arabic	mountain(s)
-järvi	Finnish	lake
jaza'ir	Arabic	islands
jazīrat	Arabic	island
jbel	Arabic	mountain
jebel	Arabic	mountain
jezero	Serbo-Croatian	lake
jezioro	Polish	lake
jiang	Chinese	river
-jima	Japanese	island
-joki	Finnish	river
-jökull	Icelandic	glacier

K

kepulauan	Indonesian	islands
khrebet	Russian	mountain range
-ko	Japanese	lake
kolpos	Greek	bay, gulf
körfezi	Turkish	bay, gulf
kryazh	Russian	ridge
kūh(ha)	Persian	mountain(s)

L

lac	French	lake
lacul	Romanian	lake
lago	Italian, Portuguese, Spanish	lake
lagoa	Portuguese	lagoon
laguna	Spanish	lagoon, lake
limni	Greek	lake
ling	Chinese	mountain(s), peak
liqeni	Albanian	lake
loch, lough	Gaelic	lake

M

massif	French	mountains
-meer	Dutch	lake, sea
mont	French	mount
monte	Italian, Portuguese, Spanish	mount
montes	Portuguese, Spanish	mountains
monts	French	mountains
muntii	Romanian	mountains
mys	Russian	cape

N

nafud	Arabic	desert
nevado	Spanish	snow-capped mountain
nuruu	Mongolian	mountains
nuur	Mongolian	lake

O

| ostrov(a) | Russian | island(s) |
| ozero | Russian | lake |

P

pegunungan	Indonesian	mountains
pelagos	Greek	sea
pendi	Chinese	basin
pesky	Russian	sandy desert
pic	French	peak
pico	Portuguese, Spanish	peak
planalto	Portuguese	plateau
planina	Bulgarian	mountains
poluostrov	Russian	peninsula
puerto	Spanish	harbour, port
puncak	Indonesian	peak
punta	Italian, Spanish	point
puy	French	peak

Q

| qundao | Chinese | archipelago |

R

ras, râs, ra's	Arabic	cape
represa	Portuguese	dam, reservoir
-rettō	Japanese	archipelago
rio	Portuguese	river
río	Spanish	river

S

sahra	Arabic	desert
salar	Spanish	salt flat
-san	Japanese, Korean	mountain
-sanmaek	Korean	mountains
sebkha	Arabic	salt flat
sebkhet	Arabic	salt marsh
See	German	lake
serra	Portuguese	range
severnaya, severo-	Russian	northern
shan	Chinese	mountain(s)
-shima	Japanese	island
-shotō	Japanese	islands
sierra	Spanish	range

T

tanjona	Malagasy	cape
tanjung	Indonesian	cape
teluk	Indonesian	bay, gulf
ténéré	Berber	desert
-tō	Japanese	island

V

vârful	Romanian	mountain
-vesi	Finnish	lake
vodokhranilishche	Russian	reservoir
volcán	Spanish	volcano

W

| wādī | Arabic | watercourse |
| Wald | German | forest |

Z

| -zaki | Japanese | cape |
| zaliv | Russian | bay, gulf |

A

Name	Page	Grid
Aachen	54	J4
Aalen	52	F8
Aalst	54	G4
Aarau	62	D3
Aare	62	C3
Aarschot	54	G4
Aba	104	F3
Ābādān	95	C1
Ābādeh	95	E1
Abadla	102	E2
Abaji	104	F3
Abakaliki	104	F3
Abakan	76	S7
Āb Anbar	95	E1
Abancay	140	C6
Abano Terme	62	G5
Abarqū	95	E1
Abashiri	82	N1
Abava	48	M8
Ābaya Häyk'	106	F2
Abay Wenz	100	G5
Abbeville, France	54	D4
Abbeville, United States	130	C4
Abd al Kūrī	90	F7
Abéché	100	D5
Abengourou	104	D3
Abenójar	60	F6
Åbenrå	52	E1
Abensberg	52	G8
Abeokuta	104	E3
Aberaeron	56	H9
Abez'	70	M1
Abhā	100	H4
Abhar	92	N5
Abidjan	104	D3
Abilene	132	G2
Abingdon, United Kingdom	54	A3
Abingdon, United States	130	E2
Abnûb	100	F2
Aboisso	104	D3
Abomey	104	E3
Abong Mbang	104	G4
Abou Déia	100	C5
Abqaiq	95	C4
Abrantes	60	B5
Abrud	66	L3
Absaroka Range	126	E1
Abū al Abayḍ	95	E4
Abu Aweigîla	94	B6
Abu Ballâs	100	E3
Abu Dhabi = Abū Ẓabī	95	F4
Abu Hamed	100	F4
Abuja	104	F3
Abumombazi	106	C3
Ābune Yosēf	100	G5
Abū Nujaym	100	C1
Abū Qarin	100	C1
Aburo	106	E3
Abu Simbel	100	F3
Abut Head	116	B6
Abuye Meda	106	F1
Abū Ẓabī	95	F4
Acaponeta	124	E7
Acapulco	134	E5
Acará	140	H4
Acarigua	140	G2
Accra	104	D3
Achaguas	134	L7
Achayvayam	78	W4
Acheng	80	H1
Achenkirch	62	G3
Achen See	62	G3
Achill Island	56	B8
Achim	52	E3
Achinsk	76	S6
Achit	70	L3
Aci Göl	68	M7
A Cihanbeyli	68	Q6
Acireale	64	K11
Acklins Island	134	K4
Aconcagua	138	D7
Açores	102	(1)B2
A Coruña	60	B1
Acquarossa	62	D4
Acqui Terme	62	D6
Acre	140	C5
Acri	64	L9
Ada, United States	130	B3
Ada, Yugoslavia	50	K12
Adak Island	132	(3)C1
Adam	90	G5
Adamas	68	G8
Adams Island	116	(2)B1
'Adan	90	E7
Adana	92	F5
Adda	62	E5
Ad Dafrah	95	E5
Ad Dahnā	95	B3
Ad Dakhla	102	B4
Ad Dammām	95	D3
Ad Dawādimī	90	D5
Ad Dawḥah	95	D4
Ad Dilam	95	B5
Ad Dir'īyah	95	B4
Addis Ababa = Ādīs Ābeba	106	F2
Ad Dīwānīyah	90	D3
Adel	128	B2
Adelaide	114	G6
Adelaide Peninsula	122	M3
Adelaide River	114	F2
Aden = Adan	90	E7
Aderbissinat	104	F1
Adh Dhayd	95	F4
Adi	87	D3
Adige	62	G5
Ādīgrat	100	G5
Adilabad	88	C5
Adin	126	B2
Adīrī	100	B2
Ādīs Ābeba	106	F2
Adi Ugri	100	G5
Adiyaman	92	H5
Adjud	66	Q3
Adler	92	H2
Admiralty Island	122	E5
Admiralty Islands	112	E6
Adoni	88	C5
Adour	58	F10
Adra	60	H8
Adrano	64	J11
Adrar	102	E3
Adrar des Ifôghas	102	F5
Adrar Tamgak	102	G5
Adria	62	H5
Adriatic Sea	64	H4
Adycha	78	P3
Adygeya	92	J1
Adygeysk	92	H1
Adzopé	104	D3
Adz'vavom	70	L1
Aegean Sea	68	H5
A Estrada	60	B2
Afghanistan	90	H3
Afgooye	106	H3
'Afif	100	H3
Afikpo	104	F3
Afmadow	106	G3
Afognak Island	132	(1)G4
A Fonsagrada	60	C1
Africa	98	F5
'Afrīn	92	G5
Afuá	140	G4
'Afula	94	C4
Afyon	68	N6
Agadez	102	G5
Agadir	102	D2
Agadyr'	76	N8
Agalega Islands	98	J7
Agan	78	B4
Āgaro	106	F2
Agartala	88	F4
Agathonisi	68	J7
Agattu Island	78	W6
Ağcabädi	92	M3
Agde	58	J10
Agen	58	F9
Agia Triada	68	D7
Ağın	92	H4
Aginskoye	76	S6
Agiokampos	68	E5
Agios Efstratios	68	H5
Agios Georgios	68	F7
Agios Nikolaos	68	H9
Agnibilekrou	104	D3
Agnita	66	M4
Agra	88	C3
Agrakhanskiy Poluostrov	92	M2
Agri	64	L8
Ağrı	92	K4
Agrigento	64	H11
Agrinio	68	D6
Agropoli	64	K8
Agryz	70	K3
Ağsu	92	N3
Agua Prieta	132	E2
Aguascalientes	134	D4
A Gudiña	60	C2
Aguelhok	102	F5
Águilas	60	J7
Agulhas Negras	140	H8
Ağva	68	M3
Ahar	92	M4
Ahaura	116	C6
Ahaus	54	K2
Ahititi	116	E4
Ahlen	54	K3
Ahmadabad	88	B4
Ahmadnagar	88	B5
Ahmadpur East	88	B3
Ahr	52	B6
Ahram	95	D2
Ahrensburg	52	F3
Ahväz	90	E3
Aichach	52	G8
Aigialousa	94	F6
Aigina	68	F7
Aigina	68	F7
Aigio	68	E6
Aigosthena	68	F6
Aiguillon	58	F9
Ahui	78	M6
Aim	78	N5
Ain	58	L7
Aïn Beïda	102	G1
'Aïn Ben Tili	102	D3
Aïn Bessem	60	P8
Aïn el Hadjel	60	P9
Ain Oussera	102	F1
Ainsa	60	L2
Aïn Sefra	102	E2
Ain Taya	60	P8
Aïn-Tédélès	60	L8
Aïn Témouchent	60	J9
Airão	140	E4
Aire	56	L8
Air Force Island	36	S3
Airolo	62	D4
Airpanas	87	C4
Aisne	54	F5
Aitape	87	F3
Aitkin	128	B1
Aitutaki	112	K7
Aiud	66	L3
Aix-en-Provence	58	L10
Aix-les-Bains	58	L8
Aizawl	88	F4
Aizkraukle	48	N8
Aizpute	48	L8
Aizu-wakamatsu	82	K5
Ajaccio	64	C7
Aj Bogd Uul	80	B2
Ajdābiyā	100	D1
Ajigasawa	82	L3
Ajka	50	G10
Ajlun	94	C4
Ajmān	95	F4
Ajmer	88	B3
Ajo	132	D2
Ajtos	66	Q7
Akanthou	94	A1
Akaroa	116	D6
Akasha	100	F3
Akashi	82	H6
Akbalyk	76	P8
Akbasty	76	L8
Akçakale	92	H5
Akçakoca	68	P3
Akdağmadeni	92	F4
Aken	52	H5
Aketi	106	C3
Akhalk'alak'i	92	K3
Akhisar	68	K6
Akhmīm	100	F2
Akhty	92	M3
Akimiski Island	36	Q6
Akita	82	L4
Akjoujt	102	C5
Akka	102	D3
Akkajaure	48	J3
Akkeshi	82	N2
'Akko	94	C4
Akmeqit	90	L2
Akobo	106	E2
Akola	88	C4
Akonolinga	104	G4
Akordat	100	G4
Akpatok Island	38	T4
Akqi	76	P9
Akra Drepano	68	G5
Akranes	48	(1)B2
Akra Sounio	68	F7
Akra Spatha	68	F9
Akra Trypiti	68	G9
Åkrehamn	48	C7
Akron	128	D2
Aksaray	92	E4
Aksarka	76	M4
Akşehir	68	P6
Akseki	68	P7
Aksha	78	J6
Akshiy	76	P9
Aksu	76	Q9
Aksuat	76	Q8
Āksum	100	G5
Aktau, Kazakhstan	46	K3
Aktau, Kazakhstan	76	N7
Aktogay, Kazakhstan	76	N8
Aktogay, Kazakhstan	76	P8
Aktuma	76	M8
Aktyubinsk	70	L4
Akula	106	C3
Akulivik	122	R4
Akune	82	F8
Akure	104	F3
Akureyri	48	(1)E2
Akwanga	104	F3
Alabama	130	D3
Alaçam	92	F3
Alaejos	60	E3
Alagoas	140	K5
Alagoinhas	140	K6
Alagón	60	J3
Al Ahmadi	95	C2
Al 'Amārah	90	E3
Alaminos	84	F3
Alamo	126	C3
Alamogordo	132	E2
Alamo Lake	132	D2
Åland	48	K6
Alanya	68	E5
Alappuzha	88	C7
Al Argoub	102	B4
Al Arṭāwīyah	90	E4
Alaşehir	68	L6
Al 'Ashurīyah	100	H1
Alaska	132	(1)F2
Alaska Peninsula	132	(1)E4
Alaska Range	132	(1)G3
Alassio	62	D6
Alatri	64	H7
Alatyr'	70	J4
Alaverdı	92	L3
Alavus	48	M5
Al 'Ayn	95	F4
Alazeya	78	S2
Alba, Italy	62	D6
Alba, Spain	60	E4
Albacete	60	J5
Alba Iulia	66	L3
Albania	68	B3
Albany, Australia	114	C6
Albany, Ga., United States	130	E3
Albany, Ky., United States	130	E2
Albany, N.Y., United States	128	F2
Albany, Oreg., United States	126	B2
Albardão do João Maria	142	L4
Al Bardī	100	D1
Al Başrah	90	E3
Albatross Bay	114	H2
Albatross Point	116	E4
Al Baydā'	100	D1
Albenga	62	D6
Albert	54	E4
Alberta	32	H5
Albertirsa	50	J10
Albert Kanaal	54	G3
Albert Lea	128	B2
Albert Nile	106	E3
Albertville	58	M8
Albi	58	H10
Albina	140	G2
Albino	62	E5
Albion	126	F1
Ålborg	48	E8
Ålborg Bugt	48	F8
Albox	60	H7
Albstadt	52	E8
Albufeira	60	B7
Āl Bū Kamāl	92	J6
Albuquerque	132	E1
Al Burayj	94	D2
Al Buraymī	90	G4
Alburquerque	60	D5
Albury	114	J7
Al Buşayyah	95	B1
Alcácer do Sal	60	B6
Alcala de Guadaira	60	E7
Alcala de Henares	60	G4
Alcalá la Real	60	G7
Alcamo	64	G11
Alcañiz	60	K3
Alcantarilla	60	J7
Alcaraz	60	H6
Alcaudete	60	F7
Alcazar de San Juan	60	G5
Alcobendas	60	G4
Alcoi	60	K6
Alcolea del Pinar	60	H3
Alcorcón	60	G4
Alcoutim	60	C7
Aldabra Islands	108	(2)A2
Aldan	78	M5
Aldan	78	N5
Aldeburgh	54	D2
Alderney	58	C4
Aldershot	54	B3
Aleg	102	C5
Aleksandrov-Sakhalinskiy	78	Q6
Aleksandrovskiy Zavod	78	K6
Aleksandrovskoye	70	Q2
Alekseyevka	76	N7
Aleksinac	66	J6
Alençon	58	F5
Aleppo = Ḥalab	92	G5
Aléria	64	D6
Alès	58	K9
Aleşd	50	M10
Alessandria	62	D6
Ålesund	48	D5
Aleutian Islands	132	(3)B1
Aleutian Range	132	(1)F4
Aleutian Trench	74	W5
Alexander Archipelago	132	(1)K4
Alexander Bay	108	B5
Alexander City	130	D3
Alexandra	116	B7
Alexandreia	68	E4
Alexandria = El Iskandarîya, Egypt	100	E1
Alexandria, Romania	66	N6
Alexandria, La., United States	130	C3
Alexandria, Minn., United States	128	A1
Alexandria, Va., United States	128	E3
Alexandroupoli	68	H4
Alexis Creek	122	G6
'Aley	94	C3
Aley	76	Q7
Aleysk	76	Q7
Al Farwāniyah	95	B2
Al Fāw	95	C2
Alfeld	52	E5
Alföld	66	H2
Alfonsine	62	H6
Alfreton	54	A1
Al Fuḥayfil	95	C2
Al-Fujayrah	95	G4
Algeciras	60	E8
Algemes	60	K5
Algena	100	G4
Alger	102	F1
Algeria	102	E3
Al Ghāt	95	A3
Al Ghaydah	90	F6
Alghero	64	C8
Algiers = Alger	102	F1
Algona	128	B2
Al Hadīthah	94	E5
Alhama de Murcia	60	J7
Al Ḥamar	95	B5
Al Ḥamīdīyah	94	C2
Al Ḥammādah al Ḥamrā'	102	G3
Al Harūj al Aswad	100	C2
Al Ḥasakah	92	J5
Alhaurmín el Grande	60	F8
Al Ḥijāz	100	G3
Al Ḥillah	90	D3
Al Ḥilwah	95	B5
Al Hoceima	102	E5
Al Ḥudaydah	100	H5
Al Hufūf	95	C4
Al Ḥumaydah	90	C4
Aliabad	95	F2
Aliağa	68	J6
Aliakmonas	68	E4
Äli Bayramlı	92	N4
Alicante	60	K6
Alice	130	B4
Alice Springs	114	F4
Alicudi	64	J10
Aligarh	88	C3
Alindao	106	C2
Alingås	48	G8
Alisos	132	D6
Aliwal North	108	D6
Al Jabal al Akhḍar	100	D1
Al Jaghbūb	100	D2
Al Jālamīd	100	G1

Al Jarah 95 B2
Al Jawf, *Libya* 100 D3
Al Jawf, *Saudi Arabia* 100 G2
Aljezur 60 B7
Al Jifārah 95 A5
Al Jubayl 95 C3
Aljustrel 60 B7
Al Kāmil 90 G5
Al Khābūrah 95 G5
Al Khālis 92 L7
Al Kharj 95 B4
Al Khaşab 95 G3
Al Khawr 95 D4
Al Khubar 95 D3
Al Khufrah 100 D3
Al Khums 102 H2
Al Khuwayr 95 D3
Al Kir'ānah 95 D4
Alkmaar 54 G2
Al Kūt 90 E3
Al Kuwayt 95 C2
Al Lādhiqīyah 92 F6
Allahabad 88 D3
Allakh-Yun' 78 P4
Alldays 108 D4
Allen 84 G4
Allendale 130 E3
Allentown 128 E2
Aller 52 E4
Aller = Cabañaquinta 60 E1
Alliance 126 F2
Allier 58 J8
Allinge 50 D2
Al Lith 100 H3
Alma, *Canada* 128 F1
Alma, *Nebr., United States* 126 G2
Alma, *Wis., United States* 128 B2
Almada 60 A6
Almadén 60 F6
Al Madīnah 100 G3
Al Mahbas 102 D3
Al Majma'ah 90 E4
Almalyk 76 M9
Al Manāmah 95 D3
Almansa 60 J6
Al Ma'qil 95 B1
Al Marj 100 D1
Almaty 76 P9
Al Mawşil 92 K5
Al Mazāḥimīyah 95 B4
Almazán 60 H3
Almeirim 140 G4
Almelo 54 J2
Almendralejo 60 D6
Almería 60 H8
Al'met'yevsk 76 J7
Almiros 68 E5
Al Mish'āb 95 C2
Almonte 60 D7
Almora 88 C3
Almosa 126 E3
Al Mubarraz 95 C4
Al Mudawwara 94 D7
Al Mukallā 90 E7
Al Mukhā 100 H5
Almuñécar 60 G8
Al Muqdādīyah 92 L7
Al Nu'ayrīyah 95 C3
Alnwick 56 L6
Alonnisos 68 F5
Alor 87 B4
Alor Setar 84 C5
Alotau 114 K2
Alpena 128 D1
Alphen 54 G2
Alpi Lepontine 62 D4
Alpine 132 E2
Alpi Orobie 62 E4
Alps 62 B5
Al Qadmūs 94 D1
Al Qalībah 100 G2
Al Qāmishlī 92 J5
Al Qar'ah 95 B3
Al Qarqar 94 E5
Al Qaryāt 100 B1
Al Qaryatayn 94 E2
Al Qaţīf 95 C3
Al Qaţrūn 100 B3
Al Qunayţirah 94 C3
Al Qunfudhah 100 H4
Al Qurayyāt 100 G1
Al Qurnah 95 B1
Al 'Quşayr, *Iraq* 95 A1
Al 'Quşayr, *Syria* 94 D2
Al Quţayfah 94 D3
Als 52 E1
Alsask 122 K6
Alsasua 60 H2
Alsfeld 52 E6
Alta 48 M2
Altaelva 48 M2
Altai Mountains 80 A1
Al Tamīnī 100 D1
Altamira 140 G4
Altamura 64 L8
Altanbulag 78 H6
Altay 76 R7
Altay, *China* 76 R8
Altay, *Mongolia* 80 B1
Altdorf 62 D4
Alte Mellum 52 D3
Altenberg 52 J6
Altenburg 52 H6
Altenkirchen 52 J2
Altkirch 62 C3
Alto Garças 140 G7
Alto Molócuè 108 F3
Alton, *United Kingdom* 54 B3
Alton, *United States* 128 B3
Altoona 128 E2
Alto Parnaíba 140 H5
Altötting 62 H2
Altun Shan 76 S10
Alturas 126 B2
Altus 130 B3
Al 'Ubaylah 90 F5
Alūksne 48 P8
Alupka 92 E1
Al 'Uqaylah 100 C1
Alushta 92 F1
Al 'Uthmānīyah 95 C4
Al 'Uwaynāt, *Libya* 100 B2
Al 'Uwaynāt, *Libya* 100 D3
Al 'Uwayqīlah 100 H1
Al 'Uzayr 95 B1
Alva 130 B2
Alvarães 140 E4
Älvdalen 48 H6
Älvsbyn 48 L4
Al Wafrā' 95 B2
Al Wajh 100 G2
Al Wannān 95 C3
Alwar 88 C3
Al Wari'ah 95 B3
Alxa Zouqi 80 D3
Alytus 50 P3
Alzey 52 D7
Alzira 60 K5
Amadi 106 E2
Amādīyah 92 K5
Amadjuak Lake 36 S4
Amadora 60 A6
Amahai 87 C3
Amakusa-Shimo-shima 82 E7
Amaliada 68 D7
Amalner 88 C4
Amamapare 87 E3
Amambaí 142 K3
Amami-Ōshima 74 S7
Amanab 87 F3
Amandola 64 H6
Amantea 64 L9
Amapá 140 G3
Amapá 140 G3
Amarante 140 J5
Amarapura 84 B2
Amareleja 60 C6
Amarillo 132 F1
Amasya 92 F3
Amay 54 H4
Amazar 78 L6
Amazon = Amazonas 138 F4
Amazonas 140 D4
Amazonas 140 E4
Ambala 88 C2
Ambanjā 108 H2
Ambarchik 78 U3
Ambato 140 B4
Ambato Boeny 108 H3
Ambatondrazaka 108 H3
Amberg 52 G7
Ambikapur 88 D4
Ambilobe 108 H2
Ambohimahasoa 108 H4
Amboise 58 G6
Ambon 87 C3
Ambositra 108 H4
Ambovombe 108 H5
Amchitka Island 132 (3)B1
Amderma 76 L4
Amdo 88 F2
Ameland 54 H1
Amengel'dy 76 M7
American Falls 126 D2
American Samoa 112 J7
Americus 130 E3
Amersfoort 54 H2
Amery 122 N5
Amery Ice Shelf 144 (2)M2
Ames 128 B2
Amfilochia 68 D6
Amfissa 68 E6
Amga 78 L5
Amga 78 N4
Amguid 102 G3
Amgun' 78 P6
Amherst 122 U7
Amiens 54 E5
Amirante Islands 108 (2)B2
Amistad Reservoir 132 F3
Amlekhganj 88 D3
Åmli 48 E7
'Amm Adam 100 G4
'Ammān 94 C5
Ammassalik 32 Z3
Ammerland 54 K1
Ammersee 62 F2
Ammochostos 92 E6
Ammochostos Bay 94 A1
Amo 84 C2
Amol 90 F2
Amorgos 68 H8
Amos 128 E1
Amourj 102 D5
Ampana 87 B3
Ampanihy 108 G4
Amparai 88 D7
Ampezzo 62 H4
Amposta 60 L4
Amrān 90 D6
Amravati 88 C4
Amritsar 88 B2
Amroha 88 C3
Amrum 52 D2
Amsterdam, *Netherlands* 54 G2
Amsterdam, *United States* 128 F2
Amstetten 62 K2
Am Timan 100 D5
Amudar'ya 76 L9
Amundsen Gulf 32 G2
Amundsen Sea 144 (2)GG3
Amungen 48 H6
Amuntai 86 F3
Amur 78 P6
Amursk 78 P6
Amvrakikos Kolpos 68 C6
Anabanua 87 B3
Anabar 78 J2
Anaconda 126 D1
Anacortes 126 B1
Anadarko 126 G3
Anadolu Dağları 92 H3
Anadyr' 78 X4
Anadyrskaya Nizmennost' 78 X3
Anadyrskiy Zaliv 78 Y3
Anafi 68 H8
'Ānah 92 J6
Anaheim 132 C2
Anáhuac 132 F3
Analalava 108 H2
Anamur 92 E5
Anan 82 H7
Anantapur 88 C6
Anan'yiv 66 T2
Anapa 92 G1
Anápolis 140 H7
Anār 95 F1
Anārak 90 F3
Anardara 90 H3
Anatolia 68 M6
Añatuya 142 J4
Anchorage 132 (1)H3
Ancona 64 H5
Ancud 142 G7
Anda 80 H1
Andalgalá 142 H4
Åndalsnes 48 D5
Andalusia 130 D3
Andaman Islands 84 A4
Andaman Sea 84 A4
Andapa 108 H2
Andarāb 90 J2
Andenne 54 H4
Andéramboukane 104 E1
Andermatt 62 D4
Andernach 54 K4
Anderson 122 F3
Anderson 130 E3
Andes 138 D5
Andfjorden 48 J2
Andilamena 108 H3
Andipsara 68 H6
Andizhan 76 N9
Andkhvoy 90 J2
Andoas 140 B4
Andong 82 E5
Andorra 60 L2
Andorra la Vella 60 M2
Andover 54 A3
Andøya 48 H2
Andradina 142 L3
Andreanof Islands 132 (3)C1
Andrews 132 F2
Andria 64 L7
Andriamena 108 H3
Andros 68 G7
Andros, *Greece* 68 G7
Andros, *The Bahamas* 130 F5
Andros Town 130 F5
Andrott 88 B6
Andrychów 50 J8
Andūjar 60 F6
Andulo 108 B2
Aneto 60 L2
Angara 78 G5
Angarsk 78 G6
Ånge 48 H5
Angel de la Guarda 132 D3
Angeles 84 G3
Ängelholm 48 G8
Angeln 52 E2
Angermünde 52 K4
Angern 62 M2
Angers 58 E6
Anglesey 56 H8
Angmagssalik = Ammassalik 32 Z3
Ango 106 D3
Angoche 108 F3
Angohrān 95 G3
Angol 142 G6
Angola 98 E7
Angola 128 D2
Angostura Reservoir 126 F2
Angoulême 58 F8
Angren 76 M9
Anguilla 134 M5
Aniak 132 (1)F3
Anina 66 J4
Ankang 80 D4
Ankara 92 E4
Ankazoabo 108 G4
Anklam 52 J3
Ankpa 104 F3
Ånn 48 G5
Anna 70 H4
Annaba 102 G1
Annaberg-Buchholz 52 H6
An Nabk, *Saudi Arabia* 94 E5
An Nabk, *Syria* 94 D2
An Nafud 100 G2
An Nāirīyah 90 E3
An Najaf 90 D3
Annapolis 128 E3
Annapurna 88 D3
Ann Arbor 128 D2
An Nāşirīyah 100 J1
Annecy 62 B5
Annemasse 62 B4
Anniston 130 D3
Annobón 104 F5
Annonay 58 K8
An Nukhayb 90 D3
Anqing 80 F4
Ansbach 52 F7
Anshan 82 B3
Anshun 80 D5
Ansley 126 G2
Anson 130 B3
Ansongo 102 F5
Antakya 92 G5
Antalaha 108 J2
Antalya 68 N8
Antalya Körfezi 68 N8
Antananarivo 108 H3
Antarctic Peninsula 144 (2)LL3
Antequera 60 F7
Anti-Atlas 102 D3
Antibes 62 C7
Antigo 128 C1
Antigua 134 M5
Antigua and Barbuda 134 M5
Antikythira 68 F9
Antiparos 68 G7
Antipaxoi 68 C5
Antipayuta 76 P4
Antipodes Islands 116 (3)A1
Antlers 130 B3
Antofagasta 142 G3
Antonito 126 E3
Antrim 56 F7
Antropovo 70 H3
Antsalova 108 G3
Antsirabe 108 H3
Antsirañana 108 H2
Antu 82 E2
Antwerp = Antwerpen 54 G3
Antwerpen 54 G3
Anuradhapura 88 D7
Anveh 95 F3
Anxi 80 B2
Anyang, *China* 80 E3
Anyang, *South Korea* 82 D5
Anyuysk 78 U3
Anzhero-Sudzhensk 76 R6
Anzi 106 C4
Anzio 64 G7
Aoga-shima 82 K7
Aomori 82 L3
Aosta 62 C5
Aoukâr 102 C5
Aoukoukar 104 C1
Apalachee Bay 130 E4
Apalachicola 130 D4
Aparri 84 G3
Apatin 66 F4
Apatity 70 F1
Ape 48 P8
Apeldoorn 54 H2
Api 88 D2
Apia 112 J7
Apoera 140 F2
Apolda 52 G5
Apollo Bay 114 H7
Aporé 140 G7
Apostle Islands 128 B1
Apoteri 140 F3
Appalachian Mountains 130 E3
Appennino 64 G5
Appennino Abruzzese 64 H6
Appennino Calabro 64 K10
Appennino Lucano 64 K8
Appennino Tosco-Emiliano 62 E6
Appennino Umbro-Marchigiano 64 H6
Appleton 128 C2
Aprilia 64 G7
Apure 140 D2
Apurímac 140 C6
Āqā 90 H3
'Aqaba 94 C7
Aquidauana 140 F8
Ara 88 D3
Arabian Sea 90 H6
Aracaju 140 K6
Aracati 140 K4
Araçatuba 140 G8
Aracuca 134 L7
Arad 66 J3
Arādah 90 F5
Arafura Sea 87 D5
Aragarças 140 G7
Araguaia 138 F4
Araguaína 140 H5
Araguari 140 H7
Araguatins 140 H5
Arāk 90 E3
Arak 102 F3
Aral Sea 76 K8
Aral'sk 70 M5
Aranda de Duero 60 G3
Aranđjelovac 66 H5
Aran Island 56 D6
Aran Islands 56 B8
Aranjuez 60 G4
Aranos 108 B4
Aranyaprathet 84 C4
Araouane 102 E5
Arapahoe 126 G2
Arapiraca 140 K5
'Ar'ar 90 D3
Araras 140 G5
Ararat 92 L4
Arauca 140 D2
Araxá 140 H7
Araz 92 L4
Arbīl 92 K5
Arbon 62 E3
Arbre du Ténéré 102 G5
Arbroath 56 K5
Arcachon 58 D9
Arcadia 130 E4
Arcata 126 B2
Archidona 60 F7
Archipelago of the Recherche 114 D6
Archipel de la Société 112 L7
Archipel des Tuamotu 112 M7
Archipiélago de Camagüey 134 J4
Archipiélago de la Reina Adelaida 142 F9
Archipiélago de los Chonos 142 F7

181

Bad Sobernheim	◙	54	K5
Bad Urach	◙	62	E2
Bad Vöslau	◙	66	D2
Bad Waldsee	◙	62	E3
Bad Wilbad	◙	62	D2
Bad Wildungen	◙	52	E5
Bad Windsheim	◙	52	F7
Bad Wurzach	◙	62	E3
Baena	◙	60	F7
Bærum	◙	48	F7
Baeza	◙	60	G6
Baffin Bay	≈	32	U2
Baffin Island	▨	36	R2
Bafia	◙	104	G4
Bafoulabé	◙	104	B2
Bafoussam	◙	104	G3
Bāfq	◙	90	G3
Bafra	◙	92	F3
Bafra Burun	⊿	92	G3
Bāft	◙	95	G2
Bafwasende	◙	106	D3
Baga	◙	100	B5
Bagani	◙	108	C3
Bagansiapiapi	◙	86	C2
Bagaroua	◙	104	E2
Bagdad	◙	132	D2
Bagdarin	◙	78	J6
Bagé	◙	142	L5
Baggs	◙	126	E2
Baghdād	■	90	D3
Bagheria	◙	64	H10
Baghlān	◙	90	J2
Bagnères-de-Bigorre	◙	58	F10
Bagno di Romagna	◙	62	G7
Bagnols-sur-Cèze	◙	58	K9
Bago	◙	84	G4
Baguio	◙	84	G3
Bagun Datuk	◙	86	C2
Baharampur	◙	88	E4
Bahawalnagar	◙	88	B3
Bahawalpur	◙	88	B3
Bahçe	◙	92	G5
Bahia	ⓐ	140	J6
Bahía Blanca	◙	142	J6
Bahía Blanca	≈	142	J6
Bahía de Banderas	≈	134	C4
Bahía de Campeche	≈	134	F4
Bahía de Manta	≈	140	A4
Bahía de Petacalco	▩	134	D5
Bahía de Pisco	≈	140	B6
Bahía de Santa Elena	≈	140	A4
Bahía de Sechura	≈	140	A5
Bahía Grande	≈	142	H9
Bahía Kino	◙	124	D6
Bahía Negra	◙	142	K3
Bahía Samborombón	≈	142	K6
Bahir Dar	◙	100	G5
Bahraich	◙	88	D3
Bahrain	Ⓐ	95	D4
Baḩrat Ḩimş	◩	94	D2
Bahr el Abiad	⧄	100	F5
Bahr el Azraq	⧄	100	F5
Bahr el Ghazal	▩	100	C5
Bahr el Ghazal	⧄	106	D2
Bahr el Jebel	⧄	106	E2
Bahr el Nîl = Nile	⧄	100	F4
Baia	◙	66	R5
Baía de Marajó	≈	140	H4
Baía de Todos os Santos	≈	140	K6
Baía do Bengo	≈	104	G6
Baia Mare	◙	66	L2
Baião	◙	140	H4
Baia Sprie	◙	66	L2
Baïbokoum	◙	106	B2
Baicheng, *China*	◙	76	Q9
Baicheng, *China*	◙	80	G1
Baie Comeau	◙	128	G1
Baie de la Seine	≈	54	B5
Baie de la Somme	≈	54	D4
Baie des Chaleurs	≈	38	T7
Baie-du-Poste	◙	122	S6
Baie St. Paul	◙	128	F1
Baiji	◙	92	K6
Baile Átha Cliath = Dublin	■	56	F8
Bailén	◙	60	G6
Bailleul	◙	54	E4
Bailundo	◙	108	B2
Bainbridge	◙	130	E3
Bairiki	■	112	H5
Bairin Youqi	◙	80	F2
Bairin Zuoqi	◙	80	F2
Bairnsdale	◙	114	J7
Bais	◙	84	G5
Baja	◙	66	F3
Baja California	⛰	124	C5
Bajram Curri	◙	68	B2
Bakchar	◙	76	Q6
Bakel	◙	104	B2
Baker	▨	112	J5
Baker, *Calif., United States*	◙	126	C3
Baker, *Mont., United States*	◙	126	F1
Baker, *Oreg., United States*	◙	126	C2
Baker Lake	◙	36	M4
Baker Lake	◩	36	N4
Bakersfield	◙	132	C1
Bakharden	◙	76	K10
Bakhta	◙	78	D4
Baki	■	90	E1
Bakkafjörður	◙	48	(1)F1
Bakkaflói	≈	48	(1)F1
Baku = Baki	■	90	E1
Balâ	◙	92	E4
Balabac	◙	84	F5
Balabac	▨	84	F5
Balabac Strait	≈	84	F5
Balagansk	◙	78	G6
Balaghat	◙	88	D4
Balaguer	◙	60	L3
Balakhta	◙	76	S6
Balaklava	◙	92	E1
Balakovo	◙	70	J4
Bālā Morghāb	◙	76	L10
Bălan	◙	66	N3
Balängir	◙	88	D4
Balashov	◙	70	H4
Balassagyarmat	◙	66	G1
Balaton	◩	66	E3
Balatonfüred	◙	66	E3
Balatonlelle	◙	66	E3
Balbina	◙	140	F4
Balčik	◙	92	C2
Balclutha	◙	116	B8
Bald Knob	◙	128	B3
Baldwin	◙	130	E3
Balearic Islands = Islas Baleares	▨	60	N5
Baler	◙	84	G3
Bāleshwar	◙	88	E4
Baley	◙	78	K6
Baléyara	◙	104	E2
Balguntay	◙	76	R9
Bali	▨	86	F4
Balige	◙	86	B2
Balıkesir	◙	68	K5
Balikpapan	◙	86	F3
Balimo	◙	87	F4
Balingen	◙	62	D2
Balintang Channel	≈	84	G3
Balkhash	◙	76	N8
Balladonia	◙	114	D6
Ballarat	◙	114	H7
Balleny Island	▨	144	(2)Y3
Ballina, *Australia*	◙	114	K5
Ballina, *Republic of Ireland*	◙	56	C7
Ballinasloe	◙	56	D8
Ballinger	◙	132	G2
Ball's Pyramid	▨	114	L6
Ballum	◙	54	H1
Ballymena	◙	56	F7
Balmazújváros	◙	66	J2
Balotra	◙	88	B3
Balranald	◙	114	H6
Balş	◙	66	M5
Balsas	⧄	134	D5
Balsas	◙	140	H5
Balta	◙	66	S2
Bălţi	◙	66	Q2
Baltic Sea	▄	48	J8
Baltimore	◙	128	E3
Baltiysk	◙	50	J3
Balvi	◙	48	P8
Balykchy	◙	76	P9
Balykshi	◙	70	K5
Bam	◙	90	G4
Bamaga	◙	114	H2
Bamako	■	104	C2
Bamba	◙	102	E5
Bambari	◙	106	C2
Bamberg	◙	52	F7
Bambesa	◙	106	D3
Bambouk	▩	102	C6
Bambouk Kaarta	▩	104	B2
Bamda	◙	80	B4
Bamenda	◙	104	G3
Bāmīān	◙	90	J3
Banaba	▨	112	G6
Bañados del Izozog	▩	140	E7
Banalia	◙	106	D3
Banana, *Australia*	◙	114	K4
Banana, *Dem. Rep. of Congo*	◙	106	A5
Banaz	◙	68	M6
Ban Ban	◙	84	C3
Ban Betong	◙	86	C1
Banbury	◙	56	L9
Banda	◙	88	D3
Banda Aceh	◙	84	B5
Bandama	⧄	104	C3
Bandarbeyla	◙	106	J2
Bandar-e 'Abbās	◙	95	G3
Bandar-e Anzalī	◙	90	E2
Bandar-e Deylam	◙	95	D1
Bandar-e Ganāveh	◙	95	D2
Bandar-e Khoemir	◙	95	F3
Bandar-e Lengeh	◙	95	F3
Bandar-e Ma'shur	◙	95	C1
Bandar-e Torkeman	◙	90	F2
Bandar Khomeynī	◙	95	C1
Bandar Seri Begawan	■	86	E2
Banda Sea	▄	87	C3
Band-e Chārak	◙	95	F3
Band-e Moghūyeh	◙	95	F3
Bandirma	◙	68	K4
Bandundu	◙	106	B4
Bandung	◙	86	D4
Băneasa	◙	66	Q5
Bāneh	◙	92	L6
Banff, *Canada*	◙	34	H6
Banff, *United Kingdom*	◙	56	K4
Bangalore	◙	88	C6
Bangangté	◙	104	G3
Bangassou	◙	106	C3
Bangbong	◙	87	B3
Banggi	▨	86	F1
Banghāzī	◙	100	D1
Bangka	▨	86	D3
Bangkalan	◙	86	E4
Bangkok = Krung Thep	■	84	C4
Bangladesh	Ⓐ	88	E4
Bangor, *N. Ire., United Kingdom*	◙	56	G7
Bangor, *Wales, United Kingdom*	◙	56	H8
Bangor, *United States*	◙	128	G2
Bang Saphan Yai	◙	84	B4
Bangued	◙	84	G3
Bangui, *Central African Republic*	■	106	B3
Bangui, *Philippines*	◙	84	G3
Ban Hua Hin	◙	84	B4
Bani-Bangou	◙	104	E1
Banī Walīd	◙	102	H2
Bāniyās	◙	92	F6
Banja Luka	◙	66	E5
Banjarmasin	◙	86	E3
Banjul	■	104	A2
Ban Khemmarat	◙	84	D3
Banks Island = Moa, *Australia*	▨	114	H2
Banks Island, *B.C., Canada*	▨	122	E6
Banks Island, *N.W.T., Canada*	▨	36	G2
Banks Lake	◩	126	C1
Banks Peninsula	▩	116	D6
Banks Strait	≈	114	J8
Bannerman Town	◙	130	F5
Bannu	◙	88	B2
Bánovce	◙	50	H9
Banská Bystrica	◙	50	J9
Banská Štiavnica	◙	50	H9
Bansko	◙	68	F3
Bantry	◙	56	C10
Banyo	◙	104	G3
Banyoles	◙	60	N2
Banyuwangi	◙	86	E4
Baode	◙	80	E3
Baoding	◙	80	F3
Baoji	◙	80	D4
Bao Lôc	◙	84	D4
Baoro	◙	106	B2
Baoshan	◙	84	B1
Baotou	◙	80	E2
Baoying	◙	80	F4
Bap	◙	88	B3
Bapaume	◙	54	E4
Ba'qūbah	◙	90	D3
Baquedano	◙	142	H3
Bar	◙	66	G7
Barabai	◙	86	F3
Baraboo	◙	128	C2
Barakaldo	◙	60	H1
Baramati	◙	88	B5
Baramula	◙	88	B2
Baran	◙	88	C3
Baranavichy	◙	70	E4
Baranof Island	▨	34	D5
Baraolt	◙	66	N3
Barbados	Ⓐ	140	F1
Barbastro	◙	60	L2
Barbate	◙	60	E8
Barbuda	▨	134	M5
Barcaldine	◙	114	J4
Barcău	⧄	66	K2
Barcellona Pozzo di Gotto	◙	64	K10
Barcelona, *Spain*	◙	60	N3
Barcelona, *Venezuela*	◙	134	M6
Barcelos, *Brazil*	◙	140	E4
Barcelos, *Spain*	◙	60	B3
Barclayville	◙	104	C4
Barco de Valdeorras = O Barco	◙	60	D2
Barcs	◙	66	E4
Bārdā	◙	92	M3
Bardai	◙	100	C3
Barddhamān	◙	88	E4
Bardejov	◙	50	L8
Bardonecchia	◙	62	B5
Bareilly	◙	88	C3
Barentin	◙	54	C5
Barents Sea	▄	76	E3
Barentu	◙	100	G4
Bareo	◙	86	F2
Barga	◙	88	D2
Bargaal	◙	106	J1
Bargteheide	◙	52	F3
Barguzin	◙	78	H6
Bar Harbor	◙	128	G2
Bari	◙	64	L7
Barikot	◙	88	B1
Barinas	◙	140	C2
Bârîs	◙	100	F3
Barisal	◙	88	F4
Barito	⧄	87	A3
Barkam	◙	80	C4
Barkava	◙	48	P8
Barkly Tableland	▩	114	F3
Barkol	◙	76	S9
Bârlad	◙	66	Q3
Bârlad	⧄	66	Q3
Bar-le-Duc	◙	54	H6
Barletta	◙	64	L7
Barmer	◙	88	B3
Barmouth Bay	≈	56	H9
Barnaul	◙	76	Q7
Barnsley	◙	56	L8
Barnstaple	◙	56	H10
Barnstaple Bay	≈	56	H10
Barpeta	◙	88	F3
Barquisimeto	◙	140	D1
Barr	◙	62	C2
Barra, *Brazil*	◙	140	J6
Barra, *United Kingdom*	▨	56	E4
Barracão do Barreto	◙	140	G5
Barracas	◙	60	K5
Barra do Bugres	◙	140	F7
Barra do Corda	◙	140	H5
Barra do Cuanza	◙	106	A5
Barra do Garças	◙	140	G7
Barra do São Manuel	◙	140	G5
Barragem de Santa Clara	◩	60	B7
Barragem de Sobradinho	◩	140	J5
Barragem do Castelo de Bode	◩	60	B5
Barragem do Maranhão	◩	60	C6
Barranca, *Peru*	◙	140	B4
Barranca, *Peru*	◙	140	B6
Barranquilla	◙	134	K6
Barreiras	◙	140	H6
Barreiro	◙	60	A6
Barretos	◙	140	H8
Barrie	◙	128	E2
Barron	◙	128	B1
Barrow	◙	132	(1)F1
Barrow Creek	◙	114	F4
Barrow-in-Furness	◙	56	J7
Barrow Island	▨	114	B4
Barrow Strait	≈	122	N2
Barshatas	◙	76	P8
Barsi	◙	88	C5
Barstow	◙	132	C2
Bar-sur-Aube	◙	58	K5
Bar-sur-Seine	◙	58	K5
Barth	◙	52	H2
Bartın	◙	92	E3
Bartle Frere	▲	112	E7
Bartlesville	◙	130	B2
Bartlett	◙	126	G2
Bartoszyce	◙	50	K3
Barus	◙	86	B2
Baruun Urt	◙	80	E1
Barwani	◙	88	B4
Barysaw	◙	70	E4
Basaidu	◙	95	F3
Basankusu	◙	106	B3
Basarabeasca	◙	66	R3
Basarabi	◙	66	R5
Basca	◙	64	C2
Basco	◙	84	G2
Basel	◙	62	C3
Bashkiriya	ⓐ	70	K4
Bāsht	◙	95	D1
Basilan	▨	87	B1
Basildon	◙	54	C3
Basiluzzo	▨	64	K10
Basingstoke	◙	56	L10
Başkale	◙	92	K4
Basoko	◙	106	C3
Bassano	◙	124	D1
Bassano del Grappa	◙	62	G5
Bassar	◙	104	E3
Bassas da India	▨	108	F4
Bassein	◙	84	A3
Basse Santa Su	◙	102	C6
Basse-Terre	◙	134	M5
Bassett	◙	126	G2
Bassikounou	◙	102	D5
Bass Strait	≈	114	H7
Bassum	◙	52	D4
Bastak	◙	95	F3
Bastānābād	◙	92	M5
Basti	◙	88	D3
Bastia	◙	64	D6
Bastogne	◙	54	H4
Bastrop, *La., United States*	◙	130	C3
Bastrop, *Tex., United States*	◙	130	B3
Bata	◙	104	F4
Batagay	◙	78	N3
Batagay-Alyta	◙	78	N3
Batak	◙	68	G3
Batamay	◙	78	M4
Batang	◙	80	B5
Batangas	◙	84	G4
Batan Islands	▨	84	G2
Batanta	▨	87	C3
Batchelor	◙	114	F2
Batemans Bay	◙	114	K7
Batesville	◙	130	D3
Bath, *United Kingdom*	◙	56	K10
Bath, *United States*	◙	128	E2
Bathinda	◙	88	B2
Bathurst, *Australia*	◙	114	J6
Bathurst, *Canada*	◙	38	T7
Bathurst Inlet	◙	36	K3
Bathurst Island, *Australia*	▨	114	E2
Bathurst Island, *Canada*	▨	36	M1
Batman	◙	90	D2
Batna	◙	102	G1
Baton Rouge	⧈	130	C3
Bátonyterenye	◙	66	G2
Batouri	◙	104	G4
Batroûn	◙	94	C2
Batticaloa	◙	88	D7
Battipaglia	◙	64	J8
Battle	⧄	122	J6
Battle Creek	◙	128	C2
Battle Harbour	◙	122	V6
Battle Mountain	◙	126	C2
Batu	▲	106	F2
Batui	◙	87	B3
Bat'umi	◙	92	J3
Batu Pahat	◙	86	C2
Baturino	◙	76	R6
Baubau	◙	87	B4
Bauchi	◙	104	F2
Baudette	◙	128	B1
Baukau	◙	87	C4
Baume-les-Dames	◙	58	M6
Bauru	◙	142	M3
Bauska	◙	48	N8
Bautzen	◙	50	D6
Bawean	▨	86	E4
Bawiti	◙	100	E2
Bawku	◙	104	D2
Bayamo	◙	134	J4
Bayanaul	◙	76	P7
Bayandelger	◙	78	H7
Bayan Har Shan	⛰	80	B4
Bayanhongor	◙	80	C1
Bayan Mod	◙	80	C2
Bayan Obo	◙	80	D2
Bayansumküre	◙	76	Q9
Bayburt	◙	92	J3
Bay City, *Mich., United States*	◙	128	D2
Bay City, *Tex., United States*	◙	130	B4
Baydhabo	◙	106	G3
Bayerische Alpen	⛰	62	G3
Bayeux	◙	54	B5
Bayfield	◙	128	B1
Bayindir	◙	68	K6
Bāyir	◙	94	D6
Baykit	◙	76	T5
Baykonur	◙	76	M8
Bay Minette	◙	130	D3
Bay of Bengal	≈	88	E5
Bay of Biscay	≈	58	C9
Bay of Fundy	≈	38	T8
Bay of Islands	≈	116	E2
Bay of Plenty	≈	116	F3
Bayonne	◙	58	D10
Bayramaly	◙	90	H2
Bayramiç	◙	68	J5
Bayreuth	◙	52	G7
Baysun	◙	90	J2
Bayt al Faqīh	◙	100	H5
Bay View	◙	116	F4
Baza	◙	60	H7
Bazas	◙	58	E9

Blanco	140	E6
Blanding	132	E1
Blangy-sur-Bresle	54	D5
Blankenberge	54	F3
Blankenburg	52	F5
Blankenheim	54	J4
Blantyre	108	F3
Blasket Islands	56	B9
Blaubeuren	62	E2
Blaye-et-Sainte-Luce	58	E8
Bled	62	K4
Blenheim	116	D5
Blevands Huk	52	D1
Blida	102	F1
Blind River	124	K2
Bloemfontein	108	D5
Bloemhof	108	D5
Blois	58	G6
Blönduós	48	(1)C2
Błonie	50	K5
Bloomfield	130	D2
Bloomington, *Ill., United States*	128	C2
Bloomington, *Ind., United States*	128	C3
Bludenz	62	E3
Blue Earth	128	B2
Bluefield	128	D3
Bluefields	134	H6
Blue Mountain Lake	128	F2
Blue Mountains	126	C2
Blue Nile = Bahr el Azraq	100	F5
Bluenose Lake	122	H3
Bluff, *New Zealand*	116	B8
Bluff, *United States*	132	E1
Blumenau	142	M4
Blythe	132	D2
Blytheville	130	D2
Bo	104	B3
Boac	84	G4
Boa Vista, *Brazil*	140	E3
Boa Vista, *Cape Verde*	104	(1)B1
Bobbili	88	D5
Bobbio	62	E6
Bobigny	54	E6
Bobingen	62	F2
Böblingen	62	E2
Bobo-Dioulasso	104	D2
Bobolice	50	F4
Bobr	50	E6
Bobrov	70	H4
Bôca do Acre	140	D5
Boca Grande	134	M7
Boca Grande	138	E3
Bocaiúva	140	J7
Bocaranga	106	B2
Bochart	128	F1
Bochnia	50	K8
Bocholt	52	B5
Bochum	52	C5
Bockenem	52	F4
Bodaybo	78	J5
Bode	52	G4
Bodélé	100	C4
Boden	48	L4
Bodham	88	C5
Bodmin	56	H11
Bodø	48	H3
Bodrog	50	L9
Bodrum	68	K7
Boende	106	C4
Boffa	104	B2
Bogale	84	B3
Bogalusa	130	D3
Boggabilla	114	K5
Boghni	60	P8
Bognor Regis	54	B4
Bogo	84	G4
Bogor	86	D4
Bogorodskoye	78	Q6
Bogotá	140	C3
Bogotol	76	R6
Bogra	88	E4
Boguchany	78	F5
Bogué	102	C5
Bo Hai	80	F3
Bohmerwald	52	H7
Bohol	84	G5
Bohumin	50	H8
Boiaçu	140	E4
Boise	126	C2
Boise City	132	F1
Bojnūrd	76	K10
Bokatola	106	B4
Boké	104	B2
Bokoro	104	H2
Bokspits	108	C5
Bokungu	106	C4
Bolbec	54	C5
Boldu	66	Q4
Bole, *China*	76	Q9
Bole, *Ghana*	104	D3
Bolechiv	50	N8
Bolesławiec	50	E6
Bolgatanga	104	D2
Bolhrad	66	R4
Bolintin-Vale	66	N5
Bolivar	128	B3
Bolivia	140	D7
Bollène	58	K9
Bollnäs	48	J6
Bolmen	48	G8
Bolnisi	92	L3
Bolobo	104	H5
Bologna	62	G6
Bolognesi	140	C5
Bolomba	104	H4
Bolotnoye	76	Q6
Bol'shaya Pyssa	70	J2
Bol'sherech'ye	70	P3
Bol'shezemel'skaya Tundra	76	J4
Bol Shirta	78	C4
Bolshoy Atlym	70	N2
Bol'shoy Osinovaya	78	W3
Bol'shoy Vlas'evo	78	Q6
Bolshoy Yugan	70	P2
Bolsover	54	A1
Bolton	56	K8
Bolu	92	D3
Bolvadin	68	P6
Bolzano	62	G4
Boma	104	G6
Bombala	114	J7
Bombay = Mumbai	88	B5
Bomili	106	D3
Bom Jesus da Lapa	140	J6
Bømlo	48	C7
Bomnak	78	M6
Bomossa	104	H4
Bonāb	92	M5
Bonaparte Archipelago	114	B2
Bonavista Bay	122	W7
Bondeno	62	G6
Bondo	106	C3
Bondokodi	114	C1
Bondoukou	104	D3
Bondowoso	86	E4
Bonerate	87	B4
Bongaigaon	88	F3
Bongandanga	106	C3
Bongao	87	A1
Bongor	104	H2
Bonifacio	64	D7
Bonn	52	C6
Bonners Ferry	126	C1
Bonneville	62	B4
Bonnie Rock	114	C6
Bonorva	64	C8
Bonthe	104	B3
Bontoc	84	G3
Bontosunggu	87	A4
Bonyhád	66	F3
Boone	128	D3
Boonville	130	C2
Boorama	106	G2
Boosaaso	106	H1
Boothia Peninsula	122	M2
Booué	104	G5
Boppard	52	C6
Bor, *Russia*	78	D4
Bor, *Sudan*	106	E2
Bor, *Turkey*	68	S7
Bor, *Yugoslavia*	66	K5
Borah Peak	126	C3
Borås	48	G8
Borāzjān	95	D2
Bordeaux	58	E9
Bordeira	60	B7
Borden Peninsula	122	Q2
Border Town	114	H7
Bordj Bou Arréridj	102	F1
Bordj Bounaam	60	M9
Bordj Flye Sante Marie	102	E3
Bordj Messaouda	102	G2
Bordj Mokhtar	102	F4
Bordj Omar Driss	102	G3
Borgarnes	48	(1)C2
Borger	132	F1
Borgholm	48	J8
Borgomanero	62	D5
Borgo San Dalmazzo	62	C6
Borgo San Lorenzo	62	G7
Borgosesia	62	D5
Borgo Val di Taro	62	E6
Bori Jenein	102	H2
Borislav	50	N8
Borisoglebsk	70	H4
Borjomi	92	K3
Borken	54	J3
Borkou	100	C4
Borkum	54	J1
Borkum	54	J1
Borlänge	48	H6
Bormida	62	D6
Bormio	62	F4
Borna	52	H5
Borne	54	J2
Borneo	86	E3
Bornholm	48	H9
Borodino	76	R5
Borodinskoye	48	Q6
Boromo	104	D2
Borongan	84	H4
Borovichi	70	F3
Borovskoy	70	M4
Borriana	60	K5
Borroloola	114	G3
Borşa	66	M2
Borshchiv	66	P1
Borshchovochnyy Khrebet	78	J7
Borðeyri	48	(1)C2
Borūjerd	90	E3
Borzya	78	K6
Bosa	64	C8
Bosanska Dubica	66	D4
Bosanska Gradiška	66	E4
Bosanska Kostajnica	62	M5
Bosanska Krupa	66	D5
Bosanski Brod	66	F4
Bosanski Novi	66	D4
Bosanski Petrovac	66	D5
Bosansko Grahovo	62	M6
Boşca	66	J4
Bose	84	D2
Bosilegrad	66	K7
Boskovice	50	F8
Bosna	66	F5
Bosnia-Herzegovina	66	E5
Bosobolo	106	B3
Bosporus = İstanbul Boğazı	68	M3
Bosporus	90	A1
Bossambélé	106	B2
Bossangoa	106	B2
Bossier City	130	C3
Bosten Hu	76	R9
Boston, *United Kingdom*	56	M9
Boston, *United States*	128	F2
Botevgrad	66	L7
Botlikh	90	E1
Botna	66	R3
Botoşani	66	P2
Botou	80	F3
Botrange	54	J4
Botswana	108	C4
Bottrop	54	J3
Bou Ahmed	60	F9
Bouaké	104	C3
Bouar	106	B2
Bouârfa	102	E2
Boufarik	60	N8
Bougainville Island	112	F6
Bougainville Reef	114	J3
Bougouni	104	C2
Bougzoul	60	N9
Bouira	102	F1
Bou Ismaïl	60	N8
Bou Izakarn	102	D3
Boujdour	102	C3
Bou Kadir	60	M8
Boukra	102	C3
Boulder	126	E2
Boulder City	132	D1
Boulia	114	G4
Boulogne-sur-Mer	54	D4
Bouna	104	D3
Boundiali	104	C3
Bounty Islands	112	H10
Bourem	102	E5
Bourg	58	E8
Bourg-de-Piage	58	L9
Bourg-en-Bresse	58	L7
Bourges	58	H6
Bourgoin-Jallieu	58	L8
Bourke	114	J6
Bournemouth	56	L11
Bou Saâda	102	F1
Bousso	100	C5
Boussu	54	F4
Boutilimit	102	C5
Bouzghaïa	60	M8
Bowbells	126	F1
Bowen	114	J4
Bowie, *Ariz., United States*	132	E2
Bowie, *Tex., United States*	132	G2
Bowkan	92	M5
Bowling Green, *Fla., United States*	130	E4
Bowling Green, *Ky., United States*	130	D2
Bowling Green, *Mo., United States*	130	C2
Bowman	126	F1
Bowman Bay	122	R3
Bo Xian	80	F4
Boxwood Hill	114	C6
Boyabat	92	F3
Boyang	80	F5
Boyarka	78	F2
Boyle	56	D8
Boysen Reservoir	126	E2
Boyuibe	142	J3
Bozcaada	68	H5
Boz Dağ	68	M7
Bozeman	126	D1
Bozkır	68	Q7
Bozoum	106	B2
Bozova	92	H5
Bozüyük	68	N5
Bra	62	C6
Brač	66	D6
Bracciano	64	G6
Bräcke	48	H5
Bracknell	54	B3
Brad	66	K3
Bradano	64	L8
Bradford	56	L8
Brady	130	B3
Braga	60	B3
Bragança, *Brazil*	140	H4
Bragança, *Portugal*	60	D3
Brahmapur	88	D5
Brahmaputra	88	F3
Brăila	66	Q4
Brainerd	128	B1
Braintree	54	C3
Brake	52	D3
Bramming	52	D1
Brampton	128	E2
Bramsche	52	D4
Branco	140	E3
Brandberg	108	A4
Brandenburg	52	H4
Brandenton	130	E4
Brandon	36	M7
Brandvlei	108	C5
Brandýs	50	D7
Braniewo	50	J3
Brasileia	140	D6
Brasília	140	H7
Braslaw	48	P9
Braşov	66	N4
Bratislava	50	G9
Bratsk	78	G5
Bratskoye Vodokhranilishche	78	G5
Brattleboro	128	F2
Braţul	66	R4
Bratunac	66	G5
Braunau	62	J2
Braunschweig	52	F4
Brawley	132	C2
Bray	56	F8
Bray Island	36	R3
Brazil	138	F4
Brazzaville	106	B4
Brčko	66	F5
Brda	50	G4
Bream Bay	116	E2
Breckenridge	132	G2
Břeclav	50	F9
Breda	54	G3
Bredasdorp	108	C6
Bredstedt	52	E2
Bredy	70	M4
Bree	54	H3
Bregenz	62	E3
Breiðafjörður	48	(1)A2
Bremangerlandet	48	B6
Bremen, *Germany*	52	D3
Bremen, *United States*	130	D3
Bremerhaven	52	D3
Bremerton	126	B1
Bremervörde	52	E3
Brenham	130	B3
Brennero	62	G4
Breno	62	F5
Brentwood	54	C3
Brescia	62	F5
Breslau = Wrocław	50	G6
Bressanone	62	G4
Bressay	56	M1
Bressuire	58	E7
Brest, *Belarus*	70	D4
Brest, *France*	58	A5
Breteuil	54	E5
Bretten	52	D7
Breves	140	G4
Brewarrina	114	J5
Brewton	130	D3
Brežice	66	C4
Brézina	102	F2
Brezno	50	J9
Bria	106	C2
Briançon	62	B6
Briceni	66	Q1
Bridgend	56	J10
Bridgeport, *Calif., United States*	132	C1
Bridgeport, *Conn., United States*	128	F2
Bridgeport, *Nebr., United States*	126	F2
Bridgetown	140	F1
Bridgewater	122	U8
Bridgwater	56	J10
Bridlington	56	M7
Brienzer See	62	D4
Brig	62	C4
Brigham City	126	D2
Brighton, *United Kingdom*	54	B4
Brighton, *United States*	126	F3
Brignoles	62	B7
Brikama	104	A2
Brilon	52	D5
Brindisi	64	M8
Brinkley	130	C3
Brisbane	114	K5
Bristol, *United Kingdom*	56	K10
Bristol, *United States*	130	E2
Bristol Bay	132	(1)E4
Bristol Channel	56	H10
British Columbia	32	F5
Britstown	108	C6
Brive-la-Gaillarde	58	G8
Briviesca	60	G2
Brixham	56	J11
Brlik	76	N9
Brno	50	F8
Broad Sound	114	J4
Broadus	126	E1
Brockton	128	F2
Brockville	128	E2
Brod	66	J9
Brodeur Peninsula	122	P2
Brodick	56	G6
Brodnica	50	J4
Broken Arrow	134	E1
Broken Bow	130	C3
Broken Hill	114	H6
Brokopondo	140	F2
Bromölla	50	D1
Bromsgrove	56	K9
Brønderslev	48	E8
Broni	62	E5
Brooke's Point	84	F5
Brookhaven	130	C3
Brookings, *Oreg., United States*	126	B2
Brookings, *S.D., United States*	126	G2
Brooks	122	J6
Brooks Range	132	(1)F2
Brooksville	130	E4
Broome	114	D3
Brora	56	J3
Brösarp	48	H9
Broughton Island	122	U3
Brovary	70	F4
Brownfield	132	F2
Browning	126	D1
Brownsville, *Tenn., United States*	130	D2
Brownsville, *Tex., United States*	130	B4
Brownwood	130	B3
Bruchsal	52	D7
Bruck, *Austria*	62	L3
Bruck, *Austria*	62	M2
Bruck an der Mur	66	C2
Brugge	54	F3
Brühl	54	J4
Bruint	88	G3
Brumado	140	J6
Brumath	62	C2
Bruneau	126	C2
Brunei	86	E2
Brunflo	48	H5
Brunico	64	F2
Brunsbüttel	52	E3
Brunswick, *Ga., United States*	130	E3
Brunswick, *Me., United States*	128	G2
Bruntál	50	G8
Brush	126	F2
Brussels = Bruxelles	54	G4
Bruxelles	54	G4
Bryan	130	B3
Bryanka	76	S6
Bryansk	70	F4
Brzeg	50	G7
Brzeg Dolny	50	F6
Brzeziny	50	J6

185

187

Dundee, *United Kingdom* 56 K5
Dunedin 116 C7
Dunfermline 56 J5
Dungarvan 56 E9
Dungeness 54 C4
Dungu 106 D3
Dungun 84 C6
Dungunab 100 G3
Dunhua 82 E2
Dunhuang 80 A2
Dunkerque 54 E3
Dunkirk 128 E2
Dunkwa 104 D3
Dun Laoghaire 56 F8
Dunnet Head 56 J3
Dunseith 126 G1
Dunsmuir 126 B2
Duque de Caxias 142 N3
Du Quoin 130 D2
Durance 58 L10
Durango, *Mexico* 132 F4
Durango, *Spain* 60 H1
Durango, *United States* 126 E3
Durankurak 66 R6
Durant 130 B3
Durazno 142 K5
Durban 108 E5
Durban-Corbières 58 H10
Düren 54 J4
Durgapur 88 E4
Durham, *Canada* 128 D2
Durham, *United Kingdom* 56 L7
Durham, *United States* 130 F2
Duri 86 C2
Durmā 95 B4
Durmanec 66 C3
Durmitor 66 G6
Durness 56 H3
Durrës 68 B3
Dursey 56 B10
Dursunbey 68 L5
D'Urville Island 116 D5
Dushanbe 90 J2
Düsseldorf 54 J3
Duvno 62 N7
Duyun 80 D5
Düzce 68 P4
Dvina 46 H2
Dvinskaya Guba 70 G1
Dwarka 88 A4
Dworshak Reservoir 126 C1
Dyat'kovo 70 F4
Dyersburg 130 D2
Dyje 62 M2
Dzamīn Üüd 78 J8
Dzavhan 76 S8
Dzerzhinsk 70 H3
Dzhalinda 78 L6
Dzhambeyty 70 K4
Dzhankoy 70 F5
Dzhardzhan 78 L3
Dzharkurgan 90 J2
Dzhetygara 70 M4
Dzhezkazgan 70 N5
Dzhigudzhak 78 T4
Dzhizak 76 M9
Dzhusaly 70 M5
Działdowo 50 K4
Dzüünbulag 80 F1
Dzuunmod 80 D1

E

Eads 126 F3
Eagle 132 (1)J3
Eagle Lake 126 B2
Eagle Pass 132 F3
East Antarctica 144 (2)P2
Eastbourne 54 C4
East Cape 116 G3
East China Sea 80 H4
East Dereham 54 C2
Easter Island 112 Q8
Eastern Cape 108 D6
Eastern Ghats 88 C6
Easter Ross 56 H4
East Falkland 142 K9
East Grinstead 54 C3
East Kilbride 56 H6
Eastleigh 54 A4
East Liverpool 130 E1
East London 108 D6
Eastmain 38 R6
Eastmain 122 S6
East Point 130 E3
East Retford 54 B1
East St. Louis 128 B3
East Siberian Sea = Vostochno-Sibirskoye More 78 U2
East Timor = Timor Timur 87 C4
Eatonton 130 E3
Eau Claire 128 B2
Ebbw Vale 56 J10
Ebensee 62 J3
Eberbach 52 D7
Ebersbach 50 D6
Ebersberg 62 G2
Eberswalde 52 J4
Ebinur Hu 76 Q9
Eboli 64 K8
Ebolowa 104 G4
Ebro 60 K3
Eceabat 68 J4
Ech Chélif 102 F1
Echinos 68 G3
Echo Bay 34 H3
Écija 60 E7
Eckernförde 52 E2
Ecuador 140 B4
Ed 100 H5
Edam 54 H2

Eday 56 K2
Ed Da'ein 100 E5
Ed Damazin 100 F5
Ed Debba 100 F4
Ed Dueim 100 F5
Ede, *Netherlands* 54 H2
Ede, *Nigeria* 104 E3
Edéa 104 G4
Edelény 50 K9
Eden, *Australia* 114 J7
Eden, *United States* 132 G2
Edendale 116 B8
Eder 52 D5
Edersee 52 E5
Edessa 68 E4
Edgecumbe 116 F3
Edgell Island 38 U4
Edinburgh 56 J6
Edineţ 66 Q1
Edirne 68 J3
Edmonds 126 B1
Edmonton 34 J6
Edmundson 124 N2
Edmundston 128 G1
Edolo 62 F4
Edremit 68 J5
Edremit Körfezi 68 H5
Edwards 132 C2
Edwards Plateau 132 F2
Eeklo 54 F3
Eemshaven 54 J1
Éfaté 112 G7
Eferding 50 D9
Effingham 130 D2
Eganville 128 E1
Eger 52 G6
Eger 66 H2
Egersund 48 D7
Eggenfelden 62 H2
Egilsstaðir 48 (1)F2
Eğridir 68 N7
Eğridir Gölü 68 N6
Egvekinot 78 Y3
Egypt 100 E2
Ehingen 62 E2
Eibar 60 H1
Eichstätt 62 G2
Eider 52 D2
Eidfjord 48 D6
Eidsvold 114 K5
Eidsvoll 48 F6
Eifel 54 J4
Eigg 56 F5
Eight Degree Channel 88 B7
Eilenburg 52 H5
Einbeck 52 E5
Eindhoven 54 H3
Eirunepé 140 D5
Eiseb 108 C4
Eisenach 52 F6
Eisenerz 62 K3
Eisenhüttenstadt 50 D5
Eisenstadt 62 M3
Eisleben 52 G5
Eivissa 60 M5
Eivissa 60 M6
Ejea de los Caballeros 60 J2
Ejido Insurgentes 124 D6
Ejin Horo Qi 80 D3
Ejin Qi 80 C2
Ejmiadzin 92 L3
Ekalaka 126 F1
Ekenäs 48 M7
Eketahuna 116 E5
Ekibastuz 76 P7
Ekimchan 78 N6
Ekonda 76 V4
Eksjo 48 H8
Ekwan 122 Q6
Elafonisos 68 E8
El 'Alamein 100 E1
El Amria 60 J9
El 'Arîsh 94 A5
Elat 94 B7
Elazığ 92 H4
El Azraq 94 D5
Elba 64 E6
El Banco 140 C2
Elbasan 68 C3
El Baúl 140 D2
Elbe 52 F3
Elbeuf 54 D5
Elbistan 92 G4
Elbląg 50 J3
El Borj 60 E9
Elbow 124 E1
Elbrus 92 K2
El Burgo de Ebro 60 K3
El Burgo de Osma 60 G3
El Cajon 132 C2
El Callao 140 E2
El Campo 130 B4
El Centro 132 C2
El Cerro 140 E7
Elch 60 K6
Elda 60 K6
El'dikan 78 P4
Eldorado 142 L4
El Dorado, *Mexico* 124 E7
El Dorado, *Ark., United States* 130 C3
El Dorado, *Kans., United States* 130 B2
El Dorado, *Venezuela* 140 E2
Eldoret 106 F3
Elefsina 68 F6
Elektrėnai 50 P3
El Encanto 140 C4
Elephant Butte Reservoir 132 E2
Eleuthera 124 L6
El Fahs 64 D12
El Faiyûm 100 F2
El Fasher 100 E5
El Geneina 100 D5

Elgin, *United Kingdom* 56 J4
Elgin, *Ill., United States* 128 C2
Elgin, *N.D., United States* 126 F1
El'ginskiy 78 Q4
El Gîza 100 F1
El Goléa 102 F2
El Homr 102 F3
Elhovo 68 J2
El Iskandarîya 100 E1
Elista 70 H5
Elizabeth 128 F2
Elizabeth City 130 F2
Elizabethton 130 E2
El Jadida 102 D2
El Jafr 94 D6
El Jafr 94 D6
Ełk 50 M4
Ełk 50 M4
El Kala 64 C12
Elk City 132 G1
El Kef 64 C12
El Kelaâ des Srarhna 102 D2
El Khandaq 100 F4
El Khârga 100 F2
Elkhart, *Ind., United States* 128 C2
Elkhart, *Kans., United States* 130 A2
El Khartum 100 F4
El Khartum Bahri 100 F4
Elkhorn 126 G2
Elkhorn 128 C2
Elkins 128 E3
Elko, *Canada* 126 C1
Elko, *United States* 126 C2
Elk River 128 B1
El Kuntilla 94 B7
Ellendale 124 G2
Ellensburg 126 B1
Ellesmere Island 120 K1
Ellice Islands 112 H6
Elliot 108 D6
Elliot Lake 36 Q7
Ellis 122 J8
Ellisras 108 D4
Elliston 114 F6
Ellsworth 128 G2
Ellwangen 62 F2
Elmadağ 68 R5
Elmali 68 M8
El Mansûra 100 F1
El Mazâr 94 A5
El Minya 100 F2
Elmira 128 E2
Elmshorn 52 E3
El Muglad 100 E5
El Nido 84 F4
El Obeid 100 F5
El Odaiya 100 E5
El Oued 102 G2
El Paso 132 E2
El Portal 128 C1
El Potosi 132 F4
El Prat de Llobregat 60 N3
El Puerto de Santa María 60 D8
El Qâhira 100 F1
El Qasr 100 E2
El Quşeima 94 B6
El Quweira 94 C7
El Reno 130 B2
El Sahuaro 132 D2
El Salvador 134 F6
Elster 52 H5
Elsterwerda 52 J5
El Sueco 132 E3
El Suweis 100 F2
Eltanin Bay 144 (2)JJ2
El Tarf 64 C12
El Thamad 94 B7
El Tigre 140 E2
El Turbio 142 G9
Eluru 88 D5
Elvas 60 C6
Elverum 48 F6
Elvira 140 C5
El Wak 106 G3
Ely, *United Kingdom* 56 N9
Ely, *United States* 126 D3
Emajõgi 48 P7
Emāmrūd 90 F2
Emba 70 L5
Emba 70 L5
Embalse de Alarcon 60 H5
Embalse de Alcántara Uno 60 D5
Embalse de Almendra 60 D3
Embalse de Contreras 60 J5
Embalse de Gabriel y Galán 60 D4
Embalse de Garcia Sola 60 E5
Embalse de Guadalhorce 60 F8
Embalse de Guadalmena 60 G6
Embalse de Guri 140 E2
Embalse de la Serena 60 E6
Embalse de la Sotonera 60 K2
Embalse del Bembézar 60 E6
Embalse del Ebro 60 G1
Embalse del Río Negro 138 F7
Embalse de Negratín 60 G7
Embalse de Ricobayo 60 E3
Embalse de Santa Teresa 60 E4
Embalse de Yesa 60 J2
Embalse Toekomstig 140 F3
Embarcación 142 J3
Emden 52 C3
Emerald 114 J4
Emi Koussi 100 C4
Emin 76 Q8
Emirdağ 68 P5
Emmeloord 54 H2
Emmen 54 J2
Emmendingen 62 C2
Emmerich 54 J3
Emory Peak 132 F3
Empalme 132 D3
Empangeni 108 E5

Empoli 62 F7
Emporia 130 B2
Empty Quarter = Rub' al Khālī 90 E6
Ems 54 J1
Ems-Jade-Kanal 52 C3
Enafors 70 B2
Encarnación 142 K4
Encs 66 J1
Ende 87 B4
Enderby Island 116 (2)B1
Energetik 70 L4
Enewetak 112 F4
Enez 68 J4
Enfida 64 E12
Enfield 54 B3
Engel's 70 J4
Enggano 86 C4
Enghien 54 G4
England 56 L9
English Channel 56 J12
Engozero 48 S4
'En Hazeva 94 C6
Enid 130 B2
Enkhuizen 54 H2
Enköping 48 J7
Enna 64 J11
Ennadai 36 L4
En Nahud 100 E5
Enngonia 114 J5
Ennis, *Republic of Ireland* 56 D9
Ennis, *United States* 126 D1
Enniscorthy 56 F9
Enniskillen 56 E7
Enn Nâqoûra 94 C3
Enns 62 K2
Enns 62 K3
Enschede 54 J2
Ensenada 132 C2
Enshi 80 D4
Entebbe 106 E3
Enterprise 126 C1
Entrevaux 62 B7
Entroncamento 60 B5
Enugu 104 F3
Enurmino 78 Z3
Envira 140 C5
Enz 62 D2
Enza 62 F6
Epanomi 68 E4
Epéna 106 B3
Épernay 58 J4
Épinal 62 B2
Episkopi 68 Q10
Epsom 54 B3
Eqlīd 95 E1
Equatorial Guinea 104 F4
Erbach 52 D7
Erçek 92 K4
Erciş 92 K4
Ercolano 64 J8
Érd 66 F2
Erdek 68 K4
Erdemli 68 S8
Erdenet 78 G7
Erding 62 G2
Erechim 142 L4
Ereğli, *Turkey* 92 D3
Ereğli, *Turkey* 92 F5
Ereikoussa 68 B5
Erenhot 80 E2
Erfurt 52 G6
Ergani 92 H4
Erg Chech 102 D4
Erg du Ténéré 102 H5
Ergel 80 D2
Ergene 68 J3
Erg Iguidi 102 D3
Er Hai 80 C5
Erie 128 D2
Erimo 82 M2
Erimo-misaki 82 M3
Eriskay 56 E4
Eritrea 100 G4
Erlangen 52 G7
Ermenek 92 E5
Ermoupoli 68 G7
Erode 88 C6
Er Rachidia 102 E2
Er Rahad 100 F5
Er Renk 106 E1
Errol 128 F2
Er Ruseifa 94 D4
Ersekë 68 C4
Erskine 128 A1
Ertai 76 S8
Ertix 76 R8
Erzgebirge 52 H6
Erzin 76 S7
Erzincan 92 H4
Erzurum 92 J4
Esan-misaki 82 L3
Esashi, *Japan* 82 L3
Esashi, *Japan* 82 M1
Esbjerg 48 E9
Escanaba 128 C1
Escárcega 134 F5
Esch 54 J5
Eschwege 52 F5
Eschweiler 54 J4
Escondido 132 C2
Eséka 104 G4
Eşfahān 90 F3
Eskifjörður 48 (1)G2
Eskilstuna 48 J7
Eskimo Lakes 34 E3
Eskişehir 92 D4
Esla 60 E3
Eslāmābād e Gharb 92 M6
Eslamshahr 90 F2
Esler Dağ 68 M7
Eslö 50 C2
Esmeraldas 140 B3

191

Fredericksburg, *Va., United States*	128	E3
Fredericktown	128	B3
Fredericton	38	T7
Frederikshåb = Paamiut	122	X4
Frederikshavn	48	F8
Frederikssund	50	B2
Frederiksværk	48	G9
Fredrikstad	48	F7
Freeport, *Ill., United States*	128	C2
Freeport, *Tex., United States*	130	B4
Freeport City	130	F4
Freer	130	B4
Free State	108	D5
Freetown	104	B3
Fregenal de la Sierre	60	D6
Freiberg	52	J6
Freiburg	62	C3
Freilassing	62	H3
Freising	62	G2
Freistadt	62	K2
Fréjus	58	M10
Fremantle	114	C6
Fremont, *Calif., United States*	132	B1
Fremont, *Nebr., United States*	124	G3
Frenchglen	126	C2
French Guiana	140	G3
French Pass	116	D5
French Polynesia	112	L7
Frenda	102	F1
Fresnes-sur-Apances	62	A3
Fresnillo	134	D4
Fresno	132	C1
Fresno Reservoir	126	E1
Freudenstadt	62	D2
Freyung	52	J8
Frias	142	H4
Fribourg	62	C4
Friedburg	62	G2
Friedrichshafen	62	E3
Friesach	62	K4
Friesoythe	52	C3
Frisian Islands	54	H1
Fritzlar	52	E5
Frobisher Bay	38	T4
Frobisher Lake	34	K5
Frolovo	70	H5
Frome	56	K10
Frontera	134	F5
Frontignan	58	J10
Frosinone	64	H7
Frøya	48	D5
Fruges	54	E4
Frýdek Místek	50	H8
Fudai	82	L4
Fuding	80	G5
Fuengirola	60	F8
Fuentesauco	60	E3
Fuerte Olimpo	142	K3
Fuerteventura	102	C3
Fugu	80	E3
Fuhai	76	R8
Fujieda	82	K6
Fujin	78	N7
Fuji-san	82	K6
Fukuchiyama	82	H6
Fukue	82	E7
Fukue-jima	82	E7
Fukui	82	J5
Fukuoka	82	F7
Fukushima	82	L5
Fukuyama	82	G6
Fulda	52	E6
Fulda	52	E6
Fuling	80	D5
Fulton	130	D2
Funabashi	82	L6
Funafuti	112	H6
Funchal	102	B2
Fundão	60	C4
Funing	84	D2
Funtua	104	F2
Furano	82	M2
Fürg	95	F2
Furmanovka	76	N9
Furmanovo	70	J5
Furneaux Group	114	J8
Furqlus	94	E2
Fürstenberg	52	J3
Fürstenfeldbruck	62	G2
Fürstenwalde	52	K4
Fürth	52	F7
Furukawa	82	L4
Fushun	82	B3
Fusong	82	D2
Füssen	62	F3
Futog	66	G4
Fuxhou	80	F5
Fu Xian	80	D3
Fuxin	80	G2
Fuyang	80	F4
Fuyu	80	G1
Fuyun	76	R8
Fuzhou	84	F1
Fyn	52	F1
Fynshav	52	F2

G

Gaalkacyo	106	H2
Gabès	102	H2
Gabon	104	G5
Gaborone	108	D4
Gabriel Strait	38	T4
Gäbrik	95	H4
Gabrovo	66	N7
Gacé	54	C6
Gacko	66	F6
Gäddede	48	H4
Gadsden	130	D3
Găeşti	66	N5
Gaeta	64	H7
Gafsa	102	G2
Gaggenau	62	D2
Gagnoa	104	C3
Gagra	92	J2
Gaildorf	62	E2
Gaillac	58	G10
Gainesville, *Fla., United States*	130	E4
Gainesville, *Ga., United States*	130	E3
Gainesville, *Mo., United States*	130	C2
Gainesville, *Tex., United States*	130	B3
Gai Xian	82	B3
Gala	88	E3
Galana	106	F4
Galanta	62	N2
Galapagos Islands = Islas Galápagos	140	(1)B1
Galashiels	56	K6
Galatas	68	F7
Galaţi	66	R4
Galdhøpiggen	48	D6
Galena	132	(1)F3
Galesburg	128	B2
Galich	70	H3
Gallabat	100	G5
Galle	88	D7
Gallipoli	64	N8
Gallipolis	130	E2
Gällivare	48	L3
Gallup	132	E1
Galtat Zemmour	102	C3
Galveston Bay	124	G6
Galway	56	C8
Galway Bay	56	C8
Gamalakhe	108	E6
Gambēla	106	E2
Gambell	78	Z4
Gambier Islands	112	N8
Gamboma	106	B4
Gamboula	106	B3
Gan	78	L7
Ganado	132	E1
Gäncä	92	M3
Gandajika	106	C5
Gander	38	W7
Ganderkesee	52	D3
Gandesa	60	L3
Gāndhīdhām	88	B4
Gandhinagar	88	B4
Gandia	60	K6
Gandu	140	K6
Ganganagar	88	B3
Gangara	104	F2
Gangdise Shan	88	D2
Ganges	58	J10
Ganges	88	E3
Gangi	64	J11
Gangtok	88	E3
Gannett Peak	126	E2
Ganta	104	C3
Ganye	104	G3
Ganzhou	80	E5
Gao	102	E5
Gaoual	102	C6
Gap	62	B6
Gapan	84	G3
Garanhuns	140	K5
Garba	104	J3
Garbsen	52	E4
Gardelegen	52	G4
Garden City	126	F3
Gardēz	90	J3
Gardone Val Trompia	62	F5
Gargždai	50	L2
Gariau	87	D3
Garies	108	B6
Garissa	106	F4
Garland	130	B3
Garlasco	62	D5
Garliava	50	N3
Garmisch-Partenkirchen	62	G3
Garnett	130	B2
Garonne	58	E9
Garoowe	106	H2
Garoua	104	G3
Garoua Boulaï	104	G3
Garry Lake	122	L3
Garsen	106	G4
Garut	86	D4
Garwa	88	D4
Garwolin	50	L6
Gary	124	J3
Garyarsa	88	D2
Garzê	80	B4
Gasan Kuli	90	F2
Gasht	90	H4
Gashua	104	G2
Gaspé	38	U7
Gastonia	130	E2
Gastre	142	H7
Gatchina	70	F3
Gateshead	56	L7
Gatesville	130	B3
Gatineau	128	E1
Gatrüyeh	95	F2
Gauja	48	N8
Gaula	48	F5
Gaurella	88	D4
Gauteng	108	D5
Gava	60	N3
Gāvbandī	95	E3
Gavdos	68	G10
Gävle	48	J6
Gawler	114	G6
Gawler Ranges	114	G6
Gaxun Nur	80	C2
Gaya, *India*	88	E4
Gaya, *Niger*	104	E2
Gaylord	128	D1
Gayndah	114	K5
Gayny	70	K2
Gaza	94	B5
Gaz-Achak	76	L9
Gazandzhyk	76	K10
Gaza Strip	94	B5
Gaziantep	92	G5
Gazipaşa	68	Q8
Gazli	76	L9
Gaz Şāleḩ	95	G2
Gbaaka	104	C3
Gbarnga	104	C3
Gdańsk	50	H3
Gdov	48	P7
Gdyel	60	K9
Gdynia	50	H3
Gebel el Tīh	94	A7
Gebel Halāl	94	A6
Gebel Katherina	100	F2
Gebel Yi'allaq	94	A6
Gebze	68	M4
Gedaref	100	G5
Gediz	68	K6
Gediz	68	M6
Gedser	52	G2
Geel	54	H3
Geelong	114	H7
Geesthacht	52	F3
Gê'gvai	88	D2
Geidam	104	G2
Geilenkirchen	54	J4
Geilo	48	E6
Geinhausen	52	E6
Geislingen	62	E2
Geita	106	E4
Gejiu	84	C2
Gela	64	J11
Geladī	106	H2
Geldern	54	J3
Geleen	54	H4
Gelendzhik	92	H1
Gelibolu	68	J4
Gelibolu Yarimadasi	68	J4
Gelsenkirchen	54	K3
Gembloux	54	G4
Gembu	104	G3
Gemena	106	B3
Gemlik	68	M4
Gemlik Körfezi	68	L4
Gemona del Friuli	62	J4
Genalē Wenz	106	G2
General Acha	142	J6
General Alvear	142	H6
General Pico	142	J6
General Pinedo	142	J4
General Roca	142	H6
General Santos	84	H5
Geneva	128	E2
Genève	62	B4
Gengma	84	B2
Genil	60	F7
Genk	54	H4
Genoa = Genova	62	D6
Genova	62	D6
Gent	54	F3
Genteng	86	D4
Genthin	52	H4
Geographe Bay	114	B6
George	108	C6
George	38	T5
George Town, *Australia*	114	J8
George Town, *Malaysia*	86	C1
George Town, *The Bahamas*	130	F5
Georgetown, *Australia*	114	H3
Georgetown, *Guyana*	140	F2
Georgetown, *The Gambia*	104	B2
Georgetown, *Ky., United States*	130	E2
Georgetown, *S.C., United States*	130	F3
Georgetown, *Tex., United States*	130	B3
George West	130	B4
Georgia	92	K2
Georgia	130	E3
Georgian Bay	128	D1
Gera	52	H6
Geraldine	116	C7
Geraldton, *Australia*	114	B5
Geraldton, *Canada*	124	J2
Gérardmer	62	B2
Gerāsh	95	F3
Gerede	92	E3
Gerefsried	62	G3
Gereshk	90	H3
Gérgal	60	H7
Gerik	84	C5
Gerlach	126	C2
Germantown	128	C3
Germany	52	E6
Germencik	68	K7
Germering	62	G2
Germersheim	54	L5
Gernika	60	H1
Gerolzhofen	52	F7
Gêrzê	88	D2
Geser	87	D3
Getafe	60	G4
Gettysburg	126	F2
Getxo	60	H1
Geugnon	58	K7
Gevaş	92	K4
Gevgelija	68	E3
Gewanē	100	H5
Geyik Dağ	68	Q8
Geyser	126	D1
Geyve	68	N4
Ghabāghib	94	D3
Ghadāmis	102	G2
Ghadīr Minqār	94	E3
Ghana	104	D3
Ghanzi	108	C4
Gharandal	94	C6
Ghardaïa	102	F2
Gharo	90	J5
Gharyān	102	H2
Ghāt	100	B2
Ghazaouet	102	E1
Ghaziabad	88	C3
Ghazipur	88	D3
Ghazn	90	J3
Gheorgheni	66	N3
Gherla	66	L2
Ghizar	88	B1
Ghotāru	88	B3
Ghōwrī	95	F2
Ghunthur	94	E2
Giannitsa	68	E4
Giannutri	64	F6
Giarre	64	K11
Gibraleón	60	D7
Gibraltar	60	E8
Gibson Desert	114	D4
Gideån	48	K5
Gien	58	H6
Gießen	52	D6
Gifhorn	52	F4
Gifu	82	J6
Gigha	56	G6
Giglio	64	E6
Giglio Castello	64	E6
Gijón	60	E1
Gila	132	E2
Gila Bend	132	D2
Gilan Garb	92	L6
Gilău	66	L3
Gilazi	92	N3
Gilbert Islands	112	H5
Gilbués	140	H5
Gilching	62	G2
Gilf Kebir Plateau	100	E3
Gilgandra	114	J6
Gilgit	88	B1
Gilimanuk	86	E4
Gillam	122	N5
Gillette	126	E2
Gillingham	54	C3
Gills Rock	128	C1
Gilroy	126	B3
Gīmbī	106	F2
Gimli	122	M6
Gimol'skoe Ozero	48	R5
Gīnīr	106	G2
Gioia del Colle	64	L8
Gioia Tauro	64	K10
Gioura	68	F5
Giresun	92	H3
Girga	100	F2
Girona	60	N3
Gironde	58	E8
Girvan	56	H6
Gisborne	116	G4
Gisenyi	106	D4
Gitega	106	D4
Giurgiu	66	N6
Givet	54	G4
Givors	58	K8
Giyon	106	F2
Gizhiga	78	U4
Gizhiginskaya Guba	78	T4
Giżycko	50	L3
Gjiri i Vlorës	68	B4
Gjirokaster	68	C4
Gjoa Haven	122	M3
Gjøvik	48	F6
Glacier Peak	126	B1
Gladstone	114	K4
Glamoč	66	D5
Glan	52	C7
Glan	87	C1
Glarner Alpen	62	D4
Glasgow, *United Kingdom*	56	H6
Glasgow, *Ky., United States*	128	C3
Glasgow, *Mont., United States*	126	E1
Glauchau	52	H6
Glazov	76	J6
Gleisdorf	62	L3
Glendale, *Ariz., United States*	132	D2
Glendale, *Calif., United States*	132	C2
Glendambo	114	G6
Glendive	126	F1
Glenmorgan	114	J5
Glennallen	132	(1)H3
Glenn Innes	114	K5
Glenrothes	56	J5
Glens Falls	128	F2
Glenwood, *Ark., United States*	128	B4
Glenwood, *Minn., United States*	128	A1
Glenwood, *N. Mex., United States*	132	E2
Glenwood Springs	126	E3
Glidden	128	B1
Glina	62	M5
Gliwice	50	H7
Glodeni	66	Q2
Głogów	50	F6
Glomfjord	48	H3
Glomma	48	F5
Glorieuses	98	H7
Gloucester, *United Kingdom*	56	K10
Gloucester, *United States*	128	F2
Głowno	50	J6
Głuchołazy	50	G7
Glückstadt	52	E3
Gmünd, *Austria*	62	J4
Gmünd, *Austria*	62	L2
Gmunden	62	J3
Gniezno	50	G5
Gnjilane	68	D2
Gnoien	52	H3
Goalpara	88	F3
Goba	106	F2
Gobabis	108	B4
Gobernador Gregores	142	G8
Gobi Desert	80	C2
Gobo	82	H7
Gobustan	90	E1
Goce Delcev	68	F3
Goch	54	J3
Gochas	108	B4
Godbout	128	G1
Godé	106	G2
Goderich	128	D2

193

Gunung Mekongga — 87 B3
Gunung Mulu — 86 E2
Gunung Pangrango — 86 D4
Gunungsitoli — 86 B2
Gunung Togwomeri — 87 D3
Günzburg — 62 F2
Gunzenhausen — 52 F7
Guoyang — 80 F4
Gura Humorului — 66 N2
Gurk — 62 K4
Gurskoye — 78 P6
Gürün — 92 G4
Gurupi — 140 H4
Gusau — 104 F2
Gusev — 50 M3
Gushgy — 90 H2
Gusinoozersk — 78 H6
Guspini — 64 C9
Güssing — 62 M3
Güstrow — 50 B4
Gütersloh — 52 D5
Guthrie, Okla., United States — 126 G3
Guthrie, Tex., United States — 132 F2
Gutsuo — 88 E3
Guttenberg — 128 B2
Guwahati — 88 F3
Guyana — 140 F2
Guyang — 80 E2
Guymon — 132 F1
Guyuan — 80 D3
Guzar — 90 J2
Gvardeysk — 50 L3
Gwadar — 90 H4
Gwalior — 88 C3
Gwanda — 108 D4
Gwardex — 64 J12
Gwda — 50 F4
Gweebarra Bay — 56 C7
Gweru — 108 D3
Gyangzê — 88 E3
Gyaring Hu — 80 B4
Gyaros — 68 G7
Gyda — 76 P3
Gydanskiy Poluostrov — 76 P3
Gyirong — 88 E3
Gyldenløves Fjord — 122 Y4
Gympie — 114 K5
Gyomaendrőd — 66 H3
Gyöngyös — 66 G2
Győr — 66 E2
Gypsumville — 122 M6
Gytheio — 68 E8
Gyula — 66 J3
Gyumri — 92 K3
Gyzylarbat — 90 G2

H

Haapajärvi — 48 N5
Haapsalu — 48 M7
Haar — 62 G2
Haarlem — 54 G2
Haast — 116 B6
Habahe — 76 R8
Habarüt — 90 F6
Habaswein — 106 F3
Habbān — 90 E7
Habbānīyah — 92 K7
Habirag — 80 F2
Habomai-Shoto — 78 R8
Haboro — 82 L1
Hachijō-jima — 82 K7
Hachinohe — 82 L3
Hachiōji — 82 K6
Hadadong — 76 Q9
Hadejia — 104 F2
Hadejia — 104 G2
Hadera — 94 B4
Haderslev — 52 E1
Ḥaḍramaut — 90 E6
Hadhunmathi Atoll — 88 B8
Hadilik — 76 R10
Hadjout — 60 N8
Haeju — 82 C4
Haenam — 82 D6
Ḥafar al Bāṭin — 95 A2
Hafik — 92 G4
Hafnarfjörður — 48 (1)C2
Haft Gel — 95 C1
Hagen — 54 K3
Hagenow — 52 G3
Hägere Hiywet — 106 F2
Hagerstown — 128 E3
Ha Giang — 80 C6
Haguenau — 54 K6
Haicheng — 82 B3
Haifa = Ḥefa — 94 B4
Haikou — 84 E3
Hā'il — 90 D4
Hailar — 78 K7
Hailey — 126 D2
Hailong — 82 C2
Hailuoto — 48 N4
Hainan — 84 D3
Haines Junction — 132 (1)K3
Haining — 80 G4
Hai Phong — 84 D2
Haiti — 134 K5
Haiya — 100 G4
Hajdúböszörmény — 66 J2
Hajdúhadház — 50 L10
Hajdúnánás — 50 L10
Hajdúszoboszló — 50 L10
Hajipur — 88 E3
Ḥājjīābād — 95 F2
Hajmah — 90 G6
Hajnówka — 50 N5
Haka — 88 F4
Hakkâri — 92 K5
Hakodate — 82 L3
Ḥalab — 92 G5

Ḥalabān — 100 H3
Ḥalabja — 92 L6
Halaib — 100 G3
Halba — 94 D2
Halberstadt — 52 G5
Halden — 48 F7
Haldensleben — 52 G4
Halifax — 38 U8
Halifax Bay — 114 J3
Hall — 62 G3
Hall Beach — 122 Q3
Halle — 54 G4
Hallein — 62 J3
Halligen — 52 D2
Hallock — 126 G1
Hall Peninsula — 122 T4
Halls Creek — 114 E3
Halmahera — 87 C2
Halmahera Sea — 87 C3
Halmstad — 50 B1
Haltern — 54 K3
Hamada — 82 G6
Hamadān — 90 E3
Hamaguir — 102 E2
Hamāh — 92 G6
Hamamatsu — 82 J6
Hamar — 48 F6
Hamarøy — 48 H2
Hamatonbetsu — 82 M1
Hambantota — 88 D7
Hamburg, Germany — 52 E3
Hamburg, Ark., United States — 130 C3
Hamburg, N.Y., United States — 128 E2
Hämeenlinna — 48 N6
Hameln — 52 E4
Hamersley Range — 114 C4
Hamhŭng — 82 D3
Hami — 76 S9
Hamīd — 100 F3
Hamilton, Australia — 114 H7
Hamilton, Bermuda — 134 M2
Hamilton, Canada — 38 R8
Hamilton, New Zealand — 116 E3
Hamilton, Al., United States — 130 D3
Hamilton, Mont., United States — 126 D1
Hamilton, Oh., United States — 128 D3
Hamina — 48 P6
Hamirpur — 88 D3
Hamm — 52 C5
Hammada du Drâa — 102 D3
Hammam Bou Hadjar — 60 K9
Hammamet — 64 E12
Hammam Lif — 102 H1
Hammelburg — 52 E6
Hammerfest — 48 M1
Hammer Springs — 116 D6
Hampden — 116 C7
Hāmūn-e Jaz Mūriān — 95 H3
Ḥanalc — 100 G2
Hanamaki — 82 L4
Hanau — 52 D6
Hancheng — 80 E3
Hancock — 128 C1
Handan — 80 E3
Handeni — 106 F5
Handerslev — 48 E9
Handlová — 50 H9
Hanford — 132 C1
Hangayn Nuruu — 76 T8
Hangu — 80 F3
Hangzhou — 80 F4
Hanīdh — 95 C3
Hanko — 48 M7
Hanksville — 126 D3
Hanna — 122 K6
Hannibal — 130 C2
Hannover — 52 E4
Hanö — 50 D2
Hanöbukten — 50 D2
Ha Nôi — 84 D2
Hanoi = Ha Nôi — 84 D2
Hanover — 128 F2
Han Shui — 80 D4
Hanson Bay — 116 (1)B1
Hanumangarh — 88 B3
Hanzhong — 80 D4
Hao — 112 M7
Hāora — 88 E4
Haouza — 102 C3
Haparanda — 48 N4
Hāpoli — 88 F3
Hapur — 88 C3
Ḥaraḍ, Saudi Arabia — 90 E5
Ḥaraḍ, Yemen — 100 H4
Haramachi — 82 L5
Harare — 108 E3
Harbin — 80 H1
Harbour Breton — 122 V7
Harburg — 52 F3
Hardangerfjorden — 48 C7
Hardangervidda — 48 D6
Hardenberg — 54 J2
Harderwijk — 54 H2
Hardin — 126 E1
Hardy — 130 C2
Haren — 54 K2
Härer — 106 G2
Hargeysa — 106 G2
Har Hu — 80 B3
Haridwar — 88 C3
Harihari — 116 C6
Harima-nada — 82 H6
Hari Rud — 90 H3
Harlan — 128 A2
Härläu — 66 P2
Harlem — 126 E1
Harlingen, Netherlands — 54 H1
Harlingen, United States — 130 B4
Harlow — 56 N10
Harlowtown — 126 E1
Harmanli — 68 H3
Harney Basin — 124 B3

Harney Lake — 126 C2
Härnösand — 48 J5
Har Nur — 78 K7
Har Nuur — 76 S8
Haro — 60 H2
Harricanaw — 122 R6
Harrisburg, Ill., United States — 128 C3
Harrisburg, Pa., United States — 130 F1
Harrison — 128 B3
Harrison Bay — 132 (1)G1
Harrisville — 128 D2
Harrogate — 56 L8
Har Saggi — 94 B6
Harsin — 92 M6
Hârşova — 66 Q5
Harstad — 48 J2
Hartberg — 62 L3
Hartford — 128 F2
Hartland Point — 56 H10
Hartlepool — 56 L7
Har Us Nuur — 76 S8
Harvey — 126 G1
Harwich — 54 D3
Harz — 52 F5
Hāsā — 94 C6
Haselünne — 52 C4
Hashtpar — 92 N5
Hāsik — 90 G6
Haskell — 130 B3
Haskovo — 68 H3
Haslemere — 54 B3
Hassan — 88 C6
Hasselfelde — 52 F5
Hasselt — 54 H4
Haßfurt — 52 F6
Hassi Bel Guebbour — 102 G3
Hassi Messaoud — 102 G2
Hässleholm — 48 G8
Hastings, New Zealand — 116 F4
Hastings, United Kingdom — 54 C4
Hastings, Minn., United States — 128 B2
Hastings, Nebr., United States — 126 G2
Haţeg — 66 K4
Hatgal — 78 G6
Ha Tinh — 84 D3
Hatteras — 130 F2
Hattiesburg — 130 D3
Hatvan — 66 G2
Hat Yai — 84 C5
Haud — 100 H6
Haud Ogadēn — 106 G2
Haugesund — 48 C7
Hauraki Gulf — 116 E3
Haut Atlas — 102 D2
Hauts Plateaux — 102 E2
Havana — 130 C1
Havana = La Habana — 134 H4
Havant — 56 M11
Havel — 50 C5
Havelock, New Zealand — 116 D5
Havelock, United States — 130 F3
Havelock North — 116 F4
Havenby — 52 D1
Haverfordwest — 56 H10
Havlíčkův Brod — 50 L8
Havre — 126 E1
Havre-St-Pierre — 38 U6
Havrylivtsi — 66 P1
Havza — 92 F3
Hawaii — 132 (2)E2
Hawaii — 132 (2)E4
Hawaiian Islands — 112 J3
Hawera — 116 E4
Hawi — 132 (2)F3
Hawick — 56 K6
Hawke Bay — 116 F4
Hawker — 114 G6
Hawr al 'Awdah — 95 B1
Hawr al Ḥammar — 95 B1
Hawthorne — 126 C3
Hay — 114 H6
Hay — 122 H5
Hayange — 54 J5
Ḥaydarābād — 92 L5
Hayden — 132 D2
Hayrabolu — 68 K3
Hay River — 34 H4
Hays — 130 B2
Hazard — 128 D3
Hazāribāg — 88 E4
Hazebrouck — 54 E4
Hazelton, Canada — 122 F5
Hazelton, United States — 128 E2
Head of Bight — 114 F6
Hearne — 130 B3
Hearst — 36 Q7
Hebbronville — 132 G3
Hebgen Lake — 126 D2
Hebi — 80 E3
Hebron, Canada — 38 U5
Hebron, Israel — 94 C5
Hebron, Nebr., United States — 126 G2
Hebron, N.D., United States — 126 F1
Hecate Strait — 34 E6
Hechi — 84 D2
Hechingen — 62 D2
Hede — 48 G5
Heerenveen — 54 H2
Heerlen — 54 J4
Ḥefa — 94 B4
Hefei — 80 F4
Hegang — 80 J1
Hegura-jima — 82 J5
Hegyfalu — 62 M3
Heide — 52 E2
Heidelberg — 52 D7
Heidenheim — 62 F2
Heilbad Heiligenstadt — 52 F5
Heilbronn — 52 E7
Heilgenhafen — 52 F2
Heimaey — 48 (1)C3
Heinola — 48 N6

Hejing — 76 R9
Hekla — 48 (1)D3
Helagsfjället — 48 G5
Helena, Ark., United States — 130 C3
Helena, Mont., United States — 126 D1
Helen Reef — 87 D2
Helensville — 116 E3
Helga — 50 D1
Helgoland — 52 C2
Helgoländer Bucht — 52 D2
Hellín — 60 J6
Helmand — 90 H3
Helmond — 54 H3
Helmsdale — 56 J3
Helmstedt — 52 G4
Helodrano Antongila — 108 H3
Helong — 82 E2
Helsingborg — 48 G8
Helsinge — 50 B1
Helsingør — 48 G8
Helsinki — 48 N6
Helston — 56 G11
Helwan — 100 F2
Hemel Hempstead — 56 M10
Henashi-zaki — 82 K3
Hendek — 68 N4
Henderson, Ky., United States — 128 C3
Henderson, Nev., United States — 126 D3
Henderson, N.C. United States — 130 F2
Henderson Island — 112 P8
Hendersonville — 128 C3
Hendijarn — 95 C1
Hengelo — 54 J2
Hengyang — 80 E5
Henichesk — 70 F5
Hénin-Beaumont — 54 E4
Hennebont — 58 B6
Hennigsdorf — 52 J4
Henryetta — 128 A3
Henzada — 84 B3
Heppenheim — 52 D7
Heppner — 126 C1
Hepu — 84 D2
Héraðsflói — 48 (1)F2
Herald Cays — 114 J3
Herāt — 90 H3
Herbert — 116 C7
Herborn — 52 D6
Herceg-Novi — 66 F7
Hereford, United Kingdom — 56 K9
Hereford, United States — 134 D2
Herekino — 116 D2
Herentals — 54 G3
Herford — 52 D4
Herisau — 62 E3
Herlen Gol — 80 E1
Hermagor — 62 J4
Herma Ness — 56 M1
Hermel — 94 D2
Hermiston — 126 C1
Hermosillo — 124 D6
Hernád — 50 L9
Herne — 52 C5
Herne Bay — 54 D3
Herning — 48 E8
Hérouville-St-Clair — 54 B5
Herrenberg — 62 D2
Hersbruck — 52 G7
Herstat — 54 H4
Hertlay — 54 E6
Hervey Bay — 114 K5
Herzberg — 52 F5
Herzliyya — 94 B4
Hesdin — 54 E4
Heshan — 84 D2
Hesselø — 50 A1
Hessisch-Lichtenau — 52 E5
Hettstedt Lutherstadt — 52 G5
Heves — 50 K10
He Xian — 84 E2
Hexigten Qi — 80 F2
Heze — 80 F3
Hezuozhen — 80 C3
Hialeah — 130 E4
Hiawatha — 130 B2
Hibbing — 128 B1
Hickory — 128 D3
Hidaka-sammyaku — 82 M2
Hidalgo del Parral — 134 C3
Hiddensee — 52 H2
Hierro — 102 B3
Higashi-suidō — 82 E7
High Point — 128 E3
High Wycombe — 54 B3
Hiiumaa — 48 M7
Hikurangi — 116 E2
Hikurangi — 116 G3
Hikutaia — 116 E3
Hildburghausen — 52 F6
Hildesheim — 52 E4
Hillsboro, Oh., United States — 130 E4
Hillsboro, Nebr., United States — 126 B1
Hillsboro, Tex., United States — 132 G2
Hillsville — 128 D3
Hillswick — 56 L1
Hilo — 132 (2)F4
Hilton Head Island — 130 E3
Hilva — 92 H5
Hilversum — 54 H2
Himalayas — 74 L6
Himarë — 68 B4
Himatnagar — 88 B4
Himeji — 82 H6
Himi — 82 J5
Himora — 100 G5
Ḥimş — 94 D2
Hîncești — 66 R3
Hindu Kush — 88 A1
Hindupur — 88 C6
Hinesville — 130 E3
Hingoli — 88 C5
Hinnøya — 48 H2

Name	Page	Grid
Hiroo	82	M2
Hirosaki	82	L3
Hiroshima	82	G6
Hirschaid	52	F7
Hirson	54	G5
Hirtshals	48	E8
Hisar	88	C3
Hischberg	52	G6
Hisdal	48	C6
Hispaniola	138	D2
Hisyah	94	D2
Hīt	92	K7
Hitachi	82	L5
Hitoyoshi	82	F7
Hitra	48	D5
Hiuchi-nada	82	G6
Hiva Oa	112	M6
Hjälmaren	48	H7
Hjalmar Lake	122	K4
Hjelmsøya	48	M1
Hlinsko	50	E8
Hlohovec	62	N2
Hlyboka	66	N1
Hlybokaye	70	E3
Ho	104	E3
Hobart, *Australia*	114	J8
Hobart, *United States*	132	G1
Hobbs	132	F2
Hobro	48	E8
Hobyo	106	H3
Hô Chi Minh	84	D4
Höchstadt	52	F7
Hockenheim	52	D7
Hódmezővásárhely	66	H3
Hodonín	50	G9
Hoek van Holland	54	G3
Hoeryŏng	82	E2
Hoeyang	82	D4
Hof	52	G6
Hofgeismar	52	E5
Höfn	48	(1)F2
Hofsjökull	48	(1)D2
Hofsós	48	(1)D2
Höfu	82	F6
Hohe	62	H3
Hohe Dachstein	50	C10
Hohe Tauern	64	G1
Hohhot	80	E2
Hoh Xil Shan	88	E1
Hôi An	84	D3
Hoima	106	E3
Hokitika	116	C6
Hokkaidō	82	N2
Holbæk	50	A2
Holbrook	132	D2
Holdrege	126	G2
Holguín	134	J4
Holíč	62	N2
Hollabrunn	62	M2
Holland	128	C2
Hollis	132	G2
Hollywood	130	E4
Holman	122	H2
Hólmavík	48	(1)C2
Holmes Reefs	114	J3
Holstebro	48	E8
Holsteinische Schweiz	52	F2
Holsteinsborg = Sisimiut	122	W3
Holton	130	B2
Holyhead	56	H8
Holy Island, *Eng., United Kingdom*	56	L6
Holy Island, *Wales, United Kingdom*	56	H8
Holyoke	126	F2
Holzkirchen	62	G3
Holzminden	52	E5
Homa Bay	106	E4
Homberg	52	E5
Hombori	102	E5
Home Bay	36	T3
Homestead	130	E4
Homewood	130	D3
Homs = Ḥimṣ	94	D2
Homyel'	70	F4
Hondo, *N. Mex., United States*	132	E2
Hondo, *Tex., United States*	132	G3
Honduras	134	G6
Hønefoss	48	F6
Honey Lake	126	B2
Honfleur	54	C5
Hon Gai	84	D2
Hong Kong = Xianggang	84	E2
Hongliuyuan	80	B2
Hongor	80	E1
Honiara	112	F6
Honjō	82	K4
Honokaa	132	(2)F3
Honolulu	132	(2)D2
Honshū	82	L5
Hooge	52	D2
Hoogeveen	54	J2
Hoogezand-Sappemeer	54	J1
Hooper Bay	132	(1)D3
Hoorn	54	H2
Hoorn Islands	112	H7
Hopa	92	J3
Hope, *Canada*	126	B1
Hope, *Ak., United States*	122	B4
Hope, *Ark., United States*	130	C3
Hopedale	122	U5
Hopetoun	114	H7
Hopin	88	G4
Hopkinsville	128	C3
Hoquiam	126	B1
Horadiz	92	M4
Horasan	92	K3
Horgo	78	F7
Horizon Depth	112	D8
Hormak	90	H4
Hormoz	95	F3
Horn	62	L2
Hornavan	48	J3
Horncastle	54	B1
Horodenka	66	N1
Horodok	50	N8
Horqin Youyi Qianqi	78	L7
Horsens	48	E9
Horsham, *Australia*	114	H7
Horsham, *United Kingdom*	54	B3
Horten	48	F7
Hortiguela	60	G2
Horton	132	(1)N2
Ḩoseynābād	95	G2
Hoshab	90	H4
Hoshangabad	88	C4
Hospet	88	C5
Hosséré Vokre	104	G3
Hotan	76	Q10
Hotan	76	Q10
Hot Springs, *Ark., United States*	128	B4
Hot Springs, *N.C., United States*	128	B4
Hottah Lake	122	H3
Houdan	54	D6
Houdelaincourt	62	A2
Houghton	128	C1
Houlton	128	G1
Houma, *China*	80	E3
Houma, *United States*	124	H6
Houmt Souk	102	H2
Houston	124	G6
Hovd	76	S8
Hövsgöl Nuur	78	F6
Hövüün	80	C2
Howard Junction	116	D5
Howland	112	J5
Höxter	52	E5
Hoxud	76	R9
Hoy	56	J3
Høyanger	48	D6
Hoyerswerda	52	K5
Hradeç Králové	50	E7
Hranice	50	G8
Hrazdan	92	L3
Hrodna	50	N4
Hron	50	H9
Hrubieszów	50	N7
Hsinchu	84	G2
Hsüeh Shan	84	G2
Hsweni	84	B2
Huacho	140	B5
Huade	80	E2
Huaibei	80	F4
Huaibin	80	F4
Huaihua	80	D5
Huainan	80	F4
Huaiyin	80	F4
Huaki	87	C4
Huallaga	140	B5
Huambo	108	B2
Huancayelica	140	B6
Huancayo	140	B6
Huang	80	F3
Huangchuan	80	F4
Huangshan	80	F5
Huangshi	80	F4
Huang Xian	80	G3
Huangyan, *China*	80	G5
Huangyan, *China*	80	C3
Huanren	82	C3
Huanuco	140	B5
Huaráz	140	B5
Huarmey	140	B6
Huasco	142	G4
Huashixia	80	B3
Huatabampo	124	E6
Hubli	88	C5
Huch'ang	82	D3
Huddersfield	56	L8
Huddinge	48	K7
Hudiksvall	48	J6
Hudson	128	F2
Hudson	128	F2
Hudson Bay	122	L6
Hudson Bay	36	P5
Hudson Strait	38	S4
Huê	84	D3
Huelva	60	D7
Huercal Overa	60	J7
Huesca	60	K2
Huéscar	60	H7
Huftaroy	48	C6
Hughenden	114	H4
Hugo	130	B3
Hugo Lake	130	B3
Huia	116	E3
Huich'ŏn	82	D3
Huila Plateau	108	A3
Huinan	82	C2
Huinca Renancó	142	J5
Huizhou	84	E2
Hulin	78	N7
Hull	128	L1
Hulst	54	G3
Hulun Nur	78	K7
Huma	78	M6
Huma	78	M6
Humaitá	140	E5
Humbe	108	A3
Humble	52	F2
Humboldt	122	L6
Humboldt	126	C2
Hümedän	90	G4
Humenné	50	L9
Humphrey	126	D2
Humpolec	50	E8
Hūn	100	C2
Húnaflói	48	(1)C2
Hunchun	82	F2
Hunedoara	66	K4
Hünfeld	52	E6
Hungary	66	F3
Hungen	52	D6
Hungerford, *Australia*	114	H5
Hungerford, *United Kingdom*	54	A3
Hüngnam	82	D4
Hunjiang	82	D3
Hunsrück	52	B7
Hunstanton	54	C2
Hunte	52	D4
Hunter Island	112	H8
Huntingburg	130	D2
Huntingdon, *United Kingdom*	54	B2
Huntingdon, *United States*	130	E2
Huntington	130	D1
Huntington Beach	132	C2
Huntly	116	E3
Huntsville, *Canada*	128	E1
Huntsville, *Al., United States*	130	D3
Huntsville, *Tex., United States*	134	E2
Hunyuan	80	E3
Ḩūr	95	G1
Hurdiyo	106	J1
Hurghada	100	F2
Huron	126	G2
Hürth	54	J4
Húsavík	48	(1)E1
Huşi	66	R3
Huslia	132	(1)F2
Husn	94	C4
Husum	52	E2
Hutag	78	G7
Hutanopan	86	B2
Hutchinson	132	G1
Hüth	100	H4
Huttwil	62	C3
Huvadu Atoll	88	B8
Huy	54	H4
Huzou	80	G4
Hvannadalshnúkur	48	(1)E2
Hvar	66	D6
Hvar	66	D6
Hvolsvöllur	48	(1)C3
Hwange	108	D3
Hyak	126	B1
Hyannis	126	F2
Hyargas Nuur	76	S8
Hyden	114	C6
Hyderabad, *India*	88	C5
Hyderabad, *Pakistan*	90	J4
Hyères	58	M10
Hyesan	82	E3
Hyndam Peak	126	D2
Hyūga	82	F7
Hyvinkää	48	N6

I

Name	Page	Grid
Iaco	140	D6
Ialomița	66	P5
Ianca	66	Q4
Iași	66	Q2
Ibadan	104	E3
Ibagué	140	B3
Ibar	66	H6
Ibb	100	H5
Ibbenbüren	52	C4
Iberia	140	C5
Ibiza = Eivissa	60	M5
Ibiza = Eivissa	60	M6
Ibotirama	140	J6
Ibrā'	90	G5
'Ibrī	95	G5
Ica	140	B6
Içana	140	D3
İçel	92	F5
Iceland	46	C1
Ichalkaranji	88	B5
Ichinoseki	82	L4
Idabel	130	C3
Ida Grove	128	A2
Idah	104	F3
Idaho	126	D2
Idaho Falls	126	D2
Idar-Oberstein	52	C7
Idfu	100	F3
Idhän Awbārī	102	H3
Idhan Murzūq	102	H4
Idiofa	106	C4
Idlib	92	G6
Idstein	52	D6
Ieper	54	E4
Ierapetra	68	H9
Ifakara	106	F5
Ifanadiana	108	H4
Ife	104	E3
Ifjord	48	P1
Igarka	76	R4
Iggesund	48	J6
Igizyar	90	L2
Iglesias	64	C9
Igli	102	E2
Igloolik	36	Q3
Ignace	128	B1
İğneada	68	K3
Igoumenitsa	68	C5
Igra	70	K3
Igrim	70	M2
Igualada	60	M3
Iguatu	140	K5
Ihosy	108	H4
Ihtiman	66	L7
Iida	82	J6
Iim	92	G2
Iisalmi	122	W3
Ijebu Ode	104	E3
IJmuiden	54	G2
IJssel	54	J2
IJsselmeer	54	H2
Ikaria	68	J7
Ikeda	82	M2
Ikela	106	C4
Iki	82	E7
Ikire	104	E3
Ikom	104	F3
Ikopa	108	H3
Ikorodu	104	E3
Ilagan	84	G3
Ïläm	90	E3
Iława	50	J4
Ilbenge	78	L4
Ilebo	106	C4
Île d'Anticosti	38	U7
Île de Jerba	102	H2
Île de la Gonâve	134	K5
Île de Noirmoutier	58	C7
Île de Ré	58	D7
Île d'Oléron	58	D8
Île d'Yeu	58	C7
Île Europa	108	G4
Ilek	70	K4
Ilek	70	K4
Île Plane	64	E11
Îles Cani	64	D11
Îles Chesterfield	112	F7
Îles Crozet	98	J10
Îles de Désappointement	112	M7
Îles de la Madeleine	38	U7
Îles d'Hyères	58	M11
Îles Duc de Gloucester	112	M7
Îles Glorieuses	108	H2
Ilesha	104	E3
Îles Kerkenah	102	H2
Îles Maria	112	L8
Îles Palliser	112	M7
Île Tidra	102	B5
Île Zembra	64	E11
Ilfracombe	56	H10
Ilgin	92	D4
Ilha da Trindade	138	H6
Ilha de Marajó	140	H4
Ilha de São Luís	140	J4
Ilha do Bazaruto	108	F4
Ilha Fernando de Noronha	140	L4
Ilha Grande	140	E4
Ilha Grande de Gurupa	140	G4
Ilharaña	108	H2
Ilhas Martin Vaz	142	Q3
Ilhéus	140	K6
Ili	76	P9
Iliamna Volcano	132	(1)G4
Iligan	84	G5
Ilkal	88	C5
Iller	62	F3
Illertissen	62	F2
Illichivs'k	66	T3
Illinois	124	H3
Illinois	124	C2
Illizi	102	G3
Illorsuit	122	W2
Ilmenau	52	F6
Ilo	140	C7
Iloilo	84	G4
Ilorin	104	E3
Ilovlya	70	H5
Il'pyrskiy	78	U4
Ilsalmi	48	P5
Iwaco	126	B1
Ilych	70	L2
Imabari	82	G6
Imatra	48	Q6
Imeni-Babushkina	76	G6
Imeni Polinyosipenko	78	P6
Imese	106	B3
Imī	106	G2
Imişli	92	N4
Immeln	52	D1
Immenstadt	62	F3
Imola	62	G6
Imotski	66	E6
Imperatriz	140	H5
Imperia	62	D7
Imperial	126	F2
Impfondo	106	B3
Imphal	88	F4
Imrali Adası	68	L4
Imroz	68	H4
Ina	82	J6
Inambari	140	C6
In Aménas	102	G3
Inangahua	116	C5
Inanwatan	87	D3
Iñapari	140	D6
Inarijärvi	48	P2
Inca	60	N5
Ince Burun	92	F2
Inch'ŏn	82	D5
Incirliova	68	K7
Indalsälven	48	H5
Independence, *Kans., United States*	130	B2
Independence, *Mo., United States*	128	B3
India	88	C4
Indiana	124	J3
Indiana	128	E2
Indianapolis	130	D2
Indian Ocean	42	J4
Indianola	128	B2
Indian Springs	126	C3
Indiga	70	J1
Indio	132	C2
Indonesia	86	D3
Indore	88	C4
Indramayu	86	D4
Indre	58	G6
Indre Sula	48	C6
Indus	90	K3
İnebolu	92	E3
İnecik	68	K4
İnegöl	92	C3
In Ekker	102	G4
Ineu	66	J3
Ingelheim	52	L5
Ingeniero Jacobacci	142	H7
Ingham	114	J3
Ingoda	78	J6
Ingolstadt	62	G2

Ingrāj Bāzār 88 E3
I-n-Guezzam 102 G5
Ingushetiya 92 L2
Inhambane 108 F4
Inhaminga 108 E3
Inírida 140 D3
Inishmore 56 B8
Inkisi-Kisantu 104 H6
Inn 62 H2
Inner Hebrides 56 F5
Inner Mongolia = Nei Monggol 80 E2
Inneston 114 G7
Innisfail 114 J3
Innsbruck 62 G3
Inongo 106 B4
Inowrocław 50 H5
In Salah 102 F3
Insein 84 B3
Inta 76 K4
Interlaken 62 C4
International Falls 128 B1
Intsy 70 H1
Inubō-zaki 82 L6
Inukjuak 36 R5
Inuvik 34 E3
Inveraray 56 G5
Invercargill 116 B8
Inverness 56 H4
Inverway 114 E3
Investigator Group 114 F6
Investigator Strait 114 G7
Inya 76 R7
Inya 78 R4
Ioannina 68 C5
Iokanga 76 F4
Iola 130 B2
Iona 56 F5
Ionești 66 M5
Ionian Sea 68 B6
Ionioi Nisoi 68 B5
Ios 68 H8
Ios 68 H8
Iowa 124 H3
Iowa City 128 B2
Iowa Falls 128 B2
Ipameri 140 H7
Ipatinga 142 N2
Ipatovo 70 H5
Ipiales 140 B3
Ipiaú 140 K6
Ipoh 86 C2
Iporá 140 G7
Ippy 106 C2
İpsala 68 J4
Ipswich 56 P9
Iqaluit 38 T4
Iquique 142 G3
Iquitos 140 C4
Iracoubo 140 G2
Irakleia 68 F3
Irakleia 68 H8
Irakleio 68 H9
Iraklion = Irakleio 46 G4
Iran 90 F3
Irānshahr 90 H4
Irapuato 134 D4
Iraq 90 D3
Irbid 94 C4
Irbit 70 M3
Irecê 140 J6
Irgiz 70 M5
Irgiz 70 M5
Irhil M'Goun 102 D2
Irian Jaya 87 E3
Iringa 106 F5
Iriri 140 G4
Irish Sea 56 G8
Irkutsk 78 G6
Iron Mountain 128 C1
Ironton 130 E2
Ironwood 128 B1
Iroquois Falls 36 Q7
Irrawaddy 88 F5
Irshava 66 L1
Irta 70 J2
Irtysh 70 P3
Irtyshsk 76 P7
Irumu 106 D3
Irún 60 J1
Irvine 56 H6
Irving 132 G2
Isabela 87 B1
Isabella 128 B1
Isabella Lake 132 C1
Ísafjarðardjúp 48 (1)A1
Ísafjörður 48 (1)B1
Isahaya 82 F7
Isar 62 G3
Ischia 64 H8
Ischia 64 H8
Ise 82 J6
Isel 62 H4
Isère 62 B5
Iserlohn 54 K3
Isernia 64 J7
Isetskoye 70 N3
Iseyin 104 E3
Isfana 90 J2
Ishikari-wan 82 L2
Ishim 70 N3
Ishim 70 N4
Ishinomaki 82 L4
Ishkoshim 90 K2
Isigny-sur-Mer 54 A5
Isiolo 106 F3
Isiro 106 D3
Iskăr 66 M6
İskenderun 92 G5
Iskitim 76 Q7
Isla Alejandro Selkirk 142 E5
Isla Campana 142 F8
Isla Clarence 142 G9
Isla Clarión 134 B5
Isla Coiba 134 H7
Isla Contreras 142 F9
Isla de Alborán 60 G9
Isla de Bioco 104 F4
Isla de Chiloé 142 G7
Isla de Coco 134 G7
Isla de Cozumel 134 G4
Isla de la Juventud 134 H4
Isla de los Estados 142 J9
Isla de Malpelo 140 A3
Isla de Margarita 140 E1
Isla de Providencia 134 H6
Isla de San Andrés 134 H6
Isla de São Francisco 142 M4
Isla de São Sebastião 142 M3
Isla Desolación 142 F9
Isla Española 140 (1)B2
Isla Fernandina 140 (1)A2
Isla Gorgona 140 B3
Isla Grande 142 N3
Isla Grande de Tierra del Fuego 142 H9
Isla Guafo 142 F7
Isla Hoste 142 G10
Isla Isabela 140 (1)A2
Isla La Tortuga 140 D1
Isla Londonderry 142 G9
Islamabad 88 B2
Isla Madre de Dios 142 F9
Isla Marchena 140 (1)A1
Islamgarh 88 B3
Islamorada 130 E5
Isla Navarino 142 H10
Island Lake 36 N6
Islands of the Four Mountains 132 (1)C5
Isla Pinta 140 (1)A1
Isla Puná 140 A4
Isla Riesco 142 G9
Isla Robinson Crusoe 142 E5
Isla San Benedicto 134 B5
Isla San Cristóbal 140 (1)B2
Isla San Salvador 140 (1)A2
Isla Santa Cruz 140 (1)A2
Isla Santa Inés 142 F9
Isla Santa María 140 (1)A2
Islas Baleares 60 N5
Islas Canarias 98 A3
Islas Canarias 102 B3
Islas Columbretes 60 L5
Islas de la Bahía 134 G5
Islas de los Desventurados 142 E4
Islas Galápagos 140 (1)B1
Islas Juan Fernández 142 E5
Islas Los Roques 140 D1
Islas Marías 134 C4
Isla Socorro 134 B5
Islas Revillagigedo 134 B5
Islas Wollaston 142 H10
Isla Wellington 142 F8
Islay 56 F6
Isle 58 F8
Isle of Man 56 H7
Isle of Wight 56 L11
Isle Royale 128 C1
Isles of Scilly 56 F12
Ismâ'ilîya 100 F1
İsmayıllı 92 N3
Isna 100 F2
Isoka 108 E2
Isola delle Correnti 64 J12
Isola di Capo Rizzuto 64 M10
Isola di Pantelleria 64 G12
Isole Égadi 64 F11
Isole Lipari 64 J10
Isole Ponziane 64 H8
Isole Tremiti 64 K6
Iso-Vietonen 48 N3
Isparta 68 N7
Ispica 64 J12
Israel 94 B5
Israelite Bay 114 D6
Issia 104 C3
Issimu 87 B2
Issoire 58 J8
Issoudun 58 H7
Issyk-Kul' 76 P9
İstanbul 92 C3
İstanbul Boğazı 92 C3
Istiaia 68 F6
Istmo de Tehauntepec 134 F5
Istra 62 J5
Istres 58 K10
Itaberaba 140 J6
Itabira 140 J7
Itabuna 140 K6
Itacoatiara 140 F4
Itaituba 140 F4
Itajaí 142 M4
Italy 64 E4
Itambacuri 140 J7
Itanagar 88 F3
Itapebi 140 K7
Itapetinga 140 J7
Itapicuru 140 K6
Itapicuru Mirim 140 J4
Itapipoca 140 K4
Itarsi 88 C4
Ithaca 128 E2
Ithaki 68 C6
Ithaki 68 C6
Itiquira 140 G7
Ituí 140 C5
Ituiutaba 140 H7
Itumbiara 140 H7
Ituni 140 F2
Ituri 106 D3
Ituxi 140 D5
Itzehoe 52 E3
Iuaretê 140 D3
Iutica 140 D3
Ivalo 48 P2
Ivanava 48 N10
Ivangrad 66 G7
Ivanhoe, *Australia* 114 H6
Ivanhoe, *United States* 128 A2
Ivano-Frankivs'k 70 D5
Ivanovo 70 H3
Ivatsevichy 48 N10
Ivdel' 70 M2
Ivittuut 122 X4
Ivohibe 108 H4
Ivosjön 50 D1
Ivrea 62 C5
Ivujivik 122 R4
Iwaki 82 L5
Iwamizawa 82 L2
Iwo 104 E3
Iyo-nadā 82 G7
Izberbash 92 M2
Izegern 54 F4
Izhevsk 70 K3
Izhma 70 K1
Izhma 70 K2
Izk 90 G5
Izkī 95 G5
Izmayil 66 R4
İzmir 92 B4
İzmir Körfezi 68 J6
İzmit 92 C3
İznik 92 C3
İznik Gölü 92 C3
Izola 62 J5
Izra' 94 D4
Izuhara 82 E6
Izumo 82 G6
Izu-shotō 82 K6

J

Jabal ad Durūẓ 94 D4
Jabal Akhḑar 95 G5
Jabal al Nuşayrīyah 94 D1
Jabal an Nabī Shu'ayb 100 H4
Jabal Ash Sham 95 G5
Jabal aẓ Ẓannah 95 E4
Jabalpur 88 C4
Jabal Shammar 100 G2
Jabal Thamar 100 J5
Jabiru 114 F2
Jablah 94 C1
Jablonec 50 E7
Jablunkov 50 H8
Jaboatão 140 K5
Jaca 60 K2
Jacareacanga 140 G5
Jackman 128 F1
Jacksboro 130 B3
Jackson, *Calif., United States* 126 B3
Jackson, *Minn., United States* 128 B2
Jackson, *Miss., United States* 130 C3
Jackson, *Oh., United States* 130 E2
Jackson, *Tenn., United States* 130 D2
Jackson Head 116 B6
Jackson Lake 126 D2
Jacksonville, *Fla., United States* 130 E3
Jacksonville, *Ill., United States* 128 B3
Jacksonville, *N.C., United States* 130 F3
Jacksonville, *Tex., United States* 130 B3
Jacmel 134 K5
Jacobabad 88 A3
Jacobina 140 J6
Jacunda 140 H4
Jacupiranga 142 M3
Jade 52 D3
Jadebusen 52 D3
J.A.D. Jensens Nunatakker 38 X4
Jādū 102 H2
Jaén 60 G7
Jaen 140 B5
Jaffna 88 D7
Jagdalpur 88 D5
Jagersfontein 108 D5
Jaggang 88 C2
Jagst 52 E7
Jahrom 95 E2
Jaipur 88 C3
Jaisalmer 88 B3
Jajce 66 E5
Jakarta 86 D4
Jäkkvik 48 J3
Jakobshavn = Ilulissat 122 W3
Jakobstad 48 M5
Jalālābād 88 B2
Jalandhar 88 C2
Jalapa Enriquez 134 E5
Jalgaon 88 C4
Jalībah 95 B1
Jalingo 104 G3
Jalna 88 C5
Jalón 60 J3
Jalpaiguri 88 E3
Jālū 100 D2
Jalūlā 92 L6
Jamaica 134 H5
Jamalpur 88 E3
Jambi 86 C3
Jambol 66 P7
James 126 G2
James Bay 36 Q6
Jamestown, *N.Y., United States* 128 E2
Jamestown, *N.D., United States* 126 G1
Jammerbugten 48 E8
Jammu 88 B2
Jammu and Kashmir 88 C2
Jamnagar 88 B4
Jämsä 48 N6
Jamshedpur 88 E4
Janakpur 88 E3
Janaúba 140 J7
Jandaq 90 F3
Jandongi 106 C3
Jane Peak 116 B7
Janesville 128 C2
Jan Mayen 120 C2
Jannatabad 76 L10
Janos 132 E2
Jánossomorja 62 N3
Janów Lubelski 50 M7
Januária 140 J7
Jaora 88 C4
Japan 82 L5
Japan Trench 112 E2
Japurá 140 D4
Jarābulus 92 H5
Jaramillo 142 H8
Jarash 94 C4
Jardim 142 K3
Jarosław 50 M7
Järpen 48 G5
Jarud Qi 80 G2
Järvenpää 48 N6
Jarvis 112 K6
Jasel'da 48 N10
Jāsk 95 G4
Jason Islands 142 J9
Jasper, *Canada* 34 H6
Jasper, *Al., United States* 130 D3
Jasper, *Fla., United States* 130 E3
Jasper, *Tex., United States* 130 C3
Jastrebarsko 62 L5
Jászberény 66 G2
Jataí 140 G7
Jatapu 140 F4
Jaunpur 88 D3
Java = Jawa 86 E4
Javarthushuu 78 J7
Java Sea 86 E4
Javoriv 50 N8
Jawa 86 E4
Jawhar 106 H3
Jayapura 87 F3
Jayrūd 94 D3
Jaza'īr Farasān 100 H4
Jazīrat Būbīyān 95 C2
Jazīrat-ye Khārk 95 D2
Jbail 94 C2
Jbel Ayachi 102 E2
Jbel Bou Naceur 102 E2
Jbel Toubkal 102 D2
Jean 126 C3
Jebba 104 E3
Jebel Bāqir 94 C7
Jebel el Atā'ita 94 C6
Jebel el Batrā 94 C7
Jebel-esh Sharqi 94 C3
Jebel Gimbala 100 D5
Jebel Ithrīyat 94 D6
Jebel Liban 94 C3
Jebel Mubrak 94 C6
Jebel Ram 94 C7
Jebel Uweinat 100 E3
Jedburgh 56 K6
Jedda = Jiddah 90 C5
Jedeida 64 D12
Jędrzejów 50 K7
Jefferson 128 B2
Jefferson City, *Mo., United States* 128 B3
Jefferson City, *Tenn., United States* 130 E2
Jeffersonville 128 C3
Jega 104 E2
Jēkabpils 48 N8
Jelgava 48 M8
Jemaja 86 D2
Jena 52 G6
Jendouba 102 G1
Jenin 94 C4
Jenkins 128 D3
Jequié 140 J6
Jequitinhonha 140 J7
Jerada 102 E2
Jeremoabo 140 K6
Jerez 132 F4
Jerez de la Frontera 60 D8
Jerez de los Caballeros 60 D6
Jericho, *Australia* 114 J4
Jericho, *Israel* 94 C5
Jerramungup 114 C6
Jersey 58 C4
Jersey City 130 G1
Jerusalem = Yerushalayim 94 C5
Jesenice 66 B3
Jesenik 50 G7
Jesi 62 J7
Jessore 88 E4
Jesup 130 E3
Jeumont 54 G4
Jever 52 C3
Jeypore 88 D5
Jezioro 50 D4
Jezioro Gardno 48 J9
Jezioro Jeziorsko 50 H6
Jezioro Łebsko 50 F3
Jezioro Śniardwy 50 L4
Jezioro Wigry 50 N2
Jezzine 94 C3
Jhang Maghiana 88 B2
Jhansi 88 C3
Jharsuguda 88 D4
Jhelum 88 B2
Jialing Jiang 80 D4
Jiamusi 80 J1
Ji'an 80 E5
Jiangle 80 F5
Jiangling 80 E4
Jiangmen 80 E6
Jiangyou 80 C4
Jianyang 80 F5
Jiaonan 80 F3
Jiaozou 80 E3
Jiaxing 80 G4
Jiayuguan 80 B3
Jibou 66 L2
Jičín 50 E7
Jiddah 90 C5
Jiesjavrre 48 N2

197

Name	Page	Ref.
Kiryū	82	K5
Kisangani	106	D3
Kisbér	66	E2
Kiselevsk	76	R7
Kishanganj	88	E3
Kishangarh, *India*	88	B3
Kishangarh, *India*	88	B3
Kishi	104	E3
Kishiwada	82	H6
Kishtwar	88	C2
Kisii	106	E4
Kiska Island	132	(3)B1
Kiskőrös	66	G3
Kiskunfélegyháza	66	G3
Kiskunhalas	66	G3
Kiskunmajsa	66	G3
Kislovodsk	92	K2
Kismaayo	106	G4
Kissidougou	104	B3
Kisumu	106	E4
Kisvárda	66	K1
Kita	104	C2
Kitakami	82	L4
Kita-Kyūshū	80	H4
Kita-Kyūshū	82	F7
Kitami	82	M2
Kitchener	38	Q8
Kitgum	106	E3
Kitimat	122	F6
Kitimat Ranges	34	F6
Kittilä	48	N3
Kitunda	106	E5
Kitwe	108	D2
Kitzingen	52	F7
Kiuruvesi	48	P5
Kivijärvi	48	N5
Kivik	50	D2
Kiya	78	D5
Kıyıköy	92	C3
Kizel	70	L3
Kizilalan	68	R8
Kızılcahamam	92	E3
Kızılırmak	92	F3
Kızılkaya	68	N7
Kizil'skoye	70	L4
Kiziltepe	92	J5
Kizlyar	92	M2
Kizlyarskiy Zaliv	92	M1
Kizyl-Atrek	76	J10
Kjustendil	68	E2
Kladanj	66	F5
Kladno	50	D2
Klagenfurt	62	K4
Klaipėda	48	L9
Klamath	126	B2
Klamath	126	B2
Klamath Falls	126	B2
Klarälven	48	G6
Klatovy	52	J7
Klaus	62	K3
Klerksdorp	108	D5
Kleve	52	B5
Klin	70	G3
Klingenthal	52	H6
Klínovec	52	H6
Klintsy	70	F4
Ključ	62	M6
Kłobuck	50	H7
Kłodzko	50	F7
Klofta	48	F6
Klosterneuburg	62	M2
Klosters	62	E4
Kluane	122	D4
Kluane Lake	132	(1)J3
Kluczbork	50	H7
Klyuchevskaya Sopka	78	U5
Klyuchi	78	U5
Kneža	66	M6
Knin	66	D5
Knittelfeld	66	B2
Knjaževac	66	K6
Knokke-Heist	54	F3
Knoxville	128	D3
Knysna	108	C6
Koba	86	D3
Kōbe	82	H6
Kobe	87	C2
København	48	G9
Kobenni	102	D5
Koblenz	52	C6
Kobo	88	G3
Kobroör	87	E4
Kobryn	50	P5
Kobuk	132	(1)F2
Kobuk	132	(1)F2
Kočani	68	E3
Koçarli	68	K7
Kočevje	66	B4
Ko Chang	84	C4
Kōch'ang	82	E6
Kochechum	78	F3
Kochi	88	C7
Kōchi	82	G7
Koch Island	36	R3
Kochki	76	Q7
Kochkorka	76	P9
Kochubey	92	M1
Kodiak	132	(1)G4
Kodiak Island	132	(1)G4
Kodino	70	G2
Kodinsk	78	F5
Kodomari-misaki	82	L3
Kodyma	66	S1
Kōflach	66	C2
Kōfu	82	K6
Køge	50	B2
Køge Bugt	50	B2
Kohat	88	B2
Kohima	88	F3
Koh-i-Qaisir	90	H3
Koh-i-Sangan	90	J3
Kohtla-Järve	48	P7
Kohumadulu Atoll	88	B8
Koidu	104	B3
Koi Sanjaq	92	L6
Koitere	48	R5
Kokenau	87	E3
Kokkola	48	M5
Kokomo	130	D1
Kokpekty	76	Q8
Kokshetau	70	N4
Koksoak	38	T5
Kokstad	108	D6
Kolaka	87	B3
Kolar	88	C6
Kolari	48	M3
Kolašin	66	G7
Kolda	104	B2
Kolding	48	E9
Kole	106	C4
Kolhapur	88	B5
Kolin	50	E7
Kolkata	88	E4
Kollam	88	C7
Köln	52	B6
Kolno	50	L4
Koło	50	H5
Kołobrzeg	50	E3
Kologriv	70	H3
Kolomna	70	G3
Kolomyya	66	N1
Kolonedale	87	B3
Kolosovka	70	P3
Kolpashevo	76	Q6
Kolpos Agiou Orous	68	F4
Kolpos Kassandras	68	F4
Kolpos Murampelou	68	H9
Kolskijzaliv	48	S2
Kolskiy Poluostrov	70	G1
Koluton	70	N4
Kolva	70	L2
Kolwezi	108	D2
Kolyma	78	R4
Kolymskaya Nizmennost'	78	S3
Kolymskaye	78	T3
Komandorskiye Ostrova	78	V5
Komárno	66	F2
Komárom	66	F2
Komatsu	82	J5
Kombe	106	D4
Komi	70	K2
Komló	66	F3
Kom Ombo	100	F3
Komotini	68	H3
Komsa	76	R5
Komsomol'skiy	78	J5
Komsomol'sk-na-Amure	78	P6
Konárka	88	E5
Konda	70	N3
Kondagaon	88	D5
Kondinskoye	70	N3
Kondoa	106	F4
Kondopoga	70	F2
Kondrat'yeva	78	V5
Kondūz	90	J2
Kong Frederik VI Kyst	122	Y4
Kongi	76	R9
Kongola	108	C3
Kongolo	106	D5
Kongsberg	48	E7
Kongur Shan	76	N10
Königsberg = Kaliningrad	48	K3
Königswinter	52	C6
Königs-Wusterhausen	52	J4
Konin	50	H5
Konispol	68	C5
Konitsa	68	C4
Köniz	62	C4
Konjic	66	E6
Konosha	70	H2
Konotop	70	F4
Konstanz	62	E3
Kontagora	104	F2
Kon Tum	84	D4
Konya	92	E5
Konz	52	B7
Kookynie	114	D5
Kootenai	126	C1
Kootenay Lake	124	C2
Kópasker	48	(1)E1
Kópavogur	48	(1)C2
Koper	62	J5
Kopeysk	70	M3
Köping	48	J7
Koplik	66	G7
Koprivnica	66	D3
Korba, *India*	88	D4
Korba, *Tunisia*	64	E12
Korbach	52	D5
Korçë	68	C4
Korčula	66	D7
Kord Sheykh	95	E2
Korea Bay	82	B4
Korea Strait	82	E6
Korf	78	V4
Korhogo	104	C3
Korinthiakos Kolpos	68	E6
Korinthos	68	E7
Köriyama	82	L5
Korkino	70	M4
Korkuteli	92	D5
Korla	76	R9
Korliki	70	C4
Körmend	66	D2
Kornat	66	C6
Koroba	87	F4
Köroğlu Dağları	68	Q4
Köroğlu Tepesi	68	P4
Korogwe	106	F5
Koronowo	50	G4
Koror	112	D5
Korosten'	70	E4
Koro Toro	100	C4
Korsakov	78	Q7
Korsør	52	G1
Korti	100	F4
Kortrijk	54	F4
Korumburra	114	J7
Koryakskiy Khrebet	78	V4
Koryazhma	76	H5
Kos	68	K8
Kos	68	K8
Kosa	70	L3
Ko Samui	84	C5
Kościan	50	F5
Kościerzyna	50	H3
Kosciusko	130	D3
Kosh Agach	76	R8
Koshoba	90	F1
Košice	50	L9
Koslan	70	J2
Kosŏng	82	E4
Kosovo	68	C2
Kosovska Mitrovica	68	C2
Kosrae	112	G5
Kostajnica	62	M5
Kostanay	70	M4
Kostenec	68	F2
Kosti	100	F5
Kostinbrod	66	L7
Kostino	78	D3
Kostomuksha	48	R4
Kostroma	70	H3
Kostrzyn	50	D5
Kos'yu	70	L1
Koszalin	50	F3
Kőszeg	66	D2
Kota	88	C3
Kotaagung	86	C4
Kotabaru	86	F3
Kota Belud	86	F1
Kota Bharu	86	C1
Kotabumi	86	C3
Kota Kinabalu	86	F1
Kotamubagu	87	B2
Kotapinang	86	B2
Kotel'nich	70	J3
Kotel'nikovo	70	H5
Köthen	52	G5
Kotido	106	E3
Kotka	48	P6
Kotlas	70	J2
Kotlik	132	(1)E3
Kotor Varoš	66	E5
Kotov'sk	70	E5
Kottagudem	88	D5
Kotto	106	C2
Kotuy	70	J2
Kotzebue	132	(1)E2
Kotzebue Sound	132	(1)D2
Kouango	104	H3
Koudougou	104	D2
Koulamoutou	104	G5
Koum	104	G3
Koumra	104	H3
Koundâra	104	B2
Koupéla	102	C6
Kourou	140	G2
Koutiala	104	C2
Kouvola	70	E2
Kovdor	48	R3
Kovel'	70	D4
Kovin	66	H5
Kovrov	70	H3
Kowanyama	114	H3
Köyceğiz	68	L8
Koygorodok	70	K2
Koykuk	132	(1)E3
Koynas	70	J2
Koyukuk	132	(1)F2
Kozan	92	F5
Kozani	68	D4
Kozheynikovo	76	W3
Kozhikode	88	C6
Kozienice	50	L6
Kozloduy	66	L6
Kozlu	68	P3
Kōzu-shima	82	K6
Kpalimé	104	E3
Kraai	108	D6
Krabi	84	B5
Kradeljevo	64	M5
Kragujevac	66	H5
Kraków	50	J7
Kraljeviča	62	K5
Kraljevo	66	H6
Kralovice	50	C8
Kramators'k	70	G5
Kramfors	48	J5
Kranj	66	B3
Krapina	66	K2
Krapinske Toplice	62	L4
Krasino	76	J3
Kráslava	48	P9
Kraśnik	50	M7
Krasnoarmeysk	70	N4
Krasnoborsk	70	J2
Krasnodar	70	G5
Krasnohrad	70	G5
Krasnokamensk	78	K6
Krasnosel'kup	76	C3
Krasnotur'insk	70	M3
Krasnoufimsk	70	L3
Krasnovishersk	70	L2
Krasnoyarsk	78	E5
Krasnoyarskoye Vodokhranilishche	76	S6
Krasnoznamensk	50	M3
Krasnystaw	50	N7
Krasnyy Chikoy	78	H6
Krasnyy Kut	70	J4
Krasnyy Yar	70	J5
Kraynka	68	E2
Kraynovka	92	M2
Krefeld	54	J3
Kremenchuk	70	F5
Kremmling	126	E2
Krems	62	L2
Kremsmünster	62	K2
Krestovka	70	K1
Krestyakh	78	K4
Kretinga	50	L2
Kribi	104	F4
Krishna	88	C5
Krishnagiri	88	C6
Kristiansand	48	E7
Kristianstad	48	H8
Kristiansund	48	D5
Kristinehamn	48	H7
Kristinestad	48	L5
Kriti	68	H10
Kriva Palanka	68	E2
Križevci	66	D3
Krk	62	K5
Krk	62	K5
Kroměříž	50	G8
Kronach	52	G6
Krŏng Kaôh Kŏng	84	C4
Kronotskiy Zaliv	78	U6
Kroonstad	108	D5
Kroper	64	H3
Kropotkin	70	H5
Krosno	50	L8
Krško	62	L5
Krugë	68	B3
Krui	86	C4
Krumbach	62	F2
Krung Thep	84	C4
Krusâ	52	E2
Kruševac	66	J6
Krychaw	70	F4
Krym'	92	E1
Krymsk	92	H1
Krynica	50	L8
Krytiko Pelagos	68	G9
Kryve Ozero	66	T2
Kryvyy Rih	70	F5
Krzna	50	N5
Ksar el Boukhari	60	N9
Ksen'yevka	78	K6
Ksour Essaf	102	H1
Kuala Kerai	86	C1
Kuala Lipis	86	C2
Kuala Lumpur	86	C2
Kuala Terengganu	86	C1
Kuandian	82	C3
Kuantan	86	C2
Kuçadasi	68	K7
Kučevo	66	J5
Kuching	86	E2
Kucovë	68	B4
Kudat	86	F1
Kudus	86	E4
Kudymkar	70	K3
Kufstein	62	H3
Kugmallit Bay	122	E2
Kühbonän	95	G1
Kühdasht	92	M7
Küh-e Alījuq	95	D1
Küh-e Bābā	90	J3
Küh-e Būl	95	E1
Küh-e Dīnär	95	D1
Küh-e Fürgun	95	G3
Küh-e Hazärän	95	G2
Küh-e Hormoz	95	F3
Küh-e Kalat	90	G3
Küh-e Kührän	95	H3
Küh-e Läleh Zär	95	G2
Küh-e Masähün	95	F1
Küh-e Safidär	95	E2
Kuh-e Sahand	92	M5
Kühestak	95	G3
Küh-e Taftän	90	H4
Kühhä-ye Bashäkerd	95	G3
Kühhä-ye Zägros	95	D1
Kuhmo	48	Q4
Kühpäyeh	95	G1
Kuito	108	B2
Kuji	82	L3
Kukës	66	H7
Kukhtuy	78	Q4
Kukinaga	82	F8
Kula	66	K6
Kulagino	70	K5
Kulandy	76	K8
Kuldīga	48	L8
Kulgera	114	F5
Kulmbach	52	G6
Külob	90	J2
Kul'sary	70	K5
Kultsjön	48	H4
Kulu	92	E4
Kulunda	76	P7
Kulynigol	78	C4
Kuma	70	N3
Kumamoto	82	F7
Kumanovo	66	J7
Kumara, *New Zealand*	116	C6
Kumara, *Russia*	78	M6
Kumasi	104	D3
Kumba	104	F4
Kumba	68	K4
Kumbakonam	88	C6
Kumeny	70	K3
Kumertau	70	L4
Kumla	48	H7
Kumluca	68	N8
Kummerower See	52	H3
Kumo	104	G3
Kumta	88	B6
Kumukh	92	M2
Kunene	108	A3
Kungälv	48	F8
Kungrad	76	K9
Kungu	106	B3
Kungur	70	L3
Kunhing	84	B2

Landstuhl 54 K5
Land Wursten 52 D3
La'nga Co 88 D2
Langarūd 92 N5
Langdon 126 G1
Langebæk 52 H1
Langeland 52 F2
Langen, *Germany* 54 L5
Langen, *Germany* 52 D3
Langenau 62 F2
Langenhagen 52 E4
Langeoog 52 C3
Langeoog 52 C3
Langfang 80 F3
Langjökull 48 (1)C2
Langkawi 84 B5
Langkon 84 F5
Langogne 58 J9
Langon 58 E9
Langøya 48 H2
Langreo 60 E1
Langres 62 A3
Langsa 84 B6
Langtry 132 F3
Langvatnet 48 G3
Länkäran 92 N4
Lannion 58 B5
L'Anse 128 C1
Lansing 128 D2
Lanxi 80 H1
Lanya 106 E2
Lanzarote 102 C3
Lanzhou 80 C3
Laoag 84 G3
Lao Cai 84 C2
Laohekou 80 E4
Laon 54 F5
La Oroya 140 B6
Laos 84 C3
Laotougou 82 E2
Lapa 142 M4
La Palma 102 B3
La Palma 134 J7
La Paragua 140 E2
La Paz, *Argentina* 142 K5
La Paz, *Bolivia* 140 D7
La Paz, *Mexico* 134 B4
La Pedrera 140 D4
La Perla 132 F3
La Pérouse Strait 80 L1
La Pesca 130 B5
La Pine 126 B2
Lapithos 94 A1
Lapland 48 M2
La Plant 126 F1
La Plata 142 K5
Lappajärvi 48 M5
Lappeenranta 48 Q6
Laptev Sea = More Laptevykh 78 L1
Lapua 48 M5
Łapy 50 M5
La Quiaca 142 H3
L'Aquila 64 H6
Lār 95 F3
Larache 102 D1
Laramie 126 E2
Laramie Range 126 E2
Larantuka 87 B4
Larat 87 D4
Larba 60 P8
Laredo, *Spain* 60 G1
Laredo, *United States* 132 G3
Largo 130 E4
L'Ariana 64 E12
Lariang 87 A3
La Rioja 142 H4
Larisa 68 E5
Larkana 90 J4
Larnaka 94 A2
Larne 56 G7
La Rochelle 58 D7
La Roche-sur-Yon 58 D7
La Roda 60 H5
La Romana 134 L5
La Ronge 122 K5
Larrimah 114 F3
Lar'yak 76 Q5
La Sarre 128 E1
Las Cabezas de San Juan 60 E7
Las Cruces 132 E2
La Serena 142 G4
La Seu d'Urgell 60 M2
La Seyne-sur-Mer 58 L10
Lashio 84 B2
Lashkar Gāh 90 H3
Las Horquetas 142 G8
Łask 50 J6
Las Lomitas 142 J3
La Solana 60 G6
Las Palmas 102 B3
Las Petas 140 F7
La Spezia 62 E6
Las Plumas 142 H7
Las Taques 140 C1
Last Chance 126 F3
Lastoursville 104 G5
Lastovo 66 D7
Las Varas 124 E7
Las Varillas 142 J5
Las Vegas, *Nev., United States* 126 C3
Las Vegas, *N. Mex., United States* 132 E1
La Teste 58 D9
Latina 64 G7
Latisana 62 J5
La Toma 142 H5
La Tuque 128 F1
Latur 88 C5
Latvia 48 M8
Lauchhammer 52 J5
Lauenburg 52 F3
Lauf 52 G7
Lau Group 112 J7
Launceston, *Australia* 114 J8
Launceston, *United Kingdom* 56 H11
La Union 60 K7
Laupheim 62 E2
Laura 114 H3
Laurel 130 D3
Lauria 64 K8
Laurinburg 130 F3
Lausanne 62 B4
Laut, *Indonesia* 86 F3
Laut, *Malaysia* 86 D2
Lauter 54 K5
Lauterbach 52 E6
Lava 50 L3
Laval, *Canada* 128 F1
Laval, *France* 58 E5
La Vall d'Uixo 60 K5
Lāvar Kabkān 95 D2
La Vega 134 K5
Laviana 60 E1
La Vila Joiosa 60 K6
Lavras 142 N3
Lavrentiya 78 Z3
Lavrio 68 G7
Lawdar 100 J5
Lawra 104 D2
Lawrence, *New Zealand* 116 B7
Lawrence, *Kans., United States* 128 A3
Lawrence, *Mass., United States* 128 F2
Lawrenceville 130 D2
Lawton 130 B3
Laya 70 L1
Laylā 100 J3
Laysan Island 112 J3
Layton 126 D2
Lazarev 78 Q6
Lázaro Cárdenas 134 D5
Lazdijai 50 N3
Lāzeh 95 E3
Lazo 78 P3
Leadville 126 E3
Leamington 128 D2
Leavenworth, *Kans., United States* 128 A3
Leavenworth, *Wash., United States* 126 B1
Lebach 54 J5
Lebanon 94 C3
Lebanon, *Mo., United States* 128 B3
Lebanon, *N.H., United States* 128 F2
Lebanon, *Pa., United States* 128 E2
Lebanon, *Tenn., United States* 128 C3
Lebel-sur-Quévillon 128 E1
Lębork 50 G3
Lebrija 60 D8
Lebu 142 G6
Lecce 64 N8
Lecco 62 E5
Lech 62 F3
Leck 52 D2
Le Creusot 58 K7
Le Crotoy 54 D4
Łeczna 50 M6
Łęczyca 50 J5
Ledmozero 48 R4
Lee 56 D10
Leech Lake 128 B1
Leeds 56 L8
Leek, *Netherlands* 54 J1
Leek, *United Kingdom* 54 A1
Leer 54 K1
Leesburg 130 E4
Leeston 116 D6
Leesville 130 C3
Leeuwarden 54 H1
Leeward Islands 134 M5
Lefkada 68 C6
Lefkada 68 C6
Lefkimmi 68 C5
Lefkonikon 94 A1
Lefkosia 68 R9
Legaspi 84 G4
Legionowo 50 K5
Legnago 62 G5
Legnica 50 F6
Leh 88 C2
Le Havre 54 C5
Lehre 52 F4
Lehrte 52 F4
Leiah 88 B2
Leibnitz 62 L4
Leicester 54 A2
Leiden 54 G2
Leie 54 F4
Leigh Creek 114 G6
Leighton Buzzard 54 B3
Leine 52 E4
Leinster 114 D5
Leipzig 52 H5
Leiria 60 B5
Leiyang 80 E5
Lek 54 G3
Lelystad 54 H2
Le Mans 58 F6
Le Mars 128 A2
Lemberg 52 D8
Lemesos 68 Q10
Lemgo 54 L2
Lemieux Islands 38 U4
Lemmer 54 H2
Lemmon 126 F1
Le Muret 58 E9
Lena 60 E1
Lena 78 L4
Lendava 62 M4
Lendinare 62 G5
Lengerich 54 K2
Lengshuijiang 80 E5
Lengshuitan 80 E5
Lenininsk-Kuznetskiy 76 R7
Leninskoye 70 J3
Lenmalu 87 D3
Lenne 54 K3
Lennestadt 54 L3
Lens 54 E4
Lensk 78 K4
Lenti 62 M4
Lentini 64 J11
Léo 104 D2
Leoben 62 L3
León, *Mexico* 134 D4
León, *Nicaragua* 134 G6
León, *Spain* 60 E2
Leonardville 108 B4
Leonberg 62 E2
Leonforte 64 J11
Leonidi 68 E7
Leonora 114 D5
Leova 66 R3
Le Palais 58 B6
Lepe 60 C7
Le Perthus 58 H11
Lepoura 68 G6
Lepsy 76 P8
Le Puy 58 J8
Léré 104 G3
Lerici 62 E6
Lerik 92 N4
Lerma 60 G2
Leros 68 J7
Lerwick 56 L1
Lešak 66 H6
Les Andelys 54 D5
Lesatima 106 F4
Lesbos = Lesvos 68 H5
Les Escaldes 58 G11
Les Escoumins 122 T7
Leshan 80 C5
Les Herbiers 58 D7
Leshukonskoye 70 J2
Leskovac 66 J7
Lesosibirsk 76 S6
Lesotho 108 D5
Lesozavodsk 82 G1
Lesparre-Médoc 58 E8
Les Sables-d'Olonne 58 D7
Les Sept Îles 58 B5
Lesser Antilles 134 L6
Lesser Slave Lake 34 H5
Lesvos 68 H5
Leszno 50 F6
Letaba 108 E4
Letchworth 54 B3
Letenye 62 M4
Lethbridge 34 J7
Lethem 140 F3
Leticia 140 D4
Letpadan 84 B3
Le Tréport 54 D4
Letterkenny 56 E7
Leutkirch 62 F3
Leuven 54 G4
Leuze 54 F4
Levadeia 68 E6
Levanzo 64 G10
Levashi 92 M2
Levaya Khetta 70 P2
Leverano 64 N8
Leverkusen 54 J3
Levice 50 H9
Levico Terme 62 G4
Levin 116 E5
Lévis 128 F1
Levitha 68 J7
Levoča 50 K9
Levski 66 N6
Lewes 54 C4
Lewis 56 F3
Lewis and Clark Lake 126 G2
Lewis Range 122 J7
Lewiston, *Id., United States* 126 C1
Lewiston, *Me., United States* 128 F2
Lewistown, *Mont., United States* 126 E1
Lewistown, *Pa., United States* 128 E2
Lexington, *Ky., United States* 128 D3
Lexington, *Nebr., United States* 126 G2
Lexington, *Va., United States* 128 E3
Lexington Park 130 F2
Leyte 84 G4
Lezhë 66 G8
Lhari 88 F2
Lhasa 88 F3
Lhazê 88 E3
Lhokseumawe 84 B5
Lian Xian 84 E2
Lianyuan 84 E1
Lianyungang 80 F4
Liao 82 B3
Liaocheng 80 F3
Liaoyang 82 B3
Liaoyuan 82 C2
Liard 122 F5
Liard River 122 F5
Libby 126 C1
Libenge 106 B3
Liberal 130 A2
Liberec 50 E7
Liberia 104 B3
Liberia 134 G6
Liberty 130 C1
Libjo 84 H4
Libourne 58 E9
Libreville 104 F4
Libya 100 C2
Libyan Desert 100 D2
Libyan Plateau 100 E1
Licata 64 H11
Lich 52 D6
Lichinga 108 F2
Lichtenfels 52 G6
Lida 48 N10
Lidköping 48 G7
Lidodi Jesolo 62 H5
Lido di Ostia 64 G7
Lidzbark Warmiński 50 K3
Liebenwalde 52 J4
Liechtenstein 62 E3
Liège 54 H4
Lieksa 48 R5
Lienz 62 H4
Liepāja 50 L1
Lier 54 G3
Liezen 62 K3
Lifford 56 E7
Lignières 58 H7
Ligueil 58 F6
Ligurian Sea 62 D7
Lihue 132 (2)B2
Lijiang 84 C1
Likasi 106 D6
Lilienfeld 62 L2
Lille 54 F4
Lillebonne 54 C5
Lillehammer 48 F6
Lillerto 62 G3
Lilongwe 108 E2
Liloy 84 G5
Lima, *Peru* 140 B6
Lima, *Mont., United States* 126 D2
Lima, *Oh., United States* 128 D2
Limanowa 50 K8
Limassol = Lemesos 68 Q10
Limbaži 48 N8
Limburg 54 L4
Limeira 142 M3
Limerick 56 D9
Limingen 48 G4
Limni Kastorias 68 C4
Limni Kerkinitis 68 E3
Limni Koronia 68 F4
Limni Trichonida 68 D6
Limni Vegoritis 68 D4
Limni Volvi 68 F4
Limnos 68 H5
Limoges 58 G8
Limon 126 F3
Limón 134 H7
Limoux 58 H10
Limpopo 108 D4
Linares, *Chile* 142 G6
Linares, *Mexico* 132 G4
Linares, *Spain* 60 G6
Linaria 68 G6
Lincang 84 C2
Linchuan 80 F5
Lincoln, *United Kingdom* 54 B1
Lincoln, *Ill., United States* 128 C2
Lincoln, *Me., United States* 128 G1
Lincoln, *Nebr., United States* 126 G2
Lincoln, *N.H., United States* 128 F2
Lindenow Fjord = Kangerlussuatsiaq 122 Y4
Lindesnes 48 D8
Lindi 106 D3
Lindi 106 F6
Lindos 68 L8
Line Islands 112 L5
Linfen 80 E3
Lingayen 84 G3
Lingen 54 K2
Lingga 86 C3
Lingshui 84 D3
Linguère 104 A1
Lingyuan 80 F2
Linhai 80 G5
Linhares 140 J7
Linhe 80 D2
Linjiang 82 D3
Linköping 48 H7
Linkou 82 F1
Linosa 64 G13
Lins 142 M3
Linton 126 F1
Linxi 80 F2
Linxia 80 C3
Lin Xian 80 E3
Linyi 80 F3
Linz 62 K2
Liobomil' 50 P6
Lipari 64 J10
Lipari 64 J10
Lipcani 66 P1
Lipetsk 70 G4
Lipin Bor 70 G2
Lipno 50 J5
Lipova 66 J3
Lippe 54 L3
Lippstadt 54 L3
Lipsoi 68 J7
Liptovský-Mikuláš 50 J8
Lipu 84 E2
Liqeni i Fierzës 66 H7
Liqeni Komanit 66 G7
Lira 106 E3
Liri 64 H7
Lisala 106 C3
Lisboa 60 A6
Lisbon = Lisboa 60 A6
Lisburn 56 G7
Liscannor Bay 56 C9
Lishi 80 E3
Lishui 80 F5
Lisieux 54 C5
Liski 70 G4
L'Isle-sur-la-Sorgue 58 L10
Lisse 54 G2
Lištica 64 M5
Listowel 56 C9
Listvyanka 78 H6
Litang 80 C5
Litani 140 G3
Litava 50 F8
Litchfield, *Ill., United States* 128 C3
Litchfield, *Minn., United States* 128 B1
Lithgow 114 K6
Lithuania 48 L9
Litke 78 Q6
Litomerice 52 K6
Litomyši 50 F8

Magdelaine Cays 114 K3
Magelang 86 E4
Magenta 62 D5
Magerøya 48 N1
Maglaj 66 F5
Maglie 64 N8
Magnitogorsk 70 L4
Magnolia 130 C3
Mago 78 P6
Magog 128 F1
Magta Lahjar 102 C5
Magu 106 E4
Magwe 84 A2
Mahābād 92 L5
Mahaboboka 108 G4
Mahagi 106 E3
Mahajamba 108 H3
Mahajanga 108 H3
Mahalapye 108 D4
Mahān 95 G1
Mahanadi 88 D4
Mahanoro 108 H3
Mahasamund 88 D4
Mahavavy 108 H3
Mahbubnagar 88 D5
Maḩḑah 95 G4
Mahé 108 (2)C1
Mahenge 106 F5
Mahesāna 88 B4
Mahia Peninsula 116 F4
Mahilyow 70 F4
Mahnomen 128 A1
Mahón 60 Q5
Mahuva 90 K5
Maicao 140 C1
Maidenhead 54 B3
Maidstone 54 C3
Maiduguri 104 G2
Mai Gudo 106 F2
Maímédy 52 B6
Main 52 E7
Mainburg 62 G2
Main-Donau-Kanal 52 G7
Maine 128 G1
Maïné Soroa 104 G2
Maingkwan 84 B1
Mainland, *Orkney Is., United Kingdom* 56 J2
Mainland, *Shetland Is., United Kingdom* 56 L1
Maintirano 108 G3
Mainz 52 D6
Maio 104 (1)B1
Majene 87 A3
Majicana 142 H4
Majuro 112 H5
Makale 87 A3
Makamba 106 D4
Makanza 106 B3
Makarora 116 B7
Makarov 78 Q7
Makarska 66 E6
Makar'yev 70 H3
Makat 70 K5
Makeni 104 B3
Makgadikgadi 108 C4
Makhachkala 92 M2
Makhorovka 76 M7
Makindu 106 F4
Makinsk 70 P4
Makiyivka 70 G5
Makkah 100 G3
Makó 66 H3
Makokou 104 G4
Makongolosi 106 E5
Makorako 116 F4
Makoua 104 H4
Maków Mazowiecka 50 L5
Makran 90 G4
Makronisi 68 G7
Mākū 92 L4
Makumbako 106 E5
Makurazaki 82 F8
Makurdi 104 F3
Makūyeh 95 E2
Makuyuni 106 F4
Malabar Coast 88 B6
Malabo 104 F4
Malack 50 F9
Malacky 62 M2
Malad City 126 D2
Maladzyechna 70 E4
Málaga 60 F8
Malaimbandy 108 H4
Malaita 112 G6
Malakal 106 E2
Malakanagiri 88 D5
Malakula 112 G7
Malamala 87 B3
Malang 86 E4
Malanje 106 B5
Malanville 104 E2
Malaryta 50 P6
Malatya 92 H4
Malaut 88 B2
Mālavi 92 M7
Malawi 108 E2
Malaya Baranikha 78 V3
Malaya Vishera 70 F3
Malaybalay 84 H5
Malāyer 90 E3
Malay Peninsula 84 C6
Malay Reef 114 J3
Malaysia 86 C2
Malbork 50 J3
Malchin, *Germany* 52 H3
Malchin, *Mongolia* 76 S8
Malden Island 112 L6
Maldives 88 B8
Maldonado 142 L5
Malé 62 F4
Male 88 B8
Male Atoll 88 B8
Malegaon 88 B4
Malé Karpaty 62 N2
Maleme 68 F9
Malesherbes 58 H5
Maleta 78 H6
Malheur 126 C2
Malheur Lake 126 C2
Mali 102 E5
Malindi 106 G4
Malin Head 56 E6
Malkara 68 J4
Malko Tărnovo 66 Q8
Mallaig 56 G4
Mallawi 100 F2
Mallorca 60 P5
Mallow 56 D9
Malmédy 54 J4
Malmesbury 108 B6
Malmö 50 C2
Malmyzh 70 K3
Maloca 140 F3
Malone 128 F2
Måløy 48 C6
Malozemel'skaya Tundra 70 K1
Målselv 48 K2
Malta 64 J13
Malta 126 E1
Malta Channel 64 J12
Maltahöhe 108 B4
Malvern 128 B4
Malý Dunaj 62 N2
Malyy Uzen' 70 J4
Mama 78 J5
Mamadysh 70 K3
Mambasa 106 D3
Mamburao 84 G4
Mamelodi 108 D5
Mammoth Hot Springs 126 D2
Mamonovo 50 J3
Mamoré 140 D6
Mamou 104 B2
Mamoudzou 108 H2
Mamuju 87 A3
Ma'mūl 90 G6
Mamuno 108 C4
Man 104 C3
Mana 132 (2)A1
Manacapuru 140 E4
Manacor 60 P5
Manado 87 B2
Managua 134 G6
Manakara 108 H4
Manali 88 C2
Mananara 108 H4
Mananara Avaratra 108 H3
Mananjary 108 H4
Manankoro 104 C2
Manantenina 108 H4
Manassas 128 E3
Manaus 140 E4
Manavgat 68 P8
Manbij 92 G5
Manchester, *United Kingdom* 56 K8
Manchester, *Ia., United States* 128 B2
Manchester, *Ky., United States* 128 D3
Manchester, *Tenn., United States* 128 C3
Manchester, *Vt., United States* 128 F2
Mand 90 H4
Mandabe 108 G4
Mandal 48 D7
Mandalay 84 B2
Mandalgovī 80 D1
Mandan 126 F1
Mandera 106 G3
Mandi 88 C2
Mandi Burewala 88 B2
Mandimba 108 F2
Manding 102 D6
Mandla 88 D4
Mandø 52 D1
Mandritsara 108 H3
Mandsaur 88 C4
Mandurah 114 C6
Manduria 64 M8
Mandvi 88 A4
Mandya 88 C6
Manfredonia 64 K7
Manga 104 G2
Manga 140 J6
Mangaia 112 K8
Mangalia 66 R6
Mangalore 88 B6
Mangareva 112 N8
Mangatupopo 116 E4
Mangaweka 116 F4
Manggar 86 D3
Mangit 90 H1
Mangnai 76 S10
Mango 104 E2
Mangoky 108 G4
Mangole 87 C3
Mangonui 116 D2
Mangrove Cay 130 F5
Manhad 88 B5
Manhattan 130 B2
Manhuaçu 140 J8
Mania 108 H3
Maniamba 108 F2
Manicoré 140 E5
Manicouagan 122 T6
Manīfah 95 C3
Manihiki 112 K7
Maniitsoq 122 W3
Manila 84 G4
Manisa 68 K6
Manistee 128 C2
Manistique 128 C1
Manitoba 32 M5
Manitou 126 G1
Manitoulin Island 36 Q7
Manitouwadge 128 C1
Manitowoc 128 C2
Maniwaki 128 E1
Manizales 140 B2
Manja 108 G4
Manjimup 114 C6
Mankato 128 B2
Manley Hot Springs 122 A4
Manlleu 60 N3
Manna 86 C3
Mannar 88 D7
Mannheim 54 L5
Manning, *Canada* 34 H5
Manning, *United States* 130 E3
Manokwari 87 D3
Manono 106 D5
Mano River 104 B3
Manosque 58 L10
Manouane 128 F1
Manp'o 82 D3
Manra 112 J6
Manresa 60 M3
Mansa 108 D2
Mansel Island 36 Q4
Mansfield, *United Kingdom* 54 A1
Mansfield, *La., United States* 130 C3
Mansfield, *Oh., United States* 128 D2
Manta 140 A4
Manteo 130 F2
Mantes-la-Jolie 54 D5
Mantova 62 F5
Manturovo 70 H3
Manú 140 C6
Manuelzinho 140 G5
Manūjān 95 G3
Manukan 84 G5
Manukau 116 E3
Manukau Harbour 116 E3
Manyberries 126 D1
Manyinga 108 C2
Manyoni 106 E5
Manzanares 60 G5
Manzanillo 134 J4
Manzhouli 78 K7
Manzil 94 D5
Manzini 108 E5
Mao 100 C5
Maoming 84 E2
Mapam Yumco 88 D2
Mapi 87 E4
Mapinhane 108 F4
Maple Creek 124 E2
Mapuera 140 E4
Maputo 108 E5
Maqueda 60 F4
Maquela do Zombo 106 B5
Maquinchao 142 H7
Maquoketa 128 B2
Māra 88 D4
Maraã 140 D4
Maraba 140 H5
Maracaibo 140 C1
Maracay 140 D1
Marādah 100 C2
Maradi 104 F2
Marāgheh 92 M5
Maralal 106 F3
Marand 92 L4
Maranhão 140 H5
Marañón 140 B4
Marans 58 E7
Marari 140 D5
Mărăşeşti 66 Q4
Marathon, *Canada* 128 C1
Marathon, *United States* 132 F2
Marbella 60 F8
Marble Bar 114 C4
Marburg 54 L4
Marcal 62 N3
Marcali 62 N4
March 54 C2
Marche 54 H4
Marchena 60 E7
Mardan 88 B2
Mar del Plata 142 K6
Mardin 92 J5
Maré 112 G8
Mareeba 114 J3
Marettimo 64 F11
Marfa 132 F2
Margate 54 D3
Margherita di Savoia 64 L7
Marghita 66 K2
Margilan 90 K1
Marguerite Bay 144 (2)KK3
María Elena 142 H3
Marianas Trench 112 E4
Marianna 130 D3
Mariańské Lázně 52 H7
Mariazell 62 L3
Mar'ib 100 J4
Maribo 52 G2
Maribor 62 L4
Maridi 106 D2
Marie Byrd Land 144 (2)FF2
Marie Galante 134 M5
Mariehamn 48 K6
Marienberg 52 J6
Mariental 108 B4
Mariestad 48 G7
Marietta, *Oh., United States* 128 D3
Marietta, *Okla., United States* 130 B3
Mariinsk 76 R6
Marijampolė 50 N3
Marília 142 M3
Marín 60 B2
Marinette 128 C1
Maringá 142 L3
Marino 64 G7
Marion, *Ill., United States* 128 C3
Marion, *Ind., United States* 128 C2
Marion, *Oh., United States* 128 D2
Maripa 140 D2
Mariscal Estigarribia 142 J3
Maritime Alps 62 C6
Mariupol' 70 G5
Marīvān 92 M6
Mariy El 70 J3
Marjayoûn 94 C3
Marka 106 G3
Markam 80 B5
Markaryd 50 C1
Marked Tree 130 C2
Marken 54 H2
Markermeer 54 H2
Market Harborough 54 B2
Markham 128 E2
Marki 50 L5
Markit 76 P10
Markkleeberg 52 H5
Markovo 78 W4
Marktoberdorf 62 F3
Marktredwitz 52 H7
Marla 114 F5
Marle 54 F5
Marmande 58 F9
Marmara Adası 68 K4
Marmara Denizi 68 L4
Marmaris 68 L8
Marmolada 62 G4
Marne 54 F5
Marne-la-Vallée 54 E6
Maro 104 H3
Maroansetra 108 H3
Marolambo 108 H4
Maroni 140 G3
Maros 87 A3
Marotiri 112 M8
Maroua 104 G2
Marquesas Islands 112 M6
Marquette 128 C1
Marradi 62 G6
Marrakech 102 D2
Marra Plateau 100 D5
Marree 114 G5
Marrupa 108 F2
Marsa Alam 100 F2
Marsabit 106 F3
Marsala 64 G11
Marsberg 54 L3
Marsden 114 J6
Marseille 58 L10
Marseille-en-Beauvaisis 54 D5
Marshall, *Ill., United States* 130 D2
Marshall, *Tex., United States* 130 C3
Marshall Islands 112 G4
Marshalltown 128 B2
Marsh Harbour 130 F4
Marsh Island 130 C4
Martapura, *Indonesia* 86 C3
Martapura, *Indonesia* 86 E3
Martigny 62 C4
Martigues 58 L10
Martin, *Slovak Republic* 50 H8
Martin, *United States* 126 F2
Martina Franca 64 M8
Martinborough 116 E5
Martinique 134 M6
Martinsburg 128 E3
Martinsville, *Ind., United States* 128 C3
Martinsville, *Va., United States* 128 E3
Marton 116 E5
Martos 60 G7
Maruchak 90 H2
Mårvatn 48 E6
Mary 90 H2
Maryborough 114 K5
Maryland 128 E3
Marysville, *Canada* 128 G1
Marysville, *Calif., United States* 132 B1
Marysville, *Kans., United States* 130 B2
Maryville 128 B2
Masai Steppe 106 F4
Masaka 106 E4
Masalembu Besar 86 E4
Masallı 92 N4
Masamba 87 B3
Masan 82 E6
Masasi 106 F6
Masbate 84 G4
Masbate 84 G4
Mascara 102 F1
Maseru 108 D5
Mashhad 90 G2
Masi-Manimba 106 B4
Masindi 106 E3
Maşīrah 90 G5
Masjed Soleymān 90 E3
Maskanah 92 H5
Mason 130 B3
Mason Bay 116 A8
Mason City 128 B2
Masqaţ 95 H5
Massa 62 F6
Massachusetts 128 F2
Massachusetts Bay 128 G2
Massafra 64 M8
Massa Marittimo 64 E5
Massawa 100 G4
Massena 128 F2
Masset 122 E6
Massif Central 58 H8
Massif de Guéra 100 C5
Massif de l'Aïr 102 G5
Massif des Écrins 62 B5
Massif du Chaillu 104 G5
Massif du Tsaratanana 108 H2
Massif Ennedi 100 D4
Massillon 128 D2
Massinga 108 F4
Masteksay 70 K5
Masterton 116 E5
Mastung 90 J4
Masty 48 N10
Masuda 82 F6

Place	Page	Ref.
Mozambique	108	E3
Mozambique Channel	108	F4
Mozdok	92	L2
Mozhga	70	K3
Mozirje	62	K4
Mpanda	106	E5
Mpika	108	E2
Mporokoso	106	E5
Mpumalanga	108	D5
Mrągowo	50	L4
Mrkonjić-Grad	62	N6
M'Sila	102	F1
Mtsensk	70	G4
Mtwara	106	G6
Muang Khammouan	84	C3
Muang Không	84	D4
Muang Khôngxédôn	84	D3
Muang Khoua	84	C2
Muang Pakxan	84	C3
Muang Phin	84	D3
Muang Sing	84	C2
Muang Xai	84	C2
Muar	86	C2
Muarabungo	86	C3
Muaradua	86	C3
Muarasiberut	86	B3
Muaratewen	86	E3
Muarawahau	86	F2
Mubarek	76	M10
Mubende	106	E3
Mubrani	87	D3
Muck	56	F5
Muckadilla	114	J5
Muconda	106	C6
Mucur	68	S5
Mudanjiang	82	E1
Mudanya	68	L4
Muddy Gap	126	E2
Mudurnu	68	P4
Mufulira	108	D2
Mughshin	90	F6
Muğla	68	L7
Mugodzhary	70	L5
Muhammad Qol	100	G3
Mühldorf	62	H2
Mühlhausen	52	F5
Muhos	48	N4
Muhu	48	M7
Muhulu	106	D4
Mukacheve	50	M9
Mukdahan	84	C3
Mukomuko	86	C3
Mukry	90	J2
Mukuku	108	D2
Mulaku Atoll	88	B8
Mulde	52	H5
Muleshoe	132	F2
Mulgrave Island	114	H2
Mulhacén	60	G7
Mülheim	54	J3
Mulhouse	62	C3
Muling	82	G1
Mull	56	G5
Mullaittivu	88	D7
Mullewa	114	C5
Müllheim	62	C3
Mullingar	56	E8
Mulobezi	108	D3
Multan	90	K3
Mumbai	88	B5
Mumbwa	108	D2
Muna	87	B4
Munaðarnes	48	(1)C1
Münchberg	52	G6
München	62	G2
Münden	52	E5
Mundo Novo	140	J6
Mundrabilla	114	E6
Munera	60	H5
Mungbere	106	D3
Munger	88	E3
Munich = München	62	G2
Munster, France	62	C2
Münster, Germany	54	K3
Munster, Germany	52	F4
Munte	87	A2
Muojärvi	48	Q4
Muonio	48	M3
Muqdisho	106	H3
Mur	62	L4
Muradiye	92	K4
Murang'a	106	F4
Murashi	70	J3
Murat	92	K4
Muratlı	68	K3
Murchison	116	D5
Murcia	60	J7
Murdo	126	F2
Mureş	66	J3
Muret	58	G10
Murfreesboro, N.C., United States	130	F2
Murfreesboro, Tenn., United States	130	D2
Murghob	90	K2
Muriaé	140	J8
Müritz	52	H3
Muriwai	116	F4
Murmansk	48	S2
Murnau	62	G3
Murom	70	H3
Muroran	82	L2
Muros	60	A2
Muroto	82	H7
Murphy	130	E2
Murray	114	H6
Murray	128	C3
Murray Bridge	114	G7
Murray River Basin	114	H6
Murska Sobota	62	M4
Murter	62	L7
Murtosa	60	B4
Murud	88	B5
Murupara	116	F4
Mururoa	112	M8
Murwara	88	D4
Murzuq	102	H3
Mürzzuschlag	62	L3
Muş	92	J4
Müša	50	N1
Musala	68	F2
Musandam Peninsula	95	D3
Musay'id	95	D4
Muscat = Masqaṭ	95	H5
Musgrave Ranges	114	E5
Mushin	104	E3
Muskegon	128	C2
Muskogee	130	B2
Musmar	100	G4
Musoma	106	E4
Mussende	106	B6
Mustafakemalpaşa	68	L4
Mut, Egypt	100	E2
Mut, Turkey	68	R8
Mutare	108	E3
Mutarnee	114	J3
Mutnyy Materik	70	L1
Mutoray	76	U5
Mutsamudu	108	G2
Mutsu	82	L3
Mutsu-wan	82	L3
Muttaburra	114	H4
Mutur	88	D7
Muyezerskiy	48	R5
Muyinga	106	E4
Muynak	76	K9
Muzaffarnagar	88	C3
Muzaffarpur	88	E3
Muzillac	58	C6
Múzquiz	132	F3
Muztagata	76	N10
Mwali	108	G2
Mwanza	106	E4
Mweka	106	C4
Mwenda	106	D6
Mwene-Ditu	106	C5
Mwenezi	108	E4
Mwenezi	108	E4
Mwinilunga	108	C2
Myanmar	84	B2
Myaungmya	84	A3
Myingyan	84	B2
Myitkyina	84	B1
Myjava	62	N2
Myjava	62	N2
Mykolayiv	50	N8
Mykonos	68	H7
Mymensingh	88	F4
Mynbulak	76	L9
Myndagayy	78	N4
Myōjin	80	K4
Myonggan	82	E3
Mýrdalsjökull	48	(1)D3
Myrina	68	H5
Myrtle Beach	130	F3
Mys Alevina	78	S5
Mys Aniva	80	L1
Mys Buorkhaya	78	N2
Mys Dezhneva	78	Z3
Mys Elizavety	78	Q6
Mys Enkan	78	P5
Mys Govena	78	V5
Mys Kanin Nos	70	H1
Mys Kril'on	80	L1
Myślenice	50	J8
Myślibórz	50	D5
Mys Lopatka, Russia	78	T6
Mys Lopatka, Russia	78	S2
Mys Navarin	78	X4
Mys Nemetskiy	48	S2
Mys Olyutorskiy	78	W5
Mysore	88	C6
Mys Peschanyy	76	J9
Mys Povorotnyy	82	G2
Mys Prubiynyy	70	F5
Mys Shelagskiy	78	V2
Mys Sivuchiy	78	U5
Mys Terpeniya	78	Q7
Mys Tolstoy	78	T5
Mys Yuzhnyy	78	T5
Mys Zhelaniya	76	M2
Myszksw	50	J7
My Tho	84	D4
Mytilini	68	J5
Mývatn	48	(1)E2
Mže	52	H7
Mzimba	108	E2
Mzuzu	108	E2

N

Place	Page	Ref.
Naalehu	132	(2)F4
Naas	56	F8
Nabas	84	G4
Naberezhnyye Chelny	70	K3
Nabeul	64	E12
Nabīd	95	G2
Nabire	87	E3
Nablus	94	C4
Nacala	108	G2
Nacaroa	108	F2
Náchod	50	F7
Nacogdoches	130	C3
Nadiad	88	B4
Nador	102	E2
Nadvirna	66	M1
Nadym	70	P1
Nadym	70	P2
Næstved	52	G1
Nafpaktos	68	D6
Nafplio	68	E7
Naga	84	G4
Nagano	82	K5
Nagaoka	82	K5
Nagaon	88	F3
Nagarzê	88	F3
Nagasaki	82	E7
Nagaur	88	B3
Nagercoil	88	C7
Nago	80	H5
Nagold	52	D8
Nagorsk	70	K3
Nagoya	82	J6
Nagpur	88	C4
Nagqu	88	F2
Nagyatád	62	N4
Nagykállš	66	J2
Nagykanizsa	62	N4
Nagykáta	50	J10
Nagykőrös	66	G2
Naha	80	H5
Nahanni	122	G4
Nahanni Butte	122	G4
Nahr en Nile = Nile	100	F2
Naiman Qi	80	G2
Nain	122	U5
Nairn	56	J4
Nairobi	106	F4
Naivasha	106	F4
Naizishan	82	D2
Najafābād	90	F3
Nájera	60	H2
Najibabad	88	C3
Najin	82	F2
Najrān	100	H4
Naju	82	D6
Nakamura	82	G7
Nakatsu	82	F7
Nakhl	94	A7
Nakhodka, Russia	76	P4
Nakhodka, Russia	82	G2
Nakhon Ratchasima	84	C3
Nakhon Sawan	84	B3
Nakhon Si Thammarat	84	B5
Nakina	122	P6
Nakło nad Notecią	50	G4
Naknek	132	(1)F4
Nakonde	106	E5
Nakskov	52	G2
Nakten	48	H5
Nakuru	106	F4
Nal'chik	92	K2
Nallihan	68	P4
Nālūt	102	H2
Namagan	76	N9
Namakzar-e Shadad	95	G1
Namangan	106	F4
Namapa	108	F2
Namasagali	106	E3
Nam Can	84	C5
Nam Co	88	F2
Namdalen	48	G4
Nam Dinh	84	D2
Namib Desert	108	A4
Namibe	108	A3
Namibia	108	B4
Namidobe	108	F3
Namlea	87	C3
Namo	87	A3
Nampa	126	C2
Nampala	104	C1
Nam Ping	84	B3
Namp'o	82	C4
Nampula	108	F3
Namsos	48	F4
Namtsy	78	M4
Namur	54	F4
Namwala	108	D3
Namwŏn	82	D6
Nan	84	C3
Nanaimo	34	C2
Nanao	82	J5
Nanchang	80	F5
Nanchong	80	D4
Nancy	62	B2
Nanda Devi	88	C2
Nānded	88	C5
Nandurbar	88	B4
Nandyal	88	C5
Nanfeng	80	F5
Nangalala	114	G2
Nangapinoh	86	E3
Nangatayap	86	E3
Nangis	58	J5
Nangong	80	F3
Nang Xian	88	F3
Nanjing	80	F4
Nankoku	82	G7
Nannine	114	C5
Nanning	84	D2
Nanortalik	122	X4
Nanpan	84	D2
Nanping	80	F5
Nansei-shotō	80	H5
Nantes	58	D6
Nanton	124	D1
Nantong	80	G4
Nanumea	112	H6
Nanuque	140	J7
Nanutarra Roadhouse	114	C4
Nanyang	80	E4
Napa	126	B3
Napalkovo	76	N3
Napamute	132	(1)F3
Napas	78	C4
Napasoq	122	W3
Napier	116	F4
Naples = Napoli, Italy	64	J8
Naples, United States	130	E4
Napo	140	C4
Napoli	64	J8
Naqb Ashtar	94	C6
Nara, Japan	82	H6
Nara, Mali	102	D5
Narathiwat	84	C5
Narbonne	58	H10
Nardò	64	N8
Nares Strait	120	J2
Narev	50	N5
Narew	50	L5
Narib	108	B4
Narmada	88	C4
Narnaul	88	C3
Narni	64	G6
Narok	106	F4
Närpes	48	L5
Narrabri	114	J6
Narrandera	114	J6
Narsarsuaq	38	X4
Narsimhapur	88	C4
Nart	80	F2
Narva	48	P7
Narva	48	Q7
Narva Bay	48	P7
Narvik	48	J2
Nar'yan Mar	70	K1
Naryn	78	F6
Näsäud	66	M2
Nashua	128	F2
Nashville	130	D2
Našice	66	F4
Nasik	88	B4
Nasir	106	E2
Nassarawa	104	F3
Nassau	130	F4
Nässjö	48	H8
Nassuttooq	38	W3
Nastapoka Islands	122	R5
Nasugbu	84	G4
Naswá	95	G5
Nata	108	D4
Natal	140	K5
Natara	78	L3
Natashquan	122	U6
Natchez	130	C3
Natchitoches	130	C3
National Park	116	E4
Natitingou	104	E2
Natori	82	L4
Natuna Besar	86	D2
Naucelle	58	H9
Nauchas	108	B4
Nauders	62	F4
Naujoji Akmenė	50	M1
Naumburg	52	G5
Na'ūr	94	C5
Nauru	112	G6
Nauta	140	C4
Nautonwa	88	D3
Navahermosa	60	F5
Navahrudak	48	N10
Navajo Reservoir	126	E3
Navalero	60	H3
Navalmoral de la Mata	60	E5
Navalvillar de Pela	60	E5
Navapolatsk	70	F3
Navlya	70	F4
Navoi	76	M9
Navojoa	124	D2
Navrongo	104	D2
Navsari	88	B4
Nawá	94	D4
Nawabshah	90	J4
Nāwah	90	J3
Naxçivan	92	L4
Naxos	68	H7
Naxos	68	H7
Nayakhan	78	T4
Nāy Band, Iran	90	G3
Nāy Band, Iran	95	E3
Nayoro	82	M1
Nazaré	60	A5
Nazareth	94	C4
Nazarovo	76	S6
Nazca	140	C6
Nazca Ridge	142	E3
Naze	80	H5
Nazilli	68	L7
Nazino	76	P6
Nazran'	92	L2
Nazrēt	106	F2
Nazwá	90	G5
Nazyvayevsk	70	P3
Ncojane	108	C4
Ndélé	106	C2
Ndjamena	100	B5
Ndjolé	104	G5
Ndola	108	D2
Nea Ionia	68	E5
Neapoli	68	F8
Nea Roda	68	F4
Nea Zichni	68	F3
Nebbi	106	E3
Nebitdag	90	F2
Nebo	114	J4
Nebraska	126	G2
Neckar	52	D7
Neckar	52	E7
Neckarsulm	52	E7
Necker Island	112	K3
Necochea	142	K6
Nédély	100	C4
Nedre Soppero	48	L3
Needles	132	D2
Nefedovo	70	P3
Nefta	102	G2
Neftçala	92	N4
Neftekamsk	70	K3
Neftekumsk	92	L1
Nefteyugansk	70	P2
Nefza	64	D12
Negage	106	B5
Negār	95	G2
Negēlē	106	F2
Negele	106	F2
Negev	94	B6
Negomane	108	F2
Negombo	88	C7
Negotin	66	K5

Nowata . . . 130 B2
Nowogard . . . 50 E4
Nowo Warpno . . . 52 K3
Nowra . . . 114 K6
Now Shahr . . . 90 F2
Nowy Dwór Mazowiecki . . . 50 K5
Nowy Sącz . . . 50 K8
Nowy Targ . . . 50 K8
Nowy Tomyśl . . . 50 F5
Noyabr'sk . . . 76 P5
Noyon . . . 54 E5
Nsombo . . . 108 D2
Ntem . . . 104 G4
Ntwetwe Pan . . . 108 C4
Nu . . . 88 C2
Nuasjärvi . . . 48 Q4
Nubian Desert . . . 100 F3
Nudo Coropuna . . . 140 C7
Nueltin Lake . . . 36 M5
Nueva Lubecka . . . 142 G7
Nueva Rosita . . . 132 F3
Nueva San Salvador . . . 134 G6
Nuevo Casas Grandes . . . 132 E2
Nuevo Laredo . . . 132 G3
Nugget Point . . . 116 B8
Nuhaka . . . 116 F4
Nuku'alofa . . . 112 J8
Nuku Hiva . . . 112 M6
Nukumanu Islands . . . 112 F6
Nukunonu . . . 112 J6
Nukus . . . 76 K9
Nullagine . . . 114 D4
Nullarbor Plain . . . 114 E6
Numan . . . 104 G3
Numata . . . 82 K5
Numazu . . . 82 K6
Numbulwar . . . 114 G2
Numfor . . . 87 E3
Numto . . . 70 P2
Nunap Isua . . . 38 Y5
Nunarsuit . . . 122 X4
Nunavik . . . 122 W2
Nunavut . . . 32 N3
Nuneaton . . . 54 A2
Nungnain Sum . . . 80 F1
Nunivak Island . . . 132 (1)D3
Nunligram . . . 78 Y3
Nuoro . . . 64 D8
Nuquí . . . 140 B2
Nura . . . 70 P4
Nurābād . . . 95 D1
Nurata . . . 90 J1
Nurmes . . . 48 Q5
Nürnberg . . . 52 G7
Nürtingen . . . 62 E2
Nurzec . . . 50 M5
Nusaybin . . . 92 J5
Nushki . . . 90 J4
Nutak . . . 122 U5
Nuuk . . . 38 W4
Nuussuaq . . . 122 W2
Nyagan' . . . 70 N2
Nyahururu . . . 106 F3
Nyala . . . 100 D5
Nyalam . . . 88 E3
Nyamlell . . . 106 D2
Nyamtumbo . . . 106 F6
Nyandoma . . . 70 H2
Nyantakara . . . 106 E4
Nyborg . . . 52 F1
Nybro . . . 48 H8
Nyda . . . 76 N4
Nyima . . . 88 E2
Nyingchi . . . 88 F3
Nyírbátor . . . 66 K2
Nyíregyháza . . . 50 L10
Nykarleby . . . 48 M5
Nykøbing . . . 52 G2
Nyköping . . . 48 J7
Nylstroom . . . 108 D4
Nymburk . . . 50 E7
Nynäshamn . . . 48 J7
Nyngan . . . 114 J6
Nyon . . . 62 B4
Nysa . . . 50 D6
Nysa . . . 50 G7
Nysted . . . 52 G2
Nyukhcha . . . 70 J2
Nyunzu . . . 106 D5
Nyurba . . . 78 K4
Nyuya . . . 78 K4
Nzega . . . 106 E4
Nzérékoré . . . 104 C3
N'zeto . . . 106 A5
Nzwami . . . 108 G2

O

Oaho . . . 132 (2)D2
Oahu . . . 112 L3
Oakdale . . . 130 C3
Oakham . . . 54 B2
Oak Lake . . . 126 F1
Oakland . . . 126 B3
Oak Lawn . . . 128 C2
Oakley . . . 130 A2
Oak Ridge . . . 128 D3
Oamaru . . . 116 C7
Oaxaca . . . 134 E5
Ob' . . . 70 N2
Obama . . . 82 H6
Oban . . . 56 G5
O Barco . . . 60 D2
Oberdrauburg . . . 62 H4
Oberhausen . . . 54 J3
Oberkirch . . . 52 D8
Oberlin . . . 130 G4
Oberndorf . . . 62 H3
Oberstdorf . . . 62 F3
Oberursel . . . 52 D6
Obervellach . . . 50 C11

Oberwart . . . 62 M3
Obi . . . 87 C3
Obidos . . . 140 F4
Obigarm . . . 90 K2
Obihiro . . . 82 M2
Obluch'ye . . . 78 N7
Obninsk . . . 70 G3
Obo, Central African Republic . . . 106 D2
Obo, China . . . 80 C3
Oborniki . . . 50 F5
Obouya . . . 104 H5
Oboyan' . . . 70 G4
Obskaya Guba . . . 76 N4
Obuasi . . . 104 D3
Ob'yachevo . . . 70 J2
Ocala . . . 130 E4
Ocaña, Colombia . . . 140 C2
Ocaña, Spain . . . 60 G5
Ocean City . . . 128 E3
Ocean Falls . . . 122 F6
Oceania . . . 112 G7
Oceanside . . . 132 C2
Och'amch'ire . . . 92 J2
Ochsenfurt . . . 52 E7
Oconto . . . 128 C2
Oda . . . 104 D3
Ōda . . . 82 G6
Ōdate . . . 82 L3
Odda . . . 48 D6
Odemira . . . 60 B7
Ödemiş . . . 68 L6
Odense . . . 52 F1
Oder = Odra . . . 50 F6
Oderzo . . . 62 H5
Odesa . . . 70 F5
Odessa = Odesa, Ukraine . . . 70 F5
Odessa, United States . . . 132 F2
Odienné . . . 104 C3
Odorheiu Secuiesc . . . 66 N3
Odra . . . 50 F6
Odžaci . . . 66 G4
Oeh . . . 80 C2
Oeiras . . . 140 J5
Oelrichs . . . 126 F2
Oelsnitz . . . 52 H6
Oeno . . . 112 N8
Oestev . . . 142 H7
Ofaqim . . . 94 B5
Offenbach . . . 52 D6
Offenburg . . . 62 C2
Ōgaki . . . 82 J6
Ogasawara-shotō . . . 74 T7
Ogbomosho . . . 104 E3
Ogden . . . 126 D2
Ogdensburg . . . 122 R8
Ogilvie Mountains . . . 122 C4
Oglio . . . 62 E5
Ogoki . . . 36 P6
Ogosta . . . 66 L6
Ogre . . . 48 N8
Ogre . . . 48 N8
O Grove . . . 60 B2
Ogulin . . . 62 L5
Ohai . . . 116 A7
Ohanet . . . 102 G3
Ohio . . . 128 C3
Ohio . . . 128 D2
Ohre . . . 52 J6
Ohrid . . . 68 C3
Ohura . . . 116 E4
Oia . . . 68 H8
Oiapoque . . . 140 G3
Oil City . . . 128 E2
Oise . . . 54 E5
Ōita . . . 82 F7
Ojinaga . . . 132 F3
Ojiya . . . 82 K5
Ojos del Salado . . . 142 H4
Oka . . . 78 G6
Okaba . . . 87 E4
Okahandja . . . 108 B4
Okanagan Lake . . . 124 C2
Okano . . . 104 G4
Okanogan . . . 126 C1
Okara . . . 88 B2
Okarem . . . 90 F2
Okato . . . 116 D4
Okavango Delta . . . 108 C3
Okaya . . . 82 K5
Okayama . . . 82 G6
Okene . . . 104 F3
Oker . . . 52 F4
Okha, India . . . 90 J5
Okha, Russia . . . 78 Q6
Okhansk . . . 70 L3
Okhotsk . . . 78 Q5
Okhtyrka . . . 70 F4
Okinawa . . . 80 H5
Okinawa . . . 80 H5
Oki-shotō . . . 82 G5
Okitipupa . . . 104 E3
Oklahoma . . . 130 B2
Oklahoma City . . . 130 B2
Okoppe . . . 82 M1
Okoyo . . . 104 H5
Okranger . . . 48 E5
Oksino . . . 70 K1
Oktinden . . . 48 H4
Oktyabr'sk . . . 70 L5
Oktyabr'skiy . . . 70 K4
Okurchan . . . 78 S5
Okushiri-tō . . . 82 K2
Ólafsvík . . . 48 (1)B2
Olancha . . . 126 C3
Öland . . . 48 J8
Olanga . . . 48 Q3
Olathe . . . 130 C2
Olava . . . 52 J7
Oława . . . 50 G7
Olbia . . . 64 D8
Olching . . . 62 G2

Old Crow . . . 34 C3
Oldenburg, Germany . . . 52 D3
Oldenburg, Germany . . . 52 F2
Oldenzaal . . . 54 J2
Oldham . . . 56 L8
Old Head of Kinsale . . . 56 D10
Olean . . . 128 E2
Olecko . . . 50 M3
Olekma . . . 78 L5
Olekminsk . . . 78 L4
Oleksandriya . . . 70 F5
Olenegorsk . . . 48 S2
Olenek . . . 78 J3
Oleněk . . . 78 L2
Oleněkskiy Zaliv . . . 78 L2
Oleśnica . . . 50 G6
Olesno . . . 50 H7
Olhão . . . 60 C7
Olib . . . 62 K6
Olinda . . . 140 L5
Oliva . . . 60 K6
Olivet, France . . . 58 G6
Olivet, United States . . . 126 G2
Olivia . . . 128 B2
Olmos . . . 140 B5
Olney . . . 130 B3
Olochi . . . 78 K6
Olonets . . . 70 F2
Olongapo . . . 84 G4
Oloron-Ste-Marie . . . 58 E10
Olot . . . 60 N2
Olovyannaya . . . 78 K6
Olpe . . . 54 K3
Olsztyn . . . 50 K4
Olt . . . 66 M4
Olten . . . 62 C3
Oltenița . . . 66 P5
Oltu . . . 92 K3
Oluanpi . . . 84 G2
Olvera . . . 60 E8
Olympia . . . 126 B1
Olympos . . . 68 E4
Olympus . . . 68 Q10
Olyutorskiy . . . 78 W4
Olyutorskiy Zaliv . . . 78 V4
Om' . . . 76 N6
Oma . . . 88 D2
Omae-saki . . . 82 K6
Omagh . . . 56 E7
Omaha . . . 126 G2
Omak . . . 126 C1
Omakau . . . 116 B7
Oman . . . 90 G5
Omapere . . . 116 D2
Omarama . . . 116 B7
Omaruru . . . 108 B4
Omba, China . . . 88 D2
Omba, Russia . . . 76 E4
Omboué . . . 104 F5
Ombrone . . . 64 F6
Omdurman = Umm Durman . . . 100 F4
Omegna . . . 62 D5
Omeo . . . 114 J7
Om Hajer . . . 100 G5
Omīdeyeh . . . 95 C1
Omineca Mountains . . . 34 F5
Omis . . . 62 M7
Ommanney Bay . . . 36 L2
Ommen . . . 54 J2
Omolon . . . 78 T3
Omoloy . . . 78 N3
Omo Wenz . . . 106 F2
Omsk . . . 76 N6
Omsukchan . . . 78 S4
Ōmū . . . 82 M1
Omulew . . . 50 L4
Ōmura . . . 82 F7
Ōmuta . . . 82 F7
Onang . . . 87 A3
Onda . . . 60 K5
Ondangwa . . . 108 B3
Ondjiva . . . 108 B3
Ondo . . . 104 E3
Ondörhaan . . . 80 E1
One and a Half Degree Channel . . . 88 B8
Onega . . . 70 G2
O'Neill . . . 126 G2
Oneonta . . . 128 F2
Oneşti . . . 66 P3
Onezhskoye Ozero . . . 70 F2
Ongjin . . . 82 C5
Ongole . . . 88 D5
Onguday . . . 76 R7
Oni . . . 92 K2
Onilahy . . . 108 G4
Onitsha . . . 104 F3
Ono . . . 82 J6
Onon . . . 78 J7
Onon . . . 78 J7
Onslow Bay . . . 134 J2
Onsong . . . 82 E2
Ontario . . . 32 P6
Ontinyent . . . 60 K6
Ontonagon . . . 128 C1
Onyx . . . 132 C1
Oodnadatta . . . 114 G5
Oologah Lake . . . 130 B2
Oostburg . . . 54 F3
Oostelijk-Flevoland . . . 54 H2
Oostende . . . 54 E3
Oosterhout . . . 54 G3
Oosterschelde . . . 54 F3
Oost-Vlieland . . . 54 H1
Ootsa Lake . . . 122 F6
Opala . . . 106 C4
Oparino . . . 70 J3
Opava . . . 50 G8
Opelika . . . 130 D3
Opelousas . . . 130 C3
Opheim . . . 126 E1
Opochka . . . 70 E3
Opoczno . . . 50 K6

Opole . . . 50 G7
Opornyy . . . 76 J8
Opotiki . . . 116 F4
Opp . . . 130 D3
Opunake . . . 116 D4
Opuwo . . . 108 A3
Oradea . . . 66 J2
Orahovac . . . 66 H7
Orai . . . 88 C3
Oran . . . 60 K9
Orán . . . 142 J3
Orange . . . 108 C5
Orange, Australia . . . 114 J6
Orange, France . . . 58 K9
Orange, United States . . . 130 C3
Orangeburg . . . 130 E3
Orangemund . . . 108 B5
Orangeville . . . 128 D2
Orango . . . 104 A2
Oranienburg . . . 52 J4
Orapa . . . 108 D4
Orăştie . . . 66 L4
Oravița . . . 66 J4
Orbec . . . 58 F4
Orbetello . . . 64 F6
Orco . . . 62 C5
Ordes . . . 60 B1
Ordes Santa Comba . . . 60 B1
Ordu . . . 92 G3
Ordway . . . 126 F3
Öreälven . . . 48 K4
Örebro . . . 48 H7
Oregon . . . 126 B2
Oregon . . . 128 A3
Orekhovo-Zuyevo . . . 70 G3
Orel . . . 70 G4
Orem . . . 126 D2
Ören . . . 68 K7
Orenburg . . . 70 L4
Orestiada . . . 68 J3
Orewa . . . 116 E3
Orford Ness . . . 54 D2
Orhei . . . 66 R2
Orihuela . . . 60 K6
Orillia . . . 128 E2
Orinoco . . . 140 D2
Orinoco Delta = Delta del Orinoco . . . 140 E2
Orissaare . . . 48 M7
Oristano . . . 64 C9
Orivesi . . . 48 Q5
Orkla . . . 48 F5
Orkney Islands . . . 56 K3
Orlando . . . 130 E4
Orléans . . . 58 G6
Orlik . . . 78 F6
Orly . . . 54 E6
Ormara . . . 90 H4
Ormoc . . . 84 G4
Ormos Almyrou . . . 68 G9
Ormos Mesara . . . 68 G9
Ornans . . . 58 M6
Örnö . . . 48 K7
Örnsköldsvik . . . 48 K5
Orocué . . . 140 C3
Orofino . . . 126 C1
Oromocto . . . 128 G1
Orona . . . 112 J6
Oronoque . . . 140 F3
Oroqen Zizhiqi . . . 78 L6
Orosei . . . 64 D8
Orosháza . . . 66 H3
Oroszlany . . . 50 H10
Orotukan . . . 78 S4
Oroville . . . 126 B3
Ororroo . . . 114 G6
Orsa . . . 48 H6
Orsay . . . 58 H5
Orsha . . . 70 F4
Orsk . . . 70 L4
Orşova . . . 66 K5
Ørsta . . . 48 D5
Ortaklar . . . 68 K7
Orthez . . . 58 E10
Ortigueira . . . 60 C1
Ortisei . . . 62 G4
Ortles . . . 62 F4
Ortona . . . 64 J6
Ortonville . . . 128 A1
Orümīyeh . . . 92 L5
Oruro . . . 140 D7
Orvieto . . . 64 G6
Orville . . . 58 L6
Ōsaka . . . 82 H6
Osăm . . . 66 M6
Osceola . . . 128 B2
Oschatz . . . 52 J5
Oschersleben . . . 52 G4
O Seixo . . . 60 B3
Osh . . . 76 N9
Oshamambe . . . 82 L2
Oshawa . . . 128 E2
Oshkosh, Nebr., United States . . . 126 F2
Oshkosh, Wis., United States . . . 128 C2
Oshogbo . . . 104 E3
Osijek . . . 66 F4
Osimo . . . 64 J7
Oskaloosa . . . 128 B2
Oskarshamn . . . 48 J8
Oslo . . . 48 F7
Oslofjorden . . . 48 F7
Osmancik . . . 92 F3
Osmaniye . . . 92 G5
Osnabrück . . . 54 K2
Osor . . . 62 K6
Osorno . . . 142 G7
Osprey Reef . . . 114 J2
Oss . . . 54 H3
Ossa de Montiel . . . 60 H6
Osseo . . . 128 B2
Ossora . . . 78 U5
Ostashkov . . . 70 F3
Oste . . . 52 E3

Osterburg 52 G4
Østerdalen 48 F6
Osterholz-Scharmbeck 52 D3
Osterode 52 F5
Östersund 48 H5
Ostfriesische Inseln 52 C3
Ostiglia 62 G5
Ostrava 50 H8
Ostróda 50 K4
Ostrołęka 50 L4
Ostrov, *Czech Republic* 52 H6
Ostrov, *Russia* 70 E3
Ostrova Arkticheskogo Instituta 76 P2
Ostrova Medvezh'i 78 T2
Ostrov Atlasova 78 S6
Ostrova Vrangelya 120 V4
Ostrov Ayon 78 V2
Ostrov Belyy 76 N3
Ostrov Beringa 78 V6
Ostrov Bol'shevik 76 V2
Ostrov Bol'shoy Begichev 78 J2
Ostrov Bol'shoy Lyakhovskiy 78 Q2
Ostrov Bol'shoy Shantar 78 P6
Ostrov Chechen' 92 M2
Ostrov Iturup 82 P1
Ostrov Karaginskiy 78 U5
Ostrov Kil'din 48 T2
Ostrov Kolguyev 76 H4
Ostrov Komsomolets 76 T1
Ostrov Kotel'nyy 78 P1
Ostrov Kunashir 82 P1
Ostrov Mednyy 78 V6
Ostrov Mezhdusharskiy 76 H3
Ostrov Morzhovets 70 H1
Ostrov Novaya Sibir' 78 S2
Ostrov Ogurchinskiy 90 F2
Ostrov Oktyabr'skoy 76 S2
Ostrov Onekotan 78 S7
Ostrov Paramushir 78 T6
Ostrov Rasshua 78 S7
Ostrov Shiashkotan 78 S7
Ostrov Shumshu 78 T6
Ostrov Simushir 78 S7
Ostrov Urup 78 S7
Ostrov Ushakova 76 Q1
Ostrov Vaygach 76 K3
Ostrov Vise 76 P2
Ostrov Vosrozhdeniya 76 K9
Ostrov Vrangelya 78 W2
Ostrowiec Świętokrzyski 50 L7
Ostrów Mazowiecka 50 L5
Ostrów Wielkopolski 50 G6
Ostuni 64 M8
Osum 68 C4
Ōsumi-shotō 82 F8
Osuna 60 E7
Oswego 128 E2
Oświęcim 50 J7
Otago Peninsula 116 C7
Otaki 116 E5
Otaru 82 L2
Oțelu Roșu 66 K4
Othonoi 68 B5
Oti 104 E3
Otira 116 C6
Otjiwarongo 108 B4
Otočac 62 L6
Otog Qi 80 D3
Otoineppu 82 M1
Otorohanga 116 E4
Otranto 64 N8
Otrøy 48 D5
Otrozhnyy 78 W3
Ōtsu 82 H6
Otta 48 E6
Ottawa 38 R7
Ottawa, *Canada* 38 R7
Ottawa, *Ill., United States* 128 C2
Ottawa, *Kans., United States* 130 B2
Ottawa Islands 122 Q5
Otterøy 48 F4
Ottobrunn 62 G2
Ottumwa 128 B2
Otukpo 104 F3
Ouachita Mountains 130 C3
Ouadâne 102 C4
Ouadda 106 C2
Ouagadougou 104 D2
Oualâta 102 D5
Ouallam 104 E2
Ouanda-Djalle 106 C2
Ouargla 102 G2
Ouarzazate 102 D2
Oudenaarde 54 F4
Oudenbosch 54 G3
Oudtshoorn 108 C6
Oued Laou 60 E9
Oued Tiélat 60 K9
Oued Zem 102 D2
Ouéléssébougou 104 C2
Ouésso 104 H4
Ouezzane 102 D2
Oujda 102 E2
Oujeft 102 C4
Oulainen 48 N4
Ould Yenjé 102 C5
Oulu 48 N4
Oulujärvi 48 P4
Oulujoki 48 P4
Oulx 62 B5
Oum-Chalouba 100 D4
Oum-Hadjer 100 C5
Ounarjoki 48 N3
Our 54 J4
Ouray 126 E3
Ourense 60 C2
Ouricurí 140 J5
Ourthe 54 H4
Oustreham 54 B5
Outer Hebrides 56 D4
Outjo 108 B4
Outokumpu 48 Q5
Out Skerries 56 M1
Ouyen 114 H7
Ovacık 68 R8
Ovada 62 D6
Ovalle 142 G5
Ovareli 92 L3
Overflakkee 54 G3
Overlander Roadhouse 114 B5
Overland Park 130 C2
Overton 126 D3
Övertorneå 48 M3
Ovidiopol' 66 T3
Oviedo 60 E1
Owaka 116 B8
Owando 104 H5
Owase 82 J6
Owatonna 128 B2
Owen River 116 D5
Owensboro 128 C3
Owens Lake 126 C3
Owen Sound 128 D2
Owerri 104 F3
Owo 104 F3
Owosso 128 D2
Owyhee 126 C2
Owyhee 126 C2
Oxford, *New Zealand* 116 D6
Oxford, *United Kingdom* 54 A3
Oxnard 132 C2
Oyama 82 K5
Oyapock 140 G3
Oyem 104 G4
Oyen 124 D1
Oyonnax 62 A4
Ózd 50 K9
Ozernovskiy 78 T6
Ozero Alakol' 76 Q8
Ozero Aralsor 70 J5
Ozero Aydarkul' 76 M9
Ozero Balkhash 76 N8
Ozero Baykal 78 H6
Ozero Beloye 70 G2
Ozero Chany 76 P7
Ozero Chernoye 70 N3
Ozero Il'men' 70 F3
Ozero-Imandra 48 R2
Ozero Inder 76 J8
Ozero Janis'jarvi 48 R5
Ozero Kamennoje 48 R4
Ozero Kanozero 48 T3
Ozero Khanka 82 G1
Ozero Kolvitskoye 48 S3
Ozero Kovdozero 48 S3
Ozero Kulundinskoye 76 P7
Ozero Kushmurun 70 N4
Ozero Lama 78 D2
Ozero Leksozero 48 R5
Ozero Lovozero 48 T2
Ozero Nyuk 48 R4
Ozero Ozhogino 78 R3
Ozero Pirenga 48 R3
Ozero Pyaozero 48 R3
Ozero Saltaim 70 P3
Ozero Sarpa 70 J5
Ozero Segozeroskoye 70 F2
Ozero Seletyteniz 76 N7
Ozero Sredneye Kuyto 48 R4
Ozero Taymyr 76 U3
Ozero Teletskoye 76 R7
Ozero Tengiz 70 N4
Ozero Topozero 48 R4
Ozero Umbozero 48 T3
Ozero Vygozero 70 G2
Ozero Yalpug 66 R4
Ozero Zaysan 76 Q8
Ozero Zhaltyr 70 K5
Ozero Zhamanakkol' 70 M5
Ozersk 50 M3
Ozhogina 78 R3
Ozhogino 78 R3
Ozieri 64 C8
Ozinki 70 J4
Ozona 132 F2
Ozurget'i 92 J3

P

Paamiut 122 X4
Paar 52 G8
Paarl 108 B6
Pabbay 56 E4
Pabianice 50 J6
Pabna 88 E4
Pacasmayo 140 B5
Pachino 64 K12
Pachuca 134 E4
Pacific Ocean 42 B3
Pacific Ranges 34 F6
Pacitan 86 E4
Packwood 126 B1
Padalere 87 B3
Padang 86 C3
Padangpanjang 86 C3
Padangsidempuan 86 B2
Padborg 52 E2
Paderborn 52 D5
Padova 62 G5
Padre Island 130 B4
Padrón 60 B2
Paducah, *Ky., United States* 128 C3
Paducah, *Tex., United States* 132 F2
Padum 88 C2
Paekdu San 82 D3
Paeroa 116 E3
Pafos 68 Q10
Pag 62 K6
Pag 62 L6
Paga Conta 140 G4
Pagadian 84 G5
Pagai Selatan 86 B3
Pagai Utara 86 B3
Pagalu = Annobón 104 F5
Pagan 112 E4
Pagatan 86 F3
Page, *Ariz., United States* 132 D1
Page, *Okla., United States* 130 C3
Pagosa Springs 126 E3
Pagri 88 E3
Pahiatua 116 E5
Paia 132 (2)E3
Paide 48 N7
Päijänne 48 N6
Painan 86 C3
Painesville 128 D2
Paisley 56 H6
Paita 140 A5
Pakaraima Mountains 140 E2
Pakch'ŏn 82 C4
Pakhachi 78 V4
Paki 104 F2
Pakistan 90 J4
Pakokku 84 A2
Pakotai 116 D2
Pakrac 62 N5
Paks 66 F3
Pakxé 84 D3
Pala 100 B6
Palafrugell 60 P3
Palagonia 64 J11
Palagruža 64 L6
Palaiochora 68 F9
Palamós 60 P3
Palana 78 U5
Palanan 84 G3
Palanga 50 L2
Palangkaraya 86 E3
Palanpur 88 B4
Palantak 90 H4
Palapye 108 D4
Palatka, *Russia* 78 S4
Palatka, *United States* 130 E4
Palau 64 D7
Palau 112 D5
Palau 112 D5
Palaw 84 B4
Palawan 84 F5
Palazzolo Arceide 64 J11
Palembang 86 C3
Palencia 60 F2
Paleokastritsa 68 B5
Palermo 64 H10
Palestine 130 B3
Palestrina 64 G7
Paletwa 84 A2
Palghat 88 C6
Pali 88 B3
Palikir 112 F5
Palimbang 84 G5
Pālkohda 88 D5
Palk Strait 88 C7
Palma del Rio 60 E7
Palma de Mallorca 60 N5
Palma di Montechiaro 64 H11
Palmanova 62 J5
Palmares 140 K5
Palmarola 64 G8
Palmas 140 H6
Palmas 142 L4
Palm Bay 130 E4
Palmdale 132 C2
Palmerston 116 C7
Palmerston Island 112 K7
Palmerston North 116 E5
Palm Harbor 130 E4
Palmi 64 K10
Palmira 140 B3
Palmyra Island 112 K5
Palojärvi 48 M2
Palopo 87 B3
Palu, *Indonesia* 87 A3
Palu, *Turkey* 92 J4
Palyavaam 78 W3
Pama 104 E2
Pamekasan 86 E4
Pamhagen 62 M3
Pamiers 58 G10
Pamlico Sound 130 F2
Pampa 132 F1
Pampas 142 J6
Pamplona, *Colombia* 134 K7
Pamplona, *Spain* 60 J2
Pana 128 C3
Panagjurište 66 M7
Panaji 88 B5
Panama 134 H7
Panamá 140 B2
Panama Canal = Canal de Panamá 134 J7
Panama City 130 D3
Panarea 64 K10
Panarik 86 D2
Panaro 62 G6
Panay 84 G4
Pančevo 66 H5
Panciu 66 Q4
Pandan 84 G4
Pandharpur 88 C5
Panevėžys 50 P2
Pangani 106 F5
Pangin 88 F3
Pangkajene 87 A3
Pangkalanbuun 86 E3
Pangkalpinang 86 D3
Pangnirtung 122 T3
Panguitch 126 D3
Pangutaran Group 84 G5
Panhandle 132 F1
Panipat 88 C3
Panjāb 90 J3
Panjgur 90 H4
Pankshin 104 F3
Pantanal 140 F7
Pantar 87 B4
Pantelleria 102 H1
Pantemakassar 87 B4
Paola 64 L9
Paoua 106 B2
Pápa 66 E2
Papa 132 (2)F4
Papakura 116 E3
Papantla 134 E4
Paparoa 116 E3
Papa Stour 56 L1
Papatowi 116 B8
Papa Westray 56 K2
Papenburg 52 C3
Papey 48 (1)F2
Papua New Guinea 112 E6
Papun 84 B3
Pará 140 G5
Para 140 H4
Parabel' 76 Q6
Paracatu 140 H7
Paracel Islands 84 E3
Paraćin 66 J6
Pará de Minas 140 J7
Paragould 130 C2
Paragua, *Bolivia* 140 E6
Paragua, *Venezuela* 140 E2
Paraguay 138 F6
Paraguay 142 J3
Paraíba 140 K5
Parakou 104 E3
Paralia 68 E8
Paralimni 94 A1
Paramaribo 140 F2
Paranã 140 H6
Paranã 140 H6
Paraná 142 J5
Paraná 142 K4
Paraná 142 L3
Paranaguá 142 M4
Paranaíba 140 G7
Paranaíba 140 G7
Paranavaí 142 L3
Paranestio 68 G3
Paraparaumu 116 E5
Paray-le Monial 58 K7
Parbhani 88 C5
Parchim 52 G3
Pardo 140 J7
Pardubice 50 E7
Pareh 92 L4
Parepare 87 A3
Parga 68 C5
Parigi 87 B3
Parika 140 F2
Parintins 140 F4
Paris, *France* 58 H5
Paris, *Tenn., United States* 130 D2
Paris, *Tex., United States* 130 B3
Parkersburg 128 D3
Park Rapids 128 A1
Parla 60 G4
Parma 62 F6
Parma, *Italy* 62 F6
Parma, *United States* 128 D2
Parnaíba 140 G7
Parnaíba 140 J4
Parnassus 116 D6
Pärnu 48 N7
Pärnu 48 N7
Paros 68 H7
Paros 68 H7
Parry Bay 122 Q3
Parry Islands 122 L1
Parry Sound 128 D2
Parsons 130 B2
Parthenay 58 E7
Partinico 64 H10
Partizansk 82 G2
Paru 140 G4
Parvatipuram 88 D5
Paryang 88 D2
Pasadena, *Calif., United States* 132 C2
Pasadena, *Tex., United States* 130 B4
Paşalimani Adası 68 K4
Pasawng 84 B3
Paşcani 66 P2
Pasco 126 C1
Pascual 84 G4
Pasewalk 52 K3
Pasig 84 G4
Pasinler 92 J3
Pasłęk 50 J3
Pasłek 50 J3
Pasleka 48 L9
Pašman 62 L7
Pasni 90 H4
Paso de Hachado 142 G6
Paso de Indios 142 H7
Paso de la Cumbre 142 H5
Paso de San Francisco 142 H4
Paso Río Mayo 142 G8
Paso Robles 132 B1
Passau 52 J8
Passo Fundo 142 L4
Passos 140 H8
Pastavy 48 P9
Pasto 140 B3
Pastos Bons 140 J5
Pasvalys 50 P1
Pásztó 66 G2
Patagonia 142 G8
Patan, *India* 88 B4
Patan, *Nepal* 88 E3
Patea 116 E4
Pate Island 106 G4
Paterna 60 K5
Paternò 64 J11
Paterson 128 F2
Pathankot 88 C2
Pathfinder Reservoir 126 E2
Patia 140 B3
Patiala 88 C2
Patmos 68 J7

Patna 88 E3
Patnos 92 K4
Patos de Minas 140 H7
Patra 68 D6
Patraikis Kolpos 68 D6
Patreksfjörður 48 (1)B2
Pattani 84 C5
Pattaya 84 C4
Patti 64 J10
Paturau River 116 D5
Pau 60 K1
Pauini 140 D5
Pauini 140 D5
Paulatuk 34 G3
Paulo Afonso 140 K5
Paul's Valley 130 B3
Päveh 92 M6
Pavia 62 E5
Pāvilosta 48 L8
Pavlikeni 66 N6
Pavlodar 76 P7
Pavlohrad 70 G5
Pavlovsk 70 H4
Pavlovskaya 70 G5
Pavullo nel Frignano 62 F6
Paxoi 68 C5
Paxson 132 (1)H3
Payerne 62 B4
Payette 126 C2
Payne's Find 114 C5
Paysandú 142 K5
Payson 132 D2
Payturma 76 S3
Pazar 92 J3
Pazardžik 66 M7
Pazin 62 J5
Peace 34 J5
Peace River 122 H5
Peach Springs 132 D1
Pearsall 130 B4
Pebane 108 F3
Pebas 140 C5
Peć 66 H7
Pecan Island 130 C4
Pechora 70 K1
Pechora 70 L1
Pechorskoye More 76 J4
Pechory 48 P8
Pecos 132 F2
Pecos 132 F2
Pécs 66 F3
Pedja 48 P7
Pedra Azul 140 J7
Pedra Lume 104 (1)B1
Pedreiras 140 J4
Pedro Afonso 140 H5
Pedro Juan Caballero 142 K3
Pedro Luro 142 J6
Peel Sound 122 M2
Peene 52 J3
Peenemünde 52 J2
Pegasus Bay 116 D6
Pegnitz 52 G7
Pegu 84 B3
Pegunungan Barisan 86 B2
Pegunungan Iran 86 F2
Pegunungan Maoke 87 E3
Pegunungan Meratus 86 F3
Pegunungan Schwaner 86 E3
Pegunungan Van Rees 87 E3
Pehuajó 142 J6
Peine 52 F4
Peiraias 68 F7
Peißenberg 62 G3
Peixe 140 H6
Pekalongan 86 D4
Pekanbaru 86 C2
Peking = Beijing 80 F3
Pelaihari 86 E3
Peleduy 78 J5
Peleng 87 B3
Pelhřimov 50 E8
Pelješac 64 M6
Pello 48 N3
Pellworm 52 D2
Pelly Bay 122 P3
Pelly Mountains 34 E4
Peloponnisos 68 D7
Pelotas 142 L5
Pelym 70 M2
Pemangkat 86 D2
Pematangsiantar 86 B2
Pemba 108 G2
Pemba Island 106 F5
Pembina 126 G1
Pembine 128 C1
Pembroke, *Canada* 128 E1
Pembroke, *United Kingdom* 56 H10
Pembroke, *United States* 130 E3
Peñafiel 60 F3
Peñaranda de Bracamonte 60 E4
Peñarroya-Pueblonuevo 60 E6
Pendik 68 M4
Pendleton 126 C1
Pendolo 86 G3
Pend Oreille Lake 126 C1
Pen Hills 128 E2
Peniche 60 A5
Península de Azuero 134 H7
Peninsula de Guajira 134 K6
Península Valdés 142 J7
Péninsule de Gaspé 38 T7
Péninsule d'Ungava 38 R5
Penmarch 58 A6
Penne 64 H6
Pennines 56 K7
Pennsylvania 128 E2
Penny Icecap 38 T3
Penrith 56 K7
Pensacola 134 G2
Penticton 34 H7
Penza 70 J4
Penzance 56 G11
Penzhina 78 V4
Penzhinskaya Guba 78 U4
Penzhinskiy Khrebet 78 V4
Peoria, *Ariz., United States* 132 D2
Peoria, *Ill., United States* 128 C2
Percival Lakes 114 D4
Peregrebnoye 70 N2
Pereira 140 B3
Pergamino 142 J5
Périers 58 D4
Périgueux 58 F8
Peristera 68 G5
Perito Moreno 142 G8
Perleberg 52 G3
Perm' 70 L3
Përmet 68 C4
Pernambuco 140 K5
Pernik 66 L7
Péronne 54 E5
Perpignan 58 H11
Perrine 130 E4
Perry, *Fla., United States* 130 E3
Perry, *Ga., United States* 130 E3
Persepolis 95 E2
Perth, *Australia* 114 C6
Perth, *United Kingdom* 56 J5
Pertuis Breton 58 D7
Peru 128 C2
Peru 140 C6
Peru-Chile Trench 138 D5
Perugia 64 G5
Pervomays'k 70 F5
Pervoural'sk 70 L3
Pesaro 62 H7
Pescara 64 J6
Pescia 62 F7
Peshawar 88 B2
Peshkopi 68 C3
Peski Karakumy 90 G2
Peski Kyzylkum 76 L9
Peski Priaral'skiye Karakumy 76 L8
Pesnica 62 L4
Pessac 58 E9
Peštera 68 G2
Petah Tiqwa 94 B4
Petalioi 68 G7
Petaluma 126 B3
Pétange 54 H5
Petare 134 L6
Petauke 108 E2
Peterborough, *Canada* 38 R8
Peterborough, *United Kingdom* 56 M9
Peterhead 56 L4
Peter I Øy 144 (2)JJ3
Petersburg 128 E3
Petersfield 54 B3
Petershagen 52 D4
Petit Mécatina 122 U6
Peto 134 G4
Petre Bay 116 (1)B1
Petrič 68 F3
Petrila 66 L4
Petrinja 62 M5
Petrolina 140 J5
Petropavlovka 78 H6
Petropavlovsk 70 N4
Petropavlovsk-Kamchatskiy 78 T6
Petrópolis 142 N3
Petroşani 66 L4
Petrovac 66 J5
Petrovsk-Zabaykal'skiy 78 H6
Petrozavodsk 70 F2
Petrun 70 M1
Petukhovo 70 N3
Pevek 78 W3
Pezinok 50 G9
Pfaffenhofen 52 G8
Pfarrkirchen 52 H8
Pflach 62 F3
Pforzheim 52 D8
Pfunds 62 F4
Pfungstadt 52 D7
Phalaborwa 108 E4
Phalodi 88 B3
Phan Rang 84 D4
Phan Thiêt 84 D4
Phatthalung 84 C5
Phet Buri 84 B4
Phichit 84 C3
Philadelphia, *Miss., United States* 130 D3
Philadelphia, *Pa., United States* 130 F2
Philippeville 54 G4
Philippines 84 G5
Philippine Trench 74 R8
Philips 122 K7
Phillipsburg 126 G3
Phitsanulok 84 C3
Phnum Penh 84 C4
Phoenix 132 D2
Phoenix 108 (1)B2
Phoenix Islands 112 J6
Phôngsali 84 C2
Phuket 84 B5
Phumĭ Sâmraông 84 C4
Piacenza 62 E5
Piadena 62 F5
Pianoro 62 G6
Pianosa 64 E6
Piatra-Neamț 66 P3
Piauí 140 J5
Piazza Armerina 64 J11
Pibor Post 106 E2
Picacho del Centinela 132 F3
Picayune 130 D3
Pichilemu 142 G5
Pico 102 (1)B2
Pico Almanzor 60 E4
Pico Cristóbal Colón 134 K6
Pico da Bandeira 142 N3
Pico da Neblina 140 D3
Pico de Itambé 142 N2
Pico de Teide 102 B3
Pico Duarte 134 K5
Picos 140 J5
Picton, *New Zealand* 116 D5
Picton, *United States* 128 E2
Pic Tousside 100 C3
Piedras Negras 132 F3
Pieksämäki 48 P5
Pielinen 48 Q5
Pierre 126 F2
Pierrelatte 58 K9
Piers do Rio 140 H7
Piešťany 50 G9
Pietermaritzburg 108 E5
Pietersburg 108 D4
Pietrasanta 62 F6
Piet Retief 108 E5
Pieve di Cadore 62 H4
Pihlájavesi 48 P6
Pik Aborigen 78 R4
Piketberg 108 B6
Pik Kommunizma 90 K2
Pik Pobedy 76 P9
Piła 50 F4
Pilaya 142 H3
Pilcomayo 140 E8
Pilibhit 88 C3
Pilica 50 J7
Pimba 114 G6
Pimenta Bueno 140 E6
Pinamalayan 84 G4
Pinamar 142 K6
Pinang 84 B5
Pınarbası 92 G4
Pinar del Río 134 H4
Pinarhisar 68 K3
Pińczów 50 K7
Pindaré Mirim 140 H4
Pindos 68 D5
Pine Bluff 128 B4
Pine Bluffs 126 F2
Pine City 128 B1
Pine Creek 114 F2
Pine Creek Reservoir 128 A4
Pinega 70 H2
Pineios 68 E5
Pine Island Bay 144 (2)GG3
Pineland 130 C3
Pinerolo 62 C6
Pineville, *Ky., United States* 128 D3
Pineville, *La., United States* 130 C3
Pingdingshan 80 E4
Pingguo 84 D2
Pingle 84 E2
Pingliang 80 D3
Pingshi 80 E5
P'ingtung 84 G2
Pingxiang, *China* 84 D2
Pingxiang, *China* 84 E1
Pinhel 60 C4
Pini 86 B2
Pinka 62 M3
Pink Mountain 122 G5
Pinneberg 52 E3
Pinsk 70 E4
Pioche 126 D3
Piombino 64 E6
Pioneer 132 D2
Pioneer Mountains 126 D1
Pionerskiy, *Russia* 50 K3
Pionerskiy, *Russia* 70 M2
Piopio 116 E4
Piotrków Trybunalski 50 J6
Piove di Sacco 62 H5
Piperi 68 G5
Pipestone 128 A2
Pipiriki 116 E4
Piqua 128 D2
Piracicaba 142 M3
Pirin 68 F3
Piripiri 140 J4
Pirmasens 52 C7
Pirna 52 J6
Pirot 66 K6
Piru 87 C3
Pisa 50 L4
Pisa 62 F7
Pisco 140 B6
Pisek 50 D8
Pishin 90 H4
Pishin 90 J3
Piska 50 L4
Pisticci 64 L8
Pistoia 62 F7
Pisz 50 L4
Pitcairn Islands 112 P8
Piteå 48 L4
Piteälven 70 C1
Pitești 66 M5
Pithara 114 C6
Pithiviers 58 H5
Pitkyaranta 70 F2
Pitlochry 56 J5
Pitlyar 70 N1
Pitt Island 116 (1)B2
Pittsburg 130 C2
Pittsburgh 128 D2
Pitt Strait 116 (1)B2
Piura 140 A5
Pivka 62 K5
Placentia Bay 38 W7
Placer 84 G4
Placerville 132 B1
Plaiamonas 68 E5
Plains 132 F2
Plainview 132 F2
Plampang 86 F4
Planalto Central 140 H6
Planalto da Borborema 140 K5
Planalto do Mato Grosso 140 G6
Plankinton 126 G2
Plano 130 B3
Plasencia 60 D5
Plast 70 M4
Plateau du Djado 102 H4
Plateau du Limousin 58 F8
Plateau du Tademaït 102 F3
Plateau of Tibet = Xizang Gaoyuan 88 D2
Plateaux Batéké 104 G5
Platinum 132 (1)E4
Plato 134 K7
Plato Ustyurt 76 J9
Platte 130 B1
Platteville 128 B2
Plattling 52 H8
Plattsburgh 128 F2
Plattsmouth 130 B1
Plau 52 H3
Plauen 52 H6
Plavnik 62 K6
Plavsk 70 G4
Playa de Castilla 60 D7
Playas 140 A4
Plây Cu 84 D4
Pleasanton 132 G3
Pleiße 52 H5
Plentywood 126 F1
Plesetsk 70 H2
Pleven 66 M6
Pljevlja 66 G6
Płock 50 J5
Pločno 66 E6
Ploërmel 58 C6
Ploiești 66 P5
Plomari 68 J6
Plön 52 F2
Płońsk 50 K5
Plovdiv 66 M7
Plumtree 108 D4
Plungė 50 L2
Plymouth, *United Kingdom* 56 H11
Plymouth, *United States* 128 C2
Plyussa 48 Q7
Plyussa 70 E3
Plzeň 50 C8
Po 62 E5
Pocahontas 134 F1
Pocatello 126 D2
Pochet 78 F5
Pochinok 70 F4
Pocking 62 J2
Pocomoke City 128 E3
Podgorica 66 G7
Podkamennaya Tunguska 78 F4
Podol'sk 70 G3
Podravska Slatina 66 E4
Poel 52 G2
Pofadder 108 B5
Pogradec 68 C4
P'ohang 82 E5
Pohnpei 112 F5
Pohokura 116 F4
Pohořelice 62 M2
Point Arena 124 B4
Point Barrow 132 (1)F1
Point Conception 132 B2
Point Culver 114 D6
Point d'Entrecasteaux 114 B6
Pointe de l'Est 38 U7
Pointe-Noire 104 G5
Point Hope 132 (1)D2
Point Hope 132 (1)D2
Point Pedro 88 D7
Point Sur 126 B3
Poitiers 58 F7
Pokaran 88 B3
Pokhara 88 D3
Poko 106 D3
Pokrovsk 78 M4
Pola de Siero 60 E1
Poland 50 G6
Polar Bluff 134 F1
Polatlı 68 Q5
Polatsk 70 E3
Police 52 K3
Polichnitos 68 J5
Policoro 64 L8
Poligny 58 L7
Poligus 76 S5
Polillo Islands 84 G4
Poliocastro 64 L9
Polis 68 Q9
Polistena 64 L10
Pollachi 88 C6
Pollença 60 P5
Polohy 70 G5
Polomoloc 84 H5
Polonnaruwa 88 D7
Poltava 70 F5
Poltavka 82 F1
Põltsamaa 48 N7
Poluostrov Shmidta 78 Q6
Poluostrov Taymyr 76 R3
Poluostrov Yamal 76 M3
Poluy 76 M4
Põlva 48 P7
Polyaigos 68 G8
Polyarnye Zori 48 S3
Polyarnyy 78 X3
Polykastro 68 E4
Polynesia 112 J6
Pombal 60 B5
Pomeranian Bay 50 D3
Pomeroy 126 C1
Pomorie 66 Q7
Pompano Beach 130 E4
Pompei 64 J8
Ponca City 130 B2
Ponce 134 L5
Pondicherry 88 C6
Pond Inlet 122 R2
Ponferrada 60 D2
Poniatowa 50 M6
Ponoy 70 H1

Pons 58 E8
Ponta Delgada 102 (1)B2
Ponta do Podrão 104 G6
Ponta do Sol 104 (1)B1
Ponta Grossa 142 L4
Ponta Khehuene 108 E5
Pont-à-Mousson 58 M5
Ponta Porã 142 K3
Pontarlier 58 M7
Pontassieve 62 G7
Ponta Zavora 108 F4
Pont-d'Alin 58 L7
Ponteareas 60 B2
Ponte da Barca 60 B3
Pontedera 62 F7
Ponte de Sor 60 C5
Pontevedra 60 B2
Pontiac 128 C2
Pontianak 86 D3
Pontivy 58 C5
Pontoise 54 E5
Pontorson 58 D5
Pontremoli 62 E6
Ponza 64 G8
Poogau 62 J3
Poole 56 L11
Poole Bay 56 L11
Pooncarie 114 H6
Poopó 140 D7
Poopó Challapata 142 H2
Poor Knights Islands 116 E2
Popayán 134 J8
Poperinge 54 E4
Popigay 76 W3
Poplar Bluff 128 B3
Poplarville 130 D3
Popocatépetl 134 E5
Popoh 86 E4
Popokabaka 104 H6
Popovača 62 M5
Popovo 66 P6
Poprad 50 K8
Poprad 50 K8
Porangatu 140 H6
Porbandar 90 J5
Porcupine 132 (1)K2
Pordenone 62 H5
Poreč 62 J5
Poret 64 H3
Pori 48 L6
Porirua 116 E5
Porlamar 134 M6
Poronaysk 78 Q7
Poros 68 F7
Porosozero 70 F2
Porozina 62 K5
Porpoise Bay 144 (2)T3
Porriño 60 B2
Porsangen 48 N1
Porsgrunn 48 E7
Portadown 56 F7
Portage 128 C2
Portage la Prairie 36 M7
Port Alberni 126 B1
Port Albert 114 J7
Portalegre 60 C5
Portales 132 F2
Port Arthur, *Australia* 114 J8
Port Arthur, *United States* 130 C4
Port Augusta 114 G6
Port-au-Prince 134 K5
Port Austin 128 D2
Port Blair 84 A4
Port Burwell 122 U4
Port Charlotte 130 E4
Port Douglas 114 J3
Portel, *Brazil* 140 G4
Portel, *Portugal* 60 C6
Port Elizabeth 108 D6
Port Ellen 56 F6
Porterville 132 C1
Port Fitzroy 116 E3
Port-Gentil 104 F5
Port Harcourt 104 F4
Port Hardy 122 F6
Port Hawkesbury 122 U7
Port Hedland 114 C4
Port Hope Simpson 122 V6
Port Huron 128 D2
Portimão 60 B7
Port Jefferson 128 F2
Portland, *Australia* 114 H7
Portland, *New Zealand* 116 E2
Portland, *Ind., United States* 128 D2
Portland, *Me., United States* 128 F2
Portland, *Oreg., United States* 126 B1
Portland Island 116 F4
Port Laoise 56 E8
Port Lavaca 130 B4
Port Lincoln 114 G6
Port Loko 104 B3
Port Louis 108 (1)B2
Port Macquarie 114 K6
Port-Menier 122 U7
Port Moresby 114 J1
Port Nolloth 108 B5
Porto, *Corsica* 64 C6
Porto, *Portugal* 60 B3
Porto Alegre, *R.G.S., Brazil* 142 L5
Porto Alegre, *Pará, Brazil* 140 G4
Porto Amboim 108 A2
Portocheli 68 F7
Porto do Son 60 A2
Pôrto Esperidião 140 F7
Portoferraio 64 E6
Pôrto Franco 140 H5
Port of Spain 140 E1
Pôrto Grande 140 G3
Portogruaro 62 H5
Porto Inglês 104 (1)B1
Portomaggiore 62 G6
Pôrto Murtinho 142 K3
Pôrto Nacional 140 H6
Porto-Novo 104 E3
Port Orford 126 B2
Porto San Giorgio 64 H5
Pôrto Santana 140 G3
Porto Santo 102 B2
Pôrto Seguro 140 K7
Porto Tolle 62 H6
Porto Torres 64 C8
Porto-Vecchio 64 D7
Pôrto Velho 140 E5
Portoviejo 140 A4
Port Pire 114 G6
Portree 56 F4
Port Renfrew 126 B1
Port Said = Bûr Sa'îd 100 F1
Port St. Johns 108 D6
Port Shepstone 108 E6
Portsmouth, *United Kingdom* 54 A4
Portsmouth, *N.H., United States* 128 F2
Portsmouth, *Oh., United States* 128 D3
Portsmouth, *Va., United States* 128 E3
Port Sudan = Bur Sudan 100 G4
Port Sulphur 130 D4
Port Talbot 56 J10
Portugal 60 B5
Portugalete 60 G1
Port-Vendres 58 J11
Port-Vila 112 G7
Port Warrender 114 E2
Posadas 142 K4
Poschiavo 62 F4
Poshekhon'ye 70 G3
Poso 87 B3
Posŏng 82 D6
Posse 140 H6
Pößneck 52 G6
Post 132 F2
Postmasburg 108 C5
Postojna 62 K5
Post Weygand 102 F4
Posušje 66 E6
Pota 86 G4
Potapovo 76 R4
Poteau 130 C2
Potenza 62 J7
Potenza 64 K8
Potgietersrus 108 D4
P'ot'i 92 J2
Potiskum 104 G2
Potlatch 126 C1
Potosí 140 D7
Potsdam, *Germany* 52 J4
Potsdam, *United States* 128 F2
Pottuvil 88 D7
Poughkeepsie 128 F2
Pourerere 116 F5
Pouto 116 E3
Póvoa de Varzim 60 B3
Povorino 70 H4
Powder 126 E1
Powder River 126 E2
Powell River 34 G7
Poyang Hu 80 F5
Požarevac 66 J5
Poza Rica 134 E4
Požega 66 H6
Poznań 50 F5
Pozoblanco 60 F6
Pozzuoli 64 J8
Prabumulih 86 C3
Prachatice 50 D8
Prachuap Khiri Khan 84 B4
Prado 140 K7
Præstø 52 H1
Prague = Praha 50 D7
Praha 50 D7
Praia 104 (1)B2
Prainha 140 G4
Prairie du Chien 128 B2
Prapat 86 B2
Praslin 108 (2)B1
Pratas = Dongsha Qundao 84 F2
Prato 62 G7
Pratt 126 G3
Prattville 130 D3
Praya 86 F4
Preetz 52 F2
Preganziòl 62 H5
Preiļi 48 P8
Premnitz 52 H4
Premuda 62 K6
Prentice 128 B1
Prenzlau 50 C4
Preobrazhenka 78 H4
Preparis Island 84 A4
Preparis North Channel 84 A3
Preparis South Channel 84 A4
Přerov 50 G8
Presa de la Boquilla 132 E3
Presa de las Adjuntas 132 G4
Presa Obregón 132 E3
Prescott 126 D4
Preševo 66 J7
Presho 126 G2
Presidencia Roque Sáenz Peña 142 J4
Presidente Prudente 142 L3
Presidio 132 F3
Preslav 66 P6
Presnogorkovka 70 N4
Prešov 50 L9
Presque Isle 128 G1
Přeštice 52 J7
Preston, *United Kingdom* 56 K8
Preston, *Minn., United States* 128 B2
Preston, *Mo., United States* 128 B3
Pretoria 108 D5
Preveza 68 C6
Priargunsk 78 K6
Pribilof Islands 132 (1)D4
Priboj 66 G6
Příbram 50 D8
Price 126 D3
Prichard 130 D3
Priego de Córdoba 60 F7
Priekule 48 L8
Prienai 50 N3
Prieska 108 C5
Priest Lake 126 C1
Prievidza 50 H9
Prijedor 66 D5
Prijepolje 66 G6
Prikaspiyskaya Nizmennost' 70 K5
Prilep 68 D3
Primolano 62 G5
Primorsk 48 Q6
Primorsko Akhtarsk 70 G5
Prince Albert 34 K6
Prince Albert Peninsula 122 H2
Prince Albert Sound 36 H2
Prince Charles Island 36 R3
Prince Edward Island, *Canada* 38 U7
Prince Edward Island, *South Africa* 98 G10
Prince Edward Island 32 U7
Prince George 34 G6
Prince of Wales Island, *Australia* 114 H2
Prince of Wales Island, *Canada* 36 M2
Prince of Wales Island, *United States* 122 E5
Prince of Wales Strait 122 H2
Prince Patrick Island 120 Q2
Prince Regent Inlet 122 N2
Prince Rupert 34 E6
Princess Charlotte Bay 114 H2
Princeton, *Canada* 126 B1
Princeton, *Ill., United States* 128 C2
Princeton, *Ky., United States* 128 C3
Princeton, *Mo., United States* 128 B2
Prince William Sound 122 B4
Príncipe 104 F4
Prineville 126 B2
Priozersk 48 R6
Priština 66 J7
Pritzwalk 52 H3
Privas 58 K9
Privolzhskaya Vozvyshennost' 70 H4
Prizren 66 H7
Probolinggo 86 E4
Proddatur 88 C6
Progreso 134 G4
Prokhladnyy 92 L2
Prokop'yevsk 76 R7
Prokuplje 66 J6
Proletarsk 70 H5
Proliv Longa 78 X2
Proliv Matochkin Shar 76 K3
Proliv Vil'kitskogo 76 U2
Prophet 122 G5
Propriano 64 C7
Prorer Wiek 52 J2
Proserpine 114 J4
Prosna 50 G6
Prosperidad 84 H5
Prostojov 50 G8
Proti 68 D7
Provadija 66 Q6
Prøven = Kangersuatsiaq 122 W2
Providence 128 F2
Providence Island 108 (2)B2
Provideniya 78 Z4
Provincetown 128 F2
Provins 58 J5
Provo 126 D2
Provost 122 J6
Prudhoe Bay 132 (1)H1
Prudnik 50 G7
Prüm 54 J4
Pruszków 50 K5
Prut 66 R4
Pružany 50 P5
Prvić 62 K6
Pryluky 70 F4
Prypyats' 46 G2
Przasnysz 50 K4
Przemyśl 50 M8
Przeworsk 50 M7
Psara 68 H6
Psebay 92 J1
Pskov 70 E3
Ptolemaïda 68 D4
Ptuj 62 L4
Pucallpa 140 C5
Pucheng 80 F5
Puch'ŏn 82 D5
Púchov 50 H8
Pucioasa 66 N4
Puck 50 H3
Pudasjärvi 48 P4
Pudozh 70 G2
Puebla 134 E5
Puebla de Don Rodrigo 60 F5
Pueblo 126 F3
Puelches 142 H6
Puelén 142 H6
Puente-Genil 60 F7
Puerto Acosta 140 D7
Puerto Aisén 142 G8
Puerto Alegre 140 E6
Puerto Angel 134 E5
Puerto Ayacucho 134 L7
Puerto Barrios 134 G5
Puerto Berrío 140 C2
Puerto Cabezas 134 H6
Puerto Carreño 134 L7
Puerto del Rosario 102 C3
Puerto de Navacerrada 60 G4
Puerto Guarini 140 F8
Puerto Heath 140 D6
Puerto Inirida 140 D3
Puerto Leguizamo 140 C4
Puerto Libertad 132 D3
Puerto Limón 140 B3
Puertollano 60 F6
Puerto Madryn 142 J7
Puerto Maldonado 140 D6
Puerto Montt 142 G7
Puerto Natáles 142 G9
Puerto Nuevo 134 K7
Puerto Páez 140 D2
Puerto Peñasco 132 D2
Puerto Princesa 84 F5
Puerto Real 60 D8
Puerto Rico 134 L5
Puerto Rico 140 D6
Puerto Rico Trench 138 E1
Puerto Santa Cruz 142 H9
Puerto Suárez 140 F7
Pukapuka 112 N7
Pukatawagen 122 L5
Pukch'ŏng 82 E3
Pukë 66 G7
Pukeuri Junction 116 C7
Pula 62 J6
Pulaski 128 E2
Puławy 50 M6
Pullman 126 C1
Puttusk 48 L10
Pułtusk 50 L5
Pulu 76 Q10
Pülümür 92 H4
Puncak Jaya 87 E3
Puncak Mandala 87 F3
Pune 88 B5
P'ungsan 82 E3
Punia 106 D4
Puno 140 C7
Punta Albina 108 A3
Punta Alice 64 M9
Punta Angamos 142 G3
Punta Arena 126 B3
Punta Arenas 142 G9
Punta Ballena 142 G4
Punta da Estaca de Bares 60 C1
Punta Dungeness 142 H9
Punta Eugenia 134 A3
Punta Galera 142 G6
Punta Gallinas 134 K6
Punta Gorda 130 E4
Punta La Marmora 64 D8
Punta Lavapié 142 G6
Punta Lengua de Vaca 142 G5
Punta Mala 140 B2
Punta Mariato 134 H7
Punta Medanosa 142 H8
Punta Negra 140 A5
Punta Norte, *Argentina* 142 J7
Punta Norte, *Argentina* 142 K6
Punta Pariñas 140 A5
Punta Rasa 142 J7
Puntarenas 134 H6
Punta San Gabriel 132 D3
Punta San Telmo 134 D5
Punta Sarga 102 B4
Puponga 116 D5
Puqi 80 E5
Pur 76 P5
Puri 88 E5
Purmerend 54 G2
Purpe 78 B4
Purukcahu 86 E3
Purus 140 E5
Puruvesi 48 Q6
Pusan 82 E6
Pushkin 70 F3
Püspökladany 50 L10
Putao 84 B1
Putaruru 116 E3
Putian 80 F5
Putna 66 P4
Puttalami 88 C7
Putten 54 G3
Puttgarden 52 G2
Putumayo 140 C4
Putusibau 86 E2
Puuwai 132 (2)A2
Puvurnituq 122 R5
Puy de Dôme 58 H8
Puy de Sancy 58 H8
Puysegur Point 116 A8
Pweto 106 D5
Pwllheli 56 H9
Pyal'ma 70 G2
Pyasina 76 R3
Pyatigorsk 92 K1
Pyè 84 B3
Pyhäjärvi 48 M6
Pyinmana 84 B3
Pylos 68 D8
Pyŏktong 82 C3
P'yŏnggang 82 D4
P'yŏngyang 82 C4
Pyramid Island 116 (1)B2
Pyramid Lake 126 C2
Pyrenees 58 E11
Pyrgos 68 D7
Pyrzyce 50 D4
Pyshchug 70 J3
Pytalovo 48 P8

Q

Qā 'Azamān 94 E5
Qadīmah 90 C5
Qādub 90 F7
Qagan Nur 80 F2
Qal'aikhum 90 K2
Qalamat Nadqān 95 D5
Qalāt 90 J3
Qal'at Bīshah 90 D5
Qal'eh-ye Now 90 H3
Qamdo 80 B4
Qamīnīs 100 C1
Qandala 106 H1
Qaraaoun 92 F7
Qardho 106 H2
Qartaba 94 C2

212

Rimava 50 J9
Rimavská Sobota 50 K9
Rimini 62 H6
Rimouski 128 G1
Rineia 68 H7
Ringe 52 F1
Ringkøbing 48 E8
Ringkøbing Fjord 48 D9
Ringsted 52 G1
Ringvassøya 48 J1
Rinteln 52 E4
Rio Branco 140 D5
Río Colorado 142 J6
Río Cuarto 142 J5
Rio de Janeiro 142 N3
Rio de Janeiro 142 N3
Río de la Plata 142 K6
Río Gallegos 142 H9
Rio Grande 132 E2
Rio Grande 142 L5
Río Grande, *Argentina* 142 H9
Río Grande, *Mexico* 132 F4
Rio Grande City 130 B4
Rio Grande do Norte 140 K5
Rio Grande do Sul 142 L4
Ríohacha 134 K6
Río Largartos 134 G4
Riom 58 J8
Río Mulatos 140 D7
Rionero in Vulture 64 K8
Río Tigre 140 B4
Rio Verde, *Brazil* 140 G7
Río Verde, *Chile* 142 G9
Rio Verde de Mato Grosso 140 G7
Ripley, *Oh., United States* 128 D3
Ripley, *Tenn., United States* 128 C3
Ripley, *W. Va., United States* 128 D3
Ripoll 60 N2
Ripon 56 L7
Rishiri-tō 78 Q7
Rishon le Ziyyon 94 B5
Risør 48 E7
Ritchie's Archipelago 84 A4
Ritzville 126 C1
Rivadavia 142 G4
Riva del Garda 62 F5
Rivarolo Canavese 62 C5
Rivas 134 G6
Rivera, *Argentina* 142 J6
Rivera, *Uruguay* 142 K5
River Cess 104 C3
River Inlet 34 F6
Riversdale 108 C6
Riversdale Beach 116 E5
Riverton, *Canada* 122 M6
Riverton, *New Zealand* 116 A8
Rivesaltes 58 H11
Rivière aux Feuilles 38 S5
Rivière-du-Loup 128 G1
Rivne 70 E4
Rivoli 62 C5
Riwoqê 88 G2
Riyadh = Ar Riyāḑ 95 B4
Rize 92 J3
Rizhao 80 F3
Roanne 58 K7
Roanoke 128 D3
Roanoke Rapids 130 F2
Robāţ 95 G1
Robe 114 G7
Robertsfors 48 L4
Robertval 128 F1
Roboré 140 F7
Robstown 130 B4
Roccastrada 64 F6
Rochefort, *Belgium* 54 H4
Rochefort, *France* 58 E8
Rochelle 128 C2
Rocher River 122 J4
Rochester, *United Kingdom* 54 C3
Rochester, *Minn., United States* 128 B2
Rochester, *N.H., United States* 128 F2
Rochester, *N.Y., United States* 128 E2
Rockall 46 C2
Rockefeller Plateau 144 (2)EE2
Rockford 128 C2
Rockhampton 114 K4
Rock Hill 128 D4
Rock Island 128 B2
Rocklake 126 G1
Rockport 126 B1
Rock Rapids 128 A2
Rock Springs 126 E2
Rocksprings 132 F3
Rocky Mount 128 E3
Rocky Mountains 32 G6
Rødby Havn 52 G2
Roddickton 122 V6
Roden 54 J1
Rodez 58 H9
Rodi Garganico 64 K7
Roding 52 H7
Rodney 128 D2
Rodopi Planina 66 M7
Rodos 68 L8
Rodos 68 L8
Roebourne 114 C4
Roermond 54 J3
Roeselare 54 F4
Roes Welcome Sound 36 P4
Rogers City 128 D1
Rogerson 126 D2
Rogliano 64 D6
Rogozno 50 G5
Rogue 126 B2
Rohrbach 62 K2
Rohtak 88 C3
Roi Et 84 C3
Roja 48 M8
Rokiškis 48 N9
Rokycany 50 C8
Rolla 128 B3
Rolleston 116 D6
Rolvsøya 48 M1
Roma 87 C4
Roma, *Australia* 114 J5
Roma, *Italy* 64 G7
Roman 66 P3
Romania 66 L4
Romans-sur-Isère 58 L8
Rombas 54 J5
Rome = Roma 64 G7
Rome, *Ga., United States* 130 D3
Rome, *N.Y., United States* 128 E2
Romney 128 E3
Romny 70 F4
Rømø 52 D1
Romorantin-Lanthenay 58 G6
Romsey 54 A3
Rona 56 G2
Ronan 124 D2
Roncesvalles 60 J2
Ronda 60 E8
Rondônia 140 E6
Rondônia 140 E6
Rondonópolis 140 G7
Rondu 90 L2
Rongcheng 80 G3
Rønne 50 D2
Ronneby 48 H8
Ronne Entrance 144 (2)JJ3
Ronne Ice Shelf 144 (2)MM2
Ronse 54 F4
Roosendaal 54 G3
Roper Bar 114 F2
Roquetas de Mar 60 H8
Roraima 140 E3
Røros 48 F5
Rosário 140 J4
Rosario, *Argentina* 142 J5
Rosario, *Mexico* 124 D6
Rosario, *Mexico* 124 E7
Rosario, *Paraguay* 142 K3
Rosário Oeste 140 F6
Rosarito 124 C6
Rosarno 64 K10
Roscommon 56 D8
Roscrea 56 E9
Roseau 134 M5
Roseburg 126 B2
Roseires Reservoir 100 F5
Rose Island 112 K7
Rosenburg 132 G3
Rosenheim 62 H3
Roses 60 P2
Rosetown 122 K6
Rosica 66 N6
Rosignano Marittimo 62 F7
Roşiori de Vede 66 N5
Rosita 66 Q6
Roskilde 48 G9
Roslavl' 70 F4
Rossano 64 L9
Ross Ice Shelf 144 (2)Z1
Ross Lake 126 B1
Rosslare 56 F9
Roßlau 52 H5
Rosso 102 B5
Rossosh' 70 G4
Ross River 34 E4
Ross Sea 144 (2)AA2
Røssvatnet 48 G4
Røst 48 G3
Rostāq 95 E3
Rosthern 122 K6
Rostock 52 H2
Rostov 70 G3
Rostov-na-Donu 70 G5
Rostrenen 58 B5
Roswell 132 F2
Rota 112 E4
Rote 87 B5
Rotenburg, *Germany* 52 E3
Rotenburg, *Germany* 52 E5
Roth 52 G7
Rothenburg 52 F7
Roto 114 J6
Rotorua 116 F4
Rott 62 H2
Rottenmann 62 K3
Rotterdam 58 K2
Rottnen 50 E1
Rottumeroog 54 J1
Rottumerplaat 54 J1
Rottweil 62 D2
Rotuma 112 H7
Roubaix 54 F4
Rouen 54 D5
Rouiba 60 P8
Round Mountain 114 K6
Round Rock 130 B3
Roundup 126 E1
Rousay 56 J2
Rouyn 38 R7
Rovaniemi 48 N3
Rovato 62 E5
Rovereto 62 G5
Rovigo 62 G5
Rovinari 66 L5
Rovinj 62 J5
Rovuma 106 F6
Rowley Island 36 R3
Rowley Shoals 114 C3
Roxas 84 G4
Roxburgh 116 B7
Royal Leamington Spa 54 A2
Royal Tunbridge Wells 54 C3
Royan 58 D8
Roye 54 E5
Royston 54 C2
Rozdil'na 66 T3
Rožňava 50 K9
Rozzano 62 E5
Rrëshen 68 B3
Rtishchevo 70 H4
Ruacana 108 A3
Ruahine Range 116 E5
Ruapehu 116 E4
Ruapuke Island 116 B8
Ruarkela 88 D4
Ruatahuna 116 F4
Ruatoria 116 G3
Ruawai 116 D3
Rub' al Khālī 90 E6
Rubeshibe 82 M2
Rubi 106 C3
Rubtsovsk 76 Q7
Ruby 132 (1)F3
Rudan 95 G3
Ruda Śląska 50 H7
Rudbar 90 H3
Rüdersdorf 52 J4
Rudkøbing 52 F2
Rudnaya Pristan' 82 H2
Rudnyy 70 M4
Rudolstadt 52 G6
Rue 54 D4
Ruffec 58 F7
Rufiji 106 F5
Rugby, *United Kingdom* 54 A2
Rugby, *United States* 124 G2
Rügen 50 C3
Ruhnu 48 M8
Ruhr 54 L3
Rui'an 80 G5
Rum 56 F5
Ruma 66 G4
Rumāh 95 B4
Rumaylah 95 B1
Rumbek 106 D2
Rum Cay 134 K4
Rumigny 54 G5
Rum Jungle 114 F2
Rumoi 82 L2
Runanaga 116 C6
Rundu 108 B3
Rundvik 48 K5
Ruoqiang 76 R10
Ruo Shui 80 C2
Rupa 62 K5
Rupat 86 C2
Rupert 122 R6
Rupert 126 D2
Rurutu 112 L8
Ruse 66 N6
Rushon 88 G3
Rushville, *Ill., United States* 128 B2
Rushville, *Ind., United States* 128 C3
Rushville, *Nebr., United States* 126 F2
Russell 126 G3
Russellville, *Ark., United States* 130 C2
Russellville, *Ky., United States* 130 D2
Rüsselsheim 52 D7
Russia 74 M3
Russoye Ust'ye 78 R2
Rust'avi 92 L3
Ruston 130 C3
Rutana 106 D4
Rute 60 F7
Ruteng 87 B4
Rutland 128 F2
Rutog 88 C2
Ruvo di Puglia 64 L7
Ruvuma 106 F6
Ruzayevka 70 H4
Ružomberok 50 J8
Rwanda 106 D4
R-Warnemünde 52 H2
Ryazan' 70 G4
Ryazhsk 70 H4
Rybinsk 70 G3
Rybinskoye Vodokhranilishche 70 G3
Rybnik 50 H7
Rychnov 50 F7
Ryde 54 A4
Rye 54 C4
Rye Patch Reservoir 126 C2
Ryki 50 L6
Ryl'sk 70 F4
Ryn-Peski 70 J5
Ryōtsu 82 K4
Rypin 50 J4
Ryukyu Islands = Nansei-shotō 80 H5
Rzeszów 50 M7
Rzhev 70 F3

S

Sa'ādatābād, *Iran* 95 E1
Sa'ādatābād, *Iran* 95 F2
Saale 52 G6
Saalfeld 52 G6
Saalfelden 62 H3
Saanen 64 B2
Saar 54 J5
Saarbrücken 54 J5
Saarburg 54 J5
Saaremaa 48 L7
Saarlouis 54 J5
Saatli 92 N4
Saatly 90 E2
Saba 134 M5
Sab' Ābār 94 E3
Šabac 66 G5
Sabadell 60 N3
Sabah 86 F1
Sabang 84 B5
Sabhā 102 H3
Sabiñánigo 60 K2
Sabinas 132 F3
Sabinas Hidalgo 132 F3
Sabine 130 B3
Sabine Lake 130 C3
Sabinov 50 L8
Sabkhet el Bardawîl 94 A5
Šabla 66 R6
Sable Island 38 V8
Sablé-sur-Sarthe 58 E6
Sabôr 60 D3
Sabres 58 E9
Sabun 76 Q5
Sabzevār 90 G2
Săcele 66 N4
Sachanga 108 B2
Sachs Harbour 34 G2
Sacile 62 H5
Säckingen 62 C3
Sacramento 126 B3
Sacramento 126 B3
Şad'ah 90 D6
Sadiqabad 90 K4
Sadiya 88 G3
Sado 60 B6
Sadon 92 K2
Sado-shima 80 K3
Sa Dragonera 60 N5
Sadūt 94 B5
Säffle 48 G7
Safford 132 E2
Safi, *Jordan* 94 C5
Safi, *Morocco* 102 D2
Safonovo, *Russia* 70 F3
Safonovo, *Russia* 70 J1
Safranbolu 68 Q3
Saga, *China* 88 E3
Saga, *Japan* 82 F7
Sagami-nada 82 K6
Sagar 88 C4
Sagastyr 76 Z3
Sage 126 D2
Saginaw 128 D2
Sagiz 70 K5
Sagiz 70 K5
Sagres 60 B7
Saguache 126 E3
Sagua la Grande 134 H4
Sagunt 60 K5
Sahāb 94 D5
Sahagún 60 E2
Sahara 98 C3
Saharah el Gharbîya 100 E2
Saharanpur 88 C3
Saharsa 88 E3
Şahbuz 92 L4
Sahel 98 C4
Sahiwal 90 K3
Sahuaripa 132 E3
Šahy 66 F1
Saïda, *Algeria* 102 F2
Saïda, *Lebanon* 94 C3
Sa'īdābād 95 F2
Saidpur 88 E3
Saigo 82 G5
Saigon = Hô Chi Minh 84 D4
Saiha 88 F4
Saihan Toroi 80 C2
Saiki 82 F7
Saimaa 48 P6
Saimbeyli 92 G4
Sä'in 95 F1
Saindak 90 H4
St. Albans 54 B3
St-Amand-Montrond 58 H7
St. Andrä 62 K4
St. Andrews 56 K5
St. Anthony 122 V6
St. Arnaud 116 D5
St. Augustin 54 K4
St-Augustin 122 V6
St. Augustine 130 E4
St. Austell 56 H11
St-Avertin 58 F6
St-Avold 54 J5
St. Barthélémy 134 M5
St-Brieuc 58 C5
St. Catharines 38 R8
St-Chamond 58 K8
St-Claude 58 L7
St. Cloud 128 B1
St. David's 56 G10
St-Denis, *France* 54 E6
St-Denis, *Réunion* 108 (1)B2
St-Dié 62 B2
St-Dizier 58 K5
Ste-Anne-de-Beaupré 128 F1
Ste-Maxime 58 M10
Ste-Menehould 54 G5
Saintes 58 E8
Stes-Maries-de-la-Mer 58 K10
St-Étienne 58 K8
St-Étienne-du-Rouvray 54 D5
St-Félicien 128 F1
St-Florent 64 D6
St-Florentin 58 J5
St-Flour 58 J8
St. Francis 126 F3
St. Gallen 62 E3
St-Gaudens 58 F10
St. George, *Australia* 114 J5
St. George, *United States* 126 D3
St. Georgen 62 D2
St. Georges 128 F1
St. George's 134 M6
St. George's Channel 56 F10
St-Germain-en-Laye 54 E6
St-Girons 58 G11
St. Helena 98 C7
St. Helena Bay 108 B6
St. Helens, *United Kingdom* 56 K8
St. Helens, *United States* 126 B1
St. Helier 58 C4
St-Hubert 54 H4
St. Ignace 128 D1
St. Ives 56 G11
St-Jean-d'Angely 58 E8
St-Jean-de-Luz 58 D10
St-Jean-de-Maurienne 62 B5

Sarbāz 90 H4
Sarbīsheh 90 G3
Sárbogárd 66 F3
Sar Dasht 92 L5
Sardegna 64 E8
Sardinia = Sardegna 64 E8
Sardis Lake 130 B3
Sar-e Pol 90 J2
Sargodha 90 K3
Sarh 104 H3
Sārī 90 F2
Saria 68 K9
Sarıkamış 92 K3
Sarıkaya 92 F4
Sarikei 86 E2
Sarina 114 J4
Sariñena 60 K3
Sarīr Tibesti 100 C3
Sariwŏn 82 C4
Sarıyer 68 M3
Sark 58 C4
Sarkad 66 J3
Sarkand 76 P8
Sarkikaraağaç 68 P6
Şarkışla 92 G4
Şarköy 68 K4
Sarmi 87 E3
Särna 48 G6
Sarnia 38 Q8
Sarny 70 E4
Sarolangun 86 C3
Saronno 62 E5
Saros Körfezi 68 J4
Sárospatak 50 L9
Sarre 58 M5
Sarrebourg 58 N5
Sarreguemines 58 N4
Sarria 60 C2
Sartène 64 C7
Sartyn'ya 70 M2
Saruhanli 68 K6
Sārur 92 L4
Sárvár 62 M3
Sarvestān 95 E2
Sarvīz 66 F2
Sarykamyshkoye Ozero 76 K9
Saryozek 76 P9
Saryshagan 76 N8
Sarysu 76 M8
Sary-Tash 90 K2
Sarzana 62 E6
Sasaram 88 D4
Sasebo 82 E7
Saskatchewan 32 K6
Saskatchewan 122 L6
Saskatoon 34 K6
Saskylakh 76 W3
Sassandra 104 C4
Sassari 64 C8
Sassnitz 52 J2
Sasso Marconi 62 G6
Sassuolo 62 F6
Satadougou 104 B2
Satara 88 B5
Satna 88 D4
Sátoraljaújhely 50 L9
Satti 88 C2
Sättna 48 J5
Satu Mare 66 K2
Satun 86 B1
Sauce 142 K5
Saudi Arabia 90 D4
Sauk Centre 128 B1
Saulgau 62 E2
Saulieu 58 K6
Sault Ste. Marie, *Canada* 36 Q7
Sault Ste. Marie, *United States* 128 D1
Saumlakki 87 D4
Saumur 58 E6
Saunders Island 138 J9
Saura 76 J9
Saurimo 106 C5
Sauðárkrókur 48 (1)D2
Sava 62 L5
Savaii 112 J7
Savalou 104 E3
Savannah 120 K6
Savannah, *Ga., United States* 130 E3
Savannah, *Tenn., United States* 130 D2
Savannakhet 84 C3
Savaştepe 68 K5
Savè 104 E3
Save 108 E4
Säveh 90 F2
Saverne 52 C8
Savigliano 62 C6
Savona 62 D6
Savonlinna 48 Q6
Savu 87 B5
Sawahlunto 86 C3
Sawai Madhopur 88 C3
Sawqirah 90 G6
Sawu Sea 87 B4
Sayanogorsk 76 S7
Sayansk 78 G6
Sayhūt 90 F6
Säylac 100 H5
Saynshand 80 E2
Sayram Hu 76 Q9
Say'ūn 90 E6
Say-Utes 76 J9
Sazan 68 B4
Sazin 90 K2
Sbaa 102 E3
Scafell Pike 56 J7
Scalea 64 K9
Scarborough 56 M7
Scargill 116 D6
Scarp 56 E3
Schaalsee 52 F3
Schaffhausen 62 D3
Schagen 54 G2
Scharbeutz 52 F2
Schärding 62 J2
Scharhörn 52 D3
Scheeßel 52 E3
Schefferville 38 T6
Scheibbs 62 L3
Schelde 54 F3
Schenectady 128 F2
Scheveningen 54 G2
Schiedam 54 G3
Schiermonnikoog 54 H1
Schiermonnikoog 54 J1
Schio 62 G5
Schiza 68 D8
Schkeuditz 52 H5
Schlei 52 E2
Schleiden 54 J4
Schleswig 52 E2
Schlieben 52 J5
Schlüchtern 52 E6
Schneeberg 52 G6
Schneeberg 52 H6
Schönebeck 52 G4
Schongau 62 F3
Schöningen 52 F4
Schouwen 54 F3
Schramberg 62 D2
Schreiber 128 C1
Schrems 62 L2
Schull 56 C10
Schwabach 52 G7
Schwäbische Alb 62 E2
Schwäbisch-Gmünd 62 E2
Schwäbisch-Hall 52 E7
Schwalmstadt 52 E6
Schwandorf 52 H7
Schwarzenbek 52 F3
Schwarzenberg 52 H6
Schwarzwald 62 D3
Schwaz 62 G3
Schwechat 50 F9
Schwedt 50 D4
Schweich 54 J5
Schweinfurt 52 F6
Schwenningen 62 D2
Schwerin 52 G3
Schweriner See 52 G3
Schwetzingen 52 D7
Schwyz 62 D3
Sciacca 64 H11
Scicli 64 J12
Scobey 126 E1
Scotia Ridge 142 K9
Scotia Sea 144 (2)A4
Scotland 56 H5
Scott City 126 F3
Scott Inlet 122 T2
Scott Island 144 (2)Z3
Scott Reef 114 D2
Scottsbluff 126 F2
Scottsboro 128 C4
Scotty's Junction 132 C1
Scranton 128 E2
Scunthorpe 56 M8
Seal 122 M5
Sea of Azov 70 G5
Sea of Galilee 94 C4
Sea of Japan 82 G3
Sea of Marmara = Marmara Denizi 68 L4
Sea of Okhotsk 78 Q5
Sea of the Hebrides 56 E4
Searchlight 132 D1
Searcy 128 B3
Seaside 126 B1
Seattle 126 B1
Sebeş 66 L4
Sebkha Azzel Matti 102 F3
Sebkha de Timimoun 102 E3
Sebkha de Tindouf 102 D3
Sebkha Mekerrhane 102 F3
Sebkha Oum el Drouss Telli 102 C4
Sebkhet de Chemchâm 102 C4
Sebnitz 52 K6
Sebring 130 E4
Secchia 62 F6
Sechura 140 A5
Secretary Island 116 A7
Secunderabad 88 C5
Sécure 140 D7
Sedalia 128 B3
Sedan 54 G5
Sedano 60 G2
Seddon 116 D5
Seddonville 116 C5
Sede Boqer 94 B6
Sedeh 90 G3
Sederot 94 B5
Sedico 62 H4
Sedom 94 C5
Seeheim 108 B5
Seelow 52 K4
Sées 58 F5
Seesen 52 F5
Seevetal 52 E3
Séez 62 B5
Seferihisar 68 J6
Segamat 86 C2
Segezha 70 F2
Seghnān 90 K2
Ségou 104 C2
Segovia 60 F4
Segré 58 E6
Séguédine 102 H4
Seguin 130 B4
Segura 60 H6
Sehithwa 108 C4
Sehnde 52 E4
Seiland 48 M1
Seiling 130 B2
Seinäjoki 48 M5
Seine 58 F4
Sekayu 86 C3
Sekondi 104 D3
Selassi 87 D3
Selat Bangka 86 D3
Selat Berhala 86 C3
Selat Dampir 87 D3
Selat Karimata 86 D3
Selat Makassar 86 F3
Selat Mentawai 86 B3
Selat Sunda 86 D4
Selawik 132 (1)F2
Selb 52 H6
Selby 126 G1
Selçuk 68 K7
Selebi-Phikwe 108 D4
Sélestat 62 C2
Selfoss 48 (1)C3
Sélibabi 102 C5
Seligman 132 D1
Seljord 48 E7
Selkirk 124 G1
Selkirk Mountains 34 H7
Sells 132 D2
Selm 54 K3
Selmer 128 C3
Selpele 87 D3
Selvas 140 C5
Selwyn Lake 36 L5
Selwyn Mountains 34 E4
Semanit 68 B4
Semarang 86 E4
Sematan 86 D2
Sembé 104 G4
Seminoe Reservoir 126 E2
Seminole, *Okla., United States* 126 G3
Seminole, *Tex., United States* 132 F2
Semiozernoye 76 L7
Semipalatinsk 76 Q7
Semiyarka 76 P7
Semois 54 H5
Semporna 86 F2
Sena Madureira 140 D5
Senanga 108 C3
Senatobia 130 D3
Sendai 82 L4
Senec 62 N2
Seneca 130 E3
Senegal 104 A2
Sénégal 104 B1
Senftenberg 52 J5
Sengerema 106 E4
Senhor do Bonfim 140 J6
Senica 50 G9
Senigallia 62 J7
Senj 62 K6
Senja 48 J2
Senlis 54 E5
Sennar 90 B7
Senneterre 128 E1
Sens 58 J5
Senta 66 H4
Seoni 88 C4
Seoul = Sŏul 82 D5
Separation Point 116 D5
Sepinang 86 F2
Sept-Îles 38 T6
Seraing 54 H4
Serakhs 90 H2
Seram 87 D3
Seram Sea 87 C3
Serang 86 D4
Serbia = Srbija 66 H6
Serdobsk 70 H4
Serebryansk 76 Q8
Sered' 66 E1
Şereflikoçhisar 68 R6
Seregno 62 E5
Serein 58 J6
Seremban 86 C2
Serenje 108 E2
Sergelen 80 E1
Sergeyevka 70 N4
Sergipe 140 K6
Sergiyev Posad 70 G3
Seria 86 E2
Serifos 68 G7
Serifos 68 G7
Serik 68 P8
Seringapatam Reef 114 D2
Sermata 87 C4
Seronga 108 C3
Serov 70 M3
Serowe 108 D4
Serpa 60 C7
Serpneve 66 S3
Serpukhov 70 G4
Serra Acari 140 F3
Serra Curupira 140 E3
Serra da Chela 108 A3
Serra da Espinhaço 140 J7
Serra da Ibiapaba 140 J4
Serra da Mantiqueira 142 M3
Serra de Maracaju 142 K3
Serra do Cachimbo 140 F5
Serra do Caiapó 140 G7
Serra do Dois Irmãos 140 J5
Serra do Roncador 140 G6
Serra dos Carajás 140 G5
Serra dos Parecis 140 E6
Serra do Tiracambu 140 H4
Serra Estrondo 140 H5
Serra Formosa 140 F6
Serra Geral de Goiás 140 H6
Serra Geral do Paranã 140 H7
Serra Lombarda 140 G3
Serra Pacaraima 140 E3
Serra Parima 140 E3
Serra Tumucumaque 140 F3
Serra da Estrela 60 C4
Serres, *France* 58 L9
Serres, *Greece* 68 F3
Serrinha 140 K6
Sertã 60 B5
Serui 87 E3
Servia 68 D4
Sêrxü 80 B4
Sese Islands 106 E4
Sesfontein 108 A3
Sesheke 108 C3
Sessa Aurunca 64 H7
Sestri Levante 62 E6
Sestroretsk 48 Q6
Sestrunj 62 K6
Sestu 64 D9
Sesvete 62 M5
Setana 82 K2
Sète 58 J10
Sete Lagoas 140 J7
Setesdal 48 D7
Sétif 102 G1
Settat 102 D2
Setúbal 60 B6
Sŏul 112 C2
Seurre 58 L7
Sevana Lich 92 L3
Sevastopol' 92 E1
Seven Lakes 132 E1
Sevenoaks 54 C3
Sévérac-le-Château 58 J9
Severn, *Canada* 122 P5
Severn, *United Kingdom* 56 K10
Severnaya Dvina 70 H2
Severnaya Osetiya 92 L2
Severnaya Zemlya 76 U1
Severn Estuary 56 J10
Severnoye 70 K4
Severnyy 76 L4
Severobaykal'sk 78 H5
Severodvinsk 70 G2
Severo-Kuril'sk 78 T6
Severomorsk 48 S2
Severoural'sk 70 M2
Severo-Yeniseyskiy 76 S5
Sevier Lake 126 D3
Sevilla 60 E7
Sevlievo 66 N7
Seward Peninsula 132 (1)E2
Seyakha 76 N3
Seychelles 108 (2)B2
Seychelles Islands 98 J6
Seydişehir 68 P7
Seyhan 92 F5
Seymchan 78 S4
Seymour, *Australia* 114 J7
Seymour, *Ind., United States* 130 D2
Seymour, *Tex., United States* 130 B3
Seyðisfjörður 48 (1)G2
Sézanne 58 J5
Sezze 64 H7
Sfakia 68 G9
Sfântu Gheorghe, *Romania* 66 N4
Sfântu Gheorghe, *Romania* 66 S5
Sfax 102 H2
's-Gravenhage 54 G2
Sha'am 95 G3
Shabunda 106 D4
Shabwah 90 E6
Shache 76 P10
Shādegān 95 C1
Shadehill Reservoir 126 F1
Shagamu 104 E3
Shagonar 76 S7
Shag Rocks 142 N9
Shahbā' 94 D4
Shahdāb 95 G1
Shahdol 88 D4
Shah Fuladi 90 J3
Shahjahanpur 88 C3
Shahrak 90 H3
Shahr-e Bābāk 95 F1
Shahrtuz 90 J2
Shakhrisabz 90 J2
Shakhtërsk 78 Q7
Shakhty 70 H5
Shakhun'ya 70 J3
Shaki 104 E3
Shakotan-misaki 82 L2
Shama 106 E5
Shamattawa 122 N5
Shamis 95 E5
Shamrock 132 F1
Shand 90 H3
Shandan 80 C3
Shandong Bandao 80 G3
Shangani 108 D3
Shangdu 80 E2
Shanghai 80 G4
Shanghang 80 F6
Shangqui 80 F4
Shangrao 80 F5
Shangzhi 80 H1
Shangzhou 80 D4
Shantarskiye Ostrova 78 P5
Shantou 80 F6
Shanwei 84 F2
Shanyin 80 E3
Shaoguan 80 E6
Shaoxing 80 G5
Shaoyang 80 E5
Shapkina 70 K1
Shaqrā' 95 A4
Sharga 76 T8
Sharjah = Ash Shāriqah 95 F4
Shark Bay 112 B8
Shark Reef 114 J2
Sharmah 100 G2
Sharm el Sheikh 100 F2
Sharūrah 90 E6
Shashe 108 D4
Shashi 80 E4
Shasta Lake 126 B2
Shatsk 70 H4
Shats'k 50 N6
Shaubak 94 C6
Shawano 128 C2

218

Name	Page	Grid
Tazovskiy Poluostrov	76	N4
Tazungdam	84	B1
T'bilisi	92	L3
Tchamba	104	G3
Tchibanga	104	G5
Tchin Tabaradene	102	G5
Tczew	50	H3
Te Anau	116	A7
Te Araroa	116	G3
Te Aroha	116	E3
Te Awamutu	116	E4
Teberda	92	J2
Tébessa	102	G1
Tebingtinggi	86	B2
Téboursouk	64	D12
Techa	70	M3
Techiman	104	D3
Tecuala	132	D4
Tecuci	66	Q4
Tedzhen	90	H2
Tees	56	L7
Tegal	86	D4
Tegernsee	62	G3
Tegina	104	F2
Teglio	62	F4
Tegucigalpa	134	G6
Tegul'det	76	R6
Te Hapua	116	D2
Te Haroto	116	F4
Tehek Lake	122	M3
Teheran = Tehrān	90	F2
Tehrān	90	F2
Teignmouth	56	J11
Tejo = Tagus	60	B5
Te Kaha	116	F3
Te Kao	116	D2
Teknaf	88	F4
Teku	87	B3
Te Kuiti	116	E4
T'elavi	92	L3
Tel Aviv-Yafo	94	B4
Telegraph Creek	132	(1)L4
Telén	142	H6
Teles Pires	140	F5
Telford	56	K9
Telfs	62	G3
Teller	132	(1)D2
Telsen	142	H7
Telšiai	50	M2
Teltow	52	J4
Teluk Berau	87	D3
Teluk Bone	87	B3
Teluk Cenderawasih	87	E3
Telukdalem	86	B2
Teluk Kumai	86	E3
Telukpakedai	86	D3
Teluk Sampit	86	E3
Teluk Sukadana	86	D3
Teluk Tomini	87	B2
Tema	104	D3
Tembenchi	76	T4
Temerin	66	G4
Temerloh	84	C6
Teminabuan	87	D3
Temirtau	76	N7
Temochic	132	E3
Tempe	132	D2
Tempio Pausaria	64	D8
Temple	132	G2
Temryuk	92	G1
Temuco	142	G6
Temuka	116	C7
Tenali	88	D5
Tendaho	100	H5
Ten Degree Channel	88	F7
Tendo	82	L4
Tendrara	102	E2
Ténéré	102	G5
Ténéré du Tafassasset	102	G4
Tenerife	102	B3
Ténès	102	F1
Tenggarong	86	F3
Tenke	108	D2
Tenkodogo	104	D2
Tennant Creek	114	F3
Tennessee	120	K6
Tennessee	124	J4
Tenojoki	48	P2
Tenteno	87	B3
Tenterfield	114	K5
Teo	60	B2
Teófilo Otoni	140	J7
Tepa	87	C4
Tepehuanes	124	E6
Tepic	124	F7
Teplice	50	C7
Ter	60	N2
Terceira	102	(1)B2
Terek	92	L2
Teresina	140	J5
Tergnier	54	F5
Terme	92	G3
Termez	90	J2
Termini Imerese	64	H11
Termoli	66	C8
Ternate	87	C2
Terneuzen	54	F3
Terni	64	G6
Ternitz	62	M3
Ternopil'	70	E5
Terracina	64	H7
Terrassa	60	N3
Terre Haute	130	D2
Terry	126	E1
Tersa	70	H4
Terschelling	54	H1
Teruel	60	J4
Tervel	92	J2
Tervola	48	N3
Teseney	100	G4
Teshekpuk Lake	132	(1)F1
Teshikaga	82	N2
Teshio	82	L1
Teslin	132	(1)L3
Teslin	132	(1)L3
Tessalit	102	F4
Tét	58	H11
Tete	108	E3
Teterow	52	H4
Teteven	68	G2
Tétouan	102	D1
Tetovo	66	H8
Teuco	142	J3
Teulada	64	C10
Tevere	64	G6
Teverya	94	C4
Tevriz	70	P3
Te Waewae Bay	116	A8
Texarkana	130	C3
Texas	124	F5
Texel	54	G1
Teya	76	S5
Teykovo	70	H3
Tfarity	102	C3
Thaba Putsoa	108	D5
Thabazimbi	108	D4
Thailand	84	C4
Thai Nguyên	84	D2
Thal	88	B2
Thale Luang	84	C5
Thamarīt	90	F6
Thames	56	L10
Thamūd	90	E6
Thane	88	B5
Thanh Hoa	84	D3
Thanjavur	88	C6
Thann	62	C3
Tharad	88	B4
Thar Desert	88	B3
Thargomindah	114	H5
Tharwāniyyah	95	E3
Thasos	68	G4
Thasos	68	G4
Thaton	84	B3
Thaya	50	E9
The Bahamas	130	F4
The Bluff	130	F4
The Dalles	126	B1
Thedford	126	F2
The Fens	54	B2
The Gambia	104	A3
The Gulf	95	C2
The Hague = 's-Gravenhage	54	G2
Thelon	122	L4
The Minch	56	F3
The Naze	54	D3
Thenia	60	P8
Theniet el Had	60	N9
Theodore Roosevelt	140	E5
Theodore Roosevelt Lake	132	D2
The Pas	122	L6
Thermaikos Kolpos	68	E4
Thermopolis	126	E2
The Sisters	116	(1)B1
The Solent	54	A4
Thessalon	128	D1
Thessaloniki	68	E4
Thetford	56	N9
Thetford Mines	128	F1
The Twins	116	D5
The Wash	56	N9
The Weald	54	B3
The Whitsundays	114	J4
Thief River Falls	128	A1
Thiers	58	J8
Thiès	104	A2
Thika	106	F4
Thimphu	88	E3
Þingvallavatn	48	(1)C2
Thionville	54	J5
Thira	68	H8
Thira	68	H8
Thirasia	68	H8
Thirsk	56	L7
Thiruvananthapuram	88	C7
Thisted	48	E8
Þistilfjörður	48	(1)F1
Thiva	68	F6
Thiviers	58	F8
Þjórsá	48	(1)D2
Tholen	54	G3
Thomasville	130	E3
Thompson	122	H6
Thompson	36	M5
Thompson Falls	126	C1
Thomson	130	C3
Thonon-les-Bains	62	B4
Þórisvatn	48	(1)D2
Þorlákshöfn	48	(1)C3
Þorshöfn	48	(1)F1
Thouars	58	E7
Thrakiko Pelagos	68	H4
Three Forks	126	D1
Three Kings Island	116	C2
Three Rivers	128	C2
Throckmorton	130	B3
Thuin	54	G4
Thun	62	C4
Thunder Bay	36	P7
Thuner See	62	C4
Thung Song	84	B5
Thüringer Wald	52	F6
Thurso	56	J3
Thusis	62	E4
Tiāb	95	G3
Tianjin	80	F3
Tianmen	80	E4
Tianqiaoling	82	E2
Tianshifu	82	C3
Tianshui	80	D4
Tianshuihai	90	L2
Tianyang	80	D6
Tiaret	102	F1
Tibati	104	G3
Tibbooburra	114	H5
Tibesti	100	C3
Tibet = Xizang	88	E2
Tiburón	134	B3
Tîchît	102	D5
Tichla	102	C4
Ticino	62	D4
Ticul	134	G4
Tidjikdja	102	C5
Tieling	82	B2
Tielongtan	88	C1
Tielt	54	F3
Tienen	54	G4
Tien Shan	76	Q9
Tien Yen	84	D2
Tierra Amarilla	126	E3
Tiétar	60	E4
Tiflis = T'bilisi	98	H1
Tifton	130	E3
Tifu	87	C3
Tighina	66	S3
Tignère	104	G3
Tigre	140	B4
Tigris	92	K6
Tijuana	124	C5
Tikanlik	76	R9
Tikhoretsk	70	H5
Tikhvin	70	F3
Tikrīt	92	K6
Tiksi	78	M2
Tilburg	54	H3
Tilichiki	78	V4
Tillabéri	104	E2
Tillamook	126	B1
Tilos	68	K8
Timanskiy Kryazh	70	K2
Timaru	116	C7
Timashevsk	70	G5
Timber Creek	114	F3
Timerloh	86	C2
Timimoun	102	F3
Timișoara	66	J4
Timmins	36	Q7
Timon	140	J5
Timor	87	C4
Timor Sea	114	E2
Timor Timur	87	C4
Tinaca Point	112	C5
Tin Alkoum	102	H4
Tinchebray	54	B6
Tindivanam	88	C6
Tindouf	102	D3
Tineo	60	D1
Tinfouchy	102	D3
Tinglev	52	E2
Tingo Maria	140	B5
Tingri	88	E3
Tingsryd	50	E1
Tiniroto	116	F4
Tinnsjø	48	E7
Tinogasta	142	H4
Tinos	68	H7
Tinos	68	H7
Tinsukia	88	G3
Tintâne	102	C5
T'i'o	100	H5
Tipperary	56	D9
Tirana = Tiranë	68	B3
Tiranë	68	B3
Tirari Desert	114	G5
Tiraspol	66	S3
Tire	68	K6
Tiree	56	F5
Tiroungoulou	106	C2
Tirschenreuth	52	H7
Tirso	64	C9
Tiruchchirāppalli	88	C6
Tirunelveli	88	C7
Tirupati	88	C6
Tiruppur	88	C6
Tiruvannamalai	88	C6
Tisa	66	H4
Ţisīyah	94	D4
Tišnov	50	F8
Tisza	50	M9
Tiszaföldvár	66	H3
Tiszafüred	66	H2
Tiszaújváros	50	L10
Tit-Ary	76	Z3
Titel	66	H4
Titlagarh	88	D4
Titova Korenica	62	L6
Titovo Velenje	64	K2
Titu	66	N5
Titusville	130	E4
Tivaouane	102	B6
Tiverton	56	J11
Tivoli	64	G7
Tiyās	94	E2
Tizi Ouzou	102	F1
Tiznit	102	D3
Tjeldøya	48	H2
Tjørkolm	48	D7
Tlemcen	102	E2
Tmassah	100	C2
Toad River	122	F5
Toamasina	108	H3
Tobago	134	M6
Tobelo	87	C2
Tobermory, United Kingdom	56	F5
Tobermory, United States	128	D1
Tobi	87	D2
Toboali	86	D3
Tobol	80	M4
Tobol	70	M4
Tobol'sk	70	N3
Tobseda	70	K1
Tocantins	140	H5
Tocantins	140	H5
Toce	62	D4
Tocopilla	142	G3
Todeli	87	B3
Todi	64	G6
Tofino	126	A1
Togo	104	E3
Toimin	64	H2
Toi-misaki	82	F8
Tōjō	82	G6
Tok	132	(1)J3
Tokar	100	G4
Tokat, Sudan	90	C6
Tokat, Turkey	90	C1
Tokelau	112	J6
Tokmak	76	P9
Tokoroa	116	E4
Tokounou	104	C3
Toksun	76	R9
Tok-tō	80	J3
Toktogul	76	N9
Tokushima	82	H6
Tokuyama	82	F6
Tōkyō	82	K6
Tolaga Bay	116	G4
Tôlañaro	108	H4
Tolbo	76	S8
Toledo, Brazil	142	L3
Toledo, Spain	60	F5
Toledo, United States	128	D2
Toliara	108	G4
Tolitoli	87	B2
Tol'ka	76	Q5
Tol'ka	76	Q5
Tollense	52	J3
Tolmezzo	62	J4
Tolmin	62	J4
Tolna	66	F3
Tolosa	60	H1
Tol'yatti	70	J4
Tolybay	76	L7
Tom'	76	R6
Tomah	128	B2
Tomakomai	82	L2
Tomamae	82	L1
Tomar, Brazil	140	E4
Tomar, Portugal	60	B5
Tomari	78	Q7
Tomaszów Lubelski	50	N7
Tomaszów Mazowiecki	50	K6
Tombouctou	102	E5
Tombua	108	A3
Tomé	142	G6
Tomelloso	60	H5
Tomini	87	B2
Tommot	78	M5
Tomo	140	D2
Tompo	78	P4
Tom Price	114	C4
Tomra	88	E2
Tomsk	76	Q6
Tomtor	78	Q4
Tomu	87	D3
Tonalá	134	F5
Tondano	87	B2
Tønder	52	D2
Tonga	106	E2
Tonga	112	J7
Tonga Islands	112	J8
Tongareva	112	K6
Tonga Trench	112	J8
Tongbai	80	E4
Tongchuan	80	D4
Tongduch'ön	82	D5
Tongeren	54	H4
Tonghae	82	E5
Tonghua	82	C3
Tongliao	80	G2
Tongling	80	F4
Tongshi	80	D3
Tongue	126	E1
Tongyu	80	G2
Tónichi	124	E6
Tonj	106	D2
Tonk	88	C3
Tonkābon	90	F2
Tônlé Sab	84	C4
Tonnay-Charente	58	E8
Tönning	52	D2
Tonopah	126	C3
Tooele	126	D2
Toora-Khem	76	T7
Toowoomba	114	K5
Topeka	124	G4
Topki	76	R6
Toplița	66	N3
Topock	132	D2
Topol'čany	50	H9
Topolobampo	124	E6
Torbali	68	K6
Torbat-e Heydarīyeh	90	G2
Torbat-e Jām	90	H2
Tordesillas	60	F3
Töre	48	M4
Torells	80	N2
Torgau	52	H5
Torgelow	50	C4
Torhout	54	F3
Torino	62	C5
Tori-shima	80	L8
Tornealven	48	L3
Torneträsk	48	K2
Tornio	48	N4
Toro	60	E3
Toronto	38	R8
Tororo	106	E3
Toros Dağları	92	E5
Torquay	56	J11
Torrance	132	C2
Torreblanca	60	L4
Torre de Moncorvo	60	C3
Torrejón de Ardoz	60	G4
Torrelapaja	60	J3
Torrelavega	60	F1
Torremolinos	60	F8

Name	Page	Grid
Torrent	60	K5
Torreón	132	F3
Torre-Pacheco	60	K7
Torres Strait	114	H2
Torres Vedras	60	A5
Torrevieja	60	K6
Torrington	126	F2
Tortolì	64	D9
Tortona	62	D6
Tortosa	60	L4
Tortum	92	J3
Torüd	90	G2
Toruń	50	H4
Tory Island	56	D6
Torzhok	70	G3
Tosa-wan	82	G7
Tostedt	52	E3
Tosya	68	S3
Totaranui	116	D5
Tôtes	54	D5
Tot'ma	70	H3
Totora	140	D7
Tottori	82	H6
Touba, *Côte d'Ivoire*	104	C3
Touba, *Senegal*	104	A2
Tougan	104	D2
Touggourt	102	G2
Tougouri	104	D2
Touil	102	C5
Toul	58	L5
Toulépleu	104	C3
Toulon	58	L10
Toulouse	58	G10
Toummo	102	H4
Toungoo	84	B3
Tourcoing	54	F4
Tournai	54	F4
Tournon-sur-Rhône	58	K8
Tours	58	F6
Touws River	108	C6
Tovuz	92	L3
Towanda	128	E2
Towari	87	B3
Towcester	54	B2
Towner	126	F1
Townsend	126	D1
Townshend Island	114	K4
Townsville	114	J3
Toxkan	76	P9
Toyama	82	J5
Toyohashi	82	J6
Toyooka	82	H6
Toyota	82	J6
Tozeur	102	G2
Tqvarch'eli	92	J2
Trâblous	94	C2
Trabzon	92	H3
Tracy	128	A2
Trail	34	H7
Traiskirchen	62	M2
Trakai	48	N9
Tralee	56	C9
Tralee Bay	56	B9
Tramán Tepuí	140	E2
Tranås	48	H7
Trancoso	60	C4
Trang	84	B5
Trangan	87	D4
Transantarctic Mountains	144	(2)B1
Trapani	64	G11
Trappes	54	E6
Traun	62	K2
Traunreut	62	H3
Traunsee	62	J3
Traversay Islands	138	H9
Traverse City	128	C2
Travnik	66	E5
Trbovlje	62	L4
Trebbia	62	E6
Třebíč	50	E8
Trebinje	66	F7
Trebišov	66	J1
Trebnje	62	L5
Trebon	62	K1
Tregosse Islets	114	K3
Trélazé	58	E6
Trelew	142	H7
Trelleborg	48	G9
Tremonton	126	D2
Tremp	60	L2
Trenčín	50	H9
Trent	56	M8
Trento	62	G4
Trenton, *Canada*	128	E2
Trenton, *United States*	128	F2
Trepassey	122	W7
Tres Arroyos	142	J6
Três Corações	140	H8
Tres Esquinas	140	B3
Tres Lagos	142	G8
Trespaderne	60	G2
Treuchtlingen	62	F2
Treviglio	62	E5
Treviso	62	H5
Triangle	108	E4
Tricase	64	N9
Trichur	88	C6
Trier	54	J5
Trieste	62	J5
Triglav	62	J4
Trikala	68	D5
Trikomon	94	K3
Trilj	62	M7
Trincomalee	88	D7
Trinidad	140	E1
Trinidad, *Bolivia*	140	E6
Trinidad, *United States*	132	G1
Trinidad, *Uruguay*	142	K5
Trinidad and Tobago	140	E1
Trinity Bay	58	W7
Trinity Islands	132	(1)G4
Trino	62	D5
Trion	130	D3
Tripoli, *Greece*	68	E7
Tripoli = Trâblous, *Lebanon*	94	C2
Tripoli = Tarābulus, *Libya*	102	H2
Trischen	52	D2
Tristan da Cunha	98	B9
Trivandrum = Thiruvananthapuram	88	C7
Trjavna	92	A2
Trjavna	68	H2
Trnava	66	E1
Trogir	66	D6
Troina	64	J11
Troisdorf	52	C6
Trois Rivières	38	S7
Troitsk	70	M4
Troitsko-Pechorsk	70	L2
Trojan	66	M7
Trollhättan	48	G7
Trombetas	140	F4
Tromsø	48	K2
Trona	126	C3
Trondheim	48	F5
Trondheimsfjörden	48	E5
Troodos	92	E6
Trotuş	66	P3
Trout Lake, *N.W.T., Canada*	34	G4
Trout Lake, *Ont., Canada*	122	N6
Troy, *Al., United States*	130	D3
Troy, *N.Y., United States*	128	F2
Troyes	58	K5
Trstenik	66	J6
Trudovoye	82	G2
Trujillo, *Peru*	140	B5
Trujillo, *Spain*	60	E5
Truro, *Canada*	38	U7
Truro, *United Kingdom*	56	G11
Trusovo	76	J4
Truth or Consequences	132	E2
Trutnov	50	E7
Trzcianka	50	F4
Trzebnica	50	G6
Tržič	62	K4
Tsetserleg	78	G7
Tshabong	108	C5
Tshane	108	C4
Tshikapa	106	C5
Tshuapa	106	C4
Tsiafajavona	108	H3
Tsimlyanskoy Vodokhranilishche	70	H5
Tsiroanomandidy	108	H3
Ts'khinvali	92	K2
Tsuchiura	82	L5
Tsugaru-kaikyō	82	L3
Tsumeb	108	B3
Tsumkwe	108	C3
Tsuruga	82	J6
Tsuruoka	82	K4
Tsushima	82	E6
Tsuyama	82	H6
Tua	60	C3
Tual	87	D4
Tuân Giao	84	C2
Tuapse	92	H1
Tubarão	142	M4
Tubas	94	C4
Tübingen	62	E2
Tubize	54	G4
Tubruq	100	D1
Tubuai	112	M8
Tubuai Islands	112	L8
Tucano	140	K6
Tuchola	50	G4
Tucson	132	D2
Tucumcari	132	F1
Tucupita	140	E2
Tucuruí	140	H4
Tudela	60	J2
Ţufayḥ	95	C3
Tuguegarao	84	G3
Tugur	78	P6
Tui	60	B2
Tuktoyaktuk	34	E3
Tula, *Mexico*	132	G4
Tula, *Russia*	70	G4
Tulare	126	C3
Tulcea	66	R4
Tulkarm	94	B4
Tullamore	56	E8
Tulle	58	G8
Tulln	62	M2
Tuloma	48	S2
Tulsa	124	G4
Tulsequah	132	(1)L4
Tulun	78	G6
Tulung La	88	F3
Tulu Weiel	106	E2
Tumaco	140	B3
Tumân	90	H2
Tumen	82	E2
Tumereng	140	E2
Tumkur	88	C6
Tumut	114	J7
Tunceli	92	H4
Tunduru	108	F2
Tundža	66	P8
Tungir	78	L5
Tungsha	86	F1
Tungsten	132	(1)M3
Tungusk	76	S5
Tunis	102	H1
Tunisia	102	E2
Tunja	140	C2
Tupelo	130	D3
Tupik	78	L6
Tupiza	142	H3
Tupper Lake	128	F2
Tuquan	80	G1
Tura, *India*	88	F3
Tura, *Russia*	78	G4
Turan	78	S7
Turangi	116	E4
Turayf	100	G1
Turbat	90	H4
Turbo	140	B2
Turda	66	L3
Turek	50	H5
Turgay	76	L8
Turgay	76	L8
Turgayskaya Stolovaya Strana	76	L7
Turgutlu	68	K6
Turhal	92	G3
Turin = Torino	62	C5
Turinsk	70	M3
Turiy Rog	82	F1
Turka	78	H6
Türkeli Adası	68	K4
Turkestan	76	M9
Turkey	92	D4
Turkmenbashi	90	F1
Turkmenistan	90	G2
Turks and Caicos Islands	134	K4
Turks Islands	134	K4
Turku	48	M6
Turma	78	N6
Turnhout	54	G3
Turnov	50	E7
Turnu Măgurele	66	M6
Turpan	76	R9
Turpan Pendi	76	S9
Turquino	138	F2
Turtas	70	N3
Turtkul'	90	H1
Turtle Island	114	K3
Turu	76	U5
Turugart Pass	76	P9
Turukhan	78	C3
Turukhansk	76	R4
Turukta	78	K4
Tuscaloosa	130	D3
Tuscola	130	D2
Tuticorin	88	C7
Tutonchany	78	E4
Tutrakan	66	P5
Tuttle Creek Reservoir	130	B2
Tuttlingen	62	D3
Tutuila	112	K7
Tuvalu	112	H6
Tuxpan, *Mexico*	124	E7
Tuxpan, *Mexico*	124	G7
Tuxtla Gutiérrez	134	F5
Tuyên Quang	84	D2
Tuy Hoa	84	D4
Tuymazy	70	K4
Tuz Gölü	92	E4
Tuz Khurmātū	92	L6
Tuzla	66	F5
Tver'	70	G3
Tweed	56	K6
Twentynine Palms	132	C2
Twilight Cove	114	E6
Twin Buttes Reservoir	132	F2
Twin Falls	126	D2
Twin Islands	36	Q6
Twizel	116	C7
Two Harbors	128	B1
Tyachiv	66	L1
Tygda	78	M6
Tyler	124	G5
Tylkhoy	78	U4
Tym	76	Q6
Tynda	78	L5
Tyne	56	K6
Tynemouth	56	L6
Tynset	48	F5
Tyra	76	S7
Tyrifjorden	48	F6
Tyrnavos	68	E5
Tyrrhenian Sea	64	F8
Tyry	78	P4
Tysa	50	N9
Tyukyan	78	K4
Tyumen'	76	M6
Tyung	78	K3
Tyva	78	F6

U

Name	Page	Grid
Uarini	140	D4
Uaupés	140	D3
Ubá	140	J8
Ubaitaba	140	K6
Ubangi	106	B3
Ube	82	F7
Úbeda	60	G6
Uberaba	140	H7
Uberlândia	140	H7
Überlingen	62	E3
Ubon Ratchathani	84	C3
Ubrique	60	E8
Ucayali	140	B5
Uchami	76	T5
Ucharal	76	Q8
Uchiura-wan	82	L2
Uchkuduk	76	L9
Uckermark	52	J3
Ucluelet	126	A1
Uda, *Russia*	78	F5
Uda, *Russia*	78	N6
Udachnyy	78	J3
Udagamandalam	88	C6
Udaipur	88	B4
Uddevalla	48	F7
Uddjaure	48	K4
Udine	62	J4
Udmurtiya	70	K3
Udon Thani	84	C3
Udupi	88	B6
Uecker	52	J3
Ueckermünde	52	J3
Ueda	82	K5
Uele	106	C3
Uelen	78	AA3
Uel'kal	78	Y3
Uelzen	52	F4
Ufa	70	L3
Ufa	70	L4
Uganda	106	E3
Ugep	104	F3
Ugine	62	B5
Uglegorsk	78	Q7
Uglich	70	G3
Ugljan	62	L6
Ugol'naya Zyryanka	78	R3
Ugol'nyye Kopi	78	X4
Ugulan	78	S4
Uh	66	K1
Uherské Hradiště	50	G8
Uherský Brod	50	G8
Uiju	82	C3
Uil	70	K5
Uil	70	K5
Uinta Mountains	126	D2
Uitenhage	108	D6
Újfehértó	66	J2
Ujiji	106	D4
Ujjain	88	C4
Ujung Pandang	87	A4
Ukerewe Island	106	E4
Ukhta	76	J5
Ukiah	126	B3
Ukmergė	50	P2
Ukraine	46	G3
Ulaanbaatar	78	H7
Ulaangom	76	S8
Ulan	80	B3
Ulan Bator = Ulaanbaatar	80	D1
Ulan-Ude	78	H6
Ulaş	92	G4
Ulchin	82	E5
Ulcinj	66	G8
Uldz	78	J7
Ulety	78	J6
Ulhāsnagar	88	B5
Uliastay	76	T8
Ulindi	106	D4
Ullapool	56	G4
Ullŭng do	82	F5
Ulm	62	F2
Ulog	66	F6
Ulongue	108	E2
Ulsan	82	E6
Ulu	78	M4
Ulubat Gölü	68	L4
Uluqqat	90	K2
Ulukışla	92	F5
Ulungur Hu	76	R8
Ulunkhan	78	J5
Uluru	114	F5
Ulu-Yul	78	D5
Ulva	56	F5
Ulverston	56	J7
Ulya	78	Q5
Ul'yanovsk	70	J4
Ulytau	76	M8
Umag	64	H3
Uman'	70	F5
Umanak = Uummannaq	122	W2
Umarkot	90	J4
Umba	70	F1
Umeå	48	L5
Umeälven	48	J4
Umfolozi	108	E5
Ummal Arānib	102	H3
Umm al Jamājim	95	A3
Umm Durman	100	F4
Umm Keddada	100	E5
Umm Lajj	100	G3
Umm Qaşr	95	B1
Umm Ruwaba	100	F5
Umnak Island	132	(1)E5
Umtata	108	D6
Umuarama	142	L3
Unalakleet	132	(1)E3
Unalaska Island	132	(1)E5
'Unayzah	94	C6
Underberg	108	D5
Ungava Bay	38	T5
Ungheni	66	Q2
Ungwana Bay	106	G4
União da Vitória	142	L4
Unije	62	K6
Unimak Island	132	(1)D5
Unim Bāb	95	D4
Unini	140	E4
Union	128	B3
Union City	134	G1
Union Springs	130	D3
United Arab Emirates	90	F5
United Kingdom	56	G6
United States	120	M5
Unna	54	K3
Unraven	132	E1
Unst	56	M1
Unstrut	52	G5
Unzha	70	H3
Upernavik	122	W2
Upington	108	C5
Upolu	112	J7
Upper Hutt	116	E5
Upper Klamath Lake	126	B2
Upper Lake	126	C2
Upper Lough Erne	56	E7
Upper Sandusky	128	D2
Uppsala	48	J7
Upsala	128	B1
'Uqlat al 'Udhaybah	95	B2
Urad Houqi	80	D2
Urakawa	82	M2
Ural	70	K5
Ural Mountains = Ural'skiy Khrebet	46	L1
Ural'sk	70	K4
Ural'skiy Khrebet	46	L1
Urambo	106	E5
Uranium City	34	K5
Uraricoera	140	E3